CUMBERLAND FAMILIES AND HERALDRY

Cumberland & Westmorland Antiquarian & Archaeological Society
Extra Series Vol. XXIII

MADE AND PRINTED IN GREAT BRITAIN BY
TITUS WILSON & SON LTD.
HIGHGATE KENDAL

The arms of Hudleston

CUMBERLAND FAMILIES AND HERALDRY

with

A SUPPLEMENT TO AN ARMORIAL FOR WESTMORLAND AND LONSDALE

by

C. ROY HUDLESTON, F.S.A.

and

R. S. BOUMPHREY, M.A.

Illustrated by J. Hughes, F.S.A., and others

Loud with names that men remember, bright with names that men forget

Printed for

THE CUMBERLAND & WESTMORLAND ANTIQUARIAN & ARCHAEOLOGICAL SOCIETY

1978

For J.H. and N.E.B.

con amore e grazie

PREFACE

Having completed *An Armorial for Westmorland and Lonsdale,* we turned to the preparation of a new edition of F. J. Field's *Armorial for Cumberland,* published by the Cumberland & Westmorland Antiquarian & Archaeological Society in 1937, and now out of print. As our task proceeded, however, we realised more and more clearly that we were producing a completely new work and that it would be fair neither to Field's memory nor to ourselves if our book were printed only as a new and revised edition of his *Armorial.*

It is true that all the Cumberland families whose arms he blazoned will be found in our volume, but we have been able to include many additional families, individuals and institutions and to provide a considerable amount of biographical, genealogical and historical information concerning them; in fact, the main emphasis of the book has turned out to be on this aspect rather than on heraldry.

It must be remembered that Field's work was largely single-handed and his book was a remarkable achievement when one considers the limited transport at his disposal – he made his journeys by bicycle – and also the fact that he was not able to study the rich store of documents in the Record Offices in Carlisle, Kendal, Preston and elsewhere, established since his day. Moreover, nearly 40 volumes of the *Transactions* of the Cumberland & Westmorland Antiquarian & Archaeological Society have appeared since he wrote, many of them containing additional genealogical and heraldic material, to say nothing of many books on these subjects. We have therefore enjoyed many advantages which were denied to him.

These things apart, it is clear that Field relied heavily upon Chancellor Ferguson's heraldic collections. We have no wish to denigrate the Chancellor's work, and we are everlastingly grateful to him, and to others such as Bell Irving, for recording many coats of arms which have since become illegible or vanished. None the less, the Chancellor's obsession with what he called "Statesman heraldry" was, we think, a snare and a delusion, and led Field astray. He repeatedly describes individuals as statesmen, but careful research has shown us that the description is wrong. Not in a single contemporary case have we found an individual so described, either in monumental inscriptions, in documents or elsewhere.

As to our own work, we have tried to record the heraldry found in houses, churches, churchyards and documents. We have travelled widely and spent many rich and happy hours in Cumberland on hot summer days and in the teeth of winter gales, and have been welcomed everywhere with help, kindness and interested co-operation; and though we know full well that such a work as this can never be complete or free from error, we have produced a reference book which will, we hope, be found useful and interesting.

That such a book as this can never be complete or free from error became clear to us even before our *Armorial for Westmorland and Lonsdale* was published, and we have taken the opportunity provided by the publication of the present work to include a Supplement to our earlier volume.

We would make it plain that we have included arms which have been either *used*, or else recorded by others as used, and we express no opinion as to whether they are or have been borne with authority.

The compilation of a book such as this is only possible with the co-operation and help of many people. The authors are very conscious of the debt they owe to many friends whose assistance has been invaluable and patience inexhaustible. Particularly do they wish to acknowledge with deep gratitude the enthusiastic help they have received at every stage from Mr. Jeremy P. Godwin, of the Record Office, Carlisle. His contributions, many and varied, have improved the book enormously. He has worked for us indoors on documents, and outdoors in churchyards, checking and re-checking, and our calls on him for help have always met with instant response. We owe him much.

We are also greatly indebted to the Rev. F. B. Swift who read the typescript and made many helpful comments. Moreover, he visited several churches and churchyards on our behalf, and allowed us to draw freely on his own extensive researches.

We likewise owe much to Miss Margaret Brander, of Tullie House, Carlisle. She has patiently answered scores of enquiries, has helped us with books, manuscripts, and bookplates, provided photostats, and made many helpful suggestions.

The Rev. J. A. Woodhead-Keith-Dixon was most helpful in the early stages of the book and allowed us to draw upon his considerable knowledge of heraldry.

Others whose help has been much appreciated, and whom we take this opportunity of thanking, are Mr. Bruce C. Jones, Archivist for Cumbria, and his staff; Mr. R. N. Bamber and Miss T. Goodman (University Library, Lancaster); Mr. Tony Behrens, who sometimes acted as our chauffeur; Mr. John R. E. Borron; Sir John Burgess; Mr. Myles Carter, Under Sheriff of Cumbria; Mrs. J. A. Clarke (Carlisle Museum); Mr. Timothy Cockerill; Miss Stella Colwell (The College of Arms); the Hon. Miss Elinor Cross; Mrs. H. Duff; Dr. T. G. Fahy; Mr. and Mrs. T. R. Fetherstonhaugh; Mr. John Fleming; Mr. R. Sharpe France, formerly Lancashire County Archivist, and the staff of Lancashire Record Office; Mrs. H. S. Greg; Mrs. G. Arden Harris; Mr. J. V. Harrison; Miss I. Hodson; the staff of Hove Area Library; Mr. and Mrs. J. P. Howard; Mr. and Mrs. Stafford Howard; Mr. Malcolm S. Howe; Mr. J. Hughes; Mr. Norman Humphreys; Mr. J. R. Hurrell (Hutton, Brentwood); Lord and Lady Inglewood and the Hon. Christopher Fletcher-Vane; Dr. Christopher Kitching (Public Record Office); Dr. L. C. Loveday; Miss Margaret McCollum (Department of Palaeography, University of Durham); Mr. R. H. McCosh; Mr. Alex McCracken; Mr. J. Melville; Mr. Roger Norris (Cathedral Library, Durham); Mr. and Mrs. George G. S. Richardson; Lady Richmond; Mr. David Scott (Under Sheriff's Office, Carlisle); Mr. Patricius Senhouse; Mr. Donald P. Sewell; Miss June W. Thompson (Local History Librarian, Newcastle upon Tyne Central Library); Dr. Robert G. Thornburgh (Long Beach, California); Mr. William Walker (Greenlands, Irton); Mr. E. R. Wilkinson (Tullie House); Miss Barbara Wilson; Mr. Paul A. Wilson (Lorton); and Dr. Robert S. Woof.

The authors acknowledge with gratitude generous financial support from the estate of the late Miss Mary C. Fair, through the good offices of Miss A. M. Armstrong, from the Lake District Museum Trust, the Cumberland and

Westmorland Antiquarian and Archaeological Society and the Curwen Trust.

Finally, it is a pleasure to pay a tribute to our printers, Messrs. Titus Wilson, and in particular to Mr. Oliver Turnbull, Mr. Raymond Fielding, Mr. Malcolm Williams and Mrs. June Inman, who have helped us in many ways. We are grateful for their patient and sympathetic co-operation, and help at every stage in the production of the book.

ABBREVIATIONS AND AUTHORITIES

AA3 & 4 = *Archaeologia Aeliana*, 3rd & 4th Series.
AGO = E. A. Greening Lamborn, *The Armorial Glass of the Oxford Diocese, 1250-1850.* 1949.
AHC = J. F. Curwen, *A History of the Ancient House of Curwen.* 1928.
AWL = R. S. Boumphrey, C. Roy Hudleston and J. Hughes, *An Armorial for Westmorland and Lonsdale.* 1975.
BBC = A. F. Borradaile, *Sketch of the Borradailes of Cumberland.* 1881.
BBE = W. K. R. Bedford, *The Blazon of Episcopacy.* 2nd ed., 1897.
BBF = L. C. W. Bullock, *Memoirs of the Bullock Family, A.D. 1166 to 1905.* 1905.
BBP = Joseph Bain, *Border Papers.* 1881-84.
BCG = Sir Bernard Burke, *A Genealogical and Heraldic History of the Colonial Gentry.* 1891-95.
BEB = J. Burke and J. B. Burke, *A Genealogical and Heraldic History of the Extinct and Dormant Baronetcies of England, Ireland, and Scotland.* 2nd ed., 1844.
BEP = Sir Bernard Burke, *A Genealogical History of the Dormant, Abeyant, Forfeited, and Extinct Peerages of the British Empire.* New ed., 1883.
BFA = H. C. Beeching, *Francis Atterbury.* 1909.
BFR = A. P. Burke, *Family Records.* 1897.
BGA = Sir B. Burke, *The General Armory of England, Scotland, Ireland and Wales.* 2nd ed., 1884.
BHC = M. Bellasis, *Honourable Company.* 1952.
BHH = Thomas Burton, *History and Antiquities of Hemingborough.* 1888.
BHI = J. B. Burke, *Heraldic Illustrations.* 1853.
BHN = Francis Blomefield, *History of Norfolk.* 1805-10.
BLG = Burke's *Genealogical and Heraldic History of the Landed Gentry.* Various eds., 1833-1972.
BLI = Burke's *Genealogical and Heraldic History of the Landed Gentry of Ireland.* 9th ed., 1899.
BP = Burke's *Genealogical and Heraldic History of the Peerage, Baronetage and Knightage.* Various eds., 1826-1970.
BPP = C. M. L. Bouch, *Prelates and People of the Lake Counties.* 1948.
BQS = J. W. T. Brey, *A Quaker Saga.* Philadelphia, N.D.
BWN = E. Bellasis, *Westmorland Church Notes.* 1888-9.
CA = College of Arms Grants.
CCC = Caesar Caine, *Cleator & Cleator Moor – Past and Present.* 1916.
CCH = G. Briggs, *Civic and Corporate Heraldry.* 1971.
CCT = J. F. Curwen, *The Castles and Fortified Towers of Cumberland, Westmorland and Lancashire North-of-the-Sands.* 1913.
CEK = W. G. Collingwood, *Elizabethan Keswick.* 1912.
CFF = Cumberland Feet of Fines.
CHC = N. Carlisle, *History of the Ancient House of Carlisle.* 1822.
CHW = T. W. Carrick, *History of Wigton.* 1949.
CKK = J. F. Curwen, *Kirkbie-Kendall.* 1900.
CME = Charles Moor, *Erminois.* 1918.

CPK = J. F. Chance, *The Pattinsons of Kirklinton.* 1899.
CVY = J. W. Clay (ed.), *Dugdale's Visitation of Yorkshire.* 1899-1917.
CW1 = *Transactions of the Cumberland & Westmorland Antiquarian & Archaeological Society,* Old Series.
CW2 = *Transactions of the Cumberland & Westmorland Antiquarian & Archaeological Society,* New Series.
CWC = Caesar Caine, *Whitehaven Churches.* 1916.
CWE = B. Bonsall, *Sir James Lowther and Cumberland and Westmorland Elections.* 1960.
CWM = R. S. Ferguson, *Cumberland and Westmorland M.P.s (1660-1867).* 1871.
DAC = R. S. Ferguson (ed.), *An Accompt of the most considerable Estates and Families in the County of Cumberland, . . . , by John Denton, of Cardew.* 1887.
DCL = Edward Hughes (ed.), *The Diaries and Correspondence of James Losh.* 1962-3.
DNB = *The Dictionary of National Biography.*
DPB = Debrett's *Peerage, Baronetage, Knightage and Companionage.* Various eds.
DRH = George Dow, *Railway Heraldry and Other Insignia.* 1973.
DSA = J. Corder, *A Dictionary of Suffolk Arms.* 1965.
DSL = A MS. List of Cumberland Sheriffs bound up with Recorder Milbourne's MS. version of Denton's *Accompt of Cumberland,* see MMD.
DVL = F. R. Raines (ed.), *Dugdale's Visitation of Lancashire.* 1872-73.
EAH = J. M. Ewbank, *Antiquary on Horseback.* 1963.
ECW = B. Nightingale, *The Ejected of 1662 in Cumberland & Westmorland – Their Predecessors and Successors.* 1911.
EDP = J. W. Clay, *The Extinct and Dormant Peerages of the Northern Counties of England.* 1913.
EGM = Edward Gibbon, *Memoirs of My Life.* Ed. by Georges Bonnard, 1966.
EHM = *Elvin's Handbook of Mottoes,* Revised with Supplement and Index by R. Pinches. 1971.
FAC = F. J. Field, *An Armorial for Cumberland.* 1937.
FBC = Fairbairn's *Book of Crests of the Families of Great Britain and Ireland.* Reprint of 4th ed., 1968.
FBK = Joseph Foster, *The Baronetage and Knightage of the British Empire.* 1883.
FCW = J. Foster, *Pedigrees Recorded at the Herald's Visitations of the Counties of Cumberland and Westmorland, 1615 and 1666.* N.D.
FD7 = A. C. Fox-Davies, *Armorial Families.* 7th ed., 1929 and 1930.
FDB = A. C. Fox-Davies, *Heraldic Badges.* 1907.
FDC = R. S. Ferguson (ed.), *Description of the County of Cumberland, by Sir Daniel Fleming of Rydal, 1671.* 1889.
FDH = A. C. Fox-Davies, *A Complete Guide to Heraldry.* Revised ed., 1925.
FFC = J. Foster, *Some Feudal Coats of Arms.* 1902.
FLP = J. Foster, *Pedigrees of the County Families of England. Vol. 1 – Lancashire.* 1873.
FMG = J. W. Clay (ed.), *Familiae Minorum Gentium, Diligentia Josephi Hunter, Sheffieldiensis. S.A.S.* 1894-96.
FVC = J. Fetherston (ed.), *The Visitation of the County of Cumberland in the Year 1615.* 1872.
FVD = J. Foster (ed.), *Pedigrees Recorded at the Visitations of the County Palatine of Durham, 1575, 1615 and 1666.* 1887.
FYP = J. Foster (ed.), *Pedigrees of the County Families of Yorkshire.* 1874-75.

FVN = J. Foster (ed.), *Pedigrees Recorded at the Heralds' Visitations of the County of Northumberland, 1615 and 1666.* N.D.

FVY = J. Foster (ed.), *The Visitations of Yorkshire, 1584/5 and 1612.* 1875.

FWE = Thomas Fuller, *The History of the Worthies of Cumberland & Westmorland.* 1841.

GA2 = C. R. Humphery-Smith, *General Armory Two.* 1973.

GEC = *The Complete Peerage.* 1910-59.

GECB = *Complete Baronetage, 1611-1800.* 1900-9.

GHF = I. Grimble, *The Harington Family.* 1957.

GM = *Gentleman's Magazine.*

GMS = William Gilpin's MS. version of John Denton's *Accompt of Cumberland* in Tullie House, Carlisle.

GOA = *Grantees of Arms.* Harl. Soc. lxviii, 1917.

GRL = W. Greenwood, *The Redmans of Levens and Harewood.* 1905.

GVL = F. R. Raines (ed.), *St. George's Visitation of Lancashire, 1613.* 1871.

HBA = C. H. Hunter Blair, *The Armorials of the County Palatine of Durham.* Archaeologia Aeliana, 4th ser., Vol. 4.

HBN = C. Hunter Blair, *The Armorials of Northumberland: An Index and Ordinary to 1666.* Archaeologia Aeliana, 3rd ser., Vol. 6.

HBO = V. C. P. Hodson, *List of the Officers of the Bengal Army, 1758-1834.* 1924-47.

HCC = W. Hutchinson, *The History of the County of Cumberland.* 1793-97.

HCF = M. E. N. Witchell and C. Roy Hudleston, *A History of the Clutterbuck Family.* 1924.

HDR = C. Roy Hudleston, *Durham Recusants' Estates, 1717-78.* Surtees Society, Vols. 173 & 175.

HHN = J. Hodgson, *A History of Northumberland.* 1827-58.

HHW = R. M. Heanley, *The History of Weyhill and Its Ancient Fair.* 1922.

HMC = MSS. of George N. Higgin, of Kendal.

HMS = J. Hill, MSS., Dean and Chapter Library, Carlisle.

HN = Howard of Naworth Muniments in Department of Palaeography, University of Durham.

HNB = C. W. Harrison, *The Harrisons of Newton and Bankfield in Lancashire.* 1939.

HNF = W. P. Hedley, *Northumberland Families.* 1968-70.

HNW = E. Hughes, *North Country Life in the Eighteenth Century: The North-West, 1700-1830.* 1965.

HS = Harleian Society publications.

HSH = Wilhelm and Walter Hoechstetter, *Stammtafel der Hoechstetter.* Munich, 1976.

HSS = H. Hornyold, *Genealogical Memoirs of the Family of Strickland of Sizergh.* 1928.

HSW = George N. Higgin, *The Heraldry of the High Sheriffs of Westmorland.* Unpublished MS., 1938 (with later additions).

IFR = Burke's *Irish Family Records.* 1976.

IOC = F. B. Swift, *Ireby Old Church.* N.D.

JAW = S. Jefferson, *The History and Antiquities of Allerdale Ward, above Derwent.* 1842.

JFP = Joseph Foster, *Penningtoniana.* 1878.

JGM = W. Jackson (ed.), *Memoirs of the Gilpin Family of Scaleby Castle, by Rev. William Gilpin.* 1879.
JLW = S. Jefferson, *The History and Antiquities of Leath Ward.* 1840.
JMP = J. H. Jesse, *Memoirs of the Pretenders.* 1890.
JMS = MS. Papers of William Jackson, F.S.A.
JPP = W. Jackson, *Papers and Pedigrees mainly relating to Cumberland and Westmorland.* Ed. by Mrs. Jackson. 1891-92.
JWC = A. J. Jewers, *Wells Cathedral.* 1892.
KEI = Rev. C. Moor, *Knights of Edward I.* 1929-32.
LAE = C. H. Hunter Blair, *Local Armorials of the Eighteenth Century.* AA4 Vol. 13, 1936.
LBA = M. E. Lacy, *A Book of Ancestors and Arms.* 1936.
LFL = A. G. Loftie, *The Family of Loftie.* 1918.
LJH = Henry Lonsdale, *Life of John Heysham, M.D.* 1870.
LMC = D. & S. Lysons, *Magna Britannia. Vol. 4, Cumberland.* 1816.
LNK = G. W. Marshall (ed.) *Le Neve's Pedigrees of the Knights made by Charles II, James II, William III & Queen Mary . . . & Queen Anne*. Harl. Soc. 1869, etc.
LTW = G. B. Longstaff, *The Langstaffs of Teesdale and Weardale.* Revised ed., 1923.
LWC = Henry Lonsdale, *Worthies of Cumberland.* 1867-75.
MCC = M. J. Ferguson, *Monumental Inscriptions in the Church and churchyard of St. Cuthbert, Carlisle.* 1889.
MCS = G. G. Mounsey, *Carlisle in 1745.* 1846.
MDF = R. E. Porter & W. G. Collingwood, *The Memoirs of Sir Daniel Fleming.* 1928.
MMD = Recorder Milbourne's MS. version of Denton's *Accompt of Cumberland* in Tullie House, Carlisle.
MMS = Rev. Thomas Machell, MSS. in Dean and Chapter Library, Carlisle.
MNH = A. W. Moore, *Nessy Heywood.* 1913.
MOM = R. Welford, *Men of Mark 'Twixt Tyne and Tweed.* 1895.
MMP = F. Warriner, *Millom People and Places.* 1937.
MSG = W. H. Chippindall, *Memoirs of Lt-Col Samuel Gledhill.* 1910.
MSN = C. H. Hunter Blair, *The Mayors and Lord Mayors of Newcastle upon Tyne 1216-1940 and the Sheriffs of the County of Newcastle upon Tyne 1399-1940.* AA4 Vol. 18, 1940.
MVC = MS. Visitation (so-called) of Cumberland 1577 or (*pace* R. S. Ferguson, CW1 i 301) 1615, in Tullie House, Carlisle.
NB = J. Nicolson & R. Burn, *The History and Antiquities of the Counties of Westmorland and Cumberland.* 1777.
NCHN = *A History of Northumberland.* 1893-1940.
NEP = L. G. Pine, *The New Extinct Peerage 1884-1971.* 1972.
NMA = R. S. Ferguson (ed.), *Miscellany Accounts of the Diocese of Carlisle, with the Terrier delivered in to me at my primary Visitation.* By W. N[icolson]. 1877.
NQ = *Notes and Queries.*
NSH = A. Nisbet, *A System of Heraldry.* 1722.
NVY = C. B. Norcliffe (ed.) *Flower's Visitation of Yorkshire.* 1881.
OBA = Papworth's *Ordinary of British Armorials.* 1874, reproduced 1961.
OCC = G. Ormerod, *The History of the County Palatine and City of Chester.* 2nd ed., 1882.

OMH = M. W. Taylor, *The Old Manorial Halls of Westmorland and Cumberland.* 1892.
PGD = C. A. Parker, *The Gosforth District.* 2nd ed., 1926.
PHY = Marshal-General G. H de S. N. Plantagenet-Harrison *(sic), The History of Yorkshire.* Vol. 1, 1879.
PJB = H. E. M. J. and W. A. J., *Extracts from the Pedigrees of James of Barrock.* 1913.
PPF = Sir John Ponsonby, *The Ponsonby Family.* 1929.
QCO = J. R. Magrath, *The Queen's College.* 1921.
RAG = J. B. Rietstap, *Armorial General,* including V. & H. V. Rolland's *Supplement.* Reproduced 1969-72.
RCC = J. W. Brown, *Round Carlisle Cross.* 1951.
RMJ = Anon., *The Genealogical Table of the Descendants of Richard and Mary Jackson, of Threaplandleas, Cumberland.* Privately printed, 1896.
RND = Rev. J. Raine, *The History and Antiquities of North Durham.* 1852.
ROW = G. F. R. Barker and A. H. Stenning, *The Record of Old Westminsters.* 1928.
RRF = Mary A. Rudd, *Records of the Rudd Family.* 1920.
RWH = C. B. Norcliffe, *Some Account of the Family of Robinson of the White House, Appleby, Westmoreland.* 1874.
SBB = J. Spedding, *St. Bega and Her Church at Bassenthwaite.* 1966.
SBR = James Wilson, *The Register of the Priory of St. Bees.* 1915.
SEB = I. J. Sandars, *English Baronies.* 1960.
SFE = Melvyn Bragg, *Speak for England.* 1976.
SGH = C. W. Scott-Giles, *Civic Heraldry of England and Wales.* Revised ed., 1953.
SHD = R. Surtees, *The History and Antiquities of the County Palatine of Durham.* 1816-40.
SOO = R. E. K. Rigbye, *Storeys of Old.* 1920.
SSF = R. Stackhouse, *The Stackhouse Family.* 1935.
TBC = G. E. Braithwaite, *The Braithwaite Clan.* 1975.
TCA = *The College of Arms, Queen Victoria Street.* The 16th and final Monograph of the London Survey Committee. 1963.
TCD = W. T. Trimble. *The Trimbles & Cowens of Dalston.* 1933.
TEV = A. E. Terrill, *Memories of a Family in England and Virginia.* 1887.
TFT = E. B. Tufnell, *The Family of Tufnell.* 1924.
TGG = J. M. Bullock, *The Gay Gordons.* 1908.
TLD = B. L. Thompson, *The Lake District and the National Trust.* 1946.
TSF = J. C. D. Spedding, *The Spedding Family.* 1909.
TTV = A late 17th or early 18th century MS. copy of Tonge's Northern Visitation of 1530 (see TVN), formerly owned by Marmaduke Tunstall, of Wycliffe, and now by A. R. Jabez-Smith.
TVN = W. H. D. Longstaffe (ed.), *Heraldic Visitation of the Northern Counties in 1530, by Thomas Tonge.* 1863.
TWH = T. W. Thompson, *Wordsworth's Hawkshead.* Ed. by R. Woof, 1970.
TWS = E. E. Moore, *Travelling with Thomas Story.* 1947.
VAC = J. & J. A. Venn, *Alumni Cantabrigensis.* 1922, etc.
VCHC = *The Victoria History of the County of Cumberland.* 1901, 1905.
VEW = J. J. Howard & F. A. Crisp, *Visitation of England and Wales.* 1894-1921.

VN = *Visitations of the North.* Surtees Society, Vols. 122, 133, 144 and 146, 1912–32.
WCF = Walford's *County Families of the United Kingdom.* Various eds.
WCW = W. Whellan, *The History and Topography of the Counties of Cumberland and Westmoreland.* 1860.
WEC = J. Woodward, *A Treatise on Ecclesiastical Heraldry.* 1894.
WG = The Westmorland Gazette.
WHC = T. D. Whitaker, *The History of Craven.* 1805.
WHR = T. D. Whitaker, *History of Richmondshire.* 1823.
WMP = G. S. H. L. Washington, *Early Westmorland M.P.s 1258–1327.* 1959.
WRC = Charles Dalton, *The Waterloo Roll Call.* 1890.
WW = Who's Who.
WWW = Who Was Who.

CUMBERLAND FAMILIES AND HERALDRY

ADAMS, Baron, of Ennerdale. John Jackson Adams, O.B.E., J.P., Hon M.A. (Dunelm), of Wybrow Terrace, Workington (1890-1960), born at Arlecdon, son of Thomas Adams, was cr. Baron Adams, of Ennerdale, 1949, but d. *s.p.* He was bur. in Arlecdon churchyard. *Arms.* Vert a torch erect between in chief two cog wheels and issuant from the base a sun rising Or thereon an open book Proper bound and clasped Gules. *Crest.* On the head of a well a fieldfare rising Proper. *Supporters.* Dexter, A miner holding in the interior hand a lamp and supporting in the exterior a pickaxe; Sinister, An agricultural labourer resting the exterior hand on a fork. *Motto.* Labore omnia vincit (NEP).

ADAMSON. Lawrence Adamson, of Whitehaven, later of 7 Windsor Crescent, Newcastle upon Tyne, H.M.'s Seneschal, Isle of Man (d. 1877, aged 73), was only son of Anthony Adamson, of Millgrove, Moresby, and Whitehaven, solicitor and banker. *Arms.* Vert gutté d'eau a cross invected in the first quarter a key in pale and in the second a talbot passant all Or. *Crest* A talbot passant Azure collared charged on the shoulder with a cross invected and holding in the dexter paw a key in pale all Or. *Motto.* Watch and ward (VEW xviii 143).

ADCOCK. See HALL.

ADDISON, of Low Wood Nook. Thomas Addison, of Delahay Street, Westminster, and of Whitehaven (b. 1641), descended from a family of yeomen of Low Wood Nook,* Torpenhow, where he was born, gave the ceiling of the nave of Torpenhow church in 1689. He marr. 1668 Isabella (d. 1671), only dau. of David Hamilton, of Whitehaven. He marr. (2) 1673 Jane Aglionby (d. 1674) and had a dau. Jane (b. 1674) who marr. 1699 Hugh Simpson, *q.v.*† He marr. (3) 1676 Jane, dau. of Sir Timothy Fetherstonhaugh, *q.v.*, and widow of Christopher Wyvill, of Winderwath, *q.v.*, by whom he had five sons, who all died young, and one dau. Bridget (1678-1707) who marr. Richard Hutton, of Hutton Hall, *q.v. Arms.* Ermine on a bend Gules three annulets Or on a chief Azure as many leopards' faces of the third. *Crest.* A unicorn's head erased pierced through the neck with an arrow (Thomas Addison's seal). Field gives: A unicorn's head erased Argent pierced through the neck with an arrow and charged on the breast with three annulets Azure (FAC).

SHELTON-AGAR. This family is descended from the Eagers of Co. Kerry. James Walter Eager (b. 1784) changed the spelling to Agar. He marr. 1835 Susan, dau. of John Shelton; their descendant Walter Richmond Shelton-Agar (1879-1952) was father of Alan Shelton-Agar, B.A. (Cantab), M.B., Ch.B. (Edin), of Melmerby Hall, Lord of the Manors of Melmerby and Gale. *Arms.* Azure a lion rampant Or gorged with an antique Irish crown

* Much of their estate was lost because Thomas' father was an officer in the King's army in the Civil War.

† In his will of 1702 (codicil 1711) Thomas Addison says that Jane "did against my will and express command marry herself to Hugh Simpson, son of Lanc. Simpson of Penrith, by which Lanc. Simpson I was most barbarously treated."

Gules a chief Ermines. *Crest.* A demi lion Azure gorged with an antique Irish crown Or and charged on the shoulder with a mullet Argent. *Motto.* Facta non verba (BLG18).

AGLIONBY, of Drawdykes and Nunnery. T. H. B. Graham in CW2 xxxiii traces the pedigree of this family which gave its name to Aglionby in Warwick. Walter Agullun appears as a witness *c.* 1130 and Lawrence son of Agyllun and Werri de Agyllunby were witnesses to a confirmation made to Wetheral Priory *c.* 1195. Adam de Agillounby was M.P. for Carlisle 1360 and 1368 and William sat in 1385 and 1387-88. Edward was M.P. 1529 and 1547, and High Sheriff of Cumberland 1544. Hugh was M.P. 1547 and Edward jun. in 1552-53. John Aglionby, of Carlisle (b. *c.* 1520), who heads the Visitation Pedigree, 1665, was M.P. 1553 and Edward sat in 1592-93,* and a later Edward 1623-25. John Aglionby (1642-1718) was Recorder of Carlisle 1679-1718, and the builder of Drawdykes Castle. He also owned Drumbrugh Castle, which he exchanged 1696 with Sir John Lowther for Nunnery, which his grandson Henry Aglionby (1684-1759) pulled down, building the present house on the site. He was M.P. for Carlisle 1721-27 and High Sheriff 1732. His son Henry Aglionby, J.P. (1715-70), High Sheriff of Cumberland 1763, marr. Anne (d. 1780), 4th dau. of Sir Christopher Musgrave, 5th Bart., and was succ. by his 3rd son Christopher, High Sheriff of Cumberland 1780, who d. unmarr. 1785, aged 33. His four sisters and coheirs were Elizabeth (d. *s.p.* 1822, aged 78), marr. Richard Bamber (d. 1808); Julia (d. unmarr. 1798, aged 53); Anne, marr. the Rev. Samuel Bateman, of Newbiggin Hall, near Carlisle, whose son Henry Aglionby Bateman (1790-1854), M.P. for Cockermouth, assumed the surname Aglionby but d. *s.p.*; and Mary, marr. John Orfeur Yates, *q.v.* Their eldest son Francis Yates (1777-1840) assumed the name Aglionby. His daus. and coheirs were Elizabeth Anne (1814-78), of Esthwaite Lodge, Hawkshead, Bellmount, Hawkshead, Wigton Hall and Grasmere; Mary (1815-82), marr. 1845 the Rev. Beilby Porteus, Vicar of Edenhall; and Jane (1820-74), marr. 1847 Charles Fetherstonhaugh, by whom she had a dau. Elizabeth (d. 1885), marr. 1871 Lt-Col Arthur Sisson Cooper, C.B., J.P., of Staffield (1832-1911), who assumed the name and arms of Aglionby 1885. Their son Capt Arthur Charles Aglionby, barrister-at-law (1872-1938), bought Nunnery 1892 from his cousin, the Rev. Francis Keyes Aglionby (see below) and sold it 1919. He left two daus. and coheirs. The line was continued by Charles Yates (1807-91), nephew of Francis Yates, later Aglionby. He also assumed the name Aglionby. His son, the Rev. Francis Keyes Aglionby, M.A., D.D. (Oxon.) (1848-1937), sold Nunnery and the manor of Aglionby 1893. His eldest son Francis Basil Aglionby, M.A., B.C.L. (Oxon), solicitor (1878-1962), was father of the present head of the family, Francis John Aglionby, M.A. (Oxon), barrister-at-law. *Arms.* Argent two bars and in chief three martlets Sable (BLG18). These arms were recorded by Dugdale at the Visitation of 1665 with the remark, "No proofe made of these armes" (FCW). NB (ii 327) record for Edward Aglionby, High Sheriff 1544: Barry of four Sable and Argent on a chief of the last three sheldrakes of the first. The monument to Major Arthur Hugh Aglionby (died of wounds received on the Scheldt 1918), 4th son of the Rev. F. K. Aglionby, displays: Argent

* Often Mayor of Carlisle "and ever ready to serve the Quene," he was murdered near Carlisle 1599.

two bars Gules in chief three martlets Sable. MMD tricks, for Aglionby: Argent two bars and in chief three martlets Azure, but adds: "But now Aglionby for his paternall coat doeth give the whole charge Sable."* *Crest.* A demi eagle displayed Or (LMC; BLG18). *Motto.* Quand Dieu playea (M.I., Ainstable church).

AINGER. The Rev. William Ainger, M.A., D.D. (Cantab) (d. 1840, aged 55), was Perpetual Curate of St. Bees 1816-40, first Principal of St. Bees Theological College 1816-40, and Canon of Chester 1827. His son, the Rev. George Henry Ainger, M.A., D.D. (Cantab) (1819-86), was tutor at St. Bees Theological College 1849-57, Principal 1858-70, Perpetual Curate of St. Bees 1858-70, Hon. Canon of Carlisle 1870-82, Rector of Rothbury (N) 1871-86, and Hon. Canon of Newcastle 1882-86. *Arms.* Ermine a griffin segreant per pale Or and Azure (Shield in chancel, Rothbury church). *Crest.* An annulet staved flory (Rev. William Ainger's seal, DRC10, R.O. Carlisle).

AINSLIE. James Ainslie, M.D., of Carlisle and Kendal (1732-90), descended from William Ainslie, of Fala, *c.* 1438, and from John de Ainslie, who acquired Dolphinton *temp.* Robert II of Scotland, was ancestor of the Ainslies, of Over Kellet and Grizedale (L). *Arms.* Argent *[sic]* a cross patonce Or (Dr. Ainslie's bookplate in Viscountess Wolseley's collection). A MS. pedigree of the family, however, gives: Or a cross flory Gules. *Crest.* An eagle's head erased Proper. *Motto.* Pietas tutissima virtus.

AINSWORTH, of The Flosh. Thomas Ainsworth, J.P., of The Flosh, Cleator (1804-81), who shared a common ancestry with the Ainsworths of Backbarrow (L) (see AWL), was a pioneer in the haematite industry in West Cumberland. He bought The Flosh *c.* 1837 and greatly enlarged the house. In 1861 he was High Sheriff. By his wife Mary Laurie (d. 1867), elder dau. of the Rev. John Stirling, D.D., he was father of David Ainsworth, D.L., J.P. (1842-1906), M.P. for West Cumberland 1880-85 and 1892-95 who succ. to The Flosh and bought Wray Castle (L) 1898. His younger brother John Stirling Ainsworth, D.L., J.P., LL.B. (London) (1844-1923), M.P. for Argyllshire 1903-18, High Sheriff of Cumberland 1891, was cr. Baronet 1917; the present holder of the title is his grandson Sir John Francis Ainsworth, 3rd Bart., M.A. (Cantab), F.R.Hist.Soc., who was Hon. General Editor of the British Record Society 1937-40. *Arms.* Gules three battle axes erect Argent. *Crest.* An eagle displayed. *Motto.* Resurgam (Shield at The Flosh; brass in Cleator church).

AISLABIE. Impaled by Denton, *q.v.*, on tablet in Sebergham church; Thomas Denton, M.A., of Warnell (d. *s.p.* 1616, aged 80), marr. (2) Anne Aislabie. *Arms.* Quarterly, 1 & 4, . . . a fess humetté . . . between three martlets . . . ; 2, . . . an eagle displayed . . . ; 3, . . . a bend . . . . *Crest.* A morion.

ALBERMARLE, Earl of – see FORZ.

ALDERSEY. A window in Aspatria church erected by Maria Aldersey Sanderson 1891, commemorates her mother, Jane Aldersey (d. 1890). *Crest.* A demi griffin segreant Gules issuing from a plume of three ostrich feathers Or.

ALDRED. Shield at Hutton-in-the-Forest; a Vane quartering. *Arms.* Argent a lion rampant double queued and crowned Gules.

* Fuller gives for Edward Allonby, Sheriff 1544-45: Azure two bars and three martlets in chief Sable; which is clearly a mistake (FWE).

ALDRICH, ALDRIDGE. The Rt. Rev. Robert Aldrich or Aldridge, M.A., D.D. (Cantab) (d. 1556), was Prebendary of Lincoln 1528, Archdeacon of Colchester 1531, Canon of Windsor 1534, Provost of Eton 1536, and Bishop of Carlisle 1537-56. *Arms.* Vert on a fess Argent between three garbs Or banded Gules two boughs of whitethorn saltirewise enfiled with a coronet between a regal orb Azure and a robin redbreast all within a bordure engrailed Or; the bordure is pommetté in one version (BBE).

ALLISON, of Pardshaw Hall. A pedigree of six generations of the Allison family, of Pardshaw Hall, Dean, headed by Tower Allysonn, appears in FCW, without dates, though it is said to have been recorded in 1615. *Arms.* Argent a fess Gules between three birds Sable a bordure of the last (FCW). MVC tricks the bordure Gules, and gives for *Crest.* A bird.

ALLISON, of Scaleby Hall. Robert Allison, of Carlisle (d. 1844), was father of Joseph Allison (d. 1842) who marr. 1836 Jane Andrew (d. 1890). Their son Sir Robert Andrew Allison, D.L., J.P., of Scaleby Hall (1838-1926), was M.P. for North Cumberland 1885-1900 and High Sheriff 1908. His elder son Wilfrid Henry Andrew Allison (1874-1921) d. *s.p.m.* and his younger son, the Rev. Herbert Allison, B.A. (Cantab) (1876-1934), was licensed preacher at Caldbeck 1924-28 and at Crosthwaite 1928-34; he d. unmarr. *Arms.* Argent on a fess Azure between three blackbirds Proper as many boars' heads couped of the field. *Crest.* In front of an eagle's head erased per fess Sable and Argent two crescents of the first. *Motto.* Vincet veritas (BLG15).

ALLONBY, of Allonby. A dau. and coheir of this family is said to have marr. William de Flimby (NB ii 162; HCC ii 295). *Arms.* Three versions have been recorded. (1) As borne by Thomas de Alanby *temp.* Edward III: Argent a chevron Azure a bordure engrailed of the last (FFC). (2) Argent a chevron engrailed Sable (Harl. vii; MMS vi 417). (3) As quartered by Martindale: . . . a chevron engrailed . . . and a bordure engrailed . . . (FAC). Field also suggests that a shield on an unidentified medieval gravestone at Kirkoswald may be for Allonby, viz. . . . a chevron engrailed . . . and a bordure . . . .

AMERICA, United States of. Amongst the shields in the east window of Upperby church commemorating the Allies of World War I, is one for the United States of America. *Arms.* Argent six pallets Gules a chief Azure.

ANNANDALE, Earl of – see MURRAY.

APPELBY, *post* DACRE, of Kirklinton. Edmund Appelby, of Askerton (d. 1698), bought Kirklinton from Sir Edward Musgrave 1661. Kirklinton Hall henceforth became the family home, and Edmund was succ. there by his son Joseph Appelby (d. 1705, aged 46) who marr. 1686 Dorothy (d. 1698), dau. of Henry Dacre, of Lanercost, *q.v.*, and half-sister and in her issue coheir of James Dacre. Their son Joseph (1690-1729), High Sheriff 1724, used the surname Dacre-Appleby, but his son Joseph, J.P., of Kirklinton Hall (1711-79), dropped the name of Appleby *c.* 1742 and he and his descendants were known as Dacre. He was High Sheriff 1738 and marr. 1736 Catherine (d. 1775, aged 58), dau. and coheir of the Rt. Rev. Sir George Fleming, 2nd Bart. He was succ. by his 2nd son William Richard Dacre, J.P. (1749-1807), who was High Sheriff 1782. His son Joseph Dacre, Madras Civil Service (1785-1828), who died in India, left two sons – Joseph, J.P. (1825-68), who succ., and the Rev. William, M.A. (Cantab) (1827-1903), who was Vicar of Irthington 1852-98. *Arms.* Azure six martlets, three, two and one, Or. *Crest.*

A martlet (M.I.s, Kirklinton church). The family later used the arms of Dacre, quartered and alone, viz. Gules three escallops Argent, sometimes with a baton sinister (M.I.s, Kirklinton church). The Rev. William Dacre, above (d. 1903), who marr. (3) Margaret, dau. of the Rev. Dr George Jeffrey, bore on his bookplate: *Arms.* Quarterly, 1 & 4, Gules three escallops Argent; 2 & 3, Azure six martlets, three and three, Argent; on an escutcheon of pretence, Paly of six Argent and Sable on a fess of the first three mullets of the second (Jeffrey). *Crest.* A bull passant Gules ducally gorged and chained. *Motto.* Fort en loialte.

APPLEBY. Thomas de Appleby, Canon of Carlisle (d. 1395), was Bishop of Carlisle 1363-95. *Arms.* . . . a chief indented . . . (BBE).

APULDERFIELD. Shield at Hutton-in-the-Forest; a Vane quartering. *Arms.* Sable a cross Or voided of the field.

ARCHBOLD – see PEARS.

ARCHDALE. The Rev. Thomas Hewan Archdale, J.P., M.A. (T.C.D.) (1843-1924), later Vicar of Tanfield (D) and Hon. Canon of Durham, was Curate of St. John, Workington, 1868-70. His younger brother, the Rev. Mervyn Archdale, M.A. (Cantab) (1846-1918), later Rector of Balmain, N.S.W., and Canon of Sydney, was Curate of St. George's, Kendal, 1869-73. *Arms.* Azure a chevron Ermine between three talbots passant Or. *Crest.* Out of a ducal coronet Or an heraldic tiger's head Proper. *Motto.* Data fata secutus (IFR).

ARCHER. Borne on an escutcheon of pretence by Howard, *q.v.*, on goblets and seals at Corby Castle; Henry Howard, of Corby Castle (1757-1842), marr. (1) 1788 Maria (d. *s.p.* 1789),* 3rd dau. and coheir of Andrew, Lord Archer, of Umberslade. *Arms.* Azure three arrows points downwards [Or].

ARCHER. John Archer, J.P., M.B. (Cantab), of Oxenholme (W) (1672-1735),† a nephew of Elizabeth Archer, wife of William Nicolson, Bishop of Carlisle, marr. (1) 1702 Dorothy, dau. and heir of William Askew, *q.v.*, and widow of Samuel Poole; and (2) 1724 Elizabeth, dau. of Sir William Pennington, 1st Bart., *q.v.* (She marr. (2) Thomas Strickland, of Sizergh.) From his first wife he inherited Standing Stones and Farmery Lands in Millom, and lands in Gosforth, Bolton, Ponsonby and Drigg. Dying *s.p.* he left these estates to his sister Marian, who marr. 1709 William Bracken. *Arms.* Azure three broad arrows Or. *Crest.* Out of a mural coronet Gules a dragon's head Argent (CW2 ix 51-52). Another version of the arms gives: Argent three arrows in pale points downwards Azure (AWL).

ARDEN. Impaled by Close on monument in Carlisle cathedral; Anne Diana (d. 1877), 3rd dau. of the Rev. John Arden, of Longcroft Hall (St), marr. 1820 as his 1st wife the Very Rev. Francis Close, Dean of Carlisle, *q.v.* *Arms.* Ermine a fess chequy Azure and Or.

ARLOSH – see LOSH.

ARMAGH, See of. The arms of the See of Armagh, impaling those of Kite, *q.v.*, are on the west front of Kite's Tower at Rose Castle. *Arms.* [Azure] an episcopal staff in pale [Argent] ensigned with a cross pattée [Or] surmounted by a pall-throughout [of the second] edged and fringed [Gold] and charged with four crosses formé fitché [Sable].

* She is commemorated by Nollekens' well-known monument in Wetheral church.

† He was son of Miles Archer, not of John Archer, as stated in AWL.

ARMSTRONG. The Armstrongs formed what can only be termed a "clan", widely spread through most of the parishes of North Cumberland, in the churchyards of which, especially at Lanercost and Bewcastle, can still be seen many examples of the arms used by individual members of the clan. These and their variants are recorded in detail by Bell Irving in ABD, and here we record only the basic achievement on which all the others are based. *Arms.* Three arms in armour embowed and couped fessways in pale. *Crest.* A like arm. The arms are sometimes vested, not armed, and sometimes neither vested nor armed; and the arm in the crest is sometimes depicted holding a sword. A late example of the arms is carved on the gravestone in All Saints' churchyard, Cockermouth, commemorating Reginald Armstrong (d. 1820, aged 40), Dinah his wife (d. 1842), and their infant son William (d. 1807), where the crest appears as: An arm embowed grasping a club.

ARMSTRONG. James Armstrong and his brother Richard are of Manor Brow, Scotland Road, Carlisle. *Arms* (on the wall of Manor Brow, Carlisle). Argent three pallets Azure. *Crest.* An arm embowed. *Motto.* Invictus maneo.

ARNISON, of High Haresceugh and Penrith. This family were landowners at High Haresceugh, Kirkoswald, as early as 1683. The property descended to George Arnison (d. 1833), and from him to his son George (d. 1869) who was succ. by his brother Nathan Arnison (1795-1886) who settled in Penrith as a linen and woollen draper. His eldest son George Arnison (d. 1883) was also in the business and was father of George Wright Arnison, J.P., M.A. (Cantab) (1875-1965), Headmaster of the Royal Grammar School, High Wycombe 1905-33. Major William Burra Arnison, of Beaumont, Penrith, solicitor (1831-96), obtained a grant of arms. He was in partnership with his younger brother Charles Nathan Arnison (1840-1911) who inherited the Haresceugh estate, which passed to his eldest son Nathan Henry Arnison, solicitor, in partnership with his brother Charles, whose sons Charles Eric Arnison, of Haresgill, Stainton, and Thomas Mitchell Arnison, of Croft House, Newton Reigny, now carry on the firm. The former sold the Haresceugh estate. *Arms.* Per pale Azure and Sable a demi lion erased between four estoiles saltirewise Or. *Crest.* In front of a fern brake a stag lodged Proper resting the dexter foot upon an estoile Or. *Motto.* Ditat servata fides.

ARTHURET. Nicholas de Arthuret and Mariota his wife were landowners in Old Salkeld. William de Arthuret (fl. 1333-69) owned half the manor of Old Salkeld which he sold 1333; he was M.P. for Carlisle 1355, 1362, 1364-5 and 1369, the year he died. Thomas de Arthuret, perhaps his son and heir, is mentioned 1377. William de Arthuret was Vicar of Arthuret 1371, and one of the same names (will pr. 1476) was Rector of Arthuret, and another William was Vicar of Aspatria 1480. The heiress marr. John Mulcaster. *Arms* (as quartered by Mulcaster). Or on a fess Sable three lozenges Argent (FAC). Field also quotes Edmondson's *Heraldry* as authority for: Argent on a fess Sable three lozenges Or.

ASBRIDGE. John Asbridge, gent., was of Kirkgate, Cockermouth, 1829 and of St. Helens there 1834, when John Asbridge jun. was living at Kirkgate. Martha, presumably his wife, died 1837 aged 28, and is bur. in All Saints' churchyard. John Asbridge senior appears to have d. 1848, leaving by Ann his wife two daus., Mary Wrangham or Asbridge, and Ann Asbridge. *Arms.* Or a fess embattled Gules between three horses' heads erased . . . . *Crest.* An arm in armour embowed flourishing a scimitar. *Motto.* Cassis tutissima virtus (Cockermouth tombstone).

ASHBRIDGE. Anne, wife of Thomas Ashbridge, of Drumburgh House, and sister of Mrs Tamar Lawson, in her will of 1885 mentions her late nephew Richard Lawson Nixon, and his sons, William and Richard Lawson Nixon, *q.v. Arms* (impaled by Nixon on house at Boustead Hill). Gules a bridge embattled of three pointed arches between three trees eradicated in chief and a like tree in base.

ASHBURN. Esther Ashburn, of Allonby, marr. Richard Hodgson, of Bowness-on-Solway, innkeeper (1741-1803). *Arms.* . . . on a fess . . . between three crescents . . . as many estoiles . . . (*Ex inf.* E. J. B. Irving, a descendant).

ASHBURNER, of Seascale Hall. The following achievement is carved on the tombstone of Martin Ashburner, of Seascale Hall (d. 1823, aged 82), in Gosforth churchyard. *Arms.* Or a chevron Gules between three bugle horns stringed . . . . *Crest.* A fox courant . . . . However, the arms and crest differ so much from any other Ashburner bearings known to the authors, and the achievement is in such an unusual situation on the tombstone, at (and now partly below) ground level, beneath the name of the mason, John Bromley, of Keswick, who marr. 1794 Elizabeth, dau. of Martin Ashburner (CW2 lxxiv 188), that it seems possible that they may be intended for Bromley.

ASHLEY. Isaac Ashley, of Great Broughton, had, *int. al.*, two sons, Joseph (d. 1740) and Jonathan. The former bought in 1703 the Ashby St. Ledgers estate, Northants., where he was succ. by his son Solomon Ashley (d. 1775), M.P. for Bridport 1734-41. He left two daus., but Ashby St. Ledgers passed to his kinsman Joseph Ashley, of Brigham* (d. 1798), grandson of the above Jonathan. He had three daus. and coheirs – Jane, marr. 1782 Thomas Gaitskell (by whom she had a son Joseph Ashley Gaitskell, M.D., see below); Mary (d. 1850), marr. Sir Joseph Senhouse, *q.v.*; and Catherine (d. 1833). Sir Joseph and Lady Senhouse had issue, *int. al.*, a dau. Maria (d. 1872), who marr. her cousin Joseph Ashley Gaitskell, above, and four sons, the youngest of whom, William Senhouse (d. 1885), inherited Ashby St. Ledgers, which he left to his cousin Humphrey Senhouse, of Netherhall, *q.v.* (*Ex inf.* P. I. King, Northamptonshire County Archivist). *Arms.* [Azure] a cinquefoil and a bordure invected† [Ermine]. *Crest.* A harpy [Proper]. (Seal of Joseph Ashley above on the marriage settlement of his dau. Mary and Sir Joseph Senhouse.)

ASKEW, of Standing Stones and Graymains. According to Denton (DAC, 17), this family descends from Thurston de Bosco, who received from the Lord of Kirksanton, Aikskeugh or Oakwood, in 1202-3. It is certain that William son of Guy Boyville granted 1309 lands in Kirksanton and Silecroft, near the two standing stones, to John son of John de Aykescowgh. Sir Robert Mulcaster and Joan his wife and Margaret de Bampton granted

* *The Cumberland Pacquet* of March and May 1775 contains an account of his setting out to take possession of the Ashby St. Ledgers estate, worth £3,000 a year, and his return, when Brigham Church bells were rung all day, and three vollies were fired outside his house. Later "a genteel treat" was given at the Seven Stars Inn by the squire, whose health was enthusiastically drunk.

† Correctly, engrailed.

1403 to Richard de Ayscogh their lands in Lacra and Scales. These estates descended to Matthew Ayscough,* who gave them to his son Richard 1478. They descended to Hugh Askew (1558-1625) who marr. Elizabeth (1560-1649), dau. and heir of Thomas Troughton, and so acquired Graymains, Muncaster. Their son William (1593-1641) succ., and was succ. by his son Hugh (1613-98), who marr. 1635 Dorothy, dau. of John Ambrose, of Lowick, and sister and coheir of the Rev. John Ambrose. Their son William Askew (1636-1717), the last male of the family, apparently sold Graymains, but retained Standing Stones and other property in Cumberland. By his wife Dorothy (1640-1705), dau. and coheir of William Musgrave, of Crookdake, *q.v.*, he had an only surviving child Dorothy, who d. *s.p.* having marr. (1) 1699 Samuel Poole, of Pontefract (Y), and (2) 1702 John Archer, of Oxenholme, *q.v.*, who inherited her estates (Unpublished account of the Askews by C. Roy Hudleston). Arms. Gules three asses' heads erased .... *Crest.* An ass passant (M.I., Kendal church, of William Askew, d. 1717, and brass in Millom church in memory of his wife Dorothy). On the tombstone in Cartmel Priory of William's sister Dorothy (1639-1719†) the arms appear as: Gules a lozenge ... charged with three asses' heads ....

ASKEW. Relying on an inaccurate statement in NB, copied in BLG, it was stated in AWL that the Askews of Kendal, Storrs and Co. Durham, were descended from the Askews of Graymains, see preceding entry. It is clear from later research that this was not so. Several members of the Storrs family have been connected with Cumberland, including the Rev. Henry Askew, M.A. (Cantab) (d. 1852, aged 87, 4th son of Dr. Anthony Askew, of Newcastle upon Tyne), Rector of Greystoke 1798-1852. His grandson, the Rev. Edmund Askew, M.A. (Cantab) (1849-1901), was Rector of Greystoke 1875-1901; his widow lived at Bushby House, Greystoke. Their elder son Capt Henry Askew, Border Regt., was killed in action at Sailly, France, 1914, aged 33.‡ His son Henry Cuthbert Adam Askew is now head of the family. The Rev. Adam Askew, M.A. (Oxon) (1724-91), younger brother of Dr. Anthony Askew, above, was Rector of Bolton (C) 1752-60, and of Plumbland 1760-87. *Arms.* Sable a fess Or between three asses passant Argent maned and unguled of the second. *Crest.* A naked arm Proper grasping a sword Argent hilt and pommel Or enfiled with a Saracen's head couped Proper wreathed about the temples Or and Sable blood issuing from the neck of the first (NB i 257; BGA). *Mottoes.* Fac et spera; Patientia casus exuperat omnes (Mausoleum, Greystoke Churchyard).

ASSEY see DACRE.

ATKINSON, of Carleton Hall. Cuthbert Atkinson (1745-1816),§ son of Thomas Atkinson, of Waverton, Wigton, was steward to the 1st Lord Muncaster. He marr. 1785 Anne, dau. of the Rev. Edward Burrough, *q.v.*,

* Matthew was ancestor of Christopher Ayscough, of Blyborough, Lincs., father of Sir Hugh Askew, of Seaton Priory (d. *s.p.* 1562), who marr. Bridget, dau. of Sir John Hudleston, of Millom. Sir Hugh was Sheriff of Cumberland 1561, and FWE and DSL record his arms as: Sable a fess Or between three asses passant Argent maned and unguled of the second.

† Not 1819, as printed in error in AWL.

‡ On a brass to his memory, erected by his wife, children, sisters and brother, in Greystoke church, it is stated that he was buried by the Germans, who inscribed on his cross the words, "Here lies a brave British officer."

§ His interesting career has been admirably described by J. R. E. Borron in CW2 lxix 189-93.

and sister and coheir of the Rev. Stanley Burrough, and so acquired an estate at Carleton, Drigg, and no doubt built Carleton Hall on the site of an earlier house. His only dau. Elizabeth (1786-1830) marr. 1807 a cousin Joseph Burrow (d. 1849) and the property was eventually inherited by her grandson Arthur Alfred Edward Burrow, who sold it 1921. *Arms.* Ermine on a fess . . . three pheons . . . . *Crest.* A pheon. *Motto.* Et nos qu . . . [the rest worn away]* (Tombstone of Cuthbert Atkinson, now at Carleton Hall).

ATKINSON, of Hornsby and Carlisle. John Atkinson was lord of the manor of Hornsby 1676 (HN 181a/7). From him presumably descended Francis Atkinson, of Brampton, who marr. 1731 Mary (d. 1760), dau. and heir of James Maxwell, *q.v.* His brother John Atkinson, Alderman of Carlisle (d. 1744), had a son James Atkinson (1734-81), a founder of the Old Brewery, Carlisle, which traded under the style of Messrs. James Atkinson for many years. His eldest son John Atkinson (1759-1813), Rouge Croix 1785-94 and Somerset Herald 1794-1813, was lord of the manor of Hornsby and was latterly of Carlisle. His brother James Atkinson, of Carlisle, attorney (1762-97), was a partner in the Old Brewery. His dau. and heir Mary (living 1880) marr. 1813 Michael Longridge, of Bedlington (N) (1785-1858) (*Ex inf.* J. V. Harrison; HN 66a/29-50). *Arms.* TCA gives no arms for John Atkinson, Rouge Croix and Somerset Herald, but Michael Longridge's bookplate shews the following for Atkinson: Paly on a fess three arrowheads points downwards on a canton a cross.

ATKINSON. John Atkinson, of Kirkcammock, yeoman, died 1758, aged 70. *Arms.* . . . a crosse pattée . . . between four roses . . . in base a fleur-de-lys (Tombstone, Walton churchyard†).

ATKINSON, post SLINGSBY. John Atkinson, of Wigton (1736-1803), was father of Thomas Atkinson, of Acorn Bank (W) and Ripley Castle (Y). His eldest dau. Emma Margaret marr. 1820 Charles Slingsby (1777-1832), son of Sir Thomas Slingsby, 8th Bart., of Scriven Park (Y); their son Sir Charles Slingsby was 10th and last Bart., and the estates descended to his first cousin, the Rev. Charles Slingsby Atkinson (1842-1912), eldest son of the Rev. Thomas Atkinson (1806-80), Rector of Kirby Sigson (Y). He assumed the name and arms of Slingsby 1899 (BLG17). *Arms.* Gules an eagle displayed with two heads Argent on a chief Or a rose between two martlets Azure (M.I., Kirby Sigston church).

ATKINSON. John Atkinson, of Whitehaven, and of Valparaiso, Chile (1821-96), was father of John Charles (b. 1867), Frederick George (b. 1873), and Henry Edward (b. 1873), all of Valparaiso and Quilpué. *Arms.* Argent on a chevron Gules between three boars' heads erased Sable as many sickles of the field. *Crest.* An eagle wings expanded and inverted Argent beaked and membered Gules holding in the dexter claw a sickle as in the arms. *Motto.* Deo et regi fidelis. *Badge.* A seahorse rampant Or (FD7).

ATKINSON, of Rampsbeck. From William Atkinson, of Temple Sowerby (*temp.* Eliz. I), descended George Atkinson, of Temple Sowerby (1730-81), Receiver-General for Cumberland and Westmorland, who was ancestor of Francis Baring Atkinson, D.L., J.P., of Rampsbeck, Watermillock, and of Morland Hall (W) (1805-64), High Sheriff of Cumberland 1853. The

* Perhaps: Et nos quoque tela sparsimus.

† On the same stone is also recorded Richard Graham, of Kirkcammock (d. 1800, aged 86).

present representative of the family is Col Francis Cuthbert Atkinson, D.L., of The Old Manse, Guestwick, Norfolk. The above George Atkinson had a younger brother Matthew, of Temple Sowerby, tanner (1736-89), who succ. him as Receiver-General. He marr. 1774 Mary (1750-1800) dau. of the Rev. George Gilbanks, of Wetheral, and had a son Matthew Atkinson, of Temple Sowerby and Staingills, Kirkland (1778-1852), who was High Sheriff 1823, and died *s.p. Arms.* Ermine an eagle with two heads displayed Gules in chief three mullets Sable a canton of the last. *Crest.* A roundle per fess Azure and Gules charged with an eagle with two heads displayed Or. *Motto.* True to the end (BLG18).

ATTERBURY. The Rt. Rev. Francis Atterbury, M.A., D.D. (Oxon) (1663-1732), was Dean of Carlisle 1704-11, Dean of Christ Church, Oxford 1711-13, Dean of Westminster 1713-23, and Bishop of Rochester 1713-23. In 1723 he was deprived of all his ecclesiastical preferments and banished the kingdom for his alleged involvement in a plot to restore the Stuarts (BFA). *Arms.* Paly of six Or and Gules a chief Vair (BBE).

AUDEN. George Augustus Auden, F.R.C.P., M.R.C.S., M.B. and B.C., M.A., M.D. (Cantab), Ph.D. (Birm), F.S.A. (1872-1957) (6th son of the Rev. John Auden, M.A. (Cantab.)), Professor of Public Health in the University of Birmingham, was of Wesco, Threlkeld. His youngest son, Wystan Hugh Auden (1907-73), was well known as a poet, and was Professor of Poetry at Oxford 1956-61. *Arms.* Argent on a cross Gules a lion passant Or between four increscents of the field. *Crest.* A caduceus in bend sinister surmounted by a scimitar in bend dexter all Proper pommel and hilt Or. *Motto.* Cresco et spero (BLG18).

AUDLEY. Shield at Hutton-in-the-Forest; a Vane quartering. *Arms.* Gules a fret Or.

AUDLEY of Walden. A Howard quartering, on shield in Great Hall of Naworth Castle; Thomas, 4th Duke of Norfolk (d. 1572), marr. (2) 1557 Margaret, dau. and heir of Thomas, Lord Audley of Walden. *Arms.* Quarterly per pale indented Or and Azure in the second and third quarters an eagle displayed wings inverted of the first over all on a bend of the second a fret between two martlets also of the first.

AUDLEY, Earl of Gloucester. A series of shields from Thornbury Castle, Glos, now in Greystoke Castle, illustrating the medieval ancestry of the Howards, includes one for Hugh, Lord Audley (d. *s.p.m.* 1347), who marr. 1317 Margaret, widow of Piers de Gaveston, Earl of Cornwall, and dau. and coheir of Gilbert de Clare, Earl of Gloucester and Hertford, *q.v.*, and was cr. Earl of Gloucester 1337. Their dau. and heir Margaret (d. 1348) marr. 1336, as his 2nd wife, Ralph de Stafford, earl of Stafford, *q.v. Arms.* Gules fretty Or.

AUMALE, Count of – see FORZ.

AUSTHWAITE. This family descended from Ketel son of Ulf who lived in the 12th century. Henry son of Arthur, Lord of Millom, gave Ketel's son Benedict, his cousin, the manor of Austhwaite (now Dalegarth) in the vill of Millom before 1215. His descendants took the name of Austhwaite, and Richard son of Thomas de Hauesthweyt released his interest in the manor to his brother Adam 1292. A later Adam (son of Thomas) was father of Constance, wife of Nicholas Stanley, *q.v.*, and to them in 1354 Thomas de Austhwait demised the manor (CW2 xli 123-52; SBR). *Arms* (as quartered by Stanley). Gules two bars and in chief three mullets Argent pierced Or (FCW). In the (so-called) Visitation of 1615, the mullets are pierced of the field (FVC). Lysons gives Gules two bars Argent in chief three mullets of six points pierced Or (LMC). GMS records the mullets as cinquefoils Argent pierced of the field.

BABER. Edward John Baber, of 7 Devonshire Terrace, Stanwix (d. *s.p.* 1935, aged 74), son of Henry Baber, manager of Hudson, Scott & Sons, Carlisle, was born in London, and joined Messrs Hudson, Scott & Sons, retiring 1929. He was an outstanding amateur actor. His nephew Henry Edward Baber was living in Leeds in 1935. *Arms.* Argent on a fess Gules three hawks' heads erased of the field. *Crest.* On a mount Vert a cock wings expanded Argent combed wattled and legged Gules (Bookplate of E. J. Baber).

BACKHOUSE. The Backhouses, said to have come from Whitrigg, held a part of the manor of Morland (W) in 1540; for their later history, see AWL. *Arms.* Or a saltire Erminois (NB i 447-8). *Crest.* An eagle volant Or "desplayed with a serpent Proper inflexing its head and tayle towards the eagle" (MMS i 613). Field quotes a member of the family as recording the following at the Visitation of London, 1568. *Arms.* Per saltire Azure and Or a saltire couped Ermine. *Crest.* An eagle Vert wings closed preying on a snake Proper. *Motto.* Confido in Deo (FAC).

BADDELEY. Impaled by Smith on flat stone in Carlisle cathedral; Anne (d. 1698, aged 67), dau. of Richard Baddeley, of North Bailey, Durham, marr. (1) 1664 the Rev. Richard Wrench, M.A. (Cantab), Prebendary of Durham (d. 1675), and (2) 1676, as his 2nd wife, the Very Rev. Thomas Smith, Dean, and later Bishop, of Carlisle. *Arms.* . . . a bend . . . between three mullets . . . . However, the will of Richard Baddeley, dated 1671, is sealed with: . . . a cross . . . in dexter chief a . ? . ; impaling, . . . a bend . . . between six crosses pattée . . . .

BAGOT. Shield at Hutton-in-the-Forest; a Vane quartering. *Arms.* Ermine two chevrons Azure.

BAIN, of Crofthead. Sir James Bain, D.L., J.P., F.R.G.S., of Crofthead, Harrington (1817-98), son of Robert Bain, of Glasgow, was Lord Provost of Glasgow 1874-77 and M.P. for Whitehaven 1891-93. His elder son, John Dove Bain, J.P. (b. 1848), was of Crofthead, and his younger son, Col James Robert Bain, J.P. (b. 1851), M.P. for West Cumberland 1900-6, was of Moresby Hall and Bolton Hall, Gosforth. *Arms.* Azure a wolf's head erased Or on a chief Argent a salmon on its back Proper with a signet ring in its mouth of the second a label of three points for difference. *Crest.* A dexter arm embowed Gules the hand grasping a dirk Proper. *Motto.* Et arte et marte (FD7).

BAINBRIDGE. Harl. MS. 1536 gives the following for a Cumberland family of this name. *Arms.* Argent on a chevron between three choughs Sable as many stags' heads cabossed Or (FVC).

BALDWIN. Shield on entrance gate pillars of Woodside, Wreay; James Losh, of Woodside, *q.v.*, marr. 1798 Cecilia, dau. of the Rev. Roger Baldwin, F.R.S., F.S.A., M.A. (Cantab) (d. 1801), Rector of Aldingham (L), Vicar of Morland (W), and Prebendary of Carlisle. *Arms.* . . . a saltire . . . . Field, presumably following BGA, gives: Argent a saltire Sable.

BALGOILL. Shield at Hutton-in-the-Forest; a Vane quartering. *Arms.* Ermine an inescutcheon Gules.

BALLANTINE, of Crookdake. Sir John Ballantine, J.P. (1632-1705), knighted 1663, son and heir of John Ballantine, of Corehouse, Lanarkshire, marr. Anne (d. 1691), dau. and heir of William Musgrave, of Crookdake, *q.v.*, and settled there in 1663; he was High Sheriff of Cumberland 1694. His son William (d. 1710), who was High Sheriff 1709, marr. without his father's "consent or privity and to my great dissatisfaction" Grizell, dau. of Sir James Johnstone, of Westerhall. Their son John Ballantine (1699-1756), High Sheriff 1726, marr. 1721 Jane (d. 1769), dau. of Frecheville Dykes, *q.v.*, and had a son John (d. 1755), whose dau. and heir Jane marr. 1764 Lawson Dykes (b. 1740) who assumed the name of Ballantine. Their son Joseph Dykes Ballantine (d. 1830), High Sheriff 1806, on his marr. 1800 to his cousin Mary Dykes, *q.v.*, resumed the surname of Dykes. *Arms.* Argent on a cross between four mullets Azure a sword erect point upwards Proper pommel and hilt Or (BGA; window in St. Bees church). Field states that the coat was also borne without the sword (FAC). *Crest.* A demi griffin Or wings expanded Argent holding in the dexter claw a sword Proper hilt and pommel Or. Field gives: A demi griffin wings expanded (FAC). *Motto.* Nec cito nec tarde (EHM).

BALLIOL. Hugh de Balliol (d. *c.* 1228) was father of John (d. 1268) and Eustace. The former, who was Lord of Barnard Castle and Regent of Scotland, was High Sheriff of Cumberland 1248-55. He marr. 1223 Devorguila (d. 1290), dau. and coheir of Alan, Lord of Galloway; they were founders of Balliol College, Oxford. Their son John (d. 1314) was King of Scotland 1292-96, and his son Edward (d. *s.p.* 1363) was King of Scotland 1332-35. The above named Eustace de Balliol (d. *s.p.* 1272) was High Sheriff of Cumberland 1261. He marr. Helewise, dau. and heir of Ralph Boyvill or de Levington, *q.v. Arms.* John de Balliol bore: Gules an orle Argent. Eustace de Balliol bore: Azure crusilly and an orle Or (FFC).

BAMPTON. Walter de Bampton, descended from Hildred de Carlisle, held the manor of Great Bampton, flourishing 1224-45. Richard de Bampton owned the manor 1331. Sir Robert de Bampton is mentioned 1338 and John de Bampton held the manor 1362, and the manor of Branthwaite 1366-69. His wife Alice and Robert de Bampton are mentioned in the will of Robert Whitrigg, *q.v.*, 1362, though no relationship is specified. *Arms.* Papworth, quoting Glover's *Ordinary,* states that the Brampton [*sic*] family bore: Argent a bend dancetté Azure (OBA). These arms were born by the Whitrigg family, who were clearly connected with the Bamptons.

BANKS, of Highmoor. William Banks, of Keswick (d. 1860), son of Joseph Banks, was father of William Banks, D.L., J.P. (1811-78) who settled in Wigton 1835, founded the firm of Banks, Henderson & Banks, linen and woollen drapers, and amassed a large fortune. He succ. the Hodge family at Highmoor House 1846, and was High Sheriff of Cumberland 1871. His sons Henry Pearson Banks, D.L., J.P., M.A. (Cantab), barrister-at-law (1844-91), and Edwin Hodge Banks, D.L., J.P., M.A. (Cantab), barrister-at-law (1847-1917), were both of Highmoor House; the former was High Sheriff 1886, and the latter 1889. The Highmoor estate was sold 1909 (BLG11; CHW). *Arms.* Sable a cross engrailed Or between in the first and fourth quarters a bear rampant of the last muzzled Gules and in the second and third quarters a fleur-de-lys also Or. *Crest.* Upon the trunk of a tree eradicated and sprouting to the dexter Proper an eagle reguardant with wings elevated Sable charged upon the breast and upon each wing with a fleur-de-lys Or. *Motto.* Dum spiro spero (FD7; achievement at Highmoor House).

BANNER. Major Robert Murray Banner, 93rd Highlanders, died of cholera at Balaclava 1854, aged 39, the year in which he marr. Anne Ferguson. *Arms.* Per pale Ermine and Or a fleur-de-lys [counterchanged] on a canton Azure a lion passant [Argent]*. *Crest.* A sinister arm embowed in armour holding in the hand a banner charged with a fleur-de-lys. *Motto.* Pro patria (M.I., Carlisle cathedral).

BARANTYNE. A Hudleston quartering, brought in by the marr. 1541 of Marie (d. 1581), dau. and coheir of Sir William Barantyne, of Haseley, Oxfordshire (b. *c.* 1481), to Anthony Hudleston, of Millom (d. 1598), *q.v.* *Arms.* Gules three eagles displayed Sable (shield at Hutton John). The correct arms are: Sable three eagles displayed Argent beaked and membered Or (AGO).

BARDSEY. The Bardseys held the manor of Bardsea (L) from the time of Ralph (or Randle) de Bardsey, living 1135, until the family failed in the male line on the death 1586 of Nicholas Bardsey, who owned the manor of Clifton (C) and lands in Greysouthen and Broughton. His daus. and coheirs were Dorothy (d. 1627), wife of James Anderton, and Elizabeth, who marr. Lancelot Salkeld, of Whitehall, *q.v.* The latter pair inherited the Cumberland estate. *Arms.* Argent two bars Gules on a canton of the last a maunch of the first (CW2 vi 175-83; VCHL viii 332-3).

BARDSLEY. John Wareing Bardsley, M.A. (T.C.D.), D.D. (Lambeth) (1835-1904), eldest son of Canon James Bardsley, was Archdeacon of Liverpool 1886-87, Bishop of Sodor and Man 1887-92, and Bishop of Carlisle 1892-1904. His brother, the Rev. Charles Wareing Endell Bardsley, M.A. (Oxon), author of *English Surnames,* was Vicar of Ulverston 1878-93 and Hon. Canon of Carlisle. Their nephew, the Rev. Joseph Udell Norman Bardsley, M.A. (Cantab) (1868-1928), was Vicar of Ulverston 1896-1909 and Hon. Canon of Blackburn. *Arms.* Argent two bars Sable on a canton of the last a maunch of the first (BBE). These arms, untinctured, are on the Bishop's monument in Carlisle Cathedral.

BARKER. The Rev. William Barker, M.A., D.D. (Oxon) (1838-1917), 3rd son of Joseph Charles Barker, of Ellicombe, Som., was Chaplain to Queen Victoria 1876-80, Canon of St. Paul's 1885-88, and Dean of Carlisle 1908-17. *Crest.* A bear muzzled (FAC).

BARKER. Brass in Great Salkeld church; Richard Lacy, of Eden Lacy (d. 1883), marr. Eliza (d. 1882), 3rd dau. of the Rev. Robert Barker, M.A. (Cantab) (1756-1816), Rector of Hollym (Y). *Arms.* Barry of ten Or and Sable a bend Gules. *Crest.* Out of a ducal coronet Or an eagle displayed Sable armed Gules. *Motto.* Servos fortuna nepotes.

BARNES. Richard Barnes, M.A. (Oxon), D.D. (Cantab) (1532-87), son of John Barnes, of Bold (L), was Chancellor of York and Prebendary of Laughton 1561, Bishop of Nottingham 1567, Bishop of Carlisle 1570-77, and Bishop of Durham 1577-87. *Arms* (as granted 1570). Azure on a bend

* Impaling, on the monument in Carlisle Cathedral: Quarterly, 1 & 4, Azure three frases [Argent]; 2 & 3, Gules three antique crowns [Argent], i.e., the arms of Fraser.

Argent between two estoiles Or* a bear passant Sable semé of estoiles of the third respecting a naked child of the fourth on a chief of the second three roses Gules radiated with rays of the sun Proper (BBE; SHD). (As granted 1580). Quarterly, 1 & 4, Quarterly Or and Vert on a fess Sable three estoiles Or (Barnes); 2 & 3, Azure on a bend Argent a bear passant Sable on a chief of the second three roses Gules radiated Or (Sanderson) (HLC xxvii 180-2). HBA gives: Quarterly, 1 & 4, Quarterly Or and Vert on a fess Sable three stars Argent; 2 & 3, Azure on a bend Argent a bear passant Sable estoiled Or seizing a naked man Proper on a chief Argent three roses Gules radiated Or. *Motto.* Crux veritati comes (FAC).

BARNES, of Aikton. Anthony Barnes, of Aikton, died 1766, aged 77. *Arms* (on tombstone). Per pale Or and Vert on a bend . . . three estoiles . . . (ABD). Field, however, who states that the family continued to be buried at Aikton as late as 1865, recorded: Per pale Or and Vert on a fess Sable three estoiles of the first (FAC).

BARNES, of Bunker's Hill and Carlisle. Thomas Barnes, J.P., M.D. (Edin) (1793-1872), a native of Aikton, who studied medicine on the continent and was present at Waterloo, was a well known Carlisle physician, who lived at Bunker's Hill. He was physician to Carlisle Dispensary and in 1820 founded Carlisle Fever Hospital. In 1842 he founded the Cumberland Infirmary, Carlisle, of which he was the first physician. He was also an author. His nephew, Henry Barnes, M.D. (Edin), LL.D. (McGill), F.R.S.E. (1842-1921), a vice president of the British Medical Association, also practised in Carlisle, and was the author of, *int. al.*, the *Medical Worthies of Cumberland,* 1905. He was physician to the Cumberland Infirmary 1873-1903 (CW2 xxi 284-5). *Arms.* Quarterly Or and Vert on a fess Sable three estoiles of the field.† *Crest.* An estoile pierced Or. *Motto.* Nec timide nec temere (BGA).

BARNES. A brass in Burgh-by-Sands church records the gift of five windows in the north aisle by his five sisters, Louisa, Ada, Ann, Mary and Kate, in memory of Thomas Kay Barnes (d. 1898). *Arms.* Quarterly Argent and Vert on a fess Sable three estoiles of the first. *Crest.* An estoile pierced Argent.

BARNES. John Barnes, of Penrith, attorney (d. 1736), marr. 1731 Anne (b. 1702), dau. of Thomas Pattenson, of Melmerby Hall, *q.v.* *Arms.* Per fess . . . and . . . in chief eight (?) billets . . . and in base a dolphin embowed . . . .

BARNFATHER. Jane, wife of Joseph Barnfather, of Cragstone, was bur. at Lanercost 1759. *Arms.* The charges are now barely visible, but Bell Irving interpreted them as: . . . a chevron . . . between three cows' heads cabossed . . . (ABD).

BARRATT, of Maiden Hill and Carleton Hall. James Barratt (d. 1869, aged 61) was of Maiden Hill, Penrith, in the 1840's and also owned Long Ashes there. Later he moved to Lymm Hall (Ch) and finally rented Carleton Hall, Drigg, where he died. He was a benefactor to the building fund of Christ Church, Penrith, opened 1850, and gave the east window in the Lady Chapel. His brother Joseph was of Greengill, Penrith. *Arms.* Barry of four Gules and Argent per pale counterchanged on a chief indented Erminois three escallops of the first. *Crest.* A wyvern Or gorged with a collar Gules

* Surtees gives this as Argent (SHD i lxxxii).

† *Sic.* this should clearly be Or.

chained also Or. *Motto.* Sans Dieu rien (East window, Lady Chapel, Christ Church, Penrith).

BARRATT. John Barratt, of Holy Wath, Coniston (1793-1866), born at Gwennap, Cornwall, came from Cornwall to Cumberland and engaged in the mining industry, opening the Hodbarrow iron mines with the help of his nephew William Barratt, J.P., of Holly How and Holy Wath (d. 1881). William was father of Alfred (d. *s.p.*); James William Henry, J.P., of Holy Wath (1850-1912), whose dau. and heir Emily, J.P.(1881-1947), marr. 1915 Major Charles William Hext; and William Isaac Barratt, J.P., of Kepplewray, Broughton-in-Furness (b. 1855). The latter's son, William Donald Barratt, J.P., of Leyfield, Millom and of Hazel Mount, Broughton-in-Furness, Major, the King's Own Royal Regt. (b. 1883), High Sheriff of Cumberland 1944, had issue *int. al.* William Barratt, of North End, North Row, Bassenthwaite, the present representative of the family; Roger Barratt, of Cowmire Hall, Crosthwaite (W); and Timothy Donald Barratt, of Hazel Mount (*Ex inf.* Roger Barratt; CW2 lxviii 151-68). *Arms.* Argent a chevron engrailed Gules between three bears' heads couped Sable muzzled Or. *Crest.* A griffin segreant reguardant. *Motto.* Et manu et corde (M.I., Coniston church; Seal of W. D. Barratt).

BARRON. Margaret, wife of John Barron, of Righead and of Horseholm, was bur. at Bewcastle 1737, aged 19. *Arms.* . . . a cross flory . . . *Crest.* A horse's head (ABD). Field recorded the crest as: A unicorn's head couped (FAC).

BARROW. William Barrow (d. 1429), Chancellor of the University of Oxford 1413-15, Bishop of Bangor 1418-23, was Bishop of Carlisle 1423-29. *Arms.* Perhaps: Argent on a chevron between three cross crosslets Sable two lions counter passant of the field (BBE); or: Argent on a fess dancetté (or indented) Sable three bezants (FAC). Both ascriptions seem doubtful.

BARTRAM, of Penrith. Dugdale's pedigree of the Bird family, of Brougham (W), shews John Bird (living 22 Edward IV) as marr. to Elizabeth, dau. of Richard Bartram, of Penrith (FCW). *Arms.* Gules semé of cross crosslets and an orle Or (HMS v 149). Burke gives for Bartram, of Cumberland: Gules an orle Or (another, adds a label of three points of the second) (BGA). For Bartrum, of Cumberland, Papworth quotes *Harl. Ms.* 1404 as authority for: Or an escutcheon Azure (OBA).

BARWICK, of Beckermet. Field recorded the following as over the door of Barwickstead, Beckermet, where the family lived in the 19th century. *Arms.* Argent a rose between three bears' heads erased Sable. *Motto.* In duris servata fides (FAC).

BARWIS, of Islekirk.* This family, said to have been cadets of de Berewyse, of Barwise Hall (W), obtained a moiety of the manor of Dearham by marr. to an heiress of de Dearham. Land in Setmurthy held by Stephen de Berwys 1399 was possessed in 1495 by Richard Berwys (d. 1507) and his son Richard Barwis (1467-*c.* 1544), who was of Hildkirk (Islekirk) 1529. His successor Anthony Barwis bought the capital messuage of Islekirk 1544 and at his death *c.* 1578 (his only son having predeceased him) it passed to his kinsman Richard Barwis (d. 1599) who marr. Mabel, widow of Anthony's son Thomas, and dau. of Thomas Dalston, of Dalston, *q.v.* His son Anthony Barwis (1580-1616) marr. Grace, dau. of William Fleming, of Rydal. John

* Contributed by the Rev. F. B. Swift.

Barwis, of Waverton (d. 1662), Anthony's brother, was High Sheriff of Cumberland 1648, 1649 and 1652, and was father of Col Thomas Barwis (1621-48), who fought on the Parliamentary side at the siege of Carlisle. Anthony was succ. by his son Richard Barwis (or Barwise) (1601-48) who marr. Frances (d. 1670), dau. of Sir Edward Musgrave, of Hayton Castle. He was M.P. for Carlisle 1627, 1639 and 1640, High Sheriff of Cumberland 1635, Mayor of Carlisle 1648, and a keen supporter of Parliament. Traditionally called "Great Richard" Barwis because of his remarkable strength, he died *s.p.* 1648. He was succ. by Richard Barwis (1644-99), son of his cousin, Col Thomas Barwis, who marr. 1669 Frances (d. 1705), dau. of Richard Musgrave, of Hayton Castle. The last male of his line to own Islekirk, his heirs were two daus., Frances (d. 1706), marr. 1700 William Kirkby, of Ashlack (L); and Anne (d. 1708), marr. John Fetherstonhaugh, of Stanhope (D), who fell at the Battle of Blenheim (CW2 l, li, lv). *Arms.* Argent a chevron between three bears' heads* couped Sable muzzled Or (FVC; LMC; Brass in Westward church). MMD shews the muzzles as Gules; and Machell shows them as Gules studded Or (MMS vi 421). *Crest.* A hand issuing in bend cutting an ostrich feather with a scimitar in saltire (BGA).

BARWIS, of Langrigg.† A branch of Barwis, of Islekirk, settled at Dryholme in Holm Cultram. In a deed of 1572 Hugh Barwis, of Dryholme, is given as heir of Islekirk if other male heirs fail. John Barwis (d. 1705), son of Anthony Barwis, of Dryholme (d. 1652), who marr. 1633 Ellen (Helen), dau. of Robert Thomlinson, of the Gill, Dalston, sold the property to Thomas Ismay, 1670.‡ The family had a number of branches (some using the spelling Barwise), including one settled at New Cowper, Holm Cultram, in 1628, from which came Thomas Barwis (1686-1766), who marr. 1710 Elizabeth (d. 1780, aged 89), dau. of Cuthbert Osmotherley, *q.v.*, from whom Thomas in 1735 bought Langrigg Hall, which he largely rebuilt. He was succ. by his son John Barwis (1711-1800), who marr. 1737 Elizabeth (d. 1814, aged 101), dau. of William Brisco, of Langrigg and Wolsty Stangs, *q.v.* Their son the Rev. John Barwis, M.A. (Oxon), Rector of Niton, Isle of Wight, succ. and died *s.p.* 1828, aged 83. His brother, William Barwis, M.D. (Leyden) (1751-91), practised in Devizes. Their sister Elizabeth Barwis (d. 1821) marr. 1776 John Dand, whose dau. Sarah Barwise Dand (d. 1901) marr. 1843 William Banks, of Highmoor (d. 1878), *q.v.* Dr. William Barwis' son, John Barwis, J.P., M.A. (Oxon) (1775-1843), barrister at law, succ. as heir to his uncle, and marr. 1818 Frances (1794-1868), dau. of the Rev. John Gutch, Registrar of Oxford University and Rector of St. Clement's, Oxford. Their surviving sons and dau. sold the estate to Joseph Bowerbank, of Cockermouth, 1876. *Arms.* Argent a chevron wavy Azure between three bears' heads erased Sable. *Crest.* A bear passant Sable muzzled Or. *Motto.* Bear and forbear (Shield on porch of Langrigg Hall: Family silver).

* Transcribed in error as boars' heads in DSL.

† Contributed by the Rev. F. B. Swift.

‡ The old rhyme has it:

> Dryholm John was much to blame
> To let th' estate go out o' th' name
> More than three hundred years complete
> Dryholm had been a Barwis seat.

BASIRE. The Rev. Isaac Basire, D.D. (Cantab) (1607-76), Prebendary of Durham and Archdeacon of Northumberland, was father of Mary (d. 1679) who marr. 1671 the Rev. Jeremy Nelson, *q.v.* *Arms* (as impaled by Nelson on M.I. formerly in Carlisle cathedral). . . . three bars wavy . . . on a chief . . . an estoile . . . (Hugh Todd's MS. *History of the Diocese of Carlisle,* f. 99v). Sharpe's MS. *Durham Pedigrees* gives a mullet instead of an estoile and for *Crest.* A demi angel affronté hands clasped.

BASSENTHWAITE. Adam de Bastunthwait is said to have been son or grandson of Gospatric, son of Waldeve, Lord of Allerdale. His descendant Sir Alexander de Bassenthwaite (*fl. c.* 1290-1327) was High Sheriff of Cumberland 1307 and 1309 and Governor of Cockermouth Castle 1317. His son Adam d. 1358,* leaving three daus. and coheirs, Joan, Agnes and Elene, one of whom apparently marr. Nicholas de Irton (*fl.* 1340-69) *q.v.* *Arms* (as quartered by Irton). Or a crescent enclosing two human hearts fessways conjoined in fess Gules (Altar frontal dated 1768 from Irton Hall chapel in the possession of Mrs. H. S. Greg of Kendal). Canon S. Taylor recorded this quartering as: Or a crescent containing two annulets conjoined Gules (CW2 xli 117).

BASSET. Shield at Hutton-in-the-Forest; a Vane quartering. *Arms.* Or three piles Gules a canton Ermine. Another shield displays: Or three piles Gules on a bordure Sable eight bezants.

BATEMAN. John Bateman, "a skilful and experienced engineer and Hon. Member of the Literary and Philosophical Society of Newcastle," died at his house in Corkickle 6 March 1816 in his 67th year (*Cumberland Pacquet,* 12 March 1816). *Arms.* Or three crescents each enclosing an estoile Gules. *Crest.* A bird close in its beak a snake (M.I. seen by Field in Holy Trinity, Whitehaven).

BATESON. Impaled by Lutwidge on tablet in Irton church; Admiral Skeffington Lutwidge, *q.v.,* marr. Catherine (d. 1810, aged 48), dau. of Richard Hardy Bateson, of Londonderry. *Arms.* Argent three bats' wings [Sable] on a chief Gules a lion passant [Or].

HARFORD-BATTERSBY. The Rev. Thomas Dundas Harford-Battersby, M.A. (Oxon) (1822-83), 2nd son of Abraham Gray Harford-Battersby, of Clifton, Bristol, was Curate of St. John, Keswick 1849-51, and Vicar 1851-83, Rural Dean of Keswick 1858-83, and Hon. Canon of Carlisle 1866-83. In 1878 he was a co-founder of the Keswick Convention. *Arms.* Quarterly, 1 & 4, Sable two bendlets Argent between three cross crosslets fitché in pale of the last (Harford); 2 & 3, Azure a saltire paly Ermine and Or between two rams passant in pale of the second and as many cross crosslets fitché in fess Argent (Battersby). *Crests.* 1, In front of flames issuant therefrom a phoenix Proper two cross crosslets fitché in saltire Argent (Harford); 2, Issuant out of fire Proper a dragon's head per pale Or and Azure between a pair of wings Ermine (Battersby). *Motto.* Inter utrumque tene (BLG 13; FD7).

BATY, of Blackford. Field states that a family of Baty claimed to have been resident at Blackford for 700 years. Thomas Batey, yeoman, was living there in 1829, but we have not traced descendants. *Arms.* (seen by Field on bookplate). Sable a chevron between three bulls passant on a chief Or a demi woodman Proper between two cinquefoils Gules. He goes on to state

* Not *temp.* Ed. II as in FAC.

that these arms are ascribed by Burke to Battie of Yorkshire, but this is not the case in our edition of BGA (FAC).

BATY. Jane, wife of William Baty, of Huds, Arthuret, d. 1720, aged 48. *Arms.* . . . a fess chequy . . . between three lozenges . . . (Arthuret gravestone).

BATY, of Roweltown. John Baty, of Roweltown in Stapleton, d. 1764, aged 75. A later John Baty, of Roweltown (1718-99), was father of John Baty (d. 1812, aged 61). *Arms.* Chequy (Stapleton gravestone). The gravestone of John Baty (1718-99) shews: Chequy except extreme base in which are three lozenges the outer ones barwise. *Crest.* Two keys saltirewise the bits down and outwards (ABD). Field recorded the crest for Baty, of Stapleton, as: Two keys in saltire bits uppermost and outwards (FAC).

BATY, of Stonehouse. Richard Baty, of Stonehouse, Arthuret, d. 1739, aged 66. *Arms.* Chequy. Above the shield is a mascle between two keys in fess wards inward. Below the shield are two lozenges.

BATY, or BEATTIE. Gravestone at Holm Cultram, details illegible. *Arms.* Five rows of chequers, 3, 2, 3, 2 and 3, touching at corners in base a lozenge and flanking the chequers at top a decrescent and an increscent; on a chief (defined by a waved figure) two keys in saltire bits down and out between two objects resembling powder horns (ABD).

BAXTER. A gravestone in Arthuret churchyard commemorates William Baxter, of Cleugh Head (d. 1752). *Arms.* . . . on a pale . . . three roundles . . . Irving recorded this as: On a pale three roundles a bordure projecting from the latter on dexter and sinister eight billets (ABD). Field recorded a *Crest.* Two stags' horns (?) (FAC).

BAXTER – see FAGAN.

BAYNES, of Cockermouth. Richard Baynes (d. 1744), Clerk of the Peace for Westmorland 1706-29, settled in Cockermouth, probably as Lord Egremont's agent. He marr. Frances (d. 1762), dau. of Robert Langton, of Cockermouth. Their son Richard Baynes (d. 1779) was also a lawyer in Cockermouth, as was his brother Robert (1717-89) who marr. Elizabeth, dau. and coheir of Col. Samuel Gledhill by Isabella, dau. of Christopher Richmond and sister and coheir of Henry Richmond, *q.v.* His sons predeceased him and his heirs were his daus. Frances (1743-1813), marr. 1772 Richmond Blamire, *q.v.*; Susannah (1745-1808); Isabella (b. 1741), marr. the Rev. Robert Stubbs; Deborah Ann (d. 1792), marr. 1781 John Armstrong, of Lancaster, merchant; and Elizabeth (1750-80), marr. 1769 Thomas Benson, of Cockermouth, *q.v.* (CW2 xxxv 30-6). *Arms* (as quartered by Benson). . . . two shin bones in saltire . . . (*Ex inf.* Canon R. A. B. Ewbank). *Crest.* An arm couped and vested Azure holding in the hand Proper a jawbone Argent (FAC).

BEATY, of Soultermoor. Soultermoor in Stapleton was bought by James Baity 1791. William Beaty, of Soultermoor, died 1849, aged 78. His dau. Elizabeth (1808-35) marr. John Denis de Vitré, *q.v.* *Arms.* . . . a pale . . . surmounted of a sword fesswise point to the sinister . . . between two keys also fesswise . . . the wards to the sinister that in chief upwards and that in base downwards in chief two mascles and another in base . . . . *Crest.* A star issuing from a crescent. *Motto.* Lumen celeste sequamur (Stapleton tombestone).

BEAUCHAMP, Earl of Warwick. A series of shields from Thornbury Castle,

Glos., now in Greystoke Castle, illustrating the medieval ancestry of the Howards, includes one for Beauchamp; Eleanor (1407-67), dau. of Richard de Beauchamp, Earl of Warwick (1382-1439), by his 1st wife Elizabeth, dau. and heir of Thomas, Lord Berkeley, marr. (2) *c.* 1436 Edmund Beaufort, Earl and Duke of Somerset, Marquess of Dorset, *q.v. Arms.* Gules a fess between six cross crosslets Or. These arms are also on the tomb of Sir John Hudleston, *q.v.*, in Millom church and on the ceiling of Carlisle Cathedral.*

BEAUCHAMP, of Little Croglin. The Beauchamps held Little Croglin till the reign of Henry VII (NB ii 426). *Arms.* Gregory King's pedigree of the Bird family shows Henry Bird, who heads it, as marrying Joan, dau. and coheir of Thomas Beauchamp, of Little Croglin, and gives: Argent on a bend Sable three plates. Elizabeth, 2nd dau. and coheir of Thomas Beauchamp, marr. 1488-89 John Hutton, of Penrith, *q.v.*, whose descendants quartered her arms as: Argent on a bend Gules three bezants. William Beauchamp, of Cumberland, *temp.* Edward III, bore: Argent on a bend Gules three plates (FFC).

BEAUCLERK. Impaled by Vane on shield at Hutton-in-the-Forest, and on tablet in Hutton-in-the-Forest church; Sir Francis Fletcher-Vane, 3rd Bart., *q.v.*, marr. 1823 Diana Olivia (d. 1875), 3rd dau. of Charles George Beauclerk, of St. Leonard's Lodge, Horsham. *Arms.* Quarterly, 1 & 4, France and England quarterly; 2, Scotland; 3, Ireland; over all a sinister baton Gules charged with three roses Argent seeded and barbed Proper.

BEAUFORT, Earl and Duke of Somerset, Marquess of Dorset. A series of shields from Thornbury Castle, Glos., now in Greystoke Castle, illustrating the medieval ancestry of the Howards, includes one for Beaufort. Sir John Beaufort, K.G., Earl and Marquess of Somerset, Marquess of Dorset (*c.* 1371-1410), eldest of the three illegitimate sons of John of Gaunt, Duke of Lancaster, marr. 1397 Margaret (d. 1439), dau. of Thomas de Holand, Earl of Kent, *q.v.*, and sister and coheir of Edmund, Earl of Kent. Their younger son, Edmund Beaufort, Earl and Duke of Somerset, Marquess of Dorset (*c.* 1406-55), marr. *c.* 1436 Eleanor (1407-67), widow of Thomas, Lord Ros, and 2nd dau. of Richard Beauchamp, Earl of Warwick, *q.v.* Their dau. Margaret marr. Humphrey, earl of Stafford, *q.v. Arms.* Quarterly, 1 & 4, Azure three fleurs-de-lys Or, 2 & 3, Gules three lions passant guardant in pale Or, all within a bordure company Azure and Argent.

BEAUMONT. The Hon. Ela Hilda Aline Beaumont, dau. of the 2nd Viscount Allendale, marr. 1945 Charles James Ruthven Howard, Viscount Morpeth, who became 12th Earl of Carlisle 1963. *Arms.* Gules a lion rampant Or armed and langued Azure between eight crescents in orle of the second.

BEDINGFELD. Col Francis Philip Bedingfeld (1763-1841), of a well known Norfolk family, was of Moorhouse Hall, near Carlisle, in 1813, and was later tenant of Kirklinton Hall, which he left in 1821 after the death there, at the age of 33, of his dau. Catherine Elizabeth. He was later of Thornton

* The present writers have experienced just as much difficulty in recording the shields on the ceiling of Carlisle Cathedral, owing to their inaccessibility and the poor light, as did Field in 1933 (CW2 xxxiv 22-29). In a number of cases we have differed from his reading of the arms; and in general we have included only those arms which we have been able to identify with a reasonable degree of certainty.

Lodge (Y). *Arms.* Ermine an eagle displayed Gules. *Crest.* An eagle displayed Or. *Motto.* Aquila non capit muscas (BLG17).

BEK. Anthony Bek (d. 1311), Bishop of Durham, 1284-1311, 3rd son of Walter, Lord of Eresby, Lincs., was lord of the Honour of Penrith. *Arms.* Gules a cross moline Ermine (BBE; FFC). His paternal arms, Gules a cross moline Argent, are on shields on the ceiling of Carlisle Cathedral. A shield at Hutton-in-the-Forest displays for Beke (a Vane quartering): Gules a cross Ermine.

BELGIUM, Kingdom of. Amongst the shields in the east window of Upperby church commemorating the Allies of World War I, is one for the Kingdom of Belgium. *Arms.* Sable a lion rampant Or.

BELL. Richard Bell, B.D. (d. 1496), Prior of Durham 1464-78, was Bishop of Carlisle 1478-96. *Arms.* BBE gives: Gules on a chief Argent three bells Sable; but there seems little authority for this. *Rebus.* A bell pendent from a capital R (BBE, and at Rose Castle and Crosby-on-Eden church).

BELL. John Bell, of Banks, Lanercost, died 1855, aged 77. *Arms.* Three bells in fess abased. Crest. A bell mouth up (ABD).

BELL. George Bell, of Bankshead, Nether Denton, died 1755. *Arms.* Three bells (Nether Denton churchyard).

BELL, of Beanlands. George Bell, of Brakenside and the Nook, Irthington (1762-1832), descended from the Bells of Low Lonning, Farlam, *q.v.,* was father of John Bell (1792-1861) who marr. Ann (1794-1876), dau. and heir of James Boustead, of Beanlands, Irthington (d. 1827), *q.v.,* and acquired that estate. His youngest dau. and coheir Barbara (1835-95) marr. 1864 James Irving, *q.v. Arms.* Azure three bells in fess Argent (Escutcheon of pretence in Irving window in Bowness-on-Solway church).

BELL, of Bellbridge. George Bell, of Fisher Street, Carlisle (*c.* 1648-1717), marr. *c.* 1680 Elizabeth (d. 1728), widow of Arthur Forster, of Kingfield, *q.v.,* and in 1685 bought Bellbridge from Mrs Mabell Younghusband. The estate was inherited by his only child Jane (d. 1744) who marr. Capt Thomas Morris (1672-1721), *q.v.* George Bell and his brothers, the Rev. Thomas Bell, M.A., and the Rev. David Bell, M.A. (Edin), were friends of Bishop Nicolson. The former was Curate of Lanercost 1679-81 and Vicar of Askham 1680-90, when he was deprived for not taking the oaths to King William and Queen Mary. The latter, who was 70 in 1728, succ. his brother at Askham, and was there until 1695, when he became Rector of Kirklinton, where he was until 1706, when he became Vicar of Aspatria. He was Rector of Great Orton 1709 until his death in 1730. *Arms.* . . . a fess Ermine between three bells . . . . *Crest.* A bird (Achievement over front door of Bellbridge).*

BELL. George Bell, of Denton Mill,† Nether Denton, died 1753. Another member of the family, William Bell, of Denton Mill (d. 1752), was late of His Majesty's Customs. *Arms.* Three bells in fess abased. *Crest.* A bell mouth up (ABD).

BELL, of Gunshole.‡ Christopher Bell, of Gunshole, yeoman (*fl.* 1663-82), and John his son conveyed Gunshole to John Carrick 1670. Mary, wife of

* The arms are on a silver tumbler, now in the Carlisle Museum, which the above George Bell gave to the Butchers' Guild, 1703.

† Field wrongly gives Denton Hall (FAC).

‡ Now Guns Hall, between Lanercost and Upper Denton.

William Bell, of Gunshole, was bur. at Lanercost 1742. Janet Bell, of the same place, was bur. there 1752. *Arms.* Three bells (Over Denton tombstone).

BELL, of Low Lonning. Joseph Bell, of Low Lonning, Farlam, formerly Officer of Excise at Hexham (d. 1766), was bur. at Farlam. *Arms.* Gules a fess Ermine between three bells Argent. *Crest.* A bird rising (ABD). Field recorded: *Arms.* Gules a chevron Ermine between three bells Argent. *Crest.* A falcon rising (FAC). A carved stone shield at Maryholme, Farlam, removed there from Low Lonning after a fire *c.* 1950 displays . . . three bells in fess abased . . . (*Inf.* Miss H. M. Bell, of Maryholme).

BELL, of Newtown, Rockcliffe. A gravestone in Arthuret churchyard commemorates John, son of Richard and Margaret Bell, of Newtown of Rockcliffe (d. 1853, aged 31); the said Margaret (d. 1855, aged 61); and the said Richard (d. 1865, aged 75). *Arms.* . . . a fess chequy . . . .

BELL. James, of Peth, Arthuret, 1723. *Arms.* Three bells in chief pendent (ABD).

BELL, Walter, of Randalinton, Arthuret, 1728. *Arms.* Three bells in fess enhanced (ABD).

BELL. Burke gives *Arms* for two Cumberland families of Bell, but gives no place of residence: 1. Sable a chevron between three bells Argent. 2. Gules on a chief Argent three bells Sable (BGA).

BELL. Jane (d. 1825, aged 82), dau. of . . . Bell and sister of George Bell, marr. 1773 Thomas Lowry, of Blackhall, Carlisle (d. 1779), *q.v.** She marr. (2) 1782 John Milbourne, of Dentonholme, Carlisle (1745-91).† *Arms* (as impaled by Lowry on tablet in St. Cuthbert's church, Carlisle). . . . a chevron reversed . . . between one bell in chief and two in base . . . .

BELL, of Wallholm. Frances Bell, wife of William Bell, of Wallholm, died 1751 and was buried at Lanercost. *Arms.* . . . three bells . . . . *Crest.* A bell mouth up (Tombstone, Lanercost churchyard).

BELL. The Rev. Henry Bell, L.Th. (Dunelm) (1838-1919), 5th son of the Rev. John Bell, Vicar of Rothwell (Y), descended from the Bells of Woolsington (N), was Vicar of Muncaster 1873-1907, Rural Dean of Gosforth 1878, Hon. Canon of Carlisle 1883, and Chaplain to Lord Muncaster. *Arms.* Sable a fess Ermine between three bells Argent. *Crest.* A hawk close Proper belled Or (BLG4; BGA).

BELL. A headstone in Caldbeck churchyard erected by their granddaughter Mary Hughes 1876, to Francis Bell, of Middleby, Scotland (d. at Upton House, Caldbeck, 1839, aged 92) and his wife Mary Head (d. at the High Height 1782, aged 29), bears the following *Arms.* . . . three bells . . . .

BELL – see SPENCER-BELL.

BELL. Thomas Bell, of Penrith, marr. before 1687 Frances . . . (d. 1737), who sealed her will with the following *Arms.* . . . three birds . . . . *Crest.* An axe erect head to the sinister.

BELLEW. A shield at Hutton John. A Hudleston quartering, brought in by Stapleton, *q.v.*; Sir Miles Stapleton (killed at Bannockburn 1314) marr.

* *The Newcastle Courant* of 3 July 1773 calls her "a handsome and accomplished girl of 25." The bridegroom is described as "a gay batchelor of 60 and a fortune of £1000 per ann."

† He remembered her in his will in the following uncomplimentary terms: "And I give to my wife only the sum of five pounds she having robbed my Chests, secreted writings, denyed her Marriage with me and swore the peace against and otherwise illtreated me."

Sibell, dau. and coheir of John de Bellew, or Bella Aqua, by Laderina, dau. of Peter de Brus, of Skelton (Y) (d. *c.* 1243), and sister and coheir of Peter de Brus (d. *s.p.* 1272). *Arms.* Sable a fret Or.

BELLINGHAM. Shield at Hutton John, a Hutton quartering; Cuthbert Hutton, of Hutton John (d. 1553), *q.v.*, marr. Elizabeth, dau. and coheir of Sir Robert Bellingham, of Burneside (W) (d. 1541). *Arms.* Argent a bugle horn Sable garnished Or stringed Gules.

BELLINGHAM. Impaled by Fetherstonhaugh on hall ceiling at Kirkoswald College; Timothy Fetherstonhaugh (d. 1728) marr. Bridget (d. 1736), dau. of James Bellingham, of Levens. *Arms.* Argent three bugle horns Sable stringed and garnished Or.

BENDLE, John, of Walton, d. 1797, aged 39. *Arms.* Three bendlets wavy Ermine on a quarter an estoile (ABD).

BENN, of Hensingham. The Rev. Caesar Caine gives, in CWC 323-4, a spurious descent of this family from Henry Benn, of Saffron Walden, *temp.* Edward IV. Mr Paul Wilson, of Lorton, has shown that the family descends from Anthony Benn who marr. at St. Bees 1598 Bridget, dau. of Henry Bellingham. Their descendant John Benn, of Hensingham House (1689-1761), High Sheriff of Cumberland 1733, who marr. (1) 1721 Bridget Patrickson (d. 1738), and (2) 1740 Margaret Benn (d. 1758), was father of Anthony Benn, J.P. (1743-99), High Sheriff of Cumberland 1775, and the builder of Hensingham church 1791. He marr. (1) 1764 Margaret (1744-79), dau. and heir of Lowther Spedding, of Whitehaven, and (2) 1781 Mary (1752-1818), eldest dau. and coheir of Robert Watters, of Whitehaven, and widow of Henry Littledale. His eldest son was the Rev. John Benn, M.A. (Oxon) (1765-1857), and his youngest son Capt Thomas Benn, R.N., of Greenbank, St. Bees (1790-1869), was father of, *int. al.*, Isabella, who marr. 1859 the Rev. James Arlosh, *q.v. Arms.* Or a fess dancetté Gules between three dragons' heads erased Proper. *Crest.* A dragon's head erased Proper (Commander Falcon-Steward's MS family History). Field blazons the arms on the gate-pillars at Woodside, Wreay, as: Argent a fess dancetté Gules between three dragons' heads erased Vert (FAC); in fact, the shield is untinctured.

BENN, *post* BENN-WALSH, Baron Ormathwaite. William Benn, of Moor Row, Egremont, marr. 1751 Mary, dau. of Timothy Nicholson, of Whitehaven, who marr. 1731 Elizabeth, sister of Dr. William Brownrigg, *q.v.* Their son John (1759-1825), having made a fortune in India, marr. 1787 Margaret (d. 1836), dau. of Joseph Fowke by Elizabeth, dau. of Joseph Walsh, Governor of Fort St. George, Madras. He assumed the additional surname and arms of Walsh 1795, and was created Baronet 1804. In 1800 he succ. to the Ormathwaite estate on the death *s.p.* of Dr. Brownrigg. His son and heir Sir John Benn-Walsh, 2nd Bart., M.P. (1798-1881), Lord Lieutenant of Radnorshire 1842-75, was cr. 1868 Baron Ormathwaite, of Ormathwaite. The present holder of the peerage and baronetcy is Sir John Arthur Charles Walsh, 6th Baron and 7th Bart. *Arms.* Argent a fess Sable cotised wavy Gules between six martlets of the second. *Crest.* A griffin's head erased per fess wavy Argent and Ermine beak and ears Or. *Supporters.* On either side a griffin Ermine gorged with a collar Vair and pendent therefrom an escutcheon Sable charged with a martlet Argent. *Motto.* Veritas et virtus vincunt (BP105; FD7).

BENSON of Cockermouth. John Benson, of Egremont, brewer (1717-89), marr. Margaret, dau. and coheir of the Rev. Christopher Denton, *q.v.*, and had a son Thomas Benson (1742-1807), a well known Cockermouth attorney, who was Lord Egremont's steward. He marr. 1769 Elizabeth (1750-80), dau. and in her issue coheir of Robert Baynes, *q.v.*, and had issue, *int. al.*, a son, the Rev. John Benson, M.A. (Cantab) (1773-1831), of St. Helen's, Cockermouth, Master of the Cockermouth Harriers, whose son Robert (1807-58) was a Cockermouth solicitor, and had daus. Catherine, marr. the Rev. Herbert Boyne Lavallin Puxley, *q.v.*, and Julia Helen, marr. the Rev. John Ewbank, *q.v.* (*Ex inf.* Canon R. A. B. Ewbank; MSG). It seems unlikely that the family is extinct in the male line, for Robert's brothers John Benson, agent to the Duke of Bedford at Tavistock, and the Rev. Christopher Benson, M.A. (Oxon) (1809-88), who was Curate of Plumbland 1832 and Vicar of Brampton 1841-73, both had sons. *Arms.* . . . on a chevron . . . between three goats passant . . . as many increscents . . . (*Ex inf.* Canon R. A. B. Ewbank).

BENSON, of Wreay Hall. Thomas Benson, of Castle Street, Carlisle (d. 1777), the Duke of Portland's chief agent in Cumberland, owned Wreay Hall, near Carlisle, and the manor of Hartrigg, Sebergham. He marr. 1752 Jane (1734-60), younger dau. of John Fletcher, of Clea Hall, *q.v.*, and had a son Thomas Benson, of Wreay Hall (1758-1825), High Sheriff of Cumberland 1814, who d. unmarr., his surviving sister Margaret, who marr. 1789 Robert Harrington, M.D., of Carlisle (1751-1837), being his heir. He left Wreay Hall to his cousin John Philip Fletcher, *q.v. Crest.* A lion's head erased (FAC).

BENTINCK (later CAVENDISH-BENTINCK), Duke of Portland. The Honour of Penrith* was given in 1694 by William III to his Dutch favourite, Hans William Bentinck, 1st Earl of Portland (1649-1709). The Honour was sold by his descendant William Henry Cavendish-Bentinck, 3rd Duke of Portland (1738-1809), to his brother-in-law, the 5th Duke of Devonshire, *q.v.* The Duke's younger brother, Lord Edward Bentinck (1744-1819), was M.P. for Carlisle 1768-74 (CWE). *Arms.* Quarterly, 1 & 4, Azure a cross moline Argent (Bentinck); 2 & 3, Sable three stags' heads cabossed Argent attired Or a crescent for difference (Cavendish). *Crests.* 1, Out of a ducal coronet Proper two arms counter-embowed vested Gules on the hands gloves Or each holding an ostrich feather Argent (Bentinck); 2, A snake nowed Proper (Cavendish). *Supporters.* Two lions double queued the dexter Or the sinister Sable. *Mottoes.* Craignez honte (BP105); Quo fata vocant (Buck's View of Penrith Castle, 1739).

BENY. Said in BGA to be of Cumberland; perhaps an error for DeAkeny. *Arms.* Azure a cross between four lions rampant Or.

BESONN. Sir Thomas de Besonn, of Cumberland, appears in the Parliamentary Roll of Edward II, and Todd records that he saw his arms in Carlisle Cathedral. *Arms.* Lozengy Argent and Sable (FFC; Todd's MS, St. Edmund Hall, Oxford, 7/1).

BEST. John Best, D.D. (Oxon) (d. 1570), Bishop of Carlisle 1561-70, received two grants of Arms. (1) *Arms* (granted 1560). Argent on a chevron Sable between in chief two doves Proper beaked and membered Gules and

* It was later claimed that the grant – though it did not specify them – included the Forest of Inglewood and the socage manor of Carlisle. The claim was upheld in 1776.

in base a book of the second garnished Or three pheons of the field. (2) *Arms* (granted 1561). Or on a chevron Sable between three books Gules as many pheons* on a chief of the third a St. Esprit issuing from a cloud* (GOA). BBE records these as: (1) Argent on a chevron Gules three pheons of the field in chief two birds russet beaks and legs Gules in base a book Gules clasped Or. (2) Or a chevron between three books Gules clasped Or on a chief Gules a holy dove descending radiated Or.

BETHOM. The Bethom family were lords of the manor of Whicham. Ralph de Bethom witnessed a charter before 1201, and a later Sir Ralph de Bethom flourished in the 1260's and 1270's. Before 1266 the King granted him the lands of John de Haile in Haile. In 1278 Sir Richard de Bethom granted estovers in Whicham to the rector (St. Bees Reg.). *Arms.* Uncertain; probably either, Argent a chief indented Azure; or else, Or three fleurs-de-lys Azure†, as quartered by Dykes (AWL). MMD gives the former.

BEWLEY, of Hesket and Woodhall. Sir Edmund Bewley's *The Bewleys of Cumberland* (Dublin, 1902) shows that the Bewleys, of Thistlethwaite, Castle Sowerby, descend from Thomas de Beaulieu, living 1332-40. Richard Bewley was M.P. for Carlisle 1459; his son William (d. *c.* 1529-32) was of Hesket Hall, and is commemorated by a brass in Greystoke Church. His descendant Thomas (d. 1632) sold the manor of Hesket 1630 to William Lawson, husband of his aunt Judith Bewley. Another branch of the family was settled at Woodhall, Caldbeck, the pedigree being headed by Matthew Bewley, living 1560. His descendant Thomas (1692-1748) was succ. at Woodhall by his son Thomas (1713-93) whose son George (1749-1828) was headmaster of the Friends' School, Stramongate, Kendal, 1772-85, and later an unsuccessful manufacturer in Whitehaven. His son Thomas (1778-1866), of Hesket and afterwards of La Praria, Canada, and Philadelphia, sold Woodhall 1833 to John Jennings, and d. in Penrith, leaving daughters. His brother George Bewley, of Hesket (1782-1813), was lost on the fells, leaving a son George, of Caldbeck (1809-52), who had sons Thomas (b. 1836) who went to Australia, and George, of Blaydon. The family is now represented in Cumberland by the Rev. Guy Patrick Bewley, R.N. (Rtd.), of Town Head, Dean, son of Edward Neville Bewley, solicitor (b. 1885, killed in action 1917), and great-grandson of John Bewley, of Liverpool and of Ash House, Cumberland (1816-96). *Arms.* The family originally bore: Argent a chevron between three choughs' or daws' heads erased Sable beaked Gules (MMD; DAC). This, slightly differenced, is now blazoned: Argent a chevron Sable between three Cornish choughs' heads erased Proper in chief an ermine spot. *Crest.* An ibex's head Or issuant from the centre of a rose Gules stalked and leaved Proper. *Motto.* Virtutis gloria merces (FD7).

BEWLEY, of Causa Grange. Edward Bewley, of Causa Grange, Westward (b. 1830), was father of John Pearson Bewley (b. 1863), Joseph Bewley (b. 1866), and Edward Bewley (b. 1876), Lieutenant, 5th Border Regt. *Arms.* Argent a chevron Sable between in chief two Cornish choughs' heads erased Proper and in base a rose Gules barbed Vert seeded Or. *Crest.* An ibex's head erased Argent attired Or and gorged with a chaplet of roses Gules. *Motto.* Virtutis gloria merces (FD7).

* No tinctures given.

† Not Sable, as stated by Field in FAC.

BIGEMS, BIGHOLMS of Longtown. A gravestone in Arthuret churchyard commemorates James Bigems, of Longtown (d. 1799, aged 67). *Arms.* On a fess between three lozenges the initials IB; impaling, A saltire engrailed between in chief a mullet in base a decrescent and in fess the initials IL.* Mary, dau. of James Bigholms, was bap. at Arthuret 13 December 1696.

BIRD, of Penrith and of Brougham. In 1681 Gregory King, Rouge Dragon, prepared a pedigree of eighteen generations of the Bird family of Brougham (W), which Dugdale certified. This shows that John Bird, of Penrith, marr. Jane, dau. and coheir of . . . Ryddings, of Brougham, and had issue, Henry (d. before 1463), who marr. Joan, dau. of John Teasdale, of Walton (N), by Joan, dau. and heir of Richard Tyndale, and so acquired a third of the manor of Brougham, which came to their descendant, James Bird, attorney and steward to Lord Tufton. He was 31 in 1668, and in 1676 acquired the other two thirds of the manor. He built Brougham Hall, which was known as Bird's Nest. By will (pr. 1714) he left a life interest in the Brougham estate to his dau. Dorothy, wife of Thomas Carleton, of Appleby, with remainder to the grandchildren of his son, John Bird. Carleton outlived the grandchildren and sold the estate to John Brougham (CW2 viii 281, 315; NB i 393-5). *Arms.* Or on a chevron engrailed Gules between three lions rampant Sable as many fleurs-de-lys of the field. *Crest.* A demi lion Pean (FCW). Lysons and Papworth tincture the field Argent but give the fleurs-de-lys as Or (LMC; OBA).

BIRKBY, of Birkby. This family, of Birkby in Crosscanonby, failed in the male line with Robert Birkby, whose dau. and heir Margery marr. Richard Orfeur who was living *c.* 1386-1405. *Arms.* Gules on a bend Argent three crosses pattée of the field (FVC).

BIRKETT, of Portinscale. John Birkett, of Portinscale (d. 1805, aged 79), was father of the Rev. Joseph Birkett, B.A. (Cantab) (1755-1833), Vicar of Stranton (D) 1796-1833, and of Thomas Birkett, of Pow House, Portinscale (1758-1831). Joseph's younger son, John Birkett, of Broomhill, brewer (d. 1884, aged 80), was father of the Rev. Thomas Birkett, M.A. (Cantab) (1835-91), Curate of Yealand Conyers (L) 1858-68. His son, the Rev. Arthur Ismay Birkett, M.A. (Cantab.) (1863-1916), was a missionary at Lusadia, where he was accidentally drowned. His brother John Stanwell Birkett, M.A. (Cantab) (1866-1916), was a member of the legal firm of Withers, Benson, Birkett and Davies, of Arundel Street, Strand, London. *Arms.* Azure a chevron between three garbs . . . .† *Crest.* A goat's head erased (Monument in Crosthwaite churchyard).

BIRLEY. The first ancestor of this family mentioned in FLP is John Birley, of Skippool, Poulton-le-Fylde (L), will dated 1732. His great-grandson Henry Birley, of Whitehaven (1771-1830), founded the Cleator Linen Thread Mills 1800, and bought The Flosh, which he considerably improved. His elder brother John (1769-1859) was of Woodend, Egremont, and his younger brother James (1784-1857) was of Low Mill, Egremont. He marr. Jane (d. 1833, aged 47), dau. of the Rev. Abraham Brown, of Egremont, one of the most celebrated wrestlers in the North of England, and widow of

* The impaled coat is for A. Little.

† Field (FAC) states that the chevron and garbs are tinctured Or, but they are not hatched and are therefore probably Argent. Papworth (OBA) gives for Berkhead, of Crestwhite, clearly a corruption of Birkett, of Crosthwaite: Sable a chevron Argent between three garbs Or.

John Richardson, of Carleton Lodge, Beckermet (d. 1811). *Arms.* Sable on a fess engrailed between three boars' heads couped Argent a mascle between two cross crosslets of the field. *Crest.* A demi boar Sable collared Argent chain reflexed over the back Or supporting a branch of burdock Proper and charged on the shoulder with a millrind Argent. *Motto.* Omni liber metu (BLG18).

BLACKBURN. John Blackburn, of Wigton (d. 1768, aged 67), marr. Susan (d. 1762, agd 65), dau. of Michael Richardson, of Wigton, and had a son John Blackburn (b. 1732), a merchant in London, who in 1784 obtained a grant of *Arms.* Azure a fess wavy Erminois between two etoiles in chief Argent and a mullet in base Or. *Crest.* A trident Sable and a cornucopia in saltire Proper (CA xv/361). *Motto.* Fide sed cui vide (Bookplate).

BLACKETT. Col Edward Umfreville Blackett, R.A., of Wylam (N) (1853-1920), lived for some years in Cumberland, first at Milton House, Brampton, and then at The Craggs, Broughton. His only son Christopher John Walter Blackett (1900-71) sold Wylam Hall 1964, and moved to a small cottage in the village. He left £500 to Great Broughton Church (*Daily Telegraph,* 4 March 1972). *Arms.* Argent on a chevron between three mullets pierced Sable three escallops of the field. *Motto.* Nous travaillerons dans l'esperance (BLG18).

BLACKETT-ORD – see ORD.

BLAICKLOCK. Robert Blaicklock, of Whitehaven, merchant (d. 1719), High Sheriff of Cumberland 1710, lent money to John Senhouse, of Seascale Hall, and the estates passed into his possession 1707. His daus. and coheirs were Mary (b. 1695, died unmarr., and admon. granted to her sister 1726), and Frances (1700-62), marr. 1726 Augustine Earle, *q.v. Arms* (as impaled by Earle). Argent on a fess Azure between three mullets Sable as many bezants (Plate facing p. 246 of vol. vi of Francis Blomefield's *History of Norfolk*).

BLAKENEY. Capt John Blakeney (d. 1749, aged 68), Royal Irish Regt., was son of John Blakeney, of Castle Blakeney, Co. Galway, whose ancestors came from Blakeney, Norfolk. He fought in Marlborough's campaigns and settled at Distington, where he was succ. by his nephew George Augustus Blakeney (1717-79) who was in Major-General Blakeney's Regiment (27th Foot). His son Robert Blakeney, D.L., J.P. (1758-1822)*, was Collector of Customs at Whitehaven and d. *s.p.,* the family becoming extinct locally (JPP i 24-32). *Arms.* Sable a chevron Ermine between three leopards' faces Or. *Crest.* Out of a ducal coronet an arm erect couped at the elbow vested Gules cuffed Argent in the hand a sword Proper hilt and pommel Or. *Motto.* Auxilium meum ab alto (BLG4; M.I., Distington church).

BLAMIRE, of Thackwood and The Oaks. Robert de Blamyr is mentioned *temp.* Edward I. His descendants flourished in Dalston parish, where they lived at the Hollinbush – which they later re-named The Oaks – Cardew Hall and Thackwood Nook. John Blamire, of The Oaks, was father of William, of Cardew Hall (1703-58), who marr. 1736 Isabel (1709-54), dau.

* He owned Fox How and Fox Ghyll, Ambleside. When the Lysons brothers were collecting data for their work on Cumberland they addressed a letter to "the Rev. Robert Blakeney." The Rev. Henry Lowther, Rector of Distington, wrote an icy letter to the brothers on 16 January 1815, observing "he has nothing whatever to do with clerical matters; being an inferior officer in the Customs at Whitehaven and clerk to the Trustees." Add. MSS. 9422.

and heir of George Simpson, of Thackwood (d. 1710), by his wife Sarah, sister and coheir of Henry Richmond, *q.v.* Their children were William (see below), Richmond (1742-97), and Susanna (1747-94), the poetess. William's grandson William Blamire, J.P., of Thackwood Nook and The Oaks (1790-1862), was High Sheriff of Cumberland 1828, M.P. for Cumberland 1831, and M.P. for East Cumberland 1832-36, when he became Chief Tithe Commissioner. He, the last male of this branch of the family, d. *s.p.* Richmond Blamire's dau. Catherine d. in Rome 1898, aged over 80. The Cumdivock branch of the family was represented in 1937 by William Blamire, of Curthwaite Mill. (DNB). *Arms.* Argent a lion rampant within an orle gules. *Crest.* A wolf sejant Proper chained Or. *Motto.* Faire sans dire (BLG4). Field states that William Blamire's seal as High Sheriff, 1828, shows the *Crest* as: A lion rampant (FAC).

BLEAMIRE, of Penrith. William Bleamire, of Grays Inn, son of Thomas Bleamire, of Penrith, only son and heir of John Bleamire, of Clifton (W), descended from a family resident for several generations at Clifton, obtained a grant of arms, 1775, for himself and his descendants and the descendants of his father. *Arms.* Argent within an orle a lion rampant gules on a canton Azure a mullet of six points pierced Or. *Crest.* A tyger sejant gutté de sang gorged with a ducal coronet and chained Or (CA xiii/86). Burke's version of this is: *Arms.* Argent a lion rampant within an orle (another, a bordure) Gules. *Crest.* A tiger sejant Gules collared and chained Or (BGA).

BLENCOWE, of Blencowe. The Blencowes for long owned Blencowe. Thomas and Simon Blencowe were jurors 1340, and Adam Blencowe (*fl.* 1344-70) received a grant of arms from his overlord 1356 (see below). His son Thomas (d. between 1406 and 1420) marr. before 1368 Elizabeth or Alice (aged 24 in 1370), dau. of Nicholas de Veteripont and sister and coheir of Robert de Veteripont, *q.v.* Sir Henry Blencowe (1562-1635)* was High Sheriff of Cumberland 1608 and 1625 and was knighted 1617. He was found dead on Newbiggin Moor, his eldest son John, a barrister (b. 1592), having d. *v.p.*, leaving two daus. and coheirs Elizabeth (b. 1623), marr. Henry Thompson, and Anne, marr. George Barwick, of Carlisle. Their uncle Christopher (1600-69) succ. and was succ. by his son Christopher (1643-78), who marr. Mary, eldest dau. and coheir of William Layton, of Dalemain, *q.v.* Their son Henry (1676-1721) was Sheriff of Cumberland 1716, and marr. (1) 1696† Dorothy (1675-1707), dau. and coheir of George Sisson, *q.v.*, and (2) 1710 Elizabeth (d. 1719), dau. of William Todd. Their son Henry (1712-65) marr. Mary, dau. and heir of Alexander Prescott of Thoby Priory, Essex. Their grandson Henry Prescott Blencowe, of Thoby Priory (d. 1847), sold Blencowe Hall to the Duke of Norfolk 1802. His son Henry Prescott Blencowe, M.A. (Cantab) (1799-1860), was succ. at Thoby by his nephew Henry Prescott George Blencowe, J.P. (1858-1921). *Arms.* The first arms recorded for the family *temp.* Edward III were: Gules a quarter Argent (FFC). This simple coat was later borne by the family when of Thoby Priory (BLG12), and is over the west door at Blencowe Hall. In 1356 William, Baron of Greystoke, granted the following to Adam de Blencowe for his services: "Sable a bend closselted (or barred) Argent and

* For Sir Henry's uncle, Anthony Blencowe (d. 1618), Provost of Oriel College, Oxford, see CW2 lx 55-65.

† The sons of this marriage died *s.p.*

Azure, with three chaplets Gules; and with a Crest closselted Argent and Azure, of my arms" (NB ii 376). Lysons, following Harl. MS. 1536, give this as: Azure on a bend Argent three chaplets Gules (LMC). At the Visitation of 1665, William Musgrave certified on behalf of Christopher Blencowe: Quarterly, 1 & 4, Gules a canton Argent; 2 & 3, Azure on a bend Or three chaplets Gules.* *Crest.* A winged heart transfixed by a sword erect point downwards (FCW). This was later blazoned: A sword in pale Argent hilt in chief Or enfiladed with a human heart Gules all between two wings expanded Argent (BLG12). *Mottoes.* Quorsum viveri mori, mori vitae (Carving at Blencowe Hall); Dulce pro patria mori (WAF); Si virtus honos (*Ex inf.* Mrs. Houlson).

BLENKINSOP, of Corby. Thomas Blenkinsop, of Helbeck (w) (d. 1501/2), marr. *c.* 1470 Margaret, dau. and coheir of Sir Richard Salkeld, *q.v.* of Corby, and so acquired a part of that estate, which their descendant Henry Blenkinsop (d. 1613) and Elizabeth his wife sold 1605 to Lord William Howard. *Arms.* Argent a fess between three garbs Sable banded Argent (MMS). NB i 586 adds a crescent for difference. Thomas de Blenkinsop, of Helbeck, *temp.* Edward III, however, bore: Gules six annulets, three, two and one Or a bordure engrailed Argent (FFC; NB i 582).

BLENNERHASSET. Alan de Blennerhasset was pardoned 1270 for murder. Next year John son of John le Fevre was pardoned for killing Henry son of Waldeve de Blennerhasset in self defence. By the time of Alan de Blennerhasset (*fl.* 1362-1400) the family had moved from the place which gave them their surname, and settled in Carlisle, where Alan Blennerhasset was Mayor 1388, and was appointed Controller of Customs 1392. His son John (living 1400) was M.P. for Carlisle 1381 and 1384, and was succ. by his son Ralph, M.P. for Carlisle 1413, who marr. Joan, dau. and coheir of Clement de Skelton, and thus acquired a third of the manor of Great Orton. Their son John (1408-72) was Mayor of Carlisle 1430, and M.P. 1441-2. His grandson Edward (d. 1532) was father of John (b. *c.* 1516, living 1550), who marr. Joan, dau. and coheir of James Martindale. In 1546 he bought Thomas Dalston's Flimby estate. His grandson Thomas Blennerhasset, of Flimby, sold his share of Great Orton 1580. He was M.P. for Carlisle 1586, and perhaps five times Mayor between 1601 and 1623, and M.P. 1603-4. He was granted Ballycarty Castle and other forfeited estates of Lord Desmond 1590. His descendant William (b. 1652) was High Sheriff of Cumberland 1676. Flimby descended to William Blennerhasset (d. 1765) who marr. 1723 Catherine (b. 1697), dau. of Timothy Wyvill, *q.v.* Their eldest son William (bap. at Penrith 1726) was a leading London attorney, and the author of *A History of England* in 6 vols., 1751, and of *The Universal and Eternal System,* 1752. He sold Flimby Hall 1772. *Arms.* The first coat recorded for the family was: Gules three dolphins embowed Argent (FFC). Another early coat was: Ermine a dolphin embowed...(Seal of Robert Blennerhasset). The family later bore: Gules a chevron Ermine between three dolphins embowed Argent (MMS vi 415; MMD; Stone shield in St Michael, Workington).

* Captain James Everard, of Lowestoft (b. 1774), who marr. Elizabeth, dau. of Henry Prescott Blencowe (d. 1787), impaled the following quarterly coat for Blencowe on his bookplate: Quarterly, 1, Gules a canton Argent; 2, Sable on a bend Argent three chaplets Gules; 3, Azure on a bend Argent three escallops Gules (Layton); 4, Sable a chevron between three owls Argent (Prescott).

LMC records: Gules a chevron between three dolphins naiant embowed Proper.*

BOAR. GMS records the following, without specifying any place of residence. *Arms.* Gules a boar statant . . . .

BOHEMIA. Impaled with France (ancient) and England in window in Carlisle Cathedral, given by the Friends of the Cathedral, 1949, and also in a clerestory window; King Richard II (1367-1400) marr. (1) 1382 Anne (1366-94), dau. of Charles IV, King of Bohemia. *Arms.* Quarterly, 1 & 4, Or an eagle displayed Sable; 2 & 3, Gules a lion rampant queue fourché and nowed Argent crowned Or.

BOHUN. Burke shews this family as of Carlisle, but we can find no reference to any family of the name in Cumberland, other than Denton's mention of Ranulph Bohun de Meschines (DAC, p. 67); and Nisbet's mention of John Bohun, *alias* Meschinas, Earl of Cumberland, *temp.* William the Conqueror (NSH). *Arms.* Or three bars Gules (BGA).†

BOILEAU. Impaled by Graham on monument in Hayton church; Reginald John Graham, of Edmond Castle, *q.v.*, marr. 1856 Ellen Leah (d. 1918, aged 80), dau. of Thomas Ebenezer John Boileau, a Judge in the H.E.I.C.S., Madras Presidency (1796-1853).‡ *Arms.* [Azure] a castle triple-towered and in base a crescent [Or].

BOLBECK. Shield in Great Hall, Naworth Castle, and quartered by Greystoke, Dacre and Howard; Ralph, Lord Greystoke (d. 1315/16), marr. Margery, dau. of Hugh de Bolbeck, of Northumberland. *Arms.* Vert a lion rampant Argent charged on the shoulder with an ermine spot.

BOLTON, of Leeming. Henry Hargreaves Bolton, J.P. (1831-1905), colliery proprietor, was of Leeming-on-Ullswater and of Newchurch-in-Rossendale (L). He was succ. at Leeming by his son Edgar Ormerod Bolton, J.P. (1862-1941), who was a director of Hargreaves Collieries Ltd. and Chairman of Penrith Cottage Hospital Committee. At Leeming he was succ. by his sister Miss Elizabeth Hargreaves Bolton (d. 1952, aged 87). *Arms.* Per pale Argent and Gules two bird bolts in saltire surmounted in the centre by a tun between three roses all counterchanged. *Crest.* Three bird bolts two in saltire and one in fess Proper thereon a falcon close belled and jessed Or. *Motto.* Sursum corda (FD7). The bookplate of H. H. Bolton shows the *Crest* as: An eagle Proper.

BOND, of Gaitsgill and Carlisle. John Bond, of Gaitsgill (1719-1801), was father of Thomas Bond, of Dalton Square, Lancaster (1758-1817), merchant. His nephew, John Bond, D.L., J.P., also of Dalton Square (1778-1856), West India merchant and Alderman of Lancaster, was son of Edward Bond, of Carlisle. He marr. 1807 Elizabeth Spooner, of Carlisle (b. 1787), by whom he had a large family, including Thomas (1808-57), who was in partnership with him. His 3rd dau., Margaret Oates, marr. James Addison

* At the Visitation of 1665, John Senhouse, of Netherhall, or Alneburgh (see Senhouse, *post* Pocklington-Senhouse, of Netherhall), shewed his arms with the following quartering, said to be for Blennerhasset: Azure on a chevron Or between three dolphins Argent five cinquefoils Gules. This coat was also quartered by Sir Joseph Senhouse, of Hensingham Hall, Arkleby Hall, and Ashby St. Ledgers (1743-1829), on his seal.

† MMD tricks two coats for Bohun, viz. Quarterly, 1 & 4, Or a lion rampant Gules, 2 & 3, Azure three garbs Or, for Radulph Bohun [*sic*]; and, Azure a bend double cotised between six lions rampant Or, for Bohun.

‡ For his brother Simeon John Boileau, see AWL.

Clarke, of Summerhill (L.). *Arms.* Argent on a chevron Sable three bezants. *Crest.* A demi pegasus (AWL).

BONNELL. James Bonnell (d. 1850, aged 73) was a chemist and druggist in Carlisle in 1799 and later. His family appears to have come from Essex. He marr. 1799 Esther (d. 1822, aged 52), dau. of Richard Lowry, of Stanwix, *q.v. Arms.* Argent a cross Gules quarter pierced and nine crosses, three, three and three, counterchanged. *Crest.* A demi lion rampant holding in the forepaws a knobstick. *Motto.* Erris peregrinus et hospe (M.I., Stanwix church).

BONNER. Thomas Bonner, of High Callerton (N) (1720-98), descended from Christopher Bonner, of Portinscale, bur. at Crosthwaite 1584, marr. 1763 Sarah (1741-74), dau. of the Rev. Thomas Maddison, by his wife Sarah Andrews, descended from a junior branch of the Warwick family. Their son Robert Bonner assumed the surname Warwick 1792; their dau. Isabella marr. 1784 John Losh, *q.v.,* who put up the Warwick, rather than the Bonner, arms at Woodside, Wreay, and Field (FAC) incorrectly attributed these to Bonner (NCHN xii 483). *Arms* (as quartered by Warwick on monument in Carlisle cathedral to the daus., d. 1823 and 1832, of Robert Warwick, of Warwick Hall (C) and High Callerton (N), formerly Bonner). Gules a lion passant between two escallops in pale Argent. *Crest.* A hand holding a sword (M.I., Holy Cross burial ground, Wallsend).

BONVILLE, Lord Bonville and Harington. Elizabeth, dau. and heir of Sir William Harington (d. 1458), *q.v.,* marr. William (killed 1460), son and heir apparent of William, 1st Lord Bonville of Chewton, and carried the Cumberland estates to the Bonville family. Their son William became Lord Harington in 1458, and he and his father were killed at Wakefield, 1460. The heiress, Cecily Bonville, marr. Thomas Grey, Marquess of Dorset, *q.v.* (GEC). *Arms.* Sable six mullets Argent pierced Gules (FFC).

BOOKER, of Langrigg. The Rev. Charles Frederick Booker, L.Th. (Dunelm), Rector of Stanningley (Y) 1864-76, marr. 1850 Sarah Jane, elder dau. of John Barwis, of Langrigg Hall, *q.v.* Their unmarr. daus. Frances Annie (1859-1940) and Mabel Constance (1863-1958) were for many years tenants of Langrigg Hall (CW2 xxxvii 106-7, 126). *Crest.* A swan close collared and chained. *Motto.* Quid non Deo juvante (Pewter formerly at Langrigg Hall).

BORRADAILE. This Cumberland family, settled at Glasson, and later at Wigton, became well known in the commercial life of London, and many members of it had prominent careers in the Indian Civil Service and Army. John Borradaile (d. 1783, aged 58), was a tanner and merchant at Wigton and marr. Mary Richardson (d. 1794, aged 69). Their eldest son William, of Lesson Hall (C) and Manor Park, Streatham, London (1750-1831), was in partnership as shipowners with his brother Richardson (1762-1835), who was chairman of the Hudson Bay Co., and M.P. for Streatham. William marr. Ann (d. 1818, aged 48), dau. of Abraham Delapierre, by Mary, dau. of the Rev. Salkeld Osmotherley. Their descendant Thomas Salkeld Borradaile (b. 1831), merchant and shipowner of Shanghai, was head of the family in 1881. *Arms.* Or three water bougets in pale Sable between two torteaux a chief Vert. *Crest.* A tower Or issuing therefrom a greyhound Sable in its dexter paw a sprig of leaves Vert. *Motto.* Integritatis ergo (BBC).

BORWICK, Baron Borwick, of Hawkshead. This old Hawkshead family gave their name to Borwick Ground in that Lancashire parish. George Borwick, of Morven, Tor Mohun, Devon, had a son, Robert Hudson Borwick, J.P., K.G.S.J. (1845-1936), who in 1893, when he was of Berkeley Square, London, obtained a grant of arms for himself, his descendants, and his brother Joseph Cooksey Borwick, and also a grant of the arms of Johnston for his wife, Caroline Smith, 6th dau. of the Rev. Richard Daniel Johnston. *Arms.* Erminois three escarbuncles fesswise Sable between three bears' heads erased of the second muzzled Or. *Crest.* Upon a mount Proper in front of a staff raguly erect Azure a stag browsing Or attired Sable. And for JOHNSTON: *Arms.* Gules on a mount Proper a lion rampant winged supporting a tilting spear erect all Argent on a chief of the last two spurs erect rowel upwards with wings elevated Gules (CA lxvii/141). In 1902 he was knighted and in 1916 cr. Bart. In 1922 he was raised to the peerage as Baron Borwick, of Hawkshead, Co. Lancaster. He lived at Eden Lacy, Great Salkeld. The present holder of the title is his grandson, Sir James Hugh Myles Borwick, M.C., of Pentwyn, Clyro, Hereford, who succ. his father as 4th Baron 1961 (BP105). On his elevation to the peerage the first Baron obtained a fresh grant of arms, with supporters, 'to distinguish him from those of inferior rank.' *Arms.* Argent three escarbuncles fesswise Sable between three bears' heads erased of the last muzzled Or. *Crest.* Upon a mount Proper in front of a staff raguly erect Azure a stag browsing Or attired Sable. *Badge.* A rose Gules between two sprigs of hawthorn in saltire all leaved and slipped Proper enfiled with a Baron's coronet Or. *Supporters.* On either side a bear Sable muzzled and charged on the shoulder with an escarbuncle Or (CA 90/36). *Motto.* Fugit (BP105).

BOSWELL. James Boswell of Auchinleck (1740-95), eldest son of Alexander Boswell, Lord Auchinleck, and famous for his Journals and as the biographer of Samuel Johnson, was Recorder of Carlisle 1788-90. His elder son, Alexander, was cr. Baronet 1821 and was killed in a duel seven months later. His son, Sir James Boswell, 2nd Bart (1806-57), died *s.p.*, when the baronetcy became extinct. He was succ. at Auchinleck by his elder dau. Julia, who died at Carlisle 1905, having marr. 1867 George Mounsey, J.P., of Kingfield, Nichol Forest, and Devonshire Street, Carlisle (b. 1819), solicitor and Superintendent Registrar of Births, Marriages and Deaths for Carlisle from 1850. He died *s.p.* at Auchinleck 1904, the estate passing on his widow's death to her nephew Lord Talbot de Malahide. She left her residuary estate to Cumberland Infirmary. *Arms.* Quarterly, 1 & 4, Argent on a fess Sable three cinquefoils of the field and on a dexter canton Azure a ship at anchor sails furled within a double tressure flory counterflory Or; 2, Argent three bars Sable; 3, Quarterly, i & iv, Argent a lion rampant Azure, ii & iii, Argent a saltire and a chief Gules (POA). *Crest.* A falcon Proper hooded Gules jessed and belled Or. *Motto.* Vraye foi (BGA).

BOTELER. Shield in Great Hall, Naworth Castle, and quartered by Greystoke, Dacre and Howard; John, Lord Greystoke (d. 1436), marr. Elizabeth (d. 1434), dau. and coheir of Sir Robert Ferrers (d. 1396), son of Robert Ferrers, Lord Le Boteler (d. 1380/1), *q.v.*, by Elizabeth (d. 1411), dau. and heir of William, Lord Le Boteler, of Wem (d. *s.p.m.* 1369). *Arms.* Gules a fess counter-company Argent and Sable between six crosses pattée fitché Or. R. S. Ferguson recorded this as: Gules a fess chequy Or and Sable between six crosses pattée fitché Or (CW1 iv 500). GEC gives: Gules crusilly Argent a fess counter-compony Or and Sable.

BOTHEL. John Bothel acquired land in Great Waverton 1302-3. *Arms.* Field interpreted the shield in MMD as: Argent a chevron Azure between three stags' heads cabossed Vert the two lower tires Or the three upper Sable (FAC). It is possible that this is what Milbourne intended, but to us it seems just as likely that he meant: Argent a chevron Azure between three blue bottle flowers slipped Vert the two lower petals Or the three upper Sable.

BOTREAUX. Stated by Burke to be of Cockermouth. *Arms.* Argent three toads erect Sable. *Crest.* A dove standing on a hill Proper (BGA).

BOUCH, of Cockermouth. A pedigree of four generations of this family, headed by Michael Bouch, is in FCW. His son Anthony Bouch, of Cockermouth (1599-1672), was High Sheriff of Cumberland 1670. He marr. (2) Elizabeth (b. 1616), dau. of William Lowther, of Ingleton (Y), and had sons Henry (b. *c.* 1638) and Thomas, who was rector of Whittington (L) 1681-1716. Henry's son Henry marr. 1689 Mary, dau. of Sir Daniel Fleming. *Arms.* Or on a cross sable five escallops Argent. *Crest.* A Saracen's head wreathed Proper. 'Respite given for proofe of these armes.' (FCW). The Rev. Thomas Bouch, however, sealed his will with: Four pellets on a cross (CHW).

BOUCH. Canon Charles Murray Lowther Bouch, M.A. (Oxon), F.S.A. (1890-1959), son of Charles Bouch, descendant of an old Cumbrian family, was Curate of St. John, Workington, 1922-23, of Maryport 1923-25, and of St. George, Barrow, 1927-31, and was Vicar of St Barnabas, Carlisle, 1932-46, and during the war years had charge of Wetheral parish. He was Rector of Clifton and Brougham 1946-59, and Hon. Canon of Carlisle from 1955. He was descended from John Bouch, who marr. 1838 Margaret, sister and coheir of William Lowther (d. 1875), a descendant of the Lowthers of Great Orton. He was President of the Cumberland & Westmorland Antiquarian & Archaeological Society 1954-57 and a prolific contributor to Transactions. In 1948 he published his *Prelates and People of the Lake Counties.* He marr. 1946 his cousin Isabella Jacquetta Lowther (now of Orchard House, King's Meaburn), 3rd dau. and coheir of the Rev. John Lowther Bouch, M.A. (Oxon), Rector of Ackworth (Y) (d. 1942, aged 70) (CW2 lix). *Arms, Crest* and *Motto.* As preceding entry. Canon Bouch also used the *Motto.* Time Deum et regem.

BOUCHER *recte* BOUCH. The Rev. Jonathan Boucher, M.A. (King's College, New York) (1738-1804), son of James Bouch, of Blencogo, was usher of St. Bees School 1756-59, and was ordained in 1762. He spent many years in America, returning to England in 1775, and was a schoolmaster in Paddington before becoming Vicar of Epsom. He contributed many articles to Hutchinson's *History of Cumberland.* From 1799 until his death he was tenant of Coledale Hall, Carlisle (CW2 xxii). *Arms.* He, having altered the spelling of his name to Boucher, adopted the arms of Bourchier: Argent a cross engrailed Gules between four water bougets Sable. *Crest.* An old man's head sidefaced Proper couped at the shoulders habited Vert collared Or on his head a ducal coronet Gold out of which is a long cap hanging forward Gules tasselled of the second. *Motto.* Non vi sed voluntate (Bookplate).

BOUMPHREY. Leslie Boumphrey, B.A. (Leeds), of Yeavering, Monkhill, Burgh-by-Sands, formerly Deputy Principal, Bishop Willis Teacher

Training College, Iganga, Uganda, is now on the staff of Morton School, Carlisle; he is son of Ernest Boumphrey, of 11 Merefield Avenue, Bolton-le-Sands (L)*. *Arms.* Or a chevron between three dragons rampant Azure. *Crest.* A demi dragon Azure. *Motto.* Jure vincimus.

BOUSTEAD, of Aglionby. William Boustead, of Aglionby, yeoman, sealed a deed dated 1688 with the following *Arms.* . . . a chevron paly . . . between three birds . . . *Crest.* A bird.

BOUSTEAD, of Cumrenton. John Boustead, of Cumrenton, Irthington, and Upper Gloucester Street, Marylebone, became Paymaster 1st Ceylon Regt. 1810 and was on the half-pay list 1856. In 1850 he obtained a grant of the following *Arms.* Per chevron Vert and Argent a chevron per chevron Or and of the first between in chief two cinquefoils of the third and in base a dexter arm embowed in chain armour couped at the shoulder and holding a cross bow in bend the bow downwards Proper. *Crest.* A lion's head Erminois issuant from a wreath of cinquefoils and holding in the mouth three cinquefoils slipped vert.

BOUSTEAD, of Slackhead. Rowland Boustead, of Cumrenton, Irthington, was grandfather of Rowland Boustead, of Slackhead (1700-81), whose son John (1734-85) was of Slackhead and Bullersyke, Irthington. He marr. Ann Robson (d. 1799, aged 66) and their son James Boustead (d. 1827) was of Beanlands, an estate inherited by his dau. and heir Ann (1794-1876), who marr. John Bell, *q.v.* *Arms.* . . . a chevron . . . between three fleurs-de-lys . . . (Tombstone of John and Ann Boustead, Irthington churchyard).

BOWEN-COLTHURST – see COLTHURST, BOWEN-.

BOWERBANK, of Johnby. William Bowerbank, of Johnby, was father of John Bowerbank, of Johnby (1695-1756). His son John Bowerbank, of Johnby (1727-1808), marr. (2) 1757 Mary Williamson (d. 1797) and had issue, *int. al.,* Isaac Bowerbank, of Johnby (b. 1758), and Hannah (1773-1866) who mar. 1797 Sir Frederick Fletcher-Vane, Bart., *q.v.* *Arms.* Two versions are impaled on shields at Hutton-in-the-Forest: (1) [Argent] on a mound in base Vert a stag lodged [Gules] in the mouth a sprig of oak leaved and fructed [Proper] a chief nebuly Azure; (2) Argent a stag lodged Gules in the mouth a sprig of oak leaved and fructed Proper.

BOWERBANK. This is one of the oldest Skelton families. William Bourbancke had sons John and Thomas bap. at Skelton, 1599. Edward Bowerbank, of Lamonby, had a 3rd son Thomas, merchant of the City of London, who, in his application for a grant of arms, said that his ancestors had been established for many generations at Lamonby. *Arms.* Thomas Bowerbank stated that his family had used: . . . on a chevron between three leopards passant three leopards' heads, the crest being a demi leopard out of a mural crown. Since these arms were not registered in the College of Arms, he obtained 1801 a grant as follows: *Arms.* Ermine on a chevron Azure between three leopards passant gardant Proper as many leopards' faces Or. *Crest.* Out of a battlement Or a demi leopard issuant gardant Proper (CA xxi/271). For the grant made to his wife, see DE JERSEY.

BOWET. The name of this family seems originally to have been Bueth. Thomas Bueth witnessed a charter of Sir Henry de Suleby *c.* 1250, and

* And shares with the co-author of this work a descent from the Boumphreys of Wirral (Ch) and of Liverpool.

Thomas Bowet owned lands in Warcop and Soulby 1283. William Bowet (d. 1359) was Rector of Dacre: his executors were Thomas Bowet and Gilbert Bowet, chaplain. The latter was chaplain at Greystoke and became first Master of the College there 1382. The former is presumably the man who d. before 1415, having marr. Margaret (living 1429), sister and heir of Sir Robert Parvyng, who in a settlement of 1386/7 named Henry Bowet clerk as trustee. The latter was Bishop of Bath and Wells 1401-7 and Archbishop of York 1407-23. In his will he mentions that his father was buried at Penrith and names his cousin Roger Bowet of Kirkby Stephen. The above Margaret Bowet succ. to the manors of Blackhall, Stainton and Botcherby, which descended to her son Sir William Bowet, of Wrentham, Suffolk, and Horsford, Burgh St. Margaret's, Norfolk. By Joan his wife, dau. and heir of Sir Robert Ufford, he had a dau. and heir Elizabeth, who marr. Sir Thomas Dacre, *q.v.* The above named Thomas Bowet marr. a sister and coheir of Robert le Brun, *q.v.*, and so acquired a third of the manor of Bothell, which his grandson Sir Nicholas Bowet sold to William Ellis 1468-69. *Arms.* On the tomb of Archbishop Bowet: Argent three reindeers' heads cabossed Sable (attired of the last). MMD gives these arms for Bowet, of Bothel. *Crest.* On a cap of maintenance Gules doubled Argent a reindeer statant (Argent attired) Sable (FVY). BBE gives for *Arms:* Argent three stags' heads cabossed Sable.* *Motto.* Honneur et joye.

BOWMAN. Anthony Bowman, of Birdoswald, died 1778, aged 89, and was buried at Lanercost; his wife Margaret died 1754, aged 37. *Arms.* . . . three long bows fully bent with arrows drawn to the head . . . (Tombstone, Lanercost churchyard).

BOWMAN. Mary, dau. of William Bowman, of Birdoswald, Lanercost, yeoman, died 1797, aged 24. William Bowman, of Birdoswald, d. 1824, aged 84. *Arms.* Or on a chevron Gules between three long bows as many ermine spots. *Crest.* A quiver of arrows bendsinisterwise hung over and before the stump of a tree from which issues a branch in leaf. *Motto.* Regem et legem arcu defendo (ABD).

BOWMAN, of Brampton. Tombstone in Brampton Old Churchyard; inscription illegible. *Arms.* . . . a bend . . . between in sinister chief a bird . . . and in dexter base three long bows . . . *Crest.* A bird.

BOWMAN. James Bowman, of Great Easby, Brampton, yeoman, d. 1751, leaving a widow Isabel. *Arms.* Three long bows with arrows on strings points to the sinister (ABD). These arms are also on the tombstone of John Bowman (d. 1767, aged 78) in Brampton old churchyard.

BOWMAN. Fragment of tombstone at Irthington of Thomas Bowman, *c.* 1730-50. *Arms.* . . . a bend . . . between two mullets of six points . . . .

BOWMAN. Thomas Bowman, of Field Garth, Kirkoswald (d. 1798, aged 53), marr. Mary (d. 1822, aged 79) and had a son John (d. 1827, aged 54), whose sons were Joseph (d. 1835, aged 17), Stephen (d. 1859, aged 35), and John (d. 1862, aged 37). *Arms.* Or a chevron Gules between three long bows erect. *Crest.* A dexter arm embowed holding an arrow (Tombstone, Kirkoswald churchyard). On the cup and patten given to Kirkoswald church by Stephen Bowman 1660, the arms appear as: . . . three long bows, two and one, ...

* Which is worked on curtains in Lanercost Priory.

BOWMAN, of Stainton. William Bowman, of Stainton, Stanwix, in his application for a grant of arms in 1780, stated that he was grandson of Robert, and son of John of the same place, and that his ancestors used a chevron between three bows and the crest a quiver of arrows, but these arms were not registered in the College of Arms, and he was granted the following: *Arms.* Azure a chevron Erminois between three archers' bows bent paleways Or stringed Argent. *Crest.* On a mount the trunk of an oak tree broken off at the top, a branch issuing from the upper part of the dexter side Proper pendant thereto by a belt Gules passing round the trunk a quiver Or filled with arrows Argent the bottom of the quiver pointing to the right of the shield (CA xiv/229).

de BOYS. Impaled by Howard on shield in hall of Greystoke Castle; Sir John Howard, Sheriff of Norfolk 1345, marr. Alice, dau. of Sir Robert de Boys, and sister and heir of Sir Robert de Boys, of Fersfield, Norfolk. *Arms.* Ermine a cross Sable.

BOWSTEAD. James Bowstead, M.A., D.D. (Cantab) (1801-43), Bishop of Sodor and Man 1838-9, and Bishop of Lichfield 1840-3, was born at Great Salkeld, 2nd son of Joseph Bowstead, of Beck Bank, Great Salkeld (1759-1835), and was descended from John Boustead, of Boustead Hill (C) (VEW Notes iii 42). *Arms.* Vert on a cross between four cinquefoils Argent a rose Gules (BBE; M.I., Great Salkeld church, where the rose appears as an annulet).

BOYVILL, of Kirklinton. Ranulph le Meschin enfeoffed Richard de Boyvill with the barony of Kirklevington (Kirklinton). By 1177 it was in the hands of his descendant Adam fitz Adam fitz Richer, from whom it came to Ralph de Boyvill or de Levington (d. 1253), the last male. His dau. and heir Helewise marr. Eustace de Balliol, *q.v.*, but dying *s.p.*, the barony descended to her father's sisters (SEB). *Arms. Constable's Roll* 1558 (TVN) gives for Levington: Or a saltire and a chief Gules the latter charged with three boars' heads Or; Field (FAC) quotes this authority for arms for this family, but it seems a dubious ascription.

BOYVILL, of Kirksanton and Thursby. The Rev. W. S. Sykes suggested (CW2 xli) that three Boyvill brothers from Boisville in Normandy acquired Millom, Kirksanton and Kirklinton. Guy de Boyvill, of Kirksanton (*fl.* 1234-55), acquired the manor of Thursby and his grandson Sir William (d. 1305) also held Ainstable manor. His son John de Boyvill (1283-1319) d. *s.p.* and was succ. by his brother Edmund, aged 30+ in 1319, who forfeited his estates for rebellion. *Arms.* Argent a fret Vert and a canton . . . (DAC). MMD tricks this as: Argent fretty Vert a canton [? Sable]. Curwen gives for Boyvill: Argent a fret Vert (CW2 vi).

BOYVILL, of Millom. Miss Mary Fair in CW2 xxxvii shows that this family came from Boisville, one of the fiefs of the Vicomte le Bussins. To one of them William le Meschin gave the great Lordship of Millom, which came to his son Godard de Boyvill, sometimes called Dapifer, the date of whose birth is surmised in CW2 xli as *c.* 1075. He was a benefactor to Furness Abbey and St. Bees (SBR) and was succ. by his son Arthur (?b. *c.* 1120), whose son Henry, sometimes known as son of Arthur, or de Millom, had two sons, William, who succ. *c.* 1200, and was succ. by 1229 by his brother Adam, whose dau. and heir Joan marr. John Hudleston, *q.v.*, and carried the Lordship of Millom to that family. *Arms.* The following are carved for

Boyvill on the tomb of Sir John Hudleston (d. 1493) in Holy Trinity, Millom: Quarterly, 1 & 4, A bugle horn stringed: 2 & 3, Two chevronels*. The Boyvill bugle horn also apparently appears on the font in Bootle church. The following is given for Gilbert de Boyvill (a kinsman of Godard, *supra*), who granted land in Orgrave to Furness Abbey in 1247, in a note in *The Coucher Book of Furness Abbey:* Sable a chevron Argent between three bulls' heads affronté of the second (Chetham Society, New Series, ix 259). The Flemings quartered, for Boyvill: Argent a chevron between three bulls' heads cabossed Sable; and, for Millom (see above): Argent a bend between two mullets Sable† (NB i 173). Field (FAC) quotes the so-called Visitation of 1615 as shewing Hudleston quartering Boyvill as: Azure a fleur-de-lys Or on a chief Argent a bugle-horn stringed Sable, but although this coat appears as a Hudleston quartering in FVC, it is not specifically assigned to Boyvill. MMD gives, for Boyvill of Millom: Argent fretty Vert a canton [?Argent]; but see Boyvill, of Kirksanton and Thursby.

BRADDYLL – see GALE, later RICHMOND-GALE-BRADDYLL.

BRADFORD. Samuel Bradford, M.A., D.D. (Cantab) (1652-1731), was Bishop of Carlisle 1718-23, and Bishop of Rochester and Dean of Westminster 1723-31. *Arms.* Argent on a fess Azure three bucks' heads erased Or (BBE).

BRANTHWAITE. Gerard de Branthayte witnessed charters *c.* 1200 and Robert de Branthwaite held Branthwaite in 1230, and was succ. by his son Robert, who held the estate 1276 and also a moiety of the manor of Hensingham. The heiress of the family carried the estates to Robert Whitrigg, *q.v.*, by marr. *c.* 1320. *Arms.* Field suggests that the Branthwaites bore: Argent fretty and a canton Gules (FAC). These are the arms attributed to Sir Thomas Whitrigg in Glover's Ordinary, but the Whitriggs undoubtedly bore, Argent a bend dancetté Azure, so Sir Thomas may have used his mother's arms. Lysons give: Or on a bend Sable three lions passant guardant of the field (LMC), but these are the arms of the much later Westmorland family of Branthwaite, of Carlingill, see AWL.

BRAOSE. A Howard quartering, on shields in Greystoke Castle and Naworth Castle; John, Lord Mowbray (1286-1322), marr. 1298 Aline, dau. and coheir of William, Lord Braose, of Gower. *Arms.* Azure crusilly and a lion rampant Or‡.

BREKIN. According to Burke, a Cumberland family, but more likely to be of Cambridgeshire, *vide* his entries under Brakyn. *Arms.* Gules a fess chequy Argent and Azure between three lozenges of the second each charged with a martlet Gules (BGA).

BRESBY, or BRISBY, of Penrith. Edward Robinson registered a pedigree of four generations of this family on behalf of Richard Bresby, of Penrith, who was then said to be 63, at the Visitation of 1665. Thomas Brisby was owner of the house Newhall, Great Dockray, Penrith, now known as the Two

* Quarters 2 & 3 are very worn and indistinct, and others have interpreted them as displaying three chevronels.

† i.e., the arms which Hudleston, of Millom, *q.v.*, quartered for Pyel. LMC assigns this coat to Millom of Millom, "a branch of the Boyvills."

‡ The shield in Greystoke Castle displays: Azure a lion rampant Or within an orle of cross crosslets Gules.

Lions, which he sold to Gerard Lowther 1584. His dau. Mabel is said to have been the mother of William Robinson, the rich grocer of London, who founded the school in Penrith which bears his name. The pedigree is headed by Richard Bresby to whom William Flower, Norroy, granted the crest 1564. His grandson Richard (1604*-75) was father of Thomas, who was 18 in 1665. *Arms.* Vairy Argent and Sable a fess Gules. *Crest.* A lamb Argent gutté de poix collared Or (FCW). Papworth records the arms as: Barry nebuly of six Argent and Sable on a fess Gules five gouttys de larmes (OBA).

BRIDGES. Shield on four-poster bed from Millom Castle, dated 1642 and with initials F[erdinand] H[udleston], now at Hutton John; William Hudleston, of Millom (d. 1628), marr. (1) Mary Bridges, of Gloucestershire. *Arms.* Argent on a cross Sable a leopard's face Or.

BRIGGS. The arms of this Westmorland family appear in glass in Ponsonby church. Thomas Briggs, of Cowmire, and Isabella his wife had a son Thomas, whose sisters Agnes and Anne were his coheirs. The former marr. Sir Richard Hutton, of Goldsborough (Y) (d. 1639), descended from the Huttons of Hutton Hall, Penrith, and the latter marr. 1591 Edward Stanley, of Dalegarth, *q.v.* *Arms.* Gules three bars gemel Or a canton Sable.

BRIGGS, of Tallantire. William Briggs (1808-77) farmed first at Lamplugh and then at Beech House, Tallantire. By Catherine (Raven) (1812-91) his wife he had seven sons and four daughters, the second son being William Briggs, see below. Three of his other sons, James, Thomas, who was head of Thomas Briggs & Sons, silk agents and importers of Oat Lane, and George (1848-1925), were Aldermen of the City of London. The last named was a silk merchant in London and Lyons, and became a Common Councilman for Cripplegate Ward 1897, was one of the Sheriffs of London 1912-13, Alderman of his Ward 1917,† a Magistrate and one of H.M.'s Lieutenants for the City. His elder son Alexander R. Briggs succ. to the business; the younger son Waldo Raven Briggs (d. 1956, aged 72), Barrister at law, was first Stipendiary Magistrate for Huddersfield 1931-56. The above named 2nd son William Briggs farmed at Highcroft, Tallantire, where he was succ. by his son William Henry Briggs, whose dau. and heir Nora Margaret, wife of William Marshall Coulthard, is now of Highcroft and is representative of the family in Cumberland (*Ex inf.* Mrs Coulthard and Mrs Buchanan, of Shooters Hill, Blackheath, descendants). *Arms.* Azure a fleur-de-lys Argent between four escutcheons of the last each charged with a pale Gules. *Crest.* In front of a sinister arm in armour embowed holding in the hand two arrows in saltire a longbow fessways all Proper. *Motto.* Fortiter et fideliter (Shield on portrait at Lorton Hall).

BRIGHAM, of Cumberland. No other details given. *Arms.* Argent a fleur-de-lys between eight martlets in orle Sable. Another: Argent three fleurs-de-lys within an orle of martlets Sable (OBA).

BRISCO, of Crofton. The Briscos are said to have been at Brisco for three generations before the reign of Edward I. Isold Brisco is said (FVC) to have marr. *temp.* Richard II Margaret, dau. and heir of Sir John Crofton, of Crofton, *q.v.*, and so acquired that manor. His son Christopher is said to

* Though said to be 63 in 1665, he was bap. at Penrith 1604.

† He resigned through ill-health when he was next in succession for the Lord Mayoralty of London.

have been taken prisoner at the burning of Wigton and forced to mortgage the manor of Brisco to the Prior of St. Mary's, Carlisle, to raise money to secure his release.* His grandson Robert marr. Katherine, dau. and heir of Clement Skelton, of Wreay. Their descendant John Brisco (d. 1583) bought two-thirds of Orton (C) manor, and his grandson John (d. 1632) bought the remaining third. This John was Bishop Nicolson's grandfather. His son and successor William Brisco, aged 58 in 1665 (d. 1688), was a strong supporter of Cromwell, High Sheriff of Cumberland 1650, and M.P. for Cumberland 1654, 1656 and 1659, and for Carlisle 1660. His grandson John was High Sheriff 1704 and was father of the Rev. John Brisco, M.A., D.D. (Oxon) (1700-71), who was Rector of Orton and Vicar of Aspatria 1730-71. He marr. Catherine (1706-56), 3rd dau. of John Hilton of Hilton (D), and sister and coheir of John Hilton (d. 1746). Their eldest son John (1739-1806), who was High Sheriff 1778, was cr. Baronet 1782. He marr. 1776 Caroline Alicia (d. 1822, agd 66), 2nd dau. and coheir of Lieut-Gen Gilbert Fane Fleming. Their grandson Sir Robert Brisco, 3rd Bart., D.L., J.P. (1808-84), was High Sheriff 1868. His grandson Sir Hylton Ralph Brisco, 5th Bart., J.P. (1871-1922), was drowned at sea on a voyage to Bombay. His twin sister and heir Hilda Cunningham Brisco (d. 1946) succ. and was Lady of the Manors of Crofton, Dundraw, Whinow, Brisco, Orton, Kirkland and Curthwaite. She sold Crofton Hall 1935 to the Land Settlement Association.† Their kinsman Sir Aubrey Hylton Brisco, 6th Bart. (1873-1957), was born in Virginia and lived in the U.S.A. He was succ. by his cousin Sir Hylton Musgrave Campbell Brisco, 7th Bart., of Hastings, Hawkes Bay, N.Z. (1886-1968), whose son Sir Donald Gilfrid Brisco, J.P. (b. 1920), is the 8th Bart. and lives at Havelock North, Hawkes Bay. The Briscos of Langrigg and of Cunninggarth and Brackenthwaite, Westward, were cadets of the Crofton family. *Arms.* Argent three greyhounds courant in pale Sable.‡ *Crest.* A greyhound courant Sable holding a rabbit Proper between his forepaws (FCW). This is now blazoned: A greyhound courant Sable seizing a hare Proper.§ *Motto.* Grata sume manu (BP105).

BRISCO, of Greenah, Langrigg, and Wolsty Stangs.‖ Anthony Brisco (d. 1577) descended from John Brisco, of Crofton, owned property at Greenah, later described as Greenah Hall, and at Langrigg. His great-grandson, Robert, was disclaimed for non-appearance at the Visitation of 1665. The family's connection with Greenah and Langrigg ended with Roger Brisco about the middle of the 18th century. Closely related and descending from a common ancestor were the Briscos of Langrigg and Wolsty Stangs, whose last representative was Gale Brisco (d. 1863, buried at Bromfield). *Arms.* As preceding entry.

* When the estates of the Dean and Chapter of Carlisle, who had inherited them from the Priory, were sold by order of the Commonwealth, William Brisco bought the manor, but had to relinquish it at the Restoration.

† For use as a smallholding estate for the unemployed of Cumberland. The Hall was pulled down and only the gatehouse and stables survive.

‡ DSL adds: collared Gules. Curwen gives another completely different coat for Brisco: Or a fess Vairy and Ermine between three cinquefoils Sable (CW2 vi), but this is surely Dykes?

§ A tablet in Lamplugh church to Mrs Margaret Brisco (1693-1731), dau. of Thomas Lamplugh and wife of Richard Brisco, with the Brisco arms impaling Lamplugh, displays not the Brisco but the Lamplugh crest, viz. A goat's head couped.

‖ Contributed by the Rev. F. B. Swift.

BROADHURST. Henry Tootal Broadhurst, of Woodhill, Prestwich (L), was father of Henry Brooks Broadhurst, J.P., of Houghton House, Carlisle (1856-1910), a director of Tootal, Broadhurst, Lee & Co., cotton spinners, manufacturers and merchants of Manchester; of Sir Edward Broadhurst, D.L., J.P., 1st and last Bart. (1858-1922), Chairman of the Company; and of Captain Arthur Brooks Broadhurst, 14th Hussars, who lived at Waterfoot, Ullswater. *Arms.* Per chevron Or and barry wavy Azure and Argent in chief two roses Gules. *Crest.* A mermaid holding in the dexter hand a sword erect and in the sinister a comb all Proper. *Motto.* Toujours prêt (FD7).

BROADLEY-SMITH – see SMITH.

BROCKHOLES. Impaled by Curwen on a wooden panel from Camerton Hall now in Camerton church dated 1625 with initials BC and HC; Henry Curwen, of Camerton (d. *c.* 1638), marr. Bridget, eldest dau. of Thomas Brockholes, of Claughton (L) (d. 1618). *Arms.* Quarterly, 1 & 4, Argent a chevron between three brocks Sable (Brockholes); 2 & 3, Vert three garbs Or.* The arms of Brockholes, but with the chevron tinctured Gules, are impaled by Howard on a fire-screen at Greystoke Castle, Charles 10th Duke of Norfolk (1720-86), having marr. 1739 Catherine (d. 1784), dau. and coheir of Thomas Brockholes, of Claughton.

BROCKLEBANK, of Hazelholm and Childwall. The Rev. Daniel Brocklebank (d. 1773, aged 68) was ordained to the curacy of Torpenhow 1735, and was Vicar of Morland 1757-73. His son the Rev. Ralph Brocklebank (d. at Egremont 1804) was born at Torpenhow 1738 and was curate of Corbridge (N). His only son John, of Hazelholm, Whitehaven (1775-1839), was Lieutenant in the West Cumberland Volunteers. His son Ralph Brocklebank, D.L., J.P., of Childwall Hall (L) (1803-92), was father of Thomas Brocklebank, D.L., J.P. (1841-1919), whose 5th son Clement Edmunds Royds Brocklebank, M.P., M.A. (Oxon) (1882-1949), was knighted 1937. His 2nd son Ralph Eric Royds Brocklebank (1870-1921) was grandfather of Ralph Wilfrid Brocklebank, B.A. (Cantab), the present head of the family. *Arms.* Azure an escallop Or between three brocks Proper on a chief engrailed of the second a cock also Proper between two escallops of the first. *Crest.* In front of a mount Vert thereon a cock as in the arms three escallops fesswise Or. *Motto.* God send grace (BLG18; VEW).

BROCKLEBANK, of Greenlands and of Irton Hall. This family began shipbuilding in Whitehaven in the 18th century. Daniel Brocklebank (d. 1801, aged 59), a younger son of the Rev. Daniel Brocklebank (see preceding entry), opened a branch in New York, but it was closed because of the War of Independence, and in 1802 the firm moved to Liverpool. The Brocklebanks were the oldest shipowning firm in the Kingdom. Daniel was succ. by his son Thomas (d. 1845, aged 71) who was of Greenlands, Irton. Dying *s.p.* he was succ. by his nephew Thomas Fisher, D.L., J.P. (1814-1906), son of his sister Anne (d. 1836, aged 58) who marr. 1812 Wilson Fisher, of Keekle (1774-1844). Thomas Fisher assumed the surname and arms of Brocklebank 1845. He was for many years head of Messrs. T. & J. Brocklebank and was High Sheriff of Cumberland 1864. He was of Greenlands and of Duddon Hall and was cr. Baronet 1885. His son and heir Sir Thomas Brocklebank, J.P., M.A. (Cantab) (1848-1911), bought Irton

* Quarters 2 & 3 were so recorded by St. George at the Visitation of Lancashire 1615, but Dugdale recorded them at the Visitation of 1665 as: Argent three garbs Gules (GVL; DVL).

Hall 1895. He was High Sheriff of Lancashire 1908. His son Sir Aubrey Brocklebank, J.P., B.A. (Cantab) (1873-1929), succ. He was High Sheriff of Cumberland 1921, and a director of the Suez Canal Co. and of the Cunard Steamship Co. His son Sir Thomas Aubrey Lawies Brocklebank, 4th Bart. (1899-1953), was of Greenlands, which was sold 1953.* His brother Sir John Montague Brocklebank, 5th Bart. (1915-74), was succ. by his son Sir Aubrey Thomas Brocklebank, the present holder of the title. *Arms.* Argent three brocks Proper each upon a mount Vert on a chief Azure as many escallops of the field. *Crest.* An anchor fesswise Sable thereon a cock Argent combed and wattled gules charged on the breast with an escallop also Sable. *Motto.* God send grace (BP105).

BROMLEY – see ASHBURNER.

BROOKSBANK, of Lamplugh. James Brooksbank, J.P., of 23 North Bailey, Durham (1786-1870), 2nd son of Benjamin Brooksbank, of Healaugh Manor (Y), marr. 1815 Ann, only dau. of John Raper (d. 1824), *q.v.,* and heir of her brothers, and had issue James Brooksbank (1816-63) whose son Walter Lamplugh Brooksbank, J.P., of Brundholme House, Keswick (1850-1916), succ. his great-uncle Henry Raper in the Lamplugh estates. These descended to his only son James Lamplugh Brooksbank (b. 1889) who sold the greater part of them, though retaining the lordship of the manor of Lamplugh (CW2 xxxviii; BLG18). *Arms.* Azure two bars wavy Argent within a bordure Or. *Crest.* A hart's head couped Argent attired Or charged on the neck with two bars wavy Azure (BP105; FD7). BGA tinctures the hart's head Proper.

BROTHERTON. A Howard quartering, on shields in Greystoke Castle and Naworth Castle; John, Lord Segrave (b. 1325, d. *s.p.m.* 1353), marr. Margaret, Duchess of Norfolk (d. *s.p.m.* 1399) dau. and heir of Thomas of Brotherton, Earl of Norfolk (1300-38), 5th son of Edward I. *Arms.* Gules three lions passant guardant in pale Or a label of three points Argent.

BROUGHAM. The manor of Brougham was held in 1264 by Christiana de Burgham, William de Crackanthorpe and Henry Ryddings, and in 1527 held by Christopher Burgham, John Crackanthorpe and William Bird. By 1563 it was owned by Henry Brougham and Thomas Bird. Thomas Brougham, the last of the family, d. 1607, and his moiety eventually came to James Bird, from whose family it was bought in 1726 by John Brougham, of Scales (C) (1677-1741), whose ancestor, Peter (d. 1570), heads the 1665 Visitation pedigree, and who is said by Field (FCW) to have marr. Anne, dau. and heir of John Southaik of Scales. John Brougham settled Brougham on the sons of his brothers Peter (1677-1732), who marr. 1718 Elizabeth, dau. of Christopher Richmond and sister and coheir of Henry Richmond; and Samuel (1681-1744). The former's son, Henry Richmond Brougham (1719-49), succ. but d. unmarr., when he was succ. by his cousin, John (d. 1756). His successor was his brother Henry (1710-82), whose son Henry (1742-1810) marr. 1777 Eleanora, only dau. of the Rev. James Syme. Their eldest son, Henry Peter Brougham, F.R.S. (1778-1868), became Lord Chancellor 1830 when he was cr. Baron Brougham and Vaux of Brougham, Westmorland. In 1860 he was cr. Baron Brougham and Vaux of Brougham and of Highhead Castle, Cumberland, with special remainder to his brother

* Irton Hall was sold 1929.

Henry Richmond Brougham, painted by Allan Ramsay in 1749, the year of his Shrievalty of Cumberland. The arms of Richmond and Brougham are on the shield. The portrait is in the possession of Mr. G. K. Galliers-Pratt and was reproduced by his permission in CW2 lxi

William (1795-1886) who became 2nd Baron. He marr. 1834 Emily Frances, only dau. and heir of Sir Charles William Taylor, Bart. His great-grandson, Victor Henry Peter, 4th Baron (1909-67), sold Brougham Hall to Geoffrey Carleton Cowper and it was demolished 1934. The present holder of the title is Michael John, 5th Lord Brougham and Vaux (GEC; BP105; DNB; CW2 lxi). *Arms.* At the 1665 Visitation respite was given 'for exhibiting the Armes and proofe.' Henry Richmond Brougham bore: Quarterly, 1 & 4, Gules two bars gemelles and a chief Or (Richmond); 2 & 3, Gules a chevron between three lucies hauriant Argent (Brougham). *Crest.* A hand and arm in armour holding a lucy fesswise (CW2 lxi facing 134). He was also entitled to quarter Vaux of Catterlen, and Delamore. The right to quarter Richmond, Vaux and Delamore died with him. Lord Brougham bears the same paternal arms as Henry Richmond Brougham, and continues to quarter Vaux and Delamore. *Crest.* A hand and arm in armour the hand holding a lucy fesswise Argent on the elbow a rose Gules. *Supporters.* Dexter, A lion Vert armed and langued Gules gorged with a Vaux collar checky Or and of the second; Sinister, a white hart antlers and hoofs Or in his mouth a rose Gules barbed and seeded Vert. *Motto.* Pro Rege lege grege (BP105). Lord Brougham is entitled to quarter Syme (*q.v.*) and Taylor.

BROUGHAM, *post* LAMPLUGH, of Cockermouth. John Brougham (d. before 1754), grandson of Thomas Brougham (d. 1648), ancestor of the Broughams, of Brougham Hall, see AWL, marr. his first cousin Mary (d. 1754), dau. of Henry Brougham, of Scales, and had issue John Brougham, attorney, of Cockermouth (1705-82), who died at Dovenby Hall, having marr. 1731 Frances (1711-40), dau. and heir of John Woodhall, *q.v.*, by his wife Elizabeth, dau. of Richard Lamplugh. His son Peter Brougham (1735-91) succ. to the manor of Dovenby 1768 and to the Hall, and in 1783 assumed the name and arms of Lamplugh. Dying unmarr., he was succ. by his niece Mary (1774-1860), who marr. 1800 Joseph Dykes Ballantine-Dykes, *q.v.* *Arms.* John Brougham, the Cockermouth attorney, above, sealed in 1748 with the arms of Brougham, of Brougham Hall, impaling Lamplugh, viz. Gules a chevron between three lucies hauriant Argent; impaling, Or a cross flory Sable.

BROUGHAM, Edward, of Burtholme, Lanercost, died 1752, aged 44. *Arms.* . . . a bird . . . and in base a rose . . . (Lanercost tombstone).

BROUGHAM, John, of Bushnook, Over Denton, yeoman, died 1780, aged 86. *Arms.* . . . a martlet [?] . . . and in base a rose . . . (Tombstone, Over Denton Churchyard).

BROUGHTON. Impaled by Irton on staircase window in Irton Hall; Richard Irton (*c.* 1440-90) marr. Margaret, dau. of John Broughton, of Broughton (L). *Arms.* Argent two bars Gules on a canton of the second a cross of the field. Field states that these arms are on the font at Millom, but this is incorrect; untinctured arms, which may be intended for Broughton, are on the sun-dial in Millom churchyard. Arms are displayed for this family on a shield at Hutton-in-the-Forest (Broughton being a Vane quartering) as: Argent two bars Gules in dexter chief a cross and in sinister chief a canton also Gules.

BROUGHTON. John Broughton, of Broughton (C), was High Sheriff of Cumberland 1435 and 1446. *Arms.* Argent a chevron between three mullets Gules (FWE). DSL describes the mullets as of six points.

BROWN, of Burnfoot. CW2 lxviii contains an account of the Browns of High and Low Burnfoot, Stapleton. Robert Brown, of Burnfoot (d. 1771), marr. Elizabeth (1706-91), sister and heir of Richard Crozier, of Burnfoot. Their sons John (1734-93) and James, of Kirkcambeck (1736-1814), are buried in Stapleton churchyard. The male line failed with James' grandson, Frederick Robert Brown (d. 1919, aged 81). *Arms.* Two different versions of their arms are carved on their gravestones, viz. (On that of John, d. 1893). . . . a chevron . . . between three bears' paws erased erect . . . on a chief . . . an eagle displayed . . . . (On that of James, d. 1814). . . . a chevron . . . between three bears' paws erased erect . . . . *Crest.* An eagle displayed head to the sinister. Field recorded the bears' paws in both cases as lions' gambs (FAC); and Irving added a bordure to James' arms (ABD).

BROWN. Barbara, wife of Johnston Brown, mariner, of Liverpool, d. in childbed 1841, aged 22; their son, Edward Johnston Brown, d. 1841, aged 10 days. *Crest.* A lion rampant holding in the dexter paw a fleur-de-lys (Gravestone in Embleton churchyard).

BROWN, post BROWN-BORTHWICK. The Rev. Robert Brown, 2nd son of William Brown, of Aberdeen, assumed the additional surname Borthwick. He was Vicar of Grange-in-Borrowdale 1869-72. *Arms* (granted 1868). Azure on a chevron Argent between two fleurs-de-lys in chief and a mascle in base Or three cinquefoils Sable. *Crest.* A hand Proper holding a fleur-de-lys Or. *Motto.* Delectat et ornat (BGA).

BROWNE, of Orthwaite Hall and Tallantire Hall. William Browne (1700-71) was of Woodhall in Caldbeck parish when his son was bap. at Greystoke 1721 and about 1723 acquired Orthwaite Hall, which came to his grandson William George Browne (1768-1813), a noted scholar and traveller, for whom see DNB. His nephew George Browne sold Orthwaite 1837. His great-uncle William Browne (1732-1802) bought Tallantire Hall 1776 and the manors of Dovenby and Papcastle, and was High Sheriff of Cumberland 1790. His son William Browne, J.P. (1780-1861) was High Sheriff 1816. He was succ. by his son William Browne, J.P., M.A. (Oxon) (1812-94),* after whose death Tallantire was sold. His son, the Rev. William Charles Browne, became Vicar of Haynes, Bedford, in 1895 (Paper by the Rev. F. B. Swift in CW2 lxx). *Arms.* Argent three martlets in pale Sable between two flaunches of the second each charged with a lion passant of the first (LMC). Papworth tinctures the lions Or (OBA). *Crest.* A griffin's head (LMC). Field gives: A griffin's head couped Vert between two wings Argent (FAC). *Motto.* Traducere saevum leniter (BGA).

BROWNE, of Matterdale. Machell recorded arms for this family, without further details. A Christopher Browne, of Matterdale Towne, was buried at Matterdale 1677. *Arms.* Argent three bars Gules over all a bend Azure (MMS vi 415).

BROWNING, of Eden Bank. John Browning, of Legh, Glos. (living 1364), marr. Alice, dau. of John Maltravers, and was father of John Browning, High Sheriff of Gloucestershire 1399, who marr. Eleanor, dau. and coheir of Sir Thomas Fitznicholl, of Hull and Berkeley, Glos. Their descendant Arrott Browning, M.Inst.C.E., chief engineer of Messrs Brassey, Wythes and Jackson for Natal Government Railways (1838-77), marr. 1866

* He was a founder member of the Cumberland & Westmorland Antiquarian & Archaeological Society.

Margaret, dau. and coheir of George Elliot, wine merchant, who built Eden Bank, Wetheral, 1834. Their only son George Elliot Browning, M.Inst.C.E., M.A.S.C.E., M.I.E., Chief Engineer Cochin Government 1896-1923 (b. 1867), inherited the property which he sold (BLG15; *Ex. inf.* Mr and Mrs G. G. S. Richardson). *Arms.* Quarterly, 1, Barry wavy of six Argent and Azure (Browning); 2, Sable a fret Or a label of three points Ermine (Maltravers); 3, Quarterly Gules and Or a bend Argent (Fitznicholl); 4, Barry wavy of six Argent and Gules (Sampford). *Crest.* On a cap of maintenance Gules turned up Ermine a pair of wings erect Or. *Motto.* Pour le roi et la loi (BLG15). FBC gives: *Crest.* A sinister arm from the elbow issuing from a cloud in the sinister the hand above a serpent's head erect from the middle and looking from the dexter Proper. *Motto.* In Deo salus.

BROWNRIGG, of Ormathwaite. Gawen Brownrigg, of Milbeck, Keswick, had three sons, of whom Giles and Henry settled in Ireland *c.* 1685. The latter was ancestor of General Sir Robert Brownrigg, K.C.B. (d. 1833), who was cr. Baronet 1816; the title is now held by his descendant, Sir Nicholas Gawen Brownrigg, 5th Bart., of California and Albuquerque, New Zealand. George Brownrigg, brother of the above Giles and Henry, marr. 1676 a dau. of Nicholas Williamson and acquired the Ormathwaite estate, which passed to his son George (1677-1760), who marr. 1705 his cousin Mary (d. 1770, aged 80), dau. of the above Henry Brownrigg. Their son William Brownrigg, M.D. (Leyden), F.R.S. (1711-1800), well known as a physician and man of science (DNB), died *s.p.* and Ormathwaite Hall passed to his great-nephew John Benn, *q.v. sub* BENN-WALSH, Lord Ormathwaite. *Arms.* Argent a lion rampant guardant Sable between three crescents gules.* *Crest.* A sword erect Proper pommel and hilt Or entwined by a serpent Vert. *Motto.* Virtute et sapientia (TSF). Sir Robert Brownrigg, above, was granted for himself, the descendants of his father and of his great uncle Henry Brownrigg, of Wingfield, Co. Wicklow, the following in 1802: *Arms.* Argent a lion rampant gardant Sable grasping in the dexter paw a sword pommel and hilt Or the blade entwined by a serpent Proper between three crescents, two and one, Gules. *Crest.* A mural crown Or thereon a sword erect entwined by a serpent as in the arms (CA xxii/7).

BROWNRIGG. Col John Newman Brownrigg, of Feura Bush, Brownrigg Road, New York, descends from Richard Brownrigg, of Co. Wicklow, whose family came from Cumberland. Richard emigrated to America 1752 and bought 6,500 acres at Edenton, North Carolina, and prospered. His grandson General Richard Thomas Brownrigg, who served in the Confederate Army in the American Civil War, moved to Mississippi 1823, and founded the town of Columbia. Later members of the family held high military rank. Col Brownrigg marr. Ida, dau. of Mr. J. Aplin, and granddaughter of Isaac Whitwell, of Garden Road, Kendal. They have a son Capt John Carter Brownrigg, U.S.A.R. and N.Y.N.G., and a daughter Dr Leslie A. Brownrigg. *Arms.* As Brownrigg, of Ormathwaite (*Ex inf.* J. P. Godwin).

* The arms on the monument to George and Mary Brownrigg in Crosthwaite church are now indecipherable.

le BRUN, of Bowness. From early times the manor of Bowness-on-Solway was held by Gamel le Brun and his descendants, often called de Feritate – i.e. "of the waste."* His descendant Sir Robert de la Ferte died *s.p.* 1300 and was succ. by a cousin Richard le Brun, Deputy Sheriff of Cumberland 1233-35, Steward of Copeland and Bailiff of Egremont. His grandson Robert le Brun, Knight of the Shire 1316, High Sheriff of Cumberland 1325-27, had licence to crenellate his dwelling house of Drumburgh 1307. His descendant John le Brun was High Sheriff 1376, and the male line ended with Robert, whose sisters and coheirs were Elena (d. *c.* 1395), marr. (1) Sir Thomas Whitrigg, *q.v.*, and (2) Sir William Curwen, *q.v.*; Margaret, marr. Sir William Lengleys; and Elizabeth, marr. Thomas Bowet. *Arms.* Azure a lion rampant Argent gutté de sang (FFC; and quartered by Curwen in window at Workington Hall). TVN shews Curwen as quartering: Azure a lion rampant Argent billetté Or; and FVC: Argent a lion rampant Sable maned and crowned Or. AHC gives for le Brun: Azure a lion rampant Argent charged with five lozenges Gules. TTV shews Curwen as quartering: Argent a lion rampant Azure charged with three billets of the field.

BRUS. Robert de Brus, Lord of Annandale (d. 1294), one of the competitors for the crown of Scotland 1291, was Sheriff of Cumberland and Governor of Carlisle 1255. His son Robert de Brus, Lord of Annandale, Earl of Carrick, *j.u.* (d. 1304), father of Robert de Brus, King of Scotland, was Sheriff of Cumberland 1283-85 and Governor of Carlisle 1295. *Arms.* Or a saltire and a chief Gules. The Earl of Carrick charged the chief with a lion passant guardant Or (FFC).

BRUS. Shield at Hutton John. A Hudleston quartering, brought in by Stapleton, *q.v.*; Sir Miles Stapleton (killed at Bannockburn 1314) marr. Sibell, dau. and coheir of John de Bellew, or Bella Aqua, by Laderina, dau. of Peter de Brus, of Skelton (Y) (d. *c.* 1243), and sister and coheir of Peter de Brus (d. *s.p.* 1272). *Arms.* Argent a lion rampant Azure.

BUBB. Captain Jeremiah Bubb (d. 1692) was M.P. for Carlisle 1689-92 and Governor of Carlisle Castle. His son Jeremiah is said to have been an apothecary in Carlisle, and was later of Weymouth. His son George Bubb† (1691-1762) was M.P. 1715-61, Lord Lieutenant of Somerset, a Lord of the Treasury, and Treasurer of the Navy. He took the name of Dodington 1717 and was cr. Baron Melcombe, of Melcombe Regis, 1761, but dying *s.p.*, the title became extinct (GEC; CWM; VCHC). *Arms.* Per pale Or and Ermine on a bend Gules three unicorns' heads erased Argent crined and attired of the first. *Crest.* On a mount Vert a unicorn sejant Argent crined and armed Gold reposing the dexter foot on a shield per pale Or and Ermine (BGA). Lord Melcombe bore for *Arms:* Argent a chevron between three bugle horns Sable (BEP).

BUDDICOM. The Rev. Robert Pedder Buddicom, M.A. (Cantab) (d. 1846, aged 66), was Vicar of St Bees and Principal of St Bees Theological College 1840-46. His 3rd and youngest dau. marr. the Rev. Joseph Empson Middleton, *q.v. Arms.* Argent a chevron between two crosses pattée in chief and a demi griffin couped in base all Gules on a chief of the last three

* The name may, however, be derived from la Ferté in France.

† He kept a famous diary, which, its editor said, showed his political conduct "to have been wholly directed by the base motives of avarice, vanity and selfishness." Another critic called him "unsteady, treacherous, vain, with no regard to truth."

escallops of the first.* *Crest.* In front of a beacon fired Proper issuant from the flames thereof a demi lion Gules gorged with a collar gemel Or holding in the dexter paw a sword in bend sinister of the first pommel and hilt Or a cross pattée between two escallops of the last. *Motto.* Virtute et vigilantia (BLG14).

BUETH. In CW2 xvi, facing p. 40, is a pedigree of Denton headed by Bueth or Boed whose son Gilles (*fl.* 1120) gave his name to Gilsland. His successor – perhaps his son – was Buethbarn, i.e. Bueth the younger, who gave Nether Denton to Lanercost. He was deprived of the lordship of Gilsland, which Henry II gave to Hubert de Vallibus. He was succ. at Bewcastle and Nether Denton by his son Robert son of Bueth, who sided with the Scots when William the Lion invaded England in 1173-74. He was a benefactor to Lanercost and Wetheral. He died *s.p.,* his sister marrying Robert son of Anketin from whom the Denton family descends. *Arms.* Almost certainly, the family bore none, but MMD attributes to Robertus fil. Bueth: Argent two bars [?Gules].

BULFELL. George Bulfell of Stonycroft, Keswick (b. 1594) son of Robert Bulfell of that place, marr. 1618 Isabel (d. 1669), dau. of John Mosse of Shundraw, and had a son Francis (b. 1619), saddler at the Sugar Loaf, Lombard Street, London. *Arms.* Ermine a mullet Sable on a chief Gules a label of five points Or. *Crest.* A demi-lion Argent (*Inf.* Dr. T. G. Fahy of Shaw End).

BULLEN. Shields at Hutton-in-the-Forest; a Vane quartering. *Arms.* Argent fretty Sable on a chief of the last three plates.

BULMAN, of Leeshill. A tombstone in Lanercost Churchyard commemorates Jeffery Bulman of Leeshill, Lanercost (d. 1710, aged 49). From him descended Christopher Bulman, yeoman, of Tenement (1804-71), who is buried in the adjoining grave. His dau. Anne (1863-1934), marr. 1884 John Forsyth *qv.,* and his son James Bulman (1856-1925) was father of Christopher Howard Bulman, of Torquay (b. 1891), the present head of the family. *Arms.* Gules three bars wavy Argent on a chief of the second an annulet between two bulls' heads cabossed Sable. *Crest.* On a mound . . . a bull passant Sable the dexter foot on a roundle. *Motto.* Pro patria. (*Ex inf.* Mrs. Dorothy Christina Carruthers, of Corner Stones, Aglionby, a descendant.)

BULTEEL. The Hon. Mary Elizabeth Bulteel (d. 1916, aged 84), Maid of Honour to Queen Victoria, eldest dau. of John Crocker Bulteel, M.P., of Flete, Devon, marr. 1861 General the Rt. Hon. Sir Henry Frederick Ponsonby, G.C.B. (1825-95). Their eldest son was Sir John Ponsonby, of Haile Hall, *q.v.* *Arms* (on oak screen in Haile church, presumably to commemorate their silver wedding 1886). Ponsonby, impaling, Quarterly, 1 & 4, [Argent] a bend between fourteen billets [Gules] (Bulteel); 2 & 3, [Argent] a chevron engrailed [Gules] between three martlets [Proper] (Crocker). With initials and date: H & M 1886.

BUNBURY. Henry William Bunbury (1750-1811), artist and caricaturist, 2nd son of the Rev. Sir William Bunbury, 5th Bart., settled in Keswick on the death of his wife 1799, and lived there until his death. His son Lt-Gen

* The arms are impaled by Middleton on the brass in St Bees church commemorating the Rev. Joseph Empson Middleton as: Or a chevron engrailed Azure between two crosses pattée in chief and a demi griffin couped in base all Gules on a chief of the last three escallops of the first.

Henry Edward Bunbury, K.C.B. (1778-1860), succ. as 7th Bart. 1821, and was great-grandfather of Lt-Col Gerald Bruce St Pierre Bunbury, I.A. (1883-1954), who marr. 1909 Frances Mary Olivia, only dau. of Francis Peter Dixon, J.P., of Blackwell Lodge, Carlisle. *Arms.* Argent on a bend Sable three chess rooks of the field. *Crest.* Two swords saltirewise passing through the mouth of a leopard's face Or the blades Proper hilted Gold. *Mottoes.* Firmum in vita nihil; Esse quam videri (BP105).

BURDETT. Mary (d. 1622), dau. of Thomas Wilson, P.C., LL.D., Secretary of State to Elizabeth I and Dean of Durham, marr. (1) Robert Burdett, of Bramcote, Warwickshire (d. 1603), and (2) Sir Christopher Lowther (d. 1617). By her 1st husband she had one son Thomas (b. 1585), cr. Baronet 1619, and daus. Elizabeth, marr. 1613 Anthony Hutton, of Hutton Hall, *q.v.*; Lettice, marr. 1623 Richard Skelton, *q.v.*; and Bridget, marr. William Whelpdale, *q.v. Arms* (as impaled by Skelton at Southwaite Hall, with date 1628). . . . two bars . . . the upper charged with three martlets . . . and the lower with one martlet . . . . Burke gives: Azure two bars Or each charged with three martlets Gules (BGA).

BURDON, of Cumberland and Nottinghamshire. No other details given. *Arms.* Azure three palmers' staves Or (BGA).

BURGESS. John Burgess (1838-1903) was editor of the *Carlisle Patriot* and of the *East Cumberland News* 1868-1903. His son Robert Nelson Burgess, F.J.I., of Evening Hill, Thursby (1867-1945) succ. him, the *Patriot* changing its name to the *Cumberland News,* of which he was editor 1910 and managing director until his death. He founded the *Cumberland Evening News.* He was a director of the Press Association (chairman 1931) and of Reuters 1925-32, and President of the Newspaper Society 1931-32. His only son Sir John Lawie Burgess, O.B.E., T.D., D.L., J.P., formerly of the Old Hall, Rockcliffe, and now of The Limes, Cavendish Terrace, Stanwix, Lt-Col Border Regt. and Hon. Col 4th Battalion 1956-68, is editor in chief and chairman of Cumberland Newspapers Ltd. and chairman of Border Television. He was a director of the Press Association 1950-57 (chairman 1954-55) and was chairman of Reuters 1959-68. He was High Sheriff of Cumberland 1969 and was knighted 1972. *Arms* (granted 1970). Barruly Argent and Sable a lightning flash and a sword point downwards in saltire Or. *Crest.* A demi bull Gules armed and unguled Or holding with the dexter hoof a quill pen resting the sinister hoof on a printer's ink ball Proper.

BURLAND. Shield at Hutton John; the Rev. William Hudleston (d. 1766) marr. 1743 Mary (d. 1795, aged 73), dau. of John Burland, of Wells, Som. *Arms.* Ermine on a chief embattled per pale Gules and Azure three roses Argent.

BURNE. Thomas Burne, of 23 Bedford Square, London, Twickenham and Alston Moor, died 1812, aged 83, and is described in the *Gentleman's Magazine* as "a true primitive Christian, and sincere friend." He may have been son of Thomas Burne, of Alston, but there is a gap in the parish registers 1727-28, and it has not been possible to find his baptism (*Ex inf.* Godfrey Thompson, City Librarian, Guildhall, and Miss J. Thompson, Local History Librarian, Newcastle upon Tyne). In 1807 he obtained a grant of the following *Arms.* Gules three fountains two and one Proper a chief nebulé Or. *Crest.* An eagle wings expanded Sable the dexter claw resting on a fountain Proper (CA xxiv/139).

BURNELL. Robert Burnell (d. 1292), Bishop of Bath and Wells 1275-92 and Lord Chancellor 1274-92, owned estates in nineteen counties, and was lord of 82 manors, including Newton Reigny, which he sold to Hugh Lowther 1290. *Arms.* Argent a lion rampant Sable crowned Or within a bordure Azure (BBE).

BURNESIDE. Shield at Hutton John; a Hutton quartering, brought in by Bellingham, *q.v.* *Arms.* Argent three bendlets Gules on a canton of the last a lion rampant of the field.

BURNYEAT, of Mill Grove. Philip Burnyeat, of Beckfoot, Ennerdale, later of Whitehaven, of a family long established in that parish, was grandfather of William Burnyeat, of Whitehaven (1819-74), whose business interests included butchery, grazing, mining and shipping. In 1865 he went to Liverpool to join his cousin Tom Dalzell in the firm of Burnyeat & Dalzell, still in existence as Burnyeat Ltd. His son William Burnyeat, J.P., of Mill Grove, Moresby (1849-1921), was father of William John Dalzell Burnyeat, J.P., M.A. (Oxon), of Moresby House, barrister-at-law (1874-1916), M.P. for Whitehaven 1906-10, who d. *s.p.* and *v.p.* (*Ex inf.* Dr. Tom Dalzell, of Egremont). *Arms.* Per pale Or and Azure on a chevron between three bears' heads couped two quatrefoils* all counterchanged. *Crest.* Issuing from flames Proper a bear's head per pale Or and Azure gorged with a collar flory counterflory counterchanged (BGA; FD7).

BURROUGH, of Brampton. William Burrough, of London (b. 1692, d. before 1727), marr. 1718 Margaret, dau. of Thomas Highmore, Serjeant Painter to William III, Queen Anne and George I, and heir to her brother John Highmore.† Their eldest son William Burrough (d. 1759, aged 37), "descended from a respectable family in the county of Suffolk," settled in Brampton and was father of Charles Burrough, Master and Commander R.N. (1753-1810), who was present as 1st Lieutenant of H.M.S. *Russell* at Camperdown, 1797. His grandson, the Rev. Charles Burrough, M.A. (Cantab) (1846-1907), was father of ten sons, of whom the eldest was the Rev. Charles James Burrough, M.A. (Oxon), Rector of Winterbourne, Glos. 1915-31, and Hon. Canon of Bristol (1872-1931), and the 9th was Admiral Sir Harold Martin Burrough, G.C.B., K.B.E., D.S.O.(1888-1977). The former's son, the Rev. John Wilson Burrough, M.A. (d. 1969), was Rector of Seale, Surrey; his only son, John Charles Wilson Burrough, of Guildford, solicitor, is now head of the family. *Arms.* On William Burrough's tombstone in Brampton Old churchyard these appear as: . . . two chevrons . . . between three chaplets . . . . *Crest.* A griffin's head couped . . . charged on the neck with two chevrons . . . . *Motto.* Vive ut vivas. The full blazon is: *Arms.* Quarterly, 1 & 4, Argent two chevronels between three chaplets Vert the roses d'Or (Burrough); 2 & 3, Argent a crossbow pointed upwards between four moorcocks Sable beaked and membered Gules (Highmore). *Crest.* A griffin's head couped Argent beaked Or charged with two chevronels as in the arms (FD7).

* Not cinquefoils, as recorded by Field (FAC).

† See DNB. Thomas was son of Abraham Highmore; his connection with the Cumberland Highmores has not been traced.

BURROUGH, or BURROW, of Carleton. Edward Burrow, of Muncaster (d. 1708), was father of the Rev. Edward Burrough (*c.* 1686-1776), schoolmaster of Carleton, Drigg, and Curate of Drigg and Irton 1730-75. His son the Rev. Stanley Burrough, M.A. (Oxon) (1725-1807), was Headmaster of Rugby 1752-78. His half-sister Anne (1745-1820) marr. Cuthbert Atkinson, *q.v.*, and their only child Elizabeth marr. 1807 her cousin Joseph Burrow, great-grandson of Joseph Burrow, younger brother of the above mentioned Rev. Edward Burrough. Joseph's son Edward (1726-1800), Collector of Customs at Port Glasgow, was M.P. for Cockermouth 1796. His younger brother Joseph (1731-74) marr. 1760 Elizabeth (d. 1773), dau. of Hugh Ashton, of Underley (W), and coheir of her brother James Ashton, and their son Joseph inherited his mother's share of the Underley estate. His son Joseph (d. 1849) marr. Elizabeth Atkinson, see above, and their grandson, Arthur Alfred Edward Burrow, the last of the family, sold Carleton Hall 1921 (J. R. E. Borron in CW2 lxix). *Arms* (as impaled by Atkinson on tombstone at Carleton Hall). . . . on a cross . . . five mullets . . . .

BURROUGHES. James Burkin Burroughes, of Burlingham Hall, Norfolk (d. 1803), was father of Mary (d. 1870), who marr. 1812 Col Sir George Charles Hoste, C.B., R.E. (d. 1845), *q.v.* Croglin Low Hall and Croglin High Hall formed part of her marriage settlement and were sold by her trustees 1873 (BP68; BLG11). *Arms.* Argent two chevronels Vert between three chaplets Gules each charged with four roses Or (Window, Kirkoswald church).

BURTHOLME, of Lanercost. Lancelot Burtholme, of Wall, Lanercost, sold his tenement in 1680 to his brother John Burtholme, or Burton, of Side House, Knaresdale (d. 1728, aged 78), who acquired two other tenements which passed to his son Lancelot Burton, of Side House, who sold them 1753. Christopher Burtholme, of Burtholme, yeoman, was bur. at Lanercost 1788, aged 89, and another branch of the family, of Hare Hill, were blacksmiths, Thomas Burtholme being representative in 1907. *Arms.* . . . a chevron . . . between three birds . . . . *Crest* (much weathered). A bird (Tombstone of John Burton, d. 1728, Knaresdale churchyard). In Lanercost churchyard on the tombstone of Christopher Burtholme (d. 1773, aged 23), the arms appear as: . . . a fess . . . between three birds' heads erased . . . . On another tombstone a chevron appears instead of a fess.

BURTON – see BURTHOLME.

BURUN – see BYRON.

BUSH. The Rev. James Bush, M.A. (Oxon) (d. 1849, aged 58), Rector of South Luffenham, Rutland, was Curate of Plumbland and Wythburn and lived at Dale Head Hall. His son the Rev. James Bush, M.A. (Oxon) (1817-89), was Rector of Ousby 1854-76, and a younger son John (1828-1908) was of Beauthorn, Watermillock, where he was succ. by his son Lt-Col John Bush, R.M.L.I. (d. 1951). His nephew Herbert E. Bush, of Gatesgarth, Watermillock, is the present head of the family. *Arms.* Argent on a fess between three boars passant Sable a fleur-de-lys between two eagles displayed Or. *Crest.* A goat's head erased Argent armed Or (VEW vi 73-4).

BUSHBY, of Greystoke. The first of this family to settle in Greystoke seems to have been Edward Bushby, who marr. 1613 Margaret Langhorne. Thomas Bushby (1716-92), son of John, of Berrier, had a large family baptised at Greystoke between 1740 and 1755. Of these, the eldest son Thomas (b. 1743) was a mariner, who d. on the coast of Guinea 1764,* and the Rev. Austin Bushby (1755-1819) was 2nd Master of Kepier School, Houghton-le-Spring (D) and was later of Harthill (Y) and Rector of Oxhill, Warwickshire, before retiring to Greystoke. His elder son† William Augustus Bushby (1793-1862) lived at Bushby House, Greystoke. *Arms.* Vair on a fess Gules five cloves Argent. *Crest.* A crow picking Proper (BGA). On the bookplate of John Bushby Gibson, *q.v.*, the arms are quartered as: Vair on a fess Argent five cloves . . . FVC & MVC, however, record for Busheby: Vair on a fess Gules three ermine spots Argent.

BUTCHERS' GUILD. Carlisle. Brigadier Thomas Stanwix, M.P., gave to the Butchers' Guild of Carlisle a silver porringer, hall marked London 1704-5, and bearing the arms of the Company. The porringer is now in Carlisle Museum. *Arms.* . . . two pole axes in saltire . . . between two bulls' heads . . . in fess and one in base on a chief . . . a boar's head erased . . . between two block brushes Vert.

BUTLER – see CLARKE-BUTLER-COLE.

BUXTON. Impaled by Ramsden on shield at Muncaster Castle; Sir John Frecheville Ramsden, 6th Bart. (1877-1958), marr. 1901 Joan, dau. of Geoffrey Fowell Buxton, C.B., of Hoveton Hall, Norwich. Of the same family, Lady Alethea Constance Dorothy Sydney Eliot, wife of the Ven. Peter Charles Eliot, *q.v.*, is dau. of the 1st and last Earl Buxton (1853-1934). *Arms.* Argent a lion rampant tail elevated and turned over the head Sable between two mullets of the second. *Motto.* Do it with thy might (NEP).

BYERS. A gravestone in Kirkandrews-on-Esk churchyard commemorates Mary, spouse to John Byers, in (?)Bonshasid (d. 1713, aged ?28). *Arms.* The whole stone is very weathered, but a shield is charged in chief with what seems to be meant for a roundle in very bold relief.

CRANMER-BYNG. Lt-Col Alfred Molyneux Cranmer-Byng, D.L., J.P. of Quendon Hall, Newport, Essex (1840-1906), marr. 1870 Caroline (d. 1887), dau. and coheir of the Rt. Hon. Henry Tufnell, *q.v.*, and in her right became Lord of the manor of Blencarn. *Arms.* Quarterly, 1 & 4, Quarterly Sable and Argent in the first quarter a lion rampant of the second (Byng); 2 & 3, Argent on a chevron Purpure between three pelicans Azure vulning themselves Proper as many cinquefoils Or (Cranmer). *Crests.* 1, An heraldic antelope passant Ermine horned tusked maned and hoofed Or (Byng); 2, A crane's head Ermine erased Gules pierced through the neck by an arrow in bend sinister Or barbed and flighted Argent. (Cranmer). *Motto.* Tuebor (BLG17).

BYRBANK. Thomas Bourbank, Archdeacon of Carlisle (d. 1520), is commemorated in the east window of Greystoke church. He was succ. by William Bourbank or Byrbank, LL.D. (Cantab), who was holding office in 1529; he was chaplain to Bishop Bell in 1488 (CW1 xv; VCHC). *Arms.* Field (FAC) quotes VCHC as authority for Archdeacon William's seal shewing: Three boars' heads couped. The shield on the seal as illustrated is a

* His M.I. in Greystoke churchyard speaks of his "regretted dissolution," and adds "He liv'd well respected with a steady and becoming Deportment and died much lamented with a fair and unblemish'd character."

† His younger son, the Rev. Frederick Ewan Bushby, M.A. (Cantab) (d. 1890, aged 94), became Fellow of Peterhouse 1825 and owned and managed the University Arms Hotel, Cambridge, where he died.

quarterly coat, and the charges in the first quarter could as well be three bears' heads as three boars' heads.

BYRON, or BURUN. *Arms* ascribed by Papworth (OBA) to these two families are on shields in Higham Hall, viz. Argent three bendlets Gules; and, Argent three bendlets sinister Gules.

CAETANI. Donna Lelia Calista Ada Caetani (d. 1977), only dau. of Roffredo Caetani, 18th Duke of Sermonetta, of Palazzo Caetani, Rome (d. 1960), marr. 1951 the Hon. Hubert John Edward Dominic Howard, of Lyulph's Tower, Ullswater, 3rd son of the 1st Baron Howard, of Penrith, *q.v. Arms.* Quarterly, 1 & 4, Argent two bendlets wavy Azure (Caetani); 2 & 3, Sable an eagle displayed Argent beaked membered and crowned Or (Aquila). *Mottoes.* Folia procumbunt; Memento quod Gibellinus es, et cum Gibellinis in cinerem reverteris (RAG).

CALDER ABBEY. Founded 1134 by Ranulph le Meschin. *Arms.* [Argent] three escutcheons, two and one, the first in dexter chief, Or a fess between two chevrons Gules; the second, Gules three lucies hauriant Argent; the third, Sable a fret Argent (TVN). These shields commemorate the three sisters and coheirs of John, 2nd Lord Multon of Egremont (d. *s.p., i.p.m.* 1335), patron of the Abbey, viz. Joan, marr. Robert FitzWalter; Margaret, marr. Thomas, Lord Lucy; and Elizabeth, marr. Robert de Harington.

CALLANDER. Impaled by Graham on monument in Arthuret church; Sir James Robert George Graham, P.C., G.C.B., LL.D., 2nd Bart., of Netherby (1792-1861), marr. 1819 Frances (d. 1857), youngest dau. of James Callander (later Campbell), of Craigforth and Ardkinglass (b. 1744). *Arms.* Quarterly, 1 & 4, Sable a bend chequy [Or and Gules] between six billets [of the second] (Callander); 2, Azure a stag's head cabossed [Or] (Mackenzie); 3, Gules three human legs in armour [Proper] flexed and conjoined in triangle at the upper part of the thigh (Kingdom of Man). The untinctured, unquartered arms are impaled by Graham on the monument to Sir J. R. G. Graham in Carlisle Cathedral.

CALTHROP. See COLLINGWOOD.

CALVERT, Thomas, of Kirkandrews-on-Esk, d. 1701. *Arms* (very weathered and indistinct). Paly of six a bend counterchanged. *Crest.* Out of (?) a coronet two flagstaffs flags to the sinister (Gravestone at Kirkandrews-on-Esk). Irving records the same arms and crest for William Calvert, of Toddbllwoad (*sic*) in North Britin (*sic*), 1721 (ABD).

CALVERT. The Rev. Frederick Calvert, M.A. (Cantab) (d. 1852, aged 59), Rector of Whatfield, Suffolk, 1823-52, had a freehold at Newby (W) in 1826. His son the Rev. Charles George Calvert, B.A. (Cantab) (b. 1833), was Vicar of Christ Church, Whitehaven, 1888-92, and was later of Duntroon Castle, Lochgilphead, and of Lowick, Argyll. He marr.* Susanna, dau. of John Warnes, by Louisa Blencowe, dau. and coheir of James Everard (see AWL). His 2nd son Charles Arthur Calvert, M.A. (Cantab) (d. 1948, aged 83), lived for many years at Lowick Hall, which he eventually bought from his cousin Francis Montagu. The representative of the family in Cumbria is his niece Mrs Margaret Everard Houlson, only surviving dau. of Rupert Harry Calvert (1878-1933) and wife of Herbert Robert Houlson, of 11 Marsh Garth, Kirkby-in-Furness. *Arms.* Paly of six Or and Sable a bend

* His brother William Sydney Calvert marr. Henrietta, another dau. of John Warnes.

counterchanged (DSA). *Crest.* Out of a ducal coronet two staves with pennons flying to the dexter side. *Motto.* Oh mon Dieu (*Ex inf.* Mrs M. E. Houlson).

CAMBRIDGE, University of. *Arms.* Gules on a cross Ermine between four lions passant guardant Or a Bible lying fesswise of the field clasped and garnished of the third the clasps in base (Shield on monument in Carlisle Cathedral to Richard Assheton, 1st Viscount Cross, *q.v.*).

CAMERTON, of Camerton. Alan de Camerton is mentioned as a Knight of Cumberland 1213-14. He was a son of Thomas de Workington, and younger brother of Patric de Curwen, who granted or confirmed to him all his lands in Camerton 1236. His descendant Robert de Camerton in 1404 released to his sister's son, Christopher Curwen, *q.v.*, land at Thornthwaite (W) and subsequently Christopher succ. to his uncle's Camerton estate (AHC). *Arms.* On a wooden panel from Camerton Hall, now in Camerton church, with date 1625 and initials H[enry] C[urwen] and B[ridget] C[urwen] the arms are quartered by Curwen as: Argent on a bend Gules three mullets pierced Or.

CAMPBELL. The Ven. Herbert Ernest Campbell, M.A. (Oxon) (d. 1930, aged 74), was Curate of Kirk Braddan, Isle of Man, 1881-82, Chaplain to the Bishop of Sodor and Man 1879-82, Vicar of St. George, Millom, 1887-95, Rector of Workington 1895-1905, Chaplain to the Bishop of Carlisle 1892-1905, Vicar of St. George, Barrow in Furness, 1905-11, Archdeacon of Furness 1905-11, Canon Residentiary of Carlisle 1911-30, Archdeacon of Carlisle 1920-30, and Chancellor of Carlisle 1920-30. His son the Ven. Donald Fitzherbert Campbell, M.A. (Oxon) (1886-1933), was Canon Residentiary and Archdeacon of Carlisle 1930-33. Another son Malcolm Drury Campbell was killed at Gallipoli 1915 aged 24. *Crest.* A boar's head erased Or armed Argent (Windows, Carlisle cathedral).

CAMPBELL. Impaled by Howard on shield in hall of Greystoke Castle; Sir Edward Stafford Howard, K.C.B., of Thornbury Castle, Glos (1851-1916), M.P. for East Cumberland 1876-85, marr. (1) 1876 Lady Rachel Campbell (d. 1906), youngest dau. of the 2nd Earl Cawdor. *Arms.* Quarterly, 1, Or a hart's head cabossed Sable; 2, Gyronny of eight Sable and Or; 3, Argent a galley oars in action Sable; 4, Per fess Azure and Gules a cross Or.

CANNING. Stained glass shield at Corby Castle; Philip Henry Howard, D.L., J.P., F.S.A., of Corby Castle (1801-83), *q.v.*, marr. 1843 Eliza Minto (1810-1865), eldest dau. of Major John Canning, H.E.I.C.S. (1775-1824), and niece and heir of Francis Canning, of Foxcote, Warwickshire (d. 1831). *Arms.* Argent three negroes' heads couped Proper wreathed about the temples Or and Azure.*

CANNING, Baron Garvagh. Leopold Ernest Stratford George Canning, 4th Baron Garvagh, of Garvagh, Co. Londonderry, D.L., J.P. (1878-1956), was for many years of The Grange, Keswick, and his widow Dora, Lady Garvagh, is now of Lyzzick Gate, Keswick. *Arms.* Quarterly of six, 1 & 6, Argent three Moors' heads in profile, two and one, couped Proper wreathed about the temples of the first and Azure (Canning); 2, Gules three spear heads erect in fess Argent (Salmon); 3, Sable a goat salient Or (Marshall); 4, Bendy Argent and Azure within a bordure Gules (Newburgh); 5, Per pale

* Correctly, Argent and Sable, as appears on an escutcheon of pretence in the library at Brunstock House.

Argent and Sable a fess nebuly between three griffins' heads erased within a bordure engrailed all counterchanged (Spencer). *Crests.* 1, A demi lion rampant Ermine holding in his paws a battle axe Proper; 2, A demi griffin segreant Sable beaked and legged Or; 3, A demi lion rampant Argent holding in his dexter paw an arrow pointing downwards Or feathered Argent. *Supporters.* Dexter, A griffin reguardant wings expanded Azure gutté d'Or beaked and legged of the last; Sinister, An eagle reguardant wings expanded Sable beaked and legged Or. *Motto.* Ne cede malis sed contra (BP105).

CANSFIELD. The *Arms* of this North Lancashire family, for further details of which see AWL, are on a shield on the ceiling of Carlisle Cathedral: Argent fretty Sable.

CANTERBURY, Archbishopric of. Window dated 1897 in Farlam church. *Arms.* Azure an episcopal staff in pale Argent ensigned with a cross pattée Or surmounted by a pall throughout of the second edged and fringed Gold and charged with four crosses formé fitché Sable. See also St. Bees School.

CAPELL. The arms of Capell are impaled by Howard, *q.v.*, on a silver loving cup, now in Carlisle Museum, given to Carlisle Corporation 1701 by Charles Howard, 3rd earl of Carlisle; he marr. 1688 Lady Anne Capell, dau. of Arthur, 1st Earl of Essex. *Arms.* [Gules] a lion rampant between three cross crosslets fitché [Or].

CARDOIL. Matthew Cardoil was Sheriff of Cumberland 1271-2. *Arms.* DSL attributes to him: Gules six annulets, two, two, and two, Argent.

CAREW. Sir Thomas Carew, 6th Bart., of Haccombe and Bickleigh, Devon (*c.* 1755-1805), marr. 1777 Jane (1754-1838), eldest dau. of the Rev. Charles Smalwood, *q.v.* Their dau. Frances marr. 1810 John Were Clarke, *q.v.*, and their granddau. Dora Frances (dau. of the Rev. Robert Baker Carew) marr. 1885 her cousin Charles Fetherstonhaugh (d. 1934), *q.v.* Jane, Lady Carew's sister Lydston Smalwood (1756-98) marr. 1785 Sir Thomas Carew's younger brother, the Rev. John West Carew. *Arms.* Or three lions passant in pale Sable (Shield in hall at The College, Kirkoswald).

CARLETON, of Carleton. The 1665 Visitation pedigree of this family is headed by Baldwyn, whose great-great-great-grandson Adam de Carleton is said to have been living 1286-87. His descendant John Carleton (d. before 1393-94) marr. Margaret, dau. and heir of John de Moston. His son, Thomas Carleton (said to be living 1399-1449) marr. Margaret, dau. and heir of George Dawbury, of Yorkshire. From them descended Thomas Carleton, of Mostyn Hall, Penrith (1514-87), who marr. Mabel, dau. and coheir of Thomas Carlyle of Carlisle. Their son Thomas Carleton (1547/8-98) marr. Barbara, dau. of Hugh Lowther, and was succ. by their son Sir Thomas Carleton (1568-1639), Recorder of Carlisle, who was knighted 1630. Dying *s.p.* he was succ. by his nephew Sir William Carleton (aged 58 in 1665, d. 1672), who was succ. by his son Robert Carleton (1656-1703), High Sheriff of Cumberland 1699,* who was the last of the family.† He marr.

* For the objection raised to his being buried in "Mr. Hutton's Quire" in St. Andrew's Church, Penrith, see Bishop Nicolson's diary.

† In St. Pancras Church, London, is a monument to John Carleton (d. 1709, aged 67), "son of Thomas Carleton Esqre who was eldest Eqvery to their Sacred Majes. King Charles the first & King Charles the second and was discended of the most Antient Family of the Carletons of Carleton Hall in the county of Cumberland." The family arms appear on the monument.

before 1698 Joan (d. 1722), 3rd dau. and coheir of John Frere, a London merchant, and the owner of an estate in Barbados, and widow of (1) Col Thomas Lewis, whom she marr. 1687, and (2) of Samuel Crisp. She marr. 4thly 1704 Robert Lowther, of Maulds Meaburn (1681-1745), Governor of Barbados, but had no issue by any of her husbands, her estates in Barbados passing to her 4th husband's family, who sold them *c.* 1916 (*Ex inf.* the late E. M. Shilstone, M.B.E., F.S.A., of the Barbados Museum and Historical Society). To a junior branch of the family belonged the Rt. Rev. Guy Carleton, M.A., D.D. (Oxon) (?1598-1685), Dean of Carlisle 1660-71, Bishop of Bristol 1671-78, and Bishop of Chichester 1678-85. *Arms.* Quarterly, 1, Ermine on a bend Sable three pheons Argent (Carleton), 2, Sable three bends* Argent in chief three plates (Moston); 3, Argent a cross between four lions rampant gules (Dawbury); 4, Or a cross moline Gules (Carlyle) (FCW). The Carleton arms, impaling Lowther, are on the ceiling of the Two Lions, Penrith. Bishop Carleton tinctured the pheons Or (BBE). *Crest.* An arm embowed Proper holding an arrow (LMC).

CARLETON, Baron Dorchester. Thomas Carleton, of Carleton (1514-87), *q.v.*, had another son Lancelot, of Brampton Foot (*c.* 1549/50-1619), who settled at Rossfad near Inniskellen. His descendant Sir Guy Carleton, K.B. (1724-1808), Governor of Canada 1775-78, was cr. Baron Dorchester, of Dorchester, 1786. His 4th son Lt-Col the Hon. George Carleton (1781-1814) marr. 1805 Henrietta, dau. of Edward King of Askham Hall, (see AWL), and their only son Guy (1811-75) succ. as 3rd Baron. He left two daus. and coheirs, Henrietta Anne (d. 1925), marr. (1) Francis Paynton Pigott, who assumed the name of Carleton, and (2) Major General Richard Langford Leir (afterwards Leir-Carleton), and was cr. Baroness Dorchester, of Dorchester, 1899; and Maria Georgiana (d. 1918), marr. 1865 Timothy Fetherstonhaugh, of The College, Kirkoswald, *q.v. Arms.* Ermine on a bend Sable three pheons Argent. On a tablet in Kirkoswald church, the pheons are tinctured Or. *Crest.* A dexter arm embowed Proper vested above the elbow Gules edged Argent the hand grasping an arrow in bend sinister point downwards also Proper. *Supporters.* Two beavers Proper, the dexter gorged with a mural coronet, the sinister with a naval coronet, both Or. *Motto.* Quondam his vicimus armis (NEP).

CARLILL, or CARLYLE. Thomas Carlill, or Carlyle, of Carlisle had a dau. and coheir Mabel, marr. Thomas Carleton, of Carleton (1514-87), *q.v. Arms* (as quartered by Carleton). Or a cross moline Gules (FCW).

CARLILL. Burke shews this family as of Cumberland and Westmorland but gives no place of residence. *Arms.* Or a cross flory Gules in the dexter chief a rose of the last. *Crest.* An arm embowed in armour holding in the hand all Proper a spear Argent (BGA).

CARLISLE. Henry I granted lands in Gamblesby and Glassonby before 1130 to Hildred de Carlisle, Sheriff of Carlisle 1129-55, and his son Odard (d. *c.* 1177) who became known as de Hoddam. His descendant Eudo de Carlisle went over to the Scots 1217 and seizin of his lands was given to Robert de Vaux. By 1225 he had regained possession (*Reg. Wetheral*), but his descendant William de Carlisle forfeited all his lands for treason 1317 (CW2 xxiv, xxxi). *Arms.* Or a cross patonce Gules (FFC).

CARLISLE, of Bridekirk. Adam Carlell or Carlyle (living 1486), brother of

* Correctly, bars.

John, 1st Lord Carlyle, *q.v.*, was ancestor of the family of Carlisle, of Bridekirk, Co. Dumfries. Herbert Carlisle (1558-1632) was father of Lancelot Carlisle, of Cairns, who marr. 1648 Barbara Johnstone and had daus. and coheirs Sara, marr. *c.* 1684 Edward Spedding (d. 1706), *q.v.*, and Mary, marr. John Gale (d. 1716), *q.v.* (CHC). *Arms.* Or a cross flory Gules. *Crest.* Two dragons' necks and heads addorsed Vert. *Motto.* Humilitate (TSF).

CARLISLE CANAL COMPANY, LTD. The seal of the Carlisle Canal* Co., Ltd., incorporated 1819, bore the following *Device.* A canal sailing-boat surmounted by a shield displaying: . . . a castle with two towers . . . on a chief . . . a lion passant guardant . . . .

CARLISLE, City of. In the *Dormont Book,* 1561, the *Arms* appear as: A cross flory between four roses. On Carlisle Cross, 1689, and on the Town Hall, 1717 and 1799, they appear as: A cross between four roses. In an alphabet of arms, *temp.* Charles II, in the College of Arms, they are given as: Gules two keys in saltire between four cross crosslets fitché Or. MMD gives: Argent a cross between four roses Gules. In Speed's *Map of Cumberland,* 1610, they appear as: Vert on a base wavy of four Argent and Azure a castle between two roses Or on a chief Gules a lion passant guardant of the fourth. These arms, but with the base wavy of six, were used from 1835 until 1924 when the city was granted the following *Arms.* Or on a cross pattée between four roses Gules a rose of the field barbed and seeded Proper. The shield ensigned by a castle triple-towered Or lined Gules the centre tower pierced by a gateway also Gules. *Supporters.* Upon a mount Vert on either side a wyvern Gules armed and langued Azure the wings semé of roses Or barbed Vert. *Motto.* Be just and fear not. The arms appeared on the City's common seal in 1462.

CARLISLE Grammar School. This old foundation, now part of Trinity Comprehensive School, originally used the arms of its patrons, the Dean and Chapter of Carlisle (see next entry). The school later used the following *Arms.* Quarterly, 1 & 4, Argent on a cross Sable a mitre Or†; 2, Or on a cross pattée between four roses Gules a rose of the field;† 3, Vert on a base wavy of six Argent and Azure a castle between two roses Or on a chief Gules a lion passant guardant of the fourth.‡ Still later it adopted the following: Argent a cross Sable between four roses Gules barbed Vert seeded Or (FAC).

CARLISLE, Priory and Deanery of. *Arms.* Argent a cross Sable (WEC; Shield on Salkeld screen in the Cathedral).

CARLISLE, See of. *Arms.* Argent on a cross Sable a mitre with labels Or (WEC). In the *Parliament Roll* of 1553, the cross is charged with a crown Or, instead of a mitre (BBE).

CARLYLE, of Cummersdale. From Robert Carlyle, of Cummersdale, Carlisle (1673-1737), descended a family of craftsmen and artists, of whom Nicholas Carlyle wrote: "They were distinguished by frankness of manners, integrity of conduct and unimpeachable veracity – and some of them exhibited a great degree of Talent." Robert's grandson Thomas Carlyle (1734-1816) was a noted wood carver and sculptor, who was responsible for

* An act to turn the bed of the canal into a railway line was secured in 1853.

† See Carlisle, See of.

‡ See Carlisle, City of.

the restoration of screens, altar piece, pulpit, pews and the bishop's throne in Carlisle cathedral. His son Thomas (b. 1762), a miniature painter, was living in Edinburgh in 1822. His sons George (b. 1797) and Robert (b. 1800) were also artists, and his younger brother Robert Carlyle, of Carlisle (1773-1825), was a well known artist, who was commissioned by William Hutchinson to illustrate his *History of Cumberland. Arms.* Or a cross flory Gules. *Crest.* A dexter arm embowed in armour Or garnished Gules the hand in a gauntlet holding a baton Or (CHC).

CARLYLE, of Torthorwald and of Carlisle. Sir William de Carlell, of Torthorwald, Co. Dumfries (d. between 1452 and 1463), had sons Sir John, of whom presently, and Adam, ancestor of the Carlyles of Bridekirk, *q.v.* Sir John (d. 1501) was cr. Lord Carlyle of Torthorwald in 1473 or 1474. His descendant Michael, 4th Lord Carlyle (d. 1575), had a son Edward, of Limekilns, whose descendant William Carlyle (d. 1744, aged 65) was a surgeon in Carlisle. His son Dr. George Carlyle (1715-84) practised in Kendal, but bought in 1772 the house in Abbey Street, Carlisle, now called Eaglesfield House. His son the Rev. Joseph Dacre Carlyle, M.A., B.D. (Cantab) (1759-1804), was Perpetual Curate of St. Cuthbert, Carlisle, Vicar of Torpenhow 1791-1801, Vicar of Castle Sowerby 1792-1801, Chancellor of Carlisle 1795-1804, Vicar of Newcastle upon Tyne 1801-4, and Professor of Arabic at Cambridge 1795-1804. His only son George d. 1798, aged 10, and his heir was his dau. Eleanor (1793-1870) who marr. Col Henry Dundas Maclean, of Lazonby Hall, *q.v.* (CHC). *Arms.* Or a cross flory Gules. *Crest.* Two dragons' heads and necks addorsed Vert (Shields in Eaglesfield House, Carlisle). POA gives for Carlyle, of Limekilns, 1736; Or a cross fleury Gules in the dexter chief point a crescent of the last. Burke adds for the Limekilns family, a *Crest.* A dexter arm holding a writing pen Proper. *Motto.* Humilitate (BGA).

CARMALT, of Langrigg. John Carmalt, of Langrigg, Bromfield, marr. Mabel, dau. and heir of Thomas Kendall, of the same place, and had a son William Carmalt, of Langrigg, who in 1740 represented to the College of Arms that his ancestors had held large estates in Cumberland, and had used as arms a dragon sejant wings elevated with crest a dragon's head erased, engraved on a silver cup about 100 years old in the family's possession. He was then granted the following: *Arms.* Vert a dragon sejant with his wings expanded between three escallop shells Or. *Crest.* A dragon's head erased party per pale Vert and Or gorged with a collar charged with three escallop shells counterchanged (CA viii/271).

CARPENTERS, Guild of. Stone shield on house in Lynns Court, Penrith, with initials R T E and date 1723. *Arms.* [Argent] a chevron engrailed between three compasses expanded [Sable].

CARR, of Carlisle. Jonathan Dodgson Carr (1806-84), son of a Kendal grocer, walked to Carlisle and established himself as a biscuit maker there. In 1841 by Royal Appointment he became biscuit maker to the Queen and at his death he had established a group of four flour mills, a small fleet of coasting vessels, and depots serving north-west England and southern Scotland, as well as bakeries. His grandson Frank Arnold Carr, of Hallsteads, Watermillock (1873-1942), chairman and managing director of Carr's Flour Mills Ltd., was High Sheriff of Cumberland 1941. His uncle James Nicholson Carr, of Cavendish Mount, Carlisle (1838-1901), was father of Lt-Col Ronald Nicholson Carr, M.C., D.L., J.P., of Newbiggin Hall, Carlisle (1894-1967), chairman of Messrs. Carr & Co., whose elder son, the Rev. Douglas Nicholson Carr, B.A. (Cantab), is now head of the family. *Arms.* Or on a pale Sable two roses over all a chevron charged with three mullets pierced all counterchanged. *Crest.* On a coronet consisting of three roses set on a plain rim a stag's head cabossed. *Motto.* Tout droit (F. A. Carr's seal as High Sheriff).

CARR. The Rev. Edmund Carr, M.A. (Cantab) (1826-1916), 2nd son of the Rev. John Edmund Carr, M.A. (Cantab), of The Outwoods (Dy), was Perpetual Curate of Casterton 1861-66, Vicar of Dalston 1866-83, Hon. Canon of Carlisle 1867-1916, Proctor in Convocation, Archdeaconry of Carlisle 1874-86, and Rural Dean of Wigton 1880-83. He was later Vicar of Holbrooke (Dy). *Arms.* Per pale Gules and Sable on a chevron invected plain cotised Argent a stag's attires Proper between two mullets of six points Sable in base a like mullet of the third. *Crest.* A stag's head erased Proper charged on the neck with a mullet of six points Or between two thistles slipped and leaved Proper. *Motto.* Tout droit (BLG18).

CARR-LLOYD. On a brass in Kirkoswald church commemorating Nancy (d. 1917, aged 40), wife of Lt-Col Timothy Fetherstonhaugh, of The College, Kirkoswald, *q.v.*, and dau. and heir of James Martin Carr-Lloyd, of Lancing Manor, Sussex, the *Arms* of Carr-Lloyd are impaled as: Quarterly, 1 & 4, Gules on a chevron Argent three estoiles of the field (Carr);* 2 & 3, Per bend sinister Ermine and Ermines a lion rampant Argent (Lloyd). On an impaled shield at The College, Kirkoswald, however, and on a silver achievement, the foregoing is replaced by: Quarterly, 1 & 4, Per bend sinister Ermine and Pean a lion rampant Or gorged with a wreath of oak Vert and holding in the dexter forepaw a sword erect Proper hilt and pommel Gold a canton Gules; 2 & 3, Per pale Argent and Sable three mullets between two chevronels all counterchanged. *Crests.* A lion's head erased gorged with a wreath and charged on the neck with a cross crosslet (Lloyd); 2, A stag's head erased charged on the neck with three roundles between two chevronels. *Motto.* Pro Deo et rege.

CARRICK, John, of Morrow, Lanercost, died 1752, aged 75. *Arms.* A fess between three dogs passant (Lanercost tombstone).

CARRICK. James Carrick, of Brampton, died 1831, aged 83 or 85. *Arms.* ... in chief two axe heads blades downwards ... in base an escutcheon ... charged with a chief the upper edge embattled ... (Lanercost tombstone).

CARRUTHERS, John, of Foultown, Arthuret, labourer, died 1783. *Arms.* ... three fleurs-de-lys ... (ABD). Field gives: Gules three fleurs-de-lys Or (FAC). Another broken tombstone at Arthuret, with no name or date visible, bore the same arms (ABD).

CARRUTHERS. William Carruthers, of Lineholme Mill, Stapleton, died 1727, aged 59. *Arms.* Three fleur-de-lys, one and two, in chief two mullets (Gravestone, Stapleton churchyard). Irving recorded the same and in addition: ... in base a millrind and below it a heart (ABD).

CARRUTHERS. John Carruthers, of Longtown, died 1719, aged 82. *Arms.* ... a chevron engrailed between three fleurs-de-lys .... *Crest.* A

* On a fine set of armorial china at The College, Kirkoswald, the Carr arms appear as: Gules on a chevron Argent three mullets Sable. *Crest.* A stag's head erased Argent attired Or.

cherub's head. *Motto.* Ready and faithful (Gravestone in Arthuret churchyard). Irving and Field incorrectly recorded the date as 1710; and Irving recorded the chevron as wavy and omitted the crest (ABD; FAC).

CARRUTHERS. Impaled by Salkeld on monument in Dalston church; David Alexander Carruthers, of Warmanbie, Annan (1789-1872), Lieutenant 30th Bengal N.I., son of James Carruthers, of Liverpool, cooper, marr. Jane, sister of Hornby Roughsedge (see AWL) and had issue *int. al.* a dau. Mary (d. 1845, aged 19) who marr. Thomas Salkeld, of Holm Hill (d. 1878, aged 71), *q.v.* *Arms.* . . . two chevronels . . . between three fleurs-de-lys . . . .

CARTMELL. This well known Carlisle and Brampton legal family is descended from Isaac Cartmell, of Broad Oak, Crosthwaite (W) (d. 1788, aged 91), whose grandson James Cartmell (1773-1821), a native of Witherslack, was a tanner in Irish Damside, Carlisle. His eldest son the Rev. James Cartmell, D.D. (Cantab) (1810-81), was Master of Christ's College, Cambridge, and his 3rd son Isaac Cartmell, of London Road, Carlisle (1814-88), was City Treasurer of Carlisle 1849 until death. He marr. 1841 Mary, dau. of William Robinson Martindale and granddau. of Joseph Studholme. Their 2nd son Studholme Cartmell, solicitor, of Westgarth, Hayton (1844-1906), was clerk to Carlisle magistrates 1880-1906. His only son Henry Studholme Cartmell, solicitor, of Woodside, Hayton, and Heads Nook Hall (1875-1946), was clerk to Carlisle and Eskdale magistrates, and steward of the Barony of Gilsland. His elder son Geoffrey Studholme Cartmell, T.D., M.A. (Cantab), solicitor, of Brampton and Kirklinton (1914-76), was clerk to Brampton and Alston magistrates. His elder son is John Cartmell, consultant engineer, and the family is represented in Cumberland by his (Geoffrey's) younger son, Timothy Henry Cartmell, T.D., M.A. (Cantab), solicitor, of The Firs, Easton, Burgh-by-Sands, who is a partner in the firm of Cartmell, Mawson & Main, of Carlisle and Brampton. *Arms* (granted to the above Isaac Cartmell of Carlisle, and the descendants of his father, 1887). Per pale nebuly Gules and Vert a lion rampant Or gutté de sang holding between the paws a tent Argent. *Crest.* A lion rampant per fess nebuly Vert and Gules gutté d'Or supporting a tent Or (CA lxiv/62).

CARUS. Impaled by Curwen, *q.v.*, on a shield carved in oak at Workington Hall; Sir Nicholas Curwen (1550-1605) marr. (2) before 1587 Elizabeth (d. 1611), dau. and heir of Thomas Carus, of Halton (L), see AWL. *Arms.* Qurterly, 1 & 4, Azure on a chevron between ten cinquefoils, six and four, Argent three mullets Gules (Carus); 2, Argent two bars Gules on a canton of the last a cinquefoil Or pierced of the field a crescent for difference (Preston); 3, . . . a goat statant . . . on a chief . . . two garbs . . . . A slightly different version of the Carus arms is impaled by Hasell on a silver two-handled cup at Dalemain, presented by the regiment 1811 to Edward Hasell, *q.v.*, Lt-Col Commandant of the West and East Wards of Local Militia, who marr. 1792 Elizabeth (1767-1810), dau. of William Carus, of Kirkby Lonsdale, viz. Azure on a chevron between nine cinquefoils [Argent] three mullets [Gules].

CASSON, of Frith Hall. The Casson family, of Kilnbank, Seathwaite (L), claimed descent from an old yeoman family of that name of Frith Hall, Ulpha; for details of the family at Seathwaite, see AWL. *Arms.* Argent on three chevrons Gules as many mullets of the first a canton of the second.

Crest. From a tower a dove rising Argent. *Motto.* Prosequor alis (BGA; OBA).

CASTELL. Said by Burke to be of Cumberland, Warwick and Devon. *Arms.* Argent three towers triple-towered Gules. *Crest.* A tower Argent flammant in the top Proper (BGA). Papworth gives the arms as: Argent three castles Gules (OBA).

CASTILE. The arms of Castile are in a window in Carlisle cathedral given by the Friends of the Cathedral, 1949; John of Gaunt, Duke of Lancaster, marr. (2) 1372 Constance (1354-94), dau. of Peter I, King of Castile. *Arms.* Quarterly, 1 & 4, Gules a castle Or; 2 & 3, Argent a lion rampant Sable; impaling, Quarterly, France (ancient) and England. The same impaled coat is in a clerestory window in the Cathedral.

CASTLE CARROCK. Eustace de Vaux was Lord of Castle Carrock *c.* 1169 and may have been ancestor of a family of that name who owned the manor. Gamel de Castlecarrock *occ.* 1160-70, and Robert *fl.* 1209-32. His son Sir Robert is mentioned 1255 and grandson Sir Richard in 1262-71. The latter's son Robert marr. Christiana, dau. of Adam de Crookdake, *q.v.*, and aunt and coheir of John de Crookdake (d. *c.* 1322). Their daus. and coheirs were Joan, marr. Thomas de Newbiggin; Christiana, marr. Michael de Appleby; and Margaret, marr. John de Eaglesfield. *Arms.* MMD records two coats: Or a fess dancetté between three mastiffs Sable; and, . . . a castle . . . . Both ascriptions seem most dubious.

CASTLEHOW, of Waterside. Thomas Castlehow, of Waterside, Watermillock, yeoman (d. 1863, aged 46), was father of Anne Elizabeth (1859-1911) and William Castlehow, M.A. (Oxon), of Waterside (1863-1918), who are described on their tombstone in Watermillock churchyard as "the last direct descendants of a line of statesmen who had unbroken connection with this parish prior to and since the year 1562." *Arms.* Azure on a mount Vert a castle Proper in chief three passion crosses Or. *Crest.* A castle Proper therefrom issuant a lion Azure supporting a passion cross Or (FD7).

CASTRE. Sir John de Castre (d. *s.p.* 1324), a Nottinghamshire landowner, had licence 1298 to marry Isabel, widow of Thomas de Multon (d. 1294-5). In 1306 he was pardoned for the death of John de Salkeld. He was a Knight banneret in 1310, the year in which he was High Sheriff of Cumberland. He filled the office again in 1311, and in 1316-18. In 1316 he was appointed Constable of Carlisle. *Arms.* Azure an eagle displayed barry of ten Argent and Gules. Another version: Sable an eagle displayed barry of twelve Argent and Gules (FFC).

CAVENDISH, Duke of Devonshire. William, 5th Duke of Devonshire, K.G. (1748-1811), son of William, 4th Duke of Devonshire (1720-64), by his wife, Charlotte Elizabeth, Baroness Clifford (1731-54), dau. and heir of Richard, Earl of Burlington and Cork, inherited his mother's Barony of Clifford (created 1628), and bought the Honour of Penrith 1787 from William Henry Cavendish Bentinck, 3rd Duke of Portland, *q.v.* He marr. (1) 1774 Georgiana (d. 1806), elder dau. of John, 1st Earl Spencer, and was succ. by his son William Spencer, 6th Duke of Devonshire, K.G. (1790-1858), who d. unmarr., when the Barony of Clifford fell into abeyance between his sisters and coheirs, Georgiana (d. 1858), wife of George, 6th Earl of Carlisle, *q.v.*, and Harriet Elizabeth (d. 1862), wife of the 1st Earl

Granville. *Arms.* Sable three bucks' heads cabossed Argent. *Crest.* A serpent nowed Proper. *Supporters.* Two bucks Proper each wreathed round the neck with a chaplet of roses alternately Argent and Azure. *Motto.* Cavendo tutus (BP105). The arms, which are quartered by Howard, are on a shield in the Great Hall of Naworth Castle with a canton, Quarterly Argent and Gules in the second and third quarters a fret Or over all on a bend Sable three escallops Argent (Spencer).

CAVENDISH-BENTINCK – see BENTINCK, CAVENDISH-.

CAVERSWELL. Shields at Hutton-in-the-Forest; a Vane quartering. *Arms.* Azure fretty Argent a fess Gules.

CHALONER, of St. Bees. Sir Thomas Chaloner (1521-65), knighted 1547 for bravery at the Battle of Musselburgh, son of Roger Chaloner, mercer, of London,* was secretary to Sir Henry Knyvett, *q.v.*, when Ambassador to the Diet at Ratisbon. In 1547 he was granted the possessions of the dissolved monastery of Gisborne (Y), and in 1553 he and his wife Joan (d. 1556), widow of Sir Thomas Leigh, notorious for his part in the suppression of the monasteries, obtained a grant of the possessions of St. Bees Priory, including the manor and rectory. He was Ambassador to Brussels 1559 and to Spain 1561. His son Sir Thomas Chaloner (d. 1615) was the founder of the alum industry in Yorkshire. In 1586 he sold the land upon which St. Bees School and the headmaster's house were built. He sold the St. Bees estate to Sir Gerard Lowther and Thomas Wybergh 1599 (JPP; Lowther documents). *Arms.* Sable a chevron between three cherubs' heads Or. *Crest.* A demi sea wolf rampant (CVY). Burke tinctures the crest Or (BGA).

CHAMBER, of Milwood. In 1707 Elizabeth Chamber, widow, was charged for unlawfully displaying arms at the funeral of her husband Thomas Chamber, of St. Andrew, Holborn, London, and for depicting arms on a hatchment set up on the front of his house in Ormond Street. She admitted using the following, being the arms of Chamber, of Milwood, Cumberland, from which family Thomas Chamber was descended. *Arms.* Argent a chevron Azure between three trefoils slipped Gules a crescent for difference. *Crest.* A bear passant Proper (Harl. Soc. cvii 105).

CHAMBER(S), of Raby Cote. Pedigrees of the Chamber(s) family are in CW2 i. One branch was of Wolsty Castle, Thomas Chamber holding the estate in 1525-38, and Robert Chamber in 1634. Raby Cote was held by Thomas Chamber (d. 1523) who is said to have been brother of Robert, Abbot of Holm Cultram. The property descended to Thomas Chamber (d. 1619) who marr. 1574 Anne Musgrave, who was murdered by Robert Beckwith 1586. He marr. (2) Jane, widow of Fergus Graham, of Nunnery, and had a son John, who was succ. 1655 by William Chamber (b. 1615), son of his sister Florence, who marr. Thomas Chamber, of Hertlawe, a distant cousin. His grandson Arthur Chamber surrendered Raby Cote 1732. A pedigree of six generations of a younger branch, settled at Knowhill, ends with George Chambers (d. 1764, aged 86) who left a dau. Frances, marr. . . . Reed, and another dau. who marr. James Edwards (CW2 i 194-234). *Arms.* Argent a chevron Azure between three trefoils slipped Gules. *Crest.* A boar passant muzzled lined and collared Or (LMC). Field gives: A bear passant Sable muzzled collared and chained Or (FAC). Robert

* The name seems to be derived from "Chalons", the material used for making blankets, which came from Chalons in France.

Chamber, or Chambers, Abbot of Holm Cultram, used for *Arms:* Quarterly, 1, . . . a cross moline . . . ; 2 & 3, In chief a mitre surmounting a pastoral staff between the letters R C and in base a chained bear (Shields at Raby Cote). *Rebus.* A bear chained to a pastoral staff enfiled with a mitre (Carvings at Holm Cultram). George Chambers, of Knowhill (d. 1764), see above, used for *Arms:* . . . in front of a post and chained thereto a bear collared (ABD).

CHAMBRE, of Whitehaven. Walter Chambre, of Lowther Street, Whitehaven (1743-1813), younger brother of Sir Alan Chambre (see AWL), was a partner in the firm of Eilbeck, Chambre and Ross, merchants in the Virginia trade.* He marr. 1767 Elizabeth (d. 1813, aged 65), eldest dau. and coheir of James Fox† by his wife Jane, dau. and heir of J. Troughear, of Aspatria and Whitehaven. His eldest son, the Rev. Alan Chambre, M.A. (Cantab) (1770-1800), Curate of Crosscrake (W), d. *v.p.*, having marr. 1799 Mary, dau. and heir of John Banks Russell, by whom he had a dau. and heir, Mary Alan Chambre (1800-61), who d. unmarr. The male line was continued by her uncle Thomas Chambre (d. 1836), barrister-at-law, who marr. Anne Grierson, dau. and heir of John Harrison; their eldest son Alan (b. 1796), Captain 17th Lancers, had an only son, Alan Francois Henri Victor Edouard Chambre (1831-1902), who marr. 1854 Beatrice, dau. of Thomas Harrison. *Arms.* Or a cross Ermine between four birds Azure on a chief of the last a serpent coronée devouring a woman Or between two roses Gules (CVY – "No proofe made of these Armes"). NB give: Or a cross Ermine between four martlets rising Sable and for an augmentation, on a chief Azure a snake coronée devouring a child Proper between two roses Gules. *Crest.* A cock Gules holding in his dexter claws three wheat-ears Or. *Motto.* En Dieu est tout (BLG 1846).

CHANCE, of Morton. From John Chaunce, yeoman, of Shepley, Bromsgrove, Worcs. (d. 1618), descended Edward Chance, D.L., J.P., of Lawnside, Great Malvern (1824-81), who marr. 1850 Maria Isabella (d. 1890), 3rd dau. of Joseph Ferguson, of Morton (1785-1863), M.P. for Carlisle 1852-57, Mayor of that city 1837, and a partner in the great firm of Ferguson Brothers, cotton spinners and manufacturers of Holme Head, Carlisle, an undertaking which was for many years carried on by the Chance family. Edward Chance's eldest son, Sir Frederick William Chance, K.B.E., D.L., J.P. (1852-1932), who was a director of Ferguson Brothers, was of Morton, and later of Lancrigg, Grasmere. He was M.P. for Carlisle 1905-9, Mayor 1907, and High Sheriff of Cumberland 1915.‡ His two elder sons, Edward Seton (b. 1881) and Andrew Ferguson (b. 1882), were killed in action in 1918 and 1916. His 3rd son, Sir Robert Christopher Chance, K.B.E., D.L., J.P., B.A. (Cantab), of Morton (1883-1960), was Mayor of

* The firm suffered serious losses in the American War of Independence.

† BLG 1849 gives among the unblazoned quarterings of the Chambre family, Fox and Troughear. James Fox, of Whitehaven, carpenter, aged 30, marr. 1747 Jane Troughear, aged 19 (*ex inf.* Mr. R. Sharpe France). BLG says that she was descended from an ancient Irish family settled in Cumberland in the 17th century, adding that J. Troughear of Whitehaven had a great nephew, the Rev. Leonard Troughear, cr. Baron Holmes in 1797; he was son of Thomas Troughear, D.D., of Northwood, IOW, by his wife Elizabeth (1696-1788), dau. of Henry Holmes, of Yarmouth, IOW, assumed the surname Holmes, and d. *s.p.m.* 1804 when the peerage became extinct (BEP). BGA does not record arms for Troughear.

‡ Other members of the family to serve as High Sheriff were Frederick Selby Chance, 1934, and Kenneth Miles Chance, 1949.

Carlisle 1929-30, High Sheriff of Cumberland 1938, Lord Lieutenant of Cumberland 1949-58, and Chairman of Ferguson Bros. His elder son, Andrew Frederick Seton Chance, J.P., of Garth House, Brampton, Vice-Chairman of Ferguson Bros., was High Sheriff of Cumberland 1965. *Arms.* Gules a saltire Vair between two fleurs-de-lys in pale and as many towers in fess Argent. *Crest.* A demi lion rampant Gules semé of annulets Or holding between the paws a sword erect entwined by a wreath of oak all Proper. *Motto.* Deo non fortuna (BLG18; FD7).

CHAPELHOW, of Lanehead. Samuel Chapelhow, of Bolton, was father of Samuel Chapelhow (1714-1806), who was grandfather of the Rev. Joseph Chapelhow, J.P. (d. 1879, aged 87), Assistant Curate of Culgaith and Curate of Kirkland 1819-45, Rector of Newton Reigny 1845-46, and Rector of Great Musgrave 1846-79. His only son, the Rev. Joseph Chapelhow, M.A., D.D. (Oxon) (1845-1914), was Curate of Kirkby Stephen 1873-75, Rector of Kirkbampton 1879-96, Rector of Great Musgrave 1896-97, and Rector of Kirkandrews-on-Esk 1897-1914. *Arms.* Ermine two flaunches Gules; on an escutcheon of pretence, . . . three crescents each enclosing a star between its tips . . . . *Crest.* A griffin's head erased gorged with a ducal coronet (Tombstone of Samuel Chapelhow, d. 1806, in Boltongate churchyard).

CHAPMAN. The Rev. Edward William Chapman, M.A. (Cantab) (1841-1919), was Vicar of Lanercost 1873-79, and of Penrith 1882-88, and Hon. Canon of Carlisle 1887-1919. He marr. 1872 the Hon. Theodosia Spring-Rice, dau. of the Hon. Stephen Spring-Rice and sister of Thomas, 2nd Lord Monteagle. Their son James Chapman, B.A. (Oxon) (1879-1952), marr. 1906 Dorothy Christian (1878-1940), 3rd dau. of the Hon. Augustus William Erskine, *q.v.*, and coheir of her brother Henry Walter Coningsby Erskine. Their son James Erskine Chapman, M.B.E., J.P., is of Leck Hill House (L). *Arms.* Per chevron Argent and Gules a crescent counterchanged. *Crest.* An arm embowed habited in mail Proper cuffed Argent holding in the hand Proper a tilting spear Or enfiled with a chaplet Vert (BFR). *Mottoes.* A cuspide corona; Resurgam (Bookplate of James Chapman).

CHARDIN. A shield in a window in the south-west corner of the nave is attributed by W. T. McIntrye in *St. Cuthbert's Church, Edenhall,* revised by W. Dodd, 1972, to Chardin; Sir Christopher Musgrave, 5th Bart (d. 1735), marr. 1711 Julia, dau. of Sir John Chardin, of Kempton Park, Middlesex. *Arms.* Per chevron Argent and Sable gutté d'Or in chief two roses Gules. The correct arms are in a window in Kirkoswald church: Argent a chevron Azure between in chief two roses Gules and in base a dove Proper.*

CHARLETON. The Rev. Charles Charleton, M.A. (Oxon) (1761-1824), 3rd son of William Charleton, of Lee Hall (N) (d. 1794), agent of the Duke of Northumberland at Alnwick, was ordained priest by the Bishop of Carlisle 1785 and was Vicar of Tynemouth (N) 1789-1824. He marr. Anna Maria, dau. of Robert Holme, a Carlisle attorney. He was constantly non-resident in Tynemouth, and lived in Abbey Street, Carlisle. He appears to have inherited from his wife a share in an estate in Calcutta, which passed to their 2nd son Charles Charleton, M.D., M.R.C.P. (Edin), of North Shields (d. 1827, aged 33). *Arms.* . . . a lion rampant . . . (Will of William Charlton, of Lee Hall, d. 1716). Probably, Or a lion rampant Gules, i.e. the arms of

* NB (i 599) give the dove as Azure.

Charlton, *q.v.*, of Hesleyside, from which family that of Lee Hall was almost certainly descended.

CHARLTON. Edward Charlton, J.P., of Hesleyside (N), marr. 1681 Margaret, dau. of Sir Francis Salkeld, of Whitehall, *q.v.* His granddau. Margaret (d. *s.p.* 1769) marr. 1737 Henry Salkeld, *q.v.*, the last male of the family. At her death the Cumberland estates, including Whitehall and the manor of Torpenhow, passed to her nephew William Charlton (1750-97). They descended to William Henry Charlton, J.P., of Hesleyside (1876-1950), who was succ. by his dau. Mary Ellen Patricia, who is Lady of the Manor of Torpenhow. She marr. 1944 her kinsman, Major Frederick John Anne, who assumed the name and arms of Charlton 1951. *Arms.* Or a lion rampant Gules a chief Ermine fretty Vert on a canton Sable a lion rampant of the field. *Crest.* A lion's face Gules between two dragons' wings elevated Proper on each a fret Sable. *Motto.* Sans varier (BLG18).

CHARLTON. Impaled by Fetherstonhaugh on shield at The College, Kirkoswald; Bronwen Alicia Mary (d. 1970, aged 87), elder dau. of St. John Charlton, of Cholmondeley, Malpas (Ch) (d. 1919), and his wife Elizabeth Bronwen (d. 1941), sister and coheir of Lt-Col Henry Bodvel Lewis Hughes, D.L., J.P., of Kinmel, N. Wales, marr. 1920 Col Timothy Fetherstonhaugh, *q.v.*, and had a son, David Henry Fetherstonhaugh, D.L., J.P., who succ. to the Kinmel estate. *Arms.* Or a lion rampant Gules armed and langued Azure.

CHAUCER. Said wrongly to be a Hudleston quartering, brought in by the marr. of Joan, dau. and coheir of Sir Miles Stapleton, *q.v.*, to Sir John Hudleston, of Millom (d. 1512), *q.v.* Joan's mother Katherine (d. 1494) was dau and heir of Sir Thomas De la Pole, brother of Michael, 1st earl of Suffolk, whose grandson William, 1st Duke of Suffolk (d. 1450), marr. Alice, dau. and heir of Thomas Chaucer, son of the poet Chaucer. Joan Stapleton, therefore, could have no right to the Chaucer quartering, though her descendants used it, as did the Fleming family who were not even descended from her. *Arms.* Per pale Argent and Gules a bend counterchanged (Shields at Hutton John and elsewhere).*

CHAUCOMBE. Shield at Hutton-in-the-Forest; a Vane quartering. *Arms.* Sable a lion rampant Argent.

CHAYTOR. Impaled by Richmond at Highhead and Catterlen; Isabella (1594-1632), dau. of Anthony Chaytor, of Croft (Y), marr. 1613 Christopher Richmond, *q.v.*, of Highhead Castle. *Arms.* Quarterly, 1 & 4, Per bend indented Azure and Argent three cinquefoils counterchanged (Chaytor); 2 & 3, Or a saltire Sable (Clervaux) (JPP i 115).

CHESTER, See of. Shields in the churches of St. Michael and St. John, Workington. *Arms.* Gules three mitres Or.

CHETTLETON. Shield at Hutton-in-the-Forest; a Vane quartering. *Arms.* Argent on a chevron Gules five bezants all within a bordure engrailed of the second.

CHETWYND. Shield at Hutton-in-the-Forest; a Vane quartering. *Arms.* Azure a chevron between three mullets Or.

CHRISTIAN, Bishop of Candida Casa or Whithorn. Thought to have consecrated Lanercost Priory, 1169 (CW1 i 100-1). *Arms.* Gules three covered cups Or (Shield on curtains in Lanercost Priory church). These

* The arms are not on the font at Millom as stated by Field (FAC).

arms, which are on a shield on the west end of the church, are, however, ascribed by Field to Lanercost Priory itself (FAC).

CHRISTIAN, of Unerigg. Ewan Christian, 10th of Milntown, Isle of Man (d. 1655), bought Unerigg, Dearham, *c.* 1638, and was succ. by his son John (1602-73), who lived mostly in Cumberland. His grandson Ewan, barrister-at-law (1651-1719), who was the friend and steward of Bishop Nicolson, built "a good house out of the shell of an old tower." His grandson Ewan (d. 1752, aged 34) was succ. by his brother John Christian, J.P. (d. 1767), who was a lawyer at Cockermouth before succeeding to Unerigg and Milntown. He was High Sheriff of Cumberland 1766. He was succ. by his son John Christian, J.P., M.H.K., 16th of Milntown (1756-1828), who was M.P. for Carlisle 1786-1812 and 1816-20, and for Cumberland 1820-28, and High Sheriff 1784. He marr. (1) 1775 Margaret (1748-78), dau. of John Taubman, and had an only son John, see below; and (2) 1782 his first cousin Isabella, dau. and heir of Henry Curwen, of Workington Hall, *q.v.*; their descendants inherited that estate. They assumed the name and arms of Curwen 1790. The above John Christian J.P., M.H.K., Deemster, M.A. (Cantab), barrister-at-law (1776-1852), succ. to Unerigg and Milntown, and was succ. by his son Henry Taubman Christian, 18th of Milntown (1810-59). He was succ. by his brother, the Rev. William Bell Christian, J.P., M.H.K., B.A. (Cantab) (1815-86), Vicar of Lezayre, IOM, 1845-61. On his death Milntown and Unerigg were sold, but his widow later rented Milntown and lived there with her daughters for many years. His eldest son Captain Ewan John Christian, Argyll and Sutherland Highlanders (1845-98), left two daus. and coheirs, Gladys Muriel (b. 1892), marr. 1916 Dr. Rupert Conrad Hewitt, and Sybil Edith (b. 1895), marr. (1) Captain Archibald Knowles Jackson, D.S.O., M.C., and (2) Col E. Gavin Byrne. To a junior branch of the family belonged Charles Christian, of Moorland Close, Brigham, attorney (1729-68), whose son Fletcher Christian (b. 1764) played the leading part in the famous Bounty Mutiny. Another cadet of the family was the Rev. Thomas Christian, B.A. (T.C.D.) (1697-1770), Vicar of Crosthwaite 1728-70. *Arms.* Azure a demi mascle between three covered cups Or. *Crest.* A unicorn's head erased Argent crined and gorged with a collar invected Or. *Motto.* Salus per Christum (BLG18). On the tomb of Charles Christian in Brigham churchyard the arms appear as: . . . a chevron between three covered cups . . . . The arms are also on the tombstones in Crosthwaite churchyard of the Rev. Thomas Christian and his 3rd wife Emma (d. 1794, aged 84).

CÎTEAUX, Abbey of. The arms of the Abbey of Cîteaux, the mother house of Holm Cultram, are on a roof corbel in Holm Cultram Abbey; the arms were used by all Cistercian houses in France. *Arms.* [Azure] eight fleurs-de-lys in orle [Or] an inescutcheon bendy of six [Or and Azure] within a bordure [Gules]. Correctly, the field should be: Azure semé-de-lys Or, the arms being: France Ancient with an inescutcheon of Burgundy Ancient.

CLARE, Earl of Hertford and Gloucester. A series of shields from Thornbury Castle, Glos., now in Greystoke Castle, illustrating the medieval ancestry of the Howards, includes one for Clare. Amice (d. 1225), dau. and coheir of William FitzRobert, Earl of Gloucester (see CONSUL), marr. Richard de Clare, Earl of Hertford (d. 1217); from them descended Gilbert de Clare, Earl of Gloucester and Hertford, "the Red Earl" (1243-95), who marr. (2)

1290 Joan of Acre (d. 1307), dau. of Edward I, and had by her a 2nd dau. and ultimately coheir Margaret (d. 1342), who marr. (2) 1317 Hugh de Audley, cr. Earl of Gloucester, *q.v.* *Arms.* Gules three chevronels Or. Correctly, Or three chevronels Gules.

CLARK, of Standingstone. John Clark, of Standingstone, Wigton (d. 1734), was father of Wilfrid (1695-1777) who marr. Jane Christian, of Milntown and Unerigg (1695-1760). Their 3rd son Ewan (1734-1811) was a well known poet. Their eldest son, the Rev. Wilfrid Clark, M.A. (Oxon), was Vicar of Wigton 1763-1802; and his son, the Rev. Wilfrid Clark, M.A. (Cantab) (1766-1825), was Vicar of Wigton 1802-4. *Arms.* Argent on a bend Gules between three pellets as many swans of the field. (The above John Clark was a subscriber to *The History & Antiquities of the Cathedral Church of Canterbury*, by the Rev. J. Dart, London, 1726, and his arms are reproduced in the list of subscribers).

CLARKE, of Armathwaite. In 1848 Walter Hutchinson Whelpdale, *q.v.*, borrowed £7,700 from Anthony William Clarke, surgeon,* of Queen Street, Cheapside, London, on the security of the estates in Penrith and Armathwaite bequeathed to him by John de Whelpdale. On his failure to repay the loan, Dr. Clarke entered into possession of the estates in 1855, and went to live at Armathwaite Hall. He d. at Pau 1875, and the Armathwaite property was sold 1890 to Edward Ecroyd, *q.v.* In 1919 Mrs. Mary Clarke, of Halden House, High Halden, Kent, and William Joseph Pearman Smith sold the Mansion House, Penrith, to Penrith Rural District Council. *Arms.* Quarterly 1 & 4, Azure three escallops in pale Or between two flaunches Ermine (Clarke); 2, Barry of six Argent and Azure three chaplets Or; 3, Sable a dove Argent between three crosses pattée Or; over all on an escutcheon of pretence, Quarterly, 1 & 4, Lozengy Or and Gules; 2, Argent on a bend cotised Sable a lion passant guardant Or; 3, Per pale Gules and Vert a fleur-de-lys Argent. *Crest.* In a gem-ring Or set with a diamond Sable a pheon Argent. *Motto.* Trust in God (Hatchment, Armathwaite Church).

CLARKE, of Langthwaite. Robert Clarke, of Langthwaite, was father of Agnes, wife of John Bird, of Brougham (d. 1587). *Arms.* Argent on a chevron Sable between three wolves' heads erased Azure as many roses of the field on a canton of the third a lion rampant of the field (Gregory King's MS. pedigree of the Bird family, R.O., Kendal).

CLARKE. Impaled by Dixon, *q.v.*, beneath a tablet in Holme Eden church; Peter Dixon, of Holme Eden (d. 1866, aged 77), marr. 1820 Sara Rebecca (d. at Ambleside 1875, aged 79), dau. of Lieutenant General Tredway Clarke, H.E.I.C.S. (1764-1858). *Arms.* Gules a chevron between three swans Argent.

CLARKE. Impaled by Fetherstonhaugh in Kirkoswald church and The College, Kirkoswald; Timothy Fetherstonhaugh, J.P., of The College, *q.v.* (1811-56), marr. 1838 Eliza Were, dau. of John Were Clarke, D.L., J.P., of Bridwell, Devon. *Arms.* Argent on a bend Gules between three pellets as many swans Proper.

CLARKE-BUTLER-COLE. For further details of this family, see AWL. The

* For an unfavourable opinion of him, see a letter of 2 June 1855 from William and Edward Bleaymire, solicitors, to Andrew Fleming Hudleston in the Hudleston muniments in the Record Office, Carlisle.

Rev. Thomas Foster Clarke (1841-1926) was father of Thomas Clarke, J.P., of Eskmeals House, Bootle (C) (1870-1952), who assumed the additional surnames of Butler-Cole 1915. He marr. 1901 Eleanor, dau. of Robert Falcon, of Eskmeals. Their son Michael Bernard Clarke-Butler-Cole is now of Eskmeals House. His son Christopher Thomas Clarke-Butler-Cole marr. 1964 the Hon. Jane Elizabeth Napier, elder dau. of the 5th Baron Napier of Magdala. *Arms.* Quarterly, 1 & 4, Vert on a fess Argent three lions' heads erased Gules charged (for distinction) in the centre chief point with a cross crosslet Or (Cole); 2, Azure a chevron between three covered cups Or charged (for distinction) in the centre chief point with a cross crosslet of the second (Butler); 3, Ermine on a pale Sable three escallops Or on a chief Argent a rose between two lions rampant Gules (Clarke). *Crests.* 1, A lion's head erased Gules pierced in the neck by an arrow in bend Argent and charged (for distinction) with a cross crosslet as in the arms (Cole); 2, A horse statant Argent pelletté bridled and reined Sable and charged (for distinction) with a cross crosslet Gules (Butler); 3, In front of a demi bull rampant Ermine horned and hoofed Sable an escallop between two fleurs-de-lys Or (Clarke). *Motto.* Deum cole regem serva.

CLAVERING. The Rev. Thomas Charles Clavering (d. 1904, aged 74), a member of an old Northumberland family, was ordained in 1856 and served as a Roman Catholic priest in Carlisle until 1858 when he went to Long Horsley (N). From 1884 until 1899, when he retired to St. Joseph's Home, Botcherby, Carlisle, he was priest at Cockermouth Roman Catholic church (*ex inf.* Dr. A. M. C. Forster). *Arms.* Quarterly Or and Gules over all a bend Sable. *Crest.* A cherub's head with wings erect. *Motto.* Ad coelus volans.

CLEATHING. John Cleathing (d. at Leghorn 1766), son of Richard Cleathing, of Scarborough, was secretary to Sir John Dick, British consul in Leghorn, and was also in partnership with Thomas Wilson, *q.v.*, whose dau. Jane (d. 1765) he marr. 1762. Their only child, the Rev. John Cleathing, M.A. (Cantab) (1765-1841), d. *s.p.*, having bequeathed £500 towards the foundation of a school at Bewcastle. *Arms.* Argent a bend wavy between two bendlets also wavy Sable; impaling, Sable a (?)dragon rampant and in chief three mullets Argent. *Crest.* A swan couchant ducally gorged (Bookplate of J. Cleathing in Viscountess Wolseley's collection in Hove Library).

CLEESBIE. Richard Cleesbie, of Ousby, yeoman, who made his will 1630, sealed it with the following *Arms.* . . . three escallops . . . within a bordure engrailed . . . . He was, presumably, using a Strickland or Milburn seal.

CLERVAUX – see CHAYTOR.

CLIBURN. Edmund Cliburn, of Cliburn (W) (d. 1546), who marr. Eleanor Layton, of Dalemain, had *int. al.* a son and heir Richard (*c.* 1531-88) and a younger son Thomas Cliburn, of Hay Close, Hesket-in-the-Forest (FVY). *Arms.* Quarterly, 1 & 4, Argent three chevronels interlaced in base and a chief Sable (Cliburn); 2 & 3, Argent a saltire engrailed Vert (Kirkbride); over all a mullet for difference (FCW).

CLIFFORD, Baron Clifford, Earl of Cumberland. The great baronial family of Clifford, which played a dominant part not only in Westmorland, but throughout the North, descended from Richard fitz Pons (d. *c.* 1138) who acquired the barony of Clifford, Herefordshire. His descendant, Roger de Clifford (drowned 1282)) marr. Isabel (d. 1291), dau. and coheir of Robert de Veteripont (*q.v.*) (d. 1264) and thus acquired half the Honour of Appleby. His son and heir Robert was summoned to Parliament and was the first holder of the Clifford barony which is now held by his descendant, the 26th Baron de Clifford. The first Baron was granted in 1308 by his aunt, Idonea de Cromwell, her moiety of Appleby and in 1310 he was granted Skipton. He was killed at Bannockburn, 1314, aged 40; Roger, his son and heir, was executed after the battle of Boroughbridge, 1322, and was succ. by his brother, Robert, 3rd Baron, a notable soldier, as were all his successors. Henry, 11th Baron (d. 1542), was cr. Earl of Cumberland, 1525. George, 3rd Earl (d. 1605), had an only surviving child, Lady Anne Clifford (1590-1676), who succ. to the barony and Hereditary Shrievalty of Westmorland and eventually to all the family estates. She marr. (1) Richard Sackville, 2nd Earl of Dorset, by whom she had a dau., Lady Margaret Sackville, who marr. John Tufton, 2nd Earl of Thanet; and (2) Philip Herbert, 4th Earl of Pembroke and Montgomery. The Earldom passed on her father's death to her uncle, Francis (1559-1641), 4th Earl, who was succ. by his son, Henry, 5th and last Earl, whose only surviving child, Lady Elizabeth (1613-91), marr. 1634 Richard Boyle, Earl of Cork, who was cr. Baron Clifford, 1644, and Earl of Burlington, 1664. (GEC; SEB; EDP). *Arms.* Chequy Or and Azure a fess Gules. *Crest.* Out of a ducal coronet Or a wyvern rising Gules. *Supporters.* Dexter, A wyvern Gules; Sinister, A monkey Proper chained Or. On the tomb of Margaret Russell, widow of the 3rd Earl, in St Lawrence's, Appleby, they appear as two wyverns Gules with wings expanded Azure. *Badges.* A dragon Sable; a raven Argent; and an annulet Or. *Motto.* Desormais.

CLOOS. Nicholas Cloos, an original Fellow of King's College, Cambridge, 1443,* was Chancellor of the University of Cambridge 1450-51, Archdeacon of Colchester, and Bishop of Carlisle 1450-52, when he was translated to Lichfield and Coventry (BPP). *Arms* (granted 1449) Argent on a chevron Sable three passion nails of the field on a chief Sable as many white roses. Another coat: Azure on a chevron Or between three falcons close Argent as many roses Gules (BBE).

CLOSE. Francis Close, M.A. (Cantab), D.D. (Lambeth) (1797-1882), a leader of the Evangelical movement, was Perpetual Curate of Cheltenham 1826-56 and Dean of Carlisle 1856-81. He was one of the founders of Cheltenham College; Dean Close School, Cheltenham, was founded in his memory.† By his wife Anne Diana Arden, *q.v.*, he had, *int. al.*, a 4th son, Major General Henry Pelham Close, Bombay Staff Corps (1830-91), who marr. 1857 Annette Charlotte (1837-1910), eldest dau. of Robert Burland Hudleston. Their three sons died *s.p.* and their only dau. Hilda Gertrude (d. 1940) marr. 1899 George Lloyd, 1st and last Baron Courthope (1877-1953). They had two daus. and coheirs, the Hon. Hilda Beryl Courthope (d. 1974) and the Hon. Elinor Daphne Courthope. *Arms.* Vert a chevron Or between three garbs . . . a martlet for difference. (M.I., Carlisle Cathedral).

CLOUGH. Dorothy Una, LL.D. (Leeds) (d. 1967), eldest dau. of George Benson Clough, of Oxshott, Surrey, marr. (1) 1909 Charles Frederick Ratcliffe, later Ratcliffe-Brotherton; (2) 1932 Captain Noel McGrigor

* He is said to have been the architect of the Chapel.

† He is commemorated in Carlisle by Close Street.

Phillips (1880-1943); and (3) 1947 Alfred Phillips. From 1922 she published volumes of verse, plays and travel books. She was patron of the Brotherton Library in the University of Leeds, President of the Yorkshire Dialect Society, and was Lady Mayoress of Leeds 1914-15. She lived for a time at Croft, Watermillock. In 1936 she bought Acorn Bank (W) (Temple Sowerby Manor), which she gave to the National Trust in 1950, retaining a life tenancy. She and her husband eventually lived in Edinburgh where she died. *Arms.* Sable a fess humetté Ermine between three leopards' faces Argent. *Crest.* A demi lion rampant Ermine holding a battle axe handled Sable headed Argent. *Motto.* Sine macula macla (Window at Acorn Bank).

CLUTTERBUCK. Richard Henry Clutterbuck, of Durran Hill House (1835-1891), son of Thomas Clutterbuck, of Stroud, Glos., attorney (d. 1872), practised as a solicitor in Carlisle for many years, in partnership with John Nanson, later Town Clerk, until 1875, and then with Sydney William Trevenen, *q.v.*, whose dau. Irene marr. 1923 his son Lt-Col Noel Stanley Clutterbuck, D.S.O., R.M. (1879-1949) (HCF). *Arms.* Azure a lion rampant in chief three escallops Argent. *Crest.* A stag sejant Gules attired Or between two branches of laurel Proper. *Motto.* Loyal (HCF). On a bookplate of Henry Clutterbuck, of this family, the stag in the crest is gorged with a plain collar.

COBBE. Col Henry Hercules Cobbe, C.M.G., D.S.O., of Loweswater Hall (1869-1939), son of Lt-Gen Sir Alexander Hugh Cobbe, K.C.B. (1825-99), was commissioned in the Royal Artillery 1888 and transferred to the Indian Army 1891. He was D.A.A.G. 1st (Peshawar) Division India 1909-12 and an A.A. and Q.M.G. 1914-20, the year in which he retired. He settled at Loweswater Hall, where he lived until his death. *Arms.* Quarterly, 1 & 4, Gules a fess Argent in chief two swans Proper (Cobbe); 2 & 3, Argent three lozenges in fess Sable each charged with a fountain between three goats' heads erased Gules collared and attired Or (Welborne). *Crest.* Out of a ducal coronet Gules a pelican's head and neck vulning itself Proper. *Mottoes.* Moriens cano; over the crest, In sanguine vita (BLG8).

COGAN. Shield in window in Kirkoswald church; a Musgrave quartering, Sir Christopher Musgrave, 4th Bart., of Edenhall (d. 1704), *q.v.*, having marr. Mary, dau. and coheir of Sir Andrew Cogan, Bart., of Greenwich. *Arms.* Gules three aspen leaves Argent.

COKE. Impaled by Salmond, *q.v.*, on monument in Dacre church; Capt James Salmond, J.P., 2nd Dragoon Guards, of Waterfoot (1805-80), marr. 1832 Emma Isabella (d. 1886, aged 75), youngest dau. of D'Ewes Coke, of Brookhill Hall, Notts. *Arms.* Gules three crescents and a canton Or.

COLDALE. A pedigree of five generations of this family is in CW2 xl, headed by Richard Coldale, a Carlisle merchant, who bought the manor of Caldcotes or Harrington Houses, Carlisle. His son John was Keeper of Inglewood Forest 1467-76 and M.P. for Carlisle 1472-75. His descendant John (d. before 1544) marr. Elizabeth (d. 1563), dau. and coheir of Roger Bertram, of Brenkley (N). Their son Richard, of Plumpton (d. 1562), was bur. in St. Andrew's church, Penrith, under a stone* bearing an inscription and two shields, one of which is blank, and the other bears his and his mother's arms. Eleanor his dau. and heir marr. 1570, when she was aged 10,

* Placed there by his nephew, John Brisco.

Robert Brisco. *Arms.* . . . a chevron . . . between three cows' heads cabossed . . . ;* impaling, . . . an orle reversed . . . (M.I., Penrith church). MMD gives: Gules three cows' heads cabossed Argent.

COLE – see CLARKE-BUTLER-COLE.

COLLINGWOOD, *olim* CALTHROP. The Rev. Robert Gordon Calthrop, J.P., M.A. (Oxon) (1825-1903), incumbent of Irton and Drigg 1855-81, marr. 1856 Arabella (d. 1898), only dau. of Edward Spencer Collingwood, formerly Stanhope, of Dissington (N), and sister and heir of Edward Collingwood, of the same and of Canada. In 1868 they assumed the surname and arms of Collingwood on succeeding to Dissington Hall. *Arms* (granted 1868). Argent a chevron between three stags' heads erased Sable and for distinction a canton of the last. *Crest.* A stag statant in front of a holly bush Proper the stag charged for distinction with a cross crosslet Sable (CA lvi/348).

BOWEN-COLTHURST. Miss Peggy Elizabeth Skeena Bowen-Colthurst, of Roblins, Kirkbampton, is 2nd dau. of Robert St. John Bowen-Colthurst, of Kelowna, British Columbia, and great-granddau. of Robert Walter Travers Bowen-Colthurst, J.P., of Oakgrove, Co. Cork (d. 1896), and his wife Georgina de Bellasis Greer Colthurst, of Dripsey Castle, Co. Cork (d. 1921). *Arms.* Quarterly, 1 & 4, Argent on a fess between three colts courant Sable as many trefoils slipped Or a crescent for difference (Coulthurst); 2 & 3, Per pale Azure and Gules a stag trippant Argent pierced in the back with an arrow and attired Or (Bowen) (IFR).

COLVILE, or COLYVILL. Burke gives this family as of Cumberland, Kent, Lincolnshire, Northamptonshire, and Northumberland, with no further particulars. *Arms.* Argent three chevrons Sable bezanté.

COLVILL. John Colvill or Colvyle marr. Isabella (1406-38), dau. of Sir Peter Tilliol, *q.v.*, and sister and coheir of her brother Robert (1415-35). Their son William (1422-79) was father of Felice (b. *c.* 1451), marr. William Musgrave, of Crookdake, *q.v.*; and Margaret (b. *c.* 1458), marr. Nicholas Musgrave, *q.v. Arms.* Or a fess Azure in chief three hurts a crescent for difference (Window in Edenhall church). In a window in the Musgrave chapel in Aspatria church, Colvill is quartered by Musgrave as: Or a cross flory Gules. On the altar below the window, however, is a Musgrave quartering apparently intended for Colvill: Argent two bars Gules on the upper one three bezants; which, according to Field, was quartered for Colvill by Dykes also. Field also states that Orfeur quartered Colvill as: Or three annulets Gules (FAC); but FVC and MVC show this quartering as: Or three hurts in chief; and not, as stated by Field, as: Or three hurts in chief and one in the fess point.

COMBER. The Very Rev. Thomas Comber, M.A., D.D. (Cantab) (1575-1654), Chaplain to James I, became Dean of Carlisle 1630 and Master of Trinity College, Cambridge, 1631, but was ejected from all his preferments by Parliament 1642 because he sent the plate of the University of Cambridge to the King (DNB). *Arms.* Or a fess dancetté Gules between three estoiles Sable. *Crest.* A lynx's head Or pelletté (BGA).

COMPTON. Quartered by Pennington in window at Muncaster Castle; Sir

* Machell recorded these arms for Cowell, viz. Gules a chevron between three cows' heads cabossed Argent (MMS vi 415); and FVC and MVC give them for Cowdnell, viz. Gules a chevron Or between three cows' heads cabossed Argent.

John Pennington, 1st Baron Muncaster (d. 1813), marr. Penelope, dau. and heir of James Compton, great-grandson of Spencer, 2nd earl of Northampton. *Arms.* Sable a lion passant guardant Or between three esquires' helmets Argent.

CONSUL, Earl of Gloucester. A series of shields from Thornbury Castle, Glos., now in Greystoke Castle, illustrating the medieval ancestry of the Howards, includes one for Robert Consul (*c.* 1090-1147), illegitimate son of Henry I, cr. Earl of Gloucester 1122. He marr. Mabel (d. 1157), dau. of Robert FitzHamon, *q.v.*, and had issue William FitzRobert, Earl of Gloucester (d. *s.p.m.s.* 1183), whose dau. and coheir Amice (d. 1225) marr. Richard de Clare, Earl of Hertford, *q.v.* *Arms.* Gules three rests Or.

CONWAY, *post* CONWAY-GORDON. Capt William Conway (1798-1882), 53rd Bengal Native Infantry, was bap. at St. Mary Abbot, Kensington, as son of William and Catherine Conway. In 1838 the widow of Lord William Gordon bequeathed him "all that mountain in Borrowdale called Castle Cragg with the building thereon erected to the memory of my husband."* In 1839 he assumed the additional surname of Gordon and in 1846 matriculated arms as "son of the deceased Right Hon. Lord William Gordon." Lord William Gordon (1744-1823), of Derwent Bay, Keswick, was 2nd son of Cosmo, 3rd Duke of Gordon, and marr. 1781 Frances (d. 1841), 2nd dau. of Charles, 9th Viscount Irvine† (HBO). *Arms.* Quarterly, 1, Azure three boars' heads couped Or a canton Ermine charged with a crescent of the second; 2, Or three lions' heads erased Gules; 3, Or three crescents within a double tressure flory counterflory Gules; 4, Azure three fraises Argent; all within a bordure company Argent and Azure (OBA). *Crest.* Issuing out of a mural crown Or a stag's head at gaze Proper attired and charged on the neck with a crescent of the first. *Mottoes.* Bydand; Animo non astutia (BLG13).

CONY. Burke (BGA, p. 223) gives arms for a family of this name of Bassingthorp, Co. Cumberland, 1612, but this place is in Lincolnshire, as is correctly stated on p. 220, *sub* CONEY.

COOKE, of Camerton Hall. Ralph Cooke, of Kendal (d. 1719, aged 63),‡ bought the manor of Camerton from Joseph Curwen 1719. He was succ. by his son Richard (1702-65), who was High Sheriff of Cumberland 1739. His son Ralph (1732-95), who marr. 1778 Frances (d. 1833), dau. and coheir of George Dawson, of Unthank House, Skelton, was an attorney in Penrith, in partnership with Thomas Simpson, *q.v.*, and lived in Bishop Yards, in the house now occupied by Messrs Little & Shepherd, solicitors. Camerton Hall was let, but by 1787 Ralph was living there. He was succ. by his son Ralph (1780-1860), whose son William (1822-66) died unmarr., and was succ. by his sister Isabel (d. 1908), who marr. Henry Falcon, *q.v.* She was succ. by her grandson Captain Ralph Falcon-Cooke, *q.v.*, son of Cmdr Tom Harrison Falcon, J.P., R.N., (1841-88). *Arms.* Or a chevron Gules between two lions

* She also left an annuity of £25 for the maintenance of her parrot Poppy.

† For Lord William's acquisition of his Derwentwater estate, see J. M. Bulloch, *The Gay Gordons*, p. 122, where it is stated "He changed the place from a wilderness to a paradise, especially by constant tree-planting. He built a beautiful villa on the margin of the bay, and beautified the place in every conceivable manner." He eventually owned all the western side of Derwentwater. Brandelhow Park, part of it, acquired by the National Trust in 1902, was the Trust's first Lakeland property.

‡ His dau. Elizabeth marr. the Rev. Curwen Hudleston.

passant reguardant Sable. (BGA). DSL blazons the lions as passant guardant.

COOKSON, of Penrith. The story of this family is told in *Cookson of Penrith and Newcastle upon Tyne,* by W. Percy Hedley and C. Roy Hudleston. This shows that the Penrith family settled there from Kendal, the first being William Cookson (1599-1666), first of a line of braziers. His grandson Thomas (1676-1721) was a mercer in which trade he was followed by his son William (1711-87) who marr. 1741 Dorothy (1719-92), dau. of Richard Crackanthorpe, *q.v.,* and sister and heir of James Crackanthorpe. Their elder son Christopher Crackanthorpe Cookson succ. to Newbiggin; their younger son, the Rev. William Cookson, M.A., D.D. (Cantab), (1754-1820) was grandfather of the Rev. Christopher Cookson (1823-74) whose senior male descendant is head of the family; and of Montagu Hughes Cookson, later Crackanthorpe, *q.v.* Ann (b. 1748), only dau. of the above William Cookson and Dorothy Crackanthorpe, marr. 1766 John Wordsworth and was mother of the poet. *Arms.* Per pale Argent and Gules two legs in fess in armour Proper couped at the thigh. *Crest.* A demi lion. *Motto.* Nil desperandum. For the arms quartered for Cookson by Crackanthorpe, see that name.

COOPER. The Very Rev. Cecil Henry Hamilton Cooper, M.A. (Oxon) (1871-1942), was Canon and Prebendary of York 1918-23, Archdeacon of York 1923, Canon of York 1926-33, Sub-Dean of York 1930-33, Dean of Carlisle 1933-38 and Dean Emeritus 1938-42. His son Martin Du Pré Cooper has been music editor of the *Daily Telegraph* since 1954. *Crest.* A stag's head erased.

COPELAND. CW2 xli traces the history of this family from Ketel son of Ulf whose son Alan owned the manor of Bootle and lands in Hensingham, Kelton, Gosforth and Santon. His grandson Sir Alan de Copeland also owned Bolton in Adgarley, a fourth part of the manor of Kirkby Lonsdale and Westhall, Whittington. His grandson Alan (*fl.* 1290) sold Westhall to John Hudleston, of Millom. His grandson Richard Copeland (d. 1393-4) was father of Katherine (d. 1428) who marr. 1393 William Denton, *q.v.,* and Alan (d. before 1432), who marr. 1393 Katherine Hudleston, of Millom. His dau. and heir Margaret marr. (1) Rowland Kirkby and (2) John Broughton, of Broughton. CW1 xii says that there was another dau. and coheir, marr. to Nicholas Senhouse. *Arms.* In the grotto at Nunnery on a stone panel, from the tomb of William Denton and Katherine his wife, formerly in St. Cuthbert's church, Carlisle, are the arms, side by side, of Denton and Copeland. The latter are shown as: . . . two bars . . . over all a bend . . . with a canton . . . . Lysons blazon the arms as: Or two bars and a canton Gules over all a bend Sable (LMC). In a window in Urswick church the arms are: Argent two bars and a canton Gules over all a bend Azure, i.e. as quartered by Irton in TVN. On an escutcheon of pretence in a window at Irton Hall, they appear as: Argent two bars Gules over all a bend Or with a canton of the second. TTV shews Irton as quartering for Copeland: Argent two bars and a canton Gules over all a bend of the second.

COPLEY. Sir Richard Copley, of Copley (Y), was father of Adam,* who

* Field, following the Visitation of Yorkshire 1584/5 pedigree, says that it was the father who marr. Margaret Denton, but the Denton pedigree says she marr. Adam Copley.

marr. Margaret, dau. and heir of Sir Richard Denton (d. 1363), *q.v.* Their grandson Richard Copley had a dau. and heir Isabel, who marr. Adam del Hall. *Arms.* Argent a cross moline Sable (FVY).

COPLEY, of Gosforth. Robert Copley (d. 1675), chief bailiff of Copeland Forest and steward to William Pennington, of Muncaster, was doubtless related to Alvarey Copley, of Batley (Y),* whose dau. Isabel marr. Joseph Pennington. He marr. 1652 Isabella (d. 1685), dau. and heir of William Tubman, of Beck Place, Gosforth (d. 1653), and so acquired that estate upon which he built Gosforth Hall. He was succ. by his son† William Copley (b. 1660), who was a prisoner for debt in Carlisle Gaol 1723, the year in which his son Robert Copley, of Ponsonby Hall (b. 1686), sold Gosforth Hall to Anthony Benn (PGD). *Arms.* Robert Copley was disclaimed at the Visitation of Cumberland, 1665. The Copleys of Batley bore: Argent a cross moline Sable.

CORBET. Shield at Hutton-in-the-Forest; a Vane quartering. *Arms.* Or a raven Proper.

CORBOILE. Shield at Hutton-in-the-Forest; a Vane quartering. *Arms.* Gules a lion rampant Argent crowned Or. Burke, however, gives this as another coat for Pershall, *q.v.* (BGA).

CORNWALL. Impaled by Howard on shield in hall of Greystoke Castle; Sir John Howard, of Wiggenhall, Norfolk (d. 1340), marr. Joan, widow of Sir Thomas Peche, and dau. of Sir Richard de Cornwall, natural son of Richard Plantagenet, Earl of Cornwall, 2nd son of King John. *Arms.* Argent a lion rampant Gules within a bordure engrailed Sable bezanté.

CORRIE, . . . , of Carlisle, 1792; formerly in Stanwix churchyard. *Arms.* Gules a saltire humetté the ends couped barwise. *Crest.* A cubit arm erect holding a curved sword bend sinisterwise (ABD).

CORRY. Walder de Corry marr. Agnes, dau. of Adam de Levington, and was succ. by his son Walter (d. 1303) who, as one of the cousins and heirs of Helewise de Balliol, inherited considerable lands in Cumberland, which descended to his son Walter de Corry (aged 22 in 1303), who was knighted at the siege of Caerlaverock. As a rebel who had joined the Scots, he forfeited his Cumberland lands 1326-27. *Arms.* Argent a saltire Sable on a chief Azure three cinquefoils Or (FFC).

CORY. John Augustus Cory, architect (1819-86), born at Borough Castle, Norfolk, was son of Robert Cory, of Great Yarmouth, and practised at 46 North Bailey, Durham, and 3 Abbey Street, Carlisle. He became County Surveyor of Cumberland 1862. His works include Bridekirk, Plumbland, Nenthead and Sebergham churches. His eldest son Robert Cory, M.B., M.A., M.D. (Cantab), F.R.C.P. (d. 1900), was founder with Sir George Buchanan of the Government animal vaccine establishment, of which he was Director 1881-1900. *Arms.* Sable on a chevron between three griffins' heads erased Or three estoiles Gules (DSA). *Crest.* Out of a ducal coronet Or a griffin's head between two wings expanded Proper. *Motto.* Virtus semper viridis (BGA).

COULTHARD, of Scotby. Thomas and Elizabeth Coulthard, of Scotby, had

*Descended from Sir Richard Copley, see previous entry.

† His younger son John Copley (1661-89) marr. 1684 Beatrix, dau. and heir of Daniel Nicholson, of Hawkshead Hall, and widow of Samuel Sandys. Their grandson the Rev. John Copley, of West Chiltington, Sussex, sold Hawkshead Hall 1756.

a son James Coulthard (b. 1718), a solicitor in Symonds Inn, London, who marr. 1754 Mary Whelpdale, of Penrith. His sister Margaret (1726-1816) marr. 1750 Thomas Graham, of Edmund Castle, *q.v.*, whose sons Thomas and Sir James Graham joined their uncle and became partners in the firm, which still exists as Lawrence, Graham & Co., New Square, Lincoln's Inn. *Arms* (granted 1784). Sable three catherine wheels Argent. *Crest.* A demi lion rampant Gules (BGA).

COULTHARD, of Lanercost. Joseph, son of Joseph and Ann Coulthard, of the Orchard House, Lanercost, d. 1787, aged 23. *Arms.* ... a chevron .... *Crest.* A lion rampant (Lanercost tombstone).

COULTHARD – see BRIGGS.

COULTHART. George Parker Knowles' *Genealogical and Heraldic Account of the Coultharts of Coulthart and Collyn,* 1855, was attacked by George Burnett, later Lyon King of Arms, in *Popular Genealogists, or the Art of Pedigree-Making,* 1865, as a fabrication and the quarterings given as spurious. The pedigree was presumably prepared for William Coulthart, of Coulthart, Co. Wigtown, and of Collyn, Co. Dumfries, or for his only son John Ross Coulthart, J.P., F.S.A. (Scot.) (b. 1807). The former, described in BLG4 as "chief of his name and family," was b. 1774 and d. at Pasture House, Cumberland, 1847. His dau. Margaret (1808-56) marr. 1833 James McGuffie, *q.v. Arms.* Quarterly of eight, 1, Argent a fess between three colts courant Sable; 2, Argent a chevron chequy Sable and Or between three water-bougets of the second (Ross of Renfrew); 3, Sable an inescutcheon chequy Argent and Or between three lions' heads erased of the third (MacKnight); 4, Quarterly Argent and Sable a cross parted per cross engrailed counterchanged (Glendonyn of Glendonyn); 5, Argent on a bend cotised nebuly Sable a tilting spear of the field (Carmichael of Carspherne); 6, Ermine a chevron chequy Argent and Sable between three boars' heads couped of the last muzzled Gules within a bordure nebuly of the third (Forbes of Pitscottie); 7, Quarterly, i & iv, Azure a stag's head cabossed Or, ii & iii, Argent three human legs armed Proper united in the centre of the upper part of the thigh triangularly flexed garnished and spurred of the second, over all an escutcheon Ermine thereon a stag's head cabossed Sable within a bordure Argent pelletté (Mackenzie of Craighall); 8, Ermine on a fess between three boars' heads erased and erect Sable a tilting spear Argent (Gordon of Sorbie). *Crest.* A war horse's head and neck couped Argent armed and bridled Proper garnished Or. *Supporters.* Dexter, A warhorse Argent armed Proper garnished Or; Sinister, A stag Proper attired and ducally gorged Or. *Motto.* Virtute non verbis (Window in Bolton church).

COURTENAY. Field recorded the arms of this ancient Devon family as on a shield formerly on the ceiling of Carlisle Cathedral. *Arms.* Or three torteaux (CW2 xxxiv 25).

COWANS. William Cowans, of Woodbank, Brisco, engineer, was father of John Cowans, a member of the famous firm of Messrs. Cowans, Sheldon & Co. He marr. Jennie Steven and was father of General Sir John Steven Cowans, G.C.B., G.C.M.G., K.C.B., M.V.O. (1862-1921), Quartermaster-General 1912-19, for whom see DNB. His younger brother was Brigadier-General Ernest Arnold Cowans, the Seaforth Highlanders. *Arms.* Argent a chevron embattled Gules between a chaplet of roses in chief of the last leaved Vert and a demi lion couped double-queued in base also Gules. *Crest.*

Issuant from a wreath of roses Argent leaved Vert a demi lion double-queued as in the arms holding between the paws a wreath of oak fructed Proper (FD7).

COWELL – see COLDALE.

COWELL-STEPNEY. Shield in library at Greystoke Castle; Sir Edward Stafford Howard, K.C.B., D.L., J.P., of Thornbury Castle, Glos., marr. (2) 1911 Catherine Meriel (1876-1952), dau. and heir of Sir Arthur Keppel Cowell-Stepney, 2nd and last Bart., of Llanelly. *Arms.* Quarterly, 1 & 4, Gules a fess chequy Or and Azure between three owls Argent (Stepney); 2 & 3, Azure a lion rampant guardant Or on a chief dovetail of the last three pallets Gules each charged with as many bezants (Cowell).*

COWEN. Thomas Cowen (d. 1720) was of Biglands, Aikton, where the family was long settled. His descendant Jacob Cowen, of Biglands (1722-1807), author of poems published 1800, was father of Jacob Cowen (b. 1758), head of Cowen, Heysham & Co., Carlisle, in partnership with his sons Robert Cowen, J.P. (1787-1862) and George Cowen, J.P. (1792-1857). The former, of 7 Devonshire Street, Carlisle, was a member of Carlisle City Council; the latter, of Mill Ellers, Dalston, was a director of the Maryport & Carlisle Railway, and partner with his brother in the cotton spinning works at Dalston. His only son Robert Watson Cowen, J.P. (1845-1905), was prominent in local affairs and was first Chairman of Carlisle Rural District Council 1894-1905. His five sons George, James, Robert, Arthur and Reginald (killed at Gallipoli) all died *s.p.m.*; his dau. Frances marr. 1892 William Tennant Trimble, *q.v.* (TCD). *Arms.* . . . three foxes' heads erased . . . . *Crest.* On a winged globe an eagle rising (Shields on tombstone of Robert Cowen erected by his niece Mary Harrington in Carlisle Cemetery).

COWPER, of Unthank and Carleton Hall. John Cowper, of Skelton, husbandman (d. 1798, aged 76), marr. 1744 Sarah Winder (d. 1814, aged 94). Their son Joseph Cowper, of Unthank (1749-1827), was steward to the Vanes of Hutton-in-the-Forest. His eldest son Joseph (1778-1841) succ. but d. *s.p.*; his brother John (1780-1851) went to London, where he made a fortune, and in 1828 he bought from Lord Wallace, Carleton Hall, near Penrith, and Kirkbarrow Hall, Barton.† The brothers were succ. by their brother Frederick Cowper, D.L., J.P. (1794-1881). His son Frederick Cowper, D.L., J.P. (1822-1899), succ. and had an elder son Frederick Carleton Cowper, J.P., of Carleton Derrick, Penrith (1858-98), who d. *v.p.*, having marr. 1886 Ella Elizabeth (d. 1941), only dau. of William Middleton Moore, D.L., J.P. (see AWL). Their only son Geoffrey Thomas Middleton Carleton Cowper, Major Westmorland and Cumberland Yeomanry (1889-1962) succ., but sold Carleton Hall‡ 1947 and went to live in Devonshire.§ His sister and heir is Mrs. Mary Ella Marjorie Burra, of Bowersyke,

* In the library at Greystoke castle is preserved the grant of arms dated 21 December 1857 to Sir John Stepney Cowell (later Cowell-Stepney), K.H., of Hertford Street, Mayfair, Middlesex, and of Llanelly, Co. Carmarthen (1791-1877), son and heir of General Andrew Cowell, of Coleshill, Bucks. (d. 1821), and father of Sir Arthur Keppel Cowell-Stepney, above, as follows: *Arms.* Cowell, as above. *Crest.* On a mount Vert a lion passant guardant Or charged on the body with three pallets Gules holding in the dexter paw a chapeau Gules turned up Ermine.

† Sold 1919.

‡ Now the Cumbria Police Headquarters.

§ He bought and demolished Brougham Hall.

Killington, who marr. 1927 Robert Burra (BLG17). *Arms.* FD7 gives: Azure a chevron paly Or and Ermine in chief an annulet between two martlets Argent. BGA, however, gives: Azure a chevron paly Or and Ermine between in chief an annulet between two martlets Argent and in base a caduceus of the second; and this coat is on a stone shield at Kirkbarrow Hall and on a brass in Skelton church to Lt-Col Malcolm Gordon Cowper, D.S.O. (1876-1931), and is prominently displayed on several shields on the exterior of Carleton Hall. *Crest.* A buffalo's head erased per fess Sable and Or armed of the last charged on the neck with a cross crosslet counterchanged in the mouth a slip of oak Proper. *Motto.* Industria et perseverantia.

CRACKANTHORPE. Further details of this family, formerly of Newbiggin Hall (W), will be found in AWL. CW2 xxxiii shows that Sir John de Crackanthorpe (d. 1436), Knight of the Shire for Westmorland 1382 and 1399, marr. Alice, dau. and heir of Roger de Salkeld, and thus acquired the manors of Ousby and Bank, which the family held for more than 500 years. Their son Thomas (d. *s.p.* 1459), who marr. Margaret, dau. and coheir of Sir Peter Tilliol, *q.v.,* was High Sheriff of Cumberland 1448, and Sir John Crackanthorpe was High Sheriff 1477-83 and 1512-14; his descendant Richard (1662-1708) was High Sheriff 1702. His dau. and heir Anne marr. Adam Askew, *q.v.,* but did not succeed to the estates. James Crackanthorpe (d. *s.p.* 1753) was the last of the male line. His sister and heir Dorothy (d. 1792) marr. 1741 William Cookson, of Penrith, *q.v.,* and had sons Christopher Crackanthorpe Cookson (1745-99) and the Rev. William Cookson (see below). The former succ. to Newbiggin and took the name and arms of Crackanthorpe 1792. His son, William Crackanthorpe, D.L., J.P., M.A. (Cantab) (1790-1888), High Sheriff of Cumberland 1822, d. unmarr. and was succ. by his cousin Montague Hughes Cookson, D.L., J.P., Q.C., D.C.L. (Oxon) (1832-1913), Chairman of Westmorland Quarter Sessions, who took the name Crackanthorpe 1888. He was grandson of the Rev. William Cookson, D.D. (Cantab), see above, and was succ. by his 2nd son Dayrell Eardley Montague Crackanthorpe, C.M.G., J.P. (1871-1950), Envoy Extraordinary and Minister Plenipotentiary and Consul General to the Central American Republics, and High Sheriff of Cumberland 1928. He was succ. by his grandson David Richard Francis Crackanthorpe, of le Village, Corbès, 30140 Anduze, France, barrister at law, who sold the Newbiggin Hall estate 1956 (BLG18). *Arms.* Or a chevron between three mullets Azure. *Crest.* A holly bush Proper (FCW). The family now bears: *Arms.* Quarterly, 1 & 4, Or a chevron between three mullets pierced Azure (Crackanthorpe); 2 & 3, Per pale Or and Gules two legs couped at the thigh in armour between as many tilting spears fesswise one in chief and one in base all counterchanged (Cookson). *Crests.* 1, A holly bush Vert fructed Proper (Crackanthorpe); 2, A demi lion Proper collared Vair holding in the dexter paw a staff raguly Gules and resting the sinister paw on a mullet pierced also Gules (Cookson). *Motto.* Mihi res subjungere conor (BLG18).

CRACKANTHORPE. Robert Crackanthorpe, of Howgill (W), a cadet of the Newbiggin Hall family, see AWL, was murdered 1438, having marr. Elizabeth (d. 1462), 2nd dau. and coheir of Sir John Lancaster, of Rydal and Howgill, see AWL. Their son John (b. 1420, living 1478) was a considerable Cumberland landowner and was Lord of the Manors of Bromfield,

Skirwith and Ousby. He was succ. by his son Ambrose (d. *s.p.* 1520), whose nieces, daus. of his brother Anthony, were coheirs – Margaret (b. *c.* 1501), wife of William Hutton, of Hutton-in-the-Forest, *q.v.*; Cecily (b. *c.* 1505), wife of Ambrose Middleton, *q.v.*; and Grace (1516-66), wife of Thomas Sandford, *q.v.* (CW2 xxxiii 70-5). *Arms* (as quartered by Middleton). Or a chevron between three mullets pierced Azure a crescent for difference (FVD).

CRAGE, of Prior Hall. A monument in Ireby Old Church, dated 1626, is in memory of "George Crage of Priour Hall Gent. who faithfullye served Queen Elizabeth, King James, Prince Henry and King Charles King of England." Prior Hall, which belonged to Carlisle priory and stood near the church, was demolished in the 19th century and rebuilt on a new site to the north-east of the church. *Arms* (on centre panel of monument). Ermine on a fess . . . three crescents . . . (IOC).

CRAKEPLACE, of Crakeplace Hall. Sandford says of this family,* "Though very ancient gentry, I never heard them of any great remark." Christopher Crakeplace (d. 1617-18) built Crakeplace Hall, Dean, recording that he did so in 1612 when he was servant to Baron Altham.† His grandson Henry (*c.* 1651-1727) marr. Jane Senhouse, and was father of Thomas Crakeplace, of Brigham (1687-1731), who marr. 1717 Margaret Christian (1689-1775). Their only son Henry, born in 1718, died in 1725, and Crakeplace Hall was inherited by his sister Christian (1721-77), who marr. (1) 1742 Lowther Spedding and (2) Peter How (d. 1772, aged 73), *q.v.* The other sisters and coheirs were Jane (b. 1726), marr. 1747 William Fletcher, of Whitehaven, and Mary (1728-88), marr. 1754 William Wybergh, *q.v.* A branch of the family was settled at Flimby. *Arms.* . . . a crow . . . (Shield over the doorway of Crakeplace Hall). Field gives: Argent (or Or) a crow Sable; but quotes no authority for the tinctures.

CRANMER-BYNG – see BYNG.

CRAWHALL, *post* CRAWHALL-WILSON. Isaac Crawhall, of Allenheads (N) and Nun Monkton (Y) (1795-1877), descended from a family of mining agents from Stanhope (D), marr. 1823 Ann, dau. of John Wilson, of Nent Hall, *q.v.*, and had issue besides an eldest son Thomas, of whom below, a 2nd son, John Bownass Crawhall, of Clifton Down, Bristol (1827-1903), whose son Walter John Crawhall, B.A. (Oxon), solicitor (b. 1865), was Lord of the Manor of Nun Monkton; and a 3rd son, George Crawhall, J.P., formerly of Allandale, later of Burton Croft and The Priory, Nun Monkton. The eldest son, Thomas Crawhall, J.P., of Alston House and Nent Hall and of Silloth (b. 1825), assumed the additional name of Wilson 1880. He marr. 1855 Fanny, younger dau. of F. F. Fothergill, and had sons Thomas Fothergill Crawhall, B.A. (Cantab) (b. 1857); the Rev. Edmund Isaac Laroche Crawhall, M.A. (Oxon) (b. 1864); and George Charles Cecil Hugh Crawhall (b. 1871). *Arms.* The family originally bore: Gules a garb Or on a chief of the last three crows Sable. *Crest.* On a garb Or a crow Sable. *Motto.* Nec careo nec curo (Bookplate of George Crawhall in Tullie House, Carlisle). The family later bore: *Arms.* Argent three battle axes chevronwise Sable between two chevronels engrailed Gules the whole between three crows also Sable. *Crest.* Upon a mount vert a crow Sable holding in the

* He calls them Craples, the way the name was pronounced.

† Sir James Altham, Baron of the Exchequer (d. 1617).

dexter claw a battle axe in bend Proper. *Motto.* Praesto et persto (FD7; BGA).

CRAWLEY. The Rev. John Lloyd Crawley, M.A. (Cantab) (1884-1951) (stepson of the Rev. George Nedham, *q.v.*), descended from Sir Thomas Crawley-Boevey, 2nd Bart. (1745-1818) was Curate of St. Mary, Windermere, 1914-21, Vicar of Aspatria, 1921-28, Vicar of Upperby, 1928-31, Rector of Harrington 1945-48, and Rector of Kirkandrews-on-Esk, 1948-51. His only surviving son, the Rev. John Lloyd Rochfort Crawley, M.A. (Cantab) is Vicar of Cockermouth. *Arms.* Erminois on a fess Azure between three cranes Proper a saltire couped between two cross crosslets fitché Or on a chief Ermine a bend Gules charged with three gouttes d'Or between two martlets Sable. *Crest.* On a mount Vert a crane Proper collared beaked and holding in the dexter foot a saltire Or. *Motto.* Esse quam videri.

CREIGHTON. Robert Creighton, timber merchant, of Carlisle (1816-1878), marr. Sarah, dau. of Thomas Mandell, of Bolton (C), and was father of the famous historian, the Rt. Rev. Mandell Creighton, P.C., M.A., D.D. (Oxon), D.D. (Cantab), LL.D. (Glasgow), D.C.L. (Oxon and Dunelm) (1843-1901), Bishop of Peterborough 1890-97, Bishop of London 1897-1901; and of James Robert Creighton, J.P., of The Snabs, Scotby, timber merchant (1845-96), an Hon. Freeman of Carlisle and Mayor 1880-81 and 1888-89. His son Robert Creighton, J.P. (b. 1873), was a director of the firm of Messrs. R. & J. R. Creighton. *Arms.* Argent a lion rampant Azure (BBE).

CREIGHTON SCHOOL, Carlisle. In 1925 the school used the following *Device.* Sable a cross fourché between four mullets of six points Gules. *Motto.* Nil sine labore.

CROCKER – see BULTEEL.

CROFT. Impaled by Curwen, *q.v.*, on tomb of Sir Christopher Curwen (d. 1453) in St. Michael, Workington; his father, Sir William Curwen (d. 1403), marr. (2) Margaret, dau. of Sir John Croft, of Claughton (L). *Arms.* Lozengy [Argent and Sable]. As quartered by Middleton, the arms were: Lozengy Or and Azure (FCW).

CROFTON, of Crofton. In CW2 xxxii T. H. B. Graham traces the descent of the Croftons of Crofton from Gilbert, whose grandson John (*fl.* 1230-50) was known as John de Dundraw or de Crofton. His descendant John (*fl.* 1300-32) was father of Clement (d. *s.p.* 1369) and John, who marr. Margaret, dau. and heir of Sir Gilbert Whinno, *q.v.*; their dau. and heir Margaret marr. Isold Brisco, *q.v. Arms.* Gules a saltire engrailed Argent (MMD). The latter authority states that Adam de Crofton sealed with: . . . a saltire couped . . . surmounted of a heart . . . on a chief . . . a spear head point downwards between two spear heads fessways . . . .* Denton states that John de Crofton, who gave lands to the priory of Carlisle, sealed with "a pelican and her young ones in her nest under her," and that Robert his son, who also gave lands to the church of Carlisle, "sealed with a lilly pot of three flowers" (DAC).

CROMPTON. The Rev. Robert Crompton (d. 1721), was Rector of Corney 1666-77, and of Whicham 1680-1720. *Arms.* The seal on his institution bond, 1680, is much worn but seems to display: Quarterly . . . and . . . a bend . . . . The seal on his will of 1718 bears: . . . three bars . . . .

* MMD also refers to Adam de Crofton being "call^{d} le Usher Sive Marshall," and tricks for Usher: Sable three lions' gambs couped and erect Argent armed Gules.

CROOKDAKE, of Crookdake. Adam de Crookdake, Justice Itinerant and Steward of Robert Bruce 1292, died 1304-5 and was succ. by his son John (d. 1305) who marr. Margaret, dau. and heir of John de Wigton, *q.v.* Their posthumous son John (1306-22) d. *s.p.*, his heirs being his father's sisters, Juliana marr. Robert de Tollesland, and Christiana marr. Robert de Castlecarrock, *q.v.* (CW2 xxi). *Arms.* Ermine three pellets (FFC). Dykes incorrectly quarters their arms as: Argent a saltire and in chief three cross crosslets Sable (Brass in Bromfield church).*

CROSLAND. John Fleming gave the church of St. Bridget, Beckermet, in marr. with his dau. Bridget to Sir Jordan Crosland, of Newby in the Liberty of Ripon (Y) (1618-70) (PGD). *Arms.* Quarterly Argent and Gules a cross botonné counterchanged (CVY).

CROSS, Viscount. Richard Assheton Cross, P.C., G.C.B., G.C.S.I., D.L., J.P., D.C.L., LL.D., F.R.S., 1st Viscount Cross, of Broughton-in-Furness (1823-1914),† is commemorated by a monument in Carlisle Cathedral, displaying the following *Arms.*‡ Gules a cross flory Argent charged with five passion nails sable a bordure of the second. *Crest.* A griffin's head erased Argent gorged with a double chain Or therefrom pendent a mullet pierced [Sable] in the beak a passion-nail also Sable. *Supporters.* On either side a pegasus Argent holding in the mouth a passion-nail Sable, the dexter gorged with a chain Or therefrom pendent a cross flory Gules, the sinister gorged with a double chain Or therefrom pendent a mullet pierced Sable. *Motto.* Crede cruci.

CROWLEY. Abraham Crowley, or Crawley (d. 1760), was a pewterer, brazier and plumber of Penrith. Examples of his church plate are at Dufton, Kirkby Thore, Temple Sowerby and Kirkland. He was churchwarden of Penrith 1743. At his death he was survived by his son Abraham Crowley, also of Penrith (*Ex inf.* Mr. M. Finley, of Castle Street, Carlisle). *Arms.* . . . a crow . . . holding in the beak a sprig . . . (Seal in Record Office, Carlisle).

CRUDDAS, of Walton. Robert Cruddas,§ of Walton, died 1747, aged 47. *Arms.* . . . an eagle displayed . . . (Walton tombstone).

CUMBERLAND COUNTY COUNCIL. *Arms.* Per fess Vert and barry wavy of six Argent and Azure in chief three Parnassus flowers Proper. *Crest.* Issuant from a mural crown Or a wreath on the dexter side of oak fructed and on the sinister side of ash in front thereof a pick and a shepherd's crook in saltire and perched upon the crown a curlew all Proper. *Supporters.* Dexter, A representation of the Dacre Bull at Naworth Gules armed unguled and collared with a chain reflexed over the back Or; Sinister, A roebuck also Gules armed and unguled Gold. The whole upon a compartment in the form of a masoned embattled wall Or. *Motto.* Perfero. Granted 1951.

CUMBERLAND, Duke of. Prince Ruprecht, or Rupert, Count Palatine of the Rhine, Duke of Bavaria (1619-82), 3rd son of Friedrich, King of

* The medieval grave-slab in Bromfield church, at one time said to be that of Adam de Crookdake, from which this quarter was derived, displays: . . . a saltire . . . on a chief . . . three cross crosslets . . . .

† To his grand-daughter, the Hon. Ellinor Frances Cross, of Ash House, Millom, we are indebted for much help and advice.

‡ The monument also displays the arms of the Universities of Oxford, Cambridge, Leeds, and St Andrews, *q.v.*

§ FAC misprints this as Crudens, and ABD as Cruders.

Bohemia, Elector Palatine of the Rhine, by the Princess Elizabeth, dau. of James I, was cr. Duke of Cumberland 1644. He d. *s.p.* *Arms.* Quarterly, 1 & 4, Sable a lion rampant ducally crowned Or; 2 & 3, Paly bendy Or and Azure. *Crest.* On a chapeau Gules turned up Ermine a lion sejant affronté Or crowned Gules between two wings paly bendy Argent and Azure. *Supporters.* Two lions guardant Or (BGA).

CUMBERLAND, Duke of. George, Prince of Denmark, Duke of Schleswig-Holstein and Count of Oldenburg, K.G. (1653-1708), youngest son of Frederik III, King of Denmark, and Consort of Queen Anne, was cr. Duke of Cumberland and Earl of Kendal, 1689. *Arms.* Or semé of hearts Gules three lions passant guardant Azure crowned Proper (BGA).

CUMBERLAND AND TIVIOTDALE, Duke of. H.R.H. Ernest Augustus, Prince of Great Britain and Ireland, King of Hanover, Duke of Brunswick-Lüneburg, K.G., K.P., G.C.B., G.C.H. (1771-1851), 5th son of King George III, was cr. Duke of Cumberland and Tiviotdale 1799. From him descends Ernest Augustus George William Christian Ludwig Francis Joseph Nicholas, Duke of Brunswick-Lüneburg (b. 1914), *de jure* Duke of Cumberland and Tiviotdale. *Arms.* These were originally, according to FAC: Quarterly, 1, England impaling Scotland; 2, France Modern; 3, Ireland; 4, Hanover, viz. Tierced in pale reversed, i, Gules two lions passant guardant in pale Or (Brunswick); ii, Or semé of hearts Gules a lion rampant Azure (Luneburg); iii (in point), Gules a horse courant Argent (Westphalia); on the centre of the fourth quarter an escutcheon Gules charged with the crown of Charlemagne Or. Over all a label of three points Argent on the central point a fleur-de-lys Azure on each of the others a cross Gules. The Dukes later bore: Quarterly, 1 & 4, England; 2, Scotland; 3, Ireland; on an escutcheon of pretence, Hanover (as above); over all, a label as above. *Crest.* On a coronet composed of crosses pattée and strawberry leaves a lion statant guardant Or crowned with a like coronet and differenced with a label of three points as in the arms. *Supporters.* Dexter, A lion rampant guardant Or crowned as the crest; Sinister, A unicorn Argent armed crined and unguled Or gorged with a coronet as in the crest a chain affixed thereto passing between the forelegs and reflexed over the back; and both differenced with a label as in the arms. The arms, crest and supporters of the 2nd Duke, King of Hanover, were further differenced with a second label of three points Gules the centre point charged with the white horse of Hanover (BGA; DPB; FDH).

CUMBRIA County Council. *Arms* (granted 1974). Per pale Azure and Or a pale wavy per pale of the last and Vert over all two bars dancetty of three points upwards countertinctured Argent Azure Argent and Vert all within a bordure of the last charged alternately with three roses Argent on each another Gules both barbed and seeded Proper and as many Parnassus flowers Argent. *Crest.* Issuant out of a mural crown Argent masoned Gules a ram's head Proper armed Or between two Parnassus flowers slipped also Proper. *Supporters.* Dexter, A representation of the Dacre Bull at Naworth Gules armed unguled and collared with a chain flexed over the back Or; Sinister, A dragon also Gules; the whole upon a Compartment composed of a section of the Roman Wall charged with two bars Gules. *Badge.* A roundle per pale Azure and Or a pale wavy per pale Or and Vert over all two bars dancetty of three points upward countertinctured Argent Azure Argent and Vert enclosed by an annulet of stonework Proper masoned Sable. *Motto.* Ad montes oculos levavi.

CUPPAGE. For an account of this family at Irton, see CW2 x 167-8. Nicholas Cuppage occurs in 1583, John in 1587, and Mungo in 1674; and Abraham Cuppage died 1774. The branch of the family settled at Drigg and Greenlands, Holmrook, bore the following *Arms.* Argent a fess between three garbs Gules. *Crest.* A dial Argent (*ex inf.* the late Rev. H. A. L. Rice).

CURWEN, of Camerton. For the earlier history of this family see CAMERTON. Alan de Camerton's line ended in a dau. who marr. John Curwen. Their grandson Thomas (d. *c.* 1500), known as Black Tom, is bur. in Camerton church, where his effigy remains. His grandson Christopher Curwen (d. 1713) was High Sheriff of Cumberland 1705, and was succ. by his brother Joseph (d. 1721) who sold Camerton Hall and manor to Ralph Cooke, *q.v. Arms.* Argent fretty Gules on a chief Azure an escallop of the first (FVC; TVN). *Crest.* A unicorn's head (Effigy at Camerton).

CURWEN, of Workington. The history of this great family, the oldest in Cumberland, has been told by J. F. Curwen in *A History of the Ancient House of Curwen;* and in JPP, CW2 xiv, and SBR. Eldred was father of Chettel or Ketel, living 1120, who was Lord of Workington and gave Workington church to St. Mary's Abbey, York. His son Gilbert was ancestor of the de Lancaster family. Orm, a younger son (living 1094), was father of Gospatrick (*fl.* 1145-79) who was father of Thomas de Workington, Orm de Ireby, *q.v.*, and Gilbert de Southaic, *q.v.* The above Thomas (d. 1200) founded Shap Abbey, and by marr. to Amabel, dau. and coheir of Thomas de Culwen, son of Uchtred, Lord of Galloway, obtained the Lordship of Culwen, now known as Colvend in Kirkcudbrightshire. His son Patrick became known as de Culwen; a younger son was Alan de Camerton, *q.v.* From Patrick descended Sir Gilbert Curwen I (d. *c.* 1290), High Sheriff of Cumberland 1278-82, and Governor of Carlisle Castle 1278. Sir Gilbert Curwen II was High Sheriff 1308, and Sir Gilbert IV served 1379. His son Sir William (d. 1403), High Sheriff 1397, marr. Elena, sister and coheir of Robert le Brun, *q.v.* Their son Sir Christopher (*c.* 1382-1453) was High Sheriff 1415, 1423, 1427, 1433, 1437 and 1444. His son Sir Christopher (d. 1499) marr. (2) Katherine, dau. and coheir of Sir Richard Salkeld.* *q.v.* By his first wife he was father of Sir Thomas (d. 1522) who, with Black Tom Curwen, of Camerton, and others, was accused of murdering Alexander Dykes 1499. He was High Sheriff 1509 and 1516, an office held in 1524-26 and 1533 by his son Sir Christopher (d. *c.* 1535) whose son Sir Thomas (*c.* 1494-1543) was Sheriff in 1536. His son Sir Henry (d. 1597) was Knight of the Shire for Cumberland 1554-56, 1563, and Sheriff 1562, 1570, 1580 and 1589. He marr. Catherine, dau. and coheir of Sir John Dalston, *q.v.*, and in 1568 he gave refuge at Workington to Mary, Queen of Scots. His son Sir Nicholas (1550-1605) was Sheriff 1600 and his son Sir Henry (1581-1623) served 1619. His three sons succ. in turn to Workington – Sir Patricius (1601-64), High Sheriff 1636, who was cr. Baronet 1626;† Thomas (1605-72), High Sheriff 1669; and Eldred, his half-brother, who d. 1673, having held the estates nine weeks. His son Henry (1661-1725), High Sheriff 1687,

* Their only child Isabella marr. 1492 Sir John Lamplugh, *q.v.*

† Sir Patricius marr. 1620 Isabella, dau. and coheir of Sir George Selby, of Whitehouse (D); their only son d. young, *v.p.*, and the baronetcy became extinct.

d. unmarr. and was succ. by Henry (1680-1727), descended from Thomas Curwen, of Sella Park (1590-1653), son of Sir Henry, above (d. 1597). He was succ. by his brother Eldred (1692-1745), High Sheriff 1729, M.P. for Cockermouth 1738-41, whose son Henry (1728-78) was the last male of the family. He was High Sheriff 1753, and M.P. for Carlisle 1761-68 and for Cumberland 1768-74. His dau. and heir Isabella (1765-1820) marr. 1782 her cousin John Christian, *q.v.* (1756-1828), who assumed the surname Curwen. Their descendant Alan de Lancy Curwen (1869-1930) was succ. by his only dau. Isabel Mary (d. 1967) who marr. 1923 Frederick Selby Chance, J.P. (d. 1946). Their elder son, Lt-Cdr Edward Stanley Chance Curwen, R.N., who assumed the surname and arms of Curwen 1956, is now of Belle Isle. *Arms.* Argent fretty Gules a chief Azure. A seal of 1257, and the Charles Roll, *temp.* Edward I, shew the arms as: Gules fretty Argent. *Crest.* A unicorn's head erased Argent armed Or. *Supporters.* Dexter, A naked woman Proper with golden hair girdled round the loins; Sinister, A unicorn Argent unguled and horned Or. *Motto.* Si je n'estoy (FCW; AHC).*

ROPER-CURZON. The Hon. John Henry Roper-Curzon (1802-86), 4th son of the 14th Baron Teynham, marr. at St. Cuthbert, Carlisle, 1829 Isabella, dau. and coheir of Col James Hodgson, H.E.I.C.S. They were of Abbot Bank, Penrith, 1835-37, and of Castelette Cottage, near Keswick, in 1847. *Arms.* Quarterly, 1 & 4, Argent on a bend Sable three popinjays Or collared Gules (Curzon); 2 & 3, Per fess Azure and Or a pale counterchanged and three bucks' heads erased of the second (Roper). *Crests.* 1, A popinjay rising Or collared Gules (Curzon); 2, A lion rampant Sable holding in the dexter paw a ducal coronet Or (Roper). *Motto.* Spes mea in Deo (BP; BGA).

CUST, of Penrith and Carlisle. Thomas Cust, apothecary, of Corn Market, Penrith (d. 1737), whose family came from Danby Hill (Y), marr. 1722 Elizabeth (d. 1779, aged 88), dau. of John Pattenson, of Penrith, *q.v.*, and had *int. al.*† a son Thomas Cust, apothecary and surgeon, of Penrith (1723-58), who had sons Capt Thomas Cust, Bengal Army (1752-95), died unmarr., and Richard Cust, a London stationer (1754-1844), who was later of 5 Abbey Street, Carlisle, and whose son Richard (1813-57) died unmarr.

* In AHC, John F. Curwen describes and illustrates a fine achievement of the Curwen arms in glass dated 1634 at Workington Hall, as follows: *Arms.* Quarterly of fifteen, 1 & 15, Argent fretty Gules a chief Azure (Curwen); 2, Azure a lion rampant Argent gutté-de-sang langued and armed Gules (le Brun); 3, Sable a bend Ermine on a chief Argent three torteaux (Broun); 4, Plain; 5, Argent a chevron engrailed between three daws' heads erased Sable billed Or (Dalston); 6, Argent a cross engrailed Vert (Kirkbride); 7, Argent two chevrons Azure within a bordure engrailed gules (Tirrell); 8, Ermine a cross Sable (Archer, alias de Boys, or for Daventre); 9, Sable three pallets Argent (?Sanderson); 10, Gules on a chevron engrailed Argent three dolphins naiant embowed Vert (Flambert, of Essex); 11, Gules [? – correctly, Argent] an eagle displayed Sable armed and langued Gules (Bruen, Broun or Tirrell); 12, Per pale Or and Sable a saltire engrailed counterchanged (de la Pole); 13, Argent a lion rampant Azure crowned Or langued and armed Gules (Pickering); 14, Ermine an escutcheon of pretence Azure (Rokeby). Impaling, Quarterly, 1 & 4, Barry of ten Or and Sable (Selby); 2 & 3, Per fess Argent and Gules Six martlets counterchanged (Fenwick). *Crest.* A unicorn's head erased Argent horned Or and Argent. *Supporters.* Dexter, A maiden Proper with golden hair girdled round the loins; Sinister, A unicorn Argent horned Or and Argent. *Motto.* SI IE N'ESTOY.

† A younger son John (b. 1725) was father of Martha (1755-1838) and Charlotte (1756-1843) who marr. 1788 Christopher Crackanthorpe Cookson, later Crackanthorpe, uncle of the poet Wordsworth, whose sister Dorothy wrote of them in 1787: "They are a mixture of Ignorance, Pride, affectation, self-conceit and affected notability . . . I could bear their ignorance well enough, if they did not think so exceedingly well of themselves" (*Letters of William and Dorothy Wordsworth, 1787-1805*, 1967).

Arms. Ermine on a chevron Sable three fountains. *Crest.* A lion's head erased collared compony Azure and Argent. *Motto.* Opera illius mea sunt. (Bookplate and Seal of Richard Cust, 1754-1844).

DACRE, of Dacre, Gilsland, Greystoke, and Naworth. This great baronial house took its name from Dacre.* William de Dacre (d. 1268) was Sheriff of Cumberland 1236-48, and his son Ranulph (d. 1286) held the office 1268-71. His grandson Sir Ranulph (*c.* 1290-1339) was summoned to Parliament as a baron 1321, was sheriff of Cumberland 1330-36, Constable of Carlisle Castle 1330, and Warden of the Marches 1333. He had licence to crenellate his home at Naworth 1335. By marr. 1317 to Margaret (whom he abducted from Warwick Castle), dau. and heir of Thomas de Multon, of Gilsland, *q.v.*, he acquired great possessions in Cumberland, including the barony of Gilsland, still held by his descendant. He was succ. in turn by his three sons, of whom Ranulph, the 2nd son, and 3rd Lord Dacre, who was in Holy Orders, was murdered at Halton (L) 1375. Thomas, the 6th Baron (1387-1458), had a son Sir Thomas who d. *v.p.*, having marr. Elizabeth, dau. and heir of Sir William Bowet, *q.v.*, and had a dau. Joan, who marr. Sir Richard Fiennes who was summoned to Parliament as Baron Dacre 1459 (see FIENNES). Joan's uncle Ranulph (killed at Towton 1461) was summoned as Baron Dacre of Gilsland 1459 and was succ. by his brother Humphrey (d. 1485) who was summoned as Baron Dacre of Gilsland 1473, the title becoming known as "of the North." His son Sir Thomas Dacre, K.G., K.B., 2nd Baron (1467-1525) was a commander at Flodden. He marr. *c.* 1488 Elizabeth (1471-1516), dau. of Sir Robert Greystoke and granddau. and heir of Ralph, 7th Lord Greystoke. Their son William, 3rd Lord Dacre (1500-63), became Lord Greystoke 1516 and was Warden of the West Marches 1527-34. He was succ. by his son Thomas, 4th Baron Dacre (*c.* 1524-66), who was M.P. for Cumberland 1553. He marr. Elizabeth, dau. of Sir James Leyburne, of Cunswick, and was succ. by their son George, 5th Baron Dacre, who was killed 1569, aged 7, by a fall from a rocking-horse, his sisters and coheirs being Anne (*c.* 1557-1630), who marr. 1571 Philip Howard, Earl of Arundel, son of her stepfather, the 4th Duke of Norfolk; Mary (b. *c.* 1563), contracted to marry Philip's brother Thomas Howard, later Earl of Suffolk; and Elizabeth (*c.* 1564-1639), who marr. Lord William Howard, *q.v.*, another son of the 4th Duke. Lady Arundel took the Barony of Greystoke and Lady William Howard that of Gilsland, though their right was bitterly contested by Leonard Dacre (d. 1573), their uncle and the male heir, whose claim to the barony of Dacre was disallowed in 1569. Joining the rising of the Northern Earls, he was defeated near Naworth 1570 and attainted, with his brother Edward (d. 1584). Their brother Francis (d. 1633) also claimed the title and was in possession of the estates *c.* 1584. His son Ranulph (1608-34) also claimed the title. He d. *s.p.*, and his sister Mary, who eloped 1635 with Marmaduke Hedworth, and died *s.p.* at a great age, was the last of her race (GEC). *Arms.* The arms of this great family – Gules three escallops Argent – are displayed in so many parts of Cumberland and Westmorland, alone and quartered by Howard, that no authority need be quoted for them. FFC records variants as follows: Azure on a cross Or five escallops Gules (Randolph Dacre, *temp.* Henry III), and Gules floretté Or three escallops Argent (Sir Edward Dacre, of Cumberland, *temp.* Edward

* And not, as legend had it, from Acre in the Holy Land.

II). *Crest.* The seal of Thomas, 6th Lord Dacre, in 1412 shewed: A bull's head issuing from a coronet. The family later used: A bull passant Gules ducally gorged, armed and chained Or. *Supporters.* Two griffins; but a stone achievement at Corby Castle, perhaps taken there from Kirkoswald Castle, displays: Dexter, A bull; Sinister, A griffin. *Badges.* An escallop Argent; An escallop and a ragged staff knotted together all Argent (but with the knot sometimes Gules); A griffin Sable armed Or; An escallop Argent within a chaplet Gules; A stag Argent. *Motto.* Fort en loyalte (Carvings, plasterwork, etc., at Naworth Castle, Carlisle Castle, etc.).

DACRE, of Lanercost. Sir Thomas Dacre (d. 1565) was illegitimate son of Thomas, 2nd Lord Dacre (d. 1525), *q.v.* In 1537 the Duke of Norfolk describes him as "a quick, sharp man, brought up in practices of such wild people" – i.e. the Borderers (BBP). He was granted by the King Lanercost Priory 1542, and in 1552 given the rectories of Lanercost, Grinsdale, Farlam, Lazonby, Brampton and Irthington. He was succ. by his son Christopher (d. 1593), who marr. 1563 Alice, dau. of Sir Henry Knyvett, *q.v.* (she marr. (2) before 1599 John Suthwicke, of Barwise (W)). Their son Henry (d. *c.* 1623), who marr. Mary Salkeld, lived at Rosgill Hall (W). His son Thomas (b. 1607, d. before 1674) was knighted 1633. He was succ. by his son Henry (d. 1696) who marr. (1) 1662 Mary, dau. and heir of the Rev. Henry Sibson, D.D., by whom he had a dau. Dorothy (d. 1698), wife of Joseph Appelby; and (2) 1675 Margaret (d. 1716), wife of William Charlton, of Hesleyside (N), by whom he had sons William (d. *s.p.* 1705), and James (d. 1716, aged 29), the last of the family.* His successor was his half-sister's son Joseph Appelby, see APPELBY, *post* DACRE. *Arms.* The family used the arms of the parent stem, sometimes alone, viz. Gules three escallops Argent; sometimes differenced with a bordure engrailed company Argent and Azure (MMS vi 425), or a bend sinister (Kirklinton church†). The Fetherstonhaughs impaled them at The College, Kirkoswald, differenced with a bordure engrailed company Or and Azure. *Crest* and *Motto*. As the parent stem.

DACRE. A differenced version of the Dacre arms is impaled by Musgrave in a window in Edenhall church, commemorating Thomas Musgrave, of Hayton (d. 1532), and his wife, Elizabeth, illegitimate dau. of Thomas, 2nd Lord Dacre, *q.v.* *Arms.* Gules three escallops Argent a bend Azure.

DACRE. John C. Dacre, of RD2, Pukehole, New Zealand, is descended from the Dacres of Cumberland. According to family tradition his ancestor Henry Dacres obtained in 1524, as representative of a younger branch of the family, a grant of the Dacre arms with certain differences. *Arms.* Argent a

* He had agreed to raise forty men for the Jacobite army, but he was "taken with a fortunate fever" and prevented from taking any part in the Rising of '15.

† There is a fine achievement of the Dacre arms in a window in Kirklinton church, viz. Quarterly of eight, 1, Gules three escallops Argent (Dacre); 2, Barry Argent and Azure three chaplets Gules (Greystoke); 3, Gules three cushions Ermine tasselled Or (Greystoke); 4, Gules a fess company Sable and Argent between six cross crosslets fitché Or (Boteler); 5, Argent three bars Gules on a canton of the last a lion passant Or (Multon); 6, Vairé Or and Gules on a canton [Gules] a lion passant Or (Ferrers); 7, Azure semé-de-lys and fretty Or (Morvill); 8, Chequy Gules and Or (Vaux); over all, a bendlet sinister Argent. *Crest.* A bull statant Gules armed unguled ducally gorged and chain reflexed over the back Or. *Motto.* Forte en loyaute. The right to the quarterings, especially Nos. 2, 3, 4 and 6, seems doubtful since the Lanercost Dacres were an illegitimate line. Field recorded Quarter No. 4 incorrectly as: Gules a fess chequy Argent and Sable between three crosses pattée fitché Or (FAC).

chevron Gules between three pellets each charged with an escallop Or. *Crest.* A dove charged on the breast with an escallop Or between two oak branches leaved and fructed. *Mottoes.* Forte en loyaute; Sic vive ut semper vivas (Bookplate).

DACRE-ASSEY, *olim* DACRE. Capt Charles Dacre (1786-1823), 12th Bengal N.I., son of William Richard Dacre, of Kirklinton Hall, see Appelby, *post* Dacre, marr. 1808 Sophia Isabella (d. 1840, aged 57, bur. Christ Church burial ground, Carlisle), sister of Charles Chaston Assey, Surgeon, H.E.I.Co. Their eldest son Charles William Dacre,* of Cavendish Place, Carlisle (d. 1842, aged 27), under the terms of his uncle's will, assumed the name and arms of Assey 1836. *Arms.* Azure on a pale Argent between two lions rampant respecting each other Or a kris Proper a chief Ermine thereon an Eastern crown Gules between two leopards' faces also Proper. *Crest.* A demi leopard erased Proper crowned with an Eastern crown and charged on the shoulder with a rose Gules the paws supporting a kris in pale as in the arms (CA xli/337).

DALRYMPLE. John Dalrymple, of Carlisle, gentleman, in his will (proved 1732), left lands in or near Carlisle to his wife Mary and mentioned his dau. Catherine, wife of Alexander Forfar, and his cousin-german Robert Dalrymple, of Edinburgh, Writer to the Signet. *Arms.* . . . on a saltire . . . nine lozenges . . . . *Motto.* Quiescam (Seal on will).

DALSTON, of Dalston Hall. Denton gives a pedigree of six generations of this family, beginning with Reginald, whose great-great-grandson Simon de Dalston (*fl.* 1271-1301) owned the manor of Little Dalston.† His descendant John Dalston (d. before 1537) marr. before 1507 Elizabeth (b. *c.* 1478), dau. and coheir of George Kirkbride, of Kirkbride, *q.v.* Their son Thomas (d. 1550), who was Sheriff of Cumberland 1540, obtained 1544 the manors of Brundholme, Uldale, and Caldbeck-Upperton, and also the manor of Temple Sowerby, which he settled on his son by his 2nd wife, Eleanor Carlile, Christopher Dalston (see Dalston, of Uldale and Acornbank). At Dalston Hall he was succ. by his eldest son Sir John (1523-80) who was M.P. for Cumberland 1556 and Sheriff 1567 and 1576. His son Sir John (1557-1633) was Sheriff 1583, 1586, 1594 and 1604-6. He marr. (1) Anne, dau. and coheir of Thomas Tyrell, of Birdbrook, Essex, and had daus. and coheirs Dorothy (b. 1577), marr. Henry Gent, and Catherine (b. 1580), marr. Sir Henry Curwen, *q.v.* He marr. (2) Frances, dau. and coheir of Thomas Warcop, and was succ. by his son Sir George (d. 1657), Sheriff 1618 and M.P. for Cumberland 1621, 1625, 1627, and 1640-41. He marr. 1604 Catherine (d. 1614), dau. and coheir of John Tamworth, of Hallstead, Leics. Their son Sir William (d. 1683), M.P. for Carlisle 1640-44, Sheriff of Cumberland 1665, was cr. Baronet 1641. By his wife Anne (d. 1639), dau. of Thomas Bolles, he was father of Sir John, 2nd Bart. (1639-1711), Sheriff 1686. His son Sir Charles, 3rd Bart. (1686-1723), Sheriff 1712, marr. Susan, dau. and coheir of Sir Francis Blake, of Witney, Oxon, and was succ. by his son Sir George (1718-65), 4th and last Bart., who was Sheriff 1752. He sold Dalston 1761. His dau. and heir Elizabeth (b. 1751) marr. Capt Theobald Dillon. The baronetcy was wrongly assumed by a distant cousin, John

* His brother, the Rev. George Dacre, B.A. (Dunelm), was Curate of Holy Trinity, Carlisle, 1843-45.

† Not the manor of Dalston, which belonged to the Bishops of Carlisle.

Dalston, Capt R.M., of the Temple Sowerby branch, who owned Beckbank, Great Salkeld, which was inherited by his dau. and heir Mary, who marr. Peter Clements (DAC; CW2 x, lviii; GEC). *Arms.* The earliest version appears to be that on a shield on the tower of Dalston Hall: . . . three daws' heads erased . . . within a bordure indented . . . FCW gives: Argent a chevron between three daws' heads erased Sable. The chevron should, however, be engrailed, see FFC; FVC; FDC; LMC; and Harl. MS. 1563. *Crest.* Out of a ducal coronet a daw's head Sable beaked Or (FCW; FVC). LMC, however, gives: On a ducal crown a falcon's head issuing Proper.

DALSTON, of Uldale and Acornbank. In 1546 Thomas Dalston (d. 1550) (see previous entry) settled the manor of Uldale on a younger son Christopher (d. 1604), who was of Acornbank (W); he was Sheriff of Cumberland 1596. The last male of the family was Sir William Dalston (1708-71), High Sheriff of Cumberland 1760. *Arms.* As Dalston, of Dalston Hall. *Crest.* Out of a ducal coronet a falcon's head Proper (FCW; NB i 385).

DALTON, of Carlisle. Thomas Dalton of Abbey Street, Carlisle, merchant (d. 1740, aged 38), was father of George Dalton, D.L., J.P., of Carlisle, grocer (1738-1784), Mayor of Carlisle 1772 and 1780, Captain, Cumberland Militia, 1760, who marr. 1773 "the amiable Miss Peggy Graham" (*Newcastle Courant*) and had an only child Elizabeth, who marr. 1800 David Kennedy, *q.v.* *Arms* (granted 1776*). Azure crusilly Argent a lion rampant guardant Or. *Crest.* A lion's head erased Or. *Motto.* Amor honor et justitia (George Dalton's bookplate in Viscountess Wolseley's collection). On the escutcheon of pretence on the arms of David Kennedy in Crosby-on-Eden church, the arms appear as: . . . a lion rampant . . . .

DALTON. Impaled by Nayler, *q.v.*, on tablet in Greystoke church; Capt Thomas Nayler, R.M. (d. 1802), marr. (2) Elizabeth Dalton, of Thurnham Hall. *Arms.* Azure crusilly and a lion rampant guardant Argent.

DALZELL. John Dalzell, of Queen Street, Whitehaven, flour dealer (1792-1867), by 1834 had begun farming at Preston Hows. Of his sons, Thomas Dalzell (b. 1826, living 1881), was of Low Wood Hall, Netherwasdale, and Joseph Dalzell, brewer (1838-1903), was of Moresby House. The latter was grandfather of Miss Dorothy Dalzell, formerly of Langdale Chase, Troutbeck, and now of The Cottage, Burton-in-Kendal. *Crest.* A dexter hand couped below the wrist grasping a scimitar. *Motto.* I dare (T. Dalzell's writing paper).

DARCY. Shields at Hutton-in-the-Forest; a Vane quartering. *Arms.* Argent three cinquefoils Gules.

DARE. Shield on tombstone of Mary (d. 1852), wife of James Dare, in St. Michael's churchyard, Workington. *Arms.* . . . a chevron Gules between three quatrefoils . . . .

DARRELL. MVC shews Lawson, of Isel, *q.v.*, as quartering the following, presumably for Darrell; Thomas Lawson, of Usworth (d. 1559), marr. Elizabeth Darrell, of Wilts (FVD). *Arms.* Azure a lion rampant Or crowned Argent.

DAVISON. John, son of William Davison, of Stapleton, d. 1734, aged 25. *Arms.* . . . a featherless arrow in pale point downwards . . . between two hearts . . . (Tombstone at Stapleton).

* For the grant, see Appendix.

DAWBURY – see CARLETON.

DAWES. The Rev. Dr Lancelot Dawes (1580-1654), Vicar of Barton 1608-54, Rector of Asby 1618-54, and Prebendary of Carlisle 1619-54, was co-founder of Barton Grammar School. His son, Thomas Dawes, of Barton Kirk (W) (d. 1684), had two sons Lancelot (d. 1675) and Thomas (d. 1733), of whom presently. Lancelot's son, Thomas Dawes (d. 1718), was Sheriff of Cumberland 1698-99, and had by Elizabeth, his wife (d. 1750), a large family. Field says that he was the last of the family, but in addition to his children, his brother Lancelot, of Sedbergh (d. 1707), also left issue, while their uncle Thomas Dawes, of Craketrees, Crosby Ravensworth (d. 1733), appears in BLG17 as ancestor of the Dawes family, of Mount Ephraim, Kent, who bear the following *Arms.* Ermine on a bend Azure cotised dancetté Gules between four battle axes erect two in chief and as many in base Sable three swans close Argent. *Crest.* In front of a demi battle axe erect Or surmounted by a dragon sans wings and legs the tail nowed Sable charged with five bezants fesswise three quatrefoils also Gold. *Motto.* Nihil sine Deo (BLG17). In the courtyard at Barton Kirk there is a shield bearing: . . . a fess . . . between three jackdaws . . . .

DAWSON, of Keswick. William Dawson, of Keswick, marr. 1787 Dinah Stainton, and died 1827, aged 73. *Arms.* . . . an eastern crown . . . . *Crest.* A hand erect couped at the wrist and holding an open book (M.I., Crosthwaite church). It seems probable that so far from these being the arms and crest of Dawson, they were a stylised form of heraldic decoration provided by the monumental mason.

DAWSON, *post* DAWSON-SCOTT, of Penrith. Robert and Isabel Dawson, of Penrith, had daus. Isabella and Margaret (1735-1821), who marr. 1766 Richard Story, *q.v.,* and a son, Thomas Dawson (1725-94), father of Robert Dawson (1776-1860), Royal Military surveyor, who made the first Ordnance Survey (DNB). His son Col Robert Kearsley Dawson, C.B., R.E. (1798-1861), is also in DNB. His son General Robert Nicholl Dawson, J.P., R.E. (1836-1922), inherited Brent House, Penrith from his uncle Thomas Scott and assumed the additional name of Scott 1872. His dau. Mary Carne Dawson-Scott d. 1951, aged 79. *Arms* (granted 1761). Azure a chevron Ermine on a chief Argent three Cornish choughs Proper. *Crest.* A demi talbot Ermine eared Azure holding an arrow Or flighted and pointed Argent (BGA). The arms are on the monument in Penrith churchyard to the above Margaret Dawson and her husband Richard Story.

DAY. Alfred Day, LL.D. (Glasgow), of Bristol (d. 1869, aged 62), mathematical writer and schoolmaster, was father of the Rev. Alfred Bloxsome Day, M.A. (Oxon) (1834-95), Vicar of Cawood (Y). His only son, the Rev. Alfred Edward Bloxsome Day, M.A., D.D. (Oxon) (1873-1951), was Precentor of Carlisle Cathedral and Master of the Choir School 1910-16, and Vicar of Rosley with Woodside 1916. The present head of the family is his son Alfred Neville Bloxsome Day, of 41 Queen's Gate Gardens, London, SW7, chartered accountant. *Arms.* . . . a chevron Sable between three mullets . . . . *Crest.* Two hands clasping each other couped at the wrist and conjoined to a pair of wings each wing charged with a mullet. *Motto.* Ad finem fidelis (Seal).

DAYMAN. The Rev. John Dayman, M.A. (Oxon), of Mambury, Devon (1802-71), Fellow of Corpus Christi College, Oxford, was Rector of

Skelton 1831-71 (BLG11). *Arms.* Gules four fusils in fess Ermine. *Crest.* A demi lion rampant ducally gorged and chained Or (BLG8). FBC gives: A demi lion holding in the dexter paw a fusil Gules charged with a fleur-de-lys Ermine. *Motto.* Toujours prest.

DEANE, of Whitehaven. The Rev. Nicholas Deane, M.A. (Cantab), Vicar of Warcop 1585-89, Vicar of Bromfield 1589-1602, Archdeacon of Carlisle 1602-22, was ancestor of a family of some importance in Appleby and Whitehaven. Richard Deane (d. 1727, aged 61) was a member of the Common Council of Appleby; his son Joseph (1701-80) was Tide Surveyor of Whitehaven *c.* 1724-77. His son, Charles Deane (1732-87), was Alderman of Appleby. The last of the family was his son, Charles Deane, solicitor, of 61 Lincoln's Inn Fields, London (d. unmarr. 1864). *Arms.* Quarterly, 1 & 4, Argent two bars and a canton Sable; 2 & 3, Per fess indented . . . and . . . three coronets counter-changed. *Crest.* A tortoise (CW2 lxxi 194-6; RWH).

DE JERSEY. Thomas Bowerbank, of London, *q.v.,* marr. Elizabeth, dau. and heir of William De Jersey, of Guernsey, merchant, and obtained in 1801 for her and her descendants a grant of the following *Arms.* Per saltire Sable and Vert an eagle with two heads displayed Or (CA xxi/271).

DE LA DENE. Shield at Hutton-in-the-Forest; a Vane quartering. *Arms.* Or a chevron engrailed Sable between three pellets. The field is usually tinctured Argent.

DELAMORE, of Cumcatch. In 1386 William de Dacre, Lord of Gilsland, and John Delamore exchanged lands, Dacre obtaining lands near Naworth, and Delamore lands at Cumcatch. Isabel, the heiress of the family, marr. William de Vaux, of Catterlen, *q.v.,* living 1481. *Arms.* John Delamore, *temp.* Edward II, bore: Gules a cross pattée (patonce in trick) and an escallop Argent (FFC). Field says that these arms, with the cross patonce, are carved on a stone panel in the porch of Brampton Old Church. At Catterlen Hall the arms are quartered by Vaux as: . . . a cross flory . . . FVC gives: Gules a cross flory Or, and also (as a Vaux quartering): Vert a cross moline Or. A shield on the ceiling of Carlisle Cathedral displaying: Gules a cross pattée Or may be intended for Delamore. In windows at Conishead Priory and Ulverston church, and on brasses and hatchments in St. Ninian's, Brougham, the arms appear as: Gules a cross patonce Or.

DELAMORE. John Delamore was Sheriff of Cumberland 1409-10. *Arms.* Argent three greyhounds courant in pale Sable collared Or (DSL).

DELAMORE. Thomas Delamore was Sheriff of Cumberland 1430. *Arms.* Argent six martlets, three, two, and one Sable (FWE).

DE LA POLE. Shield at Hutton John. A Hudleston quartering, brought in by Stapleton, *q.v.*; Sir Miles Stapleton (d. 1466) marr. Katherine, dau. and heir of Sir Thomas De la Pole. *Arms.* Azure a fess between three leopards' faces Or.

DENMAN. The Hon. Sir Richard Douglas Denman, Bart., J.P., B.A. (Oxon) (1876-1957), brother of the 3rd Baron Denman, was M.P. for Carlisle 1910-18 and for Central Leeds 1929-45, and for many years was of Staffield Hall, Kirkoswald, which was the home of his widow, who was the daughter of James Spencer, of Murrah Hall, Greystoke. He was cr. Baronet 1945, and was succ. by his son Sir Charles Spencer Denman, C.B.E.; M.C., T.D. who succ. his cousin as 5th Baron Denman 1971. *Arms.* Argent on a chevron between three lions' heads erased Gules as many ermine spots Or. *Crest.* A raven rising Proper in the beak an annulet Or. *Motto.* Prudentia et constantia (BP105).

DENTON, of Cardew. This branch of the Denton family claims descent from John Denton, brother of Sir Richard (d. before 1363), see Denton of Warnell. He was Lord of Ainstable and was succ. by his son John, Knight of the Shire for Cumberland 1368 and 1381, High Sheriff 1371 and 1374, who marr. Joan, dau. of Walter de Kirkbride. On them John de Burdon settled Cardew. Their son William marr. 1393 Katherine, dau. of Richard de Copeland, *q.v.* Their grandson John (d. 1493) was deprived of Ainstable by Thomas, Lord Dacre. He marr. Margaret (d. before 1527), eldest dau. and coheir of Sir Henry Fenwick, *q.v.*, and acquired Lowick Tower and other lands in Northumberland. Their son Henry (d. 1512) was High Sheriff of Cumberland 1490. His descendant John Denton, of Cardew (*c.* 1561-1617), was Cumberland's first historian, of whose *Accompt* the late Dr. F. W. Dendy rightly declared that "it forms the bed-rock of Cumberland History." His son and successor Henry (*c.* 1582-1627) sold Lowick and other lands in Northumberland. His grandson Col George Denton (1620-67) fell into debt and sold Ingram (N) 1647 and mortgaged Cardew, which passed to his son George* (b. *c.* 1650), who sold Dentonholme 1677 to the Forster family and Cardew to Sir John Lowther 1686. He had sons Henry (b. 1678), George (b. 1680) and Basil (b. 1682); their later history is unknown, but in 1935 Mr. Arthur Denton, of Wellington, Salop., claimed to be a representative. (CW2 xvi, lxviii; AA3 xiv). *Arms.* On the grave slab of Sir John Denton in Ainstable church these are shown as: . . . two bars . . . and in chief three martlets . . . .† The same arms are carved on the effigies in Ainstable church (taken there from St. Cuthbert's, Carlisle) of Sir John's son William and his wife Katherine de Copeland (d. 1428); and panels from this tomb are built into the grotto at Nunnery and show the same arms, with those of Copeland, and a shield . . . fretty . . . , which Field (FAC) attributes to Skelton, but which seems more likely to be Hudleston. FVC gives: Argent two bars and in chief three martlets Gules. At the Visitation of 1665 Col George Denton recorded: Quarterly, 1 & 4, Argent two bars and in chief three martlets Gules; 2, Per pale *(sic)* Gules and Argent six martlets three and three counterchanged (presumably, Fenwick); 3; Vert a lion rampant Argent (presumably, Heton, a Fenwick quartering). Dugdale added the note: "No proofe made of these armes." *Crest.* On Sir John Denton's grave slab in Ainstable church this appears as: A martlet rising; which LMC recorded as: A martlet Sable. According to John Denton, the historian, however (DAC), this crest was abandoned in favour of one used to commemorate their ancestor Sir John Denton, steward of Annandale, who "when Baliol was banished Scotland he kept still the principal house till it was fired under him, beaten and undermined until it was ready to fall, whereupon his heirs give now in remembrance thereof for their crest a castle or tower sable, flames issuing out at the top thereof and a demi-lion with a sword in his right paw issuing out of the flames." Dugdale recorded this as:

* He and Barbara his wife were charged with being papists in 1678.

† Impaling, 1. . . . a cross engrailed . . . (Kirkbride); and 2. . . . a bend dancetté . . . (Whitrigg), Sir John Denton having marr. (2) *c.* 1367 Joan de Whitrigg.

Out of turret Sable enflamed Proper a lion Or holding in its paw a sword Proper (FCW).

DENTON, of Denton and Warnell. This family, one of the oldest in Cumberland, descends from Robert son of Asketin or Asketil, living 1169, who marr. Sigrith, dau. of Buethbarn and sister and coheir of Robert son of Bueth. Their son John (living 1225) became known as de Denton and was ancestor of John de Denton, Lord of Nether Denton, who marr. Agneta, dau. and coheir of Ranulf de Halton, of Halton (N). A descendant, Sir Richard (d. by 1363), was Knight of the Shire for Cumberland 1324 and High Sheriff 1336-38 and 1350. He marr. Agnes, dau. and coheir of William de Burdon, and had a dau. and heir Margaret, who marr. Adam de Copley, of Batley (Y). Their descendant Isabel inherited Denton and marr. her kinsman Adam del Hall (d. 1408-9), who assumed the name of Denton. Their descendant John Denton (d. 1513-14) exchanged Nether Denton with Thomas, Lord Dacre, for Warnell 1507. His son Thomas (d. 1563-4) was the builder of Warnell Hall, which descended to Thomas Denton, M.A.* (d. *s.p.* 1616) who marr. (1) 1565 Elizabeth, dau. and heir of Martin Turpin and (2) Anne Aislabie. He was succ. by his great nephew Thomas Denton (b. 1610) who served as Captain in the Royal Army and died of wounds received at Hull 1643. His son Thomas Denton, M.A. (Oxon) (1638-98), barrister at law, Recorder of Carlisle and of Appleby, was the author of the well known MS. History of Cumberland. His son Thomas (1661-1736) marr. Margery (d. 1737), dau. and coheir of Lancelot Threlkeld, *q.v.*, and was succ. by their son Thomas (d. 1750) whose son John (d. 1775, aged 59) sold Warnell Hall to Lord Lonsdale 1774, reserving to himself and his son Thomas a life estate in the estate. Thomas Denton, J.P., Receiver General of Taxes for Cumberland and Westmorland, High Sheriff of Cumberland 1789, died unmarr. 1813, aged 69. The line was continued by his cousin Charles Denton, of Cockermouth, saddler (1754-1828), who had an only son, the Rev. Charles Jones Denton, M.A. (Cantab), Vicar of Askham Richard (Y) 1862-75, who died unmarr. 1877, aged 78. The line was continued by the descendants of Henry Denton, Officer of Excise (1717-1801), younger brother of John, above (d. 1775). The said Henry was of Lowthwaite, Watermillock, where his grandson Henry Denton (b. 1824) died 1900, apparently the last male of the family. *Arms.* In 1398 Richard de Copley, son and heir of John, by charter granted at Carlisle, gave to Adam Denton, son and heir of Thomas del Hall, of Carlisle, the arms of his ancestor Sir Richard Denton: Argent two bars Gules in chief three cinquefoils Sable. These arms are over the front door of Warnell Hall and also appear in Sebergham church on panels which once formed part of the monument to Thomas Denton (d. *s.p.* 1616, aged 80); and they were recorded by Thomas Denton, above (1638-98), at the Visitation of 1665. Machell recorded the cinquefoils as Sable pierced Or (MMS vi 413); and FVC and MVC trick them Gules. *Crest.* An eagle or martlet rising (Carved achievement dated 1683 over front door of Warnell Hall; M.I., Sebergham church). Burke gives: An eagle Sable (BLG 1849; BGA).

DENTON. The Rev. Thomas Denton, B.A. (d. 1702, aged 69), was Curate of Brigham 1658-61, Rector of Edenhall and Langwathby 1658-63, and Rector of Crosby Garrett (W) 1663-1702. His son, the Rev. Christopher

* Nicknamed "Tom with th' spots".

Shields on the monument to Thomas Denton in Sebergham church

John Denton's monument at Ainstable, after Lysons'
Magna Britannia. iv.

Denton, B.A. (Cantab) (1668-1738), was Rector of Gosforth 1688-1738. He marr. 1697 Isabel, dau. and coheir of John Sherwen, of Gosforth Gate, and had four daus. and coheirs – Katherine, marr. John Steele; Margaret, marr. John Benson, *q.v.*; Elizabeth; and Isabel (1703-98), marr. 1746 Thomas Poole, of Gosforth Hall (PGD). *Arms* (as quartered by Benson). Argent two bars Gules in chief three cinquefoils . . .(*Ex inf.* Canon R. A. B. Ewbank).

DERWENTWATER, of Derwentwater. This family descends from Adam (*fl.* 1210-12) whose son Sir William de Derwentwater, Lord of the manor of Derwentwater, also held land in Tallentire 1259-60. His son Thomas, M.P. for Westmorland 1295 and 1298, received a charter for a market and fair in 1276. He d. 1302-3, holding the manor of Derwentwater. A descendant, Sir John, was Sheriff of Cumberland 1375-77 and 1380, and was perhaps the John, living 1403, who was the last male. His dau. Elizabeth marr. *c.* 1417 Sir Nicholas Radcliffe, *q.v.*, and carried the Derwentwater estates to him (CW2 iv). *Arms.* Argent two bars and on a canton Gules a cinquefoil pierced of the field. In another version, the cinquefoil is Or (FFC). The shield appears with three bars Gules in a window in Bolton church (W).

DERWENTWATER, Earl of – see RADCLIFFE.

de VITRÉ. Jean Baptiste Denis de Vitré, born at Bordeaux 1757, and at the time of his death 1846, the oldest lieutenant in the Royal Navy, was of Crosby and West Knoll, Irthington, before moving to Lancaster. He marr. (1) 1791 Bridget (d. 1829), dau. of James Fawcett, of Scaleby Castle, *q.v.*, and (2) 1837 Elizabeth (d. 1844, aged 36), dau. of Arthur Forrester, or Forster, *q.v.*, of Luckens. His 3rd son John Denis (1795-1847) marr. Elizabeth, dau. of William Beaty, *q.v.*, of Soultermoor, Stapleton. *Arms.* Gules a chevron Vair in chief two griffins segreant Or and in base a bunch of grapes Proper. *Crest.* A demi griffin Or holding between its paws a bunch of grapes as in the arms issuing out of an oak wreath Proper acorned Or. *Motto.* Sans peur (BLG15; BGA).

DEYNE. Quartered by Hudleston on 17th century painting of the Hudleston arms, formerly at Millom Castle, now at Hutton John; a quartering brought in by Barantyne, *q.v. Arms.* Argent a chevron between three mullets pierced Gules.

DICKINSON, of Redhow. Joseph Dickinson, of Workington (1772-1852), son of John Dickinson, of Streetgate (d. 1802), see next entry, bought Woodend and Redhow, Lamplugh, 1817, and built the new house at Redhow 1822. His son John Dickinson, J.P. (1810-90), farmed at Havercroft and at Redhow, which he inherited 1863. His eldest son Joseph Dickinson, J.P. (1846-1909), a member of Cumberland County Council from its foundation, died *s.p.* and was succ. at Redhow by his brother George (1852-1934) who was partner with his brother John (1847-1907) in the legal firm of Hill, Dickinson of Liverpool, and was High Sheriff of Cumberland 1920. Two of his sons were killed in World War I and his surviving son George Fryer Dickinson, J.P., M.A., LL.B. (Cantab), Barrister at law, Capt The King's Liverpool Regt. (1886-1932), died *v.p.*, leaving three sons, of whom Ronald Fryer Dickinson, D.L., J.P., B.A. (Cantab), formerly Lt-Commander R.N.R., is now of Redhow, and the owner of other properties in Lamplugh. He was a member of Cumberland County Council and latterly an alderman 1940-74, and was High Sheriff 1953. He is well known as an arboriculturist and artist. *Arms.* Or a bend engrailed between two lions rampant Gules. *Crest.* A lion's head erased Gules. *Motto.* Virtutis praemium honor (*Ex inf.* R. F. Dickinson, of Redhow).

DICKINSON, of Streetgate. The Dickinsons are probably the oldest family in Lamplugh. John Dickinson, of the Streetgate (d. 1644), was father of William Dickinson, attorney (1604-78), steward to John Lamplugh, and a captain in the regiment raised by him for the King. He was at Marston Moor, was fined for his adherence to the King, and his goods were sequestrated. He built the existing house at Streetgate 1674. His son Daniel (1637-99) was a Cockermouth attorney, and High Constable for Allerdale above Derwent ward. His son John (1672-1755) was steward to Thomas Lamplugh. His youngest son, the Rev. Richard Dickinson, M.A. (T.C.D. and Cantab) (1723-1816), was Curate of Egremont 1748, Rector of Lamplugh 1768-1816 and of Castle Carrock 1778-1816, and Prebendary of York; his eldest son Daniel (1704-42) marr. 1732 Abigail Wood and died *v.p.*, the heir being his son John (1734-1802). From his son Joseph descend the Dickinsons of Redhow, *supra.* His eldest son Daniel (1759-1811) was of Ulverston, attorney. Streetgate descended to his great-grandson, Alexander Fryear Dickinson, M.C., C.E. (1886-1964), who had two daus., of whom Anne, who marr. Alan Russell, is the present owner of Streetgate (*Ex inf.* R. F. Dickinson, of Redhow). *Arms.* . . . a bend invected . . . between two lions rampant . . . .*Crest.* A lion's head erased (Tombstone, Lamplugh churchyard).

DICKINSON, of Thorncroft, later DICKINSON-STANLEY-DODGSON. William Dickinson, of Kidburngill, Workington, banker (d. 1822), was great-uncle of William Dickinson, J.P., F.L.S., of Thorncroft, Workington (d. 1882, aged 83), a well known authority on the dialect of Cumberland, and the author of *A Glossary of the Words and Phrases of Cumberland,* 1859, and *Cumbriana,* 1875. He marr. Jane (d. 1867, aged 62), dau. of John Norman, and had a son John Norman Dickinson, J.P., of Hames Hall, Cockermouth (b. 1830), who marr. 1857 Elizabeth Johnston, dau. of Stanley Dodgson, J.P. His son Stanley Dodgson Dickinson, J.P. (b. 1860), of Tarnbank, Cockermouth, and Armaside, Lorton, assumed the additional names Stanley-Dodgson 1886 and was the last of the family. *Arms.* In W. A. J. Prevost's copy of William Dickinson's *Glossary* these appear as: Or a bend engrailed between two lions rampant Gules. *Crest.* A demi lion rampant. Underneath the arms the words "Virtutis praemia honor" have been deleted and the words "Diligentia omnia vincit" substituted, followed by "These arms were given by King Edward to Dickinson his Majesty's physician. To Martha Dickinson this glossary and supplement, from her affectionate Father Wm Dickinson 1867." The crest is on a tablet in St. John, Workington to the above William Dickinson, J.P., F.L.S.

DICKSON, of Beck Bank. John Fell, of Daltongate (L) (d. 1688), marr. Ellinor, dau. of John Dickson, of Beck Bank, Millom. Thomas Sunderland, J.P., of Whittington Hall and Ulverston (L) (d. 1809), marr. Anne, dau. of William Dickson, of Beck Bank. *Arms* (as quartered by Fell). Azure a fleur-de-lys Or a chief Ermine. On his bookplate, however, Thomas Sunderland displayed them on an escutcheon of pretence as: Sable a pile Argent surmounted by a chevron Gules both flory counterflory the chevron charged with a mullet of the second. The 18th century Newcastle upon Tyne herald-painters, Ralph Waters, father and son, shewed the escutcheon of pretence on the arms of Sunderland as: Sable a chevron Gules flory counterflory between three mullets Or (LAE).

DICKSON. Edward Thompson Dickson, Surgeon, R.N. (d. 1869, aged 77), was father of, *int. al.*, Major-General Edward John Dickson, 75th Foot (Argyll and Sutherland Highlanders) (b. 1821), who was Staff Captain of the Isle of Man. His son, the Rev. Reginald Jeffcott Dickson, M.A. (Cantab) (1876-1954), was Curate of Broughton-in-Furness 1901-4, of St. Aidan, Carlisle 1905, of St. Andrew, Penrith 1905-10, and Vicar of Crosscrake 1910-21. From 1921 until 1929 he was Vicar of Ivegill, and from 1929 until 1947 Vicar of Brigham. He was Hon. Canon of Carlisle, and Hon. Canon Emeritus 1949-54. His only surviving son, Edward Mylrea Dickson, is of Cherry Holt, Abbots Leigh, Bristol. *Crest.* An arm in armour embowed holding a falchion. *Motto.* Fortes fortuna juvat.

DIGGLE. The Rt. Rev. John William Diggle, M.A., D.D. (Oxon) (1847-1920), son of William Diggle, of Pendleton (L), was Canon of Carlisle and Archdeacon of Westmorland 1896-1901, Rector of Birmingham 1901-5, Archdeacon of Birmingham 1903-5, and Bishop of Carlisle 1905-20. His sons were Major Philip Gilbert William Diggle, of Kenilworth, Cape Town (1886-1973); Percy Robert Diggle, J.P., of Deepghyll, Plumpton, later of Heads Nook and Corby Hill, Carlisle (1887-1977); and Canon Reginald Fraser Diggle, C.B.E., M.C., M.A. (1889-1975), Hon. Canon of Worcester and Vicar of St. Giles, Oxford. *Arms.* Azure on a cross between two owls in chief and as many roses in base Argent a crosier of the field (Shields in Carlisle Infirmary and Holm Cultram Abbey).

DILLON. Impaled by Irwin, *q.v.*, on brass in Wetheral church; Commander Joseph Irwin, R.N. of Wetheral Plains (1792-1890), marr. 1826 Emily dau. of John Dillon of Dublin. *Arms.* Argent a lion rampant between three estoiles issuing from as many crescents Gules over all a fess Sable.

DILLON. On an escutcheon of pretence on the arms of Kelly, *q.v.*, on brass in Carlisle cathedral; General Sir Richard Denis Kelly, K.C.B., marr. 1848 Ellen Susanna (d. 1903), elder dau. of Sir William Dillon, 4th Bart., and sister and coheir of Sir Arthur Henry Dillon, 5th Bart. (d. 1852). *Arms.* Argent a lion rampant between three crescents Gules issuant from each a mullet of six points Or.

DISTINGTON. The 1665 Visitation pedigree of Dykes records that Jane, dau. and heir of Hugh Distington (of Coupland) marr. William Dykes, 1383-84. Whellan (WCW, p. 289) calls him Sir Hugh of Distington, and adds that Jane had a sister and coheir Margaret who marr. Sir Hugh de Moresby. In 1383 William Dykes was enfeoffed of lands in Distington, which had belonged to John son of Hugh de Distington (MDF, p. 32). *Arms.* Argent four bars Gules on a canton Argent a cross crosslet Or (MMD). Dykes, however, quarters for Distington: Argent five bars Gules on a canton Sable a cross couped Or (see p. 99).

DIXON, of Knells and Holme Eden. Christopher Dixon, yeoman, of Edmund Castle (b. *c.* 1690), was grandfather of Peter Dixon, of Whitehaven, later of Tullie House, Carlisle (1754-1832), who marr. 1783 Mary, dau. of Richard Ferguson, of Carlisle, and moved to that city to assist in the management of a cotton mill at Warwick Bridge belonging to her family. The great house of Peter Dixon & Sons, the largest trading firm in Cumberland, was built up from this beginning. Peter Dixon's eldest son, John Dixon, J.P., of Knells (1785-1857), was High Sheriff of Cumberland 1838 and Mayor of Carlisle 1840-41, and was elected M.P. for Carlisle 1847, but unseated.* Knells was sold 1872 and the family's representative, Christian Dixon, was in Australia in 1937. John's younger brother† and partner, Peter Dixon, J.P. (1789-1866), built Holme Eden in 1841 and also Holme Eden church; he was Mayor of Carlisle 1838-39.‡ His eldest son Peter Sydenham Dixon, of Broadwath, was father of Francis Peter Dixon, J.P., of Wood View, Carlisle (1849-1927), four times Mayor of the city and a member of the City Council for 50 years. Two of his sons, Peter Sydenham Dixon, Lieut 7th Royal Sussex Regiment, and Arthur Edward Basil Dixon, Lieut 5th Loyal North Lancs. Regiment, were killed in action at Heilly in 1918, aged 35, and at Ypres in 1915, aged 20, respectively; another son Francis Ireland Dixon, of Blackburn, was the representative of the family in 1937. *Arms.* Azure a dove statant Proper in chief two bees volant Or on a chief of the last three pallets Gules. *Crest.* In front of an anchor in bend sinister Sable a dexter cubit arm erect Proper in the hand an olive branch also Proper. *Motto.* Peace (BLG5; M.I.s, Warwick church).

DIXON, of Rheda and of Lorton Hall. John Dixon, of the Birkes, Arlecdon (will dated 1602), was grandfather of Thomas Dixon, who acquired the Rheda estate (sold in the 1950's) by marr. 1617 to Mary, dau. of John Nicholson. From them descended Thomas Dixon, J.P., of Rheda (1808-82), who was succ. by his elder son Thomas Dixon, J.P., M.A. (Cantab), barrister at law (1861-1923), High Sheriff of Cumberland 1903. He marr. 1889 Maria Florence, only dau. and heir of Llewelyn Lewis, of Tan-y-fynwent, by whom he had two daus. and coheirs, Myfanwy Wynn Lewis, marr. 1913 Alwyn Haswell Holman, *q.v.*, and Vera Mabel Florence, marr. 1917 Capt Thomas Alexander Lacy Thompson, *q.v.* Thomas Dixon's younger brother, Anthony Joseph Steele Dixon, J.P., Capt Royal Cumberland Militia (1862-1909), was of Lorton Hall, where he was succ. by his son Anthony Thomas Steele Dixon, M.A. (Cantab) (1900-62), who sold the estate 1947 and was later of Thika, Kenya. His sister and heir Ethel Florance Nancy (d. 1975) marr. Humphrey Patricius Senhouse, *q.v. Arms.* Azure on a pale Argent a fleur-de-lys of the first a chief engrailed Ermine. *Crest.* In front of a cubit arm grasping a scimitar Proper pommel and hilt Gold a staff raguly fesswise Or. *Motto.* Quod dixi dixi. (BLG15; Grant of Arms to Thomas Dixon of Rheda, dated 1882, now at Lorton Hall; window, brasses and grave, Arlecdon church; Lorton Hall lodge).

DIXON, in Bush. A gravestone in Arthuret churchyard commemorates Thomas Dixon, in Bush, Kirkandrews-on-Esk (d. 1741, aged 66) *Arms.* . . . on a bend . . . between six roses . . . three roses . . . a chief Ermine. Irving, however, recorded: A bend and in chief three roundles a bordure Ermine (base underground) (ABD).

DIXON. The Rev. David Dixon, of Torver, Warden of Rydal Hall, is

* His eldest son Peter James Dixon, J.P., of Houghton Hall (b. 1820), was Mayor of Carlisle 1853-54.

† For his son Henry Hall Dixon (1822-70), who wrote on sporting matters under the pseudonym "The Druid," see DNB.

‡ Another brother, George Dixon, J.P., of Tullie House, Carlisle (d. *s.p.* 1860), was Mayor of the city 1843 and 1849.

descended from John Dixon, of the Birkes, Arlecdon (d. 1602), see previous entry. *Arms.* Gules a fleur-de-lys Argent and a chief Ermine a crescent for difference. *Crest.* A cubit arm grasping a scimitar Proper pommel and hilt Or. *Motto.* Quod dixi dixi.

DIXON, of Millom. Hatchment at Lorton Hall for Margaret, dau. of James Wright, of Glossop (Dy), who marr. 1911 James Dixon, of Millom, and died 1951. *Arms.* Gules a fleur-de-lys Argent on a chief Ermine a crescent Or for difference (Dixon); impaling, Sable on a chevron Argent three spearheads Gules in chief two unicorns' heads of the second erased of the third armed and maned Or in base on a pile of the last issuing from the chevron a unicorn's head erased Sable (Wright).

DIXON. Joshua Dixon, M.D., of Whitehaven (d. 1825, aged 80), a benefactor to Whitehaven and West Cumberland Infirmary, was father of the Rev. Richard Dixon, M.A. (Oxon), F.R.S. (*c.* 1780-1858), who was Fellow of The Queen's College, Oxford, 1809-22, and Rector of Niton, Isle of Wight, 1828-58. *Arms.* Argent a pale indented Vert (Shield in window of the Hall of The Queen's College).

DIXON, of Wooloaks and Calthwaite. Thomas Dixon, of Hesket-in-the-Forest and of Thomas Close, Hutton-in-the-Forest, yeoman (d. 1762, aged 89), marr. 1701 Margaret Ollivant (d. 1764, aged 81) and had *int. al.* a son, the Rev. George Dixon, M.A., D.D. (Oxon) (1709-87), Principal of St. Edmund Hall, Oxford, 1760-87, whose arms, according to Field, were . . . two bars dancetté . . . (FAC). His brother Thomas Dixon (1727-1818) bought the Wooloaks and Calthwaite estates 1791, which descended to his grandson Thomas Dixon, solicitor (1799-1846), son of his dau. Margaret, who marr. 1797 George Dixon of Calthwaite, and of Nordvue, Lazonby, "agent to several merchants in London" (1762-1822). The younger Thomas Dixon, who built Calthwaite Hall *c.* 1837 (sold *c.* 1844), marr. 1831 Mary Jane (d. 1843), eidest dau. of Christopher Parker, of Petteril Green, and had a son Thomas (b. 1833) and a dau. Sarah (b. 1835). His brother John (1802-41) succ. to Nordvue. According to Field, the last heir male, Samuel Dixon, died at New Glenelg, South Australia, 1928. *Arms.* Gules on a bend Or between six bezants three torteaux a chief Erminois. *Crest.* A cubit arm erect vested Vert semé-de-lys Sable cuffed Argent holding in the hand a roundle Ermine. *Motto.* Vincit omnia veritas (Bookplate of Thomas Dixon and will of Thomas Dixon, d. 1818).

DIXON, now WOODHEAD-KEITH-DIXON, of Lorton Hall. The Rev. James Addison Woodhead-Keith-Dixon, of Lorton Hall, Vicar of Lorton, bears the following *Arms.* Quarterly, 1 & 4, Paly Gules and Azure a fleur-de-lys Argent on a chief embattled Ermine three pallets Or (Keith-Dixon); 2 & 3, Per chevron nebuly Argent and Azure two oak trees in chief Proper and on a pile in base Or a unicorn's head erased Sable (Woodhead). *Crests.* 1, In front of a cubit arm encircled at the wrist with an annulet Or grasping a scimitar Proper pommel and hilt Or a staff raguly fesswise of the last (Keith-Dixon); 2, A unicorn's head erased Sable between on the dexter side an oak branch fructed Proper and on the sinister a rose Argent barbed and leaved Proper (Woodhead). *Mottoes.* Quod dixi dixi (Dixon); Veritas vincit (Keith); Aequo animo (Woodhead).

DOCKER. John Docker, yeoman (1794-1849), a descendant of the Docker family, of Bampton (W) (see AWL), was of Gillgrass Cottage, Gosforth, and his son Robert (1840-1915) was of Seascale. The latter's son John Singleton Docker (b. 1871) was of Calder Hall. *Arms.* Argent seven half spears Sable headed Azure, three, one, and three. *Crest.* A bridge of three arches Proper. *Motto.* Stare super antiquas vias (CW2 xviii 161-70).

DODSON. The arms of Dodson are on monuments in Loweswater church and churchyard; Joseph Skelton, of Loweswater (1774-1835), *q.v.*, and his brother, Capt Thomas Skelton, 59th Regt. (1779-1856), marr. respectively Mary (1777-1835) and Agnes (1781-1854), daus. and coheirs of John Dodson, of Woodland Hall, Kirkby Ireleth (L) (see AWL). *Arms* (as impaled by Skelton). Argent a fess nebuly Gules between six fleurs-de-lys . . . .

DONALD. The first recorded ancestor of this family in Cumberland is William Donald, of Anthorn (1632-1712), whose great-grandson William Donald, of Warwick Hall, Aspatria (1747-1809), marr. Mary, sister and heir of Matthewman Hodgson, solicitor, of Wigton (d. 1831). Their twin sons George Donald (1786-1832) and William Donald (d. 1835) were given by their uncle Solway House, Bowness-on-Solway, and Blaithwaite House, respectively. The former's eldest son William Hodgson Donald (1816-85) went to New Zealand 1842, where his descendants remain. A younger son John Reed Donald (1817-79) was a solicitor in Carlisle. The above named William Donald, of Blaithwaite House (1786-1835), had an eldest son Matthewman Hodgson Donald, of Blaithwaite and Albert Villa, Stanwix (1822-85), who marr. 1851 Henrietta Maria (d. 1876), eldest dau. of the Hon. John Henry Roper-Curzon, *q.v.* Their son the Rev. Matthewman Sidney Donald, M.A. (Cantab) (1863-1930), was Curate of Barton (W) 1887-91 and Vicar of Grinsdale 1895-99, and was later of Quarry Hill, Mealsgate. His son William George Curzon Donald, of Windyfell, Raughton Head, solicitor (1897-1955), was father of the Rev. Dennis Curzon Donald, who is now of Blaithwaite. The above named Matthewman Hodgson Donald had a younger brother John, cotton manufacturer on the West Walls and Denton Hill, Carlisle (1828-94). His only son William Nanson Donald, V.D., J.P., of Inglesham, The Scaur, Carlisle, stockbroker (1859-1936), was Lt-Col commanding the 4th Battn the Border Regiment, and Mayor of Carlisle 1907. During his year of office his elder son John Carlisle Nanson Donald, M.B.E., M.A. (Oxon), who is now of The School House, Raughton Head, was born.* He was in the Sudan Political Service 1930-54, and in the latter year was Governor of Equatoria Province. His younger brother, Commander William Spooner Donald, D.S.C., R.N., of Troutlets, Church Street, Keswick, is well known as an author. *Arms.* Quarterly, 1, Argent a lion rampant Gules; 2, Argent a dexter cubit arm couped in fess vested Azure holding in the hand Proper a cross crosslet fitché Gules; 3, Argent a lymphad oars in action sails furled Sable flags flying Gules; 4, Vert a salmon naiant Proper. *Crest.* A dexter cubit arm couped fessways vested Azure holding in the hand Proper a cross crosslet fitché Gules (Window, Aspatria church). A pedigree of the family containing the arms emblazons the field of the second and third quarters Or and shows the dexter cubit arm in the second quarter as in armour Proper,

* Only twice before in the history of the city has such an event occurred, and to mark the occasion the Mayor and Mayoress were presented with a silver epergne in the shape of a cradle. This bears the crests of Mr and Mrs Donald and the arms of Carlisle.

not vested. It shows the *Crest* as: A dexter cubit arm in armour couped fessways holding in the gauntlet Proper a cross crosslet fitché Gules. *Motto.* Pace belloque.

DONALDSON, post DONALDSON-HUDSON. Alexander Donaldson, of Wigton, watchmaker (d. 1819, aged 59), marr. Elizabeth (1767-1849), dau. of Thomas Hudson, of Wigton, *q.v.*, and sister and in her issue heir of her brother, Thomas Hudson, M.P., who left his Cheswardine, Salop., estate to her grandson Charles Donaldson, J.P., M.P. (1840-93), son of John Donaldson, of Wigton (1803-86). Mr Donaldson, who was High Sheriff of Shropshire 1886, assumed the additional name and arms of Hudson 1862. His grandson John Donaldson-Hudson, of Cheswardine Hall (1908-49), had two daus. and coheirs, Charlotte Jane and Sarah Elizabeth Ruth. *Arms.* Quarterly, 1 & 4, Hudson, *q.v.*; 2 & 3, Argent a lymphad Sable between three dolphins naiant Azure (Donaldson). *Crests.* 1, Hudson, *q.v.*; 2, In front of a saltire Azure a cubit arm erect grasping a dagger and charged with a thistle slipped all Proper (Donaldson) (BLG17).

DOUGLAS. John Douglas, M.A., D.D. (Oxon) (1721-1807), son of Archibald Douglas, of Pittenweem, Fife, was Dean of Windsor 1788, Bishop of Carlisle 1787-91, and Bishop of Salisbury 1791-1807. *Arms.* Quarterly, 1 & 4, Argent a heart Gules imperially crowned Or on a chief Azure three mullets Argent (Douglas); 2 & 3, Argent three mascles on a chief Gules three lions passant Argent (Ogston) (BBE).

DOUGLAS. William Douglas, H.E.I.C.S. (1755-1802), a Judge of the High Court of Appeal in India, 2nd son of Lt-Gen Archibald Douglas, M.P., and brother of Jane, wife of the Rt. Rev. William Van Mildert, Bishop of Durham, was father of Mary (1794-1884), who marr. 1821 Edward Stanley, of Ponsonby Hall, *q.v.* *Arms* (impaled by Stanley on tablet in Ponsonby church). Argent a human heart Gules ensigned with an imperial crown Or on a chief Azure three mullets of the field.

DOUGLAS. Joseph Douglas, of Whitehaven, captain in the merchant service, had an only son, Sir Joseph Abraham Douglas, R.N., Commander, H.E.I.Co's Maritime Service (b. 1797). In 1839, at his own expense, he armed the ship *Cambridge,* then under his command at Singapore, and proceeded to Canton to assist British subjects and defend property worth £7,500,000 and 60 vessels at Hong Kong. He also attacked Chinese junks at Kowloon where he was severely wounded. He was knighted 1841 and in 1842 obtained a grant of *Arms.* Argent a human heart Gules ensigned by a naval crown Or in chief three mullets Azure on a chief embattled of the last on the dexter a representation of the ship *Cambridge* defending a fleet of merchant vessels superinscribed "Hong Kong" in letters Gold and on the sinister side a representation of the barge belonging to the said ship engaging with three Chinese junks under a battery superinscribed "Kowloon" in letters also Gold. *Crest.* On an Eastern crown Or the rim inscribed "China" in letters Sable between two wings Argent a heart as in the arms (CA cxlv/390).

DOUGLAS of Kelhead, Marquess of Queensberry. Sir William Douglas, 2nd Bart., of Kelhead (d. 1733), had ten sons, including Sir John, his successor (d. 1778); James Douglas (d. 1756), who practised as a physician in Carlisle, and lived in the Deanery;* and Erskine (d. 1791), a Hexham physician, whose son Francis was baptised at Kirkandrews-on-Esk 1756. The above Sir John Douglas, M.P., was succ. by his son Sir William Douglas, 4th Bart. (*c.* 1730-83), M.P. for Dumfries Burghs 1768-80, who was then living at Arkleby Hall, where his sons Charles, Archibald William Johnstone, and John were born. The first named (1777-1833) succ. his kinsman as 5th Marquess of Queensberry 1810, and dying *s.p.m.*, was succ. as 6th Bart. and 6th Marquess by his brother John (1779-1856), whose descendant is the 12th Marquess of Queensberry (GEC; GECB). *Arms.* Quarterly, 1 & 4, Argent a human heart Gules ensigned with an Imperial crown Or on a chief Azure three mullets of the field (Douglas); 2 & 3, Azure a bend between six cross crosslets fitché Or (Mar); the whole within a bordure Or charged with a double tressure of Scotland. *Crest.* A human heart Gules ensigned with an Imperial crown between two wings Or. *Supporters.* On either side a pegasus Argent winged maned and hoofed Or. *Motto.* Forward (DPB; BP105).

DOUGLAS. Capt Alexander Douglas, of Newbiggin, Carlisle, made his will in 1764 (proved 1770) mentioning his son Alexander Douglas, by Nancy Moffatt, his servant. He mentions also his brother Lt-Gen Archibald Douglas and his son Alexander, and his brother Charles Douglas and his son Alexander. *Arms.* Argent a human heart . . . on a chief Azure three mullets of the first. *Motto.* Spero (Seal on Alexander Douglas' will).

DRAYTON. Shield at Hutton John; a Hudleston quartering, brought in by Barantyne, *q.v. Arms.* Argent a bend between six cross crosslets fitché Sable. *Sic*; correctly: Azure a bend between six cross crosslets fitché Or.

DUDLEY. John Sutton, of Dudley Castle (St), was father of John Sutton, or Dudley (1400-87), cr. Baron Dudley 1440. His son and heir, Sir Edmund Dudley, died *v.p.*, leaving issue *int. al.* Edward (1459-1532), 2nd Baron Dudley; Thomas, who marr. Grace, dau. and coheir of Sir Lancelot Threlkeld, *q.v.*, and so acquired Yanwath Hall, see AWL; and Alice (d. 1554), who marr. Sir John Radcliffe, of Derwentwater, *q.v.* Her niece Lucy (d. 1596) marr. (1) Albany Fetherstonhaugh, and (2) Gerard Lowther. Edmund Dudley (b. *c.* 1543, d. before 1614), a grandson of the above Thomas, marr. Catherine, sister and coheir of Thomas Hutton, of Hutton John, *q.v.*, and was Sheriff of Cumberland 1602. Their grandson Christopher (1607-60) was the last male (JPP i). *Arms.* Sir John Sutton, *temp.* Edward II and Edward III, having marr. a sister and coheir of John de Somerie, the family used the latter's arms, Or two lions passant in pale Azure, alternately with their own, Or a lion rampant double-queued Vert. On the tomb in Crosthwaite church of Sir John and Lady Radcliffe, the former coat appears, as it does in a window in the church. In the Two Lions Hotel, Penrith, the former home of Gerard Lowther, Lowther impales the latter coat.† *Crest.* Out of a ducal coronet Or a lion's head and neck Azure langued Gules (Harl. MS. 3526).

DUKINFIELD. The Rev. Charles Egerton Dukinfield, B.A. (Cantab) (1792-1840), Vicar of Edenhall 1833-40, was 5th son of Sir Nathaniel Dukinfield, 5th Bart., of Sulham, Berks. *Arms.* Argent a cross voided pointed Sable.

* The Dean being non-resident. For Dr Douglas' part in the '45 – he was arrested by the Duke of Cumberland December 1745 – see MCS.

† A shield on the ceiling of Carlisle Cathedral may well be for Dudley, but its position makes it difficult to see whether the lion is double-queued.

Crests. 1, A cubit arm Proper issuant from a ducal coronet and grasping a sun with rays Or; 2, A pelican vulning herself Or (OCC iii 817-19).

DUNN. William Allison Dunn, M.R.C.S. (1872) (b. 1848), son of William Allison Dunn, of Louth, Lincs., was house surgeon at Carlisle Dispensary and was later for over 30 years in practice in Millom. He marr. 1879 Jane, dau. of Thomas Clark, of Carlisle, and was father of William Allison Dunn, M.B., Ch.B. (Edin) (1886-1914) and Herbert Arthur Raisbeck Dunn, mining engineer (b. 1894). In 1889 he obtained a grant of the following *Arms.* Azure a wolf rampant Ermine between two serpents nowed in chief Or and a buckle in base of the last. *Crest.* In front of a bear's paw erect Proper grasping a serpent entwined around it three buckles all Or (CA lxv/47). *Motto.* Facta non verba (FD7).

DURHAM, Church and monastery of – see LINDISFARNE, See of.

DURWARD. Shield at Hutton-in-the-Forest; a Vane quartering. *Arms.* Ermine on a chevron Sable three crescents Or.

DYKES, *post* BALLANTINE-DYKES, of Dovenby. This family has a remarkable record of marrying heiresses. William Dykes marr. Agnes, dau. and heir of Hugh Waverton, of Waverton, *q.v.*, and their grandson William (living 1383-4) marr. Jane, dau. and heir of Hugh Distington, of Distington. From them descended William Dykes, of Wardhall, Plumbland (living 1481-2), who marr. Christian, dau. and coheir of Sir Richard Salkeld, of Corby, *q.v.* Their son Thomas marr. Isabel (b. *c.* 1485), dau. and heir of John Pennington, of Muncaster. Their grandson Thomas marr. Joan, dau. and heir of Lancelot Lancaster, of Sockbridge (W), and had a son Leonard (d. 1640), High Sheriff of Cumberland 1631, who marr. Anne, dau. and heir of Thomas Radcliffe, of Cockerton (D). Their son Thomas (d. 1658) marr. 1628 Joyce (b. 1610), dau. of John Frecheville and had a son Leonard, High Sheriff 1680-82, whose son Frecheville Dykes had a son Leonard (1698-1767), of Penrith, who had sons Frecheville, Captain 67th Foot (1731-84), and Lawson (b. 1740). The latter marr. 1764 Jane (d. 1821, aged 70), dau. and heir of John Ballantine, *q.v.*, and had a son Joseph (d. 1830), see below. The above Frecheville marr. 1769 Mary (1733-85), dau. of John Brougham and sister and heir of Peter Brougham. Their only dau. Mary (1774-1860) succ. to the Dykes estates and also to the Lamplugh estates, through her mother who was the eventual heiress of the Lamplughs of Dovenby. She marr. 1800 her 1st cousin Joseph Ballantine-Dykes (see above), High Sheriff 1806. Their son Frecheville Lawson Ballantine Dykes, J.P. (1800-66) was High Sheriff 1842 and M.P. for Cockermouth 1832-36, and marr. 1844 Anne Eliza (d. 1906), dau. and coheir of Joseph Gunson, of Ingwell, *q.v.* Their son Lamplugh Frecheville Ballantine-Dykes, D.L., J.P. (1854-93) was High Sheriff 1885, and was succ. by his son Col Frecheville Hubert Ballantine-Dykes, C.B., D.S.O., O.B.E., D.L., J.P. (1881-1949), High Sheriff 1923 and Lord Lieutenant of Cumberland 1944-49. He was Lord of the manors of Gilcrux, Ireby, Papcastle. Dovenby, Crookdake, Allerby and Dearham Row. He sold Dovenby Hall and was later of Kepplewray, Broughton-in-Furness. His elder son Major Thomas Lamplugh Ballantine-Dykes, Scots Guards (b. 1912), was killed in action in North Africa 1942 and he was succ. by his younger son Joseph Ballantine-Dykes, M.C., formerly Captain, R.E., of The Lodge, Redmain (BLG17; CW2 xxxix). *Arms.* Or three cinquefoils Sable (FFC; FCW). MVC shews:

Argent three cinquefoils pierced Sable. The arms appear in FVC, *sub* Brisco, as: Or a fess vairy Gules and Ermine between three cinquefoils Sable, which Papworth recorded as: Or a fess vairy Ermine and Sable between three cinquefoils of the last. (OBA).* *Crest.* A lobster Vert (FCW). *Motto.* Prius frangitur quam flectitur (BLG17).

EAGLESFIELD, of Allerby. Field gives no authority for his statement in FAC that the Eaglesfields of Allerby were an illegitimate branch of the Eaglesfields of Eaglesfield. In Dr Robert Griffith Page's papers is a pedigree which states that George Eaglesfield was a younger brother of the house of Dearham "to whom Isabell gave Alwarby mannor by will" 1610. George's grandson Thomas Eaglesfield (1618-56) marr. Judith, dau. of the Rev. Thomas Fairfax, Rector of Caldbeck, and their son Richard (1642-1705), Collector of Customs at Carlisle, registered a pedigree at the Visitation of 1665. His son Richard sold Allerby to Richard Lamplugh; another son, Thomas (d. 1699), was Collector of Excise at Newcastle upon Tyne. Their sister Grace marr. 1697 Gabriel Griffith, *q.v.* (CW2 lxiii 200). *Arms.* Argent three eagles displayed Gules a crescent for difference. (FCW). GMS gives: Or three eagles displayed Gules. *Crest.* An eagle wings expanded Argent (FCW).

EAGLESFIELD, of Eaglesfield and Alneburgh. For an account of the early history of this family, see CW2 xvi. Tristan de Eaglesfield (living 1200), who heads the pedigree, was ancestor of Thomas de Eaglesfield, living 1282-85, whose son John was father of Robert Eaglesfield, confessor to Queen Philippa and founder of The Queen's College, Oxford, 1341. Eaglesfield

* The quarterings brought in by the various heiresses whom the Dykes family married are displayed on a brass in Bromfield church, which are given here in full since our reading of some of the quarters differs somewhat from Field's version. A number of the quarterings are also in glass in Plumbland Church. 1, Quarterly, Dykes and Ballantine, *q.v.*; 2, Argent three estoiles within a bordure engrailed Gules (Waverton); 3, Argent five bars Gules on a canton Sable a cross couped Or (Distington); 4, Vert a fret Or (Salkeld); 5, Argent a bend chequy Or and Gules (Vaux); 6, Or five fusils conjoined in fess Azure (Pennington); 7, Argent two bars Gules on a canton of the last a cinquefoil Or (Preston); 8, Argent two bars Gules on a canton of the last a lion passant guardant Or (Lancaster); 9, Argent a bend engrailed Sable (Radcliffe); 10, Azure a bend between six escallops Argent (Frecheville); 11, Or two chevrons Azure (FitzRalph); 12, Gules three annulets Or (Musard); 13, Argent on a chevron Sable three crosses pattée Or (Beaufoy); 14, Gules six cocks Or (Nuttill); 15, Azure crusilly and a lion rampant Or (Braose); 16, Azure two bends one Or the other Argent (Gloucester); 17, Argent a bend Gules a bordure gyronny Azure and Or (Trehampton); 18, Or three lions Passant guardant Gules (Dyve); 19, Gules three fleurs-de-lys Argent on a chief Azure a bar nebuly of the second (Watervill); 20, Argent on a cross wavy Vert five plates (Peveril); 21, Argent a cross between four mullets Azure (Ballantine); 22, Azure six annulets Or (Musgrave, of Crookdake); 23, Gules three water-bougets Argent (Roos); 24, Azure a catherine wheel Or (Trusbut); 25, Gules three catherine wheels Argent (Espec); 26, Peveril, as No. 20; 27, Or three fleurs-de-lys Azure (Betham); 28, Argent three swords conjoined at the pommel Gules (Stapleton); 29, Or six annulets Gules (Veteripont); 30, Azure semé of fleurs-de-lys and fretty Or (Morvill); 31, Gules a lion rampant Argent over all a bend Azure (Tilliol); 32, Barry of six Gules and Argent a bend Azure (Mulcaster); 33, Or six annulets Sable (Lowther); 34, Argent a saltire and in chief three cross crosslets Sable (Crookdake); 35, Dykes, as above; 36, Waverton, as No. 2; 37, Distington, as No. 3; 38, Vaux, as No. 5; 39, Gules a chevron between three luces hauriant Argent (Brougham); 40, Per fess indented Or and Azure two bars between three crescents counterchanged (Woodhall); 41, Or a cross flory Sable (Lamplugh); 42, Per fess Gules and Argent six martlets counterchanged (Fenwick); over all, on an escutcheon of pretence, Quarterly, 1, Or three bars wavy Sable the one in chief charged with as many plates the second with two plates and the third with one on a chief Azure the barrel of a cannon Gold (Gunson); 2, Or a crescent enclosing between the horns two hearts in fess Gules (Bassenthwaite); 3, Or two bars and a bend Sable over all a canton Gules (Copeland); 4, Argent a fess Sable in chief three mullets Gules (Irton).

was inherited by the descendants of Robert's brother, of whom Gawen Eaglesfield (d. before 1528), was High Sheriff of Cumberland 1517. His son Richard (d. 1557), High Sheriff 1551 and 1556, was the last male of the family, his sisters and coheirs being Elizabeth, marr. 1528 John Senhouse, of Seascale, *q.v.*; and Anne, marr. . . . Bardsey, and was a widow in 1557. *Arms.* Argent three eagles displayed Gules (FFC; LMC). This coat is quartered by Senhouse, *q.v.*, but Dugdale recorded their Eaglesfield quartering as: Gules three eagles displayed Or (FCW). Machell recorded: Or three eagles displayed Gules (MMS), which coat was recorded for John Eaglesfield, of Leconfield (Y), at Harvey's Visitation of the North, 1552 (VN i 91), and is given by FWE and DSL for Gawen Eaglesfield, above. *Crest* (of Robert Eaglesfield, above). A dexter hand appaumé charged with an eye Proper (BGA).

EARLE. Augustine Earle, F.S.A. (d. 1762), a Commissioner of Excise, High Sheriff of Cumberland 1731, was of Carlisle and Whitehaven, and finally of Heydon, Norfolk, which manor his family owned for some centuries. He acquired the manor of Seascale by marr. 1726 to Frances, dau. and heir of Robert Blaicklock, *q.v.*, and had issue Erasmus Earle, of unsound mind (d. 1768), whose sisters and coheirs were Mary (b. 1729), marr. 1756 William Wiggett Bulwer,* and Elizabeth, marr. Henry Calder. They sold the manor of Seascale to Charles Lutwidge, of Holmrook (*Ex inf.* Mr. and Mrs. J. M. Cook of Hoveton, Norwich; PGD). *Arms.* Azure a fess between two bars gemel Or (BGA). *Crest.* A lion's paw erased Proper holding a pheon Or. *Motto.* Adversis major pars secundis (BHN vi 246).

ECROYD, of Low House. From John de Aykerode (d. *c.* 1400), Constable of Wadsworth (Y) 1381, descended William Ecroyd, of Lomeshaye (L) (1796-1876), whose 3rd son Edward Ecroyd, J.P. (1833-1914), was of Low House and Armathwaite Castle, and Lord of the manors of Ainstable and Armathwaite with Nunclose. He was succ. by his nephew Thomas Backhouse Ecroyd (1857-1945), son of William Farrer Ecroyd (see AWL). His son William Edward Bedingfeld Ecroyd (1901-51), had an only son, Edward Peter Ecroyd, who is now of Low House, and Lord of the manors of Ainstable and Armathwaite (BLG18). *Arms.* Azure on a chevron Erminois between three stags' heads erased of the last in the centre chief point a bezant charged with a rose Gules barbed and seeded Proper two oak branches slipped chevronwise also Proper. *Crest.* In front of a demi tower Proper thereon a stag's head erased Erminois three spears one in pale and two in saltire also Proper. *Motto.* In veritate victoria (FD7).

EDEN, Baron Henley. Francis Robert Eden, 6th Baron Henley (1877-1962), was of Askerton Castle. He marr. 1913 Lady Dorothy Georgiana Howard (d. 1968), 3rd dau. of the 9th Earl of Carlisle, and succ. his half-brother 1925, when he assumed the surname Eden in lieu of Henley.† He was succ. by his elder son, Michael Francis, 7th Baron Henley, M.A. (Oxon) (1914-77), who bought Scaleby Castle 1952. His son, Oliver Michael Robert (b. 1953), is the present holder of the title. His uncle the Hon. Roger Quentin Eden Eden, is now of Askerton Castle. *Arms.* Quarterly, 1 & 4, Gules on a chevron Argent between three garbs Or banded Vert

* From this marriage descend the Bulwers of Heydon Hall, and the Earls of Lytton.

† His ancestor Morton Eden, 1st Baron Henley, was son of Sir Robert Eden, 3rd Bart., of Windlestone (D); his son, the 2nd Baron, assumed in 1831 the surname of Henley only.

as many escallops Sable (Eden); 2 & 3, Azure a lion rampant Argent crowned Or within a bordure of the second charged with eight torteaux (Henley). *Crest.* A dexter arm in armour couped at the shoulder Proper and grasping a garb Or. *Supporters.* Dexter, A lion Argent semé of torteaux ducally crowned Or having a plain collar of the last rimmed Azure on the collar three escallops Sable and pendant therefrom a shield Gold charged with an eagle displayed with two heads Sable; Sinister, A stag Argent semé of torteaux attired Or and collared as the dexter supporter with the shield charged with an eagle displayed with one head Sable. *Motto.* Si sit prudentia (BP105).

EDGAR, of Buckburn, or Boggburn. David Edgar, of Buckburn, or Boggburn, died 1732, aged 53. *Arms.* . . . a lion rampant . . . within a bordure . . . (Gravestone, Kirkandrews-on-Esk churchyard).

EDGAR, of Riddings. Tombstones in Arthuret churchyard commemorate David Edgar (d. 1654, aged 53); David Edgar, in Redings (now Riddings) (d. 1691, aged 53); and Anne, spouse to David Edgar, in Redings (d. 1676). *Arms.* . . . a lion rampant . . . . A broken gravestone seen by Bell Irving in Arthuret churchyard, with date 1666– with the following shield, may perhaps also have been for Edgar: A lion rampant holding in the sinister paw a (?) sword between four roses (ABD).

EDGE. James Vernon Edge, of Wood End, Thornthwaite, Keswick (b. 1889), was 2nd son of Thomas Lewis Kekewich Edge, J.P., of Strelley Hall, Notts. (1856-1931). *Arms.* Quarterly, 1 & 4, Per fess Sable and Gules an eagle displayed Argent on a chief Or a rose between two annulets of the second (Edge); 2 & 3, Sable a fess between three cinquefoils Or (Hurt). *Crests.* 1, A reindeer's head couped Proper collared and chained Or (Edge); 2. A hart trippant Proper attired and unguled Or hurt in the haunches with an arrow of the last feathered Argent (Hurt). *Motto.* Semper fidelis (BLG18).

EDMONDSON. James Edmondson, descended from an old Greystoke family, settled at Burns, Crosthwaite. His son, the Rev. Thomas Edmondson (1720-97), was Curate of Borrowdale, Curate of Crosthwaite, and for many years Incumbent of Threlkeld and Vicar of Rodmersham, Kent. His son John Edmondson (1761-1823) practised as a surgeon in Keswick for 37 years; a younger son, Isaac (d. 1822, aged 50), was a merchant in Baltimore, America. *Arms.* Gules a pale wavy Ermine between six escallops Or, two, two, and two. *Crest.* A demi lion Argent holding an escallop Or (M.I., Crosthwaite church).

EDWARD the Confessor, King of England 1041-66. Pre-armorial, but the following *Arms* have been attributed to him: Azure a cross patonce between five martlets Or (Shield at Raby Cote). These arms are also in a window in Setmurthy church, together with a representation of the saint, placed in memory of Joseph Fisher, of Higham (1850-1921), *q.v.*

EGBERT. Shield at Hutton-in-the-Forest; a Vane quartering. *Arms.* Quarterly Azure and Or a cross couped fleury counterchanged.

EKINS. The Very Rev. Jeffery Ekins, M.A., D.D. (Cantab) (1731-91), was an assistant master at Eton, Chaplain to the Lord Lieutenant of Ireland, Rector of Morpeth (N) 1775-91, Rector of Sedgefield (D) 1777-91 and Dean of Carlisle 1782-91. His only son the Rev. Frederick Ekins, M.A. (Oxon) (d. 1842, aged 75), was Vicar of Brampton 1791-92 and Rector of Morpeth (N)

1791-1842. (VEW xiii 83-93). *Arms.* Argent a bend lozengy Sable between two cross crosslets fitché Gules. *Crest.* A lion's gamb couped Sable holding a cross crosslet fitché Gules bendwise. *Motto.* Pro rege et lege (VEW xiii 125).

ELIOT. The Ven. Peter Charles Eliot, M.B.E., T.D., M.A. (Cantab), only son of the Hon. Edward Granville Eliot (1878-1952), brother of the 8th Earl of St. Germans, was Lt-Col R.A. (T) and was admitted a solicitor 1934. Ordained in 1954, he was Vicar of Cockermouth 1957-61 and Rural Dean of Cockermouth and Workington 1960-61. He has been Archdeacon of Worcester since 1961 and Canon Residentiary since 1965. *Arms.* Argent a fess Gules between two bars gemel wavy Azure. *Crest.* An elephant's head couped Argent collared Gules. *Motto.* Praecedentibus insta (BP105).

ELLIOT. Adam Elliot, of Killah, now Kellah, Nether Denton, died 1771. *Arms.* . . . a fess . . . (Tombstone at Nether Denton; ABD).

ELLIS, of Bothel. A pedigree in the 1612 Visitation of Yorkshire shows five generations of the Ellis family, descended from Robert Ellys, of Bothel, father of John Ellis, of Bothel, who had *int. al.* sons Thomas (who marr. Mary Osmotherly and was father of John, aged 21 in 1612) and Barnard Ellis, of York, whose son John was aged 12 in 1612. *Arms.* Or on a cross Sable five crescents Argent (FVY: FVC). MMD, however, gives: Or on a cross Sable five crescents of the field. *Crest.* Field gives: A naked woman her hair dishevelled Proper (FAC). FVY records a crest for Ellis in Barwick in Elmet church as: A maiden Proper her hands affronté crined Or.

ELPHINSTONE. For reasons which are not clear, when Col Howard Elphinstone, C.B., R.E. (1773-1846), was cr. Baronet in 1815, the baronetcy was described as of Sowerby, Cumberland; the family's connection with that place is not known. Sir Howard was 6th son of Captain John Elphinstone, R.N., an admiral in the Russian Navy, who marr. Amelia, dau. of John Warburton, Somerset Herald.* The present holder of the title is Sir Maurice Douglas Warburton Elphinstone, 5th Bart., T.D., M.A. (Cantab). *Arms.* Argent gutté-de-sang on a chevron embattled Sable between three boars' heads erased Gules two swords Proper pommels and hilts Or. *Crest.* Out of a mural crown Gules a demi woman affronté habited in her dexter hand a sword erect Proper pommel and hilt Or in the sinister an olive branch Vert. *Motto.* Semper paratus (BP105).

ELWES, of Warwick Hall. Lt-Col Robert Geoffrey Gervase John Elwes, D.L., J.P., of Elsham Hall, Lincs. (1890-1966), Privy Chamberlain to Popes Pius XI and Pius XII, eldest son of Gervase Henry Elwes, D.L., J.P., of Roxby and Brigg, Lincs. (1866-1921), marr. 1919 Ailleen Mary, only child of Charles Liddell, of Warwick Hall, *q.v.* *Arms.* Or a fess Azure surmounted by a bend Gules. *Crest.* Five arrows Or barbed and feathered Argent entwined by a snake Proper. *Motto.* Deo non fortuna (BLG18).

ENGAINE, of Burgh-by-Sands. The Engaines, who owned the barony of Burgh-by-Sands, ended in the male line in William Engaine (d. before 1158), whose dau. and heir Ada marr. (1) Simon de Morville (d. 1167), *q.v.*, and (2) Robert de Vaux, of Gilsland, *q.v.* *Arms.* The family was pre-armorial, but the following have been attributed to it: Gules a fess dancetté between six cross crosslets Or (Window in Kirkoswald church); and, Gules

* Warburton, for whom see DNB, marr. 1710 Dorothy (1664-1731), dau. of Andrew Hudleston, of Hutton John; Amelia was his dau. by a later marriage.

a fess dancetté between six cross crosslets fitché Or (Shield at Naworth Castle). The Wybergh family, *q.v.*, quarter, for Engaine: Gules a fess dancetté between three cross crosslets fitché Or (FD7); and a shield on the ceiling of Carlisle Cathedral, displaying: Gules a fess dancetté between three cross crosslets Or, may be intended for Engaine. MMD gives yet another variant: Azure a fess dancetté between six escallops Or.

ERRINGTON. The gravestone of Mary, dau. of Thomas Errington, of Bridge, died aged 69, but without date, is in Irthington churchyard. *Arms.* . . . a fess . . . between three escallops . . . .

ERROLL, Earl of – see HAY.

ERSKINE, Earl of Kellie. Walter Coningsby Erskine, 12th Earl of Kellie and 15th Baron Erskine (1810-72), marr. 1834 Elise (1813-95), dau. of Lt-Col William Youngson (d. 1835, aged 75), of Bowscar, near Penrith, to which estate she succ. on the death of her brother, William Troup Youngson (1818-71). The estate was inherited by their 2nd son, the Hon. Augustus William Erskine, J.P. (1841-1919), whose sons died unmarr., the coheirs being their sisters Eveline Mary Elise (b. 1874), marr. 1896 Lt-Col Henry Lowther, I.A. (1862-1925); Agnes Helen, a sister of the Community of St. Mary The Virgin, Wantage; and Dorothy Christian (1878-1940), marr. 1906 James Chapman, *q.v.* *Arms.* Argent a pale Sable. *Crest.* On a cap of maintenance Gules turned up Ermine a dexter hand holding a skeen dhu in pale Argent hilted and pommelled Or. *Motto.* Je pense plus (BP105).*

ESCROP, or SCROPE. Philip Escrop, or Scrope, was Sheriff of Cumberland 1201-3. *Arms.* Azure a bend Or (DSL).

ESPEC. Shield in the Musgrave window in Kirkoswald church; a Musgrave quartering. *Arms.* Gules three catherine wheels Argent.† Also quartered by Dykes *q.v.*.

ESTRIVERS, or TRIVERS. Arms ascribed to this family, Barons of Burgh-by-Sands, are in the Great Hall of Naworth Castle; the barony passed to the Engaines, *q.v.*, by the marr. of Ibria (d. before 1158), dau. of Robert de Estrivers, to Ranulph de Engaine, of Isel. They were pre-armorial, and the arms were an Elizabethan fabrication. *Arms.* Argent two bears passant in pale Sable.

ETHELRED the Unready, King of England, 978-1017. Pre-armorial, but the following *Arms* have been attributed to him: Azure a cross patonce between four martlets Or (Window, Carlisle cathedral).

ETHELWULF, or ETHELRED. Shield at Hutton-in-the-Forest; a Vane quartering. *Arms.* Azure a cross potent fitché Or. On another shield, the field is sable.

EURE. Recorded by Curwen as a Pennington quartering. *Arms.* Quarterly Or and Gules over all on a bend Sable three escallops Argent (CW2 vi).

EVERDON. Silvester de Everdon, Archdeacon of Chester, was Bishop of Carlisle 1246 until his death in 1254, due to his being thrown from his horse (JPP). *Arms.* Sable a lion rampant Argent (BBE). A doubtful ascription, as is the shield on curtains in Lanercost Priory, displaying: Argent a tree Vert. *Motto.* Te rogo Virgo Dei, Sis Vigil ergo mei (BBE).

EWART, of Brampton. The Ewart family, who came from the Lowlands of

* On the wall of Bowscar are two *Crests*: 1, A demi lion reguardant, with *Motto.* Decor . . . decus addit a vito. 2, As in the text.

† Not Gules a catherine wheel Argent, as stated by Field (FAC).

Scotland, established themselves at Brampton, where they were leading members of the Presbyterian Church, and prominent as mercers and tanners. Simon Ewart, of Brampton, mercer (will dated 1745, proved 1746), was father of John Ewart, of Bysshe Court, Sussex (1719-1801), and of Simon Ewart, merchant, of Brampton (1727-53), both buried at Lanercost. Simon Ewart, of Brampton, Esq., died 1809, aged 71, and was buried at Lanercost. *Arms*. . . . two swords in saltire points upwards . . . in chief three hearts . . . . *Crest*. An arm vested and embowed the hand upwards holding a dagger in bend sinister transfixing a human heart the point towards the point of the dagger (Tombstone of the above Simon, d. 1753, in Lanercost churchyard).

EWART, of Browhead. A gravestone in Kirkandrews-on-Esk churchyard commemorates Richard, son of George Ewart, of Browhead, died 1747, aged 8, also George, died in infancy. *Arms*. . . . a fess chequy . . . in chief a heart . . . Bell Irving adds: (Within a bordure flory?) (ABD).

EWART, of Kingfield. John Ewart (1681-1735) is said to have come to Brampton from Annandale 1699. His elder son John (1730-1810) was ancestor of many bearers of the name, while his 2nd son Simon Ewart, of Brampton, brewer and tanner (1734-1803), marr. 1765 Margaret (*c*. 1739-1804), dau. of John Milbourne and sister and coheir of John Milbourne (d. 1791), and so acquired Kingfield, Cracrop and Dormansteads. The former estate was inherited by their dau. Ann (1782-1852), wife of James Mounsey (d. 1835, aged 64), and the other two properties by their son John Ewart* (1767-1821), whose son John Ewart, of Woburn Square and Sussex Square, London (1799-1871), was High Sheriff of Cumberland 1869.† He marr. his cousin Margaret (1812-76), dau. of James Mounsey, but died *s.p.* and Kingfield passed to his brother-in-law George Mounsey (see *sub* BOSWELL). *Arms* (on gravestone of Simon Ewart, d. 1770, son of Simon, above, in Lanercost churchyard). As Ewart, of Brampton.

EWBANK. The Rev. John Ewbank, B.A. (Dunelm) (d. 1927, aged 78), Rector of Bolton (C) 1888-1927, was youngest son of Joseph Ewbank, of Rosgill. He marr. 1883 Julia Helen (d. 1956, aged 98), dau. and coheir of Robert Benson, solicitor, of Cockermouth, *q.v.*, and had issue Sir Robert Benson Ewbank, C.S.I., C.I.E., I.C.S., of Tongue Ghyll, Grasmere, and The Abbey, Carlisle (1883-1967). His son, the Ven. Walter Frederick Ewbank, M.A. (Oxon), was formerly Vicar of Raughton Head, and of St. Cuthbert, Carlisle, and Archdeacon of Westmorland and Furness, and was appointed Archdeacon of Carlisle and Canon residentiary of Carlisle 1978. His dau. Clare Caroline, B.A. (Dunelm), marr. 1968 John Henry Fryer Spedding, of Mirehouse, *q.v.* *Arms*. Sable three chevronels interlaced in base Or on a chief of the second three annulets of the first (HSW).

EXETER COLLEGE, Oxford. *Arms*. Argent two bends nebuly Sable a bordure of the last charged with eight pairs of keys endorsed and interlaced in the bows Or the wards upwards (Shield in window in Carlisle cathedral commemorating Herbert Ernest Campbell, *q.v.*, Canon, Archdeacon and Chancellor of Carlisle, d. 1930).

* His great-grandson, Noel Ewart Odell, was a member, with T. H. Somervell, see AWL, of the 1924 Everest expedition.

† He was the first Sheriff of Cumberland to drive a four-in-hand to the Assizes.

MORRIS-EYTON. John Reginald Morris-Eyton, of Beckside, Whicham, Millom, is 2nd son of Robert Edward Morris-Eyton, J.P., of Calvington, Newport, Salop (1893-1936), and grandson of Sir William Lewthwaite, 1st Bart., *q.v.* *Arms.* Quarterly, 1 & 4, Or a fret Azure and for distinction a canton Argent (Eyton); 2 & 3, Sable on a fess Or between three scaling-ladders Argent a lion passant guardant of the field (Morris). *Crests.* 1, A lion's head couped holding in the mouth a ton Or and charged for distinction with a cross crosslet Sable (Eyton); 2, In front of a scaling-ladder erect Argent a boar's head erased Proper (Morris) (BLG18).

FAGAN. Major-General William Turton Fagan (1831-90), Bengal Staff Corps, had an elder dau. Beatrice Emily (b. 1871), who marr. 1901 Sir James Morton, J.P., LL.D. (St. Andrews), F.R.S.E., of Dalston Hall (1867-1943). Another member of the family, Major-General James Lawtie Fagan (1843-1919), Bombay Staff Corps, was father of Edith, O.B.E., J.P. (1867-1937), who marr. 1889 Sir George Washington Baxter, Bart., and lived at Ashness in Borrowdale. *Arms.* Per chevron Gules and Ermine in chief three covered cups Or. *Motto.* Deo patriaeque fidelis (BLG15).

FAIRFAX. The Rev. Thomas Fairfax, M.A., B.D. (Cantab), Prebendary of Carlisle 1578-95, Rector of Great Asby (W) 1578-93, Vicar of St. Michael, Appleby 1579-82, Vicar of Lowther 1579-87, Rector of Caldbeck 1583, was 3rd son of Sir Thomas Fairfax, of Walton (Y). His son, the Rev. Thomas Fairfax, M.A. (Cantab) (d. 1640), was Prebendary of Carlisle 1600-40 and Rector of Caldbeck until 1640. His eldest son, the Rev. William Fairfax, M.A. (Cantab) (d. 1665), was Vicar of Castle Sowerby 1624-46 and 1660-65 and Rector of Bolton (C) 1630-55 and 1660-65; his dau. and heir Grace marr. Richard, son of Sir Edward Musgrave, *q.v.* At the Visitation of 1665, Edward Fairfax, of Bolton (C), 7th son of the Rev. Thomas (d. 1640), recorded a pedigree on behalf of his brother, the Rev. William Fairfax; their youngest brother, Robert, the 11th son, was then of Cockermouth. *Arms.* Argent three bars gemel Gules over all a lion rampant Sable a trefoil slipped Azure for difference. *Crest.* A lion's head Sable gorged with three bars gemel Gules a trefoil Argent (FCW).

FALCON, post FALCON-COOKE. Michael Falcon, of Workington, shipbuilder (1696-1771), was grandfather of William Falcon, of Whitehaven (d. 1815, aged 43), who marr. Jane (d. 1842, aged 71), 2nd dau. of Thomas Harrison, of Stainburn, *q.v.,* and sister and coheir of John Harrison. Their eldest son John Falcon assumed the surname Harrison 1844 (see that family). Their 3rd son, Henry Falcon, of Doynton, Glos. (1805-88), marr. 1840 Isabel (d. 1890), 4th dau. of Ralph Cooke, of Camerton, *q.v.,* and sister and coheir of William Cooke (1822-66). Their son Cmdr Tom Harrison Falcon, J.P., R.N. (1841-88), succ. to Camerton Hall, which descended to his son Ralph Falcon, M.A. (Oxon), F.R.A.S., barrister at law, Capt 5th Batt. The Border Regiment (1878-1960), who assumed the additional surname Cooke 1908. His only child Olive Naomi marr. Capt H. G. T. Padfield, R.N. *Arms.* Or a chevron between three falcons close . . . each on a perch. *Crest.* A falcon rising. *Motto.* Vis, courageux, fier (M.I., Camerton church). Burke gives the following for Falcon, of Garston House, Herts., and of Workington: *Arms.* Or a chevron Azure between three falcons close Proper (BGA). Fairbairn gives for *Crest.* A falcon rising Proper (FBC).

FALCON – see STEWARD, FALCON. –

FALLOWFIELD, of Castle Sowerby. Augustine Fallowfield, of Mossband, had a dau. Mary baptised at Kirkandrews-on-Esk, 1686. A person of these names is recorded as a papist at Bolton (W) 1694-96, and is perhaps identical with Austin Fallowfield, a papist at Wetheral 1705 and bailiff to Mr. Howard of Corby *c.* 1708 (HN 1/24). He was later of Sowerby Row, Castle Sowerby, where he was bur. 1728. His son Henry (1705-58) succ., and is bur. at Castle Sowerby. He had a son Augustine, of St. Oswald's parish, Durham City (1747-73), and a dau. Elizabeth (1745-96), who marr. 1778 Charles Stapleton, M.D., of Carleton (Y) and Preston (L) (d. 1799). Their dau. Elizabeth marr. Richard Gillow, of Leighton Hall (L).* *Arms.* ... three escallops ... on a chief ... a boar's head .... *Crest.* A boar's head. *Motto.* Exitus acta probat (Tombstone at Castle Sowerby).

FALLOWFIELD, of Penrith and Castle Sowerby. John Fallowfield (1726-1802), a native of Bolton (W), settled in Corn Market, Penrith, as a druggist, acquiring in 1763 the premises which have continued ever since as a chemist's shop and over which his coat of arms still hangs. The business was carried on by his descendants for many years. He lived at Southernby House, Castle Sowerby, where he was succ. by his eldest son John (1752-1834), who was a druggist in Preston (L),† where, and at Southernby House, he was succ. by his son John (1779-1837).‡ A younger son Jonathan (1780-1860), a surgeon on the H.E.I.Co.'s Bengal establishment, was later of Watermillock and Brisco Hill. John's daus. and coheirs were Isabella Dawson (b. 1806), marr. William Sykes, of Leeds, and Mary (b. 1808), marr. 1834 Benjamin Seed. *Arms.* Sable three escallops Or. *Crest.* On a chapeau a lion guardant collared and crowned with a ducal coronet all Proper (FVC; BGA). On a shield in Corn Market, Penrith, the crest is: On a chapeau a lion statant guardant crowned Or. *Motto.* Nil sine labore. On a bookplate in the possession of Miss Charlotte Kipling, of Miller Ground, Windermere, a descendant, the escallops are Argent and the lion in the crest is not collared.

FANE. Impaled by Lowther on gallery of Moresby church; William, 1st Earl of Lonsdale, of the 2nd creation (1757-1844), marr. 1781 Augusta (d. 1838), eldest dau. of the 9th Earl of Westmorland. *Arms.* Azure three dexter gauntlets backs affronté [Or].

FANE DE SALIS. Shield in library of Greystoke Castle; Sir George Warren, 2nd Baron de Tabley, *q.v.*, marr. (1) 1832 Catharina Barbara (d. 1869), dau. of Jerome Fane de Salis, 4th Count de Salis (d. 1836), *Arms.* Quarterly, 1 & 4, Per fess the chief Or a salix or willow tree eradicated Proper the base paly of six Argent and Gules (de Salis); 2 & 3, Azure three gauntlets Or (Fane).

FARGISON, or FERGUSON. John, son of Thomas Fargison, in Crofthead, Kirkandrews-on-Esk, died 1706. *Arms.* ... three hearts ... (ABD).

* Major J. R. Reynolds, whose wife was a descendant of this marriage, tells us that at Leighton Hall is preserved a set of buttons, with the following note: "These buttons have King James II's hair in them set in gold which he gave himself to him in the year 1715, when he attended his person through Scotland and to Preston where he was commanded to be hanged on the gallows hill, but was stol out of prison by a lady, confined in a garret three days and then got out of town in the dark. I mean your Uncle Fallowfield. He was obliged to leave the Kingdom and never return till relief came, but he then came to see his friends and returned but took a fever and died."

† He was the author of essays and poems.

‡ It was "chiefly owing to his unwearied, personal exertions that the magnificient tower of Preston Parish Church was raised" *(Carlisle Patriot)*.

FARLAM. John Denton thought that this family were descendants of the Windsors, but this belief was rejected in CW2 xix by T. H. B. Graham who suggested that they were sub-feoffees of the Windsors. Solomon de Farlam gave land in Farlam to Wetheral Abbey *c.* 1220, and was perhaps the Solomon son of David who gave land in Farlam to Lanercost. Richard son of Bernard de Farlam was a contemporary. Adam de Farlam held land in Farlam in 1295, and in 1305 Christiana, aged 26 and over, wife of John de Farlam, was one of the coheirs of Christiana, widow of Robert Bruce. In 1348 John de Farlam and Margaret his wife held the manor of Farlam. Denton says that the family ended in John de Farlam, who gave the manor to Ranulph Dacre temp. Edward III. *Arms.* Gules three mullets within a bordure engrailed Argent* (MMD).

FARINGTON. The Rev. Alexander Farington, B.A. (Oxon) (*c.* 1660-99), son of Laurence Farington, of Preston (L), was Master of Kendal Grammar School 1681-94, and Vicar of Penrith 1695-99. He marr. 1684 Isabel, dau. of Hugh Forth, of Kendal, and had sons Laurence, M.A. (Oxon) (b. 1685), and Hugh, M.A. (Cantab) (1687-1739), who were both in Holy Orders. *Arms.* . . . a chevron . . . between three leopards' faces . . . (Seal on the Rev. Alexander Farington's will).

FARRER, of Carlisle. Montagu Farrer, descended from the Farrers, of Ewood (Y), was promoted Major in the Inniskilling Dragoons in 1734, and retired in 1743. He lived in Scotch Street, Carlisle, and took part in the defence of Carlisle in the '45. He was High Sheriff of Cumberland 1740-41. His son Henry Farrer, of Carlisle (will pr. 1763), d. *s.p.*, his sisters and coheirs being Elizabeth (1725-81), marr. Capt Francis Lind, 14th Foot, *q.v.*, and Margaret (b. 1731), marr. 1758 Dr. James Ainslie (see AWL). *Arms.* Argent on a bend Sable three horseshoes of the field (DSL). These arms are on a shield on the chimney piece of the dining room of a mansion on the east side of Scotch Street, Carlisle, nearly opposite the Council Chamber of the Corporation. This house belonged to Major Farrer and was inherited by his dau. Mrs. Lind.† The Farrer coat is between two shields: 1, Lind, *q.v.*; 2, . . . a cinquefoil . . . between three horses' heads erased . . . . See John Atkinson's MS. notebook, f. 161, at Tullie House, Carlisle. Burke gives for Farrer, of Ewoot [*sic*] (Y), also of Co. Hertford and London, granted 1609: *Arms.* Argent on a bend engrailed Sable three horseshoes of the field. *Crests.* 1, A horseshoe Sable between two wings Argent; 2, A horseshoe Argent between two wings Or. *Motto.* Ferré va ferme (BGA).

FARRER, of Scaleby Hall. Capt Henry Farrer, H.E.I.Co.'s maritime service, and James Farrer, solicitor, who played such important parts in the life of Mary Eleanor, Countess of Strathmore,‡ were sons of the Rev. James Farrer, Vicar of Brignall (Y) 1739-80, said to have been a native of Orton (W). Henry, who was 35 in 1782, commanded the *True Briton* East Indiaman, and died at St. Helena 1800. His only son Henry Farrer (1798-1853) marr. 1822

* Not Argent three mullets within a bordure engrailed Gules, as recorded by Field, who terms it a very dubious ascription (FAC).

† The house later belonged to William Giles and was inherited by his eldest dau. and coheir Mary, wife of Henry Hall.

‡ See Ralph Arnold, *The Unhappy Countess*, 1957. Henry's first wife, Mary Goldsmith, published in 1788 *The Appeal of an injured wife against a cruel husband written by Mrs. Farrer. Dedicated To Lady Strathmore.* The real author appears to have been Lady Strathmore's infamous husband, Andrew Robinson Bowes.

Frances (1801-86), youngest dau. of Rowland Fawcett, of Scaleby Castle, They lived in turn at Rockcliffe Hall, Kirklinton Hall, and Scaleby Hall. Of their fourteen children,* nine died *s.p.* It is believed that there are descendants of James (b. 1829) in Australia, and of John Bernard (1832-92) in South Africa (*Ex inf.* Miss Barbara Glazebrook, a descendant). *Arms.* Argent on a bend sable three horseshoes of the field. *Crest.* An arm embowed in armour holding in the hand a dagger. *Motto.* Ferré va ferme (M.I., Scaleby church).

FAWCETT, of Petteril Bank. John Fawcett, a Sedbergh hosier, was father of the Rev. John Fawcett, M.A. (Cantab) (1733-83), whose only son the Rev. John Fawcett, M.A. (Cantab) (1769-1851)†, was a leading churchman in Carlisle, where he was Perpetual Curate of St. Cuthbert's Church 1801-51, and Headmaster of Carlisle Grammar School 1795-1803; he was also Rector of Scaleby 1802-26. His eldest son John Fawcett, D.L., J.P., barrister at law (1796-1883), was of Petteril Bank, near Carlisle, and marr. (1) 1825 Catherine (d. 1829, aged 34), only dau. of John Hinchcliff, of Burley Grove, near Leeds, and (2) 1830 Sarah Grace, only dau. of Joseph Hodgson, *q.v.* Their eldest son Sir John Henry Fawcett, K.C.M.G., barrister at law (1831-98), was British Consul General at Constantinople and Judge of the Supreme Consular Court of the Levant 1877, and was a member of the Rhodope Commission after the Russian and Turkish-Bulgarian War. The above John Fawcett's 3rd son was Morris James Fawcett, J.P. (1839-99), who served as a colonel in the Turkish army and was Inspector-General of Police in Newfoundland and Jamaica. *Arms.* Or a lion rampant Sable debruised by a bend company Gules and Argent (Bookplates of John Fawcett; Shield in billiard-room of Brunstock House).‡ *Crests.* 1, A demi lion rampant; 2, A stag's head erased. *Mottoes.* Vincit veritas; Dum vivimus vivamus (Bookplates).

FAWCETT, of Scaleby Castle. James Fawcett (d. 1729) bought Broadfield, Dent, and left issue *int. al.* John, who succ. and was murdered near Sedbergh 1736. His son James Fawcett (1730-1803) marr. 1756 Agnes, dau. of Henry Stephenson, of Docker Garth (W), and sister of Rowland Stephenson, M.P., *q.v.* of Scaleby Castle, which he let in 1775 to his brother-in-law, whose descendants were tenants until 1904 when Lt-Col James Farish Malcolm Fawcett, 5th Lancers (b. 1855), left the Castle and moved to Leicestershire§ (MS. account of the owners and occupiers of Scaleby Castle in possession of Miss Barbara Glazebrook, of Pitton, Salisbury, a descendant). *Arms.* Argent on a bend Sable three dolphins naiant . . . . *Crest.* A dolphin naiant (Brass, Scaleby church). In a window in Kirkby Lonsdale church (W), the Fawcett arms appear as: Argent on a bend Azure three dolphins naiant Or.

* Their son, Charles Henry, who became a midshipman in the Indian Navy 1847, was drowned in the Solway 1860, when his boat foundered.

† One of his grandsons William Milner Fawcett, M.A. (Cantab), F.S.A., F.R.I.B.A. (1832-1908), was a distinguished Cambridge architect, one of whose buildings was the Cavendish Laboratory.

‡ On one bookplate John Fawcett, of Petteril Bank, quarters for Morris: Vert a stag statant Or; and on another, also for Morris: Azure three eagles displayed Argent on a canton Gules a tower Argent. On the latter bookplate he impales, for Hinchcliff: Or a wyvern . . . between three fleurs-de-lys . . . .

§ His cousin was Col Percy Harrison Fawcett, D.S.O., the famous South American explorer.

FEILDING. Various members of this Yorkshire family have married into Cumberland families and acquired estates in the county. Israel Feilding, of Startforth (Y) (d. 1644), marr. (4)* Frances, dau. and coheir of Simon Musgrave, of Plumpton. Their eldest son William Feilding (*c.* 1625-1708) inherited a house and lands in Plumpton Head, which he left to his son Israel (1655-1723). Israel and Frances Feilding's 3rd son, Basil Feilding, of Carlisle (d. 1697), was Collector of the Port of Londonderry. *Arms.* Argent on a fess Azure three lozenges Or a crescent for difference (CVY).

FELL, of Knells. From William Fell, of Cartmel, descended the Rev. James Alexander Fell, J.P., M.A. (Cantab) (1824-97), Vicar of Penkridge (St). He bought Knells, Houghton, where he was succ. by his eldest son Henry Walter Fell, M.A. (Cantab) (1852-1930) (BLG18). *Arms.* Quarterly, 1, Ermine† two bars nebuly Gules each charged with two crosses pattée fitché at the foot Argent between three roses in pale of the second (Fell); 2, Azure a chevron between three hanks of cotton Argent (Cotton); 3, Ermine on a fess Sable a castle Argent (Hill); 4, Or on a fess Gules between two lions passant Sable three bezants (Noble). *Crest.* Upon a rock Proper a lion sejant per pale Argent and Gules charged on the shoulder with a rose counterchanged and resting the dexter fore paw on a cross pattée fitché at the foot also Gules (FD7). *Motto.* Vigilate.

FENTON, of Castlerigg. Samuel Greame Fenton (b. 1795), descended from a Leeds family, was of Castlerigg in the 1860's. *Arms.* Argent a cross between four fleurs-de-lys Sable. *Crest.* A fleur-de-lys enfiled with a ducal coronet Or (BLG4).

FENWICK. Sir Alan Fenwick, of Fenwick (N), was father of Sir Henry Fenwick (b. 1401, d. before 14 Sept. 1459) who was High Sheriff of Northumberland 1427, and of Cumberland 1436-37 and 1458-59. He settled in Cumberland when he became Warden of Cockermouth Castle. By Joan his wife, dau. of Sir William Leigh, of Isel, he had six daus. and coheirs, all married to Cumbrians – 1. Margaret, marr. John Denton, *q.v.*; 2. Elizabeth, marr. Christopher Moresby, *q.v.*; 3. Mary, marr. Sir John Hudleston, *q.v.*; 4. Eleanor, marr. Sir Thomas Lamplugh, *q.v.*; 5. Joan, marr. John Skelton, *q.v.*; and 6. Anne, marr. John Radcliffe, *q.v.* (AA3 xiv). *Arms.* On the tomb of Sir John Hudleston and Mary Fenwick, his wife, in Millom church, the arms appear as: . . . three martlets . . . on a chief . . . three martlets . . . . FFC blazons this as: Argent a chief Gules six martlets, three, two, and one, counterchanged. Shields at Hutton John display: Per fess Gules and Argent six martlets counterchanged, three and three.

FERGUSON, of Boghall. Joseph Ferguson, of Boghall, Kirklinton, yeoman, sealed his will (pr. 1732) with the following *Arms.* . . . a chevron Or between three birds . . . . *Crest.* Out of a coronet a (?)flower.

FERGUSON, of Bush-on-Lyne and of Carlisle. Field (FAC) says that this family, which played so important a part in the commercial life of Carlisle, descends from Adam Ferguson (d. 1642) who settled at Bush-on-Lyne. A tombstone in Arthuret churchyard records that William Ferguson, of that place, died 1804, aged 94, and his brother John, of Westlinton, died 1786, aged 79. From the latter place came Richard Ferguson (d. 1787, aged 73), who settled in Carlisle in the 1740's and began the manufacture of osnaburgs

* According to JPP ii 141, another of his wives was Mary (b. 1600), dau. of Thomas Dudley.
† On a brass in Houghton Church the field is Argent.

in rooms under the Town Hall. He marr. Mary (d. 1786, aged 59), dau. and heir of Joseph Ferguson, of Harker, and so acquired that estate, which passed to his 4th son Robert (d. 1816), see Ferguson, of Harker. Three other sons, John, Richard (d. 1811, aged 57), and George, established the cotton works at Warwick, which eventually passed to their relatives, the Dixons. Of these three, John Ferguson, J.P. (1748-1802), was father of Joseph Ferguson, D.L., J.P., of Lowther Street, Carlisle (1794-1880), who marr. Margaret, dau. of Silas Saul, and was father of Richard Saul Ferguson, D.L., J.P., M.A., LL.M. (Cantab), F.S.A. (1837-1900), and Charles John Ferguson, J.P., F.S.A., F.R.I.B.A. (1840-1904). The former, perhaps the most distinguished antiquary Cumberland has produced, was a barrister-at-law, and was Chairman of Cumberland Quarter Sessions 1886-1900; Mayor of Carlisle 1881-83; and Chancellor of the Diocese of Carlisle 1887-1900. He was a founder member of the Cumberland & Westmorland Antiquarian & Archaeological Society 1866, Editor of *Transactions* 1867-1900, and President 1886-1900. He wrote extensively for *Transactions* and was the author of many books on local history.* He was succ. by his only son Major Spencer Charles Ferguson, O.B.E., J.P. (1868-1958), who was Mayor of Carlisle 1912-14. His son Major Robert Spencer Ferguson, M.V.O., Royal Northumberland Fusiliers (Rtd.), is now head of the family. The above named Charles John Ferguson (1840-1904) was a well known architect, responsible for the restoration of Naworth and Muncaster Castles. He played the leading part in the establishment of the library and museum in Tullie House. He was the first secretary of the Cumberland & Westmorland Antiquarian & Archaeological Society, serving from 1866 until 1871. *Arms.* The tombstone of William and John Ferguson, above, in Arthuret churchyard shows: . . . three hearts . . . within a bordure invected . . . . *Crest.* A fleur-de-lys. Chancellor Ferguson bore: *Arms.* Argent a lion rampant Azure between three round buckles Gules a chief Vair. *Crest.* A demi lion rampant holding in the dexter paw a thistle slipped and leaved. *Motto.* Vi et arte (Bookplate). The family now bears: *Arms.* Argent a lion rampant Azure between six oval buckles tongues erect Gules three fesswise in chief and as many in base two and one a chief Vair. *Crest.* In front of a demi lion Or collared Vair holding in the dexter paw a thistle leaved and slipped Proper three buckles fesswise as in the arms. *Motto.* Vi et arte (FD7).

FERGUSON, of Harker and of Morton House. The junior branch of the family descended from Robert Ferguson, of Harker Lodge (d. 1816), head of the firm of Robert Ferguson & Sons (see preceding entry). He was succ. by his son Richard Ferguson, D.L., J.P., of 12 Abbey Street, Carlisle (1784-1860), High Sheriff of Cumberland 1835, who d. *s.p.* and was succ. at Harker Lodge by his nephew, George Henry Hewitt, *q.v.* Richard's brother Joseph Ferguson, of Morton House (1788-1863), founded in 1825 the firm of Ferguson Bros. at the Holme Head works; he was Mayor of Carlisle 1837, and M.P. for the city 1852-57. His son Robert Ferguson, D.L., J.P., F.S.A., of Morton House (1817-98), succ. him and was senior partner of the firm. He was a distinguished antiquary and was Mayor of Carlisle 1855 and 1858 and M.P. for the city 1874-86. He d. unmarr. and the control of the firm

* "He was the heart and soul of the Society; by his energy keeping it in life and health, and by his influence and forethought fostering its prosperity, overcoming its difficulties, and controlling its activity to the success of which we have such great reason to be proud." (CW1 xvi).

passed to his nephews, the sons of his sister Maria Isabella (d. 1890) who marr. 1850 Edward Chance, *q.v. Arms.* As Ferguson of Bush-on-Lyne and Carlisle.*

FERGUSON, of Peth. John Ferguson, of Peth, died 1711, aged 71; and William Ferguson, of Peth, died 1766, aged 68. *Arms.* . . . three hearts . . . . *Crest.* A mullet (Tombstones at Kirkandrews-on-Esk).

FERITATE, de – see le BRUN.

FERRERS. On shield in the Old Library at Naworth Castle; also quartered by Dacre on an impaled coat above the entrance to the Great Hall there; and impaled by Boteler, *q.v.*, on a shield in a bedroom in Lord William's Tower; John, 6th Lord Greystoke (d. 1436) (see Greystoke, 2nd Line), marr. Elizabeth (d. 1434) dau. and coheir of Sir Robert Ferrers (d. 1396), son of Robert Ferrers, Lord Le Boteler (d. 1380/81), by Elizabeth (d. 1411), dau. and heir of William, Lord Le Boteler, of Wem, *q.v. Arms.* Vairé Or and Gules.† These arms are also on the tomb of Sir Thomas Dacre, K.G., Lord Dacre (d. 1516), at Lanercost, and in glass in the Priory church.

FETHERSTONHAUGH, of The College. Henry Fetherstonhaugh (d. 1626), High Sheriff of Cumberland 1621, a younger son of Albany Fetherstonhaugh, of Fetherstonhaugh, *q.v.*, settled at Southwaite, Dacre, and in 1590 bought for £140 the estate of the dissolved College of Kirkoswald. His son Sir Timothy (1601-51), knighted 1628, High Sheriff 1638, fought for Charles I, was captured after the battle of Wigan, charged with corresponding with Charles II, and beheaded. His son and heir Henry, said to have been knighted a few hours earlier, was killed at the battle of Worcester 1651. The line was continued by his brother Thomas (1628-86) whose dau. and heir Mary, by his first wife, marr. (1) Philip Brunskill, of Bowes, and (2) Charles Whytell, of Gilmonby Hall (Y). He was succ. by his son by his second wife, Timothy (d. 1728, aged 70), High Sheriff 1697, whose son Heneage (1693-1737) was a merchant in Bristol, and whose only son Timothy (d. 1797, aged 72), High Sheriff 1755, was the last male of the family. His sisters and coheirs were Elizabeth (d. 1809), marr. 1742 Philip Leigh, of Dartmouth, and Joyce (d. 1778, aged 50), marr. 1752 the Rev. Charles Smalwood, *q.v.* Their son Charles (1762-1839) succ. his uncle and assumed the name and arms of Fetherstonhaugh 1797. He was of the East India House, London, and was High Sheriff of Cumberland 1805. He marr. 1810 Elizabeth (1772-1823), dau. and coheir of Thomas Hartley, of Gillfoot, *q.v.* Their younger son Charles, D.L., J.P. (1812-85), was of Staffield Hall,‡ and was High Sheriff 1857; their elder son Timothy, J.P., of The College (1811-56§), was High Sheriff 1845, and was succ. by his son Timothy, D.L., J.P. (1840-1908), High Sheriff 1870. He marr. 1865 the Hon. Maria Georgiana Carleton, dau. and coheir of Guy, Lord Dorchester. Their son Col Timothy Fetherstonhaugh, D.S.O., D.L., J.P. (1869-1945), was High Sheriff 1926 and Chairman of Cumberland Quarter Sessions. He was succ.

* The arms of the Ferguson family, of Raith, Fife, are on a shield in the billiard-room of Brunstock House, near Carlisle, and may be intended for Richard Ferguson, as Sheriff of Cumberland 1835, viz. Argent a lion rampant Azure between three round buckles Gules a chief chequy of the second and first.

† A variant adds to this coat a canton Gules charged with a lion passant (sometimes passant guardant) Or, see footnote to Dacre, of Lanercost.

‡ He marr. Jane, dau. and coheir of Francis Aglionby, *q.v.*

§ He was killed in the College grounds by a falling tree.

by his son Lt-Col Sir Timothy Fetherstonhaugh, O.B.E., D.L., J.P. (1899-1969), who was knighted 1960, and was High Sheriff 1951, and Vice-Lieutenant of Cumberland 1960-69. His son, Timothy Ross Fetherstonhaugh, of The College, is now head of the family (CW2 xiv; BLG18). *Arms.* Gules a chevron between three ostrich plumes or feathers Argent.* *Crest.* An antelope's head Gules crined and armed Or (FCW). Lysons record the crest as charged on the neck with an ostrich's feather and an annulet Argent (LMC). *Motto.* Valens et volens.

FETHERSTONHAUGH, of Langwathby. Richard Fetherstonhaugh (b. 1638), 5th son of Sir Timothy Fetherstonhaugh, of Kirkoswald, *q.v.*, was of Langwathby in 1664, and of Hutton-in-the-Forest in 1670, and at the time he made his will (pr. 1693) in 1688. He marr. (1) Katherine (b. 1643), dau. of William Graham, of Nunnery, *q.v.*, by whom he had a dau. Mary (b. 1663), wife of . . . Nanson; and (2) 1670 Anne (d. 1685), dau. of Edward Walkwood, of Hutton-in-the-Forest. Of their children only Bridget (1674-1710) survived him. She marr. (1) 1699 Cuthbert Rawling, of Stainton, and (2) 1709 Robert Wilson, of Penrith (CW2 xiv). *Arms.* Burke attributes to Fetherston of "Long Wathby": Or on a fess Sable three escallops of the first with a bordure engrailed Azure. *Crest.* An antelope's head erased Gules (BGA). While the crest is that of Fetherstonhaugh, the arms appear to be a version of those borne by Richard Fetherstonhaugh's father-in-law William Graham.

FETHERSTONHAUGH, of Fetherstonhaugh. This noted Northumbrian family became landowners in Cumberland when Nicholas Fetherstonhaugh marr. 1461 Maude, dau. and coheir of Sir Richard Salkeld, of Corby, *q.v.*, and so acquired a share of the manor of Triermain, which their grandson Albany sold to William, Lord Dacre, 1553. He marr. 1543 Lucy, dau. of Thomas Dudley, of Yanwath, who marr. (2) Gerard Lowther, of Penrith. The family line at Fetherstonhaugh was continued by their eldest son Alexander (d. 1596), who marr. Anne, dau. of Sir Richard Lowther. A younger son, Henry, founded the Kirkoswald branch of the family, see Fetherstonhaugh, of The College. *Arms.* Gules a chevron between three ostrich feathers erect Argent (TVN; VN iv 131).

FETHERSTONHAUGH – see STEPHENSON.

FIDLER, of Walton Rigg. Thomas Fidler, of Walton Rigg, died 1764, aged 75 (Tombstone, Walton churchyard). On another stone is recorded Jeffrey Fidler, of the same place, died 1766. *Arms.* Per fess Argent and chequy in fess an open book (ABD). Field recorded this as: Chequy on a chief an open book.

FIENNES, Baron Dacre of the South. Thomas, 6th Lord Dacre of Gilsland, *q.v.* (d. 1458), was father of Sir Thomas Dacre (d. *v.p.*) who marr. Elizabeth, dau. and heir of Sir William Bowet, and had a dau. and heir Joan (aged 26 and more in 1459) who marr. 1446 Sir Richard Fiennes (d. 1483), who was accepted by Henry VI as Baron Dacre, the title becoming known as that of Dacre of the South. It descended to Gregory Fiennes, Lord Dacre (1539-94), who was succ. by his sister Margaret, wife of Sampson Lennard, *q.v.* *Arms.* Quartered by Lennard on shield at Dacre Castle as [Azure] three lions rampant [Or].

* MMD records two shields for the family: Gules three ostrich feathers Argent; and, Gules a chevron Ermine between three ostrich feathers Argent.

FILMER. Impaled by Musgrave on tablet in Edenhall church; Sir John Chardin Musgrave, 7th Bart. (d. 1806), marr. 1791 Mary (1761-1838), elder dau. of the Rev. Sir Edmund Filmer, 6th Bart., of East Sutton, Kent. *Arms.* Barry of six Or and Sable on a chief of the last three cinquefoils of the first.

FISHER, of Cockermouth. The Fisher family owned much land in Brackenthwaite, Lorton, and acquired the manor from the Stanley family. They also lived at Wythop Hall. From John Fisher, of Brackenthwaite (d. 1624), descended Joseph Fisher, of Cockermouth, whose son Joseph marr. 1783 Elizabeth, dau. and at length heir of Josiah Shaw, of Kendal. Their son Robert Fisher, of the Inner Temple, was ancestor of the Fishers, of Chetwynd, Salop. *Arms* (granted to Robert Fisher, 1825). Quarterly, 1 & 4, Argent on a chevron engrailed with plain cotises between three demi lions guardant Gules each supporting between the paws a dexter gauntlet Proper three bezants; 2 & 3, Paly of six Argent and Vert a chevron Erminois between three covered cups Gold. *Crest.* Issuant from a crown pallisado Or a demi lion guardant supporting a gauntlet as in the arms (CA xxxv/39). *Motto.* Virtutem extendere factis (BLG4).

FISHER, of Distington Hall. Peter Fisher, of Whitehaven and of Prospect House, Distington (1796-1863), was father of Charles Fisher, J.P. (1826-83), of Distington Hall, which he built. He marr. Ellen (d. 1904, aged 72), dau. of Edward Carr Knubley, *q.v.* Their only surviving son, Charles Edward Fisher, J.P. (1860-1947), succ. His son Charles Leslie Fisher (1890-1962) marr. 1915 Catherine, only dau. of the Hon. Sir Peter McBride (BLG15). His sisters and co-heirs are Benita Violet, widow of Walter Frederick Gaddum, of Braban House, Burneside, and Kathleen Knubley, who marr. Eric David Milligan. *Arms.* Per fess Azure and Ermines a fess bretesse Argent between two dolphins naiant in chief Or and a kingfisher in base holding in the beak a fish Proper. *Crest.* In front of a kingfisher holding in the beak a fish Proper three crosses pattée fesswise Argent. *Motto.* Virtutem extendere factis (FD7).

FISHER, of East House. John Fisher, of East House, Embleton, died 1823, aged 80; his wife, Ann, died 1831, aged 81. *Arms.* Or a chevron Gules between three demi lions rampant . . . . *Crest.* A kingfisher with an eel in its beak (Tombstone, Embleton churchyard).

FISHER, of The Cragg and Higham. The Fishers have long been established in Setmurthy. Richard Fisher left The Cragg to his son John (d. 1841, aged 71), whose grandson Joseph Fisher, J.P. (1850-1921), acquired Higham Hall. He marr. 1875 Frances Mary (d. 1911, aged 58), dau. of John Nixon Renwick, of Newcastle upon Tyne. Their son George Forster Fisher, J.P. (1878-1947), succ., and after his death the Higham estate was sold to Cumberland County Council. The present head of the family is Mr. Francis Fisher, of The Cragg. *Arms.* Argent a chevron compony countercompony Or and Gules between three demi lions rampant of the last. *Crest.* A demi lion rampant Gules holding a branch of laurel Vert (Glass at Higham Hall).

FISHER, of Nunfield. The Fishers are probably the oldest family in Cumwhitton and have been at Nunfield since at least the 17th century; their ancestor Edward Fisher (d. 1689) was father of Richard Fisher (*c.* 1635-1720) whose initials, with those of his wife, are over the door of the original house (now a grain store) with the date 1699. His eldest son Isaac succ. him at Nunfield; his 2nd son John was ancestor of the Fishers, of Cambridge, bankers; and his 3rd son Joseph was ancestor of the Fisher-Rowe family, *q.v.* From the above named Isaac descended Isaac Fisher (1887-1950), who farmed at Nunfield. The present head of the family is his eldest surviving son, Edward Isaac Fisher, of Ivy House Farm, Stoke Golding, Nuneaton, while at Nunfield are living his sister Helena Mary Florence, and brothers Pearson Hewetson Fisher, Christopher William Fisher, and Richard Fisher. Their sister Catherine marr. Canon Norman Agmondisham Vesey, *q.v.* *Arms.* . . . a chevron . . . between three demi lions rampant . . . . *Crest.* A kingfisher holding in the beak a fish. *Motto.* Vive ut vivas.

FISHER, *post* FISHER-ROWE. Joseph Fisher (d. 1751), of the Nunfield family, see preceding entry, bought Ruckcroft, Ainstable, which passed to his grandson Edward Fisher, of Dale (1736-1802), whose son Edward (1762-1833) was of Ruckcroft, Dale and Croglin Low Hall. He obtained a grant of arms 1816. His son Thomas Fisher (1790-1870) became a merchant in London, and was of Thorncombe, Surrey. He marr. 1828 Anna Berry (d. 1878), dau. of Lawrence Rowe, of Brentford, Middlesex, and heir of her brother. Their only child, Edward Rowe Fisher,* D.L., J.P. (1832-1909), Capt 4th Dragoon Guards, served in the Crimean War and in 1883 assumed the additional surname and arms of Rowe. The family is now represented by his descendant, Major David Fisher-Rowe, of Hillside Farm, Ainsty, Wilts. *Arms.* Quarterly, 1 & 4, Per pale Sable and Gules three crosses pattée in fess Or between as many lambs passant Proper each supporting with the dexter foreleg a pennon Argent charged with the cross of St. George (Rowe); 2 & 3, Ermine on a fess wavy Vert between three kingfishers Proper as many fountains (Fisher). *Crests.* 1, A lamb resting the dexter foreleg on a beehive Proper and charged on the body with a cross pattée Or (Rowe); 2, On a fountain between six bulrushes a kingfisher rising in the beak a fish all Proper (Fisher). *Motto.* Favente Deo (CA lxii/62; BLG18).

FITTON. Impaled by Howard, *q.v.,* on shield in hall of Greystoke Castle; Sir William Howard, *temp.* Edward I, marr. Alice, dau. of Sir Edward Fitton. *Arms.* Azure three cinquefoils Argent.

FITZALAN. A Howard quartering, on shields in Naworth Castle and Greystoke Castle; Thomas Mowbray, Duke of Norfolk (d. 1399), marr. (2) Elizabeth, sister and coheir of Thomas FitzAlan, Earl of Arundel (d. *s.p.* 1415); and Thomas Howard, Duke of Norfolk (1538-72), marr. (1) 1555 Mary (1540-57), dau. and in her issue heir of Henry FitzAlan, Earl of Arundel (d. 1580). *Arms.* Gules a lion rampant Or. This coat, quartering Warenne, *q.v.,* is on a shield on the ceiling of Carlisle Cathedral.

FITZALAN of Bedale. Shield at Hutton John; a Hudleston quartering, brought in by Stapleton, *q.v.*; Sir Gilbert Stapleton (d. 1321, aged 31) marr. Agnes, or Maude, dau. and coheir of Sir Brian FitzAlan, Lord of Bedale (d. 1306). *Arms.* Barry of eight Or and Gules.

FITZELYS. Shields at Hutton-in-the-Forest; a Vane quartering. *Arms.* Argent a bend between six fleurs-de-lys Gules.

FITZHAMON. A series of shields from Thornbury Castle, Glos., now in Greystoke Castle, illustrating the medieval ancestry of the Howards, includes one for Robert FitzHamon whose dau. and heir Mabel (d. 1157)

* We owe to Capt Fisher-Rowe the story of the Croglin Vampire, which he related to Augustus Hare, who recorded it in his book, *In My Solitary Life*.

marr. Robert Consul, Earl of Gloucester, *q.v. Arms.* Azure a lion rampant guardant Or.

FITZHUGH. Shield at Hutton John. Old pedigrees of Hudleston, of Millom, *q.v.*, say that Sir John Hudleston (d. 1512) marr. a dau. of Lord FitzHugh; if he did, it was before his marr. to Joan Stapleton. *Arms.* Azure three chevronels interlaced in base and a chief Argent.

FITZLANGLEY. Shield at Hutton-in-the-Forest; a Vane quartering. *Arms.* Argent a fess between six leaves Gules. Another shield displays: Argent a fess between three oak leaves Vert.

FITZWALTER. Sir Robert FitzWalter, 2nd Baron FitzWalter of Woodham Walter, Essex (*c.* 1300-28), marr. Joan (1304-63), eldest dau. of Sir Thomas Multon, Lord Multon of Egremont, and sister and coheir of John, Lord Multon, *q.v.*, and so acquired Egremont Castle and a third of the barony of Egremont, which passed to their descendant Elizabeth (b. 1430, d. *ante* 1485), who marr. before 1444 John Radcliffe, *q.v. Arms.* Or a fess between two chevrons Gules (GEC; FFC).

FITZWATER. Shield at Hutton-in-the-Forest; a Vane quartering. *Arms.* Gules two bendlets the upper Or the lower Argent.

FITZWATER. Burke gives for FitzWater, of Cumberland, with no other details, the *Arms.* Argent a chevron Sable between three buckles Gules (BGA).

FLEMING, of Beckermet and Rydal. The earliest known ancestor of the family, Reiner Flandrensis, called the dapifer, gave land in Rottington (C) to St. Bees Priory and d. before 1148. His descendant, John le Fleming, with Amabel his wife, gave land in Millom to Calder Abbey. The estates, including Beckermet and Skirwith (C) and Rydal (W), descended to Hugh Fleming (d. 1557) who marr. Joan, dau of Sir Richard Hudleston, of Millom, and sister and coheir of Richard Hudleston. Their descendant, Sir Daniel Fleming (1633-1701), knighted 1681, was perhaps the most distinguished member of the family. Scholar and antiquary, he was also prominent in public affairs and was M.P. for Cockermouth 1685-87. His eldest son William (1656-1736) was cr. Baronet 1705 with remainder failing male issue to his brothers, of whom Sir George Fleming, M.A. (Oxon), LL.D. (Lambeth) (1667-1747), Bishop of Carlisle, 1735-47, succ. him. He was Domestic Chaplain to Bishop Smith, Vicar of Aspatria 1695-1703, Prebendary of Carlisle 1700-27, Archdeacon 1705-34, and Dean 1727-34. His only son, the Ven. William Fleming, M.A., D.C.L. (Oxon) (d. *v.p.* and *s.p.m.* 1742), was Archdeacon of Carlisle 1734-42 and Prebendary 1738-42. His uncle, the Rev. Roger Fleming (1670-1736), was Vicar of Brigham 1705-36, and was ancestor of the 5th and 6th baronets, below. Sir George was succ. by his nephew William, 3rd Bart. (d. 1757), M.P. for Cumberland 1756-57. His only son, Michael le (1748-1806), 4th Bart., High Sheriff of Cumberland 1770, was succ. in the baronetcy, but not the estates, by a kinsman, Daniel, 5th Bart., who d. *s.p.* 1821 when he was succ. by his brother, the Rev. Richard Fleming, M.A. (Cantab) (1791-1857), 6th Bart. His son and successor, Michael (1828-83), 7th Bart., settled at Dalemaine, Rangiora, New Zealand. The baronetcy descended to his nephew William Hudleston le Fleming, J.P. 9th Bart. (1861-1945), grandfather of the present holder of the title, Sir William Kelland le Fleming, 11th Bart., of Kopane, RD6, Palmerston North, New Zealand (GECB; BP105; *ex inf.* John

Fleming). *Arms.* Gules a fret Argent.* *Crest.* A serpent nowed Proper holding in the mouth a wreath of olive and vine leaves Vert. *Motto.* Pax, copia, sapientia (FCW; NB i 173-4; BP105).

FLEMING, William, of Brampton, 1752. *Arms.* . . . a fret . . . (ABD).†

FLETCHER, of Clea Hall. Philip Fletcher, younger brother of Sir Richard Fletcher, of Hutton-in-the-Forest, *q.v.*, was ancestor of Richard Fletcher who marr. the heiress of the Musgraves, of Clea Hall, and so acquired that estate. His descendant John Fletcher, of Clea Hall (d. 1756), High Sheriff of Cumberland 1724-26, marr. 1717 Isabella (1693-1774), dau. and coheir of John Senhouse, of Netherhall, *q.v.*, and had six sons, four of whom were in the Army,‡ one in the Navy, and the 5th, Henry (1729-1807), in the maritime service of the H.E.I.Co., and commanded the *Middlesex* East Indiaman. He became Chairman of the H.E.I.Co., was M.P. for Cumberland 1768-1806, and was cr. Baronet 1782. He marr. 1768 Catherine (d. 1816, aged 85), dau. and heir of Henry Lintot, by Elizabeth, dau. of Sir John Aubrey, 3rd Bart. Their son,§ Sir Henry Fletcher, 2nd Bart., was High Sheriff 1810. His descendant, Sir John Henry Aubrey-Fletcher, 7th Bart., is the present holder of the title (GECB; DNB). *Arms.* Quarterly, 1 & 4, Sable a cross engrailed Argent between four plates each charged with an arrow of the first (Fletcher); 2 & 3, Azure a chevron between three eagle's heads erased Or (Aubrey). *Crests.* 1, A horse's head Argent charged with a trefoil Gules (Fletcher); 2, An eagle's head erased Or. (Aubrey). *Motto.* Martis non cupidinis (BP105).

FLETCHER, of Cockermouth and Hutton-in-the-Forest. The Fletchers of Cockermouth Hall were rich merchants. Henry Fletcher received Mary, Queen of Scots, when she came to Cumberland in 1568 and gave her sixteen ells of rich crimson velvet to replace the poor clothes she was wearing. His 6th son Thomas marr. Jane, dau. and heir of . . . Bollen, and their son Richard, High Sheriff 1615, who was knighted 1617, bought Hutton-in-the-Forest from Lancelot Hutton 1606. He d. 1637 and was succ. by his son Henry, who was High Sheriff 1641-45, and was cr. Baronet 1645. He raised a regiment for the King, and fell at the head of it at the Battle of Rowton Heath.|| He was succ. by his son¶ Sir George Fletcher (*c.* 1633-1700), who was High Sheriff 1657 and 1679, and M.P. for Cumberland, with short breaks, from 1661 until 1700. His son Sir Henry (*c.* 1661-1712) was M.P. for Cockermouth 1689-90, and having settled his estates on his cousin Thomas Fletcher, of Moresby, *q.v.*, he retired to Douay Abbey in France, where he died unmarr., the baronetcy becoming extinct. His sisters and coheirs were Lucy, marr. Francis Bowes, and Catherine, marr. 1680 Lionel Vane, of Long Newton (D), see Fletcher-Vane. *Arms.* Argent a cross engrailed Sable

* MMD gives for Fleming of Rydal: Quarterly 1 & 4, Gules fretty Argent [Fleming]; 2 & 3, Argent on a bend Sable three lozenges of the field each charged with a saltire Gules [Urswick].

† See CW2 lxxiii 300-2 for John Fleming, of Brampton, manufacturer of ginghams, etc., and a pioneer in the town's textile industry.

‡ George, the 3rd son (1723-59), Captain of Grenadiers, was shot through the heart at Quebec when serving with Wolfe.

§ Their grandson John Philip Fletcher (1815-1905) inherited Wreay Hall from his cousin Thomas Benson. It was inherited by the Rt. Hon. Sir Henry Aubrey-Fletcher, 4th Bart.

|| He marr. Catherine, dau. of Sir George Dalston, *q.v.* She marr. (2) privately Thomas Smith, Bishop of Carlisle, *q.v.*

¶ His dau. Barbara marr. Sir Daniel Fleming, *q.v.*

between four pellets each charged with a pheon of the field (FCW). *Crest.* A horse's head couped Argent charged with a trefoil slipped Gules (M.I.s, Hutton-in-the-Forest church).

FLETCHER, of Edenbrows. Ralph Fletcher, who died at Bolton (L) 1832, had a son John Fletcher, D.L., J.P., of Croft, Clappersgate, Ambleside (1808-76). His grandson, Norman Fletcher, J.P., of Edenbrows (b. 1877), was High Sheriff of Cumberland 1929. His dau. and heir Nancy marr. (1) Col Ian McInnes, and (2) John Warnford Parker, *q.v.* His brother Cyril Fletcher (b. 1881) had a son John Fletcher, of 63B Cadogan Square, London, S.W.1, who is now the senior representative of the family. *Arms.* Argent a cross engrailed and voided between four annulets engrailed on the inner edge and each enclosing a pheon Sable. *Crest.* Three arrows one in pale and two in saltire and surmounted of an estoile. *Motto.* Alta pete (FAC; Seal of Norman Fletcher, as High Sheriff).

FLETCHER, of High House and Cartgate. A family of Fletcher were at High House, Frizington, from about the middle of the 18th century and were prominent colliery owners. John Fletcher, of High House (d. 1828, aged 66), and Sarah, his wife (d. 1851, aged 73), are buried in Arlecdon churchyard. Isaac Fletcher (d. 1877), a descendant, was of High House and his son William (1851-85) was of Cartgate, Hensingham. His sister Elizabeth, wife of the Rev. Alfred Charles Higgins, Curate of Arlecdon 1884-87, built the tower of Arlecdon church, and restored the building 1903. *Arms.* Argent a cross engrailed Sable between four pellets. *Crest.* A horse's head couped (Gravestone, Arlecdon churchyard). In a window in the church to William Fletcher (d. 1885), the *Crest* appears as: A horse's erased Argent, with *Motto.* Martis non cupidinis.

FLETCHER, of Little Broughton and Allerton. Joseph Fletcher, of Little Broughton (1684-1769), was ancestor of many Cumbrians. His eldest son Abraham (1714-93) was a well known mathematician (see LWC), and his 3rd son Jacob Fletcher (1726-1808) marr. Isabella (d. 1779, aged 50), dau. of Caleb Birch, of Whitehaven, and settled in Liverpool. Their son Caleb Fletcher, a native of Whitehaven (1754-1810), was of May Place, Liverpool, and in 1802 he obtained a grant of arms. His 4th son William Fletcher (1795-1871) was of Allerton (L), where he was succ. by his 4th son Alfred Fletcher, D.L., J.P. (1841-1919), father of Lt-Col Sir Edward Lionel Fletcher, C.B.E., of Himo, Tanzania, a director of the London board of the National Bank of Australia (1876-1968). His grandson Bruce Alan Fletcher, of Bosneives Farm, Withiel, Cornwall, is now head of the family. The above Abraham and Jacob Fletcher had a younger brother David Fletcher, of Workington (1730-1817), ancestor of Henry Fletcher, J.P., of Stoneleigh, Workington (1821-85), whose only son was William Lindow Fletcher, J.P., of Stoneleigh (1864-1936), who is commemorated in the west window of St. John's Church, Workington, to which he was a benefactor. *Arms.* Azure in chief two horses' heads erased Ermine in base an anchor erect with cable Gold on a chief wavy Or three hurts each charged with a pheon point downwards Argent. *Crest.* A dexter arm embowed in armour Proper garnished Or the hand grasping a dart barbed and flighted also Proper the arm surmounting an anchor as in the arms (CA xxi/332). *Motto.* Nec quaerere nec spernere honorem (BLG18). The arms are in the west window of St. John's Church, Workington, mentioned above.

FLETCHER, of Moresby and Hutton-in-the-Forest. Henry Fletcher of Cockermouth, who entertained Mary, Queen of Scots (see Fletcher, of Cockermouth and Hutton-in-the-Forest), had an eldest son William Fletcher, of Cockermouth, who bought the Moresby estate from Sir Henry Weston 1576. His descendant William Fletcher (1644-1703) marr. (2) Mary, dau. of Sir Thomas Tyldesley, of Tyldesley (L). Their son Thomas Fletcher (d. *s.p. c.* 1735) succ. to Hutton-in-the-Forest and Moresby Hall, but sold the latter 1734. He was High Sheriff of Cumberland 1719. He marr. (1) Catherine, dau. of Somerford Oldfield (see AWL) and sister and coheir of George Middleton Oldfield, and (2) 1734 Elizabeth (b. 1708), dau and heir of Ferdinando Latus, of Cockermouth, *q.v.*; she mar. (2) 1736 William Blencowe (see AWL). Thomas Fletcher's sisters and coheirs were Ann, marr. Peter Cusack, Mary and Frances. *Arms.* Argent a cross engrailed Sable between four ogresses each charged with a pheon of the field (FDC; shield at Moresby Hall).*

FLETCHER, of Tallantire. This branch of the Fletcher family was founded by Lancelot Fletcher, of Cockermouth, brother of Henry Fletcher, Mary, Queen of Scots' host (see Fletcher, of Cockermouth and Hutton-in-the-Forest). His son George Fletcher acquired Tallantire, which descended to Henry Fletcher (d. 1712), aged 25 at the Visitation of 1665, and described by Sandford as "a great gamester." His dau. Anne (d. 1721, aged 53) marr. 1688 Matthias Partis, *q.v.*, and carried Tallantire to that family. *Arms.* Argent a cross engrailed Sable between four pellets each charged with a pheon of the field in the dexter chief a canton Gules. *Crest.* A horse's head couped Argent charged with a trefoil slipped Gules (FCW).

FLETCHER, of Tarnbank. From Lancelot Fletcher, of Mockerkin (d. 1698), descended John Wilson Fletcher, of Greysouthen and Tarnbank (1788-1857). His eldest son Isaac Fletcher, J.P., F.R.S. (1827-79), was M.P. for Cockermouth 1868-79 and Chairman of the Cockermouth, Keswick and Penrith Railway, and a prominent colliery owner. His brother Henry Allason Fletcher, J.P., of Croft Hill, Moresby (1834-84), was for 27 years managing partner of Lowca Engine Works. A third brother, William Fletcher, D.L., J.P., F.G.S., of Brigham Hill (1831-1900), was M.P. for Cockermouth 1879-80 and Chairman of Cumberland County Council 1889-92. His son Lancelot Holstock Fletcher, J.P., of Brigham Hill, colliery owner (1867-1921), died *s.p. Arms* (granted 1877 to Isaac Fletcher and the descendants of his father). Argent a cross parted and fretty and engrailed on either side Sable between four pellets each charged with a pheon Or. *Crest.* Upon a mount Vert in front of a horse's head Argent a bezant charged with a trefoil slipped Gules (CA clix/315). On the tablet to Henry Allason Fletcher in Moresby church, the *Crest* appears as: A horse's head couped charged on the neck with a roundle thereon a trefoil slipped.

FLETCHER. The Rev. Walter Fletcher, M.A. (Cantab) (d. 1846, aged 78), son of the Rev. Walter Fletcher, of Breadsall (Dy), was Vicar of Dalston 1793-1846, and of Bromfield 1799-1826, Chancellor of Carlisle 1814-46, Prebendary of York 1825-46, and Vicar of Lazonby 1826-46. *Arms.* Argent a saltire engrailed Sable between four pellets each charged with a pheon of the field (Window, Carlisle Cathedral).

FLETCHER. Impaled by Robinson on tombstone in Torpenhow chuchyard;

* The illustration in MMD adds a very small canton Gules.

William Robinson, of Bothel, *q.v.*, marr. Anne Fletcher (d. 1737, aged 69). *Arms.* . . . on a cross flory . . . between four escallops . . . a plain cross couped . . . .

FLETCHER. A coat impaled by Gilpin on wall of Scaleby Castle seems to be intended for Fletcher; William Gilpin, *q.v.*, marr. Mary, eldest dau. of Henry Fletcher, of Tallantire Hall. *Arms.* . . . a chevron . . . between three pheons . . . .

FLUDYER. Impaled by Musgrave on tablet in Edenhall church; Sir Philip Christopher Musgrave, 8th Bart. (1794-1827), marr. 1824 Elizabeth (1796-1861), 3rd dau. of George Fludyer, of Ayston, Rutland. *Arms.* Sable a cross patonce between four escallops Argent each charged with a cross patonce of the field.

FORESTERS, Ancient Order of, of Wigton. *Arms.* . . . a cross between in the first quarter two hands issuing from the dexter and sinister and clasping each other; in the second three stags in full chase in pale; in the third a chevron between in chief a Pascal lamb and in base a bugle horn stringed; and in the fourth a bugle horn stringed surmounted of an arrow in bend sinister point downwards and of a quiver palewise; on an escutcheon of pretence a bugle horn stringed surmounted of a bow fessways and three arrows points downwards two in saltire and one in pale. *Crest.* Out of a ducal coronet a stag's head. *Motto.* Unitas benevolentia et concordia (M.I. erected in Wigton church by the Ancient Order of Foresters of Wigton, 1851, in memory of W. J. Carson, M.D., d. 1849, aged 48).

FORESTER. William, son of Arthur Forester, or Foster, of Caldside, Bewcastle, died 1728, aged 27. *Arms.* . . . three hunting horns stringed mouths to sinister . . . . *Crest.* A stag (Stapleton tombstone).

FORRESTER, James, of Holmhead, Bewcastle, died 1748, aged 42. *Arms.* . . . a chevron . . . between three hunting horns mouths to the sinister . . . . *Crest.* A stag (ABD).

FORRESTER, of Sowerbys. Administration of the personal estate, valued at £126, of Nicholas or Nichol Forrester,* yeoman, of Sowerbys, Bewcastle (d. 1758, aged 71, buried at Stapleton), was granted at Carlisle to Elizabeth his widow 1758 (*Ex inf.* J. P. Godwin). *Arms.* . . . a chevron Ermine between three hunting horns mouths to the sinister . . . . *Crest.* A stag statant (*Ex inf.* A. McCracken).

FORRESTER, or FORSTER. Stapleton tombstone; no details legible. *Arms.* . . . in chief three stags' heads . . . in fess three featherless arrows points downwards . . . and in base three hunting horns, two and one, mouths to the dexter . . . (ABD).

FORRESTER, or FORSTER, of Malsgate. John Forster was owner of Malsgate, Stapleton, 1696 and d. 1724, aged 61, when he was succ. by John Forster, who marr. 1726 Christian Forster and apparently died 1756, when he was late of Malsgate. *Arms.* . . . in chief thee stags' heads couped . . . in fess three pheons points upwards . . . and in base three hunting horns mouths to the sinister . . . (Gravestone, Stapleton churchyard).

* Field (FAC, p. 173) calls him Nichol Johnson, of Sorbys, and describes him as "a Stapleton statesman." He suggests that the arms he attributes to Johnson indicate a family connection with the Forresters – as well they might, since they *are* the arms of Forrester! No Nicholas Johnson was buried at Stapleton in 1758, nor was a will of anyone of this name proved at Carlisle in the years 1757-59.

FORRESTER, or FORSTER, of the Nook. Andrew Forster, of the Nook, Nichol Forest, marr. 1665 Jane Forster. Francis Forster, of the Nook, yeoman, made his will 1750 (pr. 1751) and another Francis Forster was father of William (d. 1757, aged 27) and of Mary (d. 1757, aged 36). John Forster, of the Nook, marr. Eleanor (d. 1767, aged 50). John Forster (*c.* 1764-1832) was father of William (1794-1836) and Joseph (1804-34), both surgeons. *Arms.* . . . a chevron reversed . . . between three hunting horns mouths to the sinister . . . . *Crest.* A stag (ABD).

FORSTER, Baron Forster of Harraby. Sir John Forster, K.B.E., Q.C., 1st and last Baron Forster of Harraby, of Beckenham, Co. Kent (1888-1972), was son of John James Forster, O.B.E., of Carlisle (1858-1963), and was educated at Sedbergh. He was a leading authority on settling disputes and was Chairman of the Railway Staff National Tribunal 1940-60. He was knighted 1939, became K.B.E. 1948, and was raised to the peerage 1959. His dau. and heir, the Hon. Pamela Forster, marr. 1948 Peter Hitcham Palmer. *Arms.* Per chevron Or and Argent in chief two sprigs of clover flowered and leaved Proper and in base an oak tree eradicated and fructed also Proper. *Crest.* A dexter cubit arm Proper vested Gules the cuff Ermine the hand grasping a balance Or. *Motto.* Let peace follow my labour (BP105).

FORSTER, of Kingfield and Dormansteads. The history of this family, large landowners in Cumberland, has been set forth by C. Roy Hudleston in CW2 lxviii 72-116. Arthur Forster, of Kingfield (*c.* 1601-80), was the owner of that property and of Whiteknow, Cracrop, Dormansteads in Stapleton, Dentonholme, Carlisle, Catlowdy, Fieldfoot, etc. His son by his 1st wife, Robert (d. *v.p.* 1667), left daus. Barbara (b. *c.* 1666), marr. 1686 William Elliot, of Meikledale, Dumfriesshire, and Mary, marr. William Scott. By his 2nd wife Elizabeth (d. 1728, having remarr. George Bell, of Bellbridge, *q.v.*), Arthur had a son Arthur Forster, of Kingfield (d. 1693), who had daus. and coheirs Thomasine (1688-1753), marr. 1706 Thomas Hodgson, of Barrockfield, Hesket-in-the-Forest (d. 1745), see Hodgson, of Bascodyke; Anne; Elizabeth (d. 1745), marr. 1718 William Davison, of Elswick, Newcastle upon Tyne; and Arthuria (*c.* 1693-1713), marr. Thomas Forster, of Sinnithwaite, *q.v.* *Arms.* . . . a chevron Ermine between three bugle horns . . . . *Crest.* A stag statant (M.I., Stapleton church).

FORSTER, of the Luckens. Arthur Forster was of the Luckens in Stapleton in 1672. The property descended to his grandson Arthur (d. 1782, aged 90), whose grandson Arthur (d. 1834, aged 55) owned as well Whiteholme and Sykehead. He had *int. al.* sons Arthur and Robert (1822-75), and a dau. Elizabeth (d. 1844, aged 36), marr. 1837 John Denis de Vitré. *q.v.* *Arms.* On the tombstone in Stapleton churchyard of Elizabeth Forster (d. 1778, aged 90), wife of Arthur (see above), the arms appear as: . . . three hunting horns stringed mouths to the dexter . . . . *Crest.* A stag. On the stone to her grandson, Arthur (d. 1834), they appear as: . . . a pall reversed . . . between three hunting horns stringed . . . the mouths of those in chief being outward and of that in base to the sinister. *Crest.* A stag (ABD).

FORSTER, of Middle Kingfield and Sinnithwaite. Thomas Forster, of Middle Kingfield and Sinnithwaite, marr. clandestinely 1712 Arthuria or Arthurina (d. 1713, aged 20), dau. and coheir of Arthur Forster, of Kingfield, *q.v.*, and had by her a dau. and heir Eleanor (1712-23). He bought Upper Kingfield and was succ. 1764 by his son Thomas, who sold Upper and Middle

Kingfield 1771. *Arms.* . . . two hunting horns . . . and a stag's head . . . (Gravestone, Stapleton churchyard).

FORSTER, of Petercrook. Reginald Forster, of Petercrook, Arthuret, died 1704. *Arms.* . . . a chevron . . . between three hunting horns mouths to the sinister . . . (ABD).

FORSTER, of Roan. Robert Forster (d. 1714, aged 54) was the owner of Roan, Nichol Forest, which descended to his grandson Robert (d. 1821, aged 87) whose son John (1763-1814) was a clerk in the Bank of England. Roan eventually passed to his uncle John Forster, of Newtown, Carlisle (1739-1819), a partner in the Old Print Field, Carlisle, and an extensive landowner, his properties including Yont-the-Moss, Kirkandrews on Esk, Gibbshill and Gillespie's Luckens, Stapleton. His son and successor John (1795-1883) was of Newtown, Brampton and Moorhouse Hall, Bowness-on-Solway. His son John Forster, of the Grey House, Etterby, and the Oriental Club, London, a tea planter (1827-98), succ. He died unmarr. and the properties were sold. *Arms.* . . . three hunting horns stringed, one and two, mouths to the dexter . . . . *Crest.* A hand erect grasping a dumb-bell (ABD).

FORSTER, or FOSTER, of Salmane. In 1654 Francis Foster, of Salmane, Walton, and Margaret his wife, assigned to Charles Howard, later 1st Earl of Carlisle, their interest in Cracrop, Stapleton. *Arms.* . . . a chevron . . . between three hunting horns . . . . *Crest.* A stag's head couped (Seal on deed in HN).

FORSTER, of Stonegarthside Hall. For an account of this old Border family, see a paper by C. Roy Hudleston in CW2 lxi. The pedigree is headed by Robert Forster (b. *c.* 1570-75), whose son Arthur (aged 65 in 1665) died 1670, leaving a son and heir Nicholas who died 1673, when the estates were seized by his brother Henry (d. *c.* 1699), though the right heir was their nephew John Forster, J.P. (1669-1727), who eventually recovered them. He was succ. by his son Arthur (b. 1695) who sold the estates to Matthew Robson in 1733. Arthur's brother Henry (d. 1775), who became Excise General Accomptant, appears to have been the last male of the family. His sisters were Katherine (b. 1699), marr. (1) Thomas Stevens, and (2) Joseph Smith; Agnes (b. 1701), marr. 1734 Matthew Robson, see above; and Dorothy (b. 1706). *Arms.* At the Visitation of 1665, Nicholas Forster on behalf of his father claimed that these were: . . . a chevron . . . between three mullets . . . . Respite was given for proof, but no proof was made. Nicholas' nephew John, writing to Col James Grahame from Stonegarthside in 1704, used on his seal: . . . a chevron . . . between three bugle horns . . . . *Crest.* A stag statant. LMC (xciv) gives the arms as: Argent on a chevron Vert between three bugle horns Sable stringed Or an escallop of the last.

FORSYTH, of Carlisle. Andrew Forsyth (1789-1853) came to Cumberland from Sanquhar, Dumfriesshire, and farmed at Broadfield, and was later of Union Street, Carlisle. His eldest son John (1816-97) emigrated to America, where his descendants remain. His brother James (1826-83) served in the Royal Horse Artillery: his great grandson Andrew Forsyth (b. 1940) is of Harraby. The above named John and James Forsyth had a younger brother Andrew (1829-55), accountant and chief cashier of Messrs. Hudson, Scott of Carlisle. His son John Forsyth (1855-1934) was a noted lithographic artist in Carlisle, living at Great Corby and later at Kelsick Moss House, Abbey

Town. He marr. 1884 Anne, dau. of Christopher Bulman, *q.v.* Their son Andrew (1888-1954) had a daughter Margaret, wife of Martin Richards, of High Hesket. His sister Clara (1890-1970) marr. 1912 John Stewart Muirhead (d. 1968). Their daus. are Clara Winsome, Joan Stewart, wife of William Hayton Thompson of The Slack, Wigton, and Dorothy Christina, wife of Richard Carruthers, of Cornerstones, Aglionby. To the same family belongs Lewis Forsyth, M.B.E., of Jennet Croft, Wetheral (b. 1889), only surviving son of Tom Forsyth (1864-1917), who was son of John Forsyth of Carlisle. Mr. Forsyth was a senior executive officer of the Ministry of Pensions and National Insurance, retiring in 1954. *Arms.* Argent a chevron engrailed Gules between three griffins segreant Vert beaked and membered of the second. *Crest.* A demi griffin Vert beaked and membered Gules. *Motto.* Restaurator ruiniae. (Painting in possession of Mrs. D. C. Carruthers.)

FORWARD. Susannah, dau. and coheir of Jonathan Forward, marr. 1736 John Stephenson (1700-71), brother of Governor Edward Stephenson, *q.v.* *Arms* (as impaled by Stephenson on her husband's coffin plate found in the family vault in the chancel of Crosthwaite church). . . . a chevron engrailed . . . between three crosses pattée . . . .

de FORZ, Count of Aumale; otherwise known as de FORTIBUS, Earl of Albemarle. William de Forz (d. 1195) acquired a moiety of the barony and honour of Cockermouth by marr. *c.* 1190 to Hawise (d. 1214), dau. and heir of William le Gros, Count of Aumale, Lord of Holderness (d. *s.p.m.* 1179). He was succ. by his son William de Forz, Count of Aumale (d. 1241), father of William de Forz, Count of Aumale (d. 1260), High Sheriff of Cumberland 1255 and 1259-60. The latter's only surviving son, Thomas de Forz (1253-69), d. *s.p.*, as did his sister Aveline de Forz, Countess of Aumale (d. *s.p.* 1274), and the moiety of Cockermouth fell to the Crown (GEC; LMC). *Arms.* Gules a cross patonce Vair (FFC; GEC). FFC also records: Argent a chief Gules, as does DSL.

FOSTER, of Killhow. John Porter Foster, J.P., of Killhow, Mealsgate (d. 1878), was High Sheriff of Cumberland 1875. His only son Samuel Porter Foster, D.L., J.P., M.A. (Cantab) (1845-1909), succ. and was High Sheriff 1881. He was called to the Bar 1869 and was on the Northern Circuit. His son John Porter Foster, M.A. (Cantab) (1874-1920), was Avocat de la Cour d'Appel at Alexandria and died at Luxor (BLG8; VAC). *Arms.* Burke gives none. Field states that J. P. Foster, High Sheriff 1875, made irregular use of the arms and crest of the Porter family, of Weary Hall, *q.v.*, with the *Motto.* Vigilantia et virtute.

FOTHERGILL, of Penrith. William Fothergill, of Penrith, grocer (d. 1692), younger son of Thomas Fothergill, of Tarn House, Ravenstonedale (W), inherited Tarn House from his nephew George (1662-90), but sold it 1691. His son George Fothergill, of Penrith, merchant (1669-1740), was father of William Fothergill, of the South Sea House, London (1701-67), whose sister and heir Elizabeth marr. 1738 John Pearson, of Carlisle. *q.v.* *Arms.* Vert a stag's head couped within a bordure invected Or (MMS). *Crest.* A stag at gaze Proper. *Motto.* Thus far (HMC).

FOUNTAINS ABBEY. Alice de Romili granted Crosthwaite church to Fountains Abbey *c.* 1195. *Arms.* Gules a cross between four lions rampant

Argent. Also: Azure three horseshoes Or (Mosaic shields in chancel of Crosthwaite church; BGA).

FOWKE. The Rev. Richard Fowke, M.A. (Cantab) (d. 1693) was Rector of Greystoke 1686-93. *Arms.* Vert a fleur-de-lys Argent. *Crests.* 1. A dexter arm embowed, vested Vert, cuffed Argent, the hand Proper, grasping an arrow in bend sinister Or, barbed and flighted Silver. 2. An Indian goat's head erased Vert, ears, horns and beard Argent. *Motto.* Arma tuentur pacem. (BLG12).

FOX, of Fawe Park. Samuel Middleton Fox, B.A., LL.B. (Cantab) (1856-1941), son and heir of Samuel Lindoe Fox, marr. Adelaide (d. 1922), dau. of James Spencer-Bell, of Fawe Park, Keswick, *q.v.*, and succ. to that property, which was inherited by their elder son, Commander Frederick Middleton Fox, O.B.E., A.F.C., V.R.D., R.N.V.R., D.L. (1892-1973), who was Director for Cumberland of the British Red Cross Society 1932-52, and High Sheriff 1957. *Arms.* Ermine on a chevron Azure three foxes' heads erased Or a bordure fleuretté and over all a canton of the second charged with a cup of the third surmounted of three fleurs-de-lys Argent. *Crest.* A fox sejant Or gorged with a collar fleuretté the dexter fore paw resting on a fleur-de-lys Azure. *Motto.* Faire sans dire (BLG17).

FOX, of High House. The Fox family was settled in St. Bees as early as the 16th century. Henry Fox, of High House (1741-1806), had issue, *int. al.*, the Rev. John Fox, M.A., D.D. (Oxon) (1774-1855), who was a Fellow of The Queen's College, Oxford, 1808-27 and Provost 1827-55, and William Fox, of High House (1772-1848). The latter's 2nd son, the Rev. John Fox, M.A. (Oxon) (1806-59), was Headmaster of St. Bees School 1830-41 and Perpetual Curate of Haile 1844-59. His brother William Fox, of The Abbey, St. Bees (1800-66), was father of the Rev. Henry Fox, J.P., M.A. (Oxon), of High House (1831-1914), who was succ. by his son Philip Henry Fox, J.P., M.A. (Oxon), Paymaster Lieutenant, R.N.V.R. (1875-1936). His son William Fox, J.P., M.A. (Oxon), of High House, is now head of the family. *Arms.* Or three foxes' heads erased Gules (Shield of Provost Fox in window of The Queen's College Hall).

FOX, of Whitehaven. The arms of this family are impaled with those of Bigland and with those of Sunderland in paintings at Bigland Hall (L); Mary, dau. of John Fox, of Whitehaven, marr. (1) George Bigland, of Bigland Hall (1701-52); and (2), as his 2nd wife, Thomas Sunderland, of Bradley (Y), later of Bigland Hall (bap. 1717). *Arms.* Or on a chevron between three foxes' heads erased Gules as many fleurs-de-lys Argent.

FRANCE, Republic of. Amongst the shields in the east window of Upperby church commemorating the Allies of World War I, is one for the Republic of France. *Arms.* Per pale Azure and Gules on a pale Argent between two sprigs of laurel Vert the dexter surmounted by the letter R the sinister by the letter F both Or the Roman fasces Proper.

FRANKLYN. Impaled by Musgrave on tablet in Edenhall church; Sir Christopher Musgrave, 4th Bart. (d. 1704), marr. (2) 1671 Elizabeth, dau. of Sir John Franklyn, of Willesden. *Arms.* Argent on a bend Azure three dolphins of the field.

FRASER – see BANNER.

FRECKLETON. Lewis Goodwin Freckleton, of 25 High Portinscale, Keswick (1894-1975), was son of Arthur Freckleton, of Derby, where he was born. His only dau., Miss Margaret Mary Freckleton, is now of High Portinscale. *Arms.* Sable a chevron Ermine between three covered cups Or. *Crests.* 1, A bear's head Argent muzzled Gules; 2, A camel's head couped Proper bridled and reined Gules. *Motto.* Tien le droit (Painting in Miss Freckleton's possession).

FROGENHALL. Shield at Hutton-in-the-Forest; a Vane quartering. *Arms.* Barry of four Or and Sable a chief Argent. The correct version is: Sable two bars Or a chief Argent.

FURNESS ABBEY. A shield on the font of Millom church, which belonged to Furness Abbey, bears the latter's *Arms.* [Sable] on a pale [Argent] a crozier [of the first].

FURNESS RAILWAY COMPANY. *Device.* A facsimile of the seal used by Roger Pele, Abbot of Furness 1532, viz. Beneath a canopy the Virgin Mary holding in her dexter hand an orb and supporting with her sinister arm the Infant Jesus on either side on an escutcheon Gules three lions passant guardant in pale Or, each supported by a demi monk Proper; on a compartment in base a wyvern statant contourné. *Motto.* Cavendo tutus (DRH).

GAITSKELL. To this old Cumberland family belonged William Gaitskell, merchant, of Egremont (d. 1788), and his brother John, who in 1806 was of Surrey Place in the parish of St. George, Southwark, when he was granted arms for himself and his nephew, William Gaitskell, the younger of Egremont, silk merchant (b. 1763), who died five months later. His son Henry Gaitskell, of Yeorton Hall, Beckermet (1791-1860), was patron of the living of St. John, Beckermet. A younger brother, the Rev. John Gaitskell, B.A. (Cantab) (1800-53), was Rector of Leverton, Lincs. Henry died *s.p.* and was succ. by his nephew William. Speaking at Penrith in 1954 the Rt. Hon. Hugh Todd Naylor Gaitskell,* M.P., P.C., C.B.E., M.A. (Oxon) (1906-63) claimed descent from this family. His ancestor Henry Gaitskell, distiller, of Bermondsey, marr. 1794 Elizabeth Gandy, of Kendal, and had a son Lt-Col James Gandy Gaitskell, 26th Bengal N.I. (1813-85), who marr. 1858 Emily Todd, dau. of J. Todd Naylor, of Liverpool. Their son Arthur Gaitskell, I.C.S. (1869-1915), was father of the above Mr. Hugh Gaitskell, whose widow Anna Dora, dau. of Leon Creditor, was cr. a life peeress as Baroness Gaitskell, of Egremont, 1964. *Arms* (granted to John Gaitskell, 1806). Gules a lion passant Argent grasping with the dexter forepaw an expiring snake entwined round his body Proper on a chief embattled of the second a sword erect Proper pommel and hilt Or between two laurel branches inclined towards the point thereof. *Crest.* A rock thereon an eagle reguardant wings elevated the dexter claw resting on a cannon ball Proper gorged with a collar Azure (CA xxiii/349). The crest is on the monument to Henry Gaitskell (d. 1860) in St. John's Church, Beckermet.

GALE, of Whitehaven. The Gale family, prominent in the 17th and 18th centuries in the commercial life† of Whitehaven, was founded locally by John Gale (d. 1680) who went from Tralee in Ireland to Newcastle upon Tyne and came to Whitehaven *c.* 1665. His son John Gale, of Whitehaven (d. 1716), marr. Mary, dau. and coheir of Lancelot Carlisle, *q.v.*, and had

* There was long a Gaitskell family in Crosthwaite and Hugh Gaitskell was buried there 1573.

† They were the largest importers of tobacco from Virginia.

seven sons, of whom the 2nd, George (1671-1712), described as Colonel, settled in Virginia, and marr. (1) 1700 Mildred, widow of Lawrence Washington, and (2) Elizabeth Denwood (see CW2 lxxi) by whom he had sons Levin, John, George and Matthias, all living in Maryland 1727. If a descendant in the male line survives, he is the head of the Gale family. Col George Gale's brother William was ancestor of the Richmond-Gale-Braddyll family, *q.v.* The English line was continued by their brother Matthias Gale, of Whitehaven (d. 1751), whose youngest son Matthias Gale, of Catgill Hall, Egremont (1724-71), had a dau. and heir Jane (d. 1819) who marr. her cousin, Wilson Gale, *q.v.* The eldest son of Matthias (d. 1751), John Gale, of Whitehaven (1716-68), was father of John Gale (1751-1807), a merchant in St. Petersburgh and London. He marr. 1781 Catherine, only dau. of Henry Littledale, of Whitehaven, and had a son Lt-Col John Littledale Gale (1783-1832), 37th Bengal N.I., whose descendant Lt-Col John Ross Gale, A.P.D. (1869-1925), was head of the family (BFR). *Arms.* John Gale, above (d. 1716), obtained a grant of the following in 1712: Argent on a fess between three saltires humetté Azure an anchor between two lions' heads erased Or. *Crest.* A unicorn's head couped Argent charged with two pallets blue (*sic*) armed and crined Or over all an anchor Gold (CW1 ix 100). The family before this used the arms of Gale, of Acomb (Y) (*ib.* 98-99). viz. Azure on a fess between three saltires Argent as many lions' heads erased of the field (FVY).

GALE, later RICHMOND-GALE-BRADDYLL. William Gale, of Whitehaven (*c.* 1693-1774), 7th son of John Gale (d. 1716, see Gale, of Whitehaven), marr. 1727 Margaret (1689-1759), dau. of Christopher Richmond, of Highhead Castle, and sister and coheir of Henry Richmond. Their son* John Gale (1730-1814) was of Highhead Castle and Cleator Hall and also owned Burneside Hall (W) and Haswell (D); he was High Sheriff of Cumberland 1759. By marr. to Sarah (d. 1774), dau. and coheir of Christopher Wilson, by Margaret his wife, aunt and coheir of Thomas Braddyll, of Braddyll (L), he also acquired Bardsea Hall (L).† Their elder son Wilson Gale (1756-1818) inherited the Braddyll estates‡ and assumed that surname 1776. He was M.P. for Carlisle 1790-6 and a Groom of the Bedchamber to George III. He marr. 1776 his cousin Jane (d. 1819), dau. and heir of Matthias Gale (see Gale, of Whitehaven). Their son Col Thomas Richmond-Gale-Braddyll, D.L., J.P., Coldstream Guards (1776-1862), assumed by Royal Licence 1819 the additional surnames Richmund-Gale. He was of Conishead Priory, which he rebuilt, and which he sold 1847. He sold Cleator Hall 1842. The present representative of the family is John Richmond-Gale-Braddyll, of Prospect House, Kirkby-in-Furness. *Arms.* Quarterly, 1 & 4, Argent a cross lozengy Vert over all a bend company Ermine and Azure (Braddyll); 2, Argent on a fess between three saltires humetté Azure an anchor between two lions' heads erased Or (Gale); 3, Gules two bars gemel and a chief Or (Richmund). *Crests.* 1, A brock Or (Braddyll); 2, An unicorn's head couped Argent armed and crined Or debruised by two pallets Azure over all an anchor Gold (Gale); 3, A demi

* Their dau. Isabella (1728-76) marr. Henry Curwen, of Workington, *q.v.*

† This property was inherited by his younger son, Lt-Gen Henry Richmond Gale (1760-1814), see AWL.

‡ Including Conishead Priory.

cat of the mountains guardant Proper spotted Argent holding between the paws an esquire's helmet also Proper garnished Or (Richmund). *Motto.* Cognoies toy mesme (Grants of arms at Prospect House; shields, etc., at Conishead Priory).

GANDY, of Skirsgill. Capt Henry Gandy, D.L., J.P., 83rd Foot (1834-88), High Sheriff of Westmorland 1880, son of John Gandy, of Oakland, Windermere, was of Skirsgill Park, Penrith, which he bought 1879. He marr. 1859 Frances, younger dau. and coheir of the Rev. Edward Hartley Orme by Mary, dau. and heir of Jeremiah Garnett, of Clitheroe, and was succ. by his son, Henry Garnett Gandy, solicitor, C.B.E., D.L., M.A. (Cantab) (1860-1939), who sold Skirsgill 1925. *Arms.* Quarterly, 1 & 4, Per fess nebuly Gules and Azure in chief two pairs of swords in saltire Argent hilts and pommels Or in base a saltire couped of the last; 2, Azure an eagle displayed and in chief three battle axes Or (Orme); 3, Gules a lion rampant Argent a bordure invected Or over all a bend Ermine charged with three covered cups Azure (Garnett).

GARTH. The Rev. Richard Garth, M.A. (Oxon) (d. 1673), was Vicar of Dalston 1661-63 and of Bromfield 1663-73. In 1660 Dr. Thomas Lamplugh wrote to his friend Joseph Williamson – with whom Garth also corresponded – saying "Dick Garth is yet unprovided for & much discontented." He had petitioned unsuccessfully for the living of Workington (ECW). *Arms.* . . . two lions passant in pale . . . in chief a cross pattée fitché . . . ; impaling, . . . a chevron . . . between three pears or gouttes . . . . (Table tomb in chancel, Bromfield church).

GASKARTH, of Hill Top and Hutton Hall. The Gaskarth family lived at Hill Top, Keswick, until John Gaskarth(1708-46), High Sheriff of Cumberland 1738, bought the manor of Penrith and Hutton Hall* from Dr. Addison Hutton in 1734. He marr. 1733 Catherine (d. 1782, aged 65), dau. of the Rev. Thomas Bolton, Rector of Greystoke. His daus. Mary (b. 1737) marr. Williams Hasell, of Dalemain, *q.v.*, and Julia (1738-1819) marr. (1) 1766 Stanwix Nevinson (see AWL) and (2) 1774 John Howard, 15th Earl of Suffolk and 8th Earl of Berkshire. His only surviving son, the Rev. John Gaskarth, B.C.L. (Oxon) (1740-1812), Curate of Farnborough, Warwickshire, 1766 until 1768, when he became Vicar,† succ. to Hutton Hall, which he sold with the manor of Penrith to Lord Lonsdale 1790, though the purchase was not completed until 1804, when he sold to William, Earl of Lonsdale, The Friarage, Penrith, which he had bought in 1790. *Arms.* Or a chevron sable between three arrows Proper. *Crest.* A goat's head erased Sable armed Or (LMC). On the monument in Crosthwaite churchyard to two children of John Gaskarth, d. 1735 and 1736, the arms are so worn away that only a chevron is now discernible. On the monument to Stanwix Nevinson in the chancel of Morland church, the arms are impaled by Nevinson as: . . . a chevron . . . between three arrows . . . .

GATE, of Spring Bank House. Joseph Gate (d. 1878, aged 79), Isaac Gate, J.P. (d. 1869, aged 69), and Jonathan Gate (d. 1884, aged 81), were all of Spring

* In 1756, during the family's residence, a violent storm struck Penrith and the battlements of the pele tower at Hutton Hall were blown down and the masonry crashed into the bedroom where Mrs. Gaskarth's sister Mary Bolton was sleeping and killed her.

† *Ex inf.* Mr. M. W. Farr, County Archivist for Warwickshire.

Bank House, Braithwaite. The latter marr. Mary Stanley (d. 1866, aged 58), and was father of Jonathan (1847-99). *Arms* (as borne by Isaac Gate, above). Argent a chevron Azure between three lions rampant Gules a label of three points of the last. *Crest.* A demi lion Gules gorged with a collar Or studded of the first (Window, Thornthwaite church). Jonathan Gate, above, however, bore: *Arms.* Per pale Gules and Azure three lions rampant Argent; impaling, Argent on a bend Azure three stags' heads cabossed of the field (Stanley). *Crest.* A demi lion rampant guardant. *Motto.* Vigilo et spero* (M.I., Thornthwaite church).

GAVESTON. Sir Piers de Gaveston, Earl of Cornwall (*c.* 1284-1312), the Gascon favourite of Edward II, was Keeper of Carlisle Castle 1311/12 (GEC). and (according to Field) lord of the Honour of Cockermouth. *Arms.* Vert three eagles displayed Or. Another authority gives six eagles, and another gives the field as Azure (FFC).

HENN-GENNYS. Commander William Edward Henn-Gennys, R.N., Captain of the Coast Guard in Cumberland, died in Whitehaven 1858, aged 44. His dau. and heir Florence Cordelia (d. 1940) marr. 1875 Admiral Sir Robert Hastings Harris, K.C.B., K.C.M.G., R.N. *Arms.* Quarterly, 1 & 4, Per pale Or and Argent a lion passant guardant per pale Azure and Gules (Gennys); 2 & 3, Argent a falcon Sable bezanté belled Or in the beak a sprig of myrtle Proper (Henn). *Crests.* 1, An eagle per pale Azure and Gules the wings elevated each charged with a bezant from the beak an escroll Argent thereon the words Deo gloria (Gennys); 2, A hen pheasant Proper (Henn) (BLG17).

GENTON. Henry Genton, of whom no further details are given, bore *Arms.* Gules a chevron between three escallops Argent (FVC: MVC).

GERARD. Impaled by Howard, *q.v.*, on stone shield at Corby Castle; Francis Howard, of Corby Castle (1635-1702), marr. (1) Ann (d. 1679), dau. of William Gerard, of Bryn (L). *Arms.* [Argent] a saltire [Gules].

GIBBON. The Very Rev. Thomas Gibbon, J.P., M.A., D.D. (Cantab) (d. 1716, aged 47), son of Matthew Gibbon, a London draper, and great-uncle to Edward Gibbon, the historian, was Rector of Greystoke 1693-1716, and Dean of Carlisle 1713-16. He marr. 1697 Mary (1671-1722), dau. and coheir of William Williams, of Johnby Hall, *q.v.* His son, the Rev. Williams Gibbon, M.A. (Cantab) (1699-1758), was Rector of Dufton 1729-36.† *Arms.* Azure a lion rampant guardant between three escallops Argent. *Crest.* A demi lion rampant guardant couped Argent crowned Or holding in his paws an escallop also Or (EGM).

GIBSON, of Barfield, *post* GIBSON-ATHERLEY. Edmund Gibson, of Townend, Whitbeck (d. 1709),‡ marr. (2) 1702 Dorothy (1664-1731), dau. of Andrew Hudleston, and widow of John Parke, of Whitbeck Hall, *q.v.* Their only son Edmund Gibson (1705-80) marr. (1)§ 1731 his cousin Isabel (1707-52), dau. of Wilfrid Hudleston. He was of Workington and

* In the window commemorating Isaac Gate, this is corrupted to: Vigils et shens.

† Of him Edward Gibbon wrote: ... "in my childhood I have known his [i.e. the Dean's] son Williams Gibbon, a drunken Jacobite parson who obtained by party-interest the Rectory of Bridewell".

‡ He was originally of Parkhouse (L); his son Robert by his 1st wife was Recorder of Lancaster.

§ He marr. (2) 1753 Eleanor (1726-1807), dau. of William Watters and widow of John Littledale. Their son William Gibson was a drysalter in Newcastle upon Tyne; see details of his sons in AWL.

Whitehaven, attorney, and was steward to his kinsman William Hudleston, of Millom. In 1738 he bought Monkfoss and in 1741 Scogarbar, Whitbeck, now called Barfield, which remained with his descendants until sold 1876. HIs son Robert Gibson, J.P., of Barfield and Ulverston (d. 1831, aged 97), was gazetted Cornet in the 1st Dragoon Guards 1762, was placed on half pay 1763, and so continued until his death when he was the oldest officer in the Army List. He marr. 1776 Mary (d. 1817, aged 62), dau. and heir of the Rev. Thomas Atherley. Their son Edmund Gibson (b. 1778) assumed the additional surname Atherley and was a barrister. His only child Jane marr. Ernest Charles Jones, the Chartist (1819-69), who was also a barrister and poet (DNB). Their son Llewellyn Archer Atherley-Jones, K.C., B.A. (1851-1929), was a County Court Judge, Recorder of Newcastle upon Tyne, and M.P. for N.W. Durham. *Arms.* Azure three storks rising Proper. *Crests.* 1, A stork rising Proper in his beak an olive branch Vert; 2, A lion rampant grasping a club (LMC).

HOLLINS-GIBSON. Joseph Stephen Hollins-Gibson, of Churchtown House, Sebergham, is elder son of Joseph Gibson, of Burnside, Barbon (W), and is descended from Robert Gibson, of Barbon (d. 1669), and from Humphrey Hollins, of Ashby-de-la-Zouche, Leics. (d. 1695). See also AWL. *Arms.* Quarterly, 1 & 4, Argent on a pile Gules between two branches of holly slipped and fructed in base three storks wings expanded each holding in the beak a holly leaf slipped all Proper (Gibson); 2 & 3, Argent a chevron between in chief two crosses formé fitché at the foot and in base a cinquefoil Azure. *Crest.* On a mount a stork wings expanded holding in the beak a holly leaf between two holly branches fructed Proper.

GIBSON, of Edenhall. Rowland Gibson bought a messuage in Edenhall 1650, and Christopher Gibson is mentioned 1674. Another Christopher Gibson is mentioned in 1710, and from Bishop Nicolson's diaries it seems that he was agent to the Musgraves. He marr. Grace (d. 1757) and had a son Philip (bap. 1707), who must have died *s.p.* as his sister Mary (d. 1771, aged 63), who marr. 1732 the Rev. Richard Machell (d. 1786), *q.v.*, was heiress. *Arms.* Over the front door of Tea Rose Cottage, Edenhall, is an armorial panel, dated 1707, with initials C G G and the following arms: . . . three storks rising . . . . *Crest.* A stork rising.

GIBSON, of Stainton. John Gibson, of Stainton, near Penrith, husbandman, marr. Esther (b. 1750), dau. of Thomas Bushby, of Greystoke, *q.v.*, and had a son John Bushby Gibson (1782-1849), who became Assistant Surgeon 20th Dragoons 1803, Surgeon Sicilian Regt. 1809, and Surgeon 52nd Regt. 1810, retired on half pay 1833. He served in Sicily, Malta, Egypt, the Peninsula, and was present at Waterloo. He marr. 1820 Grace Handfield, dau. of Edward Ommaney Wrench, by Grace Kilby, dau. of William Handfield, of Chester. *Arms.* Quarterly, 1 & 4, Azure three storks rising Proper (Gibson); 2 & 3, Vair on a fess Argent five cloves . . . (Bushby); impaling, Quarterly, 1 & 4, Ermine three acorns slipped and leaved . . . on a chief Argent a lion passant guardant . . . (Wrench); 2 & 3, Argent crusilly and a lion rampant Sable (Handfield). *Crest.* A demi lion rampant. *Motto.* Fide et fiducia (Bookplate of J. B. Gibson, given by his great-grandson, the late Major Geoffrey Wrench Titherington, of Brent House, Penrith, to the Regimental Museum of the 52nd Regt. *Ex inf.* Lt-Col John Granville).

GIBSON, of Woodside. Andrew Gibson, J.P. (1864-1933), of Woodside,

Wreay, which he bought 1912, High Sheriff of Cumberland 1925, was only son of Andrew Gibson, of Liverpool (1831-98). *Arms.* Per chevron Argent and Sable in chief two oak trees eradicated and fructed Proper and in base a lymphad of the first. *Crest.* A raven Proper supporting with the dexter claw a boat hook Or. *Motto.* Semper paratus (FD7). The crest is on the lodge at Ravenside, Wreay.

GILBY. Captain John Gilby, B.A. (Cantab), of the 81st Regt., 2nd son of William Gilby, M.D., of Clifton, Bristol, was drowned on duty at Skinburness 1837, aged 31. *Arms.* Azure a fess wavy between three mullets of six points Argent a crescent for difference. *Crest.* A tower with a dragon's head issuing from the top and the tail out of the door. *Motto.* Toujours fidèle (M.I., Carlisle cathedral).

GILL, of Carlisle. Captain Joseph Gill, 51st Foot (d. 1785, aged 58), was of Whitehaven when he made his will 1773, but was later of Carlisle, where he was Alderman and Postmaster. By Thamar his wife he had issue Jane (b. 1767); Mary (d. 1849), marr. 1789 Robert Mounsey, of Rockcliffe, *q.v.* (d. 1842); and Sarah (d. 1843, aged 70), marr. John Beck, of Carlisle, banker (d. 1819, aged 43). *Arms.* Sable a pale between four fleurs-de-lys Or a canton Argent (Window in Rockcliffe church). In another window, the canton is a sinister canton.

GILL, of Cumrew. John Gill (d. 1778) built the attractive Georgian house in Cumrew, where his descendants lived until the early years of the 20th century. His grandson Capt George Gill, 89th Foot (d. 1810, aged 60), bought Leeshill, Lanercost, which descended to his brother John (d. 1829, aged 87). His son George Gill, of Cumrew (d. 1866, aged 62), was succ. by his only child John George Gill (1851-1915), who was the last of his family to live at Cumrew. He was latterly of Fernbank, Cumwhitton. His son George Gill, of Carlisle, was representative of the family in 1937. *Arms.* . . . a pale Or between four fleurs-de-lys . . . . *Crest.* A human head in profile couped at the neck crowned and collared the crown attached to the collar which is studded by a chain. *Motto.* De vallibus orti (Gravestone, Cumrew churchyard).

GILLBANKS. Joseph Gillbanks, D.L., J.P. (1780-1853), son of Joseph Gillbanks, of Scothwaite Close, Ireby, went to Jamaica in 1800 and amassed a fortune as a merchant. He returned to England in 1814 and bought Whitefield House, Orthwaite Hall, Haltcliffe Hall and other estates in the county. He marr. 1819 Mary, eldest dau. of Ralph Jackson, of Normanby (Y), and cousin and heir of W. Thomas Jackson. Their son Jackson Gillbanks, J.P., LL.B. (Cantab) (1819-78), succ. and was ordained 1844 to the curacy of Aikton and was later Curate of Gilsland. He relinquished Holy Orders and was called to the Bar 1848. He was succ. by his sisters and coheirs, Mary, marr. 1846 R. M. Lawrance, M.D., and Maria Josephine, marr. 1856 the Rev. Henry Gough. *Arms.* Azure five hearts in saltire Or on a chief Argent a rose Gules between two trefoils slipped Vert. *Crest.* A stag's head Or. *Motto.* Honore et virtute (BLG 1846; M.I. and window in Uldale church).

GILLFORD, Baron – see MEADE.

GILPIN, of Scaley and Whitehaven. For the earlier history of this family, see AWL. The Rev. Richard Gilpin, M.A. (Edin) (1625-1701), son of Isaac

Gilpin, of Strickland Kettle (W), was Rector of Greystoke *c.* 1652-60.* During that time he bought Scaleby Castle from the Musgraves and lived partly there and partly in Newcastle upon Tyne, where he was a Presbyterian preacher and a doctor. His son William Gilpin, J.P. (1657-1724), succ. and lived in Whitehaven where he was chief agent to Sir James Lowther; he became Recorder of Carlisle 1718. His son Richard (b. 1692) succ. him as Recorder, but his affairs became hopelessly involved, and Scaleby was mortgaged to Edward Stephenson, who foreclosed. His brother Capt John Bernard Gilpin, 12th Foot (1701-76), lived in retirement in Carlisle and took part in the defence of the city in 1745. His eldest son the Rev. William Gilpin, M.A. (Oxon) (1724-1804), Vicar of Boldre, was headmaster of the famous school at Cheam (DNB). His brother Sawrey Gilpin (1733-1807) was a well known painter, and was father of William Sawrey Gilpin (1762-1843), also a distinguished artist. The youngest of John Bernard Gilpin's children, Sir Joseph Dacre Appleby Gilpin, M.D. (1745-1834), was Inspector General of Hospitals, Alderman of Carlisle, and Mayor 1806, 1811, 1816 and 1820 (JGM). *Arms.* The Rev. Richard Gilpin recorded the following at the Visitation of 1665, Dugdale adding "Respite given for proofe of these armes"· Or a boar passant sable (FCW). MMD gives: Or a boar statant Sable armed and unguled Gules. *Crest.* A pine branch Vert (FCW). JGM records the crest as: A dexter arm embowed in armour Proper the naked hand grasping a pine branch fesswise Vert. *Motto.* Dictis factisque simplex.

GILSAND, *recte* GILSLAND. GMS records the following, without further details. *Arms.* Vert a stag salient Or.

GIPPS. The Rev. Henry Gipps, M.A. (Oxon) (d. 1877, aged 80), was Canon residentiary of Carlisle 1845-77, Vicar of Corbridge (N) 1829-53, and Vicar of Crosthwaite (C) 1855-77. *Crest.* Out of a mural coronet two wings elevated each charged with three mullets of six points. *Motto.* Sursum (Brass in Carlisle cathedral).

GIRD. Henry Gird, saddler (d. 1857, aged 86), freeman of Leicester 1805, became a customs house officer in 1821 and from 1824 was stationed at Whitehaven, where he died. *Arms.* Azure three garbs in fess Or between three goats' heads erased Argent attired of the second. *Crest.* An arm embowed in armour holding in the hand a sword Proper pommel and hilt Or. *Motto.* Semper constans et fidelis (Needlework in possession of Henry Gird's great-grandson, Mr. Douglas R. Wattleworth, O.B.E., formerly of Hullet Syke, Brathay and now of Feock, Cornwall.

GLADSTONE. Shield at Hutton-in-the-Forest, Sir Henry Ralph Fletcher-Vane, 4th Bart., *q.v.*, marr. 1871 Margaret, dau. of Thomas Steuart Gladstone, of Capenoch, Dumfriesshire. *Arms.* Or a savage's head affronté couped at the neck and distilling drops of blood Proper about the temples a wreath of holly Vert within a double tressure flory Gules the whole within an orle of eight martlets Azure.

GLAISTER. Field gives no authority for his statement (pp. 237 and 338) that . . . Glaister obtained lands at Bowness on Solway by marr. *temp.* Henry VII with Cicely, sister and coheir of Clement Skelton, of Wreay. Professor John Glaister in CW2 xx 210 showed that Alexander Glaister, citizen and

* It is said that he declined the Bishopric of Carlisle at the Restoration, but it seems highly unlikely that he was offered it.

shearman of London, left by will dated 1522 money to the parish church of Bowness, where he was born. The family, of Scottish origin, flourished in Holm Cultram, and Robert Glaister, of East Cote in that parish, said to have been 105 at his death 1632, fathered 19 children, from whom descended the Glaisters of East Cote, Wath, Skinburness, Blackdykes, Saltcoats, Red Flatt (sold 1918), and Penrith. The Red Flatt branch is represented by W. M. Glaister, of Stainton, near Carlisle, only son of Ernest W. Glaister (d. 1953). *Arms.* Argent three lions rampant Gules. *Crest.* A lion's head erased Argent. *Motto.* Fortis et fidelis (FAC).

GLASGOW, See of. The arms of the See of Glasgow are in a window in Caldbeck church commemorating Margaret Alice Glen (d. 1936), wife of Dr. Glen, of Barnoldswick, and portraying St. Kentigern. *Arms.* Argent on a mount in base Vert an oaktree Proper the stem at the base thereof surmounted by a salmon on its back also Proper with a signet ring in its mouth Or on the top of the tree a redbreast and in the sinister fess point an ancient hand-bell both also Proper.

GLOVERS' COMPANY. Brigadier Thomas Stanwix, M.P., gave a silver porringer, hall marked 1704-5, to the Company of Glovers of Carlisle, engraved with the Company's arms, and now in Carlisle Museum. *Arms.* Per fess Sable and Argent a pale counterchanged and three rams salient, two and one, Or. On a carved wooden panel in Carlisle Museum are two shields with the arms and motto of Carlisle, and a third shield with the arms of the Glovers.

GODBOLD. A coat quartered by Thompson, *q.v.*, on a shield above the entrance to Arkleby Hall. *Arms.* . . . two longbows interlaced in saltire . . .

GOODENOUGH. The Rt. Rev. Samuel Goodenough, M.A., D.C.L. (Oxon), F.R.S. (1743-1827), 3rd son of the Rev. William Goodenough, Rector of Broughton Pogis, Oxon, was usher at Westminster School 1766-70, Dean of Rochester 1802-8, and Bishop of Carlisle 1808-27.* His eldest son, the Rev. Samuel James Goodenough, M.A. (Oxon) (d. 1858, aged 84), was Prebendary of Carlisle 1810-58 and Rector of Aikton 1844-58. Another son, the Rev. Robert Philip Goodenough, M.A. (Oxon) (d. 1826), was Prebendary of Carlisle 1811-26, and a third, the Very Rev. Edmund Goodenough, D.D. (Oxon), F.R.S. (1785-1845), was Headmaster of Westminister 1819-28, Prebendary of Carlisle 1826-45, and Dean of Wells 1831-45. The Bishop's nephew, the Rev. William Goodenough, M.A. (Oxon) (d. 1854, aged 82), was Archdeacon of Carlisle and Rector of Great Salkeld 1827-54 (ROW). *Arms.* Or a chevron Gules between three gouttes de sang. *Crest.* A demi wolf Proper holding between his paws an escallop Argent. *Motto.* Ad sanguinem (BP105; BBE; M.I., Whittingham church (N)). The monument in Wells Cathedral to the Very Rev. Edmund Goodenough (1785-1845), Dean of Wells, shews the arms as: Argent a chevron Gules between three gouttes de sang.

GOODWIN. Harvey Goodwin, M.A., D.D. (Cantab), D.C.L. (Oxon) (1819-91), was Bishop of Carlisle 1869-91. His son Harvey Goodwin, D.L., J.P., of Orton Hall (W) (1850-1917), High Sheriff of Westmorland 1904, was succ. by his son Harvey Goodwin (1883-1942) who sold Orton Hall 1936 and went to Stratheden, Langwathby, where he died. Of his four sons, the eldest, John Wycliffe Goodwin, is the head of the family; the 2nd and

* He was the first man in England to cultivate sea-kale.

4th sons, George Archibald Wycliffe (b. 1917) and Harvey Carlisle Maxwell (b. 1920), were killed in World War II; and the 3rd son, William Henry Wakefield Goodwin, of Barco Lodge, Penrith, is the present representative in Cumbria. (BLG15). *Arms.* Or on a fess between six lions' heads erased Gules an annulet of the field (HSW). BBE blazons the fess Sable.

GOODYER. The arms of Goodyer, impaling Lowther, are on a plaster ceiling in Gerard Lowther's House, Penrith; Frances, sister of Gerard Lowther, of Penrith (d. 1596), and dau. of Hugh Lowther, of Lowther, marr. Sir Henry Goodyer, of Polesworth, Warwickshire. *Arms.* Gules a fess vairé Argent and Sable between two chevrons Or. Curwen records for Goodyer: Gules a fess between two chevrons Vairy (CW2 vi).

GORDON, of Earlston. Sir Thomas Gordon, 3rd Bart. of Earlston (1685-1769), who died at Whitehaven of "the iliack passion", marr. (2) at St. Bees Anne (d. in Roper Street, Whitehaven, 1785), dau. of . . . Gibson. He was succ. by his 8th, but 1st surviving, son by his first wife, Sir John Gordon, 4th Bart. (1720-95), who had lived for many years in Whitehaven at the time of his marriage in 1775. Sir Thomas' granddau. Anne (d. 1817, aged 35), dau. of James Gordon and wife of Jonathan Brown, of Jamaica, is commemorated by a tablet in St. James' Church, Whitehaven. *Arms.* Azure a bezant between three boars' heads erased Or. *Crest.* A dexter hand issuing out of a wreath grasping a shabble Proper. *Motto.* Dread God (BP4). Debrett gives for motto: Dominus providebit.

GORDON – see CONWAY.

GORGES. Impaled by Graham on hatchment in Arthuret Church; Charles Graham (d. 1782), eldest son of the Rev. Robert Graham, D.D., of Netherby, Rector of Arthuret (d. 1782), marr. 1781 Elizabeth, dau. of Richard Gorges, of Eye, Herefordshire. *Arms.* Lozengy Argent and Gules a chevron Azure.

GOSPATRICK. Dugdale's pedigree of the Bird family, of Brougham (W), shews William Bird, of Pireth,* living 1295, as marr. to Emme,† dau. of . . . Gospatrick, of . . . , Cumberland (FCW). *Arms.* Chequy Argent and Gules a chief Azure (HMS v 149).

LEVESON-GOWER. Impaled by Grosvenor, *q.v.,* on font in Muncaster church given by Gamel Augustus, 4th Lord Muncaster, in memory of the christening of his dau. Margaret Susan Elizabeth (d. 1871, aged 11); her grandfather, the 2nd Marquess of Westminster, marr. 1819 Elizabeth Mary Leveson-Gower, 2nd dau. of the 1st Duke of Sutherland. *Arms.* Quarterly, 1 & 4, Barry of eight [Or and Gules] over all a cross flory [Sable] (Gower); 2 & 3, [Azure] three laurel leaves [Or] (Leveson).

GRAHAM, of Ann's Hill. Charles James Graham, of Kirklinton and Ann's Hill, Etterby (d. 1847, aged 72), had an only child Mary (d. *s.p.* 1851, aged 34), who marr. 1842 John Saul, later Kirklinton-Saul, *q.v.* Ann's Hill passed to Reginald Graham (1775-1857), who was of Remenham Lodge, Henley-on-Thames, Herne Hill, and 25 Norfolk Square, Brighton before returning to Cumberland. He marr. Louisa Susanna (d. 1829), dau. of Richard

* Little Croglin in HMS.
† AEenine in HMS.

Dennison, M.D., by whom he had five daus. and four sons,* of whom only Fanny Eliza (b. 1821) survived him. She marr. 1847 William Wordsworth (d. 1883), son of the poet, and they lived at Ann's Hill and 75 Castle Street, Carlisle. *Arms* (incorrectly quartered by John Kirklinton-Saul on M.I. in Kirklinton Church). Or on a chief . . . three escallops . . . . *Crest.* An arm embowed holding a sword (Bookplate of Reginald Graham in his family Bible at Rydal Mount).

GRAHAM, of Barrock Park and Rickerby. James Graham (d. 1820, aged 73), descended from a Kirklinton family, was a partner in the banking house of Graham & Co., of Carlisle. In 1791 he bought Barrock and Ellerton and built Barrock Lodge (now Barrock Park), which he sold to the James family 1813. He was later of Rickerby House and was High Sheriff of Cumberland 1796. His eldest son William Richardson Graham (1796-1827) died unmarr. and was succ. by his brother† Major James Reginald Torin Graham, Scots Greys (1798-1865), who was at Waterloo. His daus. Harriet Elizabeth Saurin Graham (d. 1892) and Georgina Genieve (d. 1909) died unmarr.; the latter gave the reredos in Stanwix church in her family's memory. *Arms.* Or on a chief Sable three escallops of the field. *Crest.* A falcon Or preying on a heron Argent. *Motto.* Ne oublie (Brass, Stanwix church).

GRAHAM, of Brackenhill. Brackenhill, Arthuret, was bought from Sir Thomas Dacre by Fergus Graham, of the Mote, *q.v.*, and settled on his 3rd son Richard, who died 1606. His son Richard Graham (d. 1644) was transported to Ireland, but returned to Brackenhill, where his descendants remained until the estate was sold by Henry Graham (1701-69).‡ *Arms.* As Graham of the Mote, *q.v.*, with a mullet for difference (CW2 xxx 225).

GRAHAM, of Browside. Walter Graham, of Browside, Arthuret, yeoman, died 1729, leaving a widow Eleanor and a nephew, Walter Graham, of Browside. *Arms.* . . . three escallops . . . and in chief a boar's head . . . (ABD).

GRAHAM, in Burn. Bell Irving recorded the following shield for Richard Graham, in Burn, Arthuret, 1775. *Arms.* . . . a saltire engrailed . . . in chief an escallop . . . and in base two escallops . . . all within a bordure . . . (ABD).

GRAHAM, of Edmond Castle. For the early history of this family, see a paper by T. H. B. Graham in CW2 viii. Thomas Graham, yeoman, of Edmond Castle (1718-1807), was father of *int. al.* Thomas, who succ.; Sir James, of Kirkstall, *q.v.*; and Mary (b. 1756) who marr. 1791 Richard Graham, of Stonehouse, *q.v.* The said Thomas Graham, J.P., F.S.A. (1751-1813), attorney in Lincoln's Inn, was succ. by his elder son Thomas Henry Graham, D.L., J.P., M.A. (Cantab), F.S.A. (1793-1881), High Sheriff of Cumberland 1824. He was succ. by his nephew Reginald John Graham, D.L., J.P., M.A. (Cantab) (1822-97), whose son and heir was Thomas Henry Boileau Graham, J.P., M.A. (Cantab), barrister at law (1857-1937), editor of *Transactions* of the Cumberland & Westmorland Antiquarian &

* His eldest son Reginald Simpson Graham (b. 1813) marr. 1838 Emma Bellasis, and was drowned with his wife and only child, aged 6, by the upsetting of his canoe in the River Amazon near Paia, Brazil.

† Their next brother Capt John Richard Graham, 5th Bengal Cavalry (1800-30), has a monument in Carlisle cathedral, which says of him "one who living never had an enemy and dying was lamented by all who knew him."

‡ And not by his son Richard (b. 1731, d. *v.p.* 1741), as stated in CW2 xxx and FAC.

Archaeological Society 1926-34, and a frequent contributor thereto. For many years he lived in retirement in London, and Edmond Castle was uninhabited, and was eventually sold. His eldest son, Herbert Henry Cecil Graham (1896-1950), served as Sub-Lieut R.N.V.R. and was later a Special Commissioner of Taxes (BLG15). *Arms.* Per pale indented Erminois and Sable on a chief per pale of the last and Or three escallops counterchanged. *Crest.* Two armed arms Proper garnished Or embowed issuing out of the battlements of a tower also Proper holding an escallop Gold. *Motto.* N'oublie (BLG15). The monuments in Hayton church of Thomas Henry Graham and Reginald John Graham, above, display the following: *Arms.* [Or] on a chief [Sable] three escallops [of the field]. *Crest.* A tower.

GRAHAM, of Ford-sike. James, son of John Graham, of Ford-sike,* died 1741, aged 2, and John, his 2nd son, died 1763, aged 20. Ann, dau. of John Graham, of Ford-sike, was baptised at Kirklinton 1765. *Arms.* . . . on a chief . . . three escallops . . . . *Crest.* A hand cuffed at the wrist and holding a sword (Gravestone, Scaleby churchyard).

GRAHAM, of Hallside. John, son of David Graham, of Hallside, Kirklinton, died 1741, aged 19. William Graham, of Hallside, marr. 1750 . . . Lawson, of Monkwearmouth. The will dated 1792 of William Graham, yeoman, of Hallside (d. 1800, aged 88) was proved at Carlisle 1800 by his widow Ann (d. 1817, aged 88); he had a son John, whose eldest son was William, and a dau. Elizabeth, wife of John Graham. *Arms.* . . . in chief a boar's head . . . in base a quatrefoil . . . on a chief . . . three escallops . . . . *Crest.* A cubit arm holding a scimitar (Gravestone, Kirklinton churchyard). Field quotes Cowper as interpreting the scimitar as a whip (FAC).

GRAHAM, of Kirkstall. James Graham (1753-1825), a native of Hayton, 2nd son of Thomas Graham, of Edmond Castle, *q.v.,* was an attorney in Lincoln's Inn, and agent for James, 1st Earl of Lonsdale. He was M.P. for Cockermouth 1802-5 and 1807-12 and for Carlisle 1812-25. He was Recorder of Appleby and was cr. Baronet 1808. In 1781 he marr. Anne (d. 1821), only dau. of the Rev. Thomas Moore, of Kirkstall (Y), and sister and heir of Major Thomas Moore, of Kirkstall, and so acquired that estate. Their son, Sir Sandford Graham, F.S.A. (1788-1852), succ. and was succ. in turn by his first, second and third sons – Sir Sandford (1821-75), Sir Lumley (1828-90), and Sir Cyril Clerke Graham, Lt-Governor of Grenada (1834-95), all of whom died *s.p.*, and the baronetcy became extinct. *Arms, Crest,* and *Motto.* As Graham, of Edmond Castle.

GRAHAM, of Knockupworth and Ayton. Thomas Graham, of Knockupworth, Grinsdale, yeoman, mentions in his will of 1766 his sons (under 21) John and Monkhouse Graham. A later Thomas Graham, of Knockupworth (d. 1816, aged 31), had a sister Margaret, wife of Thomas Graham, who was presumably of Ayton Hall (Y) and later of Knockupworth., He d. 1865, aged 86, and was buried in Stanwix churchyard. The church contains a tablet to Eliza (d. 1852, aged 76), only dau. of John Clark, of Ormskirk (L), and wife of Thomas Graham, of Ayton Hall. *Arms.* Or on a chief . . . three escallops . . . . *Motto.* Ne oubliez (M.I., Stanwix church).

GRAHAM, of Moorhouses. Edward Graham, of Moorhouses, Kirklinton, died 1752, aged 62. Dulcibella Graham, widow, of Moorhouses, made her

* Apparently misprinted by Field as Foudike in FAC.

will 1765, proved 1772, leaving 1s. to her son William, £5 to her son Andrew, and 1s. to her son George, "if alive." *Arms.* ...on a chief... three escallops.... *Crest.* A cubit arm holding a scimitar (Kirklinton tombstone).

GRAHAM, of the Mote. Fergus Graham, of the Mote, 3rd son of "Lang Will" (see Graham, of Netherby I), was father of Arthur, who was killed by Thomas Musgrave, Captain of Bewcastle. His son William, living at the Mote 1596, was given a pension by Elizabeth I, but it was reported (see CW2 xi 73) that "if his service hereafter be no better... the pension might be better bestowed, for he is a daily abettor of evil." He was transported to Ireland 1607, but retrieved his character by brave service as a lieutenant-colonel in the Royal cause, and eventually returned to England, where he died 1657, aged 93; his tombstone in Arthuret churchyard was set up in 1662 by his nephew Capt Arthur Graham, who recorded his arms in the Office of Arms, Dublin, 1648. *Arms* (granted to Fergus Graham for service done *temp.* Henry VIII and Edward VI, 10 December 1553). Barry of six Argent and Gules over all in bend a branch of an oak root branched within a bordure engrailed Sable on the first bar Gules a boar's head couped Argent. *Crest.* An arm bendy in four pieces Gules and Azure holding in the hand charnell a branch of the bend (CW2 xiv 150). Machell recorded the arms as: Argent three bars Gules over all a bend raguly Vert leaved Or in sinister chief a boar's head couped Argent the whole within a bordure engrailed Azure (MMS vi 417).

GRAHAM, of Netherby (I). William Graham, "Lang Will" (living 1537), was banished to England from Scotland *c.* 1516, bringing with him eight sons, "whome he planted neare the... River of Eske." His eldest son Richard, called of Esk, was of Netherby, and was living 1528-41. His son Richard was given lands by Henry VIII and arms by the Duke of Norfolk. His son Walter, the "Goodman of Netherby," was banished to Ireland with his sons Richard, Arthur and Thomas, 1606, and Netherby passed eventually by sale to an unrelated Graham* (see Graham of Netherby II) (CW2 xi, xiv). *Arms.* T. H. B. Graham (CW2 xiv 149) suggests that the grant of arms by the Duke of Norfolk may have been similar to those granted to Fergus Graham, of the Mote, *q.v.*

GRAHAM, of Netherby (II) and of Esk, sometime Viscount Preston. Fergus Graham, of Plomp, had a second son Richard (d. 1654) who entered the service of George Villiers, Duke of Buckingham, and soon rose to high favour at the court of James I. He was Gentleman of the Horse to the King and M.P. for Carlisle 1626 and 1628-29, and in the latter year was cr. Baronet. He bought the Netherby estate from Lord Cumberland. By Catharine his wife (d. 1649, aged 47) he† was father of Sir George Graham, 2nd Bart (*c.* 1624-58), who marr. Lady Mary Johnstone,‡ dau. of James, 1st Earl of Hartfell. Their son, Sir Richard Graham, M.A., 3rd Bart (1648-95), was M.P. for Cockermouth 1675-81 and for Cumberland 1685-87. In 1681 he was cr. Viscount Preston and Baron Graham, of Esk, in the Peerage of

* In 1657 Netherby was unsuccessfully claimed by James Ormes, citizen and weaver of London, and Joan his wife, dau. of John Graham, son of Walter above mentioned (PRO C7. 255/72).

† His 2nd son Richard, of Norton Conyers (Y), was cr. Baronet 1662.

‡ She marr. (2) Sir George Fletcher, *q.v.*

Scotland. As an adherent of James II he was sentenced to death for high treason, his baronetcy* and estates being forfeited 1690. He was pardoned 1691. The peerage became extinct on the death *s.p.* of his grandson Charles Graham (1706-39), 3rd Viscount and perhaps 5th baronet, if the pardon of 1691 reversed the attainder. If it did so, the baronetcy passed to his cousin William Graham (1730-74) who also wrongly assumed the Preston Viscounty. The Netherby estate was inherited by the last Viscount's aunts, Mary (d. 1753) and Catherine (d. 1757), Lady Widdrington, from whom it passed to their cousin, the Rev. Robert Graham, D.D. (see Graham, of Netherby III). The baronetcy is now held by Sir Montrose Stuart Graham, 12th Bart. (b. 1904), of 45 Astor Avenue, Merrick, New York. *Arms.* About 1629 William, 7th Earl of Menteith, and Thomas Dryisdaill, Islay Herald attested the descent of Sir Richard Graham, 1st Bart., from Malise, 1st Earl of Menteith, and the arms appropriate to his family. The English Heralds, on the strength of this, allowed Sir Richard the arms of Menteith, viz. Quarterly, 1 & 4, Or on a chief Sable three escallops of the field; 2 & 3, Or a fess chequy Argent and Azure in chief a chevron Gules; with a crescent for difference, within a bordure engrailed. At the Visitation of 1665 Dugdale allowed this coat, with the bordure Azure. In 1681, when Sir Richard Graham, Bart., was cr. Viscount Preston, Lord Lyon, at the instance of the 8th Earl of Menteith, certified that he was descended from Alexander, eldest son to Earl Malise, and the Earl Marshal directed the removal of the bordure; and so the arms are now borne (CW2 xiv 153-55; FCW; BP105). *Crest.* Two wings addorsed Or (FCW). *Supporters.* An eagle and a lion both Ermine armed Gules and ducally crowned Or (BGA). *Motto.* Reason contents me (BP105).

GRAHAM, of Netherby (III). Sir Richard Graham, 1st Viscount Preston (see Graham, of Netherby II), had a younger brother,† the Very Rev. William Graham, M.A., D.D. (Oxon) (d. 1713), who was Rector of Kirkandrews-on-Esk 1682-85, Prebendary of Durham 1684-1713, Rector of Whickham (D) 1685-1713, Dean of Carlisle 1686-1704, and Dean of Wells 1704-13. His son, the Rev. Robert Graham (d. 1782, aged 79), Rector of Arthuret 1735-82, and Rector of Kirkandrews-on-Esk 1758-82, marr. 1752 his cousin Frances (d. 1801, aged 69), dau. of Sir Reginald Graham, 4th Bart. In 1757 he succ. his cousin Lady Widdrington at Netherby, which was enjoyed for a fortnight by his son Charles Graham (1760-82)‡, who had an only dau. Caroline, marr. 1811 John Joseph Webbe-Weston, of Sutton Place, Surrey (see Weston). Charles was succ. by his brother James Graham, M.A. (Oxon) (1761-1824), who was cr. Baronet 1783. He was High Sheriff of Cumberland 1786 and 1795, and M.P. for Ripon 1798-1807. In 1785 he marr. Lady Catharine Stewart (1765-1836), dau. of the 7th Earl of Galloway. Their son, the Rt. Hon. Sir James Robert George Graham, LL.D. (Cantab) (1792-1861), was M.P. for Hull 1818-20, for St. Ives 1820-21. for Carlisle 1826-29, for Cumberland 1829-32, East Cumberland 1832-37, Pembroke 1838-41, Dorchester 1841-47, Ripon 1847-52, and for Carlisle 1852-61. He

* The attainder did not affect his Scottish peerage, as no forfeiture act was passed against him in Scotland.

† For Col James Grahme, of Levens (W), another brother, see AWL.

‡ His father died on 2 February, and on 15 February Charles was in London where, in the morning, he presented the Rev. John James to the livings of Kirkandrews-on-Esk and Arthuret. At 4 o'clock Mr. James was instituted and at 6 Charles died (GM).

was first Lord of the Admiralty 1830-34 and 1852-55, and Home Secretary 1841-46. He marr. 1819 Fanny, dau. of Col James Callender, afterwards Campbell, and was succ. by their son Sir Frederick Ulric Graham (1820-88), who was High Sheriff of Cumberland 1866. In 1852 he marr. Lady Jane Hermione St. Maur (d. 1909), eldest dau. and coheir of Edward Augustus, 12th Duke of Somerset. Their son Sir Richard James Graham (1859-1932) was High Sheriff 1894. He was succ. by his son Sir (Frederick) Fergus Graham, 5th Bart., K.B.E., T.D., D.L., J.P., M.A. (Oxon), M.P. for North Cumberland 1926-35 and for Darlington 1951-59, and Lord Lieutenant of Cumberland 1958-68. His son Major Charles Spencer Richard Graham, D.L., of Crofthead, Longtown, was High Sheriff 1955. *Arms.* Quarterly, 1 & 4, Or on a chief Sable three escallops of the field (Graham); 2 & 3, Or a fess chequy Argent and Azure in chief a chevronel Gules (Stuart); in the centre of the quarters a crescent of the last and all within a bordure engrailed Azure. *Crest.* Two wings addorsed Or. *Motto.* Reason contents me (BP105).

GRAHAM, of Nunnery. William Graham, alias Carliell, 7th son of "Lang Will" (see Graham, of Netherby I), was granted the site of the Nunnery, Armathwaite, 1553. His eldest son Arthur was of Blaatwood, Dumfriesshire, but Nunnery passed to his 2nd son Fergus Graham, alias Carliell (d. before 1591). His grandson George (d. 1667) was 72 at Dugdale's Visitation 1665. His son William d. *v.p.* 1661, and Nunnery apparently passed to his (i.e. George's) grandson Richard, of Staffield, who was aged 8 in 1665 and d. 1698, leaving a dau. Anne Allison. *Arms.* Quarterly, 1 & 4, Or on a chief Sable three escallops of the field; 2 & 3, Or a fess chequy Argent and Azure in chief a chevronel Gules; all within a bordure engrailed (FCW).

GRAHAM, of Purdhamscrook. Francis Graham, of Purdhamscrook, Kirklinton, was father of George (bap. 1672). George Graham, of Purdhamscrook, died 1768, aged 52. John Graham, of the same place was father of children born between 1736 and 1743. *Arms.* . . . six escallops . . . , three and three; impaling, . . . an eagle displayed . . . and in base two roundles . . . (ABD). The Kirklinton register describes George (d, 1768) as of Blackwell Hall.

GRAHAM, of Riggfoot. Walter Graham, of Riggfoot, Kirklinton, died 1744, aged 80. *Arms* (no shield). . . . three escallops . . . , one and two, in chief a rose . . . between two hexafoils . . . (Kirklinton tombstone).

GRAHAM, of Saughtrees. Bell Irving recorded a John Graham, of Saughtrees, Stapleton, 1751. Field recorded Janie, dau. of John Graham, of Saughtrees, as born 1751. *Arms.* . . . on a fess . . . three roundles . . . in chief a rose of seven petals . . . (?). *Crest.* A boar's head to the sinister (ABD). Field, however, recorded: *Arms.* . . . on a fess . . . three escallops . . . in chief a catherine wheel . . . (FAC).

GRAHAM, of Scotchdykes. A tombstone in Kirkandrews-on-Esk churchyard commemorates Mary, dau. of John Graham, of Scotchdykes, died 1729, aged 6, and her father, died 1761, aged 59. *Arms.* . . . a boar's head couped . . . and in base a (?roundle)* on a chief . . . three escallops . . . . *Crest.* A cubit arm vested holding in the hand a sword in bend sinister.

GRAHAM, of Stonehouse. The pedigree of Graham of The Old Mill House, Micheldever, Hants., in BLG18 gives the descent of this family from the

* This charge has weathered completely smooth but may originally have been a cinquefoil, or perhaps a rose, as given by Bell Irving (ABD).

Grahams of Nunnery, but proof is lacking. Richard Graham, of Stonehouse, Hayton (1676-1746), had a son Thomas Graham, of Stonehouse and Sleddale Hall (W) (1705-87), whose eldest son Richard (1746-1807) succ. to Stonehouse. He marr. 1791 Mary Graham, of Edmond Castle, *q.v.*, and had an only child Elizabeth Margaret (b. 1792) who marr. 1816 Field Marshal Sir Hew Dalrymple Ross, G.C.B. (1779-1868); their son General Sir John Ross, G.C.B., sold Stonehouse 1899. The above Richard Graham's younger brother William (1755-1840) was of Hayton when he marr. 1789 Frances (d. 1854, aged 90), dau. of William Graham, of Wetheral Abbey; he was later of Dufton Wood and Clifton (W). His grandson William Graham, D.L., J.P., B.A. (Cantab) (1855-1934), was of Eden Grove (W), and was High Sheriff of Westmorland 1900. His great-nephew Roger Henry William Graham is the family's representative; his sister Gillian Mary Millicent marr. 1953 Sir Anthony Richard Wagner, K.C.V.O., F.S.A., Garter King of Arms. *Arms.* Quarterly, 1 & 4, Or a chief Sable thereon three escallops Gold; 2 & 3, Or a fess chequy Argent and Azure in chief a chevron Gules; over all on the fess point a bee Proper the whole within a bordure engrailed Azure. *Crest.* A sprig of oak fructed Proper between two wings Gold. *Motto.* Reason contents me (BLG18).

GRAHAM, of Westlinton. Thomas Graham, of Westlinton, died 1707, aged 70. *Arms.* . . . three crosses pattée convex . . . in chief three escallops . . . (Gravestone, Kirkandrews-on-Esk). Irving recorded the crosses as quatrefoils (ABD).

GRAHAM, of Woodhead. David Graham, of Woodhead, Kirkandrews-on-Esk, 1720. *Arms.* . . . in chief three escallops, one and two, . . . in base three quatrefoils, two and one, . . . (ABD).

GRAINGER. Impaled by Pattenson on hatchment in Melmerby church; Thomas Pattenson, of Melmerby Hall (1747-1811), *q.v.*, marr. 1768 Barbara (d. 1781), dau. of John Grainger, of Bromfield. *Arms.* Azure three ears of guinea wheat slipped and bladed Or.

GRANT, *post* MOUNSEY GRANT. Sir James Robert Grant, K.H., C.B., D.L., M.D., of the Hill, Rockcliffe (1771-1864), was son of Duncan Grant, of Lingeston, and was born at Forres, Morayshire. He was present at Waterloo as head of the Army Medical Department, and was Inspector General of Hospitals. His eldest son James Robert Grant, of the Hill and of Houghton Hall (1807-44), had an elder dau. and coheir Mary Tirzah (d. 1910) who marr. 1862 Lt-Gen Charles James Mounsey, J.P., 71st H.L.I. (1835-93), 5th son of George Gill Mounsey, *q.v.* They assumed the surname Mounsey Grant 1882, and she assumed the surname Mounsey 1896. Their only son Major Charles James Grant Mounsey Grant, J.P., of the Hill and of Chatsworth Square, Carlisle (b. 1866), was High Sheriff of Cumberland 1912. (WRC; BLG8). *Arms.* In a window in Carlisle cathedral General C. J. Mounsey Grant's arms appear as: Quarterly, 1 & 4, Gules three antique crowns Or (Grant); 2 & 3, Chequy Gules and Or on a chief of the last between two estoiles Sable a pale of the last charged with a mullet of six points gold (Mounsey). Field recorded the following on the seal of Major C. J. Mounsey Grant, High Sheriff in 1912: *Arms.* Quarterly, 1 & 4, Gules three antique crowns Or (Grant); 2 & 3, Chequy Or and Gules on a chief of the first three mullets of the second (Mounsey). *Crest.* A burning mountain.

GRAVE, of Penrith. Richard Grave, surgeon, of Penrith (d. 1760, aged 46), marr. 1750 Mary (d. 1769, aged 45), dau. of Richard Hudleston, of Penrith (1677-1758), and sister and coheir of Richard Hudleston. Their son Edward Grave (d. 1838, aged 82) was admitted on attorney 1777, and practised in Penrith for upwards of 50 years, filling the post of Under-Sheriff of Cumberland 1792.* He marr. 1782 Mary, dau. of Joseph Salkeld, of Ranbeck, but died *s.p.* His sister Mary (d. unmarr. 1841, aged 83) was the last of the family. *Arms.* Gules an eagle displayed ducally gorged Or. *Crest.* Within a ducal coronet a demi eagle Or (BGA).

GRAY, of Dalston. Charles Gray, of Dalston, gardener and yeoman (d. 1803, aged 77), had the market gardens at Dalston later in the occupation of John Walton, and also owned nurseries. His son William Gray died 1804, aged 49 (MS. note by Canon James Wilson in his copy of his *Monumental Inscriptions of Dalston,* in the possession of C. Roy Hudleston). *Arms.* Gules a lion rampant guardant within a bordure engrailed [Argent]. *Crest.* A scaling ladder (M.I., Dalston church exterior).

GRAY, of Kirkhouse. John Gray, of Kirkhouse (b. 1717), was descended from Edward Gray who marr. 1608 . . . Eliot. *Arms.* Quarterly, 1 & 4, Gules a lion rampant within a bordure engrailed Argent (Gray); 2 & 3, Gules on a bend engrailed Or a baton Azure (Eliot) (BHI).

GREEN, *post* GREEN-THOMPSON, *post* YOUNG-THOMPSON, of Bridekirk. Andrew Green, of Salmon Hall, Cockermouth (1695-1775), was grandfather of Andrew Green, of Hundith Hill, Cockermouth, and of Prestbury, Cheltenham (1774-1847), who marr. 1815 Esther (d. 1833), 2nd dau. of Henry Thompson, of Cheltenham and Bridekirk (1749-1820), descended from Thomas Thompson, of Bridekirk (d. 1586). Their son, Major Andrew Green-Thompson, 48th (Northamptonshire) Regt. (1820-89), assumed the additional surname Thompson 1885 on succeeding to Bridekirk. He was succ. by his son Lt-Col Andrew Green-Thompson, of Bridekirk (b. 1852), Inniskilling Dragoons, who died *s.p.* 1928 and was succ. by his nephew, George Eldred Young-Thompson, of Bridekirk (b. 1873), son of Robert William Young, of Colinswell, Fife, and Alexandrina Jessie Esther Green-Thompson. *Arms.* Quarterly, 1 & 4, Sable on a fess Argent between three falcons Proper as many estoiles Gules (Thompson); 2 & 3, Vert on a chevron between in chief two bucks trippant and in base a cross flory Or three mullets of the field (Green). *Crests.* 1, In front of a dexter arm embowed in armour the hand grasping a sword in bend sinister Proper pommel and hilt Or three estoiles Gules (Thompson); 2, A buck's head erased Proper charged on the neck with a cross flory Or (Green). *Motto.* Consilio et animis (BLG14, 15).

GREENALL, of Lingholm. James Fenton Greenall, V.D., J.P., of Lingholm, Keswick (b. 1836), Lt-Col 9th Lancashire Rifle Volunteers, was son of Thomas Greenall, of Grappenhall (Ch). *Arms.* Argent on a bend Sable three bugle horns Or stringed of the field. *Crest.* A bugle horn between two wings Argent. *Motto.* Alta pete (BGA).

GREENWELL, of Sleetbeck. William Greenwell† (1709-92), Sheriff of Newcastle upon Tyne 1739, marr. 1734 Anne, dau. and heir of Daniel Sowerby, *q.v.,* and inherited Sleetbeck and other lands in Bewcastle and Brampton. They built the fine house at Sleetbeck, which bears the date

* He was largely instrumental in securing the abolition of bull-baiting at Penrith.

† He and his son appear sometimes to have used Greenville as their surname.

1744, their initials, and the arms of Greenwell with Sowerby on an escutcheon of pretence. Their son John Greenwell (1755-1833) was of Ash, Bewcastle, while Sleetbeck was inherited by their eldest son William Sowerby Greenwell (1742-1811), who is sometimes called Captain, but who was buried at St. Mary's, Carlisle, as "lieut. in the Army." He sold Sleetbeck and the Brampton properties he inherited from his mother. *Arms.* Or two bars Azure between three ducal crowns Gules (AA4 xviii 91).

GREENWICH, Royal Hospital for Seamen at. The Commissioners of the Royal Hospital for Seamen at Greenwich acquired the lordship of the manor of Alston 1735. *Arms.* Argent on a cross Gules between four anchors erect Sable an Imperial crown Or. *Crest.* Out of a naval crown Or two Union flags in saltire Proper. *Supporters.* Dexter, A merman; Sinister, A sea-lion; both guardant Proper and imperially crowned Or. *Motto.* Otia tuta (Churchyard gate, Alston; *ex inf.* C. M. Dawson, Department of History, Royal Naval College, Greenwich).

GREG. The Rev. John Kennedy Greg, M.A. (Cantab), of Carlisle, is only son of Hugh Stuart Greg, of Haverthwaite (L), see AWL. He served in World War II with the R.A.C., and was invalided out of the service 1943. He was ordained 1949, and became Curate of Holy Trinity, Carlisle, 1951, Vicar of Lanercost 1955, and Vicar of Cumwhitton 1962. He is now Vicar in the team ministry of St. Barnabas, Carlisle. *Arms.* Argent a Scotch fir out of a mount Vert in base surmounted by a sword in bend Proper on a dexter canton Azure a Royal Scotch crown Proper. *Crest.* An arm embowed in armour grasping a scimitar Azure pommel and hilt Or. *Motto.* Ein doe, and spair not (BLG18).

GREY, Marquess of Dorset and Duke of Suffolk. The Grey family acquired estates in Cumberland by the marr. of Thomas Grey, Lord Ferrers of Groby, Earl of Huntingdon, and Marquess of Dorset (1451-1501), to Cicely (d. 1530), dau. and heir of William Bonville, Lord Harington, *q.v.* Their grandson Henry Grey, Duke of Suffolk, was executed for high treason 1554, and the estates reverted to the Crown. *Arms.* Barry of six Argent and Azure in chief three torteaux a label of three points Ermine (VCHL; BGA).

GREY. Shield on four poster bed from Millom Castle, dated 1642 and with initials FH, now at Hutton John; Ferdinando Hudleston, of Millom, M.P. for Cumberland 1624, marr. Jane, dau. of Sir Ralph Grey, of Chillingham (N). *Arms.* Gules a lion rampant within a bordure engrailed Argent.

GREYSTOKE, Baron Greystoke (First line). Henry I granted the barony of Greystoke to Forne son of Lyulph, whose descendants took the name de Greystoke. The family failed in the male line on the death *s.p.* 1305/6 of John, Lord Greystoke, who left his lands and lordships to his cousin Ralph FitzWilliam (see Greystoke, Second line) (EDP). *Arms.* Gules three lozenges or cushions Argent. Certain Rolls shew the cushions Or (FFC), and a shield on the ceiling of Carlisle Cathedral displays: Gules three cushions Argent tasselled Or. *Supporters.* Two wingless wyverns (GEC).

GREYSTOKE, *olim* FITZWILLIAM, Baron Greystoke (Second line). Ralph FitzWilliam, Lord Greystoke (d. 1315/6) 2nd son of William FitzRalph, Lord of Grimthorpe, by Joan, dau. of Thomas de Greystoke, of the first line, *q.v.* (d. 1246), succ. his cousin John, Lord Greystoke. His grandson Ralph (d. 1374/5) assumed the surname but not the arms of Greystoke. The barony passed to the Dacres by the marr. of Elizabeth (d. 1516), dau. of Robert de

Greystoke (d. *v.p.* 1483), and granddau. and heir of Ralph, 7th Lord Greystoke (d. 1487), to Thomas, 2nd Baron Dacre of Gilsland, *q.v.* (EDP). *Arms.* Barry Argent and Azure three chaplets Gules. *Crest.* A lion passant guardant Or. *Supporters.* Two dolphins. *Badges.* A dolphin; a lion passant guardant crowned. *Motto.* Volo non valeo (FFC; shields, carvings, etc., at Naworth, Greystoke, Lanercost, and elsewhere in Cumberland; BGA).

GRICE. An old family, long established in the Millom area, the Grices have played a prominent part in the public life of Cumberland. The name appears in Millom parish registers from the early 17th century. The Rev. John Grice (1767-1845) was Curate of Bootle, and Minister of Drigg and Irton 1797-1842. Thomas Grice, of Bootle, was father of Richard Grice, J.P.,* of Cross House in that parish (1860-1937), who was a member of Cumberland County Council 1910-32. His son Richard Gerald Grice, C.B.E., A.R.I.B.A., Dip. T.P., of Cross House, Bootle, was Chairman of the Lake District Planning Board and was for many years a member of Cumberland County Council; he was High Sheriff 1967. *Arms.* Vert a lyre Or on a chief wavy of the last a boar statant Sable between two roses Gules (Drawing supplied by R. G. Grice).

GRIFFITH. Professor Chester L. Shaver's paper on this family in CW2 lxiii shows that Gabriel Griffith, master gunner in Carlisle Castle (d. 1750), marr. (2) 1697 Grace, dau. of Richard Eaglesfield, of Allerby, *q.v.* His 3rd son by that marr., Gabriel Griffith, merchant in Whitehaven (d. 1775), marr. at Newton Reigny 1740 Ann (1713-78), dau. of Thomas Cookson, mercer, of Penrith (1676-1721), *q.v.*, and was ancestor of Robert Griffith Page, M.D., of Chicago. *Arms.* Ermins [*sic*] a lion rampant Sable (CW2 lxiii 199). This should presumably be: Ermine a lion rampant Sable.

GRIMSHAW. Impaled by Nayler, *q.v.*, on tablet in Greystoke church; Capt Thomas Nayler, R.M. (d. 1802), marr. (1) Mary Grimshaw, of Preston. *Arms.* Argent a griffin segreant Sable.

GRINDAL. Edmund Grindal, M.A., D.D. (Cantab) (1519-83), a native of St. Bees, where his family had long been established, was Master of Pembroke Hall, Cambridge, 1558-61, Bishop of London 1558-70, Archbishop of York 1570-75, and Archbishop of Canterbury 1576-83. In the year of his death, he founded St. Bees School; he died unmarr. *Arms* (granted 1559). Quarterly Argent and Azure a cross quarterly Ermines and Or between four doves collared counterchanged (BBE). This is tricked in Harl. MS 1536 as: Quarterly Or and Azure a cross quarterly Ermine and . . . between four doves counterchanged (FVC); which MVC tricks as: Quarterly Or and Azure a cross quarterly Ermine and Or between four doves collared and counterchanged. Jefferson blazons the arms on the Archbishop's monument in Croydon church, Surrey, as: Quarterly Or and Azure a cross quartered Ermine and Or between four pea-hens collared and counterchanged (JAW). MMD gives for Grindal: Quarterly Argent and Vert a cross quarterly Ermine and Argent between four birds counterchanged.†

GROSVENOR. Impaled by Pennington in window at Muncaster Castle; Gamel Augustus, 4th Baron Muncaster (1831-62), marr. 1855 Jane Louisa Octavia, 8th dau. of Richard, 2nd Marquess of Westminster. *Arms.* Azure a

* His wife, a dau. of George John Muriel, *q.v.*, was also a magistrate for Cumberland.

† The Archbishop's arms, impaled by those of the See of Canterbury, *q.v.*, are on a shield on Pow Beck Bridge, St. Bees, with date 1583, as: . . . a cross . . . between four birds . . . .

garb Or. The complete coat of Grosvenor is on a font in Muncaster church, viz. Quarterly, 1 & 4, [Azure] a portcullis with chains pendent [Or] a chief [of the last] thereon between on either side the united rose of York and Lancaster [Proper] a pallet [of the first] charged with a cross flory between five martlets [also Gold], being the arms of the City of Westminster; 2 & 3, [Azure] a garb [Or].

GUBBINS. Lt-Col Richard Rolls Gubbins, D.S.O., J.P., of The Old Hall, Rockcliffe (1868-1918), marr. 1902 Agnes, dau. and heir of George William Mounsey-Heysham, *q.v.*, and had an elder son Richard Heysham Gubbins, who assumed the additional names of Mounsey-Heysham, see that family. The younger son, Major William John Mounsey Gubbins, D.L., T.D., of Eden Lacy, was High Sheriff of Cumberland 1959. *Arms.* Argent three pallets Gules over all on a bend Sable a human heart between two escallops Or. *Crest.* A pellet charged with a demi lion rampant Argent holding in the paws a heart Gold. *Motto.* Nil sine corde (FD7).

GULDEFORD. Burke gives the following for Guldeford, of Cumberland and Northumberland. *Arms.* Argent two bars each cotised Sable (BGA). FFC gives for Sir John de Guldeford, of the North (E. II Roll): Argent two bars gemel Sable.

GULLY, Viscount Selby of Carlisle. William Court Gully, P.C., M.A., LL.D., (Cantab), D.C.L. (Oxon), Q.C. (1835-1909), son of James Manby Gully, M.D. (DNB), was a barrister at law on the Northern Circuit, and was M.P. for Carlisle 1892-1905 and Speaker of the House of Commons 1895-1905, when he was cr. Viscount Selby, of the City of Carlisle. The present holder of the title is his great-grandson Michael Guy John, 4th Viscount. *Arms.* Or a lion rampant Sable between four escallops two and two fesswise Gules on a chief of the last as many escallops of the field.* *Crest.* a cubit arm vested Sable cuff Argent the hand grasping a sword erect Proper between two wings each per pale nebuly the dexter of the last and Gules and the sinister Gules and Or.* *Supporters.* Dexter, An owl Sable charged with a balance Or; Sinister, An eagle Sable charged with a portcullis also Gold (BP105). *Motto.* Nec temere nec tarde.

GUNSON. Joseph Gunson, of Ingwell, near Whitehaven (d. 1838),† a company commander in the Peninsular War, marr. 1816 Ann Frances (b. 1783), dau. and heir of Edmund Lamplugh Irton, *q.v.*, and his wife Dorothy, dau. of Matthew Hodgson. His daus. and coheirs were Anne Eliza (d. 1906), marr. 1844 Frecheville Lawson Ballantine Dykes, *q.v.*, and Mary (d. 1885), marr. 1850 Robert Lambert Turner, J.P., Capt 87th Royal Irish Engineers (1824-1901), who assumed the additional surname Irton 1884, and left four daus. and coheirs (BLG11). *Arms.* Or three bars wavy Sable the one in chief charged with three plates the second with two and the third with one on a chief Azure the barrel of a cannon Gold (Brass in Bromfield church).

HADDOCK. Richard Haddock, of Lazonby, gentleman (d. 1686), named as executors in his will dated 1686 his cousins James Haddock, of Carlisle, and

* DPB 1948 blazons the field of the arms as Argent, and the two wings in the crest as Or.

† Writing on 27 June 1825 to her son, Elizabeth Hudleston says "Mr. Gunson return'd to Whitehaven & received by all as if nothing had happened – this shows what money will do."

William Emerson, of Lazonby. *Arms.* . . . three chevronels interlaced in base . . . on a chief . . . a (?) saltire* . . . (Seal on will).

HADDON. GMC records the following, without specifying any place of residence. *Arms.* Or a man's leg couped at the thigh Azure.

HAINES. GMS records the following for Haines, in Cumberland, without further details. *Arms.* Azure three fishes hauriant Argent.

HALE. The Rev. Bernard George Richard Hale, M.A. (Oxon) (1859-1925), only son of Bernard Hale, of Doncaster, barrister at law, was Vicar of Edenhall with Langwathby 1898-1923. His only son, Bernard John Windham Hale, Paymaster Commander, R.N.V.R., of Mell Fell House, Watermillock (b. 1905), was killed on active service 1945, and the latter's eldest son Lt-Cdr Timothy John Windham Hale, R.N., of Larkbeare House, Whimple, Devon, is the present representative of the family. *Arms.* Azure a chevron embattled counter-embattled Or. *Crest.* A snake Proper entwined round five arrows Or headed Sable feathered Argent one in pale four saltireways. *Motto.* Vera sequor (BLG4; BLG18, *sub* Hildyard).

HALL, of Gilcrux. Joseph Hall, of Gilcrux, was father of, *int. al.,* William (1756-91), Lieut Bombay Artillery; the Rev. Matthew (1760-99) who was tutor to the Senhouses at Netherhall and Curate of Ponsonby 1789-99; Samuel, of Gilcrux (1764-1836); and Henry (1770-1820), who was Deputy Master Attendant at Madras and later of Carlisle. The Rev. Matthew Hall's only son Capt Humphrey Senhouse Hall, 40th Madras N.I., died *s.p.* 1827, aged 39, and the male line failed. Samuel Hall's niece Elizabeth, eldest dau. of Joseph Hall, marr. Thomas Adcock, of Workington; they took the surname Hall and she was granted arms 1836. Their son was Henry Hall Hall. *Arms.* The Rev. Matthew Hall sealed his will with: . . . a chevron engrailed . . . between three talbots' heads erased . . . . *Crest.* Out of a ducal coronet a (?) griffin's head gorged with a collar. The arms granted to Elizabeth Hall, *olim* Adcock, and her issue were: Argent two chevronels Gules between three talbots' heads erased Sable. *Crest.* A talbot's head erased Sable surmounting an estoile irradiated Or (CA xli 343-4).

HALL, of Skirwith. The family of John Hall, of Skirwith, used before 1768 the arms of the Halls of Birtley (D), but in that year John's son William Hall, of St. Stephen, Coleman Street, London, merchant, obtained a grant of arms, very like the arms formerly used. *Arms.* Or on a chevron Sable between three demi lions passant Azure five barrulets Argent on a chief Gules the same number of chaplets as lions of the fourth. *Crest.* A crown mural Argent thereout issuant a dexter arm embowed habited Azure fretty Or cuff Argent in the hand Proper a dagger Silver hilted and pommelled Gold (CA xi/280).

HALL. John Hall, of Northsceugh, Cumwhitton, was father of John Hall, of Rock House, Walton (L). and Mollance, Kirkcudbrightshire, who in 1839 obtained a grant of arms for himself and his father's descendants. *Arms.* Per bend Argent and Or a lion rampant Proper murally crowned Gules within an orle of guttes de Sang. *Crest.* In front of a garb Vert banded Or a castle Proper (CA xliii/341).

HALLIBURTON.† John Halliburton, *alias* Burton, who may have been a Scot by birth, was a tenant-farmer in Bewcastle from about 1720 until his

* This charge is very indistinct and could be intended for two batons in saltire.

† Contributed by Roger Smith.

death in 1751. Of his four sons, three left descendants who, by the end of the 18th century, were farming in Brampton, Walton and Askerton as well as Bewcastle, while others were tradesmen in Carlisle and Alston. Subsequent generations largely gave up farming and the family became concentrated in Brampton where they were engaged in various trades for much of the 19th century. However, by the end of the century the Cumberland Halliburtons had declined to a few scattered families in Carlisle and Penrith (and some of the latter may have been of distinct origin). *Arms.* The arms displayed on the Bewcastle tombstone of Mary (d. 1791, aged 27), née Potts, of Bleatarn, Irthington, wife of John Hallyburton, of Askerton Castle (see CW2 lxxii 337), are those of the Haliburtons of Eaglescarnie, in East Lothian, a branch of the former Lords Haliburton of Dirleton: [Or] on a bend wavy [Azure] three lozenges [of the first]. *Crest.* A boar's head couped and erect [Proper]. *Motto.* Watch weel.

HALLOWES. Col John Hallowes, 56th and 58th Regiments, son of Thomas Hallowes, of Glapwell, Dethick and Mugginton (Dy) (b. 1684), and his wife Lady Catherine Brabazon, was of Penrith between 1788 and 1796, with his 2nd wife Louisa Martha, dau. of Francis Fatio, of St Augustine's, Florida (descended from the Fazios, of Pisa), and widow of George Bruere, Lt-Governor of Bermuda, to whom she was marr. at the age of 14. *Arms.* Azure on a fess between three crescents Argent as many torteaux. *Crest.* A demi griffin rampant Sable winged Argent (BLG5).

HALTON. John de Halton was Bishop of Carlisle 1292-1324. Field suggests that he may have been of the same family as the Haltons of Greenthwaite (FAC). *Arms.* (Possibly) . . . a lion rampant . . . (BBE).

HALTON, of Greenthwaite. William de Halton, of Halton (L), was also of Greenthwaite Hall, Greystoke, 1346. From him descended Miles Halton, of Greenthwaite Hall (1599-1653), Sheriff of Cumberland 1652, who marr. Dorothy Wybergh (d. 1697, aged 89). Their son Immanuel Halton, of Greenthwaite Hall, and of Wingfield Manor (Dy) (1628-99), mathematician and astronomer, was agent and auditor to the 6th Duke of Norfolk. His great-grandson, Col Winfield Halton, D.L., J.P. (1760-1831), sold Greenthwaite 1795. From a younger branch of the family descended Lt-Col Frederick William Halton, T.D., of The Grey House, Etterby, Carlisle (1872-1965), who in 1954 obtained a grant of arms for himself and the descendants of his father, John Halton, of Carlisle (1821-1911). *Arms* (as borne by Immanuel Halton, above). Quarterly, 1 & 4, Per pale Azure and Gules a lion rampant Argent (Halton)*; 2 & 3, Argent three bars between as many mullets Gules (Wybergh). *Arms* (as granted 1954). Per pale Azure and Gules a barrulet Argent over all a lion rampant Or. *Crest.* Out of a wreath of oak fructed Or a lion sejant Argent supporting with the dexter paw a broken spear Proper (BLG18). *Motto.* Tam pace quam bello (FBC). Above the entrance to Greenthwaite Hall are two shields. The smaller with initials MHD, for Miles Halton (d. 1653) and Dorothy Wybergh, his wife, date 1650, and inscription PEREGRINOS HIC NOS REPVTAMVS, displays: . . . a lion rampant guardant . . . . The larger, with date 1660, displays: . . . a lion rampant . . . ; impaling, . . . three bars . . . between as many mullets . . . . *Crest.* A demi lion rampant holding a spear.

* LMC records: Per pale Gules and Azure a lion rampant Or.

HAMILTON, of Whitehaven. The Hamilton family was one of the first to whom land was granted in Whitehaven by the Lowthers after they obtained the lordship of St. Bees. Anthony Hamilton was father of John Hamilton, a Whitehaven merchant (1669-1739), whose son Isaac Hamilton (1708-80) was a surgeon in the town and marr. 1737 Frances (d. 1792, aged 76), dau. and coheir of Isaac Langton, of Whitehaven. His eldest son John Hamilton (1739-1814) was High Sheriff of Cumberland 1799 and marr. 1790 Elizabeth, widow of James Spedding, of Summergrove, *q.v.*, and dau. of Thomas Harrington *q.v.* His younger brother Lt-Col Anthony Hamilton, Bengal Army (1752-1830), lived for many years in retirement in Roper Street, Whitehaven. *Crest.* Out of a ducal coronet an oak tree penetrated transversely by a frame-saw (Seal).

HAMMERTON. William Hammerton, of Cockermouth (d. 1811), was uncle of Mary Hammerton, who marr. John Gregory Crump, of Allan Bank, Grasmere (AWL). *Arms.* Argent three hammers Sable (M.I., Lowther church (W)).

HARCLA. Sir Michael de Harcla, of Hartley (W), was Sheriff of Cumberland 1285-98. His son Sir Andrew Harcla, Warden of the West Marches and Sheriff of Cumberland 1311, 1312-16, 1318 and 1319-23, was cr. Earl of Carlisle 1322. He was arrested on a charge of treason and executed the following year (WMP). *Arms.* Sir Michael bore: Argent a cross Gules. This coat is on the ceiling of Carlisle Cathedral. The Earl of Carlisle bore: Argent a cross Gules in the first quarter a martlet Sable (FFC).

HARDING. Christopher Harding, of Readhill, Irthington, householder (d. 1769, aged 40), bore for *Arms.* . . . on a bend . . . three martlets . . . (Harding); impaling, . . . a fess . . . and in chief a sun in splendour between two fleurs-de-lys . . . (Irthington tombstone).

HARE. Shields at Hutton-in-the-Forest; Sir George Fletcher, 2nd Bart., *q.v.*, marr. 1665 (1) Alice Hare (b. 1633), dau. of Hugh, 1st Baron Colcraine* (d. 1667, aged 61). *Arms.* Gules two bars and a chief indented Or. Other shields display (incorrectly): Barry of six Or and Gules a chief indented of the last. On a tablet in Hutton-in-the-Forest church the arms are impaled as: Gules three bars Or the upper edge of the one in chief indented. See YBD.

HARE. The Rev. Edward Christian, B.D. (Cantab) (1752-1807), a cadet of Milntown and Unerigg and Rector of Workington and Ousby, assumed the name and arms of Hare 1798, when he succ. his cousin Catherine, dau. and heir of the Hon. Hugh Charles Hare and widow of Henry Holt Henley, M.P. His descendants include Anthony Edward Christian Hare, Ph.D. (Lond), M.A. (Cantab), of the Old Rectory, Ormside, lecturer in economics in the University of Leeds 1946-71; and Major Ewan John Christian Hare, R.A., O.B.E., T.D., of Castle Park, Appleby. *Arms.* Gules two bars and a chief indented Or. *Crest.* A demi lion rampant Argent gorged with a ducal coronet Or. *Motto.* Noli altum sapere sed time (BLG17).

HARFORD-BATTERSBY – see BATTERSBY.

HARINGTON, Baron Harington. The Haringtons, who take their name from Harrington, descend from Osulph or Aculf, of Flimby, *temp.* Richard

* NB (ii 390) incorrectly shews him as Earl of Colerain, and BP58 (p. 1446) as Viscount Coleraine.

I. His descendant Sir Robert de Harington (d. 1297) marr. the heiress of the Cansfield family and was father of Sir John Harington, 1st Lord Harington (1281-1347), whose son Sir Robert (d. *v.p.* in or before 1334) marr. *c.* 1327 Elizabeth (b. *c.* 1306), dau. of Thomas de Multon, and sister of John Lord Multon of Egremont, *q.v.*, and so acquired a third of that barony. The male line failed with William, 5th Lord Harington (d. 1458), whose dau. and heir Elizabeth marr. *c.* 1442 Sir William Bonville, *q.v.* The baronies of Multon of Egremont and Harington are in abeyance, subject to attainder, between the descendants of their descendant Henry Grey, Duke of Suffolk (executed 1554) (GEC). *Arms.* Sable fretty Argent (FFC)*. *Crest.* A lion's head (GHF). *Badge.* A fret, or the Harington knot. Shields at Hutton John display the arms as borne by a younger branch of the family, viz. Sable a fret Argent; Sir Richard Hudleston, of Millom, temp. Henry V, marr. Katherine, dau. of Sir Nicholas Harington (d. 1403).

HARINGTON, of Kelston. Shield at Hutton John; the Ven. Lawson Hudleston, Archdeacon of Bath, Canon of Wells, Rector of Kelston, Som. (1678-1743), marr. 1711 Helena (d. 1748), dau. of John Harington, of Kelston. *Arms.* Sable a fret Argent and a bordure compony countercompony of the second and the first. Burke gives for Harington, of Kelston: Sable a fret humetté Argent a bordure chequy of the first and second (BGA). At Kelston the arms repeatedly occur as a simple fret, without the bordure.

HARINGTON, of Wooloaks. This family descends from the Haringtons of Wraysholme Tower (L), who were themselves descended from the Haringtons of Harrington, see Harington, Baron Harington, and AWL. William Harington, of Wraysholme, marr. Anne, dau. of Sir Thomas Parr, of Kendal, see AWL. Their son Thomas, attainted for his part in Lambert Simnel's rising 1487, forfeited Wraysholme and died *s.p.*, the line being continued by his brother Nicholas, who, marrying the dau. and heir of Richard Leyburn, acquired Yewbarrow Hall (W). Their son Thomas (d. 1542) was of Wooloaks, Hesket-in-the-Forest, where he was succ. by his son James (*c.* 1538-1606). His son and heir Thomas (*c.* 1576-1642) succ. but died *s.p. legit.* and the line was continued by his brother James. The estates were eventually inherited by Edmund Harington, of Wooloaks, Yewbarrow and Troutbeck (W) (d. 1698), whose sons died young, his daus. and coheirs being Margaret (b. 1662); Lettice (d. 1698), marr. 1677 the Rev. Henry Stephenson, Vicar of Brigham; and Katherine (d. 1690), marr. 1678 John Wilson, of Brackenburgh, Hesket-in-the-Forest (VCHL viii; FCW). *Arms.* See Harington, Baron Harington, and AWL.

HARKER. A window in Holy Trinity, Millom, given by Elizabeth Harker, 1908, in memory of her parents Jonathan and Elizabeth Harker, of Salthouse Farm, Millom, contains three roundles, as follows, which may perhaps have some heraldic significance: (i) Sable a burst of flame Gules; (ii) Argent three bars wavy Azure; (iii) Gules a chalice Argent.

HARRINGTON, of Carlisle. For a pedigree of this family, see CW2 xlvi. Thomas Harrington, of Fisher Street, Carlisle, tanner, was father of *int. al.* Elizabeth (1745-1821) who may have been his eventual heir or coheir; she marr. (1) 1779 James Spedding, of Summergrove (d. 1788), *q.v.*, and (2) 1790 John Hamilton, of Whitehaven, *q.v.* The above Thomas had a nephew

* MMD tricks for Harrington: Or a bend and a chief Gules.

Robert Harrington, M.D. (1751-1837), for whom see DNB. *Arms.* Sable a fret Argent. *Motto.* Nodo firmo (Impaled by Spedding in the west window in St. Bees Priory, and on a tablet; Shields formerly at Summergrove, on one of which the arms are quartered by Spedding).

HARRIS, of Brackenburgh and Greysouthen. Joseph Harris, J.P., of Greysouthen (1780-1860), an extensive colliery owner, was succ. by his son John Harris, D.L., J.P. (1827-63), whose son Joseph Harris, D.L., J.P., Capt and Hon. Major Westmorland and Cumberland Yeomanry (1859-1946) built Brackenburgh Tower, Calthwaite. He was High Sheriff of Cumberland 1895. His elder son John Frederick Harris, of The Old Tower, Brackenburgh (b. 1902), was High Sheriff 1936. He marr. (1) 1926 Gwendolen Arden, dau. and heir of George Colville Arden Kentish, *q.v.*, and (2) 1944 Violet Mary Arnison, younger dau. of Jacob Vickers, J.P., of Wandales, Wetheral. His only son Joseph Hugh Harris, of Brackenburgh (b. 1932), was High Sheriff of Cumbria 1976. *Arms.* Or a chevron invected Ermine between three escutcheons Azure each charged with a hedgehog Proper. *Crest.* A stag's head erased Proper gorged with a chain Or pendent therefrom an escutcheon Azure thereon a hedgehog as in the arms between the attires a chaplet of roses Gules leaved Vert. *Motto.* My prince and my country (FD7).

HARRIS. Impaled by Pattenson on hatchment in Melmerby church; John Pattenson, of Melmerby Hall (1774-1817), *q.v.*, marr. 1801 Mary Anna Frances Antoinetta (d. 1837), eldest dau.* of Stephen Harris, indigo planter, of Comilla, Bengal. *Arms.* Sable an antelope salient Argent armed crined and hoofed Or. *Crest.* A demi antelope Proper armed Or.

HARRISON, of Greystoke, Penrith and London. William Harrison, merchant, of Penrith and London, 2nd son of John Harrison, of Greystoke, obtained 1607 from Norroy a confirmation of the following *Arms.* Or on a fess Sable three eagles displayed of the first. *Crest.* On a chapeau Gules turned up Ermine an eagle's head erased Or charged with a crescent Sable (HNB).

HARRISON, of Linethwaite and Hards. Joseph Harrison, of Hards, Holm Cultram (1740-1804), had a 4th son George Harrison, of Linethwaite (1786-1861), who was principal clerk in the bank of Hartley, Potter & Co., Whitehaven, and later a merchant in Whitehaven, and High Sheriff of Cumberland 1844. He marr. 1810 Juliana, dau. and heir of Capt Thomas Barwise, of Whitehaven (d. 1823). Their son Joseph (1811-48) marr. 1837 his cousin Juliana (d. 1846), dau. and coheir of John Barwise, of Lowsay, and had a son Julian Cuthbert William Harrison, of Linethwaite (1844-71) who died unmarr. His sisters and coheirs were Juliana Georgiana (1838-69), marr. 1858 James Lumb, *q.v.*; Joanna Josephine (b. 1840); and Claudine Elizabeth (1842-67), marr. 1865 Capt J. G. M. Tulloch, 21st Fusiliers (CW2 xlvi; BLG5). *Arms.* Per pale Gules and Azure an eagle displayed Or murally gorged of the first between two pheons in fess Argent a chief indented Erminois. *Crest.* The fasces fesswise Proper banded Gules surmounted by an anchor erect entwined by a cable all Or (BGA). *Motto.* Sans devoir (M.I., Holm Cultram church).

HARRISON, of Scalesceugh and Wreay Hall. John Harrison, of Gatesgill,

* Eliza (d. 1838, aged 54), another dau., marr. 1802 Charles Pattenson, Bengal Civil Service (1776-1831), the above John Pattenson's brother.

marr. 1854 Frances (d. 1909), dau. and heir of John Robinson, of Scalesceugh, *q.v.* Their son John Robinson Harrison (1865-1923) was co-founder of the shipping firm of Messrs. Gow, Harrison of Glasgow. He inherited the Scalesceugh estate and in 1913 built the present mansion and returned to live in Cumberland. He had three sons – Ion Robinson Harrison (d. 1953), who had an elder son Iain Vittorio Robinson Harrison, of Craighat, Killearn, Stirlingshire, now head of the family; Frank Hamilton Keay Harrison, of Scalesceugh (1893-1961), High Sheriff of Cumberland 1943; and Gerald Joseph Cuthbert Harrison (1895-1954), who was M.P. for Bodmin 1924-29 and High Sheriff of Cumberland 1945. The latter's eldest son G. J. R. Harrison died 1970, and his brother Major Antony James Robinson Harrison, Scots Guards, who is of Wreay Hall (bought by his grandfather in 1919), is now representative of the family in Cumberland. *Arms.* Azure two barrulets wavy between in chief two lymphads sails furled pennons flying and in base an anchor erect all Or. *Crest.* A trident erect Sable in front of two anchors in saltire Or. *Motto.* Fear God and honour the King.

HARRISON, of Seascale. For details of this family from Matthew Harrison, of Ambleside and The Lund, Ulverston (d. 1824, aged 71), see AWL. The representation of the family devolved upon Gilbert Henry Wordsworth Harrison, Lieut 104th Bengal Fusiliers, of Manx View, Seascale (b. 1853), son of Wordsworth Harrison, J.P., of The Lund (1826-89), and grandson of Benson Harrison (see AWL). His son was Matthew Charles Coverley Harrison, Lieut 3rd Batt. The Loyal North Lancashire Regt (b. 1885), who had a son Michael Isherwood Harrison (b. 1916). *Arms.* Argent three piles two in chief and one in base Azure each charged with a demi lion couped of the field. *Crest.* A demi lion rampant Argent resting the sinister paw upon a clarion Or and charged on the shoulder with three hurts two and one each charged with a cross pattée also Argent (CA liii/276). *Motto.* Vincit qui patitur (FD7).

HARRISON. Impaled by Shaw on monument in Crosby-on-Eden church; the Rev. Henry Shaw, J.P., *q.v.*, marr. Jane Harrison (d. 1808, aged 82). *Arms.* Or on a chief Gules three eagles displayed of the field.

HARRISON, of Winscales and Stainburn. Thomas Harrison, of Winscales (d. 1812, aged 68), was father of John Harrison, D.L., J.P. (d. 1844, aged 78), and of Jane, who marr. William Falcon, *q.v.* Their son John Falcon, J.P. (1798-1866), assumed the surname Harrison 1844, and was succ. by his son William Falcon Harrison (1839-81), who left three daus. and coheirs – Ann Falcon Harrison (b. 1868), marr. . . . Carter; Violet Catherine (b. 1870); and Jane Mildred (b. 1871) (BLG5; *ex inf.* Commander Hugh Falcon-Steward). *Arms.* Quarterly, 1 & 4, Argent two bars gemel Sable between three hares courant Proper (Harrison); 2 & 3, Ermine two chevronels per pale Azure and Sable between three falcons close Proper belled Or each holding in the beak a lure also Or (Falcon). *Crests.* 1, Upon a mount Vert a stag courant reguardant Sable semé of quatrefoils attired and unguled Or holding in the mouth an arrow in bend sinister point downwards Proper (Harrison); 2, On a fret Sable a falcon rising Proper belled Or and holding in the beak a lure Or (Falcon) (*Ex inf.* Cdr Hugh Falcon-Steward). *Motto.* Vite courageux fier (FBC).

HARTLEY, of Gillfoot and Armathwaite. This family was originally of

Bridekirk, where Thomas Hartley was living 1620. His son Thomas settled in Whitehaven 1668. The family established a ropery there and later, in 1786, founded the town's first bank. In the 19th century branches of the family lived at Gillfoot, Egremont, at Linethwaite, Hensingham, and Rosehill, Moresby. In 1880 the senior representative, Thomas Hartley, D.L., J.P., of Gillfoot (1847-1929), son of Thomas Hartley, D.L., J.P. (1802-55), High Sheriff of Cumberland 1839, bought the Armathwaite estate and built the Hall, now the Armathwaite Hall Hotel; he was High Sheriff 1887. His son Thomas Milham Hartley, B.A. (Cantab) (1878-1966), sold the estate 1931 and bought Silchester House, Hants. He was the last male of the family, his only son Major Thomas Fitzhardinge Hartley, R.A. (1912-42), having died on active service. *Arms.* Argent on a cross cotised Gules four quatrefoils Or in the first and second quarters a martlet Sable (BLG11; FD7). On a monument in St. John's, Bassenthwaite, the quatrefoils are cinquefoils and the martlets are in the first and fourth quarters. On a monument in Egremont church appears the following variant: Argent on a cross quarter pierced Gules four cinquefoils Or in the first and fourth quarters a martlet Sable. There is a similar variant on shields in Kirkoswald church and in The College, Kirkoswald, except that instead of the cross being quarter pierced, it is plain* pierced, in one instance Or.† The bookplate of Hartley, of Rosehill, displays: Argent a cross Gules charged with another of the field thereon four cinquefoils Or in the first and fourth quarters a martlet Sable. *Crest.* The family originally used: A martlet Sable holding in the beak a cross crosslet fitché Or (BLG5; M.I., Egremont church‡§). They were later granted: On a chaplet of oak Proper a martlet Sable holding in the beak a cross botonny fitché Or (BLG11; FD7). *Motto.* Per crucem ad coelum.

HARTLEY, of Wodow Bank. William Hartley (d. 1815, aged 70), was of Wodow Bank, Beckermet, where his son Joseph (d. 1838, aged 44) succ. him. William Hartley, solicitor, was there in 1849-58. *Arms.* Or a cross between four martlets Azure. *Crest.* In front of a terrestrial globe a dove holding in its beak an olive branch (Tombstone, St. John's churchyard, Beckermet).

HARTNESS. John Hartness, of Cockermouth, died 1828, aged 61; his wife Jane died 1817, aged 47. *Arms.* Or semé of trefoils slipped a stag trippant reguardant . . . ; impaling, Or three crescents issuing from each a galtrap, or mullet of four points . . . on a chief Gules a greyhound courant . . . . *Crest.* A hand couped at the wrist holding a Bible. *Mottoes.* A ma puissance; Semper paratus (Gravestone, All Saints' churchyard, Cockermouth).

HASELL, of Dalemain. Sir Edward Hasell (1647-1707), descended from a Bottisham, Cambs., family, was steward to Lady Anne Clifford and High Sheriff of Cumberland 1682. He bought Dalemain 1675, was knighted 1699, and was M.P. for Cumberland 1701. He marr. (2) 1696 Dorothy, dau. and coheir of William Williams, of Johnby Hall, and was succ. by his son Edward (d. 1781, aged 83), who was High Sheriff 1727. His eldest son Williams Hasell (1736-86) succ. and was High Sheriff 1779. He marr. Mary

* I.e., the perforation is circular.

† The colours in The College are so faded and discoloured that what appears to be Or may originally have been Argent.

‡ Where the cross has been broken.

§ A family bookplate shows the crest as: A martlet Proper.

(b. 1737), dau. and coheir of John Gaskarth, *q.v.* but d. *s.p.* and was succ. by his brother Edward (1737-94), who was High Sheriff 1792. Their nephew Edward Hasell (d. 1825, aged 59) succ. and was High Sheriff 1802 and Lt-Col Commandant of the West and East Wards of local militia.* His son Lt-Col Edward Williams Hasell, D.L., J.P., M.A. (Oxon) (1795-1872) was Chairman of Cumberland and Westmorland Quarter Sessions, Chairman of the Carlisle-Lancaster Railway, and commanded the Westmorland and Cumberland Yeomanry Cavalry 1831-71. His 3rd, but eldest surviving, son John Edward Hasell, D.L., J.P., B.A. (Oxon) (1839-1910) succ. but dying *s.p.m.*† was succ. by his brother, the Rev. George Edmund Hasell, J.P., M.A. (Oxon) (1847-1932), who was Rector of Aikton 1872-1911, Rural Dean of Wigton 1888-1911, and Hon. Canon of Carlisle 1897-1932. His elder son Edward William Hasell, D.L., J.P., M.A. (Oxon), (1888-1972), Major Westmorland and Cumberland Yeomanry, succ. his father by deed of gift 1920. He was High Sheriff of Westmorland, 1927, and Vice-Lieutenant of the County. His two daus. and coheirs are Sylvia Mary, who marr. (1) 1944 Henry William Somerville Marshall, Scots Guards, killed in action 1944, and (2) 1948 Bryce Knox McCosh, of Huntfield, Biggar, Lanarkshire, and Margaret Helen, wife of Lt-Col T. J. C. Washington, M.C., *q.v.* Mrs. McCosh succ. her father in the estates and is Lady of the Barony of Barton and Lady of the Manors of Dalemain, Dacre, Barton, Martindale and Patterdale. Her cousin, Major John Antony Edward Hasell (b. 1930), who lives in Canada, is the male representative of the family. *Arms.* Or on a fess Azure between three hazel slips Proper three crescents Argent. *Crest.* A squirrel sejant cracking a nut between two oak branches all Proper (LMC). This achievement is now blazoned: *Arms.* Or on a fess Azure between three hazel nuts Proper husks stalks and leaves Vert as many crescents Argent. *Crest.* A squirrel sejant Argent cracking a hazel nut proper and encircled with two hazel branches crossing each other at the top Vert. *Motto.* Labor vincit omnia (BLG17).

HASTINGS, of Croglin. Denton says that Philip Hastings held Croglin *temp.* Henry II and a man of these names is mentioned 1214 and 1220-40. Denton adds that *temp.* Edward I the manor passed by marr. to the Wharton family, and a pedigree in CW2 xxiii confirms this, showing Nicholas Hastings as father of an heiress Emma, who marr. (1) Robert de Newbiggin, living 1329, and aged 70 and more; and (2) Gilbert de Querton (Wharton), living 1303-4; and (3) Richard le Keu (living 1322-23). The Hastings family also owned the manors of Crosby Ravensworth and Nateby (W) (CW2 xi, xx). *Arms.* Argent a maunch Sable (FFC).

HASWELL. Col John Francis Haswell, C.I.E., V.D., T.D., M.D. (Edin) (1864-1949), son of Francis Robert Newton Haswell, of Monkseaton (N), was of The Friarage, Penrith, and was a doctor in the town for many years, and Medical Officer of Health 1904-35. He served in the Boer War, and commanded the 2/4th Border Regt in World War I; he also served in the

* His splendid monument by Chantrey in Dacre church bears a long inscription, which says (*int. al.*) that he was "generous, kind, and liberal in deed and in thought and gifted in an eminent degree with all those high and good qualities which are wont to endear a man to his fellow creatures."

† His daus., who were of Dacre Lodge, were Dorothy Julia, a magistrate and County Councillor (1883-1936), and Eva Frances Hatton, M.B.E., D.D. (Lambeth) (1887-1974), founder and hon. organiser of the Canadian Sunday School Caravan Mission.

Afghan War of 1919. A Vice-President of the Cumberland & Westmorland Antiquarian & Archaeological Society, he was a frequent contributor to *Transactions* and in 1945 was elected an honorary member of the Society. His elder son Brigadier Francis William Haswell, D.S.O. (1898-1973), served in World Wars I and II and was Inspector General of the Burma Frontier Constabulary 1946-48; he died in South Africa. His brother Major Hugh Reginald Haswell, The Border Regiment (retired) (b. 1904) and sister, Miss Beatrice Haswell, are of Inglebeck, Edenhall. *Arms.* Or on a bend Gules three goats statant Argent. *Crest.* A talbot's head erased gorged with a collar. *Motto.* Fidelite (Bookplate of J. F. Haswell).

HAWTE. Shields at Hutton-in-the-Forest; a Vane quartering. *Arms.* Or a cross engrailed Gules.

HAY, Earl of Carlisle. James Hay, K.G., P.C. (*c.* 1580-1636), son of Sir James Hay, of Kingask, was cr. Baron Hay 1606, Viscount Doncaster 1618, and Earl of Carlisle 1622. He was Gentleman of the Bedchamber to the King 1603-15, Ambassador to France, Spain, Germany and Venice, and Groom of the Stole 1631-36. He was Governor of the Caribbean Islands 1627. His son, the 2nd Earl (*c.* 1612-60), established his right to the island of Barbados, then called the Carlisle Islands, 1639, but died *s.p.* and the Earldom became extinct. *Arms.* Argent three escutcheons Gules (LMC).

HAY, Earl of Erroll. Charles Gore Hay, K.T., C.B., D.L., J.P., LL.D. (Aberdeen), 19th Earl of Erroll (1852-1927), Lord High Constable of Scotland, marr. at Muncaster 1875, when he was styled Lord Kilmarnock, Mary Caroline Louisa (1849-1934), dau. of Edmund L'Estrange, of Tynte House, Leitrim. For many years Lord and Lady Erroll lived at Walls Castle, Ravenglass. *Arms.* Argent three escutcheons Gules. *Crest.* A falcon rising Proper. *Supporters.* Two men in country habits each holding an ox yoke over his shoulder all Proper (BP58). Debrett (1909 edition) gives: Two savages wreathed about the middle with laurel Proper bearing on their shoulders two oxen yokes with bows Gules. *Motto.* Serva jugum.

HAYTHORNTHWAITE. James Haythornthwaite, of Greenhead, Low Bentham (d. 1876), was father of the Rev. Richard Haythornthwaite (1838-1908), Curate of St. Paul, Silloth, 1867-72, of Workington 1872-76, Vicar of Great Broughton 1876-78, and of Cleator Moor 1878-1908. Of his sons, the eldest, the Rev. John Parker Haythornthwaite, M.A. (Cantab) (1862-1928), was Curate of St. Luke, Barrow, 1885-88, and Vicar of King's Langley 1916-28; his grandson Dr. Richard Haythornthwaite is of Cheviot, New Zealand. The Rev. Richard Haythornthwaite above named had younger sons Edward Parker Haythornthwaite (see below) and the Rev. Richard Haythornthwaite, J.P., B.A. (Cantab) (b. 1871), who was Rector of Lamplugh 1909-42, a Member of Cumberland County Council and Chairman of Ennerdale R.D.C. The above Edward Parker Haythornthwaite, B.A. (Cantab), L.R.C.P., L.R.C.S. (Edin), of Rowrah House (1869-1953), practised in Rowrah 1906-47. His elder son the Rev. Alfred Parker Haythornthwaite was Curate of Aspatria 1935-38 and of Penrith 1938-45, Chaplain to the Forces 1939-45, Rector of Kirkby Thore with Temple Sowerby 1945-57, Vicar of Seascale 1957-67, and Vicar of Allithwaite 1967-76, and is now of St. Mary's Cottage, Kirkby Lonsdale. His elder sister Constance Parker, is wife of Canon H. E. W. Turner, M.A., D.D. (Oxon), of Realands, Eskdale Green, formerly Van Mildert Professor of Divinity in the University of Durham and his younger sister Anne Rosemary Parker marr. 1947 Henry Hall of the Old Hall, Oughterside. *Arms.* Argent a chevron Gules between three hunting horns Vert stringed of the second. *Crest.* A lion rampant Gules grasping a hawthorn tree fructed and in the dexter paw a scimitar defending the same Proper. *Motto.* Suffibulatus majores sequor (*Ex inf.* Mrs. H. E. W. Turner).

HEAD, of Carlisle and Rickerby. George Head, of Cockermouth, was father of Joseph Monkhouse Head, of Carlisle, banker (1759-1841). His only son, George Head Head, J.P., of Rickerby House, Carlisle, and Sprowston Hall, Norfolk, banker (d. 1876, aged 81), was High Sheriff of Cumberland 1851. He marr. (1) 1833 Maria Woodrouffe (d. 1854, aged 59), dau. and heir of Thomas Woodrouffe Smith, of Stockwell Park, Surrey, and (2) 1858 Sarah (d. 1876, aged 64), dau. of Samuel Gurney, of Upton, Essex. *Arms.* . . . a chevron Ermine between three unicorns' heads erased . . . . *Crest.* A unicorn's head couped.* *Motto.* Study quiet (M.I., Stanwix church). The arms are on the south face of Toppin Castle, Hayton (*ex inf.* J. V. Harrison and J. P. Godwin).

HEAD, of Foxleyhenning. To this old Dalston family belonged Hugh Head, whose wife was buried 1572; John, who marr. Grace Head 1574; and John, of Foxleyhenning (d. 1599). John Head, of Foxleyhenning, Dalston (will proved 1751), was father of the Rev. Erasmus Head,† M.A. (Oxon) (1711-63), who was Vicar of Lazonby 1737-39, Rector of Newburn (N) 1738-63, Prebendary of Carlisle 1742-63, and Vicar of Whittingham (N) 1744-63. He died *s.p.* and his heirs were his sisters Dinah, wife of William Scott; Ann, marr. John Dowson; and Margaret. *Arms.* . . . a chevron . . . between three unicorns' heads couped . . . (JMS A179).

HEADLAM. The Rev. Morley Lewis Caulfield Headlam, M.A. (Oxon) (1868-1953), later Prebendary and Canon Emeritus of Chichester, was Vicar of St. John, Keswick 1906-18. *Arms.* Gules on a chevron Or between three lambs' heads erased Argent as many crosses pattée fitché Sable. *Crest.* A unicorn passant Or the dexter foreleg resting upon a cross pattée fitché Sable. *Motto.* Intellectu et innocentia (BLG18). A ceremonial trowel at All Saints', Cockermouth, used by Canon Headlam's ancestor, the Ven. John Headlam, M.A., J.P., of Gilmonby Hall (Y) (1769-1854), Archdeacon of Richmond and Chancellor of the Diocese of Ripon, in laying the chief stone of the church, 1852, is inscribed with the following: *Arms.* Gules a chevron Or between three lambs' heads erased [Argent]. *Crest.* A unicorn's head erased. *Motto.* As above.

HEATON. Recorded by Machell, with no place of residence stated. *Arms.* Vert a lion rampant Argent in dexter chief a crescent Gules (MMS vi 421).

HEBSON. Corney House, Penrith, was inherited by Catherine (1741-1811), dau. and coheir of Miles Corney. Her sister Sarah (1748-1815) marr. William Grieve and had William Douglas Grieve (1784-1807) and Mary Jean, who marr. 1806 Capt William Hebson, D.L., J.P., The Buffs, and lived at Corney House 1811-41, when they sold it. Their dau. and eventual heir Catherine Corney Hebson (1809-48) marr. William Hugh Parkin,

* The bookplate of the above G. H. Head shows a second *Crest.* A sinister arm embowed vested with leaves and holding in the hand a sprig of laurel.

† His copy of Samuel Kent's *The British Banner Display'd: A Complete System of Heraldry* . . . (1755) is now in C. Roy Hudleston's possession.

D.L., J.P., of Ravencragg, Ullswater (1801-81), a younger son of Hugh Parkin, of Skirsgill, *q.v. Arms.* Gules three cocks Argent (Impaled by Parkin on monument in Barton churchyard).

HECHSTETTER. Joachim Hochstetter, a German, employed in a Scottish mining company 1526, was perhaps father of Daniel Hechstetter (d. 1581) who was given a licence with the Rev. Thomas Thurland to search, dig, try, roast and melt mines of gold, silver, copper and quicksilver in Cumberland, Westmorland and Lancashire 1564 (CEK). He marr. Radigunda (? Stammler) and brought her and their children to England from Augsburg 1571. A son David Hechstetter, B.D. (Oxon) (d. 1623) was born at Keswick 1572 and was Vicar of Brough under Stainmore 1611-23. His son Daniel Hechstetter, M.A. (Oxon) (b. 1614), was minister of Sebergham 1648-56. David's nephew Francis was father of the Rev. Daniel Hechstetter (*c.* 1614-86), Headmaster of Carlisle Grammar School 1661-65 and Rector of Bolton (C) 1665-86, who apparently died *s.p. Arms.* Per bend engrailed Azure and Or (HSH). Joseph Hechstetter, of Keswick, however, sealed a letter of 17 Feb. 1662 to Sir John Lowther, about a mineral lease in Threlkeld, with: . . . a fess . . . and in chief three mullets . . . (D/LMS/Threlkeld/5 in R.O. Carlisle).

HELE. Warwick Hele, dental surgeon, of 11 Portland Square, Carlisle, was father of John Warwick Hele, M.R.C.S., L.R.C.P., L.D.S., J.P., of Carlisle (b. 1877), and of Thomas Shirley Hele, O.B.E., M.A., M.D. (Cantab), F.R.C.P. (1881-1953), Master of Emmanuel College, Cambridge, 1935-51, and Vice-Chancellor of the University of Cambridge 1943-45. *Arms.* Gules five fusils in bend Ermine. *Crest.* On a chapeau Gules turned up Ermine an eagle with wings expanded Argent beaked and legged Or. *Motto.* Nostra salus Christi (FAC).

HELESBY. Shield at Hutton-in-the-Forest; a Vane quartering. *Arms.* Or a saltire Sable.

HELLON. A window in St. Michael, Workington, erected by their youngest son, D. S. Hellon, 1890, commemorates John and Sarah Hellon. *Arms.* Per bend wavy Or and Sable a lion rampant counterchanged within a bordure engrailed per bend Or and Sable.* *Crest.* Out of a mural crown Argent a demi lion rampant guardant per pale Or and Argent holding in the dexter paw a sword Argent hilt and pommel Or. *Motto.* In Deo spes.

HELM, of Carlisle. Robert Dundas Helm, J.P., M.D. (Edin) (b. 1862), son of Paul Helm (1818-1902), was of 13 Portland Square, Carlisle. His eldest son Capt Henry Paul Dundas Helm, the Border Regt (1894-1918), died *v.p.*, and he was succ. by his 2nd son Lt-Cdr Leslie Robert Dundas Helm, R.N. (b. 1898). *Arms.* Sable on a bend engrailed Argent between two roses of the second barbed and seeded Proper three pheons of the first. *Crest.* A sinister and a dexter cubit arm vested Sable cuffed Or holding in the hands Proper a pheon as in the arms. *Motto.* Prospice (FD7).

HENDERSON. William George Henderson, D.C.L., D.D. (Oxon), D.D. (Dunelm) (1819-1905), *s.p.* eldest son of Admiral George Henderson, of Harbridge, Hants., and of Burton, Som. (d. 1864), was Bursar and Censor of University College, Durham 1848-50; Senior Proctor of the University of Durham 1851-2; Principal of Bishop Hatfield's Hall, Durham 1851-2;

* The bordure should doubtless be counterchanged, like the lion, but is depicted in the window as described.

Headmaster, Victoria College, Jersey 1852-62; Headmaster, Leeds Grammar School 1862-84; and Dean of Carlisle 1884-1905. His younger brother Lt-Col Sir Edmund Yeamans Walcott Henderson, K.C.B., R.E. (1821-96), Commissioner of the Metropolitan Police 1869-86, is buried in Crosthwaite churchyard. His daus. and co-heirs, of whom the second, Maude marr. Robert Slack, *q.v.*, matriculated in 1904 the arms below, with the addition of a bordure Gules. *Arms.* Until 1904 the Dean used the arms of the Hendersons of Fordell, Fife, viz. Gules three piles issuing from the sinister side Argent on a chief of the last a crescent Azure between two Ermine spots. *Crest.* A cubit arm Proper the hand holding a star Or ensigned with a crescent Azure. In 1904 he obtained a grant, as follows: *Arms.* Per bend indented Sable and Or on a chief Argent a rose Gules barbed and seeded Vert between two Ermine spots. *Crest.* A cubit arm Proper charged on the wrist with an anchor Sable the hand holding a crescent Or. *Motto.* Sola virtus nobilitas (FD7).

HENDERSON. The bookplate of Christopher Henderson, of Biglands,* bears his arms, and on the title page of one of his books his name is written with Longburgh added. There is a monument in Burgh-by-Sands churchyard to William (d. 1784, aged 5), son of G. Henderson. *Arms.* Argent three piles issuing from the dexter side Sable on a chief of the first (*sic*) a crescent between two Ermine spots of the last. *Crest.* An eagle's head couped Proper holding in its beak an Ermine spot (CW2 xii 78).

HENLEY, Baron – see EDEN.

HERBERT. Curwen gives for Herbert, of Cockermouth: *Arms.* Gules three lions rampant Or (CW2 vi).

HERSCHEL. Impaled by Marshall on brass in St. John's Church, Keswick; Reginald Dykes Marshall, D.L., J.P., of Castlerigg, *q.v.*, marr. (1) 1858 Margaret Louisa (d. 1861), 3rd dau. of Sir John Frederick William Herschel, 1st Bart. *Arms.* [Argent] on a mount [Vert] a representation of the forty-feet reflecting telescope with its apparatus [Proper] on a chief [Azure] the astronomical symbol of Uranus, or the Georgium Sidus irradiated [Or].

HETHE. Shield at Hutton-in-the-Forest; a Vane quartering. *Arms.* Argent a cross engrailed between four billets Gules.

HETHERINGTON. The arms of this well known Border family are to be found in various churchyards. Thomas, son of John Hetherington, died at Hollinstone 1752, aged 9, and has a tombstone in Brampton old churchyard, with arms (see below), and *Crest,* apparently a demi dragon, but perhaps the same as below. James Hetherington, yeoman, of the same place, whose wife Mary died 1774, aged 26, bore the same arms, as did James, of the Temonhillhead, Irthington, whose wife died 1780, aged 57, and James, of Hurtleton and the Temonhillhead, Irthington, who marr. Ann (d. 1789, aged 85). John Hetherington, of Dacre Hall, Lanercost, in 1745, and Edward Hetherington, of Walton (d. 1746), bore the same arms on their tombstones. *Arms.* ... three lions rampant ... (Irthington and other tombstones). *Crest.* A demi lion rampant (Lanercost tombstones). Bell Irving (ABD) says that James Hetherington, of the Temonhill, husband of Ann (d. 1780), bore for crest: An arm in armour embowed holding a battle axe; but there seems to be some confusion here with Warwick, *q.v.* On the

* Field states that he settled in Biglands in 1704 and later removed to Longburgh (FAC).

tombstone of James Hetherington, of Hurtleton, 1853, at Irthington, Bell Irving recorded the arms as: Per pale Argent and chequy . . . three lions rampant . . . (ABD). On an undated tombstone of Hetherington, of Orchard House, Lanercost, the arms appeared as: . . . a chevron engrailed on the upper edge . . . between three lions rampant . . . (ABD). On the tombstone at Lanercost of John Hetherington, of Orchard House (d. 1752, aged 61), the arms appear as: . . . three lions rampant . . . ; but on that of his wife Ann (d. 1740, aged 42) they are cut as: . . . a chevron . . . between three lions rampant . . . ; in both cases without crest.

HETHERINGTON. Joseph Hetherington, of London, a native of Brampton, bought the Brinkburn estate, Northumberland, from William Fenwick for £20,500 in January 1792 and died September following, leaving the estate to his only brother John Hetherington, of In-tack, near Brampton (d. 1808, aged 52), and to his sister Mrs. Elizabeth Tinniswood, of Cumcatch, Brampton. John's only child Mary (1788-1830) marr. 1809 Major Richard Hodgson, H.E.I.C.S., of Moorhouse Hall, Burgh-by-Sands, who in 1812 bought Mrs. Tinniswood's moiety and sold the whole estate to Ward Cadogan 1825 (NCHN vii 475-6). *Arms.* Per pale Argent and Sable three lions rampant [counterchanged] (Gravestone of John Hetherington, (d. 1808, Ainstable churchyard).

HEWARD, of Burdenhurst. John Heward, of Burdenhurst, Lanercost, died 1774, aged 71. Nathan Heward, of Friarwaingate, Lanercost, presumably his younger brother, was bap. at Lanercost, 1711, the son of John Heward, of Burdenhurst, and died 1786, aged 76. *Arms.* . . . . two swords in saltire points upwards . . . between four mullets . . . (Lanercost tombstone). On the gravestone of Nathan, above, the mullets appeared as cinquefoils (ABD). *Crest.* An arm embowed holding a dagger in bend sinister transfixing a human heart.

HEWARD, of Friarwaingate. Bell Irving recorded the following for Hugh Heward, of Friarwaingate, Lanercost, died 1749. *Arms.* . . . two swords in saltire points upwards . . . between four mullets, or cinquefoils . . . in chief three hearts . . . . *Crest.* An arm embowed couped below the shoulder hand to the dexter grasping a long dagger or sword bend sinisterwise over the blade of which is a heart voided (ABD).

HEWARD.* Sir Simon Heward, F.S.A., M.D., F.R.C.S., (d. 1846, aged 76), qualified as a surgeon 1793, went to Madras as assistant surgeon 1796, served for more than 30 years with the Madras Medical Service, and retired as First Member of the Medical Board in that Presidency, 1831; he settled in Castle Street, Carlisle, and died there. In India he lived with a native woman, by whom he had two natural daus., of whom Jessie Maria (d. 1877, aged 66), marr. Major Knipe of Monkstown, Co. Dublin. *Arms.* Or two swords in saltire Proper hilts and pommels Sable between two cinquefoils in fess and another in base and three hearts in chief Gules all within a bordure. Azure. *Crest.* A dexter arm embowed in armour Proper garnished Or entwined by a serpent the hand in a gauntlet holding a sword also Proper pommel and hilt Gold the blade piercing a heart as in the arms (BGA). *Motto.* Pro Deo rege et patria (M.I., Crosby-on-Eden church and churchyard).

HEWART, of Parkfoot. Simon Hewart, of Parkfoot, Stapleton, died 1736, aged 57. *Arms.* . . . two swords in saltire points upwards . . . between two

* Not Hewart, as given by Field (FAC).

roses in fess and one in base . . . in chief three hearts . . . all within a bordure . . . . *Crest.* As Heward, of Friarwaingate. *Motto.* Pro rege et patria (ABD).

HEWET, of Batenbush. A gravestone at Kirkandrews-on-Esk commemorates Christopher and Ann, children of George Hewet, of Batinbush (now Batenbush); no date is visible. *Arms.* . . . three birds . . . , one and two, that in chief to the sinister, those in base respecting each other.

HEWETSON. Henry Hewetson, a London merchant and a native of Keswick (1821-95), bequeathed money for the building and endowment of Keswick High School. *Crest.* A serpent nowed holding in the mouth a garland of laurel (M.I. Crosthwaite Church).

HEWITT. Henry Hewitt, said to be of the same family as Viscount Lifford,* marr. Mary Norman and had a son William Hewitt, of Beaumont, whose son George Hewitt, of Burgh-by-Sands, marr. Mary, dau. of John Robinson, of Longburgh, and granddau. and heir of William Hodgson, of Fauld. Their only son George Henry Hewitt assumed the surname Oliphant (see Hewitt, *post* Oliphant, *post* Oliphant-Ferguson). *Arms.* See Hewitt, *post* Oliphant, etc.

HEWITT, *post* OLIPHANT, *post* OLIPHANT-FERGUSON. A descendant of the Hewitts of Burgh-by-Sands, George Henry Hewitt, D.L., J.P., of Broadfield, Southwaite (1792-1861), High Sheriff of Cumberland 1852, assumed the name and arms of Oliphant on succeeding his cousin Henry Oliphant, *q.v.,* at Broadfield 1843. He marr. 1815 Sarah (d. 1855), dau. of Robert Ferguson, of Harker, *q.v.,* and was succ. by their only son George Henry Hewitt, D.L., J.P., B.A. (Cantab), barrister at law (1817-1900), who assumed the names Oliphant-Ferguson on succ. his uncle Richard Ferguson. He was succ. by his only dau. Mary Beatrice, who marr. Robert Stoney Sheffield, *q.v. Arms.* Quarterly, 1 & 4, Gules three crescents Argent (Oliphant); 2 & 3, Gules a chevron between three owls [Argent] (Hewitt). *Crests.* 1, An elephant (Oliphant); 2, A falcon (Hewitt) (BLG4). George Henry Hewitt Oliphant-Ferguson, above, bore: *Arms.* Quarterly, 1 & 4, Gules an elephant's head couped between three crescents Or (Oliphant); 2 & 3, Per chevron dovetailed Or and Azure three boars' heads couped counterchanged within a bordure Argent charged with six buckles . . . (Ferguson). *Crests.* 1, An elephant statant semé of crescents holding in the trunk a fer-de-moline Or (Oliphant); 2, A demi lion rampant per chevron Or and Azure the dexter paw holding a thistle and the sinister resting on a boar's head couped Azure (Ferguson) (BLG4, 8). A shield in the billard-room of Brunstock House displays the arms as: Quarterly, 1 & 4. Per fess wavy Gules and Argent three crescents counterchanged (Oliphant); 2 & 3, Gules a chevron between three owls Argent (Hewitt).

HEYSHAM. John Heysham, D.L., J.P., M.D. (Edin) (1753-1834), was son of Giles Heysham, shipowner, of Lancaster (d. 1787, aged 65). He settled in

* In St. James' Church, Piccadilly, London, is a monument to John Hewitt (d. 1788, aged 46) "of a respectable family in the county of Cumberland, a near relation, friend & many years private secretary to James Viscount Lifford, Lord High Chancellor of Ireland," and to his brother Edward Hewitt, "a very respectable merchant of the City of London" (d. 1794, aged 62), "both of them distinguished by their friendly, amiable characters, who lived united in fraternal Love, and thus in death are not divided." Lord Lifford's father William Hewitt, mercer and draper (d. 1747), was baptised at Rockcliffe as son of James Hewitt, of Churchtown, 14 September 1683; James Hewitt marr. there 1679 Mary Urwin (GEC).

Carlisle as a physician 1778 and practised there until his death, acquiring fame as the compiler of the Carlisle Bills of Mortality. He marr. 1789 Elizabeth Mary (d. 1803), dau. and heir of Thomas Coulthard, Alderman of Carlisle. Their sons, who included Thomas Coulthard Heysham, naturalist (d. 1857, aged 67); the Rev. John Heysham, J.P., M.A. (Cantab) (d. 1877, aged 85), Incumbent of Sebergham 1820-46, and Vicar of Lazonby 1846-77; and James Heysham, Lieut R. N. (d. 1870), all died *s.p.* and their heir was their sister Isabella who marr. George Gill Mounsey, *q.v.* (DNB; LJH). *Arms.* Gules an anchor in pale Or on a chief of the second three torteaux. *Crest.* On a mount Vert a stag courant Argent attired Or pierced through the neck with an arrow Proper (Monument and window, Carlisle cathedral).

HEYSHAM, MOUNSEY- – see MOUNSEY.

HEYWOOD. Peter John Heywood (1738-90), son and heir of Deemster Thomas Heywood, Speaker of the House of Keys, was a Deemster and Seneschal to the Duke of Atholl. He was of The Nunnery, Isle of Man, which he sold 1773 and went to live in Whitehaven; but later returned to the Island, living in Douglas. His 4th son Peter Heywood (1773-1831) was a midshipman on the *Bounty*, and was tried by court martial for his part in the Mutiny. He received a free pardon, and served with distinction in the Navy, rising to the rank of post captain. His younger brother Edwin Holwell Heywood (1782-1851) was a solicitor in Whitehaven and clerk to the magistrates. He marr. 1807 Elizabeth Nickle, but the family is extinct in the male line (MNH). *Arms.* Argent three torteaux between two bendlets sinister Gules (M.I., Holy Trinity, Whitehaven).

HIGHMORE, of Armathwaite. Anthony Highmore died seised of the manor of Armathwaite 1548 and was succ. by his son Robert (b. 1538). A later Robert Highmore (b. *c.* 1636) entered a pedigree of five generations at Dugdale's Visitation of 1665, on behalf of his father Robert Highmore (then aged 68), and was succ. by his son Charles Highmore (d. 1738), whose son Benson Highmore (d. 1767) was an attorney in Carlisle,* and sold Armathwaite. His nephew Daniel was living 1768. *Arms.* Ermine a cross-bow bent point downwards between three moor cocks Sable (FCW). FVC blazons the field Argent. *Crest.* A moor cock Sable wattled Gules (FCW).

HIGHMORE – see BURROUGH, of Brampton.

HIGHMORE, of Harby Brow and Westlinton. Alexander Highmore, of Harby Brow (living 1478), marr. the heiress of the Boyvills of Westlinton and acquired that estate, which was sold by a descendant, presumably Francis Highmore (d. *s.p.* 1610), who sold some of the Harby Brow estate 1595, and the manor of Westlinton to the Blencowe family *temp.* James I (LMC p. 126, on the authority of Anthony Highmore). *Arms.* Argent a cross-bow pointed upwards between four moor cocks Sable membered and beaked Gules (LMC). *Crest.* Lysons state that a cadet of the family settled in Dorset, and it was this branch of the family, presumably, which is recorded as receiving the grant of a crest in 1683: An arm armed Proper brandishing a faulchion Argent hilt and pommel Or between two leading pikes Gules headed Or (LMC).

HIGHTON. Robert Ernest Highton, J.P., Major 1st Cumberland R.G.A., of

* It was in his house in English Street, on the site of which Messrs. Marks & Spencer's store now stands, that both Bonnie Prince Charlie and the Duke of Cumberland stayed during the '45.

Newlands, Workington (b. 1858), son of Edward Highton, of Keswick, was father of Commander Mark Edward Highton, D.L., J.P., R.N., of Dunthwaite, Cockermouth (1888-1966), Chairman of the Derwent Catchment Board and High Sheriff of Cumberland 1948. His son Noel Mark Edward Highton, J.P., F.C.A., is of Birdinhand, Papcastle. *Arms.* Azure on rocks in base a (?) pigeon . . . on a chief Argent three goats' heads erased . . . . *Crest.* A pigeon. *Motto.* Occuli ad montes (Commander Highton's seal).

HILL, of Wreay Hall. Robert Hill, coalfitter of Sunderland (D) (1748-88), was grandfather of Robert John Hill, Lieut 62nd Foot (1802-72), who became House Governor of the London Hospital, and died *s.p.* at Wreay Hall, the home of his first cousin, Anne Hannah Hill (1813-1903). *Arms.* Per chevron Argent and Sable three cinquefoils counterchanged. *Crest.* A martlet Proper. *Motto.* Avancez (PJB).

HILL. Miss Beatrice Birkbeck Hill, M.A. (Oxon), of Quanterness, Portinscale, is sister and coheir of Lt-Col Sir Norman Gray Hill, M.C., M.B., B.S., R.A.M.C., 2nd and last Bart. (1894-1944), and 2nd dau. of Sir Arthur Norman Hill, 1st bart. (1863-1944), and his wife Elen Mary Stratford, elder dau. of John Towne Danson, F.S.A., of Grasmere. *Arms.* Erminois on a fess cotised Sable between two wreaths of oak Vert a castle Argent (BP96).

HILLS, of Highhead Castle. Herbert Augustus Hills, J.P., B.A. (Oxon) (1837-1907), only son of John Hills,* Recorder of Rochester, was called to the Bar 1864 and was Judge of First Instance of International Tribunals in Egypt 1875-82 and of International Courts of Appeal there 1882-94. In the early 1890's he became tenant of Corby Castle and in 1902 bought Highhead Castle, which he left to his 2nd son, the Rt. Hon. John Waller Hills, P.C., J.P., B.A. (Oxon), D.C.L. (Dunelm) (1867-1938), Major D.L.I., M.P. for Durham City 1918-22, and for Ripon 1925-38, Financial Secretary to the Treasury 1922-23. He died before the baronetcy conferred upon him had been gazetted; it was conferred upon his only son, Sir Andrew Ashton Waller Hills (1933-55), who died *s.p.* when the baronetcy became extinct. J. W. Hills' younger brother, Judge Eustace Gilbert Hills, K.C., B.A. (Oxon), of Tolson Hall, Kendal (1868-1934), was Chairman of Cumberland Quarter Sessions 1930-33. *Arms.* Quarterly, 1 & 4, Argent a bugle horn stringed Sable garnished Or on a chief Azure a trout naiant Proper (Hills); 2 & 3, Per saltire Azure and Argent a saltire per saltire counterchanged between in pale two roses of the second barbed and seeded Proper and in fess as many pierced mullets Sable (Ashton). *Crest.* On a mount Vert a talbot passant Sable resting the dexter fore paw on a cross pattée Or. *Motto.* Truth and Justice (BP99).

HILTON. The Hiltons, of Hilton Castle (D), Barons of the Bishopric of Durham, were for long lords of the manor of Alston. William Hilton, of Hilton (d. 1457), marr. shortly before January 1439 Mariota, elder dau. and coheir of William Stapleton, of Edenhall, *q.v.*, by Margaret, dau. and heir of Nicholas Veteripont, and so acquired the manor. It was mortgaged by Henry Hilton (d. 1641) to Sir Francis Radcliffe 1618 and eventually passed into the possession of that family, Earls of Derwentwater. From Henry

* His widow was of Rydal Mount (W).

Hilton's brother, John Hilton, of Hilton (d. 1655), descended John Hilton, of Hilton (d. 1712), who marr. 1694 Dorothy, dau. of Sir Richard Musgrave, 2nd Bart., of Hayton. Their son John Hilton (1699-1746), M.P. for Carlisle 1727-46, was the last of the family, his coheirs being his sisters – Anne (1697-1766), marr. 1724 her cousin Sir Richard Musgrave, 4th Bart., *q.v.*; Elizabeth (1702-51), marr. 1726 Thomas Younghusband; and Catherine (1706-56), marr. the Rev. John Brisco, D.D., of Crofton, Rector of Orton and Vicar of Aspatria, *q.v.* Lady Musgrave's son Sir Richard Musgrave, 5th Bart. (d. 1755, aged 30), High Sheriff of Cumberland 1750, succ. to the estates and took the name of Hylton. Hilton Castle was sold to Mary, Countess of Strathmore, and the Cumberland estates passed to Sir Richard's dau. Eleanor (b. 1752), marr. 1769 William Jolliffe, *q.v.* Mrs. Jolliffe and Sir John Brisco were coheirs to the supposed Barony of Hylton (GEC; GECB; NB). *Arms.* Argent two bars Azure.* *Crest.* The head of Moses affronté Proper glorified Or. *Supporters.* Two lions rampant Azure. *Motto.* Tant que je puis (FFC; FVD; SHD). Surtees gives the crest as: Moses's head, horned, or radiated.

HINDS. Samuel Hinds, M.A., D.D. (Oxon) (1793-1872), son of Abel Hinds, of Barbados, was Dean of Carlisle 1848-49, and Bishop of Norwich 1849-57, when he "resigned . . . for domestic reasons much canvassed at the time and retired into private life" *(The Times)*. *Arms.* Gules a chevron Or between three hinds trippant Argent (BBE). *Crest.* Out of a ducal coronet a cockatrice wings expanded. *Motto.* Vigilo et spero (Samuel Hinds' bookplate).

HINDSON, of Penrith. Richard Hindson, of Penrith, tanner (1721-87), was father of John Hindson, of Penrith, tanner (1761-1834), whose 2nd son Matthew Hindson, of Penrith (b. 1796), obtained a grant of arms for the descendants of his father, 1878. His elder brother, Richard Grave Hindson, of Sandgate Hall, Penrith, attorney (1795-1864), was father of the Rev. John Hutchinson Hindson, M.A. (Cantab), of Bradwall Hall, Sandbach (Ch) (1846-1919), who marr. 1891 the Hon. Lavinia Alice Julia Butler, dau. of the 16th Baron Dunboyne. Their eldest son Lt-Col Richard Eldred Hindson, Royal Welch Fusiliers (1892-1966), marr. 1921 Margaret Eacy, dau. of Sir Henry Hayes Lawrence, 2nd Bart., and had a son Christopher Eldred Hindson, M.A. (Cantab), of White House, Maresfield Park, Uckfield, Sussex. *Arms.* Azure five cross crosslets in cross between four stags' heads cabossed Or. *Crest.* In front of two cross crosslets fitché in saltire Azure a hind's head erased Or (CA lx/86).

HINTON, of Cumberland. No other details given. *Arms.* Per fess indented Sable and Or six fleurs-de-lys counterchanged Argent and Sable (BGA). FVC records Stanley, of Austhwaite, as quartering for Hinton: Per fess indented Argent and Sable six fleurs-de-lys counterchanged. Curwen records another coat: Per fess Or and Gules four fleurs-de-lys counterchanged (CW2 vi).

HODGSON, of Bascodyke. The 1665 Visitation pedigree of this family is headed by Peter Hodgson, said to have died *c.* 1644, but *recte* 1623. His son Rowland (d. 1660) was father of Peter, of Bascodyke (*c.* 1621-1701), and of William, said to be ancestor of the Hodgsons of Houghton House, *q.v.* Peter was succ. by his son Peter (1665-1701), whose half-brother William

* The arms are impaled by Veteripont in a window in Edenhall church.

(b. 1678) was one of the Landgraves and Casiques of Carolina and bought from his nephew Thomas (below) his father's lands in Ainstable. This Thomas (1685-1745) was of Barrockfield, and, in right of his wife, of Dormansteads. He marr. 1706 Thomasine (1688-1753), eldest dau. and coheir of Arthur Forster, of Kingfield and Dormansteads, *q.v.*, but left only daus. and coheirs – Dorothy (b. 1706); Mary (b. 1707); Margaret (1708-90), marr. John Milbourne; Jane, marr. 1734 William Musgrave; Mary, marr. 1736 Adam Forster; and Anne (b. 1719), marr. 1747 John Jackson. *Arms.* At Dugdale's Visitation 1665 respite was given for the showing of the arms. In 1729 the above William Hodgson, the Landgrave, applied for and obtained a confirmation of the arms which he said he had seen hanging in his father's house at Bascodyke, viz. Party per chevron engrailed Or and Azure three martlets counterchanged. *Crest* (granted to the Landgrave). A dove Azure winged Or membered and beaked Gules holding an olive branch in the beak (CW2 xxv 249; MS. 3 D14/120, College of Arms).

HODGSON, of Carlisle and Bowness. Thomas Hodgson, of Carlisle, grocer (d. 1783, aged 55), who marr. 1757 Ann, dau. of James Halton, is buried in St. Cuthbert's churchyard, Carlisle, with various members of his family, including his sons John, J.P., of Carlisle and Bowness (C) (d. 1839, aged 65), and Miles (1775-1844). John's heir was his nephew William Hodgson, M.A. (Oxon), barrister at law, son of his brother Thomas. *Arms.* . . . a chevron embattled . . . between three birds . . . . *Crest.* A bird with a sprig in its beak. *Motto.* Be ever watchful (MCC).

HODGSON, of Carlisle and Penton. John Hodgson (d. 1846, aged 77), Mayor of Carlisle 1828-29, lived at Eaglesfield House, Abbey Street, Carlisle, and Penton House, Nichol Forest. His heir was his nephew (son of his sister Ann), Dr. George Tinniswood, *q.v.* *Arms.* Per chevron embattled Or and Azure three martlets counterchanged.* *Crest.* A martlet Sable. *Motto.* Dread God (Shields in Hodgson's house in Abbey Street, Carlisle).

HODGSON, of Causeway Foot. Robert Hodgson, yeoman, of Causeway Foot, St. John's-in-the-Vale (1715-74), son of Christopher Hodgson, marr. 1755 Jane Birkett, of Hawkshead Field (d. 1816, aged 81), and had an eldest son Christopher (1756-1827), who died *s.p.*, and a 3rd son Robert Hodgson (1763-1811), a Major and barrister at law and Speaker of the House of Assembly, Prince Edward's Island. *Arms.* Per chevron engrailed Or and Azure three martlets counterchanged. *Crest.* A dove holding in the beak a sprig of laurel. *Motto.* In hoc signo spes mea (M.I., St. John's-in-the-Vale church).

HODGSON, of Cockermouth. John Hodgson, of Cockermouth, tanner (d. 1807, aged 68), and his wife Mary (d. 1824, aged 83), are commemorated by a tablet in Crosthwaite church. *Arms.* Paly of six Sable and Or on a bend Gules three mullets of four points pierced of the second. *Crest.* A spur erect between two wings Or.

HODGSON, of Easton. To this old Bowness-on-Solway family belonged Thomas Hodgson (d. 1752, aged 72), who marr. Barbara (d. 1753, aged 65) and had a son John Hodgson, who marr. 1750 Rebecca, dau. of Thomas Lowry, of Blackhall, Carlisle. Their son John Lowry Hodgson (b. 1755) was a surgeon in Carlisle and Thursby. *Arms.* Per chevron embattled . . . and . . . three martlets . . . . *Crest.* A dove with a sprig of

* The shield has been wrongly repainted and the martlets appear as Sable.

laurel in its beak (Tombstone of Thomas Hodgson in Bowness churchyard). Bell Irving records a stone to John Hodgson, 1701, at Bowness with the same arms and *Crest.* A martlet on a roundle (ABD).

HODGSON, of Houghton House. This branch of the Hodgsons of Newby Grange, *q.v.*, was founded by William Hodgson, D.L., J.P., of Houghton House (1773-1850), younger brother of Joseph Hodgson (1768-1809). He was five times Mayor of Carlisle and Clerk of the Peace for Cumberland 1809-39. In the latter office he was succ. by his eldest son Thomas Houghton Hodgson (1813-91), who served 1839-91. He was succ. at Houghton House* by his nephew, the Rev. William George Courtenay Hodgson, J.P., M.A. (Cantab) (1852-1913), Rector of Distington 1886-1913, elder son of the Rev. George Courtenay Hodgson (1821-86), Vicar of Barton (W) 1855-75, and of Corbridge (N) 1875-86. His eldest son George William (1888-1914), Lieut the Border Regt, died of wounds *s.p.* and was succ. by his brother Capt Charles Lawrence Courtenay Hodgson, Northumberland Fusiliers, of Tenters, Lorton (1893-1956), who died *s.p.* and was succ. by his brother Eldred Lowther Hodgson, M.B.E., M.C. (1896-1975), who also died *s.p.* The representation of the family is now in the descendants of the younger brother of the Rev. William George Courtenay Hodgson, above – the Rt. Rev. Henry Bernard Hodgson, M.A., D.D. (Oxon) (1856-1921), who was Bishop of St. Edmundsbury and Ipswich 1914-21. His grandson Capt Henry Peter Bascodyke Hodgson, the Border Regt (b. 1919), had a son Christopher Anthony Courtenay Hodgson (b. 1949). *Arms.* The bookplate of the Rev. William George Courtenay Hodgson displays: Per chevron engrailed Argent and Azure three martlets .... The family also bears: Sable a chevron between three martlets Or. *Crest.* A dove close Azure holding in the beak a sprig of laurel Proper.† *Motto.* Dread God (BLG8).

HODGSON, of Newby Grange. William Hodgson, of Ainstable (d. 1694), from whom this family descends, is said to have been son of Rowland Hodgson, of Bascodyke, *q.v.* His descendant William Hodgson, of Carlisle (1742-1812), was father of Joseph Hodgson and of William (see Hodgson, of Houghton House). The said Joseph (1768-1809) was an attorney and deputy Clerk of the Peace for Cumberland. His son William Nicholson Hodgson, D.L., J.P., of Newby Grange, Crosby (1801-76), was M.P. for Carlisle 1847-48, 1857-59 and 1865-68, and for East Cumberland 1868-76, and was High Sheriff 1863. Dying *s.p.* he was succ. by his nephew Thomas Hesketh Hodgson, J.P., F.S.A. (1841-1917), son of the Rev. Joseph Stordy Hodgson, M.A. (Cantab) (1805-79), Rector of Aikton and Canon residentiary of Carlisle. Mr. T. H. Hodgson marr. 1888 Elizabeth (1854-1935), only child of the Rev. Henry Wilkinson, D.D., Master of Peterhouse, Cambridge. He and his wife were prominent members of the Cumberland & Westmorland Antiquarian & Archaeological Society, of which he was President 1909-15, and of which he and his wife were honorary members, as was their dau. and heir, Katherine Sophia Hodgson, F.S.A., of Ridge House, Brampton (1889-1974), who was President of the Society 1948-51 and Chairman of Council. *Arms.* As Hodgson, of

* Sold 1921.

† The crest is on a tablet in Blackford church commemorating William Henry Hodgson, barrister-at-law, Assistant Solicitor to the Treasury (1811-81), 2nd son of the above William (d. 1850); he died at the Hill, Blackford.

Bascodyke (Brass in Carlisle Cathedral to the Rev. J. S. Hodgson, above; BGA).

HODGSON, of Salkeld Hall. Robert Hodgson, of Alston Moor (d. 1808, aged 72), was father of Robert Hodgson, J.P., LL.B. (Cantab) (d. 1855), who was High Sheriff of Cumberland 1843. He bought Salkeld Hall from Col Lacy, *q.v.*, and was succ. by his dau. Marianne, who marr. Thomas Horrocks, *q.v.* *Arms.* Per chevron engrailed Or and Azure three martlets counterchanged (Hodgson); impaling, Sable a cross engrailed Argent between four plates each charged with an arrow point downwards of the field (Fletcher) (Window, Addingham church).

HODGSON. The Very Rev. Robert Hodgson, M.A., D.D. (Cantab) (d. 1844), son of Robert Hodgson, of Congleton (Ch), was Rector of St. George, Hanover Square, London 1803-44, Dean of Chester 1815-20, and Dean of Carlisle 1820-44. *Arms.* Per chevron embattled Or and Azure three martlets counterchanged. *Crest* (formerly on railings in precincts of Carlisle cathedral). A dove close Azure holding in its beak a sprig of laurel Proper.

HODGSON. Papworth assigns to a Cumberland family of this name, 1716, *Arms.* Gules three escutcheons Argent between nine bezants (OBA). These arms are also given in Harl. MS. 1536 for Hodgson (FVC).

HOLAND, Earl of Kent. A series of shields from Thornbury Castle, Glos., now in Greystoke Castle, illustrating the medieval ancestry of the Howards, includes one for Holand; Margaret (d. 1439*), sister and coheir of Edmund de Holand, Earl of Kent (1383-1408), and dau. of Thomas de Holand, Earl of Kent (d. 1397), marr. 1397 John Beaufort, Earl of Somerset, *q.v.* *Arms.* Gules three lions passant guardant in pale Or a bordure Argent.

HOLDEN, Baron Holden, of Alston. Isaac Holden, of Gunends, Alston (d. 1826), was father of Sir Isaac Holden, D.L., J.P., 1st Bart., of Oakworth House, Keighley (Y) (1807-97), cr. Baronet 1893. He had issue (besides a younger son, Edward, father of Sir Isaac Holden, J.P., M.A. (Cantab), 5th Bart. (1867-1962), an elder son Sir Angus Holden, 2nd Bart. (1833-1912), who was cr. Baron Holden, of Alston, 1908. The barony became extinct on the death unmarr. of his grandson, Sir Angus William Eden Holden, 4th Bart. and 2nd Baron Holden (1898-1951), when the baronetcy passed to Sir Isaac Holden (see above), whose eldest son, Sir Edward Holden, M.A. (Cantab), M.R.C.S., L.R.C.P., D.A., F.F.A.R.C.S., of Croft House, Croft (Y), is the 6th and present Bart. *Arms.* Or a chief Azure over all a bend nebuly between two roses Gules. *Crest.* Issuant from a chaplet of oak Vert an eagle's head erased Or gorged with a collar gemel Azure. *Supporters.* Two rams guardant Proper armed and unguled Sable each charged on the shoulder with a rose Gules barbed and seeded also Proper. *Motto.* Extant recte factis praemia (BP105).

HOLLIDAY. John Holliday, of Hudshill, Arthuret, died 1723. Bell Irving recorded the following *Arms.* . . . a curved sword point downwards . . . in chief three crescents . . . (ABD). Field, however, recorded for John Holliday, of Hudskill, died 1723, son of Andrew Holliday: . . . a chevron . . . , but suggests that this coat was a conventional ornament supplied by a local stonemason (FAC).

HOLLINS – see GIBSON.

HOLMAN. A brass in Arlecdon church commemorates Alwyn Haswell

* See GEC xii (I) 45; not 1429, as stated in GEC xii (II) 305.

Holman, B.A. (Cantab), barrister at law, of London, Devon and Rheda, aged 50, who marr. 1913 Myfanwy Wynn Lewis, dau. and coheir of Thomas Dixon, of Rheda, *q.v.*, and his dau. Benita Rosemary Joyce, aged 17, both killed by enemy action 1940. His elder son is Peter Paul Dixon Holman, B.A. (Cantab), barrister at law, formerly Captain, the Border Regt. *Arms.* Vert a chevron Argent gutté de sang between three pheons Or. *Crest.* A bow with arrow drawn to the head and pointing to the sinister all Proper. *Motto.* Ea via (BLG18).

HOLM CULTRAM ABBEY. Founded as a daughter house of Melrose Abbey by Prince Henry, son of King David of Scotland, and by Alan fitz Waldieve, 1150 (NB ii 172; HCC ii 334). *Arms.* Azure a cross moline Or; impaling, Or a lion rampant Sable (TVN; Shields at Holm Cultram).

HOLME, of Holme Hill. John Holme, of The Hill, Hawksdale, Dalston (living 1607), was succ. by his son Percival, whose descendants continued on the estate, later known as Holme Hill. John Holme (d. 1755) was father of John (1702-69), a Carlisle attorney, who went to India and became Registrar of the Mayor's Court, Calcutta. His brother Thomas (1712-94) succ. to Holme Hill and was succ. by his niece (the dau. of John, above) Catherine* (1736-61), who marr. William Brightwell Sumner, Bengal Civil Service (*c.* 1730-96), *q.v.*, the estate passing to that family. *Arms.* Argent a buck trippant Gules. *Crest.* A hawk wings elevated Proper (BLG5, *sub* Sumner).

HOLT. Alfred Holt, of Crofton, Aigburth, Liverpool (b. 1829), was co-founder with his brother Philip Henry (1830-1914) of the Ocean Steamship Co. His 2nd son Philip Henry Holt, of Kingfield, Penton (C) (1873-1938), was High Sheriff of Cumberland 1924-25. *Arms.* Sable on a bend between two heraldic antelopes rampant Or three fleurs-de-lys Azure. *Crest.* An heraldic antelope passant Or resting the dexter hoof on a pheon Sable. *Motto.* Certum pete finem (FD7).

HOPE. Lt-Col Sir Percy Mirehouse Hope, O.B.E., D.L., J.P., L.R.I.B.A., M.I.M.C.E., of 39 Brundholme Terrace, Keswick (1886-1972), son of Joseph Fearon Hope, of Keswick, was Chairman and Managing Director, Lake District Hotels and Pape's Garages, and other companies; Alderman, Cumberland County Council; Chairman, National Council of British Hotels and Restaurants Association; Chairman of Governors, Keswick School; and Master of the Blencathra Foxhounds. *Arms.* . . . a chevron . . . between two foxes' masks . . . in chief and a roundle . . . in base. *Crest.* Issuant from an arch a lion statant. *Motto.* Esperance (Achievement in Royal Oak Hotel, Keswick).

HOPPER. Joseph Hopper, of Hole in Priorsdale, Alston (d. 1795, aged 86), was 3rd son of Humphrey Hopper, of Black Hedley (N) (1677-1760), and on the death *s.p.* of his eldest brother, John Hopper (1700-76), succ. to Black Hedley. He marr. Mary Walton, of Tynehead (d. 1782), and was father of Nicholas Hopper, of Black Hedley, an eminent agriculturalist (d. *s.p.* 1807, aged 69) (NCHN vi 296-7; *Ex inf.* J. V. Harrison). *Arms.* Argent three roses Gules (SHD iv (I) 83).

HORNE. John Horne, of Cleator, was father of Robert Horne, M.A., D.D.

* She and her husband returned to India with Lord Clive in 1765. The latter, on the voyage out, wrote to his wife that he found in Mrs. Sumner "a woman of most diabolical disposition, ignorant, ill-tempered and selfish to the highest degree. She seemed possessed of every disagreeable quality which ever belonged to the female sex."

(Cantab) (*c.* 1519-80), Dean of Durham 1551-53 and 1559-60, and Bishop of Winchester (1561-80) (DNB). *Arms.* Sable three bugle horns stringed Argent (HBA).

HORROCKS. Thomas Horrocks, D.L., J.P., of Eden Brows, barrister at law (1825-1904), was only son of James Horrocks, of Orrell Lodge (L). He marr. 1848 Marianne, eldest dau. and coheir of Robert Hodgson, of Salkeld Hall, *q.v.* They were living at Acorn Bank (W) in 1854. Their only son Robert Hodgson Horrocks, J.P., M.A. (Oxon) (1851-1913), succ. to Salkeld Hall and was High Sheriff of Cumberland 1911. He was succ. by his son Walter James Hodgson Horrocks who sold the estate. *Arms.* Or a fret Azure on a chief of the second two bees volant of the field. *Crest.* Upon a rock an eagle rising Proper. *Motto.* Spe (Seal and bookplate).

HOSKINS, of Higham. Alexander Hoskins (1722-1800), said to have been great-grandson of Sir William Hoskins, Bart., of Youghal, settled at Great Broughton Hall 1748 and was for 40 years Chairman of Cumberland Quarter Sessions. His grandson Thomas Alison Hoskins, D.L., J.P., of Higham, near Cockermouth (1800-86), was High Sheriff of Cumberland 1854. He was succ. by his eldest son the Rev. George Richard Hoskins, J.P., M.A. (Oxon) (1828-99), Curate of Cockermouth 1856-9, Perpetual Curate of St. Bridget Beckermet 1859-66, Vicar of Setmurthy 1866-92, Hon. Canon of Carlisle 1869-99, Perpetual Curate of Wythop 1873-94, and Rural Dean of Cockermouth 1872-82, who died unmarr. *Arms.* Per pale Gules and Azure a chevron engrailed Or between three lions rampant Argent. *Crest.* A cock's head erased Or pelletté combed and wattled Gules between two wings expanded Gold. *Motto.* Virtute non verbis (BLG8).

HOSTE. Col Sir George Charles Hoste, C.B., R.E. (1786-1845), a Waterloo veteran, 3rd son of the Rev. Dixon Hoste, marr. 1812 Mary (d. 1870), only dau. of James Burkin Burroughes, *q.v.* Croglin Low Hall and Croglin High Hall formed part of their marriage settlement and were sold by their trustees 1873 (BP68; BLG11; *ex inf.* the late Mr. W. H. Whitehead). *Arms.* Azure a bull's head cabossed Argent winged and armed Or (Window, Kirkoswald church).

HOUGHAM. Shield at Hutton-in-the-Forest; a Vane quartering. *Arms.* Argent five chevronels Sable.

HOUSSEMAYNE DU BOULAY. Major Thomas William Houssemayne du Boulay, The Border Regt (1875-1921), was of Threlkeld and Greystoke. He marr. 1903 Lilian, dau. of Canon Edmund Adam Askew, Rector of Greystoke, *q.v.* Their son Noel Edmund Houssemayne du Boulay marr. 1939 Henrietta Frances, 3rd dau. of John Anthony Spedding, *q.v.* (BLG18). *Arms.* Argent a fess wavy Gules. *Crest.* Out of a ducal coronet Or a dog's head collared. *Motto.* Sempre fidèle (BLG8).

HOW. John How (d. 1732), Alderman of Carlisle and Mayor 1725,* had a 2nd son Peter How, merchant of Whitehaven (d. 1772, aged 73), who marr. (2) 1755 Christian (1721-77), dau. and coheir of Thomas Crakeplace, *q.v.* Their son, the Rev. Peter How, M.A. (Cantab) (1758-1831), was Curate of Workington, Rector of Corney 1787-95, Rector of Harrington 1794-1817, Rector of Workington 1803-31, and Vicar of Isel 1814-26. He marr. 1786 his cousin Margaret, dau. of William Wybergh, *q.v.* Their son William Wybergh How, of Shrewsbury, was father of William Walsham How,

* His brother Timothy How was Mayor of Carlisle 1722 and 1730.

M.A., D.D. (Oxon) (1823-97), Bishop of Bedford 1879 and first Bishop of Wakefield 1888. His nephew Walter Wybergh How, M.A. (Oxon) (1860-1932), was Fellow of Merton College, Oxford, 1884-1932. *Arms.* John How (d. 1732) sealed with: ... a fess ... between three (?) horses' heads couped .... *Crest.* A horse statant. Bishop How bore: Argent a fess semé of escallops of the field between three wolves' heads erased Sable (BBE). Archibald Wybergh How, of Droitwich, bore for *Crest.* A wolf's head erased (FBC).

HOWARD, of Corby. Lord William Howard (see Howard, of Naworth) in 1605 bought from Henry and Elizabeth Blenkinsop, of Helbeck (W), a moiety of the manor and castle of Corby and in 1625 the other moiety from the Salkeld family. He was succ. by his son Sir Francis Howard (1588-1660), whose son Francis (1635-1702) succ. and had three daus. and coheirs – Elizabeth, marr. (1) William Errington, and (2) Michael Anne; Mary, marr. Francis Warwick, *q.v.*; and Anne, marr. Marmaduke Langdale. He was succ. by his brother William Howard (d. 1708), whose son Thomas marr. (1) Barbara, dau. of John, 1st Viscount Lonsdale and sister and in her issue coheir of Henry, 3rd Viscount Lonsdale, by whom he had issue Jane, marr. Francis Warwick, *q.v.* His son by his 2nd wife, Philip Howard (1730-1810), succeeded. His son Henry Howard (1757-1842), High Sheriff of Cumberland 1834, was succ. by his son Philip Henry Howard, D.L., J.P., F.S.A. (1801-83), M.P. for Carlisle 1830-47 and 1848-52, and High Sheriff of Cumberland 1860. He marr. Eliza Minto, dau. of Major John Canning, H.E.I.C.S., *q.v.*, and niece and heir of Francis Canning. Their son Philip John Canning Howard, J.P. (1853-1934), was the last male of the family. He was succ. by his only dau. Ursula Mary (1879-1960), who marr (1) 1899 Sir Henry Joseph Lawson, 3rd Bart., *q.v.*, and (2) 1949 Lt-Col Hugh Levin, O.B.E. Corby is now held by her grandson, John Philip Howard, formerly Lawson, son of Sir William Howard Lawson, Bart., *q.v.* *Arms.* At Dugdale's Visitation of 1665 Thomas Constable certified the following on behalf of Francis Howard, above: Quarterly, 1 & 4, Howard (as Howard, of Greystoke), a mullet for difference; 2 & 3, Gules three escallops Argent (Dacre). *Crest.* A lion guardant ducally gorged line reflexed over the back charged with a mullet for difference (FCW). The family later bore the same arms as the Howards, of Naworth, *q.v.*, without the mullet for difference. *Crest.* On a chapeau Gules turned up Ermine a lion statant guardant the tail extended Or ducally crowned Argent gorged with a label of three points of the last. *Badge.* A slip of oak Vert fructed Or charged on the stem with a crescent for difference. *Motto.* Sola virtus invicta (FD7). On receiving a Royal Licence to bear the name and arms of Howard alone, the above John Philip Howard, formerly Lawson, received a grant as follows: *Arms.* Gules on a bend between six cross crosslets fitché Argent an escutcheon Or charged with a demi lion rampant pierced through the mouth with an arrow within a double tressure flory counterflory of the first a mullet [Or] for difference and for distinction on the bend in chief a cross botonny Gules. *Crest.* On a chapeau Gules turned up Ermine a lion statant guardant the tail extended Or ducally gorged Argent charged on the shoulder with a mullet [Azure] for difference and for distinction on the body with a cross botonny also Gules.

HOWARD, of Greystoke, and HOWARD, Dukes of Norfolk. Sir Thomas

Howard, K.G., K.B., M.A. (Cantab and Oxon), 4th Duke of Norfolk, Earl Marshal of England (1538-72), marr. (3) 1567 Elizabeth, dau. of Sir James Leyburne, of Cunswick (W), and widow of Thomas, 5th Lord Dacre of Gilsland. He marr. his stepdaus. Anne and Elizabeth, sisters and coheirs of George, 6th Lord Dacre, *q.v.*, to his sons by former marriages – Philip, Earl of Arundel (1557-95), and Lord William Howard (see Howard, Earl of Carlisle). In the division of the Dacre estates, Lord and Lady Arundel acquired *int. al.* the Barony of Greystoke, still held by their descendants. It descended with the dukedom and passed to Charles Howard (d. 1713), brother of the 5th and 6th Dukes. By his wife Mary, eldest dau. and coheir of George Tattershall, *q.v.*, he was father of Henry Charles Howard, who marr. Mary, dau. and coheir of John Aylward. Their son Charles (1720-86) became 10th Duke and was succ. by his only son Charles (1746-1815) as 11th Duke. He was M.P. for Carlisle 1780-86, and marr. (1) 1767 Mariana (d. 1768), dau. and heir of John Coppinger, of Ballyvolane, Co. Cork, and (2) 1771 Frances (d. 1820, aged 70), dau. and heir of Charles Fitzroy-Scudamore, of Holme Lacy, Hereford. On his death *s.p.* the dukedom passed to his 3rd cousin Bernard Edward, 12th Duke (d. 1842), and Greystoke to Bernard Edward's younger brother, Lord Henry Molyneux-Howard (1766-1824). His son Henry Howard (1802-75) was father of *int. al.* Henry Charles Howard, see below; Sir Edward Stafford Howard, K.C.B., of Thornbury Castle, Glos.; Robert Mowbray Howard, D.L., J.P., of Bluemire, Threlkeld; and Esme William, cr. Baron Howard of Penrith, *q.v.* The said Henry Charles Howard, D.L., J.P., B.A. (Cantab) (1850-1914), High Sheriff of Cumberland 1879 and M.P. for Penrith 1885-86, was succ. by his only son Capt Bernard Henry Esme Howard, M.C., of Johnby Hall (1880-1949), the Manchester Regt. and R.F.C. His 1st cousin (son of the above Sir Edward Stafford Howard), Major Sir Algar Henry Stafford Howard, K.C.B., K.C.V.O., M.C., T.D., D.L., J.P. (1880-1970), Garter Principal King of Arms 1944-50,* succ. and was of Thornbury Castle, Glos. and Greystoke. He marr. 1921 Violet Ethel, eldest dau. and coheir of the 1st Baron Knaresborough and widow of Capt Alexander Moore Vandeleur, and had two daus. and coheirs, Anne Violet, marr. 1952 John Cahill, of Doneen, Castle Island, Co. Kerry, and Elizabeth Helen, marr. 1958 Harold William Norman Suckling. Greystoke Castle was inherited by his half-brother Stafford Vaughan Stepney Howard, formerly Captain, Coldstream Guards: his son and heir Nicholas Stafford Howard is of Johnby Hall. *Arms.* The Howards originaly bore: Gules crusilly and a bend Argent (FFC). This later became stereotyped as: Gules a bend between six cross crosslets fitché Argent (Shields at Greystoke Castle). After the augmentation granted to Thomas, 2nd Duke of Norfolk, for his victory at Flodden when Earl of Surrey, 1513, this became: Gules on a bend between six cross crosslets fitché Argent an escutcheon Or charged with a demi lion rampant pierced through the mouth by an arrow within a double tressure flory counterflory Gules. The Dukes of Norfolk, who in 1842 assumed the additional surname FitzAlan before that of Howard, now bear this on a quarterly coat, as follows: Quarterly, 1, Howard; 2, Gules three lions passant guardant in pale

* At Greystoke Castle is preserved the patent dated 6 August 1913 granting to Algar Henry Stafford Howard, when Rouge Dragon Pursuivant, the following *Badge*. A slip of oak Vert fructed Or with a crescent for distinction.

Or in chief a label of three points Argent (Brotherton, *q.v.*); 3, Chequy Or and Azure (Warenne, *q.v.*); 4, Gules a lion rampant Or (FitzAlan, *q.v.*). *Crests.* 1, Issuant from a ducal coronet Or a pair of wings Gules each charged with a bend between six cross crosslets fitché Argent; 2, On a chapeau Gules turned up Ermine a lion statant guardant with tail extended Or gorged with a ducal coronet Argent; 3, On a mount Vert a horse passant Argent holding in the mouth a slip of oak fructed Proper. *Supporters.* Dexter, A lion; Sinister, A horse; both Argent the latter holding in the mouth a slip of oak Vert fructed Proper. *Motto.* Sola virtus invicta (BP105). At Greystoke Castle is preserved the Royal Licence dated 10 August 1812, granting to Henry Thomas Howard, of Thornbury Castle and of Teversall and Wellon, Notts., see above, permission to use the additional surname Molyneux, and to quarter the arms of Molyneux with his own, as follows: *Arms.* Quarterly, 1 & 4, Azure a cross moline Or (Molyneux); 2 & 3, Howard. *Crests.* 1, On a chapeau Gules turned up Ermine a peacock's tail Proper (Molyneux); 2, Howard (i.e., as Crest No. 2 for the Dukes of Norfolk, above). At Greystoke Castle is also preserved the Royal Licence dated 1 June 1922 granting to Dame Catharine Meriel Howard, widow of Sir Edward Stafford Howard, K.C.B., of Thornbury Castle, see above, to take for herself and issue the additional surname and arms of Stepney (see COWELL-STEPNEY); her son, Stafford Vaughan Stepney Howard, see above, assumed the surname of Howard only by Deed Poll, 1950, but is entitled to retain the quartered arms (without the Ermine spot), as follows: Quarterly, 1 & 4, Gules a fess chequy Or and Azure between three owls Argent (Stepney); 2, Howard, with (for distinction) an Ermine spot. *Crests.* 1, A talbot's head erased Gules eared Or gorged with a collar chequy Or and Azure and holding in the mouth an antler Gold; 2, Howard.*.

HOWARD, of Naworth, Earls of Carlisle. Lord William Howard, of Naworth Castle (1563-1640), son of Thomas, 4th Duke of Norfolk, *q.v.*, by his 2nd wife, mar. 1577 Elizabeth, sister and coheir of George, 6th Lord Dacre, *q.v.*, and so acquired *int. al.*† the barony of Gilsland, still owned by their descendant. His great-grandson – the grandson of his eldest son, Sir Philip Howard (1581-1616) – Charles Howard, P.C., F.R.S. (*c.* 1628-85), was High Sheriff of Cumberland 1649, M.P. for Westmorland 1653, and for Cumberland 1654, 1656 and 1660. He was cr. Baron Gilsland and Viscount Howard of Morpeth 1657, and Baron Dacre of Gilsland, Viscount Howard of Morpeth and Earl of Carlisle 1661; he was Lord Lieutenant of Durham 1672-85, and Governor of Jamica 1677-81. His son Edward, 2nd Earl (d. 1692), was Lord Lieutenant of Cumberland 1668-85, Governor of Carlisle 1679-87, M.P. for Cumberland 1679-81, and for Carlisle 1681. His son Charles, 3rd Earl (1669-1738), the builder of Castle Howard (Y), was

* MMD gives for: Howard, D of Norfolk & Baron of Burgh. [Quarterly of six] 1, Gules a bend between six cross crosslets fitché Argent (Howard); 2, Gules three lions passant guardant in pale Or a label of three points [Argent] (England); 3, Chequy Or and Azure (Warren); 4, Gules a lion rampant Argent [Mowbray]; 5, Gules a lion rampant Or [FitzAlan]; 6, Argent a chief Azure [Clun]; 7, Gules a fret Or [presumably intended for Maltravers, Sable a fret Or]; 8, Argent a fess and a canton Gules (Woodville). The Crest is on a Hillock & put. [*sic* – correctly, Vert] a Horse passant arg bearing in his mouth an oak branch wth an acorn pp^r^. The Supporters are a Lyon & a Horse Arg. The word Virtutis Laus Actio.

† The Dacre estates in Yorkshire (inherited by the 9th Earl's son, the Hon. Geoffrey William Algernon Howard) and Northumberland, also fell to Lord and Lady William Howard.

Governor of Carlisle 1693-1738 and Lord Lieutenant of Cumberland and Westmorland 1694-1712 and 1714-38. Frederick, 5th Earl, K.T., P.C. (1748-1825), was Lord Lieutenant of Ireland 1780-82. His son George, 6th Earl, P.C., M.A., D.C.L. (Oxon), F.R.S.(1773-1848), was M.P. for Cumberland 1806-20, and Lord Privy Seal 1827-28 and 1834. His eldest son George William Frederick, 7th Earl, P.C., M.A. (Oxon), F.R.S. (1802-64), was Lord Lieutenant of Ireland 1855-58 and 1859-64, and died *s.p.* The 9th Earl, George James, B.A. (Cantab), D.C.L. (Dunelm), was M.P. for East Cumberland 1879-85. His great-grandson Charles James Ruthven Howard, M.C. (b. 1923), the 12th Earl, is the present holder of the title. *Arms.* Quarterly of six, 1, Gules on a bend between six cross crosslets fitché Argent an escutcheon Or charged with a demi lion rampant pierced through the mouth by an arrow within a double tressure flory counter-flory of the first a mullet for difference (Howard); 2, Gules three lions passant guardant in pale Or in chief a label of three points Argent (Brotherton); 3, Chequy Or and Azure (Warenne); 4, Gules a lion rampant Argent (Mowbray); 5, Gules three escallops Argent (Dacre); 6, Barry of six Argent and Azure over all three chaplets Gules (Greystoke).* *Crest.* On a chapeau Gules turned up Ermine a lion statant guardant the tail extended Or ducally gorged Argent a mullet Sable for difference. *Supporters.* Dexter, A lion Argent a mullet Sable; Sinister, A bull Gules armed unguled ducally gorged and lined Or. *Motto.* Volo, non valeo (BP105). In an achievement at Naworth Castle, the supporters are carved as: Two lions. On a loving cup presented by Charles 3rd Earl, to Carlisle Corporation in 1701, the supporters are: Dexter, A lion rampant; Sinister, A lion rampant crowned over the sinister shoulder a cross crosslet fitché the point held by the sinister paw.

HOWARD, Baron Howard of Penrith. Sir Esme William Howard, P.C., G.C.B., G.C.M.G., C.V.O., LL.D. (Hon.) (Washington and Hartford) (1863-1939), 4th son of Henry Howard, of Greystoke, *q.v.*, was Ambassador at Madrid 1919-24 and at Washington 1924-30. He was raised to the Peerage as Baron Howard of Penrith, of Gowbarrow, Cumberland, 1930. He was succ. as 2nd and present Baron by his eldest surviving son, Francis Philip Raphael Howard, B.A. (Cantab); and his 2nd surviving son, the Hon.

* To attempt to record all the quarterings to which the Howard family is entitled would be out of place in a work on Cumberland families and heraldry. However, no such work would be complete without a description of the stone shields above the entrances to the Inner Court and the Great Hall of Naworth Castle, displaying the achievement of Lord William Howard, above, with twenty-two quarterings. Many of these are dealt with in separate entries in this book, so we refer the reader to these and blazon here only those quarterings not dealt with elsewhere. The absence from the shield of tinctures (which we have nonetheless given) makes the identification of certain of the coats somewhat tentative, and we have followed R. S. Ferguson, CW1 iv, and FAC. *Arms.* Quarterly of twenty-two, 1, Howard, *q.v.*; 2, Fitton, *q.v.*; 3, Boys, *q.v.*; 4, Scales, *q.v.*; 5, Tendring, *q.v.*; 6, Mowbray, *q.v.*; 7, Braose, *q.v.*; 8, Segrave, *q.v.*; 9, Per pale Or and Vert a lion rampant Gules (Bigot, a Mowbray quartering); 10, Brotherton, *q.v.*; 11, Mowbray, *q.v.*; 12, Barry of eight Or and Gules (ascribed to FitzAlan by Ferguson and Field); 13, Gules a lion rampant Or (FitzAlan); 14, Azure a wolf's head erased Argent (Lupus, a Mowbray quartering); 15, Azure three garbs Or (Earl of Chester, a Mowbray quartering); 16, Wydville, *q.v.* (also a Mowbray quartering); 17, Sable a fret Or (Maltravers, a Mowbray quartering); 18, Argent a chief Azure (Clun, a Mowbray quartering); 19, Warenne, *q.v.*; 20, Tylney, *q.v.*; 21, Quarterly Or and Gules a bordure Sable bezanté (Rochfort, a Tylney quartering); 22, Azure three crescents Argent (Thorpe, a Tylney quartering). The shield above the entrance to the Great Hall impales: Quarterly of eight, 1, Dacre, *q.v.*; 2, Greystoke, 2nd Line, *q.v.*; 3, Greystoke, 1st Line, *q.v.*; 4, Multon, *q.v.*; 5, Boteler, of Wemme, *q.v.*; 6, Morville, *q.v.*; 7, Ferrers, of Wemme, *q.v.*; 8, Chequy Or and Gules (Vaux, of Gilsland, *q.v.*).

Photo] [the late Ferdinand Hudleston

The entrance door of the 1660 wing at Hutton John, now in the tower garden wall. The shield on the left bears Hudleston with Hutton on an escutcheon of pretence; the middle shield shows Hudleston and Hutton impaling Sisson; the shield on the right bears Hudleston and Hutton impaling 1 & 4, Fleming. 2, Urswick. 3, Lancaster

Hubert John Edward Dominic Howard, is of Lyulph's Tower, Ullswater. *Arms, Crests* and *Motto.* The same as those now borne by the Dukes of Norfolk, see Howard, of Greystoke. *Supporters.* Dexter, A lion Argent; Sinister, A horse also Argent holding in the mouth a sprig of oak fructed Proper; each charged on the shoulder with an escutcheon barry of six Argent and Azure three chaplets Gules (BP105).

HOWE, of Great Corby. This family, long landowners in Great Corby, appears to descend from John Howe, born *c.* 1490, died before 1555. John Howe (d. 1679) was ancestor of Joseph Howe (1791-1879), who directed in his will that his estates at Corby should be sold. His youngest son Jonah Howe, of Bolton (L) (1837-1921), was father of Joseph Hudson Howe (1882-1963), whose son Albert Howe, of Bolton (1909-60), left two sons, Malcolm Stuart Howe, M.A. (Cantab), and Graham Douglas Howe. The former, of 31 King's Court North, King's Road, Chelsea, is the senior male representative of the family, and is secretary of the Northern group of the Society of Genealogists. *Arms.* Per fess enarched Argent and Vert three crosses flory fitchy one and two counterchanged between as many roses two Gules barbed and seeded Proper and one Argent barbed and seeded Or. *Crest.* On a mount Vert semé of roses Gules and Argent as in the arms a dragon segreant Vert armed and langued Gules charged on the underside of each wing with a cross flory fitchy Argent and holding with the forelegs a fire steel striking a flint stone enflamed Proper. *Mottoes.* Malcolm Stuart Howe uses: Insignia nobilitatis astreantria dignis.* His brother Graham Douglas Howe uses: Astra castra numen lumen.

HOWE. John Howe, solicitor, of Scotch Street, Carlisle (d. 1866, aged 44), Mayor of Carlisle 1858, was of Cavendish Mount, Stanwix, where he was succ. by his son, Charles John Howe, J.P., B.A., LL.M. (Cantab), solicitor (1847-1903), a Parliamentary agent and partner in the firm of Brownlow & Howe, New Court, Carey Street, London, who lived at Matson Ground, Windermere. His son Bertram Charles Howe, B.A. (Cantab) (1871-1940), was a solicitor in Carlisle and was Deputy Clerk of the Peace for Cumberland. *Arms.* Argent a fess engrailed between three swine's heads erased Sable (FAC).

HOYLE. Sir Emmanuel Hoyle, 1st and last Bart., O.B.E., J.P., of Inglewood Bank, Penrith (1866-1939), a woollen manufacturer in Huddersfield, son of Joseph Hoyle, of Stranraer House, Longwood, near Huddersfield (1844-1920), was cr. Baronet 1922. *Arms.* Per fess Argent and Or within two flaunches Sable each charged with a rose of the first barbed and seeded Proper a mullet of the third. *Crest.* In front of a tower Proper a lion couchant Or. *Badge.* A rose Gules leaved and slipped between two sprigs of thyme Proper enfiled by a circlet Or. *Motto.* Faber quisque fortunae suae (FD7).

HUDDLESTON, Baron Huddleston. Thomas Huddleston, of Whitehaven, captain in the merchant service, later Haven Master in Dublin, probably a cadet of Huddleston of Whitbeck, was father of Sir John Walter Huddleston, Baron Huddleston (1815-90), the last created Baron of the Exchequer. Born in Dublin, called to the Bar 1839, M.P. 1865 and 1874, and Serjeant-at-law 1875, in which year he was raised to the bench of the

* This is the Latin version of the words spoken in *Macbeth* by Duncan of his son Malcolm, "Signs of nobleness, like stars, shall shine on all deservers."

Common Pleas and was knighted, he was later in the same year transferred to the Court of Exchequer.* He marr. 1872 Lady Diana de Vere Beauclerk (d. 1905), dau. of the 9th Duke of St. Albans, but died *s.p. Arms.* Quarterly, 1, Gules fretty Argent in dexter chief a portcullis Or; 2 & 3, Quarterly i & iv, France and England quarterly; ii, Scotland; iii, Ireland; over all a baton Gules charged with three roses Argent barbed and seeded Proper; 4, Gules fretty Argent.† *Crest.* Two arms counter embowed and vested Argent holding in the hands a scalp Proper. *Motto.* Solo Deo honor et gloria (Window at Gray's Inn, London, of which he was Treasurer).

HUDLESTON, of Millom. Nigel, "prepositus" of the Archbishop of York, acquired an estate in Huddleston (Y) and was ancestor of the Hudlestons of Cumberland. He was living between 1109-1112, at which time he had become a monk in Selby Abbey. His descendant Sir Richard de Hudleston succ. and in 1249 obtained a licence to hear divine service in his chapel at Huddleston and died soon after. His son Richard died *v.p.* and his younger son John, see below, was of Millom. He was succ. by his grandson Richard, who died *s.p.*, probably before 1276, when Huddleston passed to his sister Beatrix, who marr. John de Melsa. Richard's uncle John de Hudleston (d. *c* 1252) was accused by the Archbishop of York of evicting his servants from Huddleston 1250-1. He marr. Joan, dau. and heir of Adam de Boyvill, *q.v.*, and acquired the Lordship of Millom, which passed to their son Sir John Hudleston (d. before 1306), a noted soldier, who fought against the Welsh and Scots, and was present at the Battle of Falkirk and at the siege of Caerlaverock.‡ He was Governor of Galloway and Keeper of Ayr, Wigtown, Cruggleton and Botel Castles 1297. He sealed the Barons' letter to the Pope as Lord of Aneys 1301. His descendant Sir Richard, living 1433, was at Agincourt. His grandson Sir John Hudleston (d. 1493) was High Sheriff of Cumberland 1454, 1463, 1468 and 1472, and fought in the Wars of the Roses as a Yorkist, becoming Lieutenant of the Honour of Cockermouth and Constable of the castle 1461. He was Knight of the Shire for Cumberland 1467. He marr.§ Mary, dau. and coheir of Sir Henry Fenwick, *q.v.* Their eldest son Sir Richard, knighted by the Duke of Gloucester 1482, died *v.p.*, probably killed at Bosworth. He marr. 1465 Margaret, illegitimate dau. of Richard Neville, Earl of Warwick. Their son Richard (b. 1476,

* The Judicature Act of 1875 made his patent as Baron of the Exchequer the last to be issued, and as a result he used to call himself "the last of the barons."

† For comments on these arms, see CW2 lxxii 343-4.

‡ The Caerlaverock Roll has a translation of the French lines concerning him:

Likewise John de Hodleston
Who appears well and promptly
In arms at all seasons
He served the Earl [of Lincoln]
Which makes it right
That he should be named among his followers
He bore gules fretty of silver.

§ His son William (d. before October 1509) marr. before 1486 Lady Isabel Neville, 5th dau. and coheir of John, Marquess Montagu, and with her acquired the Sawston estate, Cambridgeshire, still in the possession of their descendants. To this branch of the family belong Jane Huddleston, wife of Dr. Donald Mason Chalmers Ainscow, M.A. (Cantab), of The Grange, Temple Sowerby, and dau. of Edward Henry Huddleston (1885-1934), and her cousin Barbara Huddleston, Countess of Loudoun, dau. of Capt Reginald Mowbray Chichester Abney-Hastings, formerly Huddleston (b. 1894), who marr. 1916 Edith Maud, later Countess of Loudoun, Baroness Botreaux, Stanley and Hastings.

d. before 1505) succ. to Millom, but died *s.p.** and was succ. by his uncle Sir John Hudleston (*c.* 1440/45-1512), who was High Sheriff of Cumberland 1505, but lived chiefly in Cloucestershire, where he was Constable of Sudeley Castle 1478-1512. He marr. Joan (d. 1519), dau. and heir of Sir Miles Stapleton, of Bedale (Y). Their son Sir John (*c.* 1488-1547) was made a Knight of the Bath at Anne Boleyn's Coronation 1533. He too lived chiefly in Gloucestershire where he built Southam Delabere. By his wife Joan Seymour he was father of Anthony his successor; by his 3rd wife Joyce Prickley he had a son Andrew, see Hudleston, of Hutton John. Anthony Hudleston (*c.* 1519-98) was High Sheriff of Cumberland 1563 and 1574. He marr. 1541 Marie (d. 1581), dau. and coheir of Sir William Barantyne, of Haseley, Oxon., and was succ. by their son William (1549-1628) who was Knight of the Shire for Cumberland 1601 and High Sheriff 1617. His son Ferdinando (1577-*c.* 1645) was Knight of the Shire for Cumberland 1623-24. His son Sir William Hudleston (1603-69) was a noted Royalist, who raised a regiment for the King. The estates eventually passed to his son Joseph (*c.* 1636/7-1700), who was High Sheriff 1692. He died *s.p.* and was succ. by his cousin Richard (d. 1719) whose grandson William (1699-1745) was the last male. He had two daus., Elizabeth (1728-93), who succ., and Isabella (1732-1801). The former marr. 1748 Sir Hedworth Williamson, 5th Bart., of Monkwearmouth Hall (D) (*c.* 1710-88); they sold the Lordship of Millom to Sir James Lowther, Bart., 1774. *Arms.* Gules fretty Argent (FFC). *Crest.* Two arms dexter and sinister embowed vested Argent holding in the hands a scalp Proper the inside Gules (LMC). *Motto.* Soli Deo honor et gloria (BLG18). The arms are on shields in Millom church and at Hutton John, and at Hayles Abbey, Glos., is a stone with a quarterly coat, as follows: Quarterly, 1 & 4, Hudleston; 2 & 3, FitzAlan impaling Stapleton.†

* His sisters and coheirs were Margaret (b. *c.* 1479), wife of Lancelot Salkeld, *q.v.*, and Joan (b. *c.* 1480), wife of Hugh Fleming. They succ. to their mother's manors of Blennerhasset and Upmanby.

† At Hutton John there is a fine oil painting of the Hudleston achievement, brought from Millom Castle, as follows: *Arms.* Quarterly of twenty, 1 & 20, Gules fretty Argent; 2, Argent a bend between two mullets Sable; 3, Argent a chevron between three bulls' heads cabossed Sable; 4, Per fess Gules and Argent six martlets counterchanged; 5, Argent a lion rampant Sable; 6, Argent a lion rampant Azure; 7, Barry of eight Or and Gules; 8, Sable a fret Or; 9, Azure a fess between three leopards' faces Or; 10, Per pale Or and Vert a cross moline Gules; 11, Per pale Argent and Gules a bend counterchanged; 12, Gules three eagles displayed Sable (*sic*; correctly, Sable three eagles displayed Argent armed Or); 13, Argent a bend between six cross crosslets fitché Sable (*sic*; correctly, Azure a bend between six cross crosslets fitché Or); 14, Ermine two bars and in chief a demi lion rampant issuant Gules; 15, Argent on a chief Or two bucks' heads cabossed Proper (*sic*; correctly, Argent on a chief Gules two bucks' heads cabossed Or); 16, Azure a chevron Or between ten bezants; 17, Ermine on a fess Or three billets Sable; 18, Argent a chevron between three mullets pierced Gules; 19, Azure three chevronels gules (*sic*; correctly, Azure three chevronels Argent). *Crest.* Two arms dexter and sinister embowed vested Argent holding in the hands a scalp Proper the inside gules. *Motto.* Soli Deo honor et gloria. *Legend.* The Paternal Arms of Ferdinand Hudleston of Millum Castle in the County Cumberland Esqr. Who Quarters, the Arms of Millom, Pyell, Boyvil, Fenwick, Stapleton, Falkinbridge, Fits-Allon, Harrington, Dela-pole, Ingham, Chaucer, Barington, Drayton, Popham, Zouch, Malyn, &c.

It seems very probable that the marshalling of the above quarters was undertaken by Sir Daniel Fleming, of Rydal (1633-1701) (see AWL), the well known scholar and antiquary, who was a close friend and a kinsman of Ferdinand Hudleston, of Millom (d. 1687). Despite the interpretation placed on certain of the quarters by Sir Daniel Fleming (see MDF, p. 90), the key to them appears to us to be: 1 & 20, Hudleston; 2, Pyel; 3, Boyvill; 4, Fenwick, 5, Stapleton; 6, Brus; 7, FitzAlan, of Bedale; 8, Bellew; 9, De la Pole; 10, Ingham; 11, Chaucer; 12, Barantyne;

HUDLESTON, of Hutton John. Andrew Hudleston, of Farington Hall (L) (*c.* 1532-1601), son of Sir John Hudleston, of Millom (d. 1547), *q.v.*, marr. 1564 Mary, dau. of Cuthbert Hutton, of Hutton John, *q.v.*, and sister and coheir of Thomas Hutton. Their son* Joseph Hudleston, of Farington Hall and Hutton John (1565-1646), bought Hutton John from his uncle Thomas Hutton 1615. His son and heir† Andrew Hudleston (1603-72) served in the Royalist army and was fined as a papist and delinquent. His son Andrew (1638-1706) was the first Protestant in the family and was Receiver General of Cumberland and Westmorland and High Sheriff of Cumberland 1683.‡ He had, *int. al.*, sons Wilfrid (1673-1729), who succ. him, and Lawson (see Hudleston, of Kelston and Hutton John). The former had, *int. al.*, sons Andrew and the Rev. Curwen (see below). The former, who was D.L., J.P., was born 1705 and died 1780. He was called to the Bar 1728, was Recorder of Carlisle and Chairman of Cumberland Quarter Sessions for nearly 40 years. He marr. 1731 Mary (d. 1796), dau. and heir of the Rev. Richmond Fenton, of Plumpton Hall, and had a son and heir Andrew Hudleston, barrister at law (1734-1821), who was Bencher of Gray's Inn 1770 and Treasurer 1775. He sold part of the Hutton John estate to his friend Charles, 11th Duke of Norfolk,§ in 1787. He marr. 1794 Elizabeth (d. 1830, aged 77), 4th dau. of Sir William Fleming, 3rd Bart., and sister and, in her issue, coheir of Sir Michael le Fleming, 4th Bart. Their son Andrew Fleming Hudleston, J.P., H.E.I.C.S. (1796-1861), High Sheriff of Cumberland 1849, was the last of the male line. A few months before his death he succ. his cousin Lady le Fleming in the Rydal estates. He bequeathed Hutton John to his kinsman William Hudleston, see Hudleston, of Kelston and Hutton John. His great-uncle the Rev. Curwen Hudleston, M.A. (Oxon) (1709-71), was incumbent of St. Nicholas, Whitehaven 1735-71, and was succ. by his son the Rev. Wilfrid Hudleston, B.A. (Cantab) (1745-1829), who held the living until 1811. He was succ. by his only son the Rev. Andrew Hudleston, M.A., D.D. (Cantab) (1779-1851), who held the living till his death, and was Rector of Moresby 1821-23, and of Bowness-on-Solway 1828. Dying unmarr., his surviving sisters Mary, Elizabeth, Joyce, who marr. James Kiero Watson, and Dorothy were his coheirs. All died without surviving

13, Drayton; 14, Segrave; 15, Popham; 16, Zouche; 17, Maylyngs, or Molyns; 18, Deyne; 19, Lewknor.

We are indebted to the late E. St. John Brooks, of 121 St. George's Square, London, S.W.1, for help in identifying some of these.

* A younger son Richard, O.S.B. (1583-1655), was a well known priest, author of *A Short and Plain Way to the Faith and Church.* See DNB.

† His 2nd son John Hudleston, O.S.B. (1608-98), was the priest who aided Charles II's escape after the Battle of Worcester and received him into the Roman Catholic church on his death bed (DNB).

‡ He played a prominent part in promoting the Revolution of 1688.

§ Many stories are told of the two friends. One relates how, when they were in their cups at Greystoke Castle, the Duke always lost the power of speech and Hudleston the use of his limbs. When the third bottle was finished, the Duke, by this time speechless, would rise from the table, walk across the dining-room, and ring the bell for the footman, who would be told by Hudleston, by now unable to move, to bring them another bottle. It is also said that on one occasion at Greystoke Castle, Hudleston fell under the table and the Duke attempted to pick him up. "Never," said Hudleston, "shall it be said that the Head of the House of Hudleston was helped to his feet by a Howard." "In that case," replied the Duke, "the Head of the House of Howard will have to lie down by the side of the Head of the House of Hudleston," and the two friends spent the rest of the evening side by side on the floor.

issue, but their sister Eleanor (1775-1851), who marr. 1807 Thomas Ward, had a dau. Elizabeth (1807-78) who marr. 1827 John Simpson, M.D., J.P. (1793-1867), who assumed the surname and arms of Hudleston 1867. His elder son, Wilfrid Hudleston Hudleston, J.P., M.A. (Cantab), F.R.S., F.G.S. (1828-1909), see DNB, was succ. by his brother the Rev. John Henry Hudleston, M.A. (Cantab) (1834-1912), who was of Cayton Hall, South Stainley, Yorks. His grandson Nigel Andrew Hudleston, M.A. (Cantab), is now of Cayton Hall and Rectory Farm, Rillington. *Arms, Crest* and *Motto.* As Hudleston, of Millom.

HUDLESTON, of Kelston and Hutton John. The Ven. Lawson Hudleston, M.A. (Oxon) (1678-1743), 5th son of Andrew Hudleston, of Hutton John, *q.v.,* was Rector of Kelston, Som., 1710-43, Prebendary of Wells 1712-43, Vicar of St. Cuthbert, Wells, 1736-41, and Archdeacon of Bath 1733-43. From his elder surviving son descended Lt-Col Ivor Robert Hudleston, D.S.O., R.A.M.C. (1886-1951), whose elder son Major Guy Lawson Harington Hudleston, R.A., of Hinton Martell, Dorset, is now head of this branch of the family. The Archdeacon's younger son, the Rev. William Hudleston, M.A. (Cantab) (1716-66), was father of John Hudleston, M.P., H.E.I.C.S., of Bath (1749-1835), a director of the East India Company 1803-26.* His grandson William Hudleston, C.S.I., J.P., Madras Civil Service (1826-94), was Member of Council at Madras 1877-82, and Acting Governor 1881. In 1861 he succ. his kinsman Andrew Fleming Hudleston, *q.v.,* in the Hutton John estate and was succ. by his eldest son Andrew John Hudleston, J.P. (1856-1912), whose daus. and coheirs were Gertrude Dorothy, of Knowe Crag, Threlkeld (1896-1970), Margaret Jessie, and Honoria Joan. He was succ. at Hutton John by his brother Ferdinand Hudleston, J.P. (1857-1951), well known as a writer on antiquarian subjects, and an honorary member of the Cumberland & Westmorland Antiquarian & Archaeological Society.† His son and heir Nigel Ferdinand Hudleston (1901-69) was also a prominent member of the Society, a member of Cumberland County Council, and first Chairman of the Joint Archives Committee. His son John Andrew Hudleston (b. 1931), who works for the World Health Organisation in Geneva, is head of this branch of the family, which is represented in Cumberland by his son Roland Andrew Hudleston (b. 1965), who is now the owner of the Hutton John estate. *Arms, Crest* and *Motto.* As Hudleston, of Millom.

HUDLESTON, of Rainors. Daniel Hudleston (d. 1832, aged 99) bought Rainors, Gosforth, 1771 and he and his son John (1772-1834) built up the estate. Of John the *Cumberland Pacquet* of 8 July 1834 said "probably there is not one person in England to whom the enclosure of so many commons was entrusted." His daus. and coheirs were Hannah (1799-1845), marr. 1820 William Wright, surgeon, of Gosforth; Mary (b. 1801), marr. 1821 John Hetherington, of Branthwaite Hall; and Faith (1807-55), marr. 1831 the Rev. John Fox (d. 1859), Headmaster of St. Bees School, *q.v. Arms.* Gules

* (Note by R. S. Boumphrey.) From him descends also the distinguished Northern genealogist, C. Roy Hudleston, F.S.A., with whom it has been such a privilege and a pleasure to collaborate in compiling this book, a work which could never have been brought to fruition without his unrivalled knowledge of Cumbrian families and relationships.

† Before succeeding to the estate he was a civil engineer in Liverpool and London, one of his chief works being the Central London Tube Railway.

fretty Argent. *Crest.* An arm embowed in armour grasping a sword (Tombstone, Gosforth churchyard).

HUDSON. John Hudson, of Lane Foot, Caldbeck, and of Haltcliffe Hall (d. 1764, aged 84), was father of the Rev. Joseph Hudson (1719-1811), Prebendary of Carlisle, and of Christopher (b. 1718). The latter's son, the Rev. Joseph Hudson (1762-1839), was Vicar of Stanwix 1808-39. He was father of the Rev. Samuel Hudson (1802-34), Vicar of Castle Carrock, and of the Rev. Joseph Hudson (1793-1891) who was vicar of Chillingham (N). The latter's son the Rev. Joseph Hudson, M.A. (Cantab) (1834-1919), was vicar of Troutbeck (W) 1870-77, and of Crosby-on-Eden 1879-95. His elder son, Canon Ernest Hudson, M.A. (Cantab) (1869-1958), was Vicar of Barton (W) 1931-58. *Arms* (granted to the Rev. Joseph Hudson and the descendants of his father 1786). Or three falchions barwise in pale Sable on a chief per pale Gules and Azure a cross moline between two cross crosslets fitché Argent. *Crest.* A falcon wings displayed Proper beaked membered and belled Or collared Azure reposing the dexter claw on an escutcheon Gules charged with a cross crosslet fitché Argent (CA xvi/189).

HUDSON. Thomas Hudson, of Wigton (d. 1807, aged 66), was 4th son of Christopher Hudson, of Lonning Foot, and was Clerk to the Dean and Chapter of Carlisle. His eldest son Robert, Midshipman, R.N. (b. 1764), was killed in action on H.M.S. *Magicienne* 1783; his 2nd son Thomas Hudson (1772-1852), M.P. for Evesham 1831-35, bought Cheswardine Hall, Salop, 1835, died *s.p.,* and left the estate to his great nephew Charles Donaldson, *q.v.* *Arms* (as quartered by Donaldson). Or on a fess dancetté between two boars' heads couped in chief and a lion rampant in base Gules two martlets of the field.

HUDSON, Viscount Hudson of Pewsey. Robert Spear Hudson, P.C., C.H., 1st Viscount Hudson of Pewsey, Co. Wilts (1886-1957), who was Minister of Pensions 1935-36, Minister of Shipping 1940, and Minister of Agriculture 1940-45, was M.P. for Whitehaven 1924-29, and lived at Ingwell Moor Row. He was cr. Viscount 1952, and was succ. by his only son Robert William (1924-63), who died *s.p.m.* when the title became extinct. *Arms.* Gules a cross moline between two garbs and two dolphins in saltire Or. *Crest.* An East African crowned crane Proper. *Supporters.* Dexter, A Friesian bull; Sinister, A sable antelope Proper; each gorged with a chain pendant therefrom a portcullis Gold. *Motto.* Animo non astutia (NEP).

HUGHES – LE FLEMING. Major-General George Cumberland Hughes, D.L., J.P., Madras Native Infantry (1807-77), succ. his cousin Andrew Fleming Hudleston in the Beckermet, Skirwith, Rydal and other estates in 1861. He was eldest son of John Cumberland Hughes, of Bath, who marr. 1805, Elizabeth (d. 1856, aged 75), dau. and coheir of George Edward Stanley by his marr. 1774 to Dorothy (d. 1786), dau. of Sir William Fleming, 3rd Bart., and sister and in her issue coheir of Sir Michael le Fleming, 4th Bart. General Hughes assumed 1862 the additional surname and arms of le Fleming, and was succ. by his son, Stanley Hughes le Fleming, D.L., J.P. (1855-1939), whose elder son Michael George Hughes le Fleming, J.P. (1900-66), succ. The present representatives of the family are his sisters, Mrs. Joan Isabel Curwen, of Manor Cottage, Rydal, and Mrs. Diana Elizabeth Stockley. *Arms.* Quarterly, 1 & 4, Gules a fret Argent (Fleming); 2 & 3, Quarterly Or and Argent a lion rampant Azure between three fountains (Hughes). *Crests.* 1, A serpent nowed holding in the mouth a wreath of olive and vine leaves all Proper (Fleming); 2, Upon a mount Vert a lion couchant Or gutté de larmes the dexter paw resting on a fountain Proper (Hughes). *Motto.* Pax, copia, sapientia (BLG17).

HULTON. The Rev. Arthur Emilius Hulton, M.A. (Cantab) (1812-68), was Incumbent of Threlkeld 1849-53, and Incumbent of Ivegill 1853-68. He built Ivegill church and vicarage, and gave to Crosthwaite church the north-east window in memory of his brother; he also gave the church a silver gilt communion set. *Arms.* Quarterly, 1 & 4, Argent a lion rampant Gules; 2 & 3, Quarterly Sable and Or in the first quarter a lion passant of the last (Window in Crosthwaite church).

HUME. The Rev. Robert Hume, M.A. (Edin) (d. 1706), was Vicar of Crosby-on-Eden 1672-80, of Lazonby 1680-1703, and of Aspatria 1703-6. His brother, the Rev. George Hume, M.A. (Edin) (d. 1703), was Rector of Beaumont with Kirkandrews-on-Eden 1692-1703. *Arms.* Quarterly, 1 & 4, . . . a lion rampant . . . ; 2, . . . three popinjays . . . ; 3, . . . a cross engrailed . . . (Seal of the Rev. Robert Hume – Haresceugh deeds).

HUNTINGTON. John Huntington, apothecary, was admitted a freeman of Carlisle as a member of the Merchants' Guild on Low Sunday, 1717. *Arms.* Ermine on a bend Argent cotised Or three water bougets Gules. *Crest.* A stag's head couped Proper attired Or transfixed with an arrow Or (Painting in Tullie House, Carlisle).

HUTCHINSON, of Carlisle and Itonfield. This family descends from Nicholas Hutchinson, of Durham (d. 1630). John Hutchinson, of Framwellgate, Durham (d. 1715), was Mayor of the city 1714. His son John Hutchinson (1708-49) marr. 1732 Isabella (d. 1746), dau. and coheir of Christopher Richmond, of Highhead Castle and Catterlen, *q.v.*, and had a son John (d. 1776) who was of Skirsgill, also of Newbiggin Hall (W) and Appleby. His son Christopher William Hutchinson (1769-1822), the last male of the family, was of Carlisle and Itonfield. His heir was his sister Elizabeth (1765-1836), who mar. 1785 Capt John Nickleson Martin, *q.v.*, (SHD iv (II) 155; BLG4). *Arms.* The monument in Carlisle Cathedral to Christopher William Hutchinson, above, displays: Quarterly, 1 & 4, Azure a lion rampant within an orle of cross crosslets Argent (Hutchinson); 2, Gules two bars gemel and a chief Or (Richmond); 3, Gules a fess chequy Or and Gules between three garbs [Or] (Vaux). *Crest.* A lion rampant. In 1836 Capt Thomas Martin, RN., of the Wilderness, Reigate, eldest surviving son of John Nickleson Martin, above, petitioned the College of Arms for a grant of arms for Hutchinson, stating that the family, long resident in Durham City, used the Hutchinson arms as recorded at the 1666 Visitation of Durham. The grantee had done research to discover the common ancestor of the two Hutchinson families without success, and therefore sought a new grant to be quartered with the Martin arms. He was granted the following *Arms.* Per pale Gules and Azure semé of cross crosslets Or a lion rampant Argent a canton Ermine (CA xli/380). Burke records the *Crest* as: Out of a ducal coronet Or a cockatrice wings endorsed Azure beaked combed and wattled Gules (BGA).

HUTCHINSON, of Ousby. Robert Hutchinson, of Ousby, had a dau. Margaret who marr. William Bird, of Brougham (W) (living 6 Henry VIII) (FCW). *Arms.* Per pale, dexter Gules crusilly Or, sinister Azure, over all a lion rampant Argent (HMS v 149; MS. pedigree in the Record Office, Kendal, compiled 1681 by Gregory King, Rouge Dragon, and certified by Dugdale).

HUTCHINSON. Sir Joseph Turner Hutchinson, J.P., M.A. (Cantab) (1850-1924), was 2nd son of Isaac Hutchinson, of Braystones. He was Chief Justice of the Gold Coast 1889-95, of Grenada 1895-97, of Cyprus 1897-1906, and of Ceylon 1906-11. He was knighted 1895 and was High Sheriff of Cumberland 1918-19. For a time he lived at Lorton Hall, and latterly at Newtown, Ravenglass. *Arms.* Azure a lion rampant . . . between six annulets . . . , two, two and two. *Crest.* A griffin sejant its dexter foreclaw resting on an annulet. *Motto.* Sursum corda (Seal).

HUTHWAITE. In 1266-67 Thomas de Hotewayt and Beatrix de Lowther were parties to a fine concerning the advowson of Brigham, and a man of the same names made a settlement of the manor of Hothwayt (Huthwaite) and half the manor of Brigham 1337-38. By 1398 the estates had passed to the Swinburne family, *q.v. Arms.* Sable fretty Ermine (MMD).

HUTTON, of Hutton-in-the-Forest. The history of this family is in CW2 xi, xxv and xxx. The Huttons were hereditary foresters of Plumpton Hay, Edmund having been granted Hutton-in-the-Forest, held by the service of keeping Plumpton Hay. His grandson Adam succ. 1168, the male line ending with Thomas Hutton whose dau. and heir Cecily marr. Nicholas le Venur. Thomas de Hoton, who may have been descended from Edmund, died 1319, owning Hutton. His descendant Thomas (d. 1362) bought land from John de Rachton 1348, holding it by the service of holding the stirrup when the King mounted his horse in Carlisle Castle. His descendant William Hutton (1493-1557) marr. Margaret, dau. and coheir of Anthony Crackanthorpe, *q.v.* His grandson Thomas Hutton (1549-1601) marr. Barbara, dau. and coheir of Thomas Middleton, *q.v.*, and by this marriage acquired large estates in the county. He sold most of these estates, including the manors of Bromfield, Langrigg, Mealrigg and Ousby. His son Lancelot (b. 1582) sold the remaining estates, including the manors of Skirwith in 1604 and Hutton 1606. *Arms.* FFC records, for William Hutton, "of the Forest": Gules a fess Sable between three cushions tasselled Argent. Machell recorded: Argent a bugle horn Sable stringed Gules and garnished Or on a canton of the third a martlet Argent (MMS vi 419). FVC records for Hoton, of Cumberland: Gules on a canton Argent a martlet Sable; and for Hutton, of the Forest: Ermine on a fess Gules three bucks' heads couped Argent attired Or.

HUTTON, of Hutton John. John son of Adam of Hutton is mentioned 1250 and in 1296 the Sheriff of Cumberland was ordered to deliver to Dougal de Geveleston custody of the land at Hutton John which belonged to William de Hoton until William's heir should come of age. In 1316-17 William de Hoton held Hutton John and a later bearer of the name occurs 1421-22. In 1461 the Kingmaker granted a pension of £5 a year (confirmed by Richard, Duke of Gloucester, 1473) to Thomas de Hoton, presumably the man who "mayd" the two slabs now in the dining-room at Hutton John, on one of which his arms, quartered with Thirlwall, appear, see below. Henry Hutton was a free tenant of the barony of Greystoke 1488, and Hugh Hutton (d. 1522) was Sheriff of Cumberland 1506 and 1508. His son Cuthbert (*c.* 1504-53), who succ., was Sheriff 1534 and M.P. for Cumberland 1545.

He marr. Elizabeth (d. between 1556 and 1559), dau. and coheir of Sir Robert Bellingham, and by her, who was mistress of the maids of honour at the court of her friend Queen Catherine Parr, had a son and heir Thomas Hutton (*c.* 1538-*c.* 1628), who became involved in debt,* was persecuted as a Roman Catholic, and spent 50 years in prison. His sisters and coheirs were Marie (god-dau. of Princess, later Queen, Mary), who marr. Andrew Hudleston, *q.v.*; Catherine, who marr. Edmund Dudley, of Yanwath, *q.v.*; and Anne, who marr. (1) Thomas Sandford, of Askham (d. 1574), *q.v.*, and (2) 1576 John Middleton, of Carlisle, *q.v.* (CW2 xxx). *Arms.* A stone tablet in the dining-room at Hutton John displays: Quarterly, 1 & 4, [Gules] a fess [Or] between three cushions [Argent] (Hutton); 2 & 3, [Gules] a chevron between three boars' heads couped [Argent] (Thirlwall); accompanied by a griffin segreant to the sinister, a Thirlwall supporter, and the legend "Thys mayd Thomas" [Hutton], see above. Machell recorded: Gules a fess Or between three cushions Argent tasselled Or each charged with a fleur-de-lys of the field (MMS vi 419). GMS gives: Gules a fess between three lozenges Argent each charged with a fleur-de-lys of the field. The family later bore: *Arms.* Gules a fess Or between three cushions Argent each charged with a fleur-de-lys of the field on a canton Azure a falchion of the third hilt and pommel Gold (Shields at Hutton John). *Crest.* Two eagles' heads erased in saltire endorsed Sable enfiled with a coronet Or (LMC).

HUTTON. The Rev. Richard Hutton, B.D. (d. 1704, aged 71), was Rector of Bootle 1664-1704. *Arms.* Argent on a fess Sable three stags' heads cabossed Or (Hutton); impaling, Argent three greyhounds courant in pale Sable (Hatchment, Bootle church).

HUTTON. Machell recorded the following for a Cumberland family of this name, without specifying a place of residence. *Arms.* Ermine on a fess Gules three stags' heads couped Or (MMS vi 419). GMS gives an almost identical coat for Hutton, of Penrith, *q.v.*, viz. Ermine on a fess Gules three stags' heads cabossed Or, with the note "? if the field be Erm for tis only arg in the windows of thier house at Penrith And the glass is Sable."

HUTTON, of Hutton Hall, Penrith, and Gale. John de Hoton was grandfather of John Hutton, of Penrith, who marr. 1488-89 Elizabeth, 2nd dau. and coheir of Thomas Beauchamp, of Croglin, *q.v.* Their grandsons were Sir William Hutton, of Hutton Hall (d. 1623), and Sir Richard Hutton, of Goldsborough (Y), Justice of the Common Pleas (1564-1639), who marr. Agnes, dau. and coheir of Thomas Briggs, of Cowmire (W). The above mentioned Sir William Hutton, a Commissioner of the Middle Shires, who was prominent in Border affairs,† was steward to George, Earl of Cumberland, and was High Sheriff of Cumberland 1603 and 1609 and was knighted 1604. For many years he lived at Shank Castle, Solport. He was succ. by his son Anthony Hutton (1582-1637), a Master in Chancery, whose effigy and that of his wife Elizabeth Burdett is in St. Andrew's church, Penrith. He was succ. by his brother Bernard Hutton, of Huddlesceugh, Kirkoswald (d. 1645), whose son William Hutton, also of Gale, Melmerby,

* He was obliged to sell a great deal of his property, including the manor of Crook (W), which he inherited from his mother. He sold Hutton John to his nephew Joseph Hudleston, *q.v.*, 1615.

† For Lord William Howard's strictures on Sir William, see *The Household Books of Lord William Howard* (Surtees Society).

certified his pedigree at Dugdale's Visitation of 1665, when he was aged 39. He was succ. by his son Anthony (b. 1648), who had a son Richard (1675-1717), High Sheriff of Cumberland 1708. His son Dr Addison Hutton (b. 1706) sold Hutton Hall to John Gaskarth 1734, and died *s.p.* (will dated 1741, proved 1742). His coheirs appear to have been his father's sisters, Elizabeth (b. 1672); Katherine (b. 1675), marr. Timothy Wyville, *q.v.*; Dorothy, and a sister who marr. Thomas Richardson, *q.v. Arms.* Argent on a fess Sable three bucks' heads cabossed Or (FCW). FVC gives the same coat (with a crescent for difference), quarterly with, Argent on a bend gules three bezants. (Beauchamp). *Crest.* Three broad arrows two in saltire one in pale Sable enfiled with a ducal coronet Or (FCW). The arms of Hutton impaling Briggs are in a window in Ponsonby church.

INGHAM. Shield at Hutton John; a Hudleston quartering, brought in by Stapleton, *q.v.*; Sir Miles Stapleton, of Bedale and Ingham (d. 1364), who fought at Crècy, marr. Johanna, dau. and heir of Sir Oliver de Ingham. *Arms.* Per pale Or and Vert a cross moline Gules.

INGLEWOOD, Baron – see VANE, FLETCHER-.

INGLIS. Thomas Inglis, M.D., H.E.I.C.S. (1796-1874), descended from the Inglis family of Mannerhead, near Peebles, was father of Col Henry Alves Inglis, C.M.G., R.A. (1859-1924), who marr. Ethel (1875-1975), 2nd dau. and coheir of George Robinson, of Green Lane, Dalston (1817-1908). Their son Major-General George Henry Inglis, C.B., C.B.E., D.L., J.P., R.A., of Crosby House, Crosby-on-Eden, was G.O.C. Nigeria District 1952-56, and Colonel Commandant R.A. 1960-67. He was High Sheriff of Cumberland 1961. In 1940 he marr. Margaret Edith, dau. of Charles Henry Shaw, of Rampsbeck, *q.v. Arms.* Azure a lion rampant Argent within a bordure of the last on a chief Or three mullets of the field. *Crest.* A demi lion rampant Argent. *Motto.* Nobilis est ira leonis (Bookplate).

IREBY, of Ireby. Orme, son of Gospatrick of Workington (see Curwen), was granted High Ireby before 1184 by his father. His descendants were known as de Ireby. One of them, John, was Knight of the Shire for Cumberland 1384, 1387-8 and 1396-7, and High Sheriff 1388, 1391 and 1395. A junior branch became Lords of Low or Market Ireby. To it belonged William de Ireby (d. 1257), who had a grant of a market in Ireby 1237-8. He marr. Christian, dau. and coheir of Odard, Lord of Bolton, Glassonby and Gamblesby, and had two daus. and coheirs – Eva, marr. Robert de Avenel, Robert de Stuteville and Alan de Charters; and Christiana,* who marr. (1) Thomas de Lascelles, *q.v.,* (2) Sir Adam de Jesmond, and (3) Robert Brus (JPP i 320-4). *Arms.* FFC records two coats: Argent fretty and a canton Sable; and, Argent fretty Sable on a canton Gules a cinquefoil Or. DSL records for John Ireby, the Sheriff: Argent fretty Sable a canton Gules. Papworth records: Argent fretty Gules a canton Azure (OBA). A shield on Moothill Hall, Ireby, displays, presumably for Ireby: . . . fretty . . . and a canton . . . .†

IRTON, of Irton. The Irtons were at Irton for at least six and a half centuries. The pedigree is headed by Thomas de Irton (*fl.* 1225-50) whose descendant

* At her *i.p.m.* at Carlisle 1305 the heirs to her Cumberland lands were found to be Joan (30+), wife of Roger de Edneham; Joan (28+), wife of Robert de Hudleston; Christiana (26+), wife of John de Farlam; and Isabel (25+), wife of Hugh de Bochardby.

† The illustration in MMD gives for Ireby: Argent a chevron Argent [*sic*] between three trefoils Or.

Nicholas (*fl.* 1340-70) appears to have married a Bassenthwaite coheir. A later Nicholas (*fl.* 1428-55) is said to have been Sheriff of Cumberland 1453. His descendant Richard (d. 1534), Sheriff in 1530, was grandfather of Christopher, whose younger son Christopher was Lieutenant of Cockermouth Castle and ancestor of the Irtons of Threlkeld Hall. The line at Irton was continued by his elder brother Richard Irton (1557-1608), whose descendant George (1667-1749) marr. 1695 Elizabeth Poole, of Knottingley (Y) (d. 1744, aged 75).* Their son George (1700-62), High Sheriff 1751, marr. 1732 Elizabeth (1701-75), dau. and heir of Thomas Lamplugh, but their only child Frances died 1733, a baby. He was succ. by his brother Samuel Irton, of Crown Court, Old Soho, London, merchant (1714-66), who was High Sheriff of Cumberland 1765. He marr. 1752 Frances (d. 1802), dau. and heir of Robert Tubman, of Cockermouth. Their son George Irton (1759-81) died unmarr. and was succ. by his brother Edmund Lamplugh Irton (1761-1820), High Sheriff 1791, who is described as handsome and extravagant, a friend of the Prince Regent. By his 1st wife he had a dau. and heir Anne Frances (b. 1783), who marr. Joseph Gunson, *q.v.* He was succ. by his son of his 2nd marr., Samuel Irton, D.L., J.P. (1796-1866), M.P. for West Cumberland 1833-47 and 1852-57. He marr. 1825 Eleanor,† dau. and coheir of Joseph Tiffin Senhouse, *q.v.*, but died *s.p.* Though he had nearer relatives, he left his estates to his cousin Elizabeth Fell, who marr. John Oldham Ryder *q.v.*, (CW2 xli). *Arms.* Argent a fess Sable in chief three mullets Gules (FFC). FVC records these arms quarterly with: Argent two bars and a canton Gules over all a bend Sable (Copeland). *Crests.* 1, A Saracen's head and bust affronté Proper (M.I.s, Irton church); 2, A demi lion Sable collared Argent holding in his dexter paw a mullet Gules (LMC). *Motto.* Semper constans et fidelis (M.I.s, Irton church).‡

IRVING, of Carlisle. Col Paulus Aemilius Irving, of Woodhouse, Dumfries (d. 1796, aged 84), 9th son of William Irving, of Bonshaw Tower, commanded the 15th Regt of Foot at the capture of the Heights of Abraham, Quebec, 1759; he died at Brough under Stainmore and is buried there. His son General Paulus Aemilius Irving, of Fisher Street, Carlisle (1751-1828), was cr. Baronet 1809. He was a distinguished soldier and commander of the forces in the West Indies (DNB). His son Sir Paulus Aemilius Irving, of Carlisle (1792-1838), succ. and was succ. by his brother Sir Thomas St. Lawrance Irving, of Carlisle, 3rd and last Bart (1795-1866). *Arms.* Argent three holly leaves Vert. *Crest.* An arm embowed in armour fessways holding in the hand a trefoil. *Motto.* Haud ullis labantia ventis (AWL).

IRVING, of Carlisle. Robert Irving, of Brunton Place, Warwick Road,

* Their monument in Irton church says of them, "in a long life spent in the greatest industry they retrieved an estate almost lost."

† In a letter to her son Elizabeth Hudleston wrote on 27 June 1825: "Miss Senhouse of Calder Bridg, report says, is going to be married to Mr Irton – this by no means what can . . . be considered a good business for either. A large House & distant from every place cannot be kept in repair for a trifle & where there is little on either side cannot promise much comfort in the present day."

‡ A wax seal impression in the possession of Mrs. H. S. Greg, of Little Aynam, Kendal, displays the following: *Arms.* . . . two bars the bottom edge of the lower one angled . . . in chief three mullets . . . ; impaling, . . . a lion rampant . . . within an orle of eight fleurs-de-lys . . . . *Crest.* A Saracen's head in profile. This differs somewhat from the description of the seal given by Canon S. Taylor in CW2 xli 92.

Carlisle, and of Stanwix (d. 1853, aged 54), and Mary his wife (d. 1851, aged 50), were buried in Christ Church burial ground, Botchergate. *Arms* (on tombstone). . . . three bunches of holly-leaves tied with ribbon . . . .

IRVING, of Jerriestown. John Irving, of Jerriestown, Kirklinton, died 1772, aged 87. *Arms.* . . . a chevron . . . between in chief three holly leaves . . . and in base a segment of a circle with beaded edge . . . (Kirklinton tombstone).

IRVING, of Kelsick Moss House. Clark Irving, J.P., of Kelsick Moss House, Bromfield, of Hyde Park Square, London, of Ashby Park, district of Clarence river, and of Casino, district of the Richmond river, Australia, was a member of the Legislative Assembly for New South Wales. He was born at Bromfield 1808, son of Thomas Irving, farmer, and died 1865. (*Australian Dictionary of Biography* iv 462). In 1863 he obtained a grant of the following *Arms.* Argent on a chevron Gules between three holly leaves Vert as many mullets of six points of the field a bordure of the second upon a chief Azure a fleece Or between two emus respectant Proper. *Crest.* A cornucopia fesswise Proper in front of an arm embowed in armour also Proper holding a holly leaf Vert (CA lv/12). *Motto.* Sub sole, sub umbra, virens (BGA).

IRVING, of Port Carlisle. James Irving, of Bowness-on-Solway, sea captain and mariner (1776-1833), descended from Edward Irving, of Bonshaw, Dumfriesshire (d. *c.* 1522), had a 3rd son Peter Irving, of Port Carlisle, ship owner and merchant (1804-69), father of James Irving, of Blackhall House, Carlisle, and of Solway House, Port Carlisle, shipowner, stockbroker and insurance agent (1835-77). His eldest son, John Bell Irving, of Blackhall House, also of Beanlands and of Balmacneil, Ballinluig (1864-1916), had a 2nd son John Bell Irving, now of Angerton Farm, Kirkbride (BLG18). *Arms* (of Peter Irving, of Port Carlisle, and his son James, see above). Argent three holly leaves slipped Vert within a bordure of the last. *Crest.* A dexter arm armed and embowed Proper the hand holding two holly leaves slipped Vert. *Motto.* Nullis cadentia ventis (Window in Bowness-on-Solway church). *Arms* (as matriculated by John Bell Irving, 1959). Argent three holly leaves slipped Vert within a bordure per pale dexter invected Sable sinister Or charged with five gouttes of the third (Extract of matriculation, also shield above entrance to Angerton Farm). *Crest* and *Motto.* As above.

IRWIN. William Irwin, of Highrow, Nether Denton, died 1763, aged 71, and Jane died 1764, aged 72. *Arms.* . . . three bunches each of three holly leaves . . . two in saltire and one in pale. *Crest.* Five arrows points downwards banded (Gravestone, Nether Denton churchyard). The gravestone of John Irwin, of Lowrow, Nether Denton, died 1779, aged 44, and Mary his wife, died 1784, aged 38, bears the same arms and crest, but Field recorded the latter as: A garb (FAC).

IRWIN. Andrew Irwin, of Troddermain, Lanercost, died 1769, aged 90. *Arms.* . . . three bunches each of three holly leaves slipped and banded . . . (ABD). *Crest.* A bunch of holly leaves (Lanercost tombstone).

IRWIN, of Justicetown and Calder Abbey. Thomas Irwin, of Justicetown (1757-1832), who marr. 1788 Jane, 2nd dau. of John Senhouse, of Calder Abbey, was High Sheriff of Cumberland 1808. His eldest son Capt Thomas Irwin, D.L., J.P., the Inniskilling Dragoons (1789-1877), was High Sheriff 1836.* He marr. 1823 his cousin Mary (1793-1884), eldest dau. and coheir of

* He built St. Bridget's church, Calderbridge.

Joseph Tiffin Senhouse, *q.v.*, and was of Calder Abbey *jure uxoris.* He died *s.p.* and was succ. at Justicetown by his great nephew Col Thomas Angelo Irwin, D.L., J.P., of Lynehow, near Carlisle (1845-1913). He was High Sheriff 1897, and was succ. by his eldest son Col Thomas Strutt Irwin, D.L., J.P. (b. 1881), who sold Justicetown 1946. His three daus. and coheirs were Mary Frances, marr. 1944 Ronald Mackintosh Robertson; Diana, marr. 1938 Rupert Langley Smithers; and Suzanne marr. 1942 David, 4th Lord Terrington. The male representative is the Colonel's nephew Major Arthur Francis Reginald Irwin. *Arms* (as borne by Capt Thomas Irwin). Argent three holly leaves Proper. *Crest.* A dove holding in the beak an olive branch all Proper. *Motto.* Haud ullis labentia ventis (Window, Calderbridge church). The family now bears: *Arms.* Quarterly, 1, Per pale Or and Argent three annulets in fess between as many holly leaves slipped and pendent Vert (Irwin); 2, Or a green parrot Proper in the sinister chief a cross crosslet fitché Sable (Senhouse); 3, Argent on a chevron between three lions' heads erased Gules as many battleaxes of the field (Tiffin); 4, Gules a fess Ermine between three boars' heads couped Argent (Towerson). *Crest.* Upon a mount between two holly leaves Vert a dove Argent holding in the beak an olive branch Proper and an ear of wheat Or (FD7). *Motto.* As above.

IRWIN, of The Plains. Commander Joseph Irwin, R.N., of The Plains, Wetheral (1792-1890), 3rd son of Thomas Irwin, of Justicetown, *q.v.*, marr. 1826 Emily, dau. of John Dillon, of Dublin, and had, *int. al.*, a son, the Rev. John Irwin, M.A. (T.C.D.) (b. 1830), who was Rector of Hurworth (D) 1875-1905. *Arms.* Argent three holly leaves in pale Vert. *Crest.* A dove holding in its beak an olive branch (Brass, Wetheral church).

ISMAY. Thomas Ismay, of Dundraw (1704-88), was grandfather of Thomas, of Uldale, who was captured by the French and died a prisoner in Guadaloupe 1795. His son Henry Ismay, of Maryport (1777-1862), was father of Joseph Ismay, shipbuilder and shipowner of Maryport (1804-50). His eldest son Thomas Henry Ismay, D.L., J.P. (1837-99), was educated at Croft House School, Brampton, and apprenticed to a shipping firm in Liverpool. In 1869 he founded the White Star Line. His eldest son Joseph Bruce Ismay (1862-1936) was chairman of the White Star Line and of the Asiatic Steam Navigation Co. (BLG17; Window, Maryport church; M.I.s, Maryport churchyard). *Arms.* Azure a chevron between in chief a cross pattée between two bezants and in base a cross pattée fitché all Or. *Crest.* An esquire's helmet Proper in front thereof a cross pattée fitché Or. *Motto.* Be mindful (FD7).

ITALY, Kingdom of. Amongst the shields in the east window of Upperby church commemorating the Allies of World War I, is one for the Kingdom of Italy. *Arms.* Gules a cross Argent.

JACKSON, of Armboth. John Jackson, of Armboth,* was father of Wilson Jackson (1756-1844) whose son Edward Washington Jackson, of Keswick, attorney, died *v.p.* 1825, aged 33, leaving an only child Mary (d. 1902, aged 81), who marr. 1839 Count Vladimir Boris Ossalinsky (d. 1859, aged 51), of Chestnut Hill, Keswick (see Ossolinski). Manchester Corporation acquired Armboth from the Countess in 1879. Her son Vladimir Boris Jackson Ossalinsky, of Skiddaw View, Keswick (1840-93), assumed the surname

* For anecdotes of the ghosts of Armboth, see A. G. Bradley: *Highways and Byways in the Lake District*, 1901.

Jackson. His dau. Ethel Beatrice died 1949, aged 76; his sister Nathalie marr. 1862 William Harrison, of Penrith, solicitor, and had issue. *Arms.* Or on a chevron Sable between three eagles' heads erased [Azure] as many cinquefoils Argent. *Crest.* A horse courant Argent. *Motto.* Retinens vestigia famae (M.I., Crosthwaite church).

JACKSON, of Carlisle. Thomas Jackson, of Carlisle, a trooper in Cromwell's army and nicknamed "Trooper Tom" (d. 1700), owned property in the city. He marr. 1671 Mary Johnston, presumably an heiress, and had a son Joseph Jackson, merchant, of Carlisle (d. 1733), who marr. 1710 Isabella, dau. of William Nicholson, of Carlisle, a cousin of Bishop Nicolson. Their sons the Rev. William Nicholson Jackson, of Croglin Hall, and of Scotch Street, Carlisle (*c.* 1712-76), Curate of Bromfield 1736-76, Joseph Jackson (d. 1746), and Jerome Jackson (d. 1751), all died *s.p.*, and were succ. by their sister Margery (d. unmarr. 1812, aged 90), the well known Carlisle miser, noted for her eccentricities and love of litigation (RCC).* *Arms.* The Rev. William Nicholson sealed his will (proved 1776) with the following, the impression however being very worn: Quarterly, 1 & 4, . . . on a chevron . . . between three (?) fish urinant . . . as many roundles . . . ; 2 & 3, . . . a saltire . . . on a chief . . . two cushions . . . (Johnston). *Crest.* A horse courant.

JACKSON, of Gosforth. Isaac Jackson, of The Broom, Gosforth (d. 1878), was father of Lt-Col Edwin Jackson, J.P., of The Broom, and of Threlkeld Leys, Cockermouth (b. 1858), Lt-Col commanding the 3rd Volunteer Battn the Border Regt. His son Edwin Harley Jackson was born 1888. *Arms.* Azure three pheons points downwards in fess Or between as many eagles' heads erased Ermine. *Crest.* In front of a mount Vert thereon a horse courant Argent three caltraps Or. *Motto.* Celer et audax (FD7).

JACKSON, of Greta Hall. William Jackson, carrier (d. 1809, aged 61), son of Thomas Jackson, carrier, of Low Wood, Ambleside, was of Greta Hall, Keswick, where he was landlord of Robert Southey,† poet laureate, and of the Coleridge family. He acquired a third of the advowson of Alston, to which in 1790 he presented his brother, the Rev. Benjamin Jackson, J.P., who was Vicar till he died 1834, aged 72. *Arms.* Per fess Gules and Or in chief a greyhound courant . . . and in base three mullets each issuing from a crescent . . . . *Crest.* A hand couped at the wrist holding an open Bible. *Motto.* Semper paratus (Gravestone, Crosthwaite churchyard).

JACKSON, of Keswick. John Jackson, of the Queen's Head Inn, Keswick, died 1837, aged 62. *Arms.* Quarterly, 1 & 4, Or on a chevron Sable between three eagles' heads erased . . . as many cinquefoils . . . ; 2, Gules three boars' heads erased . . . ; 3, Azure three oak trees . . . . *Crest.* An arm in armour embowed holding a falchion. *Motto.* Retinens vestigia famae (Tombstone Crosthwaite churchyard).

JACKSON. William Jackson, J.P., F.S.A., son of Samuel Jackson, who died at Whitehaven in 1829, was born at Barkstone, Lincs., 1823 and died in

* Burke (BP105) gives *sub* Jackson, of Arlsey, Baronets, a pedigree which at first sight seems to be connected with this family, but if Burke's facts are correct, the similarities can only be coincidental.

† See Ernest Betham: *A House of Letters*, p. 113. In a letter of 19 September 1808 Robert Southey says that Jackson, formerly a waggoner, but now retired for some years, built Greta Hall – "two houses under one roof . . . [he] lives in one & I am his tenant in the other. A worthier hearted man never breathed than this my Landlord."

London 1890. He was a founder member of the Cumberland & Westmorland Antiquarian & Archaeological Society 1866, a vice-president of the Society, and one of the most valued contributors to its *Transactions.* An expert in genealogy, he wrote papers on the history of most of the leading Cumberland families, still much consulted today, as are his MSS. in Tullie House, Carlisle, to which he left his valuable library. He lived in turn at Aspatria, Newton Reigny and Fleatham House, St. Bees (CW1 xi). *Arms.* Vert a jack naiant in fess Or on a chief Azure the sun in his splendour. *Crest.* The sun in his splendour surmounted by a jack naiant Proper. *Mottoes.* Apollo jactat lucem; Lux lucis (Bookplate).

JACKSON, of Rockcliffe. Bishop Nicolson recorded an inscription on a tombstone in Rockcliffe churchyard to Jean (d. 1694), wife of William Jackson, of the New Town, with beneath it the following *Arms.* . . . a chevron . . . between three bucks' heads erased . . . (NMA p. 14).

JACKSON. The Ven. William Jackson, J.P., M.A., D.D. (Oxon) (1792-1878), younger son of the Rev. Thomas Jackson (d. 1821, aged 65), Rector of Grasmere, was Vicar of St. James, Whitehaven, 1821-33, and of Penrith 1833-41, Rector of Lowther 1828-78, Chancellor of Carlisle 1846-55, Archdeacon of Carlisle 1856-62, and Canon Residentiary 1856-62, and Provost of The Queen's College, Oxford, 1862-78. *Arms.* Argent on a fess between three cocks' heads erased Sable combed and wattled Gules a greyhound courant between two pheons Or* all within a bordure Azure semé of plates. *Crest.* A cock's head as in the arms. *Motto.* Virtute vigila (AWL).

JACKSON, of Threaplandleas. Richard Jackson (d. 1742) removed from Broadlees, Haile, to Threaplandleas, Torpenhow. His son Richard (d. 1769, aged 56) marr. Mary, dau. and heir of John Voake, and had *int. al.* sons Richard (b. 1749) and Daniel (b. 1763), see *post.* Richard marr. Fanny Starkie and had sons Richard (b. 1780) and the Rev. John Starkie Jackson (1781-1822), Perpetual Curate of Holm Cultram 1814-22 and Vicar of Kingston and Iford, Sussex. His brother Richard Jackson, of Moss-side, Holm Cultram, marr. 1813 Jane Fletcher and had a dau. and heir Mary (b. 1814), who marr. 1835 Ashley Henry Wilson (see Wilson, of The Gale). The above named Daniel Jackson (b. 1763) had a 4th son, the Rev. Richard Jackson, M.A. (Oxon) (d. 1865), who was Curate of Borrowdale 1828, Curate of Ainstable 1832-35, and Perpetual Curate of Wreay 1835-65. His son Thomas Watson Jackson, M.A. (Oxon), was Fellow, Lecturer, Dean and Vice-President of Worcester College, Oxford. *Arms.* Ermine a spearhead in pale Azure embrued Gules headed Or. (Painting in possession of Ashley Fletcher Story Wilson, see WILSON, of the Gale.) *Crest.* A sun in his splendour between two branches of laurel (RMJ).

JACKSON. A window in St. John-in-the-Vale church commemorates Henry Corrie Jackson (1879-1900), son of the Rev. Corrie Jackson, M.A. (Cantab) (1853-95), Chaplain of the Foundling Hospital, London, and his wife Elizabeth (d. 1891, aged 40), dau. of Joseph Hall, of Beckthorns, Keswick. A scholar of Merchant Taylors School and Sir Thomas White and Pusey and Ellerton Hebrew Scholar of St. John's College, Oxford, he served with the 59th Company, Imperial Yeomanry, and died on active service at Boshof, South Africa. *Arms.* Argent a greyhound courant Ermines between

* Perhaps Argent.

three eagles' heads erased Sable (Shield in window). *Crest.* A demi horse Argent gutté-de-sang maned and hoofed Sable (VEW).

JACKSON. Harl. MS. 1536 gives the following for a family of Jackson, of whom no details are known.* *Arms.* Argent on a chevron Sable between three eagles' heads erased Azure as many cinquefoils of the first (FVC).

JACKSON. Major William Jackson, of St. Mary's Vale, Lanercost, is son of William Jackson, of Leighton Court, Neston (Ch) (1870-1951), and great-grandson of Sir William Jackson, M.P., 1st bart., of the Manor House, Birkenhead. He marr. (1) 1927 Lady Ankaret Howard (d. 1945), 2nd dau. of the 10th Earl of Carlisle, and (2) 1966 Ina Pattinson, dau. of James Leonard Joyce, F.R.C.S., of Reading. His son by his 1st wife, William Thomas Jackson, C.L.A., is of Roughton, Ennerdale. *Arms.* Azure a fess between two goats' heads couped in chief and a fleur-de-lys in base Argent two flaunches of the last. *Crest.* Upon a ragged staff Sable a goat's head couped Argent semé of trefoils Vert. *Motto.* Fortiter fideliter feliciter (BP105).

JAMES, of Barrock Park. The ancestor of this family was Thomas James, of Culgaith (d. 1668), whose son John James (1664-1747) was of West Auckland (D). From him descended William Evans James (1764-95), father of William James, D.L., J.P., M.A. (Cantab) (1791-1861), who bought Barrock Park 1813. He was M.P. for Carlisle 1820-26 and 1831-34, and for East Cumberland 1836-47. He was High Sheriff of Cumberland 1827, Chairman of the Carlisle Canal Co., and owner of large estates in Jamaica. His eldest son Capt William Edward James, D.L., J.P., 34th Regt (1816-79), High Sheriff 1867, was father of William Edward Ashton James, J.P., H.E.I.C.S. (1842-84), who was succ. by his eldest son Capt William Wybergh James, 20th Hussars (1873-1906), whose daus. and coheirs were Lorna Ashton, marr. 1927 Rupert Francis James Brooke, and Millicent Dora, of Redmain Gill, Cockermouth, marr. 1928 Cdr Frank Reginald Woodbine Parish, D.S.O., R.N., *q.v.* The above William Wybergh James was succ. at Barrock by his brother Lt-Col Charles Ashton James, J.P., Indian Army (1876-1960), who was High Sheriff 1931. His son Major Peter Charles James, M.C., K.R.R.C. (b. 1916), died on active service 1944, and his dau. Rosemary Evelyn, who marr. Edmund Selwyn Powell, succ. to Barrock Park, which she sold (BLG18). *Arms.* Quarterly, 1 & 4, Azure a dolphin embowed Proper (James); 2 & 3, Argent three boars' heads couped Sable langued and armed Gules (Evans). *Crest.* A bull passant Proper. *Motto.* Vincit amor patriae (BLG11).

JAMES. Field (see FAC, p. 196, footnote 3) states: "A monument in the Musgrave chapel at Aspatria Church gives the arms of Sir Richard Musgrave (d. 1710) of Hayton as Or a dolphin Sable between three crosslets Gules, and his crest as A goat or lion head erased." This is incorrect, for the arms, those of James, with the crest above, are quite clearly impaled with the arms of Musgrave, of Hayton, *q.v.* As now painted, the arms on the monument are: Or on a fess between three cross crosslets Gules a dolphin Sable. As stated by Field, the arms, untinctured and without the fess and crest, are on a stone fragment now at the west end of the church. Sir Richard Musgrave, Bart. (d. 1710, aged 61), marr. 1670 Dorothy (1649-1718), dau. and eventually coheir of William James, of Washington (D).

* Field states that they were of Loweswater.

JAMES. The Rev. Octavius James, J.P., M.A. (Cantab) (1818-89), was 8th son of William James, of Deckham Hall (D), and a descendant of Thomas James, of Cargo. He was Rector of Kirkhaugh (N) 1846-89, and lived at Clargill Hall, where he was burnt to death. His dau. Wilhelmina Martha was a novelist, writing under the pseudonym of Austin Clare. *Arms.* Sable on a chevron Argent between three dolphins embowed Erminois as many cross crosslets Gules. *Crest.* A buffalo passant Gules armed Proper the dexter forefoot resting on an escutcheon Argent charged with a pheon Sable. *Motto.* Deo semper confido (BLG4).

JAMES, of Thornbarrow. Thomas James, of Thornbarrow, Plumpton, marr. 1723 Mary Dawson and was father, *int. al.,* of Thomas (1727-97) and the Rev. John James, M.A., D.D. (Oxon) (1729-85), who was Headmaster of St. Bees 1755-71, Vicar of Kirkoswald 1771-74, Rector of Arthuret 1782-85, and Rector of Kirkandrews-on-Esk 1782-85. His brother Thomas James, of Mostyn Hall, Penrith, succ. to Thornbarrow, which descended to his son Thomas James, of Hensingham House (1759-1835). Some of his descendants are believed to be in South Africa. *Arms.* . . . a dolphin embowed . . . . *Crest.* A bull's head couped in the mouth a (?) human arm erased. *Motto.* Esse et videre (M.I., Carlisle Cathedral, to Hugh James, M.D. (1771-1817), son of the Rev. Dr. John James, *ut supra*).

JAMESON. Joseph Jameson, of Heywood Hall (L), cotton manufacturer (d. 1898, aged 75), was also of Nord Vue, Armathwaite, which he bought in 1862 for £6,300.* He was father of Lt-Col John Bland Jameson, C.I.E., I.M.S., of Morton House, Kingsworthy, Hants. *Arms.* Or a saltire Azure between two roses Gules barbed and seeded Proper in pale and as many hanks of cotton also Proper in fess on a canton of the second a caduceus of the first. *Crest.* Issuant out of a mural crown Or a galley Proper. *Motto.* Acta non verba (FD7).

JEFFERSON. The Rev. Jacob Jefferson, M.A., D.D. (Oxon) (1720-82), son of Thomas Jefferson, of Rosley, was Fellow of The Queen's College, Oxford, 1756, and Vicar of Carisbrooke, Isle of Wight, 1768-82. *Arms.* Gules a griffin segreant Argent within a bordure of the second (Shield in window of The Queen's College Hall).

JEFFERSON. The Rev. Thomas Jefferson, B.A. (Oxon),† M.A. (Cantab) (d. 1768, aged 94‡), was son of the Rev. Robert Jefferson, of Denbigh, and was ordained to the curacy of Torpenhow and Ireby 1703. He was Minister of Cockermouth 1705-68, Vicar of Holm Cultram 1715-30, and Rector of Lamplugh 1730-68. He marr. 1705 Dorothy, dau. of John Winder, of Lorton Hall, *q.v.* His dau. and heir Mary marr. 1737 the Rev. Joseph Ritson, *q.v. Arms.* . . . a lion rampant . . . (Seal in Record Office, Carlisle, DRC 10).

JEFFERSON, of Bulman Hill. Benjamin Jefferson, of Bulman Hill and Caldew Beck, Sebergham (d. 1727), said to be descended from a family settled at Ripon, was father of Robert Jefferson (d. 1790, aged 85), who had *int. al.* sons Robert (1749-1829) and Thomas (1752-1825). The latter was of

* He won the Ascot Stakes with Dan Dancer in 1888.

† It is said that his career at The Queen's College, Oxford, came to an untimely end when his father visited him in Oxford, and proudly said, "Is not my Tom a fine lad, begotten in Cumberland, born in Wales, and bred in Scotland?" The admission that his son was not a native of Cumberland ended his career at Queen's.

‡ He died from exposure as the result of a fall from his horse, which lamed him, so that he had to lie out all night on a common.

Caldew Beck and had *int. al.* a son Thomas Robert Jefferson, M.D. (1796-1867), of Gloucester Square, Bayswater, who erected the monument to his forbears in Sebergham church. By Margaret his wife (1799-1862), dau. and heir of John Nixon, *q.v.*, he had a son D'Oyly Ramsay Jefferson, M.A. (Oxon), barrister at law (1839-1911), who died *s.p.*, and daus. Emily (d. 1900, aged 68), marr. Lt-Col Hugh Somerville S. Burney, 51st Regiment (d. *s.p.* 1897), and Laura de Blair, marr. 1864 Edmund Lionel Wells-Dymoke, Captain Royal Cumberland Militia (1814-92).* The above Robert Jefferson (d. 1829) had a large family of sons, of whom Christopher died 1842, aged 46. *Arms.* Azure on a saltire Argent between four bezants a leopard's face of the field. *Crest.* A demi griffin segreant Azure collared Or holding in the claws a bezant (M.I., Sebergham church). Field recorded the saltire in the arms as Or (FAC). The Ven. Joseph Jefferson, M.A. (Cantab), F.S.A., Archdeacon of Colchester (died 1821, aged 61) (son of Robert Jefferson, died 1790, above), bore: Azure a saltire Or between four bezants (BGA).

JEFFERSON, of Springfield and Rothersyke. This family came from Aikton where Robert Jefferson (1704-79), captain of a ship in the Virginia trade, was born. His grandsons were Robert Jefferson, J.P., of Springfield, Bigrigg and Keekle Grove (d. 1848), and Henry Jefferson, J.P. (1800-77), who built Rothersyke, Egremont, where he was succ. by his son Robert, D.L., J.P. (b. 1826), who died unmarr. The Springfield line was continued by Henry Jefferson, D.L., J.P. (1823-96), High Sheriff of Cumberland 1890, who was succ. by his elder son Robert Jefferson, J.P. (1857-1942). His elder son, Henry Jefferson, of Howman, St. Bees, is the present owner of the Springfield estate (BLG17). *Arms.* Azure on a saltire Or between four bezants a leopard's face of the field. *Crest.* A griffin's head erased. *Motto.* Manu forte (Seal of Henry Jefferson, as High Sheriff). On the monument in St. Bees church to Henry Jefferson, of Rotherskye (d. 1877) the crest is: A dragon's head couped.

JEFFERSON. A gravestone in Arthuret churchyard commemorates George Jefferson, of Moorstown (d. 1711, aged 89); his wife Mary (d. 1696, aged 50); and Margaret, wife of John Jefferson, of Moorstown (d. 1723/4, aged ?51). *Arms.* . . . a cross . . . in the first quarter a hunting horn . . . .†

JEFFREY – see APPELBY.

JOHNSON, of Castlesteads. William Johnson, of Whitehaven, was father of John Johnson (d. 1800, aged 58), who, on his return from India, bought the Castlesteads estate, including the remains of the Roman fort, and "erected a handsome mansion," Walton House (HCC i 118). He marr. 1786 Elizabeth (d. 1792, aged 33), dau. of John Ponsonby, of Whitehaven, and had issue William Ponsonby Johnson, B.A. (Oxon), of Walton House (1789-1865). His eldest son George John Johnson, D.L., J.P. (1816-96), was High Sheriff of Cumberland 1876, and his son Frederick Ponsonby Johnson, D.L., J.P., B.A. (Oxon) (1843-1918), was High Sheriff 1907. He marr. 1901 Frances Mary, dau. and heir of Col William Gray, D.L., J.P., M.P., of Farley Hill,

* Their grandson Anthony Powell, the author, has some interesting notes on the Jeffersons in *Infants of the Spring*, 1976. He is inclined to doubt the Yorkshire origin of the family which rests on the statement on the monument put up by his great-grandfather in Sebergham church.

† There was certainly another charge in the 3rd quarter, and probably in the 2nd and 4th also, but the stone is so weathered that these are now indecipherable.

Berks., and was succ. by his son Major General Sir George Frederick Johnson, K.C.V.O., C.B., C.B.E., D.S.O., D.L., B.A. (Cantab), who was High Sheriff 1966. To the same family belonged Sir Robert Arthur Johnson, K.B.E., T.D., M.A. (Oxon), Deputy Master and Controller of the Royal Mint (1874-1938) (BLG17). *Arms.** Argent on a saltire Sable five bezants on a chief Gules an Eastern crown between two woolpacks Or. *Crest.* An estoile within a spur erect between two wings elevated Or (CA xvi/324; Monument in Carlisle Cathedral; Engraving of Walton House in HCC). *Motto.* Numquam non paratus (FD7).

JOHNSON, JONSON. According to Joseph Hunter's *Pedigrees* (*Harl. Soc.* lxxxviii 140), ... Johnson, of Annandale, Scotland, removed to Carlisle *temp.* Henry VIII. His son, who died 1574, a sufferer under Queen Mary, when he was imprisoned and lost his estate, was father of Ben Jonson, playwright and poet. *Arms.* ... three spindles or rhombi ... (DNB).

JOHNSON. The Rev. William Johnson, B.D. (Cantab) (1784-1864), a pioneer of education and a native of Kirklinton, son of Anthony Johnson, of Scaleby, was Curate and Schoolmaster of Grasmere 1811-12, and was later Superintendent of the National Society's Central Schools, retiring in 1840. From 1820 until his death he was Rector of St. Clement Eastcheap with St. Martin Orgar, London. He was a friend of Wordsworth and Southey (DNB). *Arms* (granted 1838). Argent a chevron Azure between three pheons Gules on a chief of the second an open book representing the Holy Bible Proper edged and sealed Or thereon inscribed Proverbs Chapter xxii v. 6 between two crosses flory of the last. *Crest.* A pheon as in the arms surmounted by a star of eight points Or (CA xlii/324).

JOHNSON. For "Nichol Johnson", a mythical person who appears in FAC (p. 173), see FORRESTER.

JOHNSTON, of Hayton. George Johnston, of Hayton, husbandman, marr. 1810, when he was 24, and she 23, Elizabeth Hetherington, spinster, of Irthington (d. at Stanwix 1853, aged 67). *Arms.* Argent a saltire Sable on a chief ... three cushions ... ; impaling, Per pale Argent and Sable three lions rampant ... (Hetherington) (Tombstone of Elizabeth Johnston in Irthington churchyard).

JOHNSTON, in Rosetrees. Thomas Johnston, in Rosstreis, or Rosetrees, died 1699, aged 72. *Arms.* ... a saltire ... and in chief three cushions ... (Gravestone, Kirkandrews-on-Esk churchyard). Field recorded the cushions as on a chief (FAC).

JOHNSTON, of Soulterfoord. A gravestone in Stapleton churchyard commemorates Jane (d. 1711, aged 7), John (d. 1716, aged 4), and Jane (d. 1716, aged 1), children of John Johnstoun, of Soulterfoord. *Arms.* ... three cushions ... in chief.

JOHNSTON, of Wampool. George Johnston, of Wampool, Aikton, yeoman (d. 1834, aged 43), marr. 1817 Mary Pearson and had issue George (d. 1840, aged 21), Robert and Jane. James Johnston, of Wampool (d. 1840, aged 80), marr. Jane ... (d. 1834, aged 82), and had issue Richard (d. 1802, aged 17). *Arms.* ... a saltire ... on a chief ... three cushions .... *Crest.* A winged spur. *Motto.* Nunquam non paratus (Gravestones in Aikton churchyard).

JOHNSTON – see BORWICK.

* Granted 1788, but Burke nevertheless shews the family as bearing: *Arms.* Argent on a saltire Sable five bezants (BGA).

JOHNSTONE, Earl of Hartfell. Mary, eldest dau. of James Johnstone, 1st Earl of Hartfell,* marr. (1) Sir George Graham, 2nd Bart., of Netherby (d. 1658), *q.v.*, and (2) before 1665 Sir George Fletcher, 2nd Bart., of Hutton-in-the-Forest (d. 1700), *q.v.* *Arms.* [Argent] a saltire [Sable] on a chief [Gules] three cushions [Or]. *Crest.* A winged spur [Or]. *Supporters.* Two horses [Argent furnished Gules] (M.I., Arthuret church). The arms are impaled on a portrait of Sir George Fletcher at Hutton-in-the-Forest. On a tablet in Hutton-in-the-Forest church they are impaled as: Argent a saltire Sable on a chief Gules three lions passant guardant Or.

JOLLIFFE, of Hayton. William Jolliffe, M.P. (d. 1802), marr. 1769 Eleanor, dau. and heir of Sir Richard Hylton, formerly Musgrave, Bart, *q.v.*, and so acquired the Cumberland estates of that family, including Hayton castle. His son Col Hylton Jolliffe (1773-1843) was M.P. for Petersfield for more than 40 years, and declined Lord Liverpool's offer of a baronetcy. He was succ. by his son Charles Jolliffe, D.L., whose son was Charles Hylton Jolliffe (1864-1926), Lord of the manor of Hayton, High Sheriff of Cumberland 1905. *Arms.* Argent on a pile Vert three dexter gauntlets two and one of the field. *Crest.* A cubit arm erect vested Vert cuffed and the sleeve charged with a pile Argent the hand grasping a sword in bend. *Motto.* Tant que je puis (Seal).

KAYE, of Millbeck Towers. Cecil William Kaye, M.A. (Oxon), (1865-1941), was Headmaster of St. Bees School 1917-26, and was later of Millbeck Towers, Underskiddaw, now the home of his son Brigadier James William Kaye, R.A., commissioned in 1918, and retired in 1949. *Arms.* Argent two bendlets Sable. *Crest.* A goldfinch Proper. *Motto.* Kynd kynn knawne kepe (Bookplate of C. W. Kaye).

KEARNEY. John Kearney,† 3rd son of James Kearney, of Blanchville, Co. Kilkenny, and Dublin, was of Upper Grange, Ireland, and later of Castlerigg, Keswick, where his dau. Letitia Georgina was born 1807. *Arms.* Argent three lions rampant Gules on a chief Azure between two pheons Or a gauntleted hand in fess of the last holding a sword of the first. *Crest.* A gauntleted hand Or holding a dagger Argent. *Motto.* Sustine et abstine (BLG5).

KELLY. General Sir Richard Denis Kelly, K.C.B. (1815-97), was Colonel, 1st Battn. the Border Regt. He marr. 1848 Ellen Susanna, dau. of Sir William Dillon, 4th Bart., and sister and coheir of Sir Arthur Henry Dillon, 5th Bart. *Arms.* Azure two lions rampant combattant Argent chained Or supporting a tower triple-turretted of the second; on an escutcheon of pretence, Dillon, *q.v.* *Crest.* An enfield passant Vert. *Motto.* Turris fortis mihi Deus (Brass, Carlisle Cathedral).

KELLY – see WILMER.

KEMBLE. Stephen George Kemble, of The Grove, Durham (1758-1822), a well known actor and brother of Mrs. Siddons, was grandfather of the Rev. Nicholas Freese Young Kemble, M.A. (Dunelm) (1825-1909), who was Rector of Sebergham 1852-65, Vicar of Hesket-in-the-Forest 1865-76 and Vicar of All Hallows, Allerton, Liverpool, 1876-1902. His son, the Rev.

* The tablet in Hutton-in-the-Forest church and also NB (ii 390) shew her as dau. of the Earl of Annandale, but she was in fact sister of James, Earl of Annandale.

† His sister Anne marr. 1815 the Rev. Theobald Butler and was mother of the Rev. Theobald Butler, *q.v.* p. 386.

Hulton Henry Kemble, M.A. (Oxon), was Curate of Ambleside 1893-95 and Vicar of Low Wray from 1895. *Arms.* Azure on a bend Or cotised Argent a rose Gules between two leopards' faces Sable. *Crest.* Between a branch of laurel on the dexter side and a branch of palm on the sinister Proper a boar's head and neck Sable erased Gules and charged on the neck with an estoile irradiated Argent. *Motto.* Suaviter fortiter (Bookplate of Stephen George Kemble in the possession of his great-great-grandson Roger K. Slater, of Windyfell, Raughton Head).

KEMP, Baron and Viscount Rochdale. George Kemp, C.B., D.L., J.P., B.A. (Cantab), of Lingholm, Keswick (1866-1945), Chairman of Kelsall & Kemp, Rochdale, M.P. for S.E. Lancashire 1895-1906 and for N.W. Manchester 1910-12, was knighted 1909 and was cr. Baron Rochdale, of Rochdale, 1913. For some 40 years he lived at Lingholm, Keswick, which is now the home of his only son John Durival Kemp, 2nd Baron Rochdale, O.B.E., T.D., D.L., B.A. (Cantab), who was cr. Viscount Rochdale, of Rochdale, 1960. *Arms.* Argent a chevron engrailed Gules between two estoiles in chief Azure and a rose of the second in base barbed and seeded Proper. *Crest.* A cubit arm erect vested Argent cuffed Azure the hand Proper grasping a chaplet Vert encircling a rose as in the arms. *Supporters.* On either side a ram Or charged on the shoulder with a rose Gules slipped and leaved Proper. *Motto.* Lucem spero (DPB).

KENNEDY, of Crosby Lodge. David Kennedy, D.L., J.P. (d. 1819, aged 41), was of Craig, Ayrshire, when he marr. 1800 Elizabeth (d. 1845), only child of George Dalton, *q.v.* They lived in Abbey Street, Carlisle, and later at Crosby Lodge, which he built and where he died as a result of a fall from his horse. Their eldest son David Dalton Kennedy was born 1808, and their youngest son George died 1838, aged 25. *Arms.* . . . a chevron . . . and in chief a heart . . . between two cross crosslets fitché . . . . *Crest.* A dolphin naiant. *Motto.* Avise la fin – Behold the end (Tombstone of David Kennedy in Crosby-on-Eden churchyard).

KENNEDY. Capt William George Ainslie Kennedy, R.N., of Church House, Greystoke (1873-1938), was 5th son of Myles Kennedy, of Hill Foot, Stone Cross, Ulverston (see AWL). His only son, Major Myles Harold William Kennedy, 4/7th Rajputs, is of 24 Ladies Mile Road, Bergvliet, Cape Town. *Arms.* Sable on a fess Or between three esquires' helmets Proper an escallop of the field. *Crest.* In front of a dexter cubit arm holding in the hand a sprig of oak fructed Proper two escallops Or. *Motto.* Adhaereo virtuti (BLG18).

KENTISH, of Wigton Hall and Bowscar. John Kentish, Bombay Civil Service (1796-1861), was father of the Rev. John George Kentish, LL.B. (Cantab) (1828-59), who marr. (2) 1852 Agnes, dau. of the Very Rev. Francis Close, *q.v.* She and her daughters were of Wigton Hall for more than 30 years from 1882, and later the daughters were of Bowscar, Penrith, which was also the home of their brother George Colville Arden Kentish, J.P. (1856-1933), from 1924. He was succ. by his surviving dau. Gwendolen Arden, who marr. 1926 John Frederick Harris, of Brackenburgh, *q.v.* *Arms.* Gules a pair of wings conjoined Argent over all a bendlet Azure. *Crest.* A demi ostrich wings endorsed Sable holding in the beak a horsehoe Or.* *Motto.* Nihil sine labore (Family silver). On a *prie-dieu* in Wigton church the

* John Kentish, above, of the Bombay Civil Service, used for *Crest.* An oak tree.

Arms appear as: Gules two wings conjoined and inverted over all a bend Sable. *Crest.* A demi ostrich wings expanded and inverted holding in the beak a horseshoe.

KEY. William Key, described as of Mirehouse in 1726, and later of Frankishow, Crosthwaite (d. 1739), had by Sarah, his wife (living 1741), four daus., of whom Ann (1731-1809) marr. Isaiah White, *q.v. Arms.* Sable a chevron between three hedgehogs passant Argent (Impaled by White on tablet in Crosthwaite church).

KEYME. The arms of Gilbert Keyme (d. 1452, aged 72), are painted on a framed canvas at Garth House, Burgh-by-Sands, brought there from his home in Cornwall by John Hodgson Read (d. 1971). *Arms.* Gules in chief two mullets of eight points Or and in base a crescent Argent. *Crest.* A demi lion Or. *Motto.* In bellis gerebat pro patria die et nocte.

KILLINGHALL. Harl. MS. 1536 attributes to this family, without any further details, the following *Arms.* Gules a bend raguly Argent between three garbs Or (FVC). These are the arms of Killinghall, of Middleton St. George (D), see FVD and SHD.

KING. John King sealed a letter dated 11 March 1757 from Whitehaven to Mr. Armitage, agent at Lowther, about land at Threlkeld, with the following *Arms.* . . . on a bend . . . three escallops . . . ; impaling (apparently*), . . . three mullets in fess . . . between six fleurs-de-lys . . . . *Crest.* Two (?) elephants' tusks in saltire points downwards (D/Lons/L/Threlkeld/10 in Record Office, Carlisle).

KING. John King, of Fieldhead, yeoman, marr. at Hesket-in-the-Forest 1781, when a widower aged 65, Ann Hodgson, aged 49. He died *s.p.* 1790, and was buried at Hesket-in-the-Forest, his heir at law being his nephew William Cartmel, son of William Cartmel, of Rockcliffe (John King's will, dated 1789, proved 1790). *Arms.* Field states that he "bore the arms and crest of King, Earl of Lovelace, to which he may have had some right; as well as the supporters, to which he certainly had no right at all," and that these were displayed on his tombstone. In the drastic re-arrangement and destruction of tombstones in Hesket-in-the-Forest churchyard since Field's day, this monument has disappeared. Field recorded the achievement as: *Arms.* Sable three spear heads erect Argent embrued Gules on a chief Or as many poleaxes Azure their edges to the sinister. *Crest.* A dexter arm erect couped at the elbow vested Azure thereon three Ermine spots in fess Or cuffed Argent grasping a truncheon Sable the top broken off the bottom couped of the third. *Motto.* Labor ipse voluptas. *Supporters.* Two mastiffs reguardant (FAC).

KINGSCOTE. John Kingscote (d. 1463) was appointed Bishop of Carlisle 1462, in recompense of £600 due to him from the King's father and the King. *Arms.* Argent ten escallops in pile Sable on a canton Gules a mullet pierced Or (BBE).

KIRKBRIDE, of Kirkbride and Ellerton. In CW2 xv, T. H. B. Graham traced the descent of this family from the de Wigtons, Lords of Wigton. Adam de Wigton II (d. 1225) is said to have given the manor of Kirkbride to his younger son Adam, who adopted the surname de Kirkbride. His son Richard (d. *c.* 1267) marr. Euphemia de Levington, one of the coheirs of her niece Helewise de Balliol (see Levington). Their son Sir Richard Kirkbride

* Part of shield is missing from the seal impression.

(d. 1330) was a noted soldier, who was present at the siege of Caerlaverock.* He marr. his cousin Christina, dau. of Walter de Wigton, and aunt and, in her issue, heir of Margaret de Weston, dau. of John de Wigton. Their son Sir Walter Kirkbride (*c.* 1287-1336) was Knight of the Shire for Cumberland 1316. His descendant George Kirkbride (d. 1511) left three daus. and coheirs – Elizabeth (b. *c.* 1478), marr. John Dalston, of Dalston, *q.v.*; Isabel (b. 1482), marr. (1) Thomas Beauchamp and (2) Gilbert Weddale; and Emmotte (b. 1490), marr. Robert Cliburn (see AWL). The uncle of these ladies, Richard Kirkbride, living 1486, marr. Christina Whitfield and founded the family long settled at Ellerton, Hesket-in-the-Forest. His great-grandson Richard Kirkbride, who heads the 1665 Visitation pedigree, marr. his kinswoman Eleanor, dau. of Edmund Cliburn. Their grandson Richard (d. 1659) was Colonel of a regiment of foot in the Royal army. He marr. Bridget, dau. and coheir of the Rev. Edward Maplet, Vicar of Addingham and Prebendary of Carlisle. Their son Bernard Kirkbride, J.P., of Ellerton and Braithwaite Hows (*c.* 1629-77), High Sheriff of Cumberland 1672-74, was the last male† of the family. He marr. Jane (1629-95), eldest dau. of Sir Timothy Fetherstonhaugh, *q.v.*; but had no issue; she marr. (2) Sir Edward Hasell, *q.v.* Bernard's sisters and coheirs were Mary, wife of William Graham, of Nunnery, *q.v.*, and Barbara, wife of (1) Leonard Barrow, of Ainstable, and (2) . . . Haggett. *Arms.* Sir Richard Kirkbride (d. 1330) who bore, according to the *Caerlaverock Roll,* see above, Argent a cross engrailed Vert, is also said to have borne; Argent a saltire engrailed Vert (FFC), which are the arms recorded at the Visitation of Yorkshire, 1564 (NVY), and quartered by Cliburn (see AWL). The Dalstons quartered the arms as: Argent a cross engrailed Vert between four annulets Sable (FVC). At Dugdale's Visitation of Cumberland, 1665, Bernard Kirkbride recorded: Argent a cross engrailed Sable a label of three points for difference (FCW), and this coat, without the label, is on his monument in Hesket church. MMD records three variants: (1) Argent a cross Vert; (2) Argent a cross engrailed Vert; (3) Argent a cross engrailed Sable. DSL records for Bernard Kirkbride, as High Sheriff: Argent a saltire Vert.

KIRKBY. John de Kirkby, Prior of Carlisle (d. 1352), was Bishop of Carlisle 1332-52. *Arms.* Argent on a fess Vert three crescents Or (BBE). Field, however, suggests that he was a cadet of Kirkby, of Kirkby in Furness, for whose arms, see next entry.

KIRKBY. The arms of Kirkby are on a shield at Hutton John; Sybel (living 1343), dau. of Lawrence de Cornwall or de Kirkby, marr. before 1279 Sir John Hudleston, of Millom (d. before 1306). They are impaled by Irton in a window in Irton Hall; Richard Irton (1557-1608) marr. Dorothy, dau. of Roger Kirkby, of Kirkby Ireleth (L), who was living aged 95 at St.

* The Caerlaverock Roll records of him: "Many a heavy and crushing stone did he of Kirkbride receive, but he placed before him a white shield with a green cross engrailed."

† There was long a yeoman family of this name in Hesket-in-the-Forest parish. Isaac Kirkbride marr. 1713 Elizabeth Robinson and had *int. al.* a son the Rev. William Kirkbride (1724-1809) who was Curate of Armathwaite 1749-62, of Nicholforest 1763-4, and of Kirkandrews-on-Esk 1772-82. He was Perpetual Curate of Hesket-in-the-Forest 1764-1809. His brother John (1727-1815) was of Trough Foot, Hesket. His descendants included Isaac Kirkbride, of Holly House, Nun Close (1858-1918), and William Kirkbride, of Low Street House, Plumpton, widely known as "the Duke of Plumpton" (1792-1865). He was father of John Kirkbride (d. 1897, aged 64), whose widow Jane died at Keswick 1937.

George's Visitation of Lancashire, 1613. They are impaled by Senhouse on a pew in Cross Canonby church; Humphrey Senhouse, of Netherhall (d. 1738), marr. Eleanor, dau. of William Kirkby, of Ashlack (L) (aged 29 at Dugdale's Visitation of Lancashire 1664), 4th son of Roger Kirkby, of Kirkby Ireleth (d. 1643), great-grandson of Roger Kirkby, above. They are also on a shield on the ceiling of Carlisle Cathedral. *Arms.* Argent two bars Gules on a canton of the last a cross moline Or.

KIRKLINTON – see SAUL.

KITE. The Most Rev. John Kite (d. 1537), Archbishop of Armagh 1513-21, was Bishop of Carlisle 1521-37. He was present at the Field of the Cloth of Gold 1520, and was made Archbishop of Thebes 1521 (DNB; NB). *Arms.* Azure on a chevron between three kites' heads erased Or three gillyflowers or roses Gules slipped Vert (BBE; shields formerly at Rose Castle and on Dalston Cross, destroyed 1815).

KNIGHT, of Papcastle. Thomas Knight (d. 1853, aged 74), 2nd son of John Knight, of Lea Castle, Worcs., settled in Cumberland, first at Keswick and then at Papcastle. His son Edward (1806-76) was father of Edward Frederick Knight, B.A. (Cantab) (1852-1925), the well known war correspondent (WWW; BLG4). *Arms.* Argent three pales Gules within a bordure engrailed Azure on a canton of the second a spur Or. *Crest.* On a spur lying fessways Or an eagle per fess Argent and Azure wings expanded of the first beaked and legged Gules (BLG4).

KNIGHTLEY. Various shields at Hutton-in-the-Forest represent either Knightley or Pershall, two Vane quarterings, as follows. *Arms.* Quarterly, 1 & 4, Ermine; 2 & 3, Paly of six Or and Gules; all within a bordure Azure. Also, Quarterly, 1 & 4, Paly of six Or and Azure; 2 & 3, Ermine; all within a bordure Azure.

KNIGHTON. A shield at Hutton-in-the-Forest; a Vane quartering. *Arms.* Barry of eight Argent Azure Argent and Vert two lions passant Or. Another shield displays: Vert two lions passant Or.

KNUBLEY, of Finglandrigg. Edward Knubley, of Finglandrigg, Bowness-on-Solway, marr. 1748 Anne Stoddart and was father of Edward Knubley, D.L., J.P. (1756-1815), who succ. him and was High Sheriff of Cumberland 1785. He was Collector of Customs at Whitehaven and was twice elected M.P. for Carlisle, in 1786 and 1790, but on both occasions was unseated. His son Edward Carr Knubley, of Whitehaven, attorney (1785-1850), marr. 1817 Mary Ponsonby, by whom he had a son, the Rev. Miles Ponsonby Knubley, LL.B. (Cantab) (1826-58), who was Curate in charge of Plumbland 1851-58. He left a son, the Rev. Edward Ponsonby Knubley, M.A. (Cantab) (1850-1931), Canon of Salisbury, whose son Edward Miles Knubley, M.A. (Cantab), died at Newcastle, Natal, 1950. *Arms.* . . . a lion rampant guardant . . . on a chief . . . an estoile . . . between two crescents . . . (Tombstone, Bowness-on-Solway churchyard).

KNYVETT. Sir Henry Knyvett, of Charlton, Wilts., marr. Anne (d. 1582), dau. and heir of Sir Christopher Pickering, *q.v.* Their son Thomas (d. 1622), cr. Baron Knyvett 1607, joined with his mother and stepfather John Vaughan in selling Moresby to William Fletcher 1577. His sister Alice marr. 1563 Christopher Dacre, of Lanercost, *q.v.* *Arms* (impaled by Dacre on overmantel from Kirklinton Hall, to which it was removed from Dacre

Hall, Lanercost, now in the Bowes Museum, Barnard Castle). Argent on a bend Sable a crescent of the field a bordure engrailed of the second.

LACI. Roger de Laci, Constable of Chester (d. 1211 or 1212), Sheriff of Yorkshire 1206-11, was Sheriff of Cumberland 1204.* *Arms.* Or a lion rampant Purpure (DSL).

LACY, of Eden Lacy. Samuel Lacy, master and mariner (1690-1762), a native of Great Yarmouth, was of Tynemouth (N). His son Richard Lacy (1744-78) marr. 1765 Dorothy (b. 1741), dau. of Joseph Dacre, *q.v.* Their son Lt-Col Samuel Lacy, Royal Cumberland Militia (1766-1847), left Northumberland *c.* 1790, and bought Salkeld Lodge or Hall, where he lived until 1836, when he sold the property and bought an estate† at Great Salkeld, on which he built the house which he called Eden Lacy. It was inherited by his 2nd son Richard Lacy (1796-1883), who marr. 1821 Eliza Barker, and had a son Augustus Dacre Lacy (after whose death the family papers were sent to his son in Australia, who has been lost sight of), and two daus. – Gertrude (1834-1904), marr. 1856 Lt-Col Thomas Charles Thompson, of Milton Hall, Brampton (d. 1888), *q.v.*, and Georgina, died unmarr. *Arms.* The family originally bore: Quarterly Argent and Sable on a bend Gules three martlets Or and a label Ermine (Tombstones in Tynemouth Priory burial ground). In 1802 Samuel Lacy obtained a new grant, as follows: *Arms.* Quarterly Ermine and Sable the latter charged with an acorn Or on a bend Gules three martlets Or. *Crest.* An arm mailed embowed the hand holding a branch of mistletoe.‡ *Motto.* Non in visco fides sed in Deo (Monument in Addingham church to Col Lacy erected by his grandson Samuel Lacy William Sanderson).

LACY. The arms of the Lacy family, of Enfield, Middx., are on a wooden panel in Layton House, Greystoke. *Arms.* Quarterly, 1 & 4, [Gules] two bars wavy Ermine; 2 & 3, . . . on a bend . . . an escutcheon . . . ; in the first quarter a mullet for difference; impaling, Lucas, *q.v.* *Crest.* Out of a ducal coronet [Or] a lion sejant [Ermine].

LAMB, of Seat Hill and Temon. From David Lamb, of the Riddings (d. 1626), descended David Lamb, of Seat Hill, Irthington, and Temon, Upper Denton (1651-1719). He was father of Richard Lamb, of Seat Hill (1685-1746), whose sons were prominent in the commercial life of Newcastle upon Tyne, and included Joseph Lamb, J.P., of Ryton Hall (D) (1732-1800), father of Joseph Lamb, D.L., J.P., of Temon (1781-1859), whose 2nd son Richard Westbrook Lamb, D.L., J.P., of West Denton (N) (1826-95), was father of Stephen Eaton Lamb (1860-1928), who inherited Temon from his cousin Capt Everard Joseph Lamb, Northumberland Fusiliers (b. 1885), who was killed in action *s.p.* 1914, son of Robert Ormiston Lamb, J.P., of Hayton House, How Mill and Temon (1836-1912). The said Stephen's elder son was the Very Rev. Monsignor Joseph Cuthbert Lamb, M.A. (Cantab) (1909-64), Vice-Rector of the Beda College, Rome, who served in World War II with the Border Regt and on the General

* His ferocity against the Welsh earned him the nickname "Roger of Hell."

† The estate included the prehistoric monument Long Meg.

‡ In 1802 Samuel Lacy wrote that he had adopted the crest "from my being in possession of Long Meg, and wishing the family ever to remain in Cumberland." He associated acorns and mistletoe with the Druids, whom he imagined to have ceremoniously cut mistletoe from an oak tree at Long Meg (LBA).

Staff. The present head of the family is his brother Major Richard Anthony Lamb, R.A., M.A. (Oxon), of Knighton Manor, Broadchalke, Wilts (BLG18). *Arms.* Richard Lamb, above (d. 1746), bore: . . . two mullets . . . in fess between in chief a fleur-de-lys . . . and in base a rose . . . .* *Crest.* In front of a Latin cross a lamb (Tombstone, Irthington churchyard). The family now bears: *Arms.* Sable on a fess Ermine between three cinquefoils Argent two mullets of the field. *Crest.* A Paschal lamb Proper between two mullets as in the arms. *Motto.* Palma non sine pulvere (BLG18; Brass in Hayton church).

LAMBERT. John Lambert, of Wattsfield, Kendal (1735-1801), see AWL, was father of Josias Lambert (1763-1841) who practised as an attorney at Lazonby for 30 years until 1828, and was later of Storth Cottage, near Kendal, where he died. *Arms.* Argent a chevron Gules between three lambs Sable a chief chequy Azure and of the first (CKK).

LAMBERT. A brass in Carlisle cathedral commemorates John Oswald Lambert, Captain, 5th (Princess Charlotte of Wales) Regt. of Dragoon Guards (d. 1880, aged 30, bur. at Rockcliffe). He was descended from John Lambert, of Alnwick (1783-1849), who marr. 1812 Juliana (d. 1859), dau. of Robert Mounsey, of Castletown. *Arms.* Gules a chevron Ermine between three lambs statant Argent a chief chequy Or and Azure.

LAMBERT. Sybil, wife of William Lambert, farmer, died at Brockley Moor, Plumpton, 1880, aged 31, and was buried at Hesket-in-the-Forest. In the drastic re-arrangement and destruction of tombstones in Hesket-in-the-Forest churchyard since Field's day, her tombstone has disappeared, but Field recorded it as displaying: *Arms.* . . . a bend sinister company . . . (FAC).

LAMBTON, DAWSON-. Nicholas Lambton (d. 1778) was succ. at South Biddick Hall (D) by his dau. and heir Mary, who d. 1814 leaving the estate to John Dawson, who assumed the additional surname Lambton and died 1815, aged 44. He was presumably father of George Dawson Lambton, of Old Elvet, Durham, whose will was proved 1829 by his brother John Dawson-Lambton, of Low House, Wetheral. *Arms.* Gules on a fess engrailed Ermine between two lambs passant in chief Argent and a mascle in base Or three mullets of the field. *Crest.* A torteau charged with a lamb's head in profile couped at the neck Ermine within two branches of oak Or (FD7).

LAMPLUGH, of Lamplugh. Robert de Lamplugh held Lamplugh of Gospatrick son of Orme, Lord of Workington (who may have been his father), *temp.* Henry II and Richard I. His descendant Sir John Lamplugh was High Sheriff of Cumberland 1419 and 1432 and was succ. by his son Sir Thomas, High Sheriff 1464, who marr. Eleanor, dau. and coheir of Sir Henry Fenwick, *q.v.* Their son Sir John Lamplugh,† High Sheriff 1537 and 1549, was succ. by his son John (d. 1604, aged 76), who built Lamplugh Hall, burnt down in the 18th century.‡ He was High Sheriff 1572 and 1579. He was succ. by his nephew John (1585-1636), High Sheriff 1620, whose son

* Field recorded this as: A fleur-de-lys between two mullets pierced in chief and a rose in base.

† He marr. (2) Catherine, dau. and coheir of Sir Guy Forster, who, according to FVC, was of "Alderwyke" (C). Their three daus. and coheirs were Mary, marr. Thomas Skelton; Frances, marr. William Porter; and Mabel.

‡ Only the gateway, dated 1595, survives.

Col John Lamplugh (1618-89), High Sheriff 1663, marr. 1654 Frances, dau. of Thomas Lamplugh, of Ribton, *q.v.* Their dau. Grace marr. 1706 her cousin Robert Lamplugh, of Ribton, *q.v.*, and their son Thomas (1656-1737), High Sheriff 1700-2, M.P. for Cockermouth 1701-8, was the last male.* He marr. Frances (d. 1746), dau. and coheir of Abraham Moline (see Lamplugh, of Dovenby), and had an only surviving dau. Elizabeth (1701-75), who marr. 1732 George Irton, *q.v.*, and died *s.p.* The Lamplugh estate passed eventually in 1766 to the Rev. Thomas Lamplugh (1727-83), Rector of Copgrove and grandson of Thomas Lamplugh, Archbishop of York, whose relationship to the family is not clear, though one certainly existed; on the Rev. Thomas Lamplugh's death *s.p.* the manor of Lamplugh passed to his sisters, of whom Ann mar. 1750 John Raper, *q.v.*; their son John Lamplugh Raper assumed the surname and arms of Lamplugh 1825 (CW2 xxxviii, xxxix†). *Arms.* FFC gives for Sir John de Lamplewe, of Cumberland: Or (another, Argent) a cross florettė at the points Sable. At Dugdale's Visitation of Cumberland 1665, Col John Lamplugh, above, recorded: Or a cross flory Sable; and this coat is on a shield on the ceiling of Carlisle Cathedral.‡§ *Crest.* A goat's head Proper (FCW). FVC records the crest as: A goat's head Sable attired and bearded Or; whilst Lysons give: A goat's head Argent attired and bearded Or (LMC). A fine achievement of the arms and crest is on the gateway to Lamplugh Hall, dated 1595.

LAMPLUGH, of Dovenby. Thomas Lamplugh, of Dovenby (b. *c.* 1488, living 1532) was a kinsman of Sir John Lamplugh, of Lamplugh, *q.v.* His son Robert Lamplugh was High Sheriff of Cumberland 1545 and 1557. His son Francis (d. 1602) served 1578, and was succ. by his eldest son, Sir Thomas Lamplugh (*c.* 1577-1632), who was High Sheriff 1613 and died *s.p.*, his eventual heir being the descendants of his niece Frances (d. before 1638) who marr. William Bullock and had an only dau. Frances (d. 1676), wife of Abraham Moline, by whom she had two daus. – Frances (d. 1745, aged 80), marr. Thomas Lamplugh, of Lamplugh, *q.v.*, and Mary, marr. Richard Lamplugh, of Ribton, *q.v.* (CW2 xxxix). *Arms.* As Lamplugh, of Lamplugh. Harl. MS. 1536, however, gives for Francis Lamplugh, of Dovenby: Argent a cross engrailed Vert (FVC), as does MVC.

LAMPLUGH, of Ribton and Dovenby. Thomas Lamplugh (d. 1670) is said to have come to Cumberland from Beverley (Y), and to have bought the Ribton estate before 1636, on which he began building the house which his son Richard (*c.* 1633-1705) completed; the latter was M.P. for Cumberland 1679 and High Sheriff 1690. He marr. (1) 1667 Frances, dau. of Sir Christopher Lowther, of Sockbridge, by whom he had Richard Lamplugh (1668-1724) who died *s.p.*, having sold Ribton 1722; and Jane (b. 1663), marr. (1) John Senhouse, *q.v.*, and (2) Charles Orfeur, *q.v.* Richard Lamplugh, senior, marr. (2) Mary, dau. and coheir of Abraham Moline (see Lamplugh, of Dovenby) and so acquired a part of the Dovenby estate, which passed to their son Robert (1686-1763), High Sheriff 1718. He marr.

* If one excepts his feeble minded cousin Josiah Lamplugh, buried at Lamplugh 1739, *s.p.*

† These papers should be used with caution; they contain many errors.

‡ The cross is so drawn in the illustration in MMD that the shield could be blazoned: Or a cross potent flory Or.

§ Fuller recorded for Sir John Lamplugh, Sheriff 1419 and 1432: Or two crosses floury Sable (FWE). DSL gives: Or a cross patonce Sable.

1706 his cousin Grace Lamplugh, of Lamplugh, *q.v.* Their son Richard (1707-64) died unmarr., leaving his estate to his niece Elizabeth Falconer (d. unmarr. 1768). Dovenby then passed to her cousin Peter Brougham (1735-91) who took the name and arms of Lamplugh 1783. He died unmarr. and was succ. by his niece Mary (b. 1774), the only dau. of his sister who had marr. 1769 Frecheville Dykes, *q.v.* (CW2 xxxviii, xxxix). *Arms.* As Lamplugh, of Lamplugh.

LANCASTER. The Rev. Thomas Lancaster, M.A. (Glasgow) (1718-89), was son of John Lancaster, of Pooley, Barton (W), a cadet of the Lancasters, of Sockbridge. He was Curate of Culgaith 1745, Curate of Alston and Garrigill 1754-56, and Vicar of Alston 1756-89. *Arms.* Argent two bars Gules on a canton of the second a lion passant Or* (M.I., Alston church). NB (i 402) record for Lancaster, of Sockbridge: Argent two bars Gules on a canton of the second a lion passant guardant Or.† Fleming, however, recorded the canton as charged with a mullet Or (FDW); and elsewhere the mullet is Argent and untinctured (CW2 vi 212; FCW).

LANERCOST PRIORY. *Arms.* Woodward gives: Or two flaunches Gules (WEC; see also CW1 i 113-14). Field, however suggests that a shield on the west end of the priory church, displaying: . . . three covered cups . . . , may be the arms of the Priory (FAC).

LANGLANDS. John Langlands, of Stapleton, died 1767, aged 74. *Arms.* . . . three leopards' faces in bend . . . in sinister chief three cocks . . . , two and one (ABD).

LANGRIGG. Adam (son of Dolfin de Langrigg) and Christiana his wife granted land in Blencogo to Holm Cultram Abbey *c.* 1250-60. Contemporary with him was Thomas de Langrigg, living 1280, whom Field, quoting no authority, says was son of Hugh de Langrigg. He also says that he was the last of the family, leaving daus. and coheirs, Agnes, marr. Ranulph de Osmotherley, and Alice, marr. Thomas del Lathes. Margaret and Roger Langrigg, however, were landowners in Langrigg, Bromfield and Uldale as late as 1391 (DAC; FAC; Holm Cultram Register). *Arms.* Field quotes VN i 42 as authority for Martindale quartering Langrigg in 1552 as: Argent six billets, three, two and one, Sable; but this is a very tentative ascription.

LANGTON, of Cockermouth. Robert Langton, of Cockermouth, "housekeeper" (d. 1709, aged *c.* 60), had a son John (d. 1721) who marr. Anne, niece and heir of Thomas Benson, of Coat How, Rydal. Through this marr. a large estate, including the manor of Baysbrowne (W), came to the family. Their only son John Langton (1713-77), High Sheriff of Cumberland 1761, marr. 1746 Barbara (1718-72), dau. and coheir of Gawen Wren, *q.v.,* and so acquired Castlerigg and other properties in Keswick. Their three sons John (1750-81), Gawen Wren (d. 1790, aged 38), and Thomas (b. 1754), all died *s.p.* Of them, John marr. Frances (1758-86), dau. of John Borradaile, of Wigton; she marr. (2) 1784 Samuel Kenyon (1747-1819), and they sold Coat How and other Westmorland lands to Sir Michael le Fleming, Bart. The above Robert (d. 1709) had a 2nd surviving son Isaac Langton, merchant, of Whitehaven, and of The Howe, Ennerdale

* Fuller records the same arms for Sir John Lancaster, Sheriff of Cumberland 1416-17, for whom see AWL.

† DSL records these arms for William de Lancaster, Sheriff of Cumberland 1358-9.

(1685-1741), who marr. 1708 Frances (1683-1767), 2nd dau. and in her issue coheir of Anthony Patrickson, *q.v.* Their sons Robert, Mocha, and Anthony (d. 1746, aged 28), left no issue, and their five daus. and coheirs were Mary (d. 1754), marr. 1733 Joseph Littledale, *q.v.*; Frances, marr. 1737 Isaac Hamilton; Elizabeth, marr. . . . Watts; Isabella, marr. 1747 the Rev. Thomas Spedding; and Anne (d. unmarr. 1792, aged 71) (CW2 xxv). *Arms.* Per pale Argent and Or three chevronels Gules (BLG4, *sub* Littledale). These arms, quartered with Littledale and Patrickson, are impaled with Royds on a shield in the Shire Hall, Lancaster.*

LANGTON, of Keswick. Skinner Zachary Langton, J.P. (1797-1884), descended from the Langtons of Broughton Tower, near Preston, was of Barrow House, Keswick, where he lived for many years; he is buried in St. John's churchyard. His sons Walter Langton, J.P., M.A. (Cantab) (b. 1840), and Leyland Langton, J.P., succ. him at Barrow House. The former was father of Stephen Hamilton Langton, M.A. (Cantab) (b. 1871), an assistant master at Charterhouse 1900-9. *Arms.* Argent three chevronels Gules a canton Vair. *Crest.* An eagle displayed with two heads Vert charged on the breast with a trefoil Or (DVL; FLP).

LANGTON. A pedigree in FVC shews William Langton, descended from the Langtons, Barons of Newton (L), as of Herton† in Cumberland in 1591. *Arms.* Argent three chevrons Gules in dexter chief an annulet Sable. The younger branch of the family to which William belonged substituted a fleur-de-lys for the annulet (FVC).

LASCELLES. As GEC says (vii 444), there were several families of Lascelles in the North in the 12th and 13th centuries. In Cumberland Duncan Lascelles (d. 1211) marr. before 1200 Christiana, dau. and heir of Walter de Windsor (d. 1195), and acquired the manor of Bolton. Their grandson Thomas Lascelles (d. before October 1260) was the last male. He marr. before 1257 Christiana (d. 1305), dau. and coheir of William de Ireby, *q.v.*, and had a dau. and heir Ermina (living 1314), who marr. Sir John de Seton, *q.v.* Her mother marr. (2) before August 1261 Sir Adam de Jesmond (d. 1270) and (3) 1273 Robert Brus the Competitor (d. 1295), *q.v.* another family of Lascelles were Cumberland landowners. Alan Lascelles witnessed the foundation charter of Holm Cultram 1150, and a namesake marr. before 1265 Isabella de Corby, widow of Roald Fitz Alan. This Alan is apparently the man who owned Waverton (which included Lessonhall, said to be a corruption of Lasselhall) in 1277. His line appears to have ended in an heiress Isabel, who marr. Walter Routhbury. *Arms.* MMD gives those of Lassell, of Sowerby (Y): Sable a cross flory Or.‡

* Shields with the Langton arms in Brigham church are now much worn and barely decipherable. On the tablet to John Langton (d. 1777) and his wife Barbara they appear with an escutcheon of pretence, from which all tinctures and charges have disappeared. On the tablet to their sons John and Gawen Wren Langton, they appear impaling: . . . on a bend . . . three fleurs-de-lys . . . .

† We can trace no place of this name in Cumberland. Papworth spells it Heton (DBA); and Curwen attributes to Laughton, of Heton: Argent three chevronels Sable in dexter chief an annulet for difference (CW2 vi).

‡ In the section dealing with Lessonhall, MMD gives for Lasenhall: Ermine a mullet of six points pierced Gules, but adds, "[as the coat of the Lascells of Sowerby P340]." It seems clear, however, either that Lasenhall is a misreading of Hassenhull, see BGA, or *vice versa.*

LATHOM. Shield at Hutton-in-the-Forest; a Vane quartering. *Arms.* Or on a chief indented Azure three plates.

LATIMER. William de Latimer, 2nd Baron Latimer (*c.* 1277-1327), was granted two parts of the manor of Lamonby with its hamlets of Gamelsby and Unthank. His son William, 3rd Baron (1302-35), succ. and was succ. by his son William, 4th Baron (1330-81), who had a dau. and heir Elizabeth (d. 1395), who marr. 1381 John, Lord Neville, of Raby (d. 1389), father of Ralph, Lord Neville, of Raby, *q.v.* (GEC; CW2 xxi). *Arms.* Gules a cross patonce Or (FFC; shield on the ceiling of Carlisle Cathedral*). *Crest.* Burke gives: A plume of feathers Or (BGA).

LATIMER. A gravestone in Arthuret churchyard commemorates Thomas Latimer (d. 1745, aged 27), for eleven years a merchant in Virginia. *Arms.* Or a cross patonce . . . over all a bend . . . charged with three fleurs-de-lys . . . . Bell Irving recorded a tombstone at Arthuret commemorating John Latimer, of Arthuret, without date, as follows: . . . a cross botonné (?) . . . and three fleurs-de-lys . . . in bend (ABD).

LATIMER, David, of Clift, Kirklinton, 1736. *Arms.* . . . three fleurs-de-lys . . . and a bordure . . . (ABD).

LATUS, of The Beck and Whicham Hall. Richard Latus was steward to Sir John Hudleston, of Millom (d. 1547). His son Ralph Latus (*c.* 1535-1603) was of The Beck, Millom, and marr. Anne (b. *c.* 1537), dau. of the above Sir John. Their grandson Anthony (d. 1669) marr. 1614 his cousn Margaret (d. 1631), dau. of William Hudleston. Their son William (1615-98) was of The Beck and Whicham Hall, and marr. Agnes, dau. of John Ambrose, of Lowick Hall. Their son John Latus, J.P. (*c.* 1640-1702), acquired Lowick from his uncle, the Rev. Dr. John Ambrose; he was High Sheriff of Cumberland 1696. He marr. (1) Catherine (d. 1693), dau. of William Orfeur, and (2) Agnes (1642-1725), dau. of Andrew Hudleston, of Hutton John. His son John (b. 1674) marr. Dorothy, dau. of . . . Hudleston, whilst his dau. Bridget (b. 1666) marr. Richard Hudleston, of Millom. He was succ. by his son Ferdinando Latus (1670-1738), barrister-at-law, Collector of Customs at Whitehaven, Steward to Lord Carlisle. His sons died *v.p.*, as did his dau. Henrietta, who marr. (1) John Hudleston, and (2) John Robertson, of Cleator. His successor was his dau. Elizabeth (b. 1708) who marr. (1) 1734 Thomas Fletcher, of Hutton-in-the-Forest, and (2) 1736 William Blencowe, who thus acquired Lowick Hall. *Arms.* Ferdinando Latus, above, in 1731 sealed with: Quarterly, 1, . . . a chevron . . . between three garbs . . . ; 2, . . . fretty . . . (? Hudleston); 3, . . . a cross . . . ; 4, . . . a cross . . . on a canton . . . a mullet . . . (Orfeur).

DYSON-LAURIE. Col Julius Dyson Dyson-Laurie (1839-1909), 34th Foot, Colonel commanding the Border Regt 1881-86, assumed the additional surname Dyson 1869. He marr. 1869 his cousin Beatrice Margaret (d. 1879), elder dau. of Peter Northall-Laurie, LL.D. (Cantab) (1808-77), who assumed the additional surname and arms of Northall 1850 (BLG18). *Arms.* Sable a cup Argent issuing therefrom a wreath of oak between two branches of laurel Vert (Laurie); impaling, Quarterly, 1 & 4, Laurie; 2 & 3, Vert three dexter hands couped at the wrist Or a chief chequy of the last and of the first (Northall). *Crest.* An arm embowed in armour holding in the hand

* MMD shews the cross as a cross flory, and also records: Gules a cross flory Or over all three fleurs-de-lys bendwise in bend Sable.

an acorn between two branches of laurel. *Motto.* Deeds shew (Brass, Carlisle Cathedral).

LAW, Baron Ellenborough, Earl of Ellenborough. For the earlier history of this family, see AWL. Edmund Law, D.D. (Cantab) (1703-87), was Rector of Greystoke 1739-87, Archdeacon of Carlisle 1743-56, Master of Peterhouse, Cambridge, 1756-69, and Bishop of Carlisle 1769-87. His 3rd son Edward (1750-1818), was Lord Chief Justice 1802-18 and was cr. Baron Ellenborough, of Ellenborough, 1802. His eldest son Edward (1790-1871), was Governor-General of India 1841-44, and was cr. Earl of Ellenborough 1844. The Earldom became extinct on his death *s.p.s.,* but the barony descended to his nephew and is now held by Richard Edward Cecil Law, 8th Baron. *Arms.* Burke gives for the Bishop: Argent on a bend between two cocks Gules three mullets of the field (BGA). BBE ascribes to him the arms of the Lords Ellenborough, viz. Ermine on a bend engrailed between two cocks Gules three mullets pierced Or. *Crest.* A cock Gules chained round the neck and charged on the breast with a mitre Or. *Supporters.* Two eagles wings elevated Sable the dexter chained round the neck and pendent therefrom on the breast a mitre Or; the sinister with a like chain and pendent therefrom a covered cup of the second. *Motto.* Compositum jus fasque animi (BP105).

LAW. Elizabeth Law, of Irthington, spinster, died 1745, aged 22. *Arms.* . . . a horse passant the tail over the back . . . (Tombstone in Irthington churchyard).

LAWSON, of Isel and Brayton. Sir Wilfrid Lawson (1545-1632), son of Thomas Lawson, of Usworth (D) (d. 1559), was Sheriff of Cumberland 1582, 1597, 1606 and 1612. In 1591 the Earl of Northumberland made him Lieutenant of the Honour of Cockermouth. He marr. *c.* 1572 Matilda (d. 1624), dau. of Richard Redman, *q.v.,* and widow of Christopher Irton (d. before 1567) and of Thomas Leigh, of Isel., *q.v.,* by which marriage he acquired the manor of Isel and other estates, which he settled on his nephew William Lawson, son of his brother Gilfrid. William's son Wilfrid (d. 1689) is said variously to have been born in 1609, 1610 and 1615. He was Sheriff of Cumberland 1635, 1645-47, 1652-57 and 1678, was knighted 1641, and was M.P. for Cumberland 1659 and for Cockermouth 1661-78. He was cr. Baronet 1688. He was succ. by his grandson Sir Wilfrid Lawson (*c.* 1665-1705)* who was Sheriff 1689 and M.P. for Cockermouth 1690-95. He marr. Elizabeth (d. 1734), dau. and heir of George Preston, of Holker, and was succ. by his son Sir Wilfrid Lawson, 3rd Bart., F.R.S. (1696-1737). He was Groom of the Bedchamber to George I, and M.P. for Boroughbridge 1718-22 and Cockermouth 1722-37.† He was succ. in turn by his sons‡ Sir Wilfrid (1731-39) and Sir Mordaunt (1735-43). The latter was succ. by his cousin Sir Gilfrid Lawson§ (1675-1749), son of Wilfrid (d. 1710) (2nd son of the first Bart.) who marr. 1665 Sarah, dau. and coheir of William James, of Washington (D). He was M.P. for Cumberland 1702-5 and 1708-34. The

* On discovering that his estate had been under-taxed, he sent £600 to the Treasury (Wotton's *Baronetage*).

† He was first elected for Cockermouth when he was a minor, and was unseated on the petition of his opponent, Lord Percy.

‡ His dau. Elizabeth (d. 1759), Maid of Honour to the Princess of Wales, was loved by General Wolfe, but refused him.

§ His father acquired the Brayton estate, Aspatria.

baronetcy passed eventually to his nephew Sir Wilfrid, 8th Bart. (1712-1762), who was Sheriff 1756 and M.P. for Cumberland 1762. His brother, Sir Gilfrid, 9th Bart. (1713-94), was Sheriff 1768, and was succ. by his son Sir Wilfrid Lawson, 10th and last bart., M.A. (Cantab) (*c.* 1764-1806),* who was Sheriff 1801. He marr. 1787 Anne (d. 1811, aged 47), 2nd dau. of John Hartley, of Whitehaven, but died *s.p.*, bequeathing his estates to his wife's nephew Thomas Wybergh, see Lawson, *olim* Wybergh (GECB; CW2 xxiv). *Arms.* Per pale Argent and Sable a chevron counterchanged. *Crest.* Out of clouds Proper two arms embowed couped at the elbow vested Ermine cuffed Argent supporting in the hands Proper a sun in splendour Or (FCW).

LAWSON, *olim* WYBERGH. Sir Wilfrid Lawson, 10th Bart., died *s.p.* 1806 (see Lawson, of Brayton and Isel), leaving his estates to his wife's nephew Thomas Wybergh (1788-1812), 2nd son of her sister Isabel Hartley, who marr. Thomas Wybergh. He took the name of Lawson 1806, but died *s.p.* and *v.p.* at sea on his way home from Madeira, when he was succ. by his brother Wilfrid (1795-1867), who assumed the name Lawson 1812 and was cr. Baronet 1831. He was High Sheriff of Cumberland 1820. His son Sir Wilfrid Lawson, J.P. (1829-1906), M.P. for Carlisle 1859-65 and for Cockermouth 1886-1900 and 1906, was the well known temperance reformer (DNB). He was succ. by his son Sir Wilfrid Lawson, D.L., J.P., B.A. (Oxon) (1862-1937), M.P. for Cockermouth 1910-16, who was succ. by his nephew Sir Hilton Lawson, 4th and last Bart. (1895-1959), High Sheriff of Cumberland 1952. His aunts were Ellen (1864-1949), marr. 1884 the 3rd Viscount Knutsford; Mabel (1870-1918), marr. 1895 Alan de Lancey Curwen, *q.v.*; and Lucy (1872-1942), marr. 1896 Lt-Col Edmund Heathcote Thruston, *q.v. Arms.* Per pale Argent and Sable a chevron counterchanged a canton Sable charged with two bars Or. *Crest.* Out of clouds Proper two arms embowed vested Erminois cuffs Sable holding a sun also Proper. *Motto.* Quod honestum utile (BP99). This achievement is carved in stone on the entrance to Brayton Hall.

LAWSON. Sir Henry Joseph Lawson, 3rd Bart., of Brough Hall (Y) (1877-1947), marr. 1899 Ursula Mary, dau. and heir of Philip John Canning Howard, of Corby Castle, *q.v.* Their son Sir Ralph Henry Lawson, 4th Bart. (1905-75), was of Raventhorpe, Carmel Road, Darlington, and later of Wood House, Catterick. He died *s.p.m.* and was succ. by his brother Sir William Howard Lawson, 5th Bart., formerly of Heighington House, Heighington (D), and now of Wood House, Warwick Bridge. His elder son John Philip Lawson, who has assumed the surname Howard, is now of Corby Castle. *Arms.* Argent a chevron between three martlets Sable. *Crest.* On a cap of maintenance Gules turned up Ermine a martlet Sable. *Motto.* Leve et reluis (BP105).

LAWSON. The Hon. Lucia Edith Lawson, only dau. of the 4th Baron Burnham, of Hall Barn, marr. (2) 1966 John William Whitehead, of The Hill, Gilsland. *Arms.* Quarterly, 1 & 4, Azure three bars gemel Argent over all a winged morion Or; 2 & 3, Gules a saltire double parted and fretted Or

* Elizabeth Hudleston wrote on 27 June 1825: "Sir Wilfred Lawson's Heir at Law is making his claim to a part of the Brayton Property in which general success is wished for his succeeding in regaining his right, who is said to be a respectable young Man, a grocer in Newcastle".

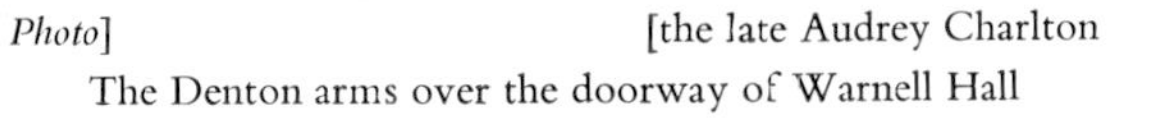

Photo] [the late Audrey Charlton

The Denton arms over the doorway of Warnell Hall

Photo] [the late John Dixon-Johnson

The Lamplugh arms over the gateway at Lamplugh Hall

between two rams' heads couped in fess Argent. *Motto.* Of old I hold (BP105).

LAWSON, *recte* LOWSON. John Lowson, of Renwick in 1823, left Moorside, Haresceugh, to William Lowson, of Owlet Ash, Milnthorpe (W) (1772-1824), who changed the spelling of his name to Lawson. He was succ. by his son, the Rev. William de Lancy Lawson, M.A. (Cantab) (1809-84), who was patron of Renwick. Moorside was inherited by Charlotte, wife of the Rev. William Smith. *Crest.* On the monument in Beverley Minster to William Lawson's youngest son, Major Barclay Lawson, R.A. (1823-62), appears the crest of Lawson, of Isel, viz. Out of clouds Proper two arms embowed vested Erminois cuffed Sable holding a sun in his splendour.

LAYTON, of Dalemain. A pedigree of five generations of this family was certified by William Layton, then its head and aged 40, at the Visitation of 1665. It is headed by Anthony Layton, whose son William, High Sheriff of Cumberland 1628, marr. Anne, dau. of Sir Thomas Sandford, of Howgill Castle (W). Their descendant, the above named William (1625-75), who was High Sheriff 1667, marr., probably in 1649, Margaret (d. 1699), dau. of Sir Thomas Layton, or Laton, of Laton (Y). After William's death the Dalemain estate was sold to Sir Edward Hasell, *q.v.*, whose descendants still own it. In CW2 xliv it is shewn that William had six daus. and coheirs – Isabella (b. 1651); Mary, marr. Christopher Blencowe, *q.v.*; Katherine (b. 1655), marr. William Dawes; Anne (d. 1706), marr. 1682 George Lewin, of Newcastle upon Tyne; Margaret, marr. the Rev. Richard Tickell, *q.v.* and Elizabeth (b. 1662), marr. 1681 Timothy Tyzack, of Gateshead (D). *Arms.* Sable on a bend Argent three escallops Gules (FCW; MMS vi 419). MMD gives: Argent on a bend Gules three escallops of the field; which may have been the family's original arms, see FFC. DSL gives for William Layton, High Sheriff 1628: Or on a bend Azure three escallops of the first. Field states that the family originally bore: Argent a fess between six cross crosslets fitché Sable (FAC). These arms, however, which are a slight variant of those of the Yorkshire family of Layton, of West Layton,* and which are quartered by Layton on a stone panel dated 1649 above the entrance to Layton House,† Greystoke, the home of Mr. and Mrs. H. C. Gill, seem to have been brought in as a quartering by the marr. of William Layton, above, to Margaret, dau. of Sir Thomas Layton, or Laton. *Crest.* the Visitation pedigree gives: A lion's head erased collared . . . (FCW). Lysons record: A lion's head erased Argent gorged with a collar Sable charged with three bezants (LMC), which is carved on the panel referred to above; at the top of the latter are carved two lions passant reguardant, and also the *Motto.* Tam pace quam bello.

LAZONBY, of Calthwaite. The Lazonbys farmed at Calthwaite for many years. William Lazonby was father of Joseph Lazonby, of Calthwaite House and later of Fern How, Braithwaite (1849-1932), two of whose sons, Joseph Lionel (b. 1881) and Julian (killed in World War I), died *v.p.* His eldest son William St. George Lazonby, who farmed at Calthwaite House, died *s.p.*,

* Who bore: Argent a fess between six crosses botonné fitché Sable. The Latons, of Sexhow (Y), bore: Argent a fess between six cross crosslets Sable; and the Laytons, of Barrowby (Y), bore: Argent a fess between six cross crosslets fitché Sable with a difference (FVY).

† Formerly known as Greystoke Mid Farm. It is suggested that the panel was brought to Greystoke from Dalemain when the latter was rebuilt by the Hasells (CW2 xliv 93-9).

and the family is now represented by Joseph Lancelot Lazonby, of Hawthorne, Florida, U.S.A., an attorney, who is son of Joseph Lancelot Lazonby, attorney, of Gainesville, Florida (d. 1969), who was only son of Joseph Lionel Lazonby, above named. In England the family is represented by the descendants of Annie Josephine, dau. of the above named Joseph Lazonby, who marr. 1908 George Messenger, *q.v.* *Arms.* Gules a fess Argent between three cushions Azure tasselled Or on a bend Sable three guttes d'Or (*Ex inf.* Mrs. Mary Underwood of Silloth, a descendant). Field recorded: Gules a fess between three cushions Argent tasselled Or over all a bend Sable gutté d'Or (FAC).

LEATHES, later STANGER-LEATHES. The Laythes, later Leathes, family was of Laythes, Aikton. Adam Laythes, of Laythes (d. 1621), marr. 1571 Alice Blencow, of Blencow, and bought Dalehead and the manor of Legburthwaite in 1577. His descendant Joshua Leathes, J.P. (1661-1724), was High Sheriff of Cumberland 1721. His grandson Thomas, an attorney in London (1726-1806), returned to Dalehead where he died *s.p.,* leaving his estates to Thomas Stanger, son of his sister Mary, who marr. 1752 Thomas Stanger, a Keswick mercer. On succeeding to the estates Thomas Stanger, junior, assumed the name and arms of Leathes. His son Thomas Leathes Stanger-Leathes (d. 1876, aged 85) succ. and was succ. by his son George Stanger-Leathes (b. 1827) who sold Dalehead to Manchester Corporation 1879 (CW2 lx 109-119). *Arms.* Azure on a bend between three fleurs-de-lys, one and two, Argent as many mullets Gules. *Crest.* A lion's head affronté (LMC). Burke gives: A lion's head affronté Proper (BGA). The arms appear on the seal of Thomas Leathes, of Wythburn (d. 1759), on a deed of 1748, but on the seal of Joshua Leathes, above, they are: ... on a bend ... three mullets of six points ... (Writ of 1721, R.O., Carlisle).

LEDIARD. Henry Ambrose Lediard, J.P., M.D. (Edin), of Wood View, Chatsworth Square, Carlisle (d. 1932, aged 84), son of Samuel Lediard, of Cirencester, Glos., solicitor (d. 1852), was in general practice in Carlisle and surgeon to the Cumberland Infirmary for over 50 years. An obituary notice described him as "one of the most distinguished members of the older school of medical and surgical practitioners."* His dau. Mary was well known locally as a solo pianist and lecturer on musical subjects. *Arms.* Gules on a fess between three wolves' heads erased Or five lilies slipped and inverted Pean. *Crest.* A wolf's head erased per pale Pean and Gules (BGA). *Motto.* In spe et silentio (Bookplate of the Henry Ambrose Lediard Memorial Music Library† in Tullie House).

LEE, or LEIGH, of Cumberland. No other details given. *Arms.* Ermine three bezants, two and one (OBA).

LEEDS, University of. *Arms.* Vert an open book Proper edged and clasped Or inscribed with the words "Et augebitur scientia" between in chief three mullets Argent and in base a rose of the last barbed and seeded Proper (Shield on monument in Carlisle Cathedral to Richard Assheton, 1st Viscount Cross, *q.v.,* who was Hon. LL.D., Leeds).

LEEMING, of Skirsgill. James Whiteside Leeming, J.P. (1865-1946), 4th son

* He drove about "in a horse-drawn phaeton – probably the last of its type in the city and district."

† On the bookplate the arms are depicted as: Per pale ... and ... on a fess ... between three wolves' heads erased Ermine five lilies slipped and inverted ....

of Richard Leeming, J.P., of Greaves House, Lancaster (1817-88), bought the Skirsgill estate, Penrith, 1924. He marr. 1911 Thérèse (d. 1976), dau. of Baron de Pfyffer Altishofen, of Lucerne, and had, *int. al.*, twin sons, born 1912 – Gerard de Pfyffer Leeming, of Field Hall, Holt, Norfolk, and Richard Whiteside Leeming, of Skirsgill (d. 1976), whose eldest son Antony Richard Leeming, M.A., D.Phil. (Oxon), is now of Skirsgill. *Arms.* The family bore: Ermine a cross patonce Azure. *Motto.* In hoc signo vinces. The above Richard Leeming obtained a grant of the following: *Arms.* Per chevron Argent and Azure a wreath of oak Vert between in chief two estoiles of the second and in base a cross patonce of the first. *Crest.* Upon a rock Proper a cross patonce Or between two ostrich feathers Argent (BGA). *Motto.* Garde bien la foy (FD7).

LEESON. The Hon. Robert Leeson (1772-1842), 3rd son of Brice, 3rd Earl of Milltown, was of Crosby Lodge, near Carlisle, and later of The Thorn, Penrith, where he died.* His son, the Rev. Joseph Leeson, M.A. (TCD) (1813-50), was assistant Curate of St. Giles, Durham, and Vicar of Fishlake (Y); he was father of Robert William Frederick Leeson (1842-1906), who claimed the Earldom of Milltown, which has been dormant since 1891. *Arms.* Gules a chief Argent on the lower part a cloud the rays of the sun issuing therefrom Proper. *Crest.* A demi lion rampant Gules holding between the paws the sun Or. *Motto.* Clariori e tenebris (BP105).

LEGH, of Cumberland; no other details given. *Arms.* Argent a fess Sable in chief three mullets of the second (BGA).

LEGH, or LEIGH, of Cumberland; no other details given. *Arms.* Ermine on a chevron Sable three bezants (another, plates) (OBA).

LEIGH, of Isel. Hubert de Multon, of Isel in 1292, had a son William, whose dau. and heir Margaret marr. Sir William Leigh, who thus acquired the estate. In her widowhood she was given licence for a chapel at Isel, 1360. Her son Sir William Leigh (d. 1428) was High Sheriff of Cumberland 1399, 1412 and 1423, and Constable of Cockermouth 1403. He marr. Agnes, dau. and coheir of Sir Clement Skelton, *q.v.* Their son Sir William (b. 1394) was M.P. for Cumberland 1423, and was succ. by his son Sir William (1420-62), who was M.P. for Cumberland 1459 and was beheaded. His son Sir William (d. 1484) was High Sheriff 1469 and 1473. He marr. 1474-5 Elizabeth (d. 1526), dau. of Sir John Hudleston, of Millom, *q.v.* Their son Sir John Leigh (*c.* 1486-*c.* 1563) was Sheriff 1548 and 1557. His son Thomas Leigh, the last of his family to own Isel, was Sheriff 1553, and died 1573, having marr. (1) Agnes, dau. of Roger Tempest, and had a dau. Jane, marr. Christopher Danby; and (2) Matilda (d. 1624), dau. of Richard Redman and widow of Christopher Irton (d. 1562), and subsequently wife of Sir Wilfrid Lawson, *q.v.* Thomas's heir was his nephew John (b. *c.* 1551, d. before 1632),† whose brother Robert was father of Matilda (1600-68) who was heiress of the family, but did not inherit Isel. She marr. Wilfrid Irton, grandson of Matilda Irton, see above. *Arms.* . . . two bars . . . over all a bend counter-company . . . (Tombs at Millom and Isel). Lysons blazon this as: Azure two bars Argent over all a bend counter-compony Or and Gules (LMC). MMD gives: Argent two bars Azure over all a bend counter-

* His dau. Alicia Anne marr. 1849 Peter Vickers, of Carleton Terrace, Penrith, and had a dau. Emily Honoria Neve, who marr. 1884 Frederick Maurice Dickson, of Levenside, Haverthwaite.

† It was said that he was an idiot and attainted for taking part in the Rising of the North.

compony Or and Gules. FVC gives, for Henry Leigh, of Isel: Azure two bars Or over all a bend counter-compony of the last and Gules. DSL gives for Sir William Leigh, the Sheriff: Argent two bars Sable over all a bend Gules. A shield on the ceiling of Carlisle Cathedral, which Field (FAC) read as: Argent two bars Sable a bend counter-compony Argent and Gules, but the present writers as: Argent two bars Sable a bend lozengy Or and Gules, may be intended for Leigh.*

de la LEKE. Shields at Hutton-in-the-Forest; a Vane quartering. *Arms.* Azure a chief Argent over all a lion rampant Or crowned Gules.

L'ENGLEYS, or ENGLISH, of Highhead. Sir William L'Engleys, descended from the family who held Little Asby (W), acquired Highhead Castle. He was Chief Forester of Inglewood from 1328, and was succ. by his son† Sir William (d. 1369) whose dau. and heir Isabel, aged 24 in 1369, marr. Sir Nicholas Harington, of Farleton (d. 1403) (CW2 xii). *Arms.* Sable three lions rampant Argent (FFC; and so quartered by Sandford, of Askham, see FCW). NB (i 425) gives: Sable three lions rampant caud inflexed (i.e. coward) Argent.

LENNARD, Baron Dacre of the South, Earl of Sussex. Margaret (1541-1612), sister and heir of Gregory Fiennes, Lord Dacre, *q.v.*, marr. 1564 Sampson Lennard, M.P., Sheriff of Kent (d. 1615). Their son Henry (1570-1616) succ. as Lord Dacre, and the title descended to Thomas Lennard (1654-1715), who was cr. Earl of Sussex 1674. His daus. and coheirs were Barbara (d. *s.p.* 1741), wife of Lt-Gen Charles Skelton, and Anne (1684-1755), who marr. (1) 1716 her cousin Richard Barrett, (2) Henry, 8th Baron Teynham, and (3) 1725 the Hon. Robert Moore. She and her sister sold their Cumberland estates, including the castles at Dacre and Kirkoswald 1716, and she succ. to the title on her sister's death. The title was inherited by her descendant Thomas Henry Brand, C.M.G., 4th Viscount Hampden and 26th Baron Dacre (1900-65), at whose death the barony of Dacre fell into abeyance between his two daus. and was called out of abeyance 1970 in favour of the elder, the Hon. Rachel Leila Douglas-Home, wife of the Hon. William Douglas-Home, the playwright. *Arms.* Or on a fess Gules three fleurs-de-lys of the field. *Crest.* Out of a ducal coronet Or an heraldic tiger's head Argent maned and tufted Gold. *Supporters.* Dexter, A wolf Argent gorged with a spiked collar chain reflexed over the back Or; Sinister, A bull Gules armed ducally gorged and chain reflexed over back Or. *Motto.* Pour bien desirer (BGA). The arms, quartering Fiennes, Dacre and Multon, the supporters and the motto are carved over the entrance to Dacre Castle.

L'ESTRANGE. Impaled by Pennington in window at Muncaster Castle; Josslyn Francis, 5th Baron Muncaster (1834-1917), marr. 1863 Constance (1839-1917), 2nd dau. of Edmund L'Estrange, of Tynte House, Leitrim. Her sister Mary Caroline Louisa (b. 1849) marr. at Muncaster 1875 the 19th Earl of Erroll, *q.v.* Their cousin Col Paget Walter L'Estrange was father of Rhoda Ankaret (b. 1867), who marr. at Muncaster 1894 the 10th Earl of Carlisle. *Arms.* Gules two lions passant guardant in pale Or.

* The tomb of Sir William Leigh (d. 1484) in Isel churchyard displays: . . . two bars . . . over all a bend . . . between two fleurs-de-lys in pale . . . and two lions rampant in bend sinister . . . . The tomb was formerly in the church and the blocks of stone which support the top of the table-tomb, and on which the heraldry is displayed, have been arranged in such a way as to produce this hybrid coat.

† His dau. Juliana (marr. Ralph Restwold, *q.v.*) inherited Highhead Castle.

LEVESON-GOWER – see GOWER.

LEVINGTON. King Henry I granted the barony of Levington (Kirklinton) to Richard de Boyvill, *q.v.*, whose descendants were known as de Levington. Ranulph de Levington (d. 1253) was succ. by his dau. Helewise (d. *s.p.* 1272), who marr. Eustace de Balliol. Her heirs were the descendants of her aunts – Euphemia, marr. Richard de Kirkbride *q.v.*; Isabella, marr. Walter de Twynham; Eva, marr. Patrick de Southaic; Agnes, marr. Walter de Corry; Margery, marr. Robert de Hampton; and Juliana, marr. . . . Carrick. *Arms.* Or a saltire Gules on a chief of the second three boars' heads fesswise couped of the field (OBA).

LEWIS. Impaled by Howard on shield in hall of Greystoke Castle; Murray Bernard Cyprian Neville Howard (b. 1942) marr. 1969 Lavinia Zara, dau. of Lt-Col Philip Lewis, of Meon House, Droxford, Hants. *Arms.* Or a lion rampant Sable.

LEWIS – see ORD.

LEWKNOR. Quartered by Hudleston on shield from Millom Castle, now at Hutton John; brought in by Barantyne, *q.v.* *Arms.* Azure three chevronels Gules. *Sic*; correctly, Azure three chevronels Argent.*

LEWTHWAITE, of Broadgate. This family was settled in Whicham until Thomas Lewthwaite (1588-1667) bought Broadgate in Thwaites parish 1642. His descendant William Lewthwaite, D.L., J.P. (1853-1927), was cr. Baronet 1927. His grandson Sir William Anthony Lewthwaite, B.A. (Cantab), solicitor, 3rd Bart, is the present holder of the title. His brother and heir presumptive, Brigadier Rainald Gilfrid Lewthwaite, C.V.O., M.C., O.B.E., B.A. (Cantab), Defence and Military Attaché in Paris 1964-68, is owner of the Broadgate estate. *Arms.* Ermine a cross flory Azure fretty Or. *Crest.* A garb Or bound by a serpent nowed Proper holding in the mouth a cross crosslet fitché Gules. *Motto.* Virtus ad aethera tendens (BP105).

LEVY. The Rev. Thomas Bayley Levy, M.A. (Oxon) (1812-72), elder son of Capt Abraham Levy, of Temple Sowerby, Mostyn Hall, and Hutton Hall, Penrith (d. 1834, aged 65), was Curate of Kirkby Thore 1838-42 and Fellow of Queen's College, Oxford, 1846-72. In 1846 he obtained a grant of arms for himself, his brother the Rev. George Levy, M.A. (Oxon) (d. 1853, aged 40), and his sister Mrs. Mary Jane Peters. *Arms.* Per chevron nebuly Or and Sable in chief three estoiles and in base a cross pattée counterchanged. *Crest.* A demi eagle displayed Sable semé of crosses pattée fitché Or (CA xlviii/143).

LEY, of Lazonby. Sir Francis Ley, J.P., 1st Bart (cr. 1905) (1846-1916), was son of George Phillips Ley, of Winshill, Burton-on-Trent. He was Lord of the manors of Lazonby, Staffield, Glassonby, and Kirkoswald, and was succ. by his son Sir Henry Gordon Ley, of Lazonby Hall (1874-1944). His elder son Sir Gerald Gordon Ley, T.D., B.A. (Oxon), the 3rd and present baronet, was High Sheriff of Cumberland 1937. *Arms.* Argent a bend lozengy Gules between two broken tilting spears erect of the last. *Crest.* In front of a cubit arm in armour holding in the hand a broken tilting spear in bend sinister Proper four lozenges conjoined fessways Gules. *Motto.* Post mortem spero vitam (BP105).

* Curwen wrongly attributes this quartering to Barrington, and blazons it: Argent three chevronels Gules (CW2 vi).

LEYBURNE. Roger Leyburne, of the family of Cunswick (W) (will dated 1507), Master of Pembroke College, Cambridge, Rector of Sedgefield (D), Archdeacon and Chancellor of Durham, Master of Kepier Hospital, Durham, and Prebendary and Archdeacon of York, was Bishop of Carlisle 1503-7. *Arms.* Azure six lions rampant, three, two and one, Argent (NB i 146; BBE). The arms are also on the shield of an effigy in Calder Abbey, thought to be that of either Sir Roger Leyburne (d. 1283), or Robert Leyburne, of Elliscales (d. before 1328) (PGD).

LIDDELL, of Moorhouse. John Liddell, of Moorhouse, Burgh-by-Sands, was father of Catherine, who marr. 1755 John Losh, *q.v.*, and Joseph Liddell, B.A. (Cantab), of Moorpark, barrister-at-law (1736-1820). The latter, who was a commissioner in bankruptcy, was lessee of Cox Lodge and Kenton collieries and had interests in the Carlisle Bank and in the Newcastle bank of Messrs. Surtees & Liddell* (DCL; VAC). *Arms.* ... fretty ... on a chief ... three leopards' faces ... (Gate pillars at Woodside). *Crest.* Field quotes BGA as authority for: A lion rampant Sable billetté and crowned with an eastern crown Or; Burke, however, gives this not for Liddell, of Cumberland, but for Liddell, Earl of Ravensworth and Baron Ravensworth.

LIDDELL, of Warwick Hall. Charles Liddell, J.P., of Warwick Hall (1856-1922), High Sheriff of Cumberland 1917, was 4th son of John Liddell, of Benwell Hall (N) (1811-88). He marr. 1894 Madeline (d. 1936), dau. of James Arthur Dease, of Turbotston, Co. West Meath. He acquired the Warwick Hall estate from the Parker family at the beginning of the 20th century and it passed to his only child, Ailleen Mary (b. 1894) who marr. 1919 Lt-Col Robert Geoffrey Gervase John Elwes, *q.v.* Her cousin Peter John Liddell, D.S.C., F.Z.S., who is Chairman of the North West Water Authority, is of Moorhouse, Warwick. *Arms.* Argent fretty Gules two flaunches Or on a chief of the second an estoile between two leopards' heads erased and affronté of the third. *Crest.* Two hands clasped Proper surmounted by a cross crosslet Gules between two wings Or. *Motto.* Constans et fidelis (BLG18).

LIGHTFOOT. Robert Lightfoot, Doctor of Physic, on a quitclaim to Sir John Lowther, of Whitehaven, 1682, sealed with the following *Arms.* Barry of six ... and ... on a bend ... three escallops .... *Crest.* A griffin's head erased and gorged with a collar charged with three mullets (D/Lons/W/Whvn Town/41; *ex inf.* J. P. Godwin).

LIND. Capt Francis Lind, of Carlisle, 14th Foot, marr. Elizabeth (1725-81), sister and coheir of Henry Farrer, *q.v.* Letters of administration were granted to Elizabeth at Carlisle 1759. Their son Edward George Lind, of Burton (W) and London, marr. 1786 his first cousin Elizabeth Ainslie. Their son Montague (1788-1815), Captain 1st Life Guards, was killed at Waterloo. *Arms.* ... two swords in saltire ... between a mullet ... in chief and a crescent ... in base (John Atkinson's MS. notebook, folio 161, Tullie House, Carlisle).

LINDESAY. The Rev. Robert Thomas Mauleverer Lindesay, M.A. (Oxon) (b. 1870), 5th son of Frederick Lindesay, D.L., J.P., M.A., of Loughry, Co. Tyrone, by his 2nd wife Charlotte Murphy, was Vicar of Walton 1907-38.

* James Losh records of him that at the age of 76, in 1812, he married his first wife's servant maid.

He was a descendant of William Nicolson, Bishop of Carlisle. *Arms.* Gules a fess chequy Argent and Azure between three mullets in chief of the second and a crescent Proper in base. *Crest.* A swan wings closed Proper (BLG8).

LINDISFARNE, See of. The arms of the church and monastery of Durham are attributed to the See of Lindisfarne in a window in Caldbeck church commemorating Margaret Alice Glen (d. 1936), wife of Dr. Glen, of Barnoldswick, and portraying St. Cuthbert, Bishop of Lindisfarne. *Arms.* Azure a cross patonce Or between four lions rampant Argent.

LINDOW, *post* BURNS-LINDOW, of Ehen Hall and Irton Hall. Jonas Lindow, member of an old Cleator family, marr. Agnes Matson, of Tytup Hall (see AWL). Their grandson, Jonas Lindow (1770-1846), became the largest bacon factor in Cumberland, and also owned the spade forge in Cleator. His sons Samuel Lindow, D.L., J.P., of Ingwell (1799-1871), High Sheriff of Cumberland 1862, and John Lindow, D.L., J.P., of Ehen Hall (1804-78), High Sheriff 1874, were two of the foremost pioneers of the haematite industry in West Cumberland. John's only son Jonas, D.L., J.P., M.A. (Oxon), of Ehen Hall, later of Ingwell (1847-1904), was High Sheriff 1883, and died *s.p.* At the death of his uncle Samuel, his cousin Jonas Lindow Burns-Lindow, of Irton Hall, son of Dr. Isaac Burns, of Black How, Cleator, Whitehaven and Ingwell (1809-70), who had marr. 1834 Samuel's sister Agnes, assumed the additional surname and the arms of Lindow; he was High Sheriff 1877. His younger son Samuel Lindow Burns-Lindow, J.P., M.A. (Oxon), of Ingwell and Greenlands, Holmrook (b. 1869), was High Sheriff 1906, and his elder son Lt-Col Isaac William Burns-Lindow, D.S.O., J.P. (b. 1868), was High Sheriff 1935. *Arms.* Ermine on a chevron dovetailed between three sinister hands couped at the wrist Gules as many fountains. *Crest.* A lion rampant Gules semé of buckles Or and holding between the paws a fountain. *Motto.* Vi et virtute (BLG14; FD7; Shields at Ehen Hall, Irton Hall and Mill Place, Irton; seal of Jonas Lindow Burns-Lindow).

LINDSAY. The Rev. Robert Lindsay, M.A. (Dunelm), was Curate of St. Mary, Gateshead, 1939-43; Curate in charge of Sacriston 1943-45; Curate of Benfieldside 1945-46; Vicar of Lanercost 1946-55; Vicar of Hawkshead 1955-70; Rector of Dean 1970-74; Vicar of Loweswater with Buttermere 1974; and Hon. Canon of Carlisle 1972. *Arms.* Gules a fess chequy Argent and Azure (Shield on curtains in Lanercost Priory church).

LINDSEY. Alan, 2nd Baron of Allerdale, gave Blennerhasset and Upmanby to his sister Ochtred and her husband Ranulph de Lindsey, *temp.* Henry II. Ranulph also owned Loweswater, which descended to William Lindsey *temp.* Richard I (DAC). *Arms.* Burke gives for Lindsey, of Cumberland, without further details: Or an eagle displayed Purpure membered Gules (BGA). These are the arms given by FFC for Sir Philip Limsey, or Lindesey, "of the North."

LINTOT. Sir Henry Fletcher, 1st Bart. (d. 1807), *q.v.*, bore the following on an escutcheon of pretence on his arms, presumbably for his wife Catherine (d. 1816), dau. and heir of Henry Lintot, of Southwater, Sussex. *Arms.* . . . a lion rampant . . . .

LINTHORNE. Mrs. Gertrude Adele Roope Thom-Postlethwaite (1890-1974), wife of Andrew Cecil Scott Thom-Postlethwaite, *q.v.*, was dau. and coheir of Sir Richard Roope Linthorne, O.B.E., J.P., solicitor (1864-1935),

Town Clerk of Southampton 1899-1929. *Arms.* Ermine on a cross Sable fimbriated Or three pheons in pale between two crescents of the last.

LITTLE, of Brunstock. A gravestone in Arthuret churchyard commemorates Ann (d. 1741, aged 65), espoused wife of William Little, of Brunstock, Crosby. *Arms.* . . . a chevron engrailed . . . between in chief a mullet . . . and in base a crescent reversed . . . .

LITTLE, of Conhess. A gravestone in Arthuret churchyard commemorates John Little, of Conhess (d. 1737, aged 33) and his brother, Ringn *(sic)* Little (d. 1718, aged 23); erected by Agnes, spouse of John. *Arms.* . . . a saltire . . . between two mullets . . . in pale.

LITTLE, of Crofthead. Andrew Little, of Crofthead, died 1734, aged 57. *Arms.* . . . a saltire engrailed . . . (Gravestone, Kirkandrews-on-Esk).

LITTLE, of Green. Thomas Little, of Green, Stapleton, died 1747, aged 66; John Little, of Green, died 1772, aged 40. *Arms.* Chequy . . . and . . . (ABD).

LITTLE, of Harperhill. Bell Irving recorded, for Thomas Little, of Harperhill, Stapleton, 1763, the following *Arms.* . . . a chevron . . . in chief a square and compass . . . (ABD).

LITTLE, of Raise House. John Little, of Raise House, Alston, died 1821, aged 47; his widow, Sarah, died 1857, aged 80. *Arms.* Sable a saltire engrailed Gules.* *Crest.* A cock Sable combed and wattled Gules. *Motto.* Magnum in parvo (M.I., Garrigill church).

LITTLEDALE, of Ennerdale and Whitehaven. The Littledale family, which played so important a part in the commercial life of Whitehaven in the 18th and 19th centuries, was for long settled in Ennerdale. Joseph Littledale, merchant, of Whitehaven (d. 1749, aged 69), was father of Joseph Littledale, of Whitehaven (1710-44), who marr. 1733 Mary, eldest dau. and coheir of Isaac Langton, *q.v.* From their son Isaac (1735-91) descended John Bolton Littledale, D.L., J.P., B.A. (Oxon), of Bunbury House (Ch) (b. 1868), who had an only son Ronald (b. 1902). Isaac's younger brother Henry Littledale, a Whitehaven mercer (1741-96), removed to Eton House, Lancaster. His elder son, the Rt. Hon. Sir Joseph Littledale, Judge of the Queen's Bench (1767-1842), died *s.p.* and the line was continued by his younger brother Anthony Littledale, of Liverpool (1777-1820), who marr. 1809 Mary, elder dau. of Pudsey Dawson, of Langcliffe Hall and Bolton Hall (Y); the latter estate she inherited. In 1897 the head of the family was Commander Henry William Assheton Littledale, R.N. (b. 1846), who had a son, Henry Ambrose Pudsey, (b. 1881) (BFR; BLG4). *Arms.* Argent a lion passant Gules on a chief Azure three cross crosslets of the field. *Crest.* A demi lion rampant Gules gorged with a collar gemel and holding in the dexter paw a cross crosslet Argent. *Motto.* Fac et spera (BFR).

LITTLER. Sir Ralph Daniel Makinson Littler, C.B., K.C., D.L., J.P., B.A. (London), barrister at law (1835-1908), was of Petteril Bank, Upperby. He was Chairman of Middlesex County Council and of Middlesex Quarter Sessions, and one of H.M. Lieutenants for the City of London. *Arms.* Argent

* *Sic:* perhaps the result of repainting.

a chevron Sable between three squirrels sejant Gules (Glass in window at Petteril Bank).*

LOCH. James Loch (1775-1828), son of James Loch, joint King's Remembrancer for Scotland, was of Keswick when he marr. 1804 Agnes (1780-1863), dau. of Joseph Langstaff. Their son John Dickson Loch was born at Portinscale 1805. James Loch became chief architect to the King of Oudh. *Arms.* Or a saltire engrailed Sable between two swans naiant in fess in a loch Proper. *Crest.* A swan with wings endorsed devouring a perch both Proper. *Motto.* Assiduitate non desidia (LTW).

LOFTIE. John Henry Loftie, of Tanderagee, Co. Armagh (1808-60), was father of Canon Arthur Gershom Loftie, M.A. (TCD) (1843-1922), Rector of Great Salkeld 1894-1904 and of Wetheral and Warwick 1904-16, and of Rowley Crozier Loftie (1840-1915), Government Resident at Albany, W. Australia. The latter's only son Capt John Henry Loftie, R.N., of Beulah, Pooley Bridge (1874-1940), marr. 1913 Madeleine Elizabeth (1883-1960), 3rd dau. of Robert Thompson, of Inglewood, Penrith. Their son, Lt-Cdr William Henry Paule Loftie, R.N., of Bowerbank, Pooley Bridge, died 1976, aged 57. *Arms.* Sable a chevron Ermine between three trefoils slipped Argent. *Crest.* A boar's head erect and erased Argent tusked Or. *Mottoes.* Prend moy tel que je suis; Loyal au mort (LFL).

LOMAS. William Lomas, M.D. (d. 1822, aged 51), a native of Aspatria, was of Allonby, and practised as a doctor for nearly 30 years. His only dau. Jane Agnes (d. 1839, aged 19) marr. William Thompson, of Workington, *q.v.* *Arms.* Argent three fleurs-de-lys in pale Sable between two pallets Gules a chief Azure. *Crest.* On a cap of maintenance Gules turned up Ermine a pelican vulning herself Argent (Window in Aspatria church).

LONDON (QUAKER) LEAD COMPANY, The. The arms used by the London (Quaker) Lead Company, or The Corporation for Smelting Lead with Pitcoal and Seacoal, 1692-1905,† have recently been re-erected as the sign of the Miners' Arms Inn, Nenthead, by the licensee, Mr. Keith Hey. *Arms.* Or on a chevron between three oval fetter links fesswise Sable as many bezants.‡ *Crest.* In front of a bell two bursts of flame Proper. *Supporters.* Dexter, A lead smelter holding in the exterior hand a pair of smelting tongs; Sinister, A miner holding in the exterior hand a miner's pick; all Proper. *Motto.* Spectatur in igne.

LONG. Impaled by Howard on shields in hall of Greystoke Castle; Lord Henry Molyneux-Howard (1766-1824) marr. 1801 Elizabeth (d. 1834), dau. of Edward Long, Chief Judge of the Vice-Admiralty Court, Jamaica, and their son Henry Howard, of Greystoke Castle and of Thornbury Castle, Glos. (1802-75), marr. 1849 Charlotte Caroline Georgiana (d. 1896), eldest dau. of Henry Lawes Long, of Hampton Lodge, Surrey, by his wife, the Lady Catherine Walpole, dau. of the 2nd Earl of Orford. *Arms.* Sable a lion passant Argent holding in the dexter paw a cross crosslet fitché Or on a chief of the second three cross crosslets of the field.

* Next to this coat of arms in the window is a shield bearing the following arms which we have not been able to identify: Azure a bend sinister Or between in chief on a wreath Argent and Sable a dove close holding in the beak a sprig of olive and in base an anchor erect all of the second. *Motto.* Spes sibi quisque.

† See A. Raistrick, *Two Centuries of Industrial Welfare,* Revised ed., 1977.

‡ The illustration in Raistrick's book gives no tinctures; these have been devised by the sign painter, and it seems highly probable that the bezants should be plates.

On a hatchment in Greystoke church, the arms are impaled as: Quarterly, 1, Sable a lion passant Argent on a chief of the last three cross crosslets fitché at the foot of the field (Long); 2, Per fess Or and Gules a pale counterchanged and three Cornish choughs Proper (Tate); Gules ten bezants, four, three, two and one, and a canton Ermine (Zouche); 4, Argent two chevronels Gules in chief a label of five points Azure (St. Maur).*

LONGRIGG. John Hemsley Longrigg, of Broadstone, Dorset, formerly of Cumwhitton and of India (1890-1974), who was descended from Isaac Longrigg, farmer, of Ireland House, Hesket-in-the-Forest, perhaps baptised at Lowther 1744, obtained in 1945 a grant of the following *Arms.* Per pale Gules and Azure three fleurs-de-lys Or on a chief of the last two gaurs' heads cabossed Proper. *Crest.* Out of an eastern crown Or an arm embowed vested Azure cuffed Gules the hand Proper holding a garb also Or. *Motto.* Aestiva persequor (BLG18).

LONSDALE. Earl of – see LOWTHER.

LOSH, formerly and later ARLOSH, of Woodside. According to Henry Lonsdale (see LWC), William Arlosh alias Losh, yeoman, was of Woodside, Wreay, in the 1570's. The estate descended to John Losh (d. 1789), who marr. 1755 Catherine, dau. of John Liddell, of Moorhouse, Burgh-by-Sands, *q.v.* Their eldest son John Losh (d. 1814, aged 59) succ. to Woodside, was a partner in the Walker Alkali Works, Newcastle upon Tyne, and was High Sheriff of Cumberland 1811. He marr. Isabella, dau. of Thomas Bonner, of Callerton (N), and was succ. by their dau. Sarah (1785-1863), a generous benefactor to Wreay, and the builder of Wreay church. Her uncle James Losh, of Jesmond Grove, Newcastle upon Tyne (1763-1833), who marr. Cecilia, dau. of the Rev. Roger Baldwin, *q.v.*, was a distinguished lawyer and Recorder of Newcastle. He was also well known as a philanthropist and political reformer. His eldest son James Losh, M.A. (Cantab) (1802-58), was a County Court Judge. Another son Lt-Col John Joseph Losh, Madras Army, was of Wreay Syke, where he died 1862. Woodside was inherited by his brother William Septimus Losh who marr. his first cousin Cecilia, dau. of George Losh by his wife Frances, dau. of Joseph Wilkinson of Carlisle, *q.v.*† Their only son the Rev. James Losh, J.P., M.A. (Dunelm), of Woodside (1834-1904), resumed the name of Arlosh 1870. He was incumbent of Ponsonby 1861-71, and Diocesan Inspector of Schools in Carlisle diocese. He became a Unitarian and occasionally officiated in the Unitarian Chapel, Carlisle. He was a generous benefactor to Manchester College, Oxford. In 1859 he marr. Isabella, youngest dau. of Capt Thomas Benn, R.N., *q.v.*; their only son Godfrey died *v.p. Arms.* Argent a fess Gules between three griffins' heads erased Azure (LWC). On the gateposts at Woodside, however, the griffins' heads are couped. *Crest.* Two ostrich feathers erect Proper. *Motto.* Persevere (LWC; Seal of John Losh, Sheriff in 1811).

LOUGH. Thomas Lough, junior, bought lands in Sebergham and Langholme from Roger Salkeld 1539 and the manor of Blencarn from Edward and Agnes Restwold 1540. Nicholas Lowghe was a juror 1574 and in 1598

* See R. M. Howard: *Records and Letters of the family of the Longs of Longville, Jamaica, and Hampton Lodge, Surrey.* 1925.

† Her sister Alice marr. 1798 George's brother William Losh, and a third sister was wife of William Richard Dacre, *q.v.*, *sub* Appelby.

Thomas Lough and Frances his wife joined with Adam and Julia Denton in selling the Sebergham and Langholme lands to John Denton. Thomas Lough, of Blencarn, died 1717.* Mary Lough marr. 1724 John Carleton, of Skirwith Hall, and Blencarn descended to their son Lough Carleton (d. *s.p.* 1792, aged 68) who was articled to his mother's brother, an attorney in London, to whose extensive practice he succeeded. His heirs to Blencarn and Tynehead, Alston, were his three nieces, daus. of his brother Thomas Carleton, agent to Lord Monson; one of them, Mary, marr. 1804 William Tufnell, *q.v.* (NB ii 444; HCC i 259). *Arms.* Or a maunch Gules on a chief of the last three fleurs-de-lys of the field (MMS vi 401; FVC).

LOWNDES. Richard Lowndes, Lieut R.N., marr. 1751, when he was 32, Bridget (b. 1727), dau. of William Dalston, of Great Salkeld. They lived in the house in Bishop Yards, Penrith, now occupied by Messrs. Little & Shepherd, solicitors. Their elder son William (b. 1752) was Commissioner of the Board of Taxes, and their younger son Richard (b. 1756), an attorney in London, marr. 1787 Rebecca, dau. of Henry Brougham. The said Bridget, a widow in 1766, sold the house in Bishop Yards 1786. *Arms.* Fretty Argent and Sable on a canton Gules a leopard's head erased Or wreathed Vert. *Crest.* A leopard's head erased Or with a chaplet Vert (BLG3).

LOWRY, of Blackhall and Durran Hill. Thomas Lowry, of Blackhall, Carlisle, yeoman (d. 1764), marr. 1717 Rebecca (d. 1767), dau. of . . . Simpson, of Sebergham. Their elder son Thomas (d. *s.p.* 1779, aged 61) marr. 1773 Jane Bell, *q.v.*, and their younger son John (d. 1785) was of Durran Hill, Wetheral, where he was succ. by his son Richard Lowry, a Carlisle attorney, who was killed by a fall from his horse 1841, aged 66. His son John died *v.p.* 1831, aged 26, and he was succ. by his daus. Mary Anne and Eliza, who were also coheirs of their mother Mary, née Porter. *Arms.* On the tablet in St. Cuthbert's church, Carlisle, commemorating the above Thomas and Rebecca Lowry and their son Thomas, the arms (impaling Bell) appear as: . . . a chevron . . . between three roses . . . . *Crest.* A unicorn's head couped contourné. On the tomb of John Lowry (d. 1785) at Wetheral, however, the arms appear as: . . . a cup . . . issuing therefrom a garland between two branches . . . . *Crest.* Two branches crossing in saltire near the base. *Motto.* Virtus semper viridis. The same arms and crest are on the obelisk to his son Richard's memory in Wetheral churchyard.

LOWRY, of Botcherby and Crosby. The Rev. Thomas Lowry, M.A., D.D. (Cantab) (d. 1832, aged 70), son of Richard Lowry, of Botcherby and Stanwix, was Curate of Armathwaite 1789-91, Vicar of Crosby-on-Eden 1791-1832 and Rector of Ousby 1807-32, and was five times Mayor of Carlisle. His eldest son, the Rev. John Stamper Lowry, M.A. (Cantab) (1804-54), was Curate of Ousby 1829-31, and incumbent of Crosscrake (W) 1840-41. Another son, Thomas (1814-81), settled at Okawa, New Zealand; Lowry Bay and Lowry Peaks are named after him. *Arms.* Sable a cup Argent issuing therefrom three branches of laurel. *Crest.* Two sprigs of laurel in orle Proper. *Motto.* Virtus semper viridis (M.I. in Stanwix church to Esther (d. 1822, aged 52), dau. of Richard and Jane Lowry, wife of James Bonnell, and sister of the Rev. Dr. Thomas Lowry, above).

* Elizabeth, dau., and heir of John Lough, of Blencarn, marr. 1706 John Pattenson, *q.v.*, but did not apparently succeed to Blencarn.

LOWTHER, Earl of Lonsdale. One of the oldest families in Westmorland, whose descent is traced by the late Canon C. M. Lowther Bouch from Geoffrey de Lowther, living 1247, great-grandson of Dolfin, the Lowther family from the 17th century also had extensive interests in Cumberland, especially in Whitehaven. Geoffrey's son, Sir Hugh de Lowther (*i.p.m.* 1317), was M.P. for Westmorland 1299-1300 and 1304-5. His descendant Sir John Lowther (1605-75) was cr. Baronet *c.* 1638, and his grandson John Lowther, P.C. (1655-1700), was cr. Viscount Lonsdale 1696. The Viscounty became extinct on the death unmarr. 1751 of Henry, 3rd Viscount Lonsdale, when the baronetcy passed to his kinsman Sir James Lowther (d. *s.p.* 1802), who was cr. 1784 Baron Lowther of Lowther, Baron Kendal, Baron Burgh, Viscount Lonsdale, Viscount Lowther, and Earl of Lonsdale (of the first creation). Having no issue, he obtained a new patent 1797, creating him Baron and Viscount Lowther, with remainder to the heirs male of his cousin, the Rev. Sir William Lowther, 1st Bart., of Swillington (1707-88), cr. Baronet 1764. The latter's eldest son William, 2nd Baron and Viscount Lowther, K.G. (1757-1844), was cr. Earl of Lonsdale (of the 2nd creation) 1807. From him descended James William, Viscount Ullswater, *q.v.*; Hugh Cecil, 5th Earl of Lonsdale (1857-1944), 'The Yellow Earl';* and the present holder of the title, James Hugh William, 7th Earl of Lonsdale, of Askham Hall, elder son of Anthony, Viscount Lowther, D.L., J.P. (1896-1949) (CW2 xvi 108-68, xlviii 114-24; BP105). *Arms.* Or six annulets, three, two, and one, Sable. *Crest.* A dragon passant Argent. NB (i 437) give: A griffin passant Argent. *Supporters.* Two horses Argent each gorged with a wreath of laurel Vert. *Motto.* Magistratus indicat virum (BP105).

LOWTHER, Viscount Ullswater. James William Lowther, P.C., G.C.B., J.P., LL.M. (Cantab) (1855-1949), Speaker of the House of Commons 1905-21,† nephew of the 3rd Earl of Londale, was cr. Viscount Ullswater, of Campsea Ashe, Suffolk, 1921. He was for several years tenant of the Hudleston family at Hutton John. The present holder of the title is his great-grandson, Nicholas James Christopher, 2nd Viscount, whose aunt, the Hon. Jennifer Lowther, dau. of Major the Hon. Christopher Lowther (d. 1935) marr. (1) 1954 the 7th Earl of Lonsdale; (2) Wing Commander William Edward Clayfield, D.F.C.; (3) the Rev. Oswald Dickon Carter, formerly Rector of Lazonby, and now of Linden Cottage, Cromwell Crescent, Carlisle. *Arms, Crest,* and *Motto.* As Lowther, Earl of Lonsdale. *Supporters.* Two horses Argent each gorged with a wreath of laurel Vert and charged on the shoulder with a portcullis chained Or. *Badge.* A mace enfiled by a Viscount's coronet Or (BP105).

LOWTHER, of Cockermouth. William Lowther, of Ingleton (Y), a younger son of the Lowthers, later Earls of Lonsdale, marr. Eleanor, youngest dau. of Anthony Welbury, of Ingleton and of Castle Eden (D), and had issue *int. al.*, besides a 7th son, the Rev. Robert Lowther, Bachelor of Laws (d. 1671), Chancellor of Carlisle 1660-66, Rector of Bewcastle 1663-71, an eldest son Richard Lowther, of Ingleton, counsellor-at-law (1602-45), who was

* Better known in Cumbria as "Lordy."

† *The Spectator*, 1st April, 1949, printed the following characteristic story about him as Speaker. During a debate a member, who insisted on challenging one of his rulings, asked finally: "Mr. Speaker, what appeal is there from your decision?" "None," came the calm and instantaneous answer. "Like the Pope, I am infallible." (Sir Clement Jones, *Walks in North Westmorland.* 1955.)

Governor of Pontefract Castle for Charles I. His 5th son Henry Lowther, of Cockermouth, certified a pedigree at Dugdale's Visitation 1665, when he was aged 32 and his son Gerard aged 2. *Arms.* Or six annulets, three, two and one, Sable a canton Gules. *Crest.* A dragon passant Argent charged with a trefoil Gules (FCW). The above Robert Lowther, as Chancellor of Carlisle, bore on his seal the undifferenced arms of Lowther, i.e. without the canton.

LOWTHER, of Threlkeld and Dornock. Grayham, son of Anthony Lowther, of Midhall, was baptised at Threlkeld 1582. The Rev. Tristram Lowther was ordained in 1663 to the Curacy of Threlkeld and was there until his death 1698. George Lowther, perhaps his son, marr. at Threlkeld 1692 Ellinor Drurie and had sons Tristram (b. 1693) and William (b. 1694). The latter, described as "in Dornock," died 1728, and is buried at Dornock, Dumfriesshire, where his arms appear. A later member of the family, Tristram Lowther, died at Eden Terrace, Carlisle, 1835 "advanced in years," having several years before selected a place in Dornock churchyard for his burial place and erected a tombstone with an inscription, omitting only the date of his death (WG 14 February 1835). *Arms.* . . . six annulets, three, two and one, . . . between in chief a (?) heart . . . and in base a rose . . . (Tombstone of William Lowther, at Dornock).

LOWTHIAN, of Staffield. The Lowthians are one of the oldest families in the Kirkoswald-Renwick area. George Lowthian, of Staffield (d. 1735, aged 70), marr. 1683 Bridget, dau. of Leonard Barrow, of Ainstable. Though a considerable landowner in Cumberland, he spent the last 30 years of his life at Leadhills, Dumfriesshire, where he also owned land; he was buried in St. Michael's churchyard, Dumfries. His eldest son John (1687-1742) succ. to Staffield, but died unmarr. and was succ. by his brother, the Rev. Richard Lowthian (1696-1784), who was of St. John's College, Cambridge, and was ordained in 1723 by a non-juring bishop. He marr. 1738, when of Dumfries,* Sarah (d. 1797), dau. of Henry Aglionby, *q.v.*, but died *s.p.*, his sisters and coheirs being Mary (b. 1685), marr. Alexander Ross; Barbary (1691-1777), marr. 1730 John Tinkler; Dorothy, marr. (1) 1727 Robert Wilson, of Hole House, Wolsingham (D), and (2) . . . Maughan; and Bridget (b. 1700), marr. 1722 William Bird, of Glassonby. Staffield was inherited by George Ross, *q.v.* (TMF). *Arms.* Argent on a mount Vert a pine tree Proper hanging from the branches thereof a bugle horn Sable garnished Or and chained to the trunk a hound of the third all within a bordure of the second. *Crest.* A bugle horn Sable garnished and stringed Or. *Motto.* Non dormit qui custodit (FAC).

LUCAS. Impaled by Lacy, *q.v.*, on wooden tablet in Layton House, Greystoke. *Arms.* . . . a fess . . . between six annulets . . . .

LUCY, Baron Lucy. Reynold de Lucy (d. 1199) was associated with Cumberland as early as 1158. He marr. Amabel, 2nd dau. and coheir of William Fitz Duncan, and acquired the lordships of Egremont and

* It was in his house in Dumfries, now the Commercial Hotel, that Prince Charles Edward Stuart stayed in December 1745, on the march from Derby to Scotland. Mr. Lowthian "though well affected to the Prince's cause, . . . judged it prudent not to appear in his company, and yet neither did he wish to offend him by . . . deliberately going out of his way." He solved the dilemma by getting so drunk that he had to be kept from the Royal presence. "His wife, who could not well be taxed with treason, did the honours of the house without scruple." (JMP, pp. 229-30).

Copeland. His son Richard (d. 1213) marr. between 1200 and 1204 Ada, elder dau. and coheir of Hugh de Morville, *q.v.* Their daus. were Mabel, marr. Lambert de Multon, and Alice (d. 1288), marr. Alan de Multon, sons of their mother's 2nd husband Thomas de Multon, *q.v.*, by his first wife. Alice and her husband took the name of Lucy and were succ. by their son Thomas (d. 1305), whose son Anthony (aged 50 and more in 1331, d. 1343) was summoned by writ to Parliament 1321, and so became Baron Lucy. His grandson Anthony, 3rd Lord Lucy (d. 1368), left a dau. Joan (d. 1369, aged 2). Her heir was her aunt Maud (26 and more in 1369, d. 1398), who marr. (1) Gilbert de Umfraville, Earl of Angus, *q.v.*, and (2) Henry Percy, Earl of Northumberland, *q.v.* She settled her estates on her 2nd husband's son by his first wife, on condition that he quartered the Lucy arms with his own, which the Percies have done since then. *Arms* (as quartered by Percy). Gules three luces hauriant Argent (FFC). These arms, alone and quartered by Percy, are on shields on the ceiling of Carlisle Cathedral.

LUMB, of Brigham Hall. Robert Lumb, of Lowther (d. 1819, aged 54), was for many years agent to Lord Lonsdale. His son William Lumb, D.L., J.P., of Brigham Hall and of Meadow House, near Whitehaven, was father of James Lumb, D.L., J.P., of Homewood (formerly called Chapel House), Hensingham, and Cunsey, Windermere (1826-1901), High Sheriff of Cumberland 1880, who marr. 1858 Juliana Georgina (d. 1869), dau. and coheir of Joseph Harrison, of Linethwaite, *q.v.* Their son, Capt Edward James Machell Lumb, J.P. (b. 1863), was of Northcroft House, Englefield Green, Surrey. *Arms.* Or three escutcheons Sable each charged with a mullet pierced of the field. FD adds: A martlet for difference. *Crest.* A blackamoor's head in profile couped at the shoulders Proper wreathed about the temples Or and Sable and charged on the neck with a mullet of six points Gold all within a wreath in arch Or and Sable. *Motto.* Respice finem (BLG4; FD7).

LUMLEY. Marmaduke Lumley (d. 1451), a younger son of Sir Ralph Lumley, of Lumley (D), was Chancellor of the University of Cambridge 1428/9, Bishop of Carlisle 1429-50, and Bishop of Lincoln 1450-51. *Arms.* Argent on a fess [Gules] between three popinjays Vert collared Gules a mitre (BBE).

LUPUS, Hugh, Earl of Chester (d. 1101). Shields at Hutton-in-the-Forest; a Vane quartering. *Arms.* Azure a wolf's head erased Argent.

LUSHINGTON. The Rev. James Stephen Lushinton, J.P., M.A. (Cantab) (1734-1801), Vicar of Crosthwaite 1770-80, and Prebendary of Carlisle 1777-1801, marr. (1) 1764 Mary, dau. of Edmund Law, Bishop of Carlisle, *q.v.* *Arms.* Quarterly, 1 & 4, Or a fess wavy Vert charged with three Ermine spots Gold between three lions' heads erased of the second (Lushington); 2 & 3, Sable a chevron between three pelicans' heads erased Or vulning themselves Proper (Godfrey). *Crest.* A lion's head erased Vert ducally gorged Argent charged on the erasure with three Ermine spots Or. *Motto.* Fides nudaque veritas (BLG15).

LUTWIDGE, *post* LOWTHORPE-LUTWIDGE, of Holmrook Hall. Thomas (1670-1745) and Walter Lutwidge, of Irish extraction, were prominent 18th century Whitehaven merchants. The latter was High Sheriff of Cumberland 1748, and the former served in 1726. He marr. 1721 Lucy (d. 1780), youngest dau. of Sir Henry Hoghton, 4th Bart., of Hoghton

Tower (L), by Mary, his wife, eldest dau. of John Skeffington, 2nd Viscount Massereene. Their eldest son Charles Lutwidge, D.L., J.P. (1722-84), Surveyor and Comptroller General of the coasts of Cumberland and Westmorland, bought Holmrook Hall, and the manors of Seascale and Bolton 1759. His brother and heir Henry, of Walton le Dale (1724-98), succ. By Jane his wife, dau. and coheir of Rigby Molyneux, of Preston, he was father of Major Charles Lutwidge (1768-1848), Collector of Customs at Hull, who sold the Cumberland estates to his uncle, Admiral Skeffington Lutwidge* (1737-1814), who left Holmrook to his nephew Major Skeffington Lutwidge, D.L., Madras Army (1779-1854). He was succ. by his brother Henry Thomas Lutwidge, of Ambleside (1780-1861), see AWL, whose successor was his great-nephew Charles Robert Fletcher Lutwidge,† D.L., J.P., M.A. (Cantab) (1835-1907) (grandson of Charles, see above). He was succ. by his cousin Lt-Col Ernest Frederick Lowthorpe, D.L., J.P. (b. 1865), High Sheriff of Cumberland 1922, grandson of Elizabeth Frances, dau. of the above Charles Lutwidge. He assumed the additional surname and arms of Lutwidge 1909. His son was Ernest Cecil Fletcher Lowthorpe-Lutwidge (1896-1971) (BLG13). *Arms.* Quarterly, 1 & 4, Azure three caps of maintenance Or turned up Ermine (Lutwidge); 2 & 3, Gules six lioncels rampant, three, two and one, Argent between two flaunches of the last a chief invected Or thereon two cinquefoils of the first (Lowthorpe). *Crests.* 1, A lion rampant per pale Argent and Gules collared Or (Lutwidge); 2, Upon a lion's gamb erased fesswise a wyvern wings elevated Proper charged with a trefoil Or (Lowthorpe). *Motto.* Deo patriae amicis (FD7). The Lutwidge arms and motto are engraved on a chalice in Gosforth church with the inscription "Ex dono Car. Lutwidge Arm. Patr. Ecclesiae Gosforthiae Anno 1784."

LUXMOORE. Mrs. Sylvia Jane Westoll, M.B.E., wife of James Westoll, D.L., J.P., of Dykeside, Longtown, *q.v.*, whom she marr. 1946, is 3rd dau. and coheir of the Rt. Hon. Sir Arthur Fairfax Charles Coryndon Luxmoore, a Lord Justice of Appeal (d. 1944). *Arms.* Argent two chevronels Gules between three moorcocks close Proper all within a bordure nebuly Sable charged with eight bezants. *Motto.* Securis fecit securum.

LYDSTON. Impaled by Fetherstonhaugh, *q.v.*, on hall ceiling at The College, Kirkoswald; Heneage Fetherstonhaugh (1693-*c.* 1737) marr. 1715 Jane, dau. of . . . Lydston, of Dartmouth, Devon. *Arms.* Or two bars Vair. These tinctures, however, like all the shields on the ceiling, are very faded, and the correct blazon could be: Or two bars vairy Argent and Sable, which Burke gives for Litcott or Lydcotte (BGA).

LYTTELTON. The Rt. Rev. Charles Lyttelton, D.C.L. (Oxon), F.R.S., F.S.A., (d. unmarr. 1768), 3rd son of Sir Thomas Lyttelton, 4th Bart., of Hagley and Frankley, Worcs., was ordained 1742, became Dean of Exeter 1747, and was Bishop of Carlisle 1762-68. *Arms.* Argent a chevron between three escallops Sable (BBE). *Crest.* A Moor's head in profile couped at the shoulders Proper wreathed about the temples Argent and Sable. *Motto.* Ung Dieu, ung roy (BGA).

* He commanded H.M.S. *Carcass* on a voyage of discovery towards the North Pole, 1773 (M.I., Irton church).

† His aunt Frances Jane marr. 1827 her cousin, the Ven. Charles Dodgson, Rector of Croft, and was mother of Charles Lutwidge Dodgson (Lewis Carroll).

MACAN. Arthur Henry Macan, of Greystoke and The Oaks House, Dalston (b. 1883), was son and heir of Arthur Macan, D.L., J.P., of Drumcashel, Co. Louth (1852-1938), and marr. 1914 Helen, dau. of Joseph E. Carter Wood, of Skinburness Tower, Silloth. *Arms.* Azure fretty Or on a fess Argent a boar passant Gules.* *Crest.* A salmon naiant Proper. *Motto.* Virtus sub pondere crescit (BLG8).

McCOSH. Bryce Knox McCosh, of Huntfield, Lanarkshire, Member of the Royal Company of Archers (Her Majesty's Bodyguard for Scotland), eldest surviving son of Robert McCosh, O.B.E., M.C., W.S., of Hardington, Lanarkshire (d. 1959), and great-grandson of James McCosh, of Merksworth and Parkhill, Ayrshire (1809-80), marr. 1948 Sylvia Mary, Lady of the Barony of Barton and Lady of the Manors of Dacre, Barton, Martindale and Patterdale, and dau. and coheir of Edward William Hasell, of Dalemain, *q.v.* Their 2nd son, Robert Hasell McCosh, F.S.A. (Scot.), lives at Dalemain. *Arms* (as matriculated 1964 by the above Bryce Knox McCosh). Gules issuant from a fess wavy barry wavy of four Azure and Argent a circular tower Argent turret cap Vert ball finial Or accompanied by two oak leaves slipped in dexter and sinister chief also Argent and in base a falcon rising of the last a bordure indented Or for difference. *Crest.* A squirrel sejant holding in its dexter claw a hazel nut all Proper accompanied on the other side by a branch of oak leaves vert fructed Or. *Motto.* Celeritate. In 1977 the above named Robert Hasell McCosh matriculated *Arms* as follows: Quarterly, 1 & 4, McCosh, as above, the bordure indented per fess Or and Azure; 2 & 3, Or on a fess Azure between three hazel nuts Proper husks stalks and leaves Vert as many crescents Argent (Hasell).

McDONNELL. Impaled by Howard on shield in hall of Greystoke Castle; Henry Charles Howard, D.L., J.P., B.A. (Cantab), of Greystoke Castle (1850-1914), High Sheriff of Cumberland 1879, marr. 1878 the Lady Mabel McDonnell (d. 1942), 2nd dau. of the 6th Earl of Antrim. *Arms.* Quarterly, 1 & 4, Quarterly, i, Or a lion rampant Gules; ii, Or a dexter arm issuant from the sinister fess point out of a cloud Proper in the hand a cross crosslet fitché Azure; iii, Argent a lymphad sails furled Sable; iv, Per fess Azure and Vert a dolphin naiant in fess Proper; 2 & 3, Quarterly, i & iv, Azure a sun in splendour Or; ii, Gules on a chevron Argent three mullets of the field; iii, Sable on a chevron between three unicorns' heads erased Argent as many mullets of the field.

MacGEORGE. William MacGeorge, Lt-Col 71st Bengal N.I., Deputy Judge Advocate General of India (1799-1873), descended from a Galloway family, acquired the Hames Hall, Cockermouth, estate by marr. 1850 to his 3rd wife Dora Fagan (d. 1893, aged 69), dau. of Col James Steel, C.B., who inherited it from her uncle, John Steel, M.P. for Cockermouth, *q.v.* Their son William Henry MacGeorge (b. 1851), Major 6th Dragoon Guards, was adjutant of the Westmorland and Cumberland Yeomanry Cavalry (HBO). *Arms.* Per pale indented Or and Gules in chief two mullets counterchanged. *Crest.* A dexter cubit arm the hand grasping a sabre all Proper and charged with a fess indented Azure. *Motto.* Dread God (BLG7).

* The arms are impaled on the bookplate of Humphrey Pocklington-Senhouse, D.L., J.P., of Netherhall (1843-1903), *q.v.*, who marr. 1879 Florence Catherine (d. 1920), eldest dau. of Turner Arthur Macan, of Carriff, Co. Armagh, and 2nd cousin of the above Arthur Henry Macan. Her sister Mary Camilla (d. 1939) marr. 1891 Sir Wilfrid Lawson 3rd bart., *q.v.*

McGUFFIE, of Cross Hill and Isel Mill. James McGuffie, of Crossmichael, later of Crosshill, near Wigton (1800-88), marr. 1833 Margaret (1808-56), only dau. of William Coulthart, and sister and in her issue heir of John Ross Coulthart, *q.v.* They had issue, *int. al.,* William (1835-1917); John Ross Coulthart (1839-1916); James (1841-1924); and Alexander (1851-1934). The eldest son, William McGuffie, of Isel Mill (1835-1917), had issue, besides a 5th son Thomas (1885-1965), an eldest son John Ross Coulthart McGuffie, of Isel Mill (1871-1961), whose son John Ross Coulthart McGuffie, of Thornbrae, Laversdale, Irthington (b. 1902), the present head of the family, has a son John (b. 1934). The 5th son, Thomas McGuffie (1885-1965), was father of Ross Coulthart McGuffie, now of Isel Mill. The above mentioned John Ross Coulthart McGuffie (1839-1916), was of Crosshill, Wigton, and of Carlisle, and at the age of 70 succ. to his uncle's estate of Greenlaw, Castle Douglas. For his younger brother, James McGuffie, of Penrith (1841-1924), see AWL; and for Alexander (1851-1934), see next entry. *Arms.* The west window of Boltongate church, to the memory of the above Margaret Coulthart, wife of James McGuffie, displays these as: Argent a fess between three boars' heads couped Sable. In 1874 the said James McGuffie obtained from the Lord Lyon King of Arms a grant of arms, as follows: *Arms.* Argent two croziers saltirewise Sable between a man's heart in chief Gules and three boars' heads couped of the second in flank and base. *Crest.* A boar's head as in the arms. *Motto.* Arma parata fero (Lyon Register ix/60). In 1969 Ross Coulthart McGuffie, above, of Isel Mill, matriculated the above arms differenced by a bordure embattled Gules (Lyon Register liv/38).

MacGUFFIE. Alexander McGuffie (1851-1934), 5th son of James McGuffie, of Cross Hill, *q.v.,* was father of Lt-Col the Rev. Alexander Henley MacGuffie, M.B.E., who served in the Royal Engineers 1907-35, and was Lt-Col Pioneer Corps 1939-45. He was ordained 1944, and was Curate of St. George, Millom, in charge of St. Luke 1952-56, and Vicar of Mungrisdale 1956-73. In 1931 he matriculated arms, as follows: *Arms.* Argent two croziers saltirewise Sable between a man's heart in chief Gules and three boars' heads couped of the second in flank and base a bordure engrailed Azure. *Crest.* A boar's head as in the arms. *Motto.* Arma parata fero (Lyon Register).

MACKENZIE. Hugh Munro Mackenzie, J.P. (1825-85), brother of Katherine, wife of James Robertson-Walker, *q.v.,* was of Belle Vue, Distington, and later of Prospect House in that parish. His niece Helen Mary marr. 1883 Dr. John MacDougall, of Carlisle, and of The Hill, Midlothian and his nephew, her brother, John Hugh Munro Mackenzie, O.B.E., J.P., of Mornish, Isle of Mull (1849-1937), succ. him at Belle Vue. *Arms.* Quarterly, 1 & 4, Azure a stag's head cabossed Or (Mackenzie); 2, Azure three cinquefoils Argent (Fraser); 3, Or an eagle's head erased Gules within a bordure wavy of the second charged with three cross crosslets fitché of the first (Monro of Erribol); all within a bordure per pale dexter engrailed Ermine sinister Or. *Crest.* A hand Proper holding a chaplet of laurel leaves within which chaplet is a gauntlet fessways all Proper. *Motto* (above the crest). Virtute et valore (BLG18).

MACLAREN. Roderick Maclaren, M.D. (Edin), of 23 Portland Square, Carlisle (d. 1913), who was for nearly 40 years on the staff of Cumberland Infirmary, was father of Norman Maclaren, see below, and Douglas

Maclaren, B.A. (Cantab), solicitor, of Carlisle and of Watch Hill, How Mill (b. 1878). Norman Maclaren, M.A., B.C., M.B. (Cantab), F.R.C.S., T.D. (1876-1937), practised in Carlisle, and was consulting surgeon and Treasurer of the Cumberland Infirmary. He served as Lt-Col, R.A.M.C., in World War I. His elder son Roderick Maclaren, M.A. (Cantab), F.R.G.S. (1908-73), was an assistant master at Clifton College 1929-48 and later a schoolmaster in Rhodesia, where he died. His brother Henry Colin Maclaren, B.A. (Cantab), M.R.C.S., L.R.C.P. (b. 1911), practised in Carlisle. *Arms.* Or two chevronels between a fleur-de-lys accompanied with two shepherd's crooks in chief and a boar's head erased Sable langued Gules armed Argent in base. *Crest.* An esculapian rod and a shepherd's crook in saltire Proper. *Motto.* Bi 'se mac na cromaige (Be thou the son of a shepherd's crook) (FAC).

MACLEAN, of Lazonby. Lt-Col Henry Dundas Maclean, D.L., J.P. (1800-63), High Sheriff of Cumberland 1848, 5th son of Lt-Col Alexander Maclean, 13th of Ardgour, built Lazonby Hall. He marr. 1840 Eleanor* (d. 1870), dau. and heir of the Rev. Joseph Dacre Carlyle, Chancellor of Carlisle, *q.v.*, but died *s.p.* and was succ. by his nephew John Dalrymple Maclean, I.C.S., J.P., a member of the Eden Fishery Board. He d. 1897 and was succ. by his uncle Major-General Peter Maclean, R.A. (d. 1901), who was succ. by his grandson Allan Somerset Hope Maclean (1870-1908), who was succ. by his brother Commander Henry Hugh Maclean, R.N. (1871-1955), 18th heir male of the Macleans of Ardgour, who sold Lazonby 1920 to Sir Henry Gordon Ley, Bart., *q.v.* *Arms.* Quarterly, 1, Argent a lion rampant Gules; 2, Azure a triple-turreted tower Argent masoned Sable windows and portcullis Gules; 3, Or a ten-oared galley sails furled oars in action Sable flagged Gules in a sea in base Vert a salmon naiant Proper; 4, Argent a dexter hand couped fessways Gules holding a cross crosslet fitché Azure.† *Crest.* A branch of laurel and cypress in saltire surmounted by a battle-axe in pale all Proper. *Supporters.* Two golden eagles wings elevated Or beaked and membered Gules. *Motto.* Altera merces. *Badge.* Holly (BLG17).

MACLEAN OF DOCHGARROCH. Allan Maclean of Dochgarroch (1827-1909) was father of the Rev. Allan Mackinstosh Maclean, B.A. (Lampeter) (1872-1944), and of the Rev. Hector Maclean, B.A. (Lampeter) (b. 1873), who assumed the additional surname of Sykes and was Rector of Watermillock 1906-14. The former was Rector of Greystoke 1905-14, and was father of the Rev. Donald Allan Lachlan Maclean of Dochgarroch, M.A. (Oxon) (b. 1905), who was Rector of Greystoke 1950-53, and is now of Seafield House, via Inverness. He marr. 1950 Loraine Murray, dau. and heir of Capt Hedley Murray Calvert, J.P., and has issue Allan Murray (b. 1950). *Arms.* Per fess Or and Azure in dexter chief a dexter hand appaumé Gules and in sinister chief a galley sails furled oars in saltire Sable and in base a castle triple towered Argent masoned of the fourth windows and portcullis

* She built Lazonby church, employing Anthony Salvin as architect, 1865.

† A variant of these arms is on a shield in the billiard-room of Brunstock House, as follows: Quarterly, 1, Or a lion rampant Gules; 2, Azure a castle triple-towered Argent; 3, Or issuing from the sinister an arm in armour fessways holding in the hand Proper a cross crosslet fitché Argent on a chief of the last two griffins' heads erased Gules; 4, Per fess Argent and Sable in chief a lymphad sails furled in base a fish naiant counterchanged. Over all, on an escutcheon of pretence, Or a cross flory Gules (Carlyle).

Gules. *Crest.* A battle axe erect in pale between a branch of laurel and another of cypress all Proper. *Mottoes.* 1 (above the crest), Vincere vel mori; 2 (below the shield), Virtue mine honour (BLG17).

MADDISON. John Maddison, of Newcastle upon Tyne (d. *s.p.* 1784), son of the Rev. Thomas Maddison, and grandson of John Maddison, of Newcastle (1656-1722), by his 2nd wife Mary, dau. of Thomas Warwick, inherited Warwick on the death *s.p.* 1772 of Francis Warwick, of Warwick Hall. *Arms.* Quarterly, 1 & 4, Argent on a chevron between three martlets Sable as many mullets Or; 2 & 3, Argent two battle-axes in saltire Sable. *Crest.* A dexter hand Proper sleeve Erminois grasping a battle-axe Sable (SHD ii 135; HCC i 154-5). The second and third quarters, with the field tinctured Or, are on shields at Hutton-in-the-Forest.

MADDISON. Pamela Mary, wife of Ronald Fryer Dickinson, *q.v.*, is only dau. of the Rev. William Maddison, M.A. (Oxon) (b. 1883), Vicar of Haltwhistle 1930-39 and of Hartburn (N) 1939-55, and Hon. Canon of Newcastle, and granddau. of the Rev. William Maddison, M.A. (Dunelm) (1853-1920), Vicar of Gosforth (N) 1893-1920, whose nephew the Rev. Thomas Rowland Story Maddison, B.A. (Cantab) (1877-1920), was Curate of St. John, Barrow-in-Furness, 1912-13, and of Christ Church, Cockermouth, 1913-15. *Crest.* Out of a crown flory an arm in armour Proper garnished Or holding in the gauntlet a battle axe Proper charged with a cross Gules the staff Sable (*Ex inf.* the above Mrs. Dickinson).

MAJENDIE. Ann, elder sister and heir of John Routledge, of Cumcrook, Stapleton (d. 1811), carried this estate to her husband, Henry William Majendie, B.A., D.D. (Cantab) (1754-1830), Bishop of Chester, 1800-9, and of Bangor 1809-30. Of Huguenot descent, he was son of the Rev. John James Majendie, D.D. (1709-83), Canon of Windsor, and brother of Lewis Majendie, of Hedingham Castle, Essex. His grandson owned Cumcrook in 1873. *Arms.* Or on a mount in base Vert a tree between a serpent erect on the dexter and a dove close on the sinister all Proper. *Crest.* An arm embowed in armour the hand holding a scimitar all Proper (BBE; BGA).

MALING. John Maling, of the Grange, Bishopwearmouth (D), a banker in Sunderland (1746-1823), had issue, by his 1st wife, William Maling, of the Grange, also of Kidside Lodge, Heversham (W) (1769-1857), who marr. 1800 Elizabeth (1777-1827), dau. and heir of Capt William Haygarth, R.N., of Kidside Lodge. Their youngest son Christopher Maling, M.R.C.S., of Abbey Holme (1815-49), had issue a dau. and heir Margaret (b. 1843), who marr. Joseph Addison, of The Banks (FYP). *Arms.* Ermine on a chevron Vert between three hawks Proper as many roses Argent. *Crest.* A hawk with wings expanded Proper (FYP; BGA).

MALTON. Henry de Malton held land in Kirklinton 1296. One of the same names, a knight by 1320, took part in the defence of Carlisle when the city was besieged by Bruce 1314 and was Sheriff of Cumberland 1323-25. He was a considerable landowner and acquired William de Mulcaster's lands in Threapland 1316. He also owned lands in Little Waverton, Leversdale and Bewcastle. Before 1322 he marr. Margaret . . . and both were living 1362. One of their daus. and coheirs marr. Thomas Skelton, *q.v. Arms.* Henry de Malton bore: Sable a lion rampant within an orle of annulets Argent. Sir Henry de Malton bore: Sable a lion rampant Argent crowned Or a bordure of the second charged with annulets of the first (FFC). MMD gives Ermine a cross Gules surmounted by another cross Argent.

MALTRAVERS. Shield at Greystoke Castle, a Howard quartering, brought in by Mowbray, *q.v.*, from FitzAlan, *q.v.*; John d'Arundel, summoned to Parliament 1377-79, younger son of Richard FitzAlan, Earl of Arundel (*c.* 1313-76), marr. Eleanor, granddau. and coheir of John, Lord Maltravers of Mautravers (*c.* 1290-1364). *Arms.* Sable a fret Or.

MAN, Kingdom of. The *Arms* of the Kingdom of Man are on a shield on the ceiling of Carlisle Cathedral: Gules three legs embowed and conjoined in fess point in armour Proper garnished and spurred Or.

MANSEL. Sir Philip Mansel, 15th Bart., who succ. his father in 1947 at the age of four, was educated at Grosvenor College, Carlisle, and Carlisle Grammar School, and was of Hall Flatt, Scaleby, in 1969 and of Greenfields, Rockcliffe, in 1971. *Arms.* Argent a chevron between three maunches Sable. *Crest.* A cap of maintenance Gules turned up Ermine enflamed on the top Proper. *Motto.* Quod vult valde vult.

MARK. Sir John Mark, J.P., of Greystoke, Didsbury (1832-1909), was 4th son of Joseph Mark, of Bowscale, Greystoke, by Hannah, dau. of Joseph Wilson, of Greysouthen; he was Mayor of Manchester 1890 and 1891 and was knighted 1901. He had three daus. – Ethel Louisa, marr. 1884 Frederick William Lee; Maud Constance, marr. Robert Frederick Lee; and Florence, marr. 1891 Robert Arthur Lord Hutchinson. *Arms.* Azure on a rock in base Proper a lion of St. Mark sejant with wings addorsed Or resting the dexter paw upon an escutcheon of the last charged with a bee volant of the second on a chief also Or a terrestrial globe also Proper between two saltires couped gules. *Crest.* A lion as in the arms semé of bees volant Proper resting the dexter paw upon a rose Gules barbed and seeded Proper. *Mottoes.* Manu et corde; Hoc mihi sit signum (FD 1895; FBC; Sir John Mark's bookplate). On the bookplate, the head of the lion in arms and crest is irradiated.

MARKHAM. The Ven. Robert Markham, M.A. (Oxon) (1768-1837), Prebendary of York, Archdeacon of the West Riding of Yorkshire, Chancellor of Richmond, Rector of Bolton Percy, Vicar of Bishopsthorpe, and Residentiary Canon of York, was Prebendary of Carlisle 1801-37. He was 5th son of William Markham, Archbishop of York (1719-1807), for whom see AWL. *Arms.* Azure on a chief Or a demi lion rampant issuing Gules. *Crest.* A lion of St. Mark passant holding a pair of hames Or (BLG1846). The family later used: A lion of St. Mark sejant guardant and resting his paws on a pair of hames Or (AWL).

MARLEY. Shield in window at Hutton-in-the-Forest; a Vane quartering. *Arms.* Argent on a chevron between three martlets Sable as many mullets Or. Another shield displays the following variant of the same arms: Or on a chevron between three merles Sable as many mullets of the field. Still another shield displays: Sable a fleur-de-lys Argent.

MARSHALL, of Keswick. John Marshall, M.P. for Leeds (1797-1836), 2nd son of John Marshall, of Patterdale Hall, *q.v.*, bought from Greenwich Hospital, *q.v.*, the Derwentwater estates in Keswick 1832. He was the builder of St. John's church, Keswick, but died before it was completed. His son Reginald Dykes Marshall, D.L., J.P., of Castlerigg Manor, Keswick (1832-1913), succ. This branch of the family is extinct in the male line. Henry Cowper Marshall, D.L., J.P. (1808-84), younger brother of John, was of Derwent Island, Keswick, and of Weetwood Hall, Leeds, and was succ. by his son John Marshall, J.P., M.A. (Cantab), of Derwent Island (1840-94), father of Denis Marshall, J.P., B.A. (Oxon), of Derwent Island and of Brackensgill, Sedbergh (b. 1876), a master at Sedbergh 1901-36. This branch of the family is also extinct in the male line. *Arms, Crest* and *Motto.* As Marshall, of Patterdale and Hallsteads.

MARSHALL, of Patterdale and Hallsteads. John Marshall, of Headingley, Leeds (1765-1845), a wealthy Leeds linen manufacturer, M.P. for Yorkshire 1826-30 and High Sheriff of Cumberland 1821, marr. 1795 Jane (1771-1847), 6th dau. and coheir of William Pollard, of Halifax,* and bought Patterdale Hall 1825.† His children included William, see below, John and Henry Cowper Marshall (see Marshall of Keswick) and Arthur, who succ. to his aunts' estate, Hallsteads, Watermillock. The above William Marshall, D.L., J.P., B.A. (Cantab) (1796-1872), succ. to Patterdale Hall and was M.P. for Carlisle 1835-47 and for East Cumberland 1847-68. He was succ. in turn by his three sons – John William Marshall, J.P. (1829-81), who also succ. to Hallsteads, George Hibbert Marshall, J.P. (1832-87), and Walter James Marshall, D.L., J.P. (1837-99), of Patterdale Hall and Hallsteads, whose grandson William Martin Walter Marshall, of Mariners, Courtlands, Esher, Surrey, who sold the Patterdale estate 1937, is now head of the family. In Cumberland the family is now represented by his brother, the Rev. Godfrey Hibbert Marshall, M.A. (Cantab), Vicar of Hayton with Talkin 1965-73, and now of Ruckcroft, Johnby. *Arms.* The family originally bore: Argent three bars Sable a canton Ermine. *Crest.* A man in armour Proper (BLG 1851). The Marshalls now bear: *Arms.* Barry of six Sable and Argent on a pale Ermine three horseshoes palewise Or. *Crest.* A man in armour affronté Proper holding in his dexter hand a javelin and supporting with his sinister hand a flagstaff Proper having a banner Sable charged with two horseshoes Or. *Motto.* Nec cito nec tarde (BLG17; FD7).

MARTIN, of Itonfield. Capt John Nickleson Martin (b. 1758) marr. 1785 Elizabeth (1765-1836), only dau. of John Hutchinson, of Skirsgill, Penrith, Crossfield House, Kirkoswald, and Appleby, *q.v.*, and heir of her brothers John and Christopher William Hutchinson. Their son and heir was Admiral Thomas Martin, R.N., of Itonfield, and of The Wilderness, Surrey (1787-1868), whose son and heir was Admiral Thomas Hutchinson Mangles Martin, J.P., R.N., of Tryermayne, Bitterne, Hants (b. 1829); his younger brother John Nickleson Martin (1839-57) was murdered at Cawnpore during the Indian Mutiny. *Arms.* Paly of six Or and Gules on a chevron Argent an anchor erect Sable on a chief of the second three martlets of the first. *Crest.* In front of a garb Or a marten cat statant Proper. *Motto.* Fide et clementia (BLG 1846; WCF).

MARTIN, of Pattentown. Francis Martin, F.S.A., of Pattentown, Kirkandrews-on-Esk, and of Cambridgeshire (*c.* 1767-1848), 3rd son of Francis Martin, Secretary of the Bank of England, by Margaret Pearce, of Cressage, Salop.; was Bluemantle Pursuivant of Arms 1797; Windsor Herald 1819; Norroy King 1839; and Clarenceux King of Arms 1846. *Arms.* Quarterly, 1 & 4, Argent two bars engrailed Gules and in chief a mantle

* The Pollard daughters, close friends of Dorothy Wordsworth, lived at Hallsteads on Ullswater.

† From about 1815 he began buying estates in the Lake District.

Azure lined Ermine* between two roses Gules (Martin); 2 & 3, Per pale indented Or and Azure on a fess Ermine between three pelicans with wings raised and pecking their breasts counterchanged three annulets Sable (Pearce). *Crest.* On a tree-stump eradicated Or a marten cat sejant erect Proper with collar and chain and holding in its forepaws a flaming cresset Proper. *Motto.* Poursuivant mon devoir (TCA).

MARTIN. Samuel Martin, of Lowther Street, Whitehaven (will proved 1800), is described by Professor E. Hughes in HNW as the doyen of the merchants of that port. A man of great wealth, he owned estates in Virginia valued at over £30,000, and his 110 slaves were worth £6,600. He also had estates in the West Indies and Ireland. He was on the High Sheriff's roll for Cumberland in 1775, but was ruined by the American War of Independence, his Virginian estates confiscated by the General Assembly and he was declared a bankrupt. He therefore never served as Sheriff. *Arms.* Vert a chevron between three crescents Argent. *Crest.* A cubit arm erect brandishing a scimitar. *Motto.* Pro patria (Samuel Martin's seal).

MARTINDALE, of West Newton. Roger Martindale marr. the dau. and heir of Thomas Newton, *q.v., temp.* Edward III and acquired West Newton, which descended to James Martindale, who died *s.p.m.,* his estates being divided between his five daus., of whom Joan marr. John Blennerhasset, Isabel marr. William Musgrave, of Hayton, *q.v.,* and Elizabeth marr. Thomas Middleton, *q.v. Arms* (as quartered by Musgrave, of Hayton, in window and on altar tomb in Aspatria church). Barry of six Gules and Argent a bend Azure.† The arms are also quartered by Musgrave on a shield carved above the entrance to Johnby Hall, with date 1583, and the names William Musgrave and Isabel Martendal. They were quartered by Middleton, of Skirwith, *q.v.,* as: Argent two bars Gules over all a bend Sable. MMD gives: Argent two bars Gules over all a bend Or; and also: Argent two bars Gules over all a bend Azure.

MARTINDALE. Henry Martindale, of Town Yeat, Crosthwaite (W) (d. 1888), was County Treasurer of Westmorland 1860-88. His son James Henry Martindale, F.S.A., F.R.I.B.A., of Moor Yeat, Wetheral (1856-1931), was a distinguished architect and was Surveyor of Carlisle Cathedral and Diocesan Surveyor from 1905. A Vice-President of the Cumberland & Westmorland Antiquarian & Archaeological Society, he contributed many papers to *Transactions.* He was succ. as Cathedral and Diocesan Surveyor by his son Christopher James Fawcett Martindale, F.R.I.B.A. (1888-1966), whose son Christopher Bernard Martindale, F.R.I.B.A. (b. 1914), formerly of Moor Yeat, Wetheral, was Cathedral and Diocesan Surveyor 1946-62; he is now of Bradwell House, Wolverton, Bucks. *Arms.* Argent two bars Gules over all a bend Azure. *Crest.* A wolf courant Proper.

MARTINDALE. Field recorded the following as on a doorway in Allonby, with initials N.M.I., and date 1766, for Nicholas and Jane Martindale. *Arms.* Barry Argent and Gules a bend Sable (FAC).

MARYPORT, Town of. The following was included as the first quarter of the arms used by the Maryport & Carlisle Railway Company, *q.v.,* for the town of Maryport. *Arms.* In front of clouds and the sky and on waves of the sea in base a three-masted vessel sails furled all Proper.

* "In allusion to his pursuivantship" (TCA).

† Not Sable, as stated by Field (FAC).

MARYPORT & CARLISLE RAILWAY Co. Ltd. Incorporated 1837, completed 1845. *Arms.* Quarterly, 1, the town of Maryport, *q.v.*; 2, Or a popinjay Vert (Senhouse); 3, Per pale Argent and Sable a chevron counterchanged (Lawson); 4, Vert on a base wavy Argent and Azure a castle between two roses Or on a chief Gules a lion passant guardant of the fourth (Carlisle). Joseph Pocklington Senhouse, of Netherhall (1804-74), and Sir Wilfrid Lawson, 2nd Bart. (1829-1906), were the first and fourth chairmen of the company (DRH).

MASSICKS, *post* BARLOW-MASSICKS, of The Oaks. Thomas Massicks, J.P. (1832-1908), was Inspector of Cargoes, Whitehaven, 1857, and acquired an interest in haematite mines in West Cumberland. In 1865 he was a founder, and in turn secretary, general manager and managing director of the Cumberland Iron Mining & Smelting Co., Ltd., which on his advice built its works at Millom, where he became chairman of the Local Board of Health. He lived at Duddon Villa, Millom, and latterly at The Oaks, Thwaites; and assumed the additional surname of Barlow 1883 (CW2 lxvi 455). *Arms.* Per pale Or and Azure on a fess between four leopards' faces jessant-de-lys three in chief and one in base two quatrefoils all counterchanged. *Crest.* A cross pattée Azure surmounted by a leopard's face jessant-de-lys. Or. *Motto.* Vestigia nulla retrorsum (BGA).

MATHEWS. The Rev. William Arnold Mathews, M.A. (Oxon) (1839-1924), son of William Mathews, J.P., M.D. (Edin), of Hatfield (Y) (1800-69), was Vicar of Dacre 1871-77, Rector of Skelton 1877-79, Vicar of St. Mary, Carlisle, 1879-83, Vicar of St. Lawrence, Appleby, 1883-96, Hon. Canon of Carlisle, and Rector of Bassingham, Lincs., 1896-1913 and Vicar of Wendron, Cornwall, 1913-24. For his son, Dr. T. G. Mathews, of Green Close, Kirkby Lonsdale (1869-1919), and other members of the family in that town, see AWL. *Arms.* Gules three chevronels Or. *Crest.* On an escallop Gules between two wings a cross flory Or. *Motto.* Aequam servare mentem.

MATTHEWS, of Wigton Hall. Joseph Matthews, of Burgh-by-Sands, settled at Wigton Hall, where he was succ. by his son John (1739-99), Lieutenant R.N., who marr. Jane (d. 1796), elder dau. of the Rev. Francis Yates, *q.v.* Their son the Rev. Richard Matthews, J.P., M.A. (Cantab) (1771-1846), a keen botanist, an early meteorologist, and a student of anatomy and medicine, died unmarr. and was succ. by his sisters Jane (d. unmarr. 1854) and Mary (d. 1854), who marr. 1814 her cousin Francis Yates, later Aglionby, *q.v.* Their eldest dau. Elizabeth Anne (d. 1878) inherited Wigton Hall. *Arms.* . . . a lion rampant . . . (Shield above entrance to Wigton Hall).

MAUCLERK. Walter Mauclerk (d. 1248), Bishop of Carlisle 1223-46, was one of the outstanding rulers of the See, to whose foresight it owes Rose Castle. He was Sheriff of Cumberland 1223-25. He resigned the See and became a mendicant at Oxford. *Arms.* Or a chevron Ermine between three lions rampant Sable (BBE).

MAXWELL. James Maxwell, of Naworth, Irthington and Boothby (d. 1731), was steward to Lord Carlisle. His dau. Mary (b. 1703) marr. 1731 Francis Atkinson, of Brampton (see Atkinson, of Hornsby and Carlisle). *Arms.* . . . a saltire . . . and a bordure engrailed . . . (Seal).

CONSTABLE MAXWELL. Impaled by Howard, *q.v.*, on an embroidered cushion at Corby Castle; Philip John Canning Howard, J.P., of Corby

Castle (1853-1934), marr. 1875 Alice Clare (d. 1941), youngest dau. of Peter Constable Maxwell, and niece of the 10th Baron Herries. *Arms.* Quarterly, 1, Argent an eagle displayed with two heads Sable beaked and membered Gules on his breast an escutcheon of the first charged with a saltire of the second and surcharged with a hedgehog Or (Maxwell); 2, Quarterly, i & iv, Or a saltire Sable, ii & iii, Argent three hedgehogs Sable (Herries); 3, Quarterly Gules and Vair a bend Or (Constable); 4, Azure on a bend cotised Argent three billets Sable (Haggerston).*

HERON-MAXWELL. Sir John Robert Heron-Maxwell, D.L., J.P., 7th Bart. (1836-1910), was of Evening Hill, Thursby, in 1873, and later of Durran Hill, Scotby, until he succ. to the baronetcy 1885. *Arms.* Quarterly, 1 & 4, Argent on a saltire Sable an annulet Or stoned Azure in base a crescent of the second all within a bordure Gules charged with eight bezants (Maxwell); 2 & 3, Gules on a bend Argent a rose between two lions passant of the field (Heron). *Crest.* A dexter hand Proper holding up an eagle's neck with two heads erased Sable. *Supporters.* Two eagles close reguardant Sable. *Motto.* Revirescat (BP58).

MAYLINGS, or MOLYNS. Shield at Hutton John; a Hudleston quartering, brought in by Barantyne, *q.v.* *Arms.* Ermine on a fess Or three billets Sable.

MEADE. Richard Charles Meade, styled Lord Gillford (1868-1905), eldest son of Richard James, 4th Earl of Clanwilliam, died *v.p.* and *s.p.m.* at Whelprigg, Kirkby Lonsdale, and was buried at Torpenhow (GEC; windows in Torpenhow church). He was Captain 3rd Volunteer Battn. The Border Regt. *Arms.* Gules a chevron Ermine between three trefoils slipped Argent. *Crest.* An eagle displayed with two heads Sable armed Or. *Motto.* Toujours prest (BP105).

MELROSE ABBEY. Arms on a roof corbel in Holm Cultram Abbey, said to be those of Melrose Abbey, the mother house of Holm Cultram, are those used unofficially by the Burgh of Melrose until 1931. *Arms.* [Azure] a hind's head erased issuant therefrom the head of a bishop's crozier in dexter chief a mason's mell and in sinister chief a rose.

MERCATUS, Earl of Carlisle. A legendary figure, to whom arms are ascribed on Speed's Map of Cumberland, 1610, and on Blaeu's Map of Cumberland, 1662. *Arms.* . . . three spears bendwise in bend sinister . . . .†

MERCHANT TAYLORS SCHOOL. In a window in St. John's-in-the-Vale church, commemorating Henry Corrie Jackson, *q.v.*, Scholar of Merchant Taylors School, who died at Boshof, South Africa, 1900, aged 20. *Arms.* Argent a pavilion Purpure garnished Or lined Ermine between two mantles of the second lined of the fourth on a chief Azure a lion passant guardant Or.

MERCIA. Shield at Hutton-in-the-Forest; a Vane quartering. *Arms.* Sable an eagle displayed Or. Another shield displays: Or an eagle displayed Sable, which Papworth attributes to, *int. al.*, Leofric, Earl of Mercia (OBA).

MERCIER. The Rev. Philip Brandon Mercier, M.A. (Oxon) (1878-1958), son of the Rev. Jerome John Mercier (1835-1901), Rector of Kemerton, Glos., and descended from François Mercier (born at Hardivillers, Beauvais, Picardy, 1725), was Curate of St. John, Windermere, 1902-7, Curate of

* The embroidery is very worn, faded and difficult to decipher, so we have recorded the correct blazon although this seems to differ slightly from the arms on the cushion.

† Modern colouring of the maps shews the spears Or and the field of the shield sometimes Azure, sometimes Gules.

St. James, Barrow-in-Furness, 1907-8, and Perpetual Curate of Seascale 1908-19. *Arms.* Gules a chevron between three cherubim Or. *Motto.* Fais ce que dois advienne que pourra (*Ex inf.* Mr. Christopher P. Mercier, of Halkyn, North Wales, son of the foregoing).

MERKES. Thomas Merkes, a monk of Westminster (d. 1409), was Bishop of Carlisle 1397-1400, in which year he was deprived of his see and imprisoned in the tower of London for his support of Richard II. He was Rector of Todenham, Glos., 1404-9. *Arms.* ... a canton ... and a label of five points ... (BBE).

MERLAY. A shield in the Great Hall, Naworth Castle, and quartered by Greystoke, Dacre, and Howard; William, Lord of Greystoke (*i.p.m.* 1289), marr. Mary, eldest dau. and coheir of Roger de Merlay, of Morpeth (N). *Arms.* Barry Argent and Gules on a bordure Azure eight martlets Or.

MERTON COLLEGE, Oxford. Shield in window in Carlisle Cathedral, commemorating John William Diggle, Bishop of Carlisle 1904-20, *q.v.* *Arms.* Or three chevronels per pale the first and third Azure and Gules the second of the same counterchanged.

le MESCHIN. Randolph or Ranulph le Meschin, Vicomte de Bayeux and Earl of Chester (d. *c.* 1129), often but incorrectly described as Earl of Carlisle and Earl of Cumberland, held in fact only the Lordship of Carlisle (GEC). His younger brother, William le Meschin (d. *c.* 1134), was Lord of Copeland and founded St. Bees Priory *c.* 1125. *Arms.* Pre-armorial, but the following coats have been attributed to Randolph le Meschin: 1, Or a lion rampant Gules (LMC); 2, Barry Or and Gules (Speed's Map of Cumberland, 1610); 3, Or three bars Gules (Nisbet's Armories). The first coat was recorded by Whitaker (WHC) in a window in Kildwick church (Y) as the arms of Walter de Meschines (correctly, William le Meschin, above), and impales the third coat as the arms of his wife, Cecily de Romilli.

MESSENGER, of Cow Lane. William Messenger, yeoman, of Cow Lane, Silloth (1827-1903), was father of, *int. al.,* Dr. Thomas Messenger, of Kirkbride (1863-1932) (whose twin grandsons, Frank Ord Messenger, of Jesmond, and Eric William Messenger, of Goschen Road, Carlisle, are the senior representatives of the family), and George Messenger, of Cow Lane (1873-1943), father of William Lazonby Messenger (1909-69), whose daus. Anne and Julia are of Standing Stone, Wigton (*Ex inf.* Mrs. Messenger, of Crag End, Braithwaite, daughter-in-law of Dr. Messenger, above, and Mrs. Josephine Mary Underwood, dau. of George Messenger, above, and wife of Mr. Tom Underwood, of North House, Silloth). *Arms.* Argent a chevron Sable between three esquires' helmets Proper. *Crest.* A lion rampant Gules holding in the dexter paw a sword erect Argent hilt and pommel Or. *Motto.* Vincit veritas (painting in possession of the family).

MESSENGER, of Wheyrigg. John Messenger, yeoman (will dated 1732, proved 1735) marr. Frances Penrice, of Holm Cultram, and settled at Wheyrigg, Bromfield, owned by his descendants until it was sold *c.* 1900. Robert Messenger inherited from a cousin Lessonhall near Wigton *c.* 1860, which is now the property of his grandson John L. Messenger, of Stonehaven, Wormley, Godalming, Surrey, son of Sidney John Messenger, of Gordon House, Beckenham, Kent, whose widow Mrs. Katherine Alice Messenger obtained a grant of arms 1942, the family having formerly used the same arms as the Messengers of Cow Lane, which were not recorded in the College of Arms. *Arms.* Per chevron Sable and Argent three helmets counterchanged. *Crest.* A pegasus rampant Argent winged crined queued and unguled Or resting the sinister foreleg upon a helmet also Argent.

METCALFE. The Rev. Francis Metcalfe, M.A. (Cantab) (1752-1822), 7th son of the Rev. Thomas Metcalfe, M.A. (Cantab), of Northallerton (Y) (1706-74). descended from the Metcalfes, of Nappa (Y), was Rector and Patron of Kirkbride.* He was father of the Rev. Francis Metcalfe, M.A. (Cantab) (d. *s.p.* 1834), Rector of Kirkbride 1823-34. *Arms.* Argent three calves passant Sable a canton Gules (BLG18; CVY).

MEY. The Rt. Rev. John Mey, M.A., B.D. (Cantab), who came from Suffolk, was ordained 1557, was Prebendary of Ely 1564-82, Archdeacon of the East riding of Yorkshire 1569-88, and Bishop of Carlisle 1577 until he died 1598. William Mey, B.A. (Cantab), M.A. (Oxon) (d. 1626), was ordained 1585 and was Rector of Great Orton (C) 1585-1626 and of Cliburn (W) 1587-1626, and Prebendary of Carlisle 1595-1626. *Arms.* Sable a chevron Or between three cross crosslets fitché Argent on a chief of the second as many roses Gules (BBE). Machell recorded: Vert a chevron between three cross crosslets fitché Argent on a chief of the last as many roses Gules barbed Vert seeded Or (MMS vi 413).

MEYSEY-THOMPSON. Impaled by Howard on shield in hall of Greystoke Castle; Sir Algar Henry Stafford Howard, K.C.B., K.C.V.O., M.C., T.D., D.L., J.P. (1880-1970), Garter Principal King-of-Arms, marr. 1921 the Hon. Violet Ethel Meysey-Thompson (d. 1960), widow of Capt A. M. Vandeleur, and dau. and coheir of the 1st and last Baron Knaresborough. *Arms.* Quarterly, 1 & 4, Per fess Argent and Sable a fess embattled counter-embattled between three falcons counterchanged belled and jessed Or (Thompson); 2 & 3, Argent a fess between three cinquefoils Sable (Meysey).

MIDDLETON, of Skirwith and Barnard Castle. Thomas Middleton, of Barnard Castle (living 1488), marr. Joan, dau. and heir of Sir John Headlam, of Nunthorpe (Y). Their grandson Ambrose Middleton marr. Cecily, dau. and coheir of Anthony Crackanthorpe, *q.v.*; she inherited the manor of Skirwith from her uncle Ambrose Crackanthorpe. Their 3rd son John Middleton, of Carlisle, Sheriff of Cumberland 1584, marr. (2) 1576 Anne, sister and coheir of Thomas Hutton, of Hutton John, *q.v.* His elder brother Thomas Middleton (d. 1580) succ. to Skirwith, and marr. Elizabeth, dau. of James Martindale, *q.v.* Their daus. and coheirs were Barbara (b. *c.* 1555), marr. Thomas Hutton, of Hutton-in-the-Forest, *q.v.*, and Grace (b. *c.* 1557), wife of George Hussey. *Arms.* Quarterly of eight, 1, Argent a saltire engrailed Sable an annulet for difference (Middleton); 2, Gules a chevron Or between three lambs' heads couped Argent an annulet for difference (Headlam); 3, Or a chevron between three mullets pierced Azure a crescent for difference (Crackanthorpe); 4, Argent two bars Gules on a canton of the second a lion passant guardant Or (Lancaster); 5, Argent two bars Gules over all a bend Sable (Martindale); 6, Argent on a chevron Or [*sic*] three garbs Sable (Newton); 7, Argent six billets Sable, three, two, and one (Langrigg); 8, Argent a chevron and a bordure engrailed Sable (Allonby) (FVD).

* The Rev. Thomas Metcalfe bought the living of Kirkbride from Sir George Dalston for £240 in 1763. In 1787, when the living was offered for sale, it was stated "the occasional duty is so trifling that it has for many years past been performed by a curate at about £14 per annum."

MIDDLETON. Impaled by Irton, *q.v.*, on staircase window in Irton Hall; Richard Irton (d. 1534) mar. (2) Ann, dau. of Sir William Middleton, of Stokeld (Y). *Arms.* Argent fretty and a canton Sable. See FVY.

MIDDLETON. The Rev. Joseph Empson Middleton, M.A. (Cantab) (d. 1885, aged 78), Vicar of Belton, Leics., was Curate of St. Bees 1845-71, and Lecturer and Tutor in the Theological College there. He marr. Caroline, 3rd and youngest dau. of the Rev. Robert Pedder Buddicom, *q.v.* *Arms.* Or a saltire engrailed Sable. *Motto.* Servire deo regnare est (Brass in St. Bees church).

MIDDLETON. Shield in Gerard Lowther's house, Penrith; his father Sir Richard Lowther, of Lowther (d. 1607, aged 77), marr. Frances, dau. of John Middleton, of Middleton Hall (W). *Arms.* Argent a saltire engrailed and couped Sable. Correctly, Argent a saltire engrailed Sable.

MILBOURNE, of Armathwaite Castle. On the death *s.p.* 1741 of Robert Sanderson, *q.v.*, Armathwaite Castle passed to his great-nephew William Milbourne (1717-69), son of Thomas Milbourne, feltmaker and hatter of Newcastle upon Tyne, and grandson of Henry Milbourne, hostman of Newcastle, who marr. 1679 Margaret Sanderson. He was Recorder of Carlisle, steward to Lord Carlisle, and much interested in local history. He died unmarr. and Armathwaite passed to his sister Margaret (1715-75), and then to his cousin Robert Milbourne, a Newcastle merchant (1729-82). He was succ. by his son William Henry Milbourne (1756-1808), High Sheriff of Cumberland 1794, whose son Robert Sanderson Milbourne (1796-1822) marr. 1817 Mary, dau.* of Isaac Parker, formerly Field (see Parker, of Moorhouse Hill), but died *s.p.* and was succ. by his sister Isabella Agnes (1791-1846) who marr. the Rev. John Raper Hunton (1783-1838). *Arms.* Sable a chevron between three escallops Argent. *Crest.* A griffin's head erased Proper beaked Or (Hatchment in Armathwaite church).

MILBURN, of Hullerbank and Townend. Families of this name were of Hullerbank and Townend in Talkin. The latter family was represented in 1880 by John Milburn, joiner, owner of the plate mentioned below. From Hullerbank came the brothers Leonard and Richard Milburn; the former, who was ordained 1588 and died 1635, was Rector of Castlecarrock 1589-1635, and the latter, who was M.A., D.D. (Cantab), was Dean of Rochester 1611-15, Chaplain to Prince Henry, Bishop of St. Davids 1615-21, and Bishop of Carlisle 1621 until he died 1624. His son Leonard (d. 1672) was Rector of Ousby 1622-72, and Rector of Skelton 1623-47 and 1660-72. The last of the Hullerbank family, Thomasine, is said to have died 1723. *Arms.* Azure three escallops Argent within a bordure engrailed of the last semé of cross crosslets fitché Gules (GMS). BBE gives the same arms for Bishop Milburn with the cross crosslets plain, not fitché, but GMS† states that he bore the bordure engrailed but not semé of cross crosslets. The Townend family possessed in 1880 a plate inscribed with the names of Thomas and Mary Milburn, the date 1671, and the arms: . . . a chevron . . . between three escallops . . . (CW1 iv 444).

MILLER, of Plumpton. In 1590 Richard Miller, of Plumpton, was granted the following *Arms.* Ermine three wolves' heads erased Azure "woonded and

* Field describes her as daughter and heir of Isaac Parker (FAC), but this is wrong.
† GMS also states: "The family is now very much decayed."

langued" Gules. *Crest.* A caltrap Or pointed Gules (MS ZDVX. 39 in North Riding Record Office, Northallerton).

MILLER. Claiming that his family had been settled at Bampton (W) for 200 years, Thomas Miller, Mayor of Preston, applied for a grant of arms 1821. He was son of Henry Miller, of Whitehaven, merchant, who appears to have been baptised at Bampton 1739, son of Thomas Miller, of Hegdale, Shap. The younger Thomas (d. 1840, aged 73) became a partner in the great firm of Horrockses, Miller & Co., cotton manufacturers, Preston, *c.* 1801. He was Mayor of Preston 1820, 1826 and 1835, an alderman and magistrate, and the owner of estates in Cumberland and Westmorland. His sons* Thomas and Henry Miller succeeded him in the firm, but the family interest was bought out after the death of the former 1864 (*Ex inf.* Keith Bishop, Lancashire County Archivist). *Arms.* Azure on a fess Argent between two bees volant in chief Proper and in base a wolf's head couped Or a wheel-shuttle in fess also Proper. *Crest.* A demi wolf Erminois gorged with a collar gobony† Argent and Azure supporting with the paws a spindle erect Proper (CA xxii/347).

MILLER – see REYNOLDSON.

MILLOM – see BOYVILL, of Millom.

MILNER. The Very Rev. Isaac Milner, M.A., D.D. (Cantab) (1750-1820), a native of Leeds, was Dean of Carlisle 1791-1820. For his nephew, the Rev. Joseph Milner, M.A. (Cantab) (1793-1864), see AWL. *Arms.* Sable a chevron between three bits all within a bordure Argent (Portrait of Dean Milner). *Crest.* A horse's head bridled (HMS i 182).

MIREHOUSE, of Miresyke. John Myrehouse, of Miresyke and Mosergh, is said to have relinquished lands to the King at the Dissolution of the Monasteries. His descendant John Mirehouse, of Miresyke (d. 1771, aged 92), had issue John, of Miresyke (1705-1807), and the Rev. Thomas Mirehouse, see below. John had issue John (d. *s.p.* 1814, aged 76), the Rev. Jonathan Mirehouse (1746-1806), Curate of Bolton (C) and of Ryton and Winston (D), and Joseph Mirehouse (d. 1828, aged 88), who succ. to Miresyke. His son John Mirehouse (1800-39) was father of John Mirehouse (d. 1913, aged 85), Captain in the Merchant Service,‡ the last of the male line in Cumberland. He was succ. by his sister Anne Marie (d. 1913, aged 78), who marr. James Mawson, shipowner, of Barrow-in-Furness, whose grandson Horace Wills Mawson, solicitor, of Carlisle (1897-1966), was father of David John Williams Mawson, of Calees, Banks, Brampton, solicitor, and John A. Mirehouse Mawson, of Houghton House, Carlisle, solicitor. The above named Rev. Thomas Mirehouse (1716-69) was schoolmaster and curate of Millom in 1740 and later Rector of Eton and Canon of Peterborough. His son John Mirehouse, D.L., J.P., of Angle and Brownslade, Pembs. (1753-1823), was ancestor of the family long settled

* His daughter Eliza (d. 1872) mar. 1827 Samuel Horrocks, junior, of Lark Hill, Preston (d. *s.p.* 1846).

† The grant has a pencilled note: "counter compony in docket."

‡ A contemporary newspaper stated that: "He carved his own way to independence, capacity, and perseverance. When his father died the fortunes of his family were at a low ebb, and in the early days of her widowhood his mother had a very hard struggle to maintain herself and her two children until Capt Mirehouse was old enough to assist her . . . ." He retired *c.* 1883, when he was high in the service of the Inman Line, and "realised the great ambition of his life which was to redeem the fortunes of his ancestral days," and live at Miresyke.

there, the present representative being Major John Newton Seymour Allen-Mirehouse, of the Hall, Angle (BLG18). *Arms.* Gules a bend Argent billetté Sable (Painting on parchment in possession of Mr. J. A. M. Mawson, above). Burke, however, gives: Gules a bend Argent billetté of the field (BGA). *Crest.* An arm embowed in armour holding a sword all Proper. *Motto.* Qualis ab incepto (BGA).

MITCHINSON, of Carlisle. John Mitchinson (d. *c.* 1810), a leading Carlisle attorney, and a member of the Society of Friends, was an extensive landowner, in Cumberland, and Lord of the manor of Crosby. His heirs were his daus. Ruth (d. 1849, aged 76), marr. 1792 Jacob Maude, of Selaby Hall (D); Mary (d. 1834, aged 58), marr. William Calvert, J.P., of Windy Brow, Keswick; and Abigail (d. 1831), marr. (1) 1809 Col Thomas Salkeld, *q.v.*, and (2) John Staig, of Dumfries. *Arms.* Argent three rainbows each with clouds at each end [Proper] in chief a ram's head erased . . . (Bookplate of John Mitchinson). On an escutcheon of pretence on the shield of Col Salkeld in Kirkland church, the ram's head is couped. On a tablet in Gainford church (D), the arms appear as: . . . three rainbows in pale each with clouds at each end . . . . *Motto.* Otium fuge (Bookplate).

MITTON. The Rev. Lancelot Edgar Dury Mitton, M.A. (Cantab) (1880-1955), was Curate of St. Andrew, Penrith 1907-8, Rector of Bowness-on-Solway 1908-53, and Hon. Canon of Carlisle 1949-53. *Arms.* Per pale Gules and Azure a double-headed eagle displayed Or within a bordure chequy of the third and first. *Crest.* A double-headed eagle displayed Azure legged Gules charged on each wing with a rose Argent barbed and seeded Proper. *Motto.* Semper fidelis (BLG17).

MOISES. The Rev. Hugh Moises, M.A. (Cantab) (1722-1806), Master of the Royal Grammar School, Newcastle upon Tyne, 1749-87, was Rector of Greystoke 1787-98. *Arms.* Gules a fess Erminois between three bulls' heads Argent horned Or. *Crest.* Bullrushes Proper. *Motto.* Nisi virtus vilior alga (LAE).

MOLESWORTH. Robert Molesworth (d. 1783, aged 44), grandson of the 1st Viscount Molesworth, was Postmaster of Carlisle. His grandson, Sir Robert Molesworth, M.A. (TCD) (1806-90), was Judge of the Supreme Court at Victoria, Australia 1856-86. *Arms.* Gules an escutcheon Vair between eight cross crosslets in orle Or. *Crest.* A dexter arm embowed in armour Proper holding a cross crosslet Or. *Motto.* Vincit amor patriae (BCG).

MOLEYNS. Impaled by Howard on shield in hall of Greystoke Castle, and in window in Lord William's Oratory in Naworth Castle; Sir John Howard, K.G., 1st Duke of Norfolk (killed at Bosworth 1485), marr. (1) Katherine (d. 1465), dau. of William, Lord Moleyns. *Arms.* Paly wavy of six Or and Gules.

MÖLLING. Impaled by Kirklinton and borne on an escutcheon of pretence on tablets in Kirklinton church; John Kirklinton-Saul, of Kirklinton Hall and St. Ann's Hill (1815-68), *q.v.*, marr. (2) Mary Frederica (1814-91), dau. of Godfrey Mölling. *Arms.* Azure on a rock in base . . . a dove . . . in the beak a sprig of olive . . . .

MOLYNEUX. The Hon. Thomas Joseph Molyneux (1689-1756), younger son of the 4th Viscount Molyneux, brother of the 5th, 6th and 7th Viscounts, and father of the 1st Earl of Sefton, was of Warwick (C) in 1728. *Arms.* Azure a cross moline Or. *Crest.* A chapeau Gules turned up Ermine adorned with a plume of peacock's feathers Proper. *Motto.* Vivere sat vincere (BP105).

MOLYNEUX. Impaled by Howard on shield in hall of Greystoke Castle; Henry Howard, of Glossop (1713-87), marr. 1764 Juliana (d. 1808), 2nd dau. of Sir William Molyneux, Bart., of Wellow, Notts. *Arms.* Azure a cross moline Or.

MOLYNEUX-SEEL – see SEEL.

MOLYNS – see MAYLYNGS.

MONCEAUX, MOUNCEAUX. Shields on the ceiling of Carlisle Cathedral may be intended for Amand or Hamond Monceaux, or Mounceaux, Sheriff of Cumberland 1381, 1383 and 1385. *Arms.* Gules a cross moline Or. FFC gives his arms as: Gules a cross recercelé (tricked moline) and an escallop Or. DSL, however, attributes to him: Gules a maunch Or.

MONINS. William Godfrey Clerke Monins (1813-60), Major Royal Cumberland Militia, marr. 1841 Dorothy Anne (d. 1854, aged 39), eldest dau. of the Rev. John Raper Hunton, of Armathwaite Castle (see Milbourne). In 1841 he was of the Abbey, Carlisle, and he and his wife later lived in Fisher Street, Carlisle. *Arms.* Gules three crescents Or. *Crest.* An increscent Or. *Motto.* Mediocria maxima (BLG4).

MONTE ALTO. Sir Adam de Monte Alto (dead by 1290) was a Keeper of Yorkshire, Northumberland, Cumberland, Westmorland and Lancashire 1263. *Arms.* Argent three bars gemel Sable over all a lion rampant Gules (KEI; Shield in Shire Hall, Lancaster).

de MONTMORENCY. Harvey Francis William de Montmorency, L.R.C.P., L.R.C.S. (Edin) (d. 1936, aged 69), of Boroughgate, Appleby, practised in the town for over 30 years. His son Trevor R. C. de Montmorency, of Wordsworth Street, Penrith, was father of S. T. L. de Montmorency, of Purley, Surrey. *Crest.* On a ducal coronet Or a peacock in his pride Proper (*Ex inf.* S. T. L. de Montmorency).

MOON. From Robert Moone, of Newsham, Woodplumpton (L) (d. 1616), descended Sir Richard Moon (1814-99), Chairman of the London North-Western Railway, who was cr. Baronet 1887. He marr. 1840 Eleanor (d. 1891), dau. of John Brocklebank, of Hazelholm (C). His niece Constance Mary marr. 1889 the Rev. Dr. Charles Moor, *q.v. Arms.* Argent an eagle displayed Gules and two flaunches of the last each charged with a fleur-de-lys of the field on a chief of the second three crescents of the first (Bookplate of the Rev. Dr. Moor). *Crest.* A fleur-de-lys Argent in front of a demi eagle displayed Gules charged on the breast with an escutcheon of the first bearing a crescent also Gules. *Motto.* Vincit omnia veritas (DPB).

MOOR, of Irton. In his book *Erminois,* the Rev. Dr. Charles Moor traces his descent from Nicholas Moor, of Cragg, Irton, who died before 1583-4. His descendant Christopher Moor, of Cragg (1694-1774), was father of the Rev. Christopher Moor, B.A. (Oxon) (1730-1803), who was assistant master at Rugby when his fellow Cumbrian, the Rev. Stanley Burrough, was headmaster. His son the Rev. James Knight Moor, M.A. (Cantab) (1767-1810), marr. 1794 Selina (d. 1818), only child of the Rev. John Frewen. From them descended the Rev. Charles Moor, M.A., D.D. (Oxon), F.S.A., F.R.Hist.S. (1857-1944), Vicar of Gainsborough and Canon of Lincoln, author of *Erminois* and contributor to the *Transactions* of the Cumberland &

Westmorland Antiquarian & Archaeological Society. *Arms* (granted 1816). Erminois on a chevron engrailed Sable between three moorcocks Proper a mitre between two crosses pattée Or. *Crest.* A Moor's arm embowed Proper the hand grasping two javelins the points towards the dexter broken Or. In 1917 Dr. Moor was granted, to perpetuate the memory of his eldest son, Lieut Christopher Moor, B.A. (Cantab), the Hampshire Regt (1892-1915), who was killed in action at Gallipoli, a *Badge.* A crux ansata (or ankh) Or (i.e. the ancient Egyptian sign of Life, not before used in English heraldry) (FD7). On his bookplate, Dr. Moor quartered: 1, Moor, as above; 2, Ermine four bars Azure a demi lion rampant Gules issuant in chief (Frewen); 3, Argent a cross crosslet fitché Sable (Scott*); 4, Azure three congers' heads erased Or (Congherst); the whole impaling, Moon, *q.v. Motto.* Non eget Mauris jaculis (CME).

MOORE. Francis Moore, of Skelton (d. 1754), had sons John (b. 1722) and Francis Moore (b. 1730), who was a merchant of St. Vedast alias Foster, London, and in 1786 obtained a grant of arms for himself and the descendants of his father. *Arms.* Or a chevron engrailed Pean between three moorcocks Sable beaks combs wattles and legs Gules. *Crest.* An eagle rising Or gorged with a collar Gules pendant thereto an escutcheon Azure charged with a bezant (CA xvi/155).

MOORE, *post* PARKIN-MOORE, of Whitehall. George Moore (1806-76), the great philanthropist, who made a fortune from the lace industry, was born at Mealsgate, descended from a family long established at Overgates, Torpenhow. In 1858 he bought the Whitehall estate and commissioned Anthony Salvin to re-build the mansion; he was High Sheriff of Cumberland 1872. Dying *s.p.*, he was succ. by his great-nephew William Parkin, D.L., J.P. (1865-1937), grandson of William Parkin, of Blaithwaite. He assumed the additional surname of Moore 1889 and was High Sheriff 1899. His elder son George Parkin-Moore marr. 1923 Grace Mary, dau. of Theodore Arnold, and granddau. of Dr. Arnold of Rugby. Their son William Arnold Parkin-Moore (1935-74) was accidentally drowned in Buttermere. *Arms.* Quarterly, 1 & 4, Ermine on a chevron between three moorcocks Sable an escallop between two cross crosslets Argent (Moore); 2 & 3, Argent on a pile Sable between two fir cones erect slipped and leaved in base Proper an eagle displayed of the field each wing charged with a cross crosslet of the second (Parkin). *Crests.* 1, A Moor's head couped at the shoulders in profile Proper wreathed round the temples Or and Gules and suspended from the neck by a double chain Gold an escutcheon Argent charged with a cross crosslet sable (Moore); 2, On a mount Vert a fir cone as in the arms between two wings Sable. *Motto.* Aut nunquam tentes aut perfice (BLG17; FD7).

MORDAUNT. Impaled by Lawson, *q.v.*, on the seal of Sir Wilfrid Lawson, F.R.S., 3rd Bart., of Isel (d. 1737), who marr. Elizabeth Lucy, dau. of Lt-Gen Harry Mordaunt, and niece of Charles, Earl of Monmouth and Peterborough. *Arms.* [Argent] a chevron between three estoiles [Sable] (Q/11/1730 Mids/2/14, R.O., Carlisle).

MORESBY. This family is descended from Dolfin son of Ailward. His son Alan gave Brackenthwaite to Waldeve son of Dolfin, who was the first to

* Stephen Frewen marr. 1629 Katherine, dau. and coheir of Thomas Scott, of Northiam, Sussex, who was descended from a Congherst heiress.

assume the surname of Moresby. From him descended Sir Hugh de Moresby, who having assisted in the capture of Sir Andrew de Harcla, was granted three quarters of the manor of Culgaith 1323. He marr. Margaret (d. 1380), dau. and heir of Robert de Askeby, and acquired Asby Winderwath (W). He was Sheriff of Cumberland 1341-44 and died 1349, when his son Sir Christopher, High Sheriff 1360-61 and 1363-64, was of age. His descendant Sir Christopher was High Sheriff 1424-26 and 1438-39, and was succ. by Sir Christopher Moresby who marr. Margaret, dau. and coheir of Peter de Tilliol, *q.v.* Their son Sir Christopher (1429-61) was High Sheriff 1460. His son Sir Christopher (d. 1499), High Sheriff 1471, 1485 and 1487, was the last heir male. By Elizabeth, 2nd dau. and coheir of Sir Henry Fenwick, *q.v.*, he had a dau. and heir Anne (aged 30 and more in 1499), who marr. Sir James Pickering, of Killington (W), *q.v. Arms.* Sable a cross Or a cinquefoil pierced Argent (FFC). MMD gives: Sable a cross and in the first quarter a cinquefoil Argent. Lysons give: Sable a cross Argent in the first quarter a cinquefoil Or (LMC). Fuller recorded, for Sir Christopher Moresby, Sheriff 1424-26 and 1438-39: Argent a cross Sable in the first quarter a cinquefoil of the second (FWE); which is recorded for Moresby by FVC & MVC. The arms are on two memorial tablets in St. Andrew's, Penrith. On one, commemorating Sir Christopher Moresby and Elizabeth his wife, they appear as: Quarterly, 1, . . . a cross couped . . . in dexter chief a cinquefoil . . . , impaling, . . . three water bougets . . . ; 2, . . . a lion rampant . . . ; 3, . . . a lion rampant . . . over all a bend. . . (Tilliol); 4, . . . six martlets . . . , three, two, and one, a label of three points . . . (Fenwick). On the other commemorating Sir Christopher Moresby (d. 1499), appears the simple coat, . . . a cross . . . in dexter chief a cinquefoil . . . . On another tablet in the church, the arms are quartered by Pickering, *q.v.*, as: Quarterly, 1, . . . a cross couped . . . in dexter chief a cinquefoil . . . ; 2, . . . six martlets, three and three, . . . ; 3, . . . two lions rampant in bend . . . and two octofoils in bend sinister . . . over all a bend . . . ; 4, . . . a lion rampant . . . .

MORRIS, of Bellbridge. Capt Thomas Morris, 17th Foot (1672-1721), marr. Jane (d. 1744), dau. and heir of George Bell, of Bellbridge, *q.v.*, and acquired that estate, which descended to their eldest son, Capt Thomas Morris, 17th Foot, who sold it 1745. His younger brother Lt-Col Arthur Morris, of the same regiment, was of Fisher Street, Carlisle, and of Mellguards, Hesket-in-the-Forest. Capt Thomas's sons, Thomas (b. 1732), 17th Foot, and Capt Charles Morris, 17th Foot (1745-1838), are in DNB, both having been noted song writers; Charles, who was a friend of the Prince Regent and punch-maker and bard of the Beefsteak Society, marr. 1773 Ann Hussey. *Arms.* Azure a battle-axe in bend sinister surmounted of another in bend dexter between four cannons Or on a chief of the second a fleur-de-lys between a demi-rose couped in pale Gules radiated Gold and the stump of a tree eradicated and couped at the top as the third (Brass formerly in Sedbergham church, see FAC).

MORRIS-EYTON – see EYTON.

MORRISON, of Alston. John Morrison, who came from Sleekburn (N), was buried at Alston as of Alston Brewery 1810, as was his eldest son John Morrison (d. 1816, aged 56). A tablet in Alston church commemorates also the latter's 3rd son, William Hampson Morrison, of the Royal Mint,

Sir Thomas Musgrave, Bart.
The shield displays 1 & 4, Musgrave. 2 & 3 Hilton

London (d. 1840, aged 39). *Arms.* Argent on a fess wavy Azure between three Moors' heads couped at the shoulders Proper and each wearing a flat-topped hat of the second as many roses Or. *Crest.* A Moor's head couped at the shoulders and wearing a flat-topped hat (M.I., Alston church).

MORSHEAD. Sir Frederick Treise Morshead, 2nd Bart. (1783-1828), Coldstream Guards, was of Pigmy Hall and later of Derwent Lodge, Keswick, where he died. He was buried in Wetheral churchyard, having marr. 1821 Jane (1799-1832), 3rd dau. of Robert Bonner Warwick, *q.v.* Their only child, Sir Warwick Charles Morshead, 3rd Bart. (1824-1905), was born at Derwent Lodge.* He died *s.p.,* when the baronetcy became extinct (*Ex inf.* Sir Owen Morshead, G.C.V.O.). *Arms.* Azure a cross crosslet Argent between four martlets Or on a chief of the second three escallops Gules. *Crest.* A demi wyvern rampant reguardant Vert collared Or supporting an escutcheon Azure charged with a bezant (DPB).

MORTIMER. Shields on ceiling of Carlisle Cathedral. *Arms.* Barry of six Or and Azure on a chief of the first two pallets between two base esquires of the second over all an inescutcheon Gules (correctly, Argent).

MORTON – see FAGAN.

MORTON – see MOSTON.

MORVILLE, of Burgh-by-Sands. By marriage to Ada,† dau. and heir of William Engaine, *q.v.,* Simon de Morville (d. 1167) acquired the barony of Burgh, in which he was succ. by his son Hugh (d. 1202), whose daus. and heirs were Ada, who marr. (1) Richard de Lucy, *q.v.,* and (2) Thomas de Multon; and Joan (d. 1246), who marr. Richard de Gernon (CW2 xi). *Arms.* Pre-armorial, but later ages devised for them a beautiful shield: Azure semé-de-lys and fretty Or (Shields at Naworth Castle; LMC; a Dacre quartering).

MOSCROP, or MOSSOP. John Moscrop, of Whole House, Seascale (b. 1713), was father of the Rev. Henry Mossop (1748-1822), Curate of Cleator 1772-1821, and of the Rev. John Mossop (1754-1834), Curate of Deeping St. James, Lincs., whose great-grandsons were Arthur George Mossop, M.R.C.S., L.R.C.P., of Maldon, Essex (1863-1923), and George Augustus Mossop, M.A. (Cantab) (1864-1921); the latter was a master at Appleby Grammar School in 1885. The former obtained in 1918, for the descendants of his father, a grant of *Arms.* Vert a sword in pale point upwards surmounted by two sickles in saltire between in chief two acorns slipped and leaved all Or. *Crest.* Two swords in saltire points upwards Proper pommelled Gules hilted Or interlaced by a sickle also Proper. *Motto.* Pax quaeritur armis (FD7).

MOSELEY. Impaled by Shaw on gravestone in Edenhall churchyard; Charles Henry Shaw, of Edenhall and Rampsbeck, *q.v.,* marr. 1900 Edith (1870-1941), 2nd dau. of Joseph Moseley, of Cringle Hall (L). *Arms.* [Azure] a fess [Or] between three trefoils slipped [Erminois].

MOSSOP. The Rev. John Mossop, M.A. (Oxon) (1774-1849), was son of Clement Mossop, of Rottington, where he was born. He was Rector of Hothfield, Kent, 1802-49, and was father of John Henry Mossop, of St. Leonard's-on-Sea, who in 1869 obtained a grant of *Arms.* Argent two chevronels between in chief two fleurs-de-lys Sable and in base a passion

* Offered for sale 1830.

† She marr. (2) 1170 Robert de Vaux.

cross Gules. *Crest.* In front of a cubit arm Proper holding a fleur-de-lys Sable three annulets interlaced fesswise Or. *Motto.* Fides atque veritas (CA records).

MOSSOP – see also MOSCROP.

MOSTON,* MOSTYN. John de Moston, who presumably gave his name to Mostyn Hall, Penrith, was father of Margaret, his heir, who marr. John de Carleton, *q.v.* (NB ii 403). Mostyn Hall was inherited by their descendant Thomas Carleton (1514-87). *Arms* FCW gives as a Carleton quartering: Sable three bends Argent in chief three plates. The Carletons in fact quartered: Sable three bars Argent in chief three plates, as given by Jefferson (JLW), which Papworth ascribed to Moston, of Northumberland (OBA).

MOUNCEAUX – see MONCEAUX.

MOUNSEY, of Patterdale Hall. George Mounsey (d. 1624) was steward at Greystoke Castle to Anne, Countess of Arundel, and his widow Joan bought the lordship of Patterdale and gave it to her son, whose descendants were at Patterdale Hall until the estate was sold 1825. A descendant, John Mounsey, of Eamont Lodge, near Penrith (1845-1925), was agent for the Carleton Hall estate. His grandson, Geoffrey Mounsey, of South Ruislip, eldest surviving son of Thomas William Mounsey, of Portland Place, Penrith (d. 1962, aged 72), is now head of the family. *Arms.* Chequy Or and Sable on a chevron Ermine two lions passant addorsed Azure (HMS).

MOUNSEY, *post* MOUNSEY-HEYSHAM, *post* GUBBINS-MOUNSEY-HEYSHAM. The Rev. Robert Mounsey (1695-1780), Curate and schoolmaster of Uldale and Ireby and Curate of Ravenstonedale, was father of George Mounsey (d. 1803, aged 75), a leading Carlisle attorney, whose firm† continues today. His 2nd son Robert (d. 1842) succ. and was Deputy Registrar of the diocese of Carlisle and Secretary to the Bishop. He built Castletown, Rockcliffe, where he was succ. by his son George Gill Mounsey (1797-1874) who also succ. to his father's legal and ecclesiastical offices; he was the author of the valuable *Carlisle in 1745* (1846), and was Mayor of Carlisle 1836, 1841 and 1861. By Isabella (d. 1848), his wife, dau. of John Heysham, M.D., of Carlisle, *q.v.*, and sister and coheir of James Heysham, of Borrans Hill, Sebergham, he was father‡ of George William Mounsey, D.L., J.P., M.A. (Cantab), barrister at law (1831-1910), who succ. to Borrans Hill and assumed the additional surname Heysham 1871; he was High Sheriff of Cumberland 1893. His dau. Agnes marr. 1902 Lt-Col Richard Rolls Gubbins, D.S.O., J.P., of The Old Hall, Rockcliffe (d. 1918), whose elder son Major Richard Gubbins-Mounsey-Heysham§ (1904-60) succ. to Castletown. His only son Giles Herchard Gubbins Mounsey-Heysham is now head of the family. *Arms.* The family originally bore: Chequy Or and Gules on a chief of the second three mullets of the first.||

* Though Nicolson & Burn and Hutchinson give the name correctly, later writers, including Field, have wrongly converted it into Morton.

† As Mounsey, Bowman & Sutcliffe.

‡ He was succ. at Castletown by his eldest son Robert Heysham Mounsey, M.A. (Cantab) (1828-81), on whose death unmarr. the estates passed to his brother.

§ His younger brother Major William John Mounsey Gubbins, D.L., T.D., of Eden Lacy, was High Sheriff 1959.

|| A brass in Carlisle Cathedral to Robert Heysham Mounsey, of Castletown (d. 1881), Registrar of the diocese, displays: Chequy Or and Gules on a chief of the first three mullets of the second.

Crest. An arm in armour flourishing a sword (Windows and M.I., Rockcliffe church). They later bore: *Arms.* Chequy Or and Gules on a chevron Ermine two lions passant counter-passant Azure. *Crest.* A demi griffin gorged with a wreath of oak and holding with the claws a banner erect (BLG11). They now bear: *Arms.* Chequy Or and Gules a chief of the first thereon between two estoiles Sable a pale also Sable charged with a mullet Gold. *Crest.* A demi griffin Gules collared and chained Or holding in the dexter claw a flagstaff in bend Proper therefrom flowing to the sinister a pennon Azure and resting the sinister claw on a mullet Sable (FD7). *Motto.* Semper paratus.

MOWBRAY. A Howard quartering, on shield in Great Hall of Naworth Castle, also impaled by Howard in hall of Greystoke Castle; Sir Robert Howard (d. 1436) marr. Margaret, dau. and in her issue coheir of Thomas de Mowbray, 1st Duke of Norfolk, Lord Mowbray and Segrave (1366-99), by his 2nd wife Elizabeth, dau. of Richard FitzAlan, Earl of Arundel (1346-97), and sister and coheir of Thomas FitzAlan, Earl of Arundel (d. *s.p.* 1415, aged 34). *Arms.* Gules a lion rampant Argent. This coat is on the ceiling of Carlisle Cathedral; and was borne by Robert de Mowbray, Sheriff of Cumberland 1372-73 (DSL).

MULCASTER. This family takes its name from Muncaster and DAC states that Benedict de Pennington was father of David de Mulcaster, whose descendant Sir Robert Mulcaster, Sheriff of Cumberland 1260, died 1281-2, leaving a son Sir Walter, of Arthuret, who was Knight of the Shire for Cumberland 1290, and died *s.p.* He was succ. by his brother Sir William Mulcaster (b. *c.* 1253) who was Sheriff 1298-1303, and Knight of the Shire 1309 and 1311.* He died before March 1319 and was succ. by his son Sir Robert (b. *c.* 1296, living 1346) who was Knight of the Shire 1325. His grandson Sir Robert, living 1408, who was Knight of the Shire 1388, "became an unthrift" and sold much of his lands (CW2 xviii). His wife Joan was perhaps dau. and coheir of Sir Robert de Bampton. Their dau. and heir marr. Sir Piers de Tilliol (KEI iii). *Arms.* Sir Walter Mulcaster bore: "Burele de argent e de goul a une bende de sable e iii escalops de or" (Parl. Roll). Sir Robert (b. *c.* 1296) bore: Barry of six Argent and Gules a bend Azure (FFC). The seal on Sir Robert Mulcaster's charter of 1403 shows: . . . barry of ten . . . over all a bend . . . . MMD, FVC and MVC give: Barry of ten Argent and Gules a bend Azure.

MULCASTER. The Rev. John Scott Mulcaster, M.A. (TCD) (1809-79), a native of Laversdale, was 2nd son of Richard Mulcaster and Margaret (Scott) his wife. He was Curate of Mungrisdale 1836 and of Greystoke 1836-55, and Rector of Great Salkeld 1855-79. Another member of the family, the Rev. Richard Mulcaster, M.A. (Dunelm) (1830-87), a native of Lanercost, son of Richard and Margaret (Calvert), was Curate of Grinsdale 1854, of Great Salkeld 1855, of Bothal (N) 1856-60, of Barnard Castle 1863-66, of Ulverston 1866-70, and of Aspatria 1870-71. *Arms* (in window of Great Salkeld church recording the restoration of the chancel by the Rev. J. S. Mulcaster). Argent four bars Gules a bend Azure. *Crest.* A lion rampant Azure ducally gorged Or holding a sword erect Argent pommel and hilt of the second the point embrued Gules (BGA).

MULTON, Baron, of Egremont and of Gilsland. Thomas de Multon, of

* A contemporary John de Mulcaster died before 1302 seised of Threapland, having marr. the heiress of the Arthuret family.

Moulton, Lincs., *temp.* Henry I, was grandfather of Thomas de Multon, of Lincolnshire (d. 1240), Sheriff of Lincolnshire 1206, and of Cumberland 1233-36, who marr. (2) Ada, dau. and coheir of Hugh de Morville, *q.v.*, and widow of Richard de Lucy, of Egremont (d. *c.* 1213), *q.v.* His eldest son by his 1st wife, Lambert de Multon (d. 1246), acquired Egremont by marr. to Amabel, elder dau. and coheir of the above Richard de Lucy, and was grandfather of Thomas de Multon, 1st Lord Multon of Egremont (d. 1321), whose son John, 2nd Lord Multon, died *s.p.* 1334, leaving three sisters and coheirs, of whom Joan marr. Sir Robert FitzWalter, *q.v.*, and Elizabeth marr. Sir Robert Harington, *q.v.* By his 2nd wife Ada, the above Thomas de Multon (d. 1240) was father of Thomas de Multon (d. 1271) who acquired Gilsland by marr. to Maud, dau. and heir of Hubert de Vaux. From them descended Thomas de Multon, 1st Lord Multon of Gilsland (d. 1313), whose dau. and heir marr. Ranulph de Dacre, *q.v.* (EDP; SEB). *Arms.* Argent three bars Gules (FFC; Matthew Paris, *Chronica Majora*). Some rolls blazon this as: Barry Argent and Gules, or Gules three bars Argent. The Gilsland Multons at one time bore the Vaux coat, Chequy Or and Gules; and the Dacres and Howards quartered Multon of Gilsland as: Argent three bars Gules on a canton of the last a lion passant guardant Or (Shield at Naworth Castle; banner held by the Multon beast, a sheep, or 'mouton,' in the Great Hall, Naworth Castle). On the shield on the gatehouse at Naworth the field is barry, and Field records: Barry of six Argent and Gules on a canton of the second a lion passant Or (FAC). In a window in Kirkoswald church the arms appear as: Barry of six Gules and Or on a canton of the first a lion passant guardant of the second.*

MUMBERSON. The Mumberson family, of the Keswick area, originated from West Cumberland; John Mumberson (d. 1880, aged 83) is buried in Crosthwaite churchyard. *Arms.* Argent a lion rampant Sable charged on the shoulder with a dolphin Or. *Crest.* A plume of ostrich feathers Or. *Motto.* Ma foi en Dieu seulement (*Ex inf.* the late Rev. H. A. L. Rice, of Kirkby Lonsdale). These are the bearings of Mompesson, of Norfolk, of which name Mumberson may be a corruption.

MUNCASTER, Baron – see PENNINGTON.

MURIEL. George Bertram Muriel, J.P., M.B., B.Ch. (Cantab), of Greenbank, Whitehaven (1871-1956), was son of George John Muriel, J.P., M.R.C.S., of Glenfield, Whitehaven (1842-1923), and was descended from the Rev. Thomas Muriel, B.D. (d. 1629), Vicar of Soham, Rector of Hildersham, and Archdeacon of Norfolk. His dau., Miss Margaret Ritson Muriel, B.Sc. (London), who was born at Whitehaven, is now of 24 Fairgarth Drive, Kirkby Lonsdale. *Arms.* Or a bend and in base a cross crosslet Gules the bend charged with a crescent for difference. *Crest.* A boar passant Proper. *Motto.* Firmum in vita nihil.

MURRAY, Earl of Annandale. In 1605 James I granted a 40 years' lease of Plumpton Park to James Murray (d. 1640), later 1st Earl of Annandale. In 1625 Charles I made a grant of Plumpton in fee to Lord Annandale, whose son James, 2nd Earl (d. 1658), sold the estate 1653 to Sir John Lowther. *Arms.* Azure a crescent between three stars Argent a tressure† flory

* A shield on the ceiling of Carlisle Cathedral which the present writers read as: Argent two bars Gules, but Field as: Argent three bars Gules, is doubtless Multon.

† BEP records the tressure as a double tressure flory counterflory.

counterflory of the last on a canton of the last a thistle Vert crowned Or. *Crest.* An angel Proper. *Motto.* Noctesque diesque praesto (BGA).

MURRAY, of Longtown. Margaret, wife of John Murray, of Longtown, died 1692, aged 35. *Arms.* . . . three mullets . . . , two and one, and in base a buglehorn . . . (Gravestone, Arthuret churchyard).

MURRAY. A tombstone in Matterdale churchyard commemorates Thomas Murray (d. 1848, aged 82); Anne, his wife (d. 1838, aged 70); John, their son (d. 1873, aged 73); and Sarah, his widow (d. 1891, aged 80). *Arms.* . . . a chevron . . . between three roundles . . . in chief and one in base.

MURRAY. Shield in library at Greystoke Castle; Sir John Stepney Cowell-Stepney, *q.v.*, marr. (2) Euphemia Jamina (d. 1874), dau. of General John Murray, of Glenalla, Co. Donegal. *Arms.* Azure three stars Argent.*

MUSGRAVE, of Crookdake. A branch of the Musgrave family acquired large estates in Cumberland and Co. Durham when William Musgrave, of Crookdake and Penrith (d. 1487), son of Thomas Musgrave, of Eden Hall, *q.v.*, and Joan Stapleton his wife, marr. Felicia (b. *c.* 1451), dau. and coheir of William Tilliol or Colville, *q.v.* Their† son Cuthbert (1474-1533) marr. Joan, dau. and coheir of Richard Launder, and had a son Mungo (*c.* 1503-41), whose descendant William Musgrave (d. 1664) was the last male, leaving three daus. and coheirs – Anne, marr. (1) 1657 John Senhouse, of Seascale, and (2) Sir John Ballantine, *q.v.*; Mary, marr. . . . Charter; and Dorothy (d. 1705, aged 65), marr. William Askew, *q.v. Arms.* Azure six annulets Or, three, two, and one, a crescent for difference (MMS vi 423).

MUSGRAVE, of Edenhall. The Musgraves, long one of the leading families in Cumberland and Westmorland, take their name from Musgrave (W). Thomas de Musgrave (d. *c.* 1246) was amerced at the Cumberland Assizes 1242, and in 1243 was one of four knights serving on a jury. Thomas Musgrave (d. 1385), deputy Sheriff of Westmorland and M.P. for the county 1340-44, was summoned to Parliament 1350, whereby he is held to have become Lord Musgrave, though his descendants never used the title. After the marr. of Thomas Musgrave (d. before 1457/8) to Joan, elder dau. and coheir of William Stapleton, of Edenhall, *q.v.*, the family made that place their chief seat; the Hall was sold and demolished 1934. Sir Thomas Musgrave (d. *c.* 1407), grandfather of the said Thomas, was High Sheriff of Cumberland 1391. His descendant Sir Edward (1461-1542) was High Sheriff 1514, 1519 and 1527, and his son Sir William (1509-44) served in 1532 and 1541. His son Sir Richard (1524-55) was High Sheriff 1554. His line failed with his dau. Eleanor (*c.* 1546-1623), *de jure* Baroness Musgrave, wife of Robert Bowes. She was succ. by her cousin Sir Philip Musgrave (1607-78), son of Sir Richard Musgrave, K.B. (d. 1615), who was cr. Baronet 1611. His son Sir Richard, 3rd Bart. (1635-87), died leaving a dau. Mary (1661-1728), who marr. John Davison, of Blakiston (D), in whose descendants the barony is now vested. Her uncle Sir Christopher (d. 1704, aged 72), 4th Bart., was M.P. for Carlisle, Westmorland, Appleby, Oxford University and Totnes. His grandson Sir Christopher, 5th Bart. (1688-1736), was M.P. for Carlisle 1713-15 and for Cumberland 1722-27. Sir Philip, 8th Bart. (1794-1827), High Sheriff 1817, was M.P. for Carlisle 1825-27. His brother

* They are depicted as three mullets of four points irradiated.

† In FCW Cuthbert is said to have been a son of William's 2nd wife Margaret, dau. of . . . Thornton and widow of . . . Middleton.

Sir George, 10th Bart. (1799-1872), was High Sheriff 1840. The estates in Cumberland and Westmorland were sold by his grandson Sir Richard George Musgrave, 12th Bart. (1872-1926). The present holder of the title is Sir Christopher Patrick Charles Musgrave, 15th Bart., of Talwrn Glas Farm, Llanfair Clydogan, Cardiganshire (GEC; GECB). *Arms.* Azure six annulets, three, two, and one, Or (FFC; FCW; Shield on ceiling of Carlisle Cathedral). *Crest.* Two arms in armour gauntleted Proper and grasping an annulet Or. *Motto.* Sans changer (NB i 599; BP105).

MUSGRAVE, of Fairbank and Musgrave Hall. A branch of the Musgraves, descended from Thomas Musgrave, of Edenhall, and Joan (Stapleton) his wife, was of Fairbank, Plumpton, and Musgrave Hall, Penrith, but whether descended from Sir John Musgrave, Sheriff of Cumberland 1489 and 1493, or from his brother William, who was ancestor of the Musgraves, of Crookdake, *q.v.*, and who is described as of Penrith, it is impossible to say. Simon Musgrave (d. 1658), who marr. Susan (d. 1622), dau. of Sir William Hutton, *q.v.*, was probably baptised at Penrith 1579, son of Cuthbert Musgrave. His son William Musgrave (d. 1686) left only daus., of whom Marie (b. 1643) marr. 1662 Lancelot Simpson, *q.v.*, who thus acquired Fairbank and Musgrave Hall (CW1 xv 82-104). *Arms* and *Crest.* As Musgrave, of Edenhall (Lintels at Musgrave Hall and Fairbank, the latter being a curious mixture of the Musgrave and Stapleton arms).

MUSGRAVE, of Hayton. Thomas Musgrave, by Joan (Stapleton) his wife, was father of, *int. al.*, Richard, of Edenhall (see that family); Sir John, Sheriff of Cumberland 1489 and 1493; William, ancestor of Musgrave of Crookdake; and Nicholas, who marr. Margaret, dau. and coheir of William Tilliol, and was ancestor of the Musgraves of Hayton Castle. His grandson William Musgrave, of Johnby Hall (1518-96), was Sheriff of Cumberland 1573 and 1592. He marr. Isabel, dau. and heir of James Martindale, and had a son Thomas, who died *v.p.*, leaving a dau. Isabel (b. 1579) who marr. (1) her cousin John Musgrave, of Catterlen, and (2) John Vaux, of Catterlen, *q.v.* The estates were inherited by her uncle Sir Edward Musgrave (living 1628), who bought Scaleby Castle. He marr. Catherine Penruddock and had a son William, who marr. Catherine, dau. of Hugh Sherburne, of Esholt and Guiseley (Y). Their son Sir Edward Musgrave (1621-73) was cr. Baronet 1638, and was fined £960 for his loyalty to the Royalist cause. His son Sir Richard (*c.* 1650-1710) was Sheriff of Cumberland 1684 and Vice-Admiral of Cumberland and Westmorland. He marr. 1670 Dorothy (d. 1718, aged 69), dau. and coheir of William James, of Washington (D), *q.v.* Their son Sir Richard Musgrave, M.A. (Edin) (*c.* 1675-1711), was M.P. for Cumberland 1700-2 and 1705-8. He marr. Elizabeth, dau. and coheir of Joseph Finch, of Leeds. Their son Sir Richard, M.A. (Oxon), 4th Bart. (*c.* 1701-39), was Sheriff 1730 and marr. 1724 Anne, 2nd dau. of John Hylton, of Hylton Castle (D), and sister and coheir of John Hylton, M.P. Their son Sir Richard Musgrave (1724-55) took the name of Hylton 1746 on inheriting Hylton Castle. He marr. 1746 Eleanor, dau. and coheir of John Hedworth, and had a dau. and heir Eleanor (b. 1752), who marr. 1769 William Jolliffe, *q.v.* Her uncle Sir William Musgrave, F.R.S. (1735-1800), who succ. as 6th Bart. but did not inherit the estates, was the compiler of Musgrave's *Obituary*. He was succ. by his brother General Sir Thomas Musgrave (1737-1812), who died unmarr. On the death of the 10th baronet, the Rev. Sir William Augustus Musgrave, M.A. (Oxon), in 1875, the baronetcy became dormant or extinct (GECB). *Arms.* Azure six annulets Or, three, two, and one, a martlet for difference. *Crest.* Two arms counter embowed armed and gauntleted Proper holding an annulet Or, a martlet for difference (LMC; Monuments in Aspatria church). *Supporters.* These appear on the monuments in Aspatria church to the 2nd and 4th Baronets as: Dexter, A unicorn Argent armed gorged with a ducal coronet and chained Or; Sinister, A woodman Proper wreathed about the loins and temple Vert holding in the sinister hand a club also Proper. On the monument to General Sir Thomas Musgrave, 7th Bart., the sinister supporter appears as: A lion rampant guardant imperially crowned and chained Or. DPB (1868) gives: Dexter, A stag Proper gorged with a ducal coronet and chained Or; Sinister, A lion rampant gorged and chained as the dexter. *Mottoes.* Munit haec et altera vincit; Teres et rotundus (M.I., Aspatria church; DPB).

MUSGRAVE, of Stapleton. Jane, wife of Richard Musgrave, of Stapleton, died 1729, aged 49. *Arms.* . . . six annulets . . . (ABD). These arms, charged with the Red Hand of Ulster, are on a stone in the church.

MYERS, of Po House. For this old Whicham family, see MPP. Thomas Myers, of Groupes (1687-1741), was father of, *int. al.*, Mary (b. 1713), who marr. Miles Postlethwaite, of Po House, *q.v.*; John Myers, of Rallies (d. 1786); and the Rev. Thomas Myers, J.P., LL.B. (Lambeth) (1735-1826), who was Curate of Barton (W), Rector of Croglin 1780-1804, and Vicar of Lazonby 1783-1826 (see AWL). His younger son John Myers. M.A. (Cantab) (1767-1821), succ. his cousin John Postlethwaite (d. 1813) at Po House, Millom, but dying *s.p.m.*, he was succ. by his cousin William (1774-1835), whose son Joshua Sayer Myers (1802-93) left the estate with Lacra and Lowscales to his children William (1831-98), George (1838-1917) and Elizabeth Ann (1830-1919). Their nephew William Benn Myers, J.P., of Gateside, Silecroft (1875-1949) succ. and sold Po House 1919. His younger brother George Birkett Myers, of Stone House, Penrith (1879-1962), played a prominent part in the life of that town. His only son is Dr. George Graham Myers, who represents this branch of the family. The senior male representative is John Myers, of Geneva, grandson of John Postlethwaite Myers, of Fairfield, Silecroft (d. 1915, aged 82), 2nd son of Joshua Sayer Myers, above (*Ex inf.* Mrs. Elizabeth Barraclough, elder dau. of G. B. Myers). *Arms.* Gules a fess Ermine between three water bougets Argent. *Crest.* A peacock's tail Proper encircled with a wreath Argent and Gules (RWH).

MYERS. Lt-Gen Sir William Myers (1751-1805) was son of Christopher Myers, who went from Whitehaven to Monkstown, Dublin. He had a distinguished military career, having been Governor of Tobago and Commander-in-Chief of the forces in the Leeward Islands. He was cr. Baronet 1804, and died in Barbados* the following year, when he was succ. by his only son, Lt-Col Sir William James Myers (1783-1811), who was killed *s.p.* at the Battle of Albuera, the title becoming extinct (M.I.s at St. Michael's Cathedral, Barbados, and St. Paul's Cathedral, London; *Ex inf.* Mr. Taylor, Director of the Barbados Museum and Historical Society and Barbados Department of Archives). *Arms.* Argent a lymphad with her sails

* He was the fourteenth out of 18 members of his family to die after their arrival in the West Indies. "Most fortunately his lady staid in England."

furled a flag at head and stern Gules a double headed pennant at each top of the last on a canton also Gules a baton sinister Or surmounted by a sword Argent hilt Or in saltire over both a mural crown Argent. *Crest.* A mermaid Proper finned Gules comb and mirror Or charged with a mural crown Or (DBP). *Motto.* Non dormit qui custodit (BEP).

NANSON. Thomas Nanson, J.P., of English Street, Carlisle, hatter and furrier (b. *c.* 1802), was Mayor of Carlisle 1865. His son Major John Nanson, D.L., J.P. (b. 1841), was agent at Appleby of the Carlisle & Cumberland Bank, and lived at The Friary there; he was Vice-Chairman of Westmorland County Council and Major, 2nd Volunteer Battn The Border Regiment. His eldest son Ernest Lonsdale Nanson, J.P., solicitor, of Nethercliffe, Seascale (1868-1938), was agent to the Lowther Estates. His son Philip Lonsdale Nanson (1900-50) was a master at Sandroyd School for 25 years. Laurence Donald Nanson, a younger son of the above Major John Nanson, was of Haverbrack, Milnthorpe. *Crest.* A ducal coronet surmounted by a martlet (FBC).

NANSON. In 1791 William Nanson gave to the Guild of Butchers a standing cup, hall marked 1776-7, which is now in Carlisle Museum, and on which are engraved his *Arms.* Sable a chevron between three annulets Argent. *Crest.* A bull's head couped.

NAYLOR. Captain Thomas Naylor, Royal Marines (d. 1802, aged 44), was of Ennim Bank, Blencowe.* He marr. (1) Mary Grimshaw, of Preston, and (2) Elizabeth (d. 1816), dau. of Robert Dalton, of Thurnham Hall (L), and sister of the wife of Sir James Fitzgerald, 7th Bart. (see AWL). *Arms.* Or a pale between two lions rampant Sable. *Crest.* A lion's head erased Sable charged on the neck with a saltire couped Or (M.I., Greystoke church).

NEAVE. Impaled by Howard, *q.v.,* on goblets and seals at Corby Castle; Henry Howard, of Corby Castle (1757-1842), marr. (2) 1793 Catherine Mary (d. 1849), 2nd dau. of Sir Richard Neave, 1st Bart., of Dagnam Park, Essex. *Arms.* Argent on a cross Sable five fleurs-de-lys Or.

NEDHAM. George Nedham, son of Sir Robert Nedham, of Pool Park (Dy), who was knighted 1630, fled to Jamaica after the Battle of Worcester 1651, and his descendant Capt Henry Nedham, D.L., J.P. (b. 1814), of Mount Olive, Jamaica, was father of the Rev. George Nedham (1856-1940), who was Rector of Kirkbride 1911-40. His dau. Beatrix Gwendoline Harriet marr. 1914 Canon M. H. Banister, Rector of Greystoke. *Arms.* Argent a bend Azure between two bucks' heads cabossed Sable. *Crest.* A phoenix in flames Proper. *Motto.* Nunc aut numquam (BLG 1849). On a shield on the font cover in Kirkbride church, the bend in the arms is engrailed.

NELSON, of Penrith and Virginia. Hugh Nelson,† of Penrith, grocer (1591-1674), marr. 1619 Marian Nelson (d. 1657, aged 58). Their descendant Hugh Nelson (1643-1708) had a son Thomas Nelson (1678-1745) who, after making several voyages to Virginia, finally settled there and was the founder of Yorktown. He was known as "Scotch Tom." His son, the Hon. William Nelson (d. 1772, aged 61), became President of the Council and acting Governor of Virginia. By Elizabeth Burwell his wife he had a son Thomas Nelson (1738-89), who was at school in Hackney, going up to

* The house, now called Ennim, is the home of the Rt. Hon. William Whitelaw, M.P.

† Nelson was a common surname in Penrith. There are 720 entries, as against 326 Robinson entries, in the registers between 1556 and 1700.

Christ's College, Cambridge, 1758 and residing until 1761. He was on H.M. Council of Virginia 1764 and was one of the signers of the Declaration of Independence. He became Commander in Chief in the Virginia Commonwealth and was elected Governor 1781. As Major-General of the Virginia forces he joined Washington in the siege of Yorktown, but resigned through ill-health (CW2 i; VAC). *Arms* (formerly on Thomas Nelson's monument at Yorktown). . . . a bar . . . between three fleurs-de-lys . . . (CW2 i).

NELSON. The Rev. Jeremy Nelson, M.A. (Cantab) (d. 1685), son of the Rev. Jeremy Nelson, M.A. (Cantab), Rector of Elsdon (N), became Curate of Stanhope (D) 1662, and was Prebendary of Carlisle 1667-85, Vicar of Stanwix 1667-76, and Vicar of Corbridge (N) 1674-85. He marr. 1671 Mary, dau. of the Rev. Dr. Isaac Basire, *q.v.*, Prebendary of Durham and Archdeacon of Northumberland. By her he had four children – John (b. 1673), who was in Barbados 1703; Frances (b. 1672), marr. . . . Grundy; Mary (b. 1676); and Margaret. The two last were mutes and Margaret was blind as well (Dean and Chapter of Carlisle lease book). *Arms.* . . . a chevron . . . between three fleurs-de-lys . . . (Monument formerly in Carlisle Cathedral mentioned in Hugh Todd's MS. *History of the Diocese of Carlisle*).

NELSON THOMLINSON SCHOOL, Wigton. The Nelson Thomlinson School was formed by the amalgamation in 1952 of the Nelson School (established 1896 with money left by Joseph Nelson, of Moor Row, Dundraw, who died 1893) and the Thomlinson Girls' Grammar School (established 1898, when the former Wigton Grammar School, founded in the period 1714-30 by the Rev. John Thomlinson, M.A., and his brother, the Rev. Robert Thomlinson, D.D., was re-constituted as a Grammar School for Girls). The Nelson School used the following *Arms.* Per pale Argent and Sable a chevron between three fleurs-de-lys all counterchanged. *Crest.* The school originally used: A cubit arm quarterly Argent and Sable holding in the hand Proper a fleur-de-lys per pale Argent and Sable. This later became: A cubit arm holding in the hand a fleur-de-lys all per pale Argent and Sable. *Motto.* Faith and works. The Thomlinson Girls' Grammar School used the following *Arms.* Per pale wavy Argent and Vert three greyhounds courant in pale counterchanged a chief indented Azure. *Crest.* A demi savage wreathed about the middle and holding in both hands a spear all Proper. The Nelson Thomlinson School uses the following *Arms.* Per pale Argent and Azure a chevron between three fleurs-de-lys all counterchanged.* *Crest.* A cubit arm holding in the hand a fleur-de-lys all Argent. *Motto.* Fide et operis (*Ex inf.* Dr. L. C. Loveday, of Wigton, Clerk to the Governors of the Nelson Thomlinson School; writing paper, bookplates, etc.).

NEVILLE. Hugh de Neville was Sheriff of Cumberland 1209-13. *Arms.* DSL attributes to him: Argent a lion rampant Azure in chief a pile (or label) of three points Gules.

NEVILLE, Baron Neville of Raby, Earl of Westmorland. Ralph, 4th Lord Neville, of Raby (D) (*c.* 1364-1425), received a grant of Penrith and

* It is clear from information received from Dr. Loveday, to whom we are indebted for much help with this entry, that the narrow blue surround to the present arms is meant to be an outline of the shield, and not a bordure. It is unfortunate that the bookplate at present in use hatches the arms incorrectly.

Inglewood forest from Richard II in 1397, in which year he was cr. Earl of Westmorland. The Cumberland lands descended to his younger son (by his 2nd wife), Richard, Earl of Salisbury (d. 1460), father of Richard, Earl of Warwick (d. 1471, aged 42), who forfeited them. The 1st Earl of Westmorland's eldest son, John de Neville (d. *v.p.* 1420), was father of Ralph, 2nd Earl of Westmorland (*c.* 1406-84), whose son John died *v.p.* and *s.p.* 1450 and who was succ. by his nephew Ralph, 3rd Earl of Westmorland (1456-99), son of John, Lord Neville (d. 1461). From him descended Charles, 6th Earl of Westmorland (*c.* 1542-1601), who joined the earl of Northumberland in the rising of the North 1569, and was attainted 1571 when all his honours were forfeited (GEC; EDP; SHD iv (i) 158-61). *Arms.* Gules a saltire Argent (FFC; GEC; Shields in Carlisle Cathedral).* *Crest.* Out of a ducal coronet Or a bull's head Sable armed Or. The crest sometimes issued from a chapeau, not a coronet (SHD). Burke gives; Out of a ducal coronet Or a bull's head pied (BGA), *Supporters.* Two pied bulls armed unguled collared and chained Or (SHD). Burke gives; Two greyhounds collared (BGA). *Badges.* A galley Sable; A dun bull; An annulet; A fret Or; A ship's buoy; Staples (FDB). *Mottoes.* Esperance me comfort (SHD); Moys Droyt, Moys Droyt (TVN).

NEVILLE. Impaled by Howard on shield in hall of Greystoke Castle; Stafford Vaughan Stepney Howard, now of Greystoke Castle, marr. (2) 1940 Mary Gracia, dau. of George Wilder Neville, of Portsmouth, Virginia, U.S.A. *Arms.* Or fretty Gules on a canton Sable a lymphad Or sails furled Argent flags and pennon flying Gules.

NEVINSON. The Rev. Thomas Nevinson, B.A. (Oxon) (1658-1728), son of Edward Nevinson, of Newby, Morland (see AWL), was Rector of Uldale 1684-97, Curate of Bassenthwaite 1693 and of Ireby 1693-1728, Vicar of Addingham 1697-98, and Vicar of Torpenhow 1699-1728. He marr. 1690 Grace, sister of Bishop Nicolson, and their son, the Rev. Thomas Nevinson, M.A. (Oxon) (1696-1744) was Headmaster of Appleby Grammar School 1721-23 and Vicar of Whittingham (N) 1722-44. *Arms.* Argent a chevron between three eagles displayed Azure. *Crest.* A talbot Proper collared and with chain reflexed over the back Or (AWL).

NEWCASTLE & CARLISLE RAILWAY CO. Incorporated 1829, amalgamated with the North Eastern Railway Co. 1862. *Arms.* Sable two escutcheons the dexter Gules three castles triple-towered Argent (Newcastle upon Tyne), the sinister Vert on a base wavy Argent and Azure a castle between two roses Or on a chief Gules a lion passant guardant of the fourth (Carlisle). *Crest.* A castle as in the dexter escutcheon issuing therefrom a demi lion guardant supporting a flagstaff Or flying therefrom a forked pennon of the arms of St. George. *Supporters.* On either side a sea horse Proper crined and finned Or (DRH).

NEWELL OF STAFFA. The Watson family, *q.v.*, long established at Easton, Bowness-on-Solway, is now represented by the Rev. Gerald Frederick Watson Newell of Staffa, Rector of Spennithorne, Finghall and Hauxwell 1967-69. He is son of Group Captain Frederick Rusden Newell (1904-63), who marr. Kathleen, dau. of the Rev. Sidney Montague Watson, and his family owned Staffa until 1974. *Arms.* Or three cross crosslets fitché

* The arms are also in a window in the Cathedral differenced in one case with a martlet gules, in another with a label Or.

Gules in chevron on a chief engrailed Sable three roses Argent barbed and seeded Proper. *Crest.* In front of a lion's head couped Sable gorged with a mural coronet Argent four garbs Or. *Motto.* Hold fast.

NEWMARCH. Shield at Hutton-in-the-Forest; a Vane quartering. *Arms.* Gules on a fess Or five fusils of the field. The correct version is: Gules five fusils conjoined in fess Or.

NEWTON, of West Newton and Grinsdale. Alan, 2nd Lord of Allerdale, gave West Newton to Odard de Wigton (living 1130), from whom it passed to his son Ketill de Newton, ancestor of Sir Richard Newton, living 1262, whose grandson Thomas, *temp.* Edward III, was the last male; his dau. and heir marr. Roger Martindale, *q.v.* *Arms.* Argent on a chevron Azure three garbs Or (LMC).*

NICHOLSON, of Brampton. Isaac Nicholson, flaxdresser, of Brampton, died 1765. *Arms.* Bell Irving recorded these, on his tombstone in Brampton Old churchyard, as: . . . a fess . . . on a chief . . . three roses . . . (ABD). Field recorded them as: Barry of four Azure and Ermine in chief three suns in their splendour (FAC).

NICHOLSON. The Rev. Henry Nicholson (1755-1812), son of the Rev. John Nicholson, was born in Whitehaven and was Curate of Gosforth 1778 and of Ponsonby 1780-89, and Rector of Moresby 1789-1812. He became Headmaster of Whitehaven Grammar School 1775, and later of Moresby Classical Academy which he founded. His son, the Rev. Patrick Charles Nicholson, B.D. (Cantab) (1809-88), was Curate of Ulverston 1832-35 and of Maryport in 1837, Chaplain to Lord Carlisle 1849-65, and Rector of St. Philip, Salford (L), 1849-88. *Arms* (granted to the Rev. P. C. Nicholson 1842). Sable two bars chequy Or and Azure in chief a stag's head cabossed between two suns in splendour of the second. *Crest.* A lion's head erased Ermine charged on the neck with a burning heart Or within two branches of palm Proper (CA xlvi/26).

NICHOLSON. Charles Nicholson, of Cockermouth, was grandfather of Sir Charles Nicholson, D.C.L. (Oxon), LL.D. (Cantab) (1808-1903), Speaker of the Legislative Council of New South Wales and Provost of the University of Sydney. He was knighted 1852 and cr. Baronet 1859. His 3rd son Sir Sydney Hugo Nicholson, M.V.O., M.A., Mus.B. (Oxon), Mus.D. (Cantab), F.R.C.O. (1875-1947), organist of Westminster Abbey 1918-27, who was knighted 1938, was acting organist of Carlisle Cathedral 1904-8, and lived at 161 Warwick Road, Carlisle. *Arms.* Azure two bars nebuly Argent in chief a sun in splendour Proper between two stars of eight points Or. *Crest.* On a rock Proper a lion's head Azure charged with a star as in the arms. *Motto.* Virtus sola nobilitas (BP105).

NICHOLSON. The 1634 Visitation of Essex contains the pedigree entered by Francis Nicholson, of Chappell in that county, descended from Nicholas Nicholson, of Cumberland, whose grandson Thomas Nicholson, of Woodhall (L), obtained a grant of arms 1585. The grant was exemplified 1596 to his son Otho Nicholson, of London, an Examiner in Chancery.

* Field quotes VN i (not ii) 42 as authority for Martindale quartering this coat for Newton, but it should be noted that in the authority quoted, it is ascribed tentatively to Cradock. See I. M. Roper: *Effigies of Gloucestershire,* p. 29, where it is stated that Lord Chief Justice Sir Richard Cradock changed his name to Newton.

Arms. Azure two bars Ermine on a chief Argent three suns Proper. *Crest.* A lion's head erased Gules ducally gorged Or.* *Motto.* Per castra ad astra.

SCOTT-NICHOLSON – see SCOTT, *post* SCOTT-NICHOLSON.

NICOLSON. Joseph Nicolson, of Averas (now Ambrose) Holme, Wetheral, marr. Radigunda Scott, heiress of Park Broom, and had a son Joseph Nicolson, B.A. (Oxon), who was Rector of Plumbland 1647-49 and 1661-86 and of Great Orton 1657-63, and Vicar of Crosby-on-Eden 1658-65 and of Stanwix 1659-60. His son, William Nicolson, M.A., D.D. (Oxon) (1655-1727), became Carlisle's most famous Bishop. He was Fellow of The Queen's College, Oxford, Vicar of Torpenhow 1681-98, Prebendary of Carlisle 1681-1702, Archdeacon of Carlisle and Rector of Great Salkeld 1682-1702, Vicar of Addingham 1699-1702, Bishop of Carlisle 1702-18, Bishop of Derry 1718-27, and Archbishop of Cashel 1727. His son the Rev. Joseph Nicolson, D.D. (Oxon), Chancellor of Lincoln, died 1728, leaving two daus., one of whom died 1734 and the other was living 1741. Descendants of the Bishop's dau. Elizabeth, wife of the Rev. Bellingham Mauleverer, exist. The Bishop's brother John Nicolson (d. 1727) was Registrar of Carlisle Diocese, Chapter Clerk and Steward to Bishop Rainbow, with whom he lived at Rose Castle. His eldest son Thomas Nicolson, D.C.L. (Oxon) (1700-35), was Vicar of Crosthwaite 1727-28 and curate of Ireby and vicar of Torpenhow 1728-35. His 2nd son William Nicolson, M.A. (Oxon) (1703-31), was Vicar of Dalston 1727-31, and his 3rd son Joseph Nicholson, J.P. (1706-77), Alderman of Carlisle and Steward to Lord Carlisle, was author with Dr. Richard Burn of *The History and Antiquities of the Counties of Westmorland and Cumberland,* 1777. All three brothers died *s.p.* and the line was continued by their sister Mary (b. 1695) who marr. 1718 Clement Nicholson, of Whitehaven (d. 1758); one of their sons, John (1723-95), owned Linstock Castle (DNB; CW2 i). *Arms.* Barry of six Azure and Ermine in chief three suns Or (BBE). The above named Joseph Nicolson, of Hawkesdale, Dalston, sealed a letter dated 15 January 1749 to Andrew Hudleston with the following Arms. . . . two bars Ermine in chief three suns in their splendour. *Crest.* Out of a coronet a lion's gamb erect holding a sun in his splendour.

NIXON, of Boustead Hill. Richard Lawson Nixon, of Boustead Hill, Burgh-by-Sands, nephew of Mrs. Anne Ashbridge, *q.v.,* was father of William Nixon, of Boustead Hill (1868-1937), who was born at Longburgh House, and was joint master of the Thurstonfield Hounds 1896-1900, and of Richard Lawson Nixon-Lawson, land agent, of 52 English Street, Carlisle, and Drumburgh House (b. 1870), who assumed the additional surname of Lawson 1891. *Arms.* Gules two garbs in fess . . . between in chief an ox yoke . . . and in base two sickles in saltire . . . . *Crest.* A cubit arm holding a scythe. *Motto.* Nec sibi nec aliis (Stone shield on house at Boustead Hill).

NIXON, of Noblestown. James Nixon was recorded as of Noblestown, Bewcastle, in 1744, by Bell Irving. *Crest.* A cherub with long wings on a small pyramid. *Motto.* Haud dulces labentia ventos (ABD).

NIXON, of Slacks. William Nixon, of Slacks, Bewcastle, died 1723, aged 43. His dau. and heir Isabel marr. Andrew Dodgson, of Dodgsonstown, and the

* Burke gives a variant of this achievement for Nicholson, of Cumberland & Lancashire, as follows: *Arms.* Azure two bars Ermine in chief three suns in splendour Or. *Crest.* Out of a ducal coronet Gules a lion's head Ermine (BGA).

Dodgson heirs still held the Slacks in 1934 (MS. notes on *Cumberland Armorials* by J.V.H.). *Arms.* ... a chevron ... between in chief two lozenges ... and in base a heart ... (ABD). Field recorded: A chevron between three lozenges (FAC).

NIXON. A tablet in Carlisle Cathedral to John Nixon, of West Lodge, Clapham, Surrey (d. 1841, aged 82), erected by his son-in-law Thomas Robert Jefferson, *q.v.*, states that he was a native of Carlisle, was elected an alderman of the city in 1827, and was a benefactor publicly and privately. The inscription adds that "after more than half a century of his useful and honourable life he was actively engaged as a Merchant in the City of London." His son George Burrell Nixon died 1837; his dau. Margaret (1799-1862) marr. the above named T. R. Jefferson (*Ex inf.* Anthony Powell, a descendant, and J. P. Godwin). *Arms* (quartered by Jefferson). Sable five bezants on a chief Argent a battle axe Proper (*Ex inf.* Anthony Powell).

NOBLE. The Rev. William Noble, M.A. (Oxon) (b. 1691), was son of the Rev. Gawen Noble (d. 1693), schoolmaster at Appleby 1673-76, and at Cockermouth 1676, Minister of Cockermouth 1678-91, and Rector of Orton (C) 1691-93. He became Fellow of The Queen's College, Oxford, 1719 and was later Vicar of Sparsholt, Berks. *Arms.* Ermine three leopards' faces crowned Or (Glass in The Queen's College Hall).

NOBLE, of Holmhead. Irving Bell records James Noble as late of Holmhead, Bewcastle, in 1768. *Arms.* ... on a fess ... between two lions passant ... three annulets ... all within a bordure .... *Crest.* A (?) greyhound salient couped at the thigh and transfixed by an arrow (ABD). Field omits the bordure from the arms and describes the lions as passant guardant; and interprets the crest as a demi lion rampant (FAC).

NOBLE, of Kirklinton. Field quotes H. S. Cowper's MS as authority for the following arms for this family on an 18th century Kirklinton tombstone. *Arms.* ... on a fess ... three annulets ... (FAC).

NOEL; or, NEVILLE. Shield at Hutton-in-the-Forest. *Arms.* Or fretty Gules a canton Ermine.

NORFOLK, Duke of – see HOWARD, of Greystoke.

NORMAN. Robert Norman, son of John Norman, of Carlisle, left Cumberland *c.* 1790, settled in London, and bought property in Kent. *Arms.* Quarterly, 1 & 4, Argent on a bend Gules three bucks' heads cabossed of the field; 2 & 3, Gules on waves of the sea a ship of three masts Proper in chief three mullets Argent. *Crest.* A sea lion sejant resting its dexter paw on an anchor. *Motto.* Deus dabit vela (BHI).

NORMAN. The Rev. John Burton Norman, M.A. (Oxon) (d. 1906), only son of Robert Norman, of Kirkandrews-on-Eden, was Curate of Bowness-on-Solway 1853-56, Perpetual Curate of Grinsdale 1856-65, and Curate-in-charge and Rector of Little Stanmore, Middlesex, 1865-97. *Crest.* A stag's head erased Proper. *Motto.* Frangas non flectes (FBC).

NORTHBURGH. Roger de Northburgh, Bishop of Lichfield and Coventry 1322-58, became Rector of Bowness-on-Solway 1307. *Arms.* Crusilly three cinquefoils ... (BBE).

NORTHUMBERLAND. Shield at Hutton-in-the-Forest; a Vane quartering. *Arms.* Azure a lion rampant Argent. An unidentified shield at Hutton-in-the-Forest, displaying: Azure a lion rampant guardant Or, may also be intended for Northumberland.

NORTHUMBERLAND, Earl of – see PERCY.

NOWELL. John Nowell, aged 66 in 1767 (d. 1770), was for many years principal agent to Lord Carlisle, and lived in Naworth Castle, and latterly at Hepscott. He was son of Leonard Nowell, of Whalley (L). His dau. Maria Dorothea (b. 1733) marr. 1755 Richard Radcliffe, merchant of Cockermouth. *Arms.* . . . three covered cups . . . . *Crest.* An arm embowed in armour holding in the hand [a bomb fired] (Seal in HN).

NURSE. The Ven. Charles Euston Nurse, M.A. (Cantab), was Curate of Holy Trinity, Carlisle, 1932-37, Vicar of St. Nicholas, Whitehaven, 1937-48, Vicar of St. George, Barrow-in-Furness, 1948-58, Rural Dean of Dalton 1949-58, Archdeacon of Carlisle 1958-70, and Canon Residentiary of Carlisle 1958-73. *Arms.* Argent on a fess Gules between two chevrons of the second three crowns Or. *Crest.* An arm couped Proper issuant from a crown Or holding three snakes Vert. *Motto.* Justitia.

OGLE. The Rev. John Ogle, B.A. (Oxon), was vicar of Holm Cultram 1695-1715. A relative of the same names was headmaster of Blencow Grammar School 1688-97 and Curate of Hutton-in-the-Forest 1694. Another member of the family, the Rev. Henry Ogle, M.A. (Edin) (b. 1668), was Rector of Egremont 1692 until 1700, when he resigned. *Arms.* Argent a fess between three crescents Gules (HNF ii 192-4).

OGLE. Robert de Ogle, of Ogle (N) (d. 1362), after his marriage to Joan (d. 1365), dau. of Robert de Hepple, was seised of the manor of Thursby, which was demised to Richard Denton. It descended to his grandson Sir Robert Ogle (*c.* 1351/54-1410), whose descendant Robert, 1st Lord Ogle, died seised of it 1469 (HNF). *Arms.* Argent a fess between three crescents Gules (FFC; HBN).

OGLETHORPE. Owen Oglethorpe, D.D. (Oxon), said to have been illegitimate son of Owen Oglethorpe, of Newton Kyme (Y), was Vice-Chancellor of Oxford 1551, Dean of Windsor 1554, and Bishop of Carlisle 1557-59, when he was deprived, shortly before his death, for refusing to take the oath under the new Act of Uniformity. He has a place in history as the Bishop who crowned Elizabeth I (BPP). *Arms.* Quarterly Argent and Sable a cross quarterly Ermines and Ermine between four boars' heads couped counterchanged in the mouth of each an oak branch (BBE).

OLIPHANT, or OLLIVANT. John Oliphant, or Ollivant, a Penrith attorney (d. 1717), was father of Capt Thomas Ollivant, 21st Royal North British Fusiliers (1699-1747), who was at Dettingen, Fontenoy and Culloden. In 1724 he killed a brother officer in a duel at the Mitre tavern, Charing Cross. His will shows that he had houses and land in Hesket-in-the-Forest (CW2 xlvii). *Arms.* . . . three crescents . . . . *Crest.* An elephant (Seal on will of John Oliphant).

OLIPHANT, of Broadfield House. Lancelot Oliphant, of Itonfield, later known as Broadfield House, Hesket-in-the-Forest (d. 1809, aged 63), bought that estate together with Colt Close and Hay Close 1793. He was succ. by his son Henry Oliphant, of Broadfield House, Moorhouse Hill and Tally-ho Cottage, Hesket, who died 1843, leaving all his real estate to his relative, George Henry Hewitt, *q.v.* *Arms.* Gules three crescents Argent.

Crest. An elephant statant (BLG3; tombstone, Hesket-in-the-Forest churchyard).

OLLIVANT. In VEW vi 15-19 there is a pedigree of Ollivant, "formerly of Hutton-in-the-Wold, Cumberland." It is stated that John Ollivant, of that place, who marr. Elizabeth Bullough, was later of Manchester. Their son William Ollivant, of Ancoat's Hall, Manchester (1773-1847), formerly a clerk in the Admiralty, was father of Alfred Ollivant, B.A., D.D. (Cantab) (1798-1882), Bishop of Llandaff 1849-82. *Arms.* Gules three crescents Argent. *Crest.* A unicorn's head couped Argent armed and maned Or. *Motto.* Tout pourvoir (VEW). BBE, however, records that Bishop Ollivant bore: *Arms.* Gules a chevron between three crescents Argent.

BLACKETT-ORD. Mrs. Anne Dillingham Lewis, wife of Lt-Col St. Hilary Wilfred Tamar Lewis, of Reigny House, Newton Reigny, whom she marr. 1951, is 2nd dau. of Major John Reginald Blackett-Ord, J.P., of Whitfield Hall (N). *Arms.* Quarterly, 1 & 4, Per pale Sable and Azure three salmons hauriant Argent within a bordure engrailed Ermine (Ord); 2 & 3, Argent on a chevron between three mullets pierced Sable as many escallops of the field (Blackett). *Motto.* Nous travaillerons dans l'espérance (BLG18).

ORFEUR, of High Close. The history of this family will be found in JPP ii 190-218, which records that Thomas Orfeur, of Plumbland, was living *temp.* Edward II. Richard Orfeur was M.P. for Carlisle 1366; his descendant of the same name, living 1405, marr. Margery, dau. and heir of Robert Birkby, of Birkby. Their son Richard (living 1416) marr. Margaret, dau. and heir of Sir John Lamplugh, of Lamplugh, and his son Richard marr. Alice, dau. and coheir of Thomas Colville, of Hayton Castle. Their descendant William (d. 1614) was High Sheriff 1602, and his son William (d. 1660) was High Sheriff 1633. He was succ. by his son William (*c.* 1618-81) who was High Sheriff 1676. His son Charles Orfeur, J.P., of High Close (d. 1726), marr. 1695 Jane* (1663-1720), dau. of Richard Lamplugh, of Ribton, and widow of John Senhouse, of Netherhall. Their children were born there but in 1705 they left Netherhall and returned to Plumbland. Their daus. and coheirs were Anne (1696-1773), who marr. the Rev. Francis Yates, *q.v.*; Bridget (b. 1698), marr. 1723 Ralph Musgrave; Phoebe, d. an infant; Catherine (1701-75); Margaret (b. 1703), marr. 1736 the Rev. Lancelot Pattenson, *q.v.*; and Eleanor (d. 1745). The male line was continued by Charles' brother Philip Orfeur, of Kirkland, Kendal (d. 1733), whose son Capt John Orfeur left daus. only, of whom Catherine marr. Matthew Cavanagh and left issue. To a junior branch belonged Charles Howard Orfeur (1844-1931) and Richard Cuthbert Orfeur, of Manor Court, High Street, London, N.14, who died 1970, aged 89, leaving sons, Cyril and George; the latter had sons David and Peter. *Arms.* Sable a cross Argent a mullet of the second for difference (FCW). The mullet is sometimes pierced (JPP). DSL gives: Sable a cross Argent on a canton of the last a mullet Gules. *Crest.* A woman's bust Proper on her head a cross pattée fitché Or (FCW).

ORMATHWAITE, Baron – see BENN.

ORME – see GANDY.

ORTON, of Orton. Orton (C) was held by Simon de Orton, Justice of Assize 1225, and Coroner for Cumberland 1232. His descendant Sir John Orton

* She had two sons and six daus. by her 1st husband, and the same number by her 2nd husband. Her four sons died young.

was Knight of the Shire for Cumberland 1323, as was his son John (d. 1365) in 1360. His son Giles Orton (d. 1369) left a dau. and heir Joan, who marr. Sir Clement de Skelton, *q.v.*, and had four daus. and coheirs (CW2 xxxii, xl). *Arms.* FFC gives: Azure a lion rampant Argent. DAC and LMC give: Vert a lion rampant Argent crowned and armed Gules.

OSBALDESTON. Richard Osbaldeston, M.A., D.D. (Cantab) (1691-1764), 2nd son of Sir Richard Osbaldeston, of Hunmanby (Y) (d. 1728), was Vicar of Hunmanby 1715-62, Dean of York 1728-47, Bishop of Carlisle 1747-62, and Bishop of London 1762-64. *Arms.* In a window at Fulham these appear as: Argent a mascle Sable between three pellets (BBE). At the Visitation of Yorkshire 1665 Dugdale recorded: Argent a mascle Sable between three pellets a canton Gules. *Crest.* A knight on horseback in complete armour brandishing a sword on his shield the arms of Osbaldeston (CVY). The Bishop's arms are also on his monument in Hutton Buscel church (Y).

OSMOTHERLEY, of Langrigg and Dubmill. For the early history of this family, see CW2 xvi. Ranulph de Osmunderlaw by marr. *c.* 1290 to Agnes, dau. and coheir of Thomas de Langrigg, acquired that estate and Langrigg was the family home for many centuries. William de Osmunderlaw, a knight by 1402, was M.P. for Carlisle 1382/3, Knight of the Shire for Cumberland 1397-98, and High Sheriff 1402 and 1417. His descendant William Osmotherley (d. 1590) had sons Cuthbert (d. 1599), who succ. him, and William (d. 1618), for whom see below. From the said Cuthbert descended Cuthbert Osmotherley (d. 1745), who sold Langrigg Hall 1735 to Thomas Barwis, *q.v.,* husband of his dau. Elizabeth (1690-1780). His son the Rev. Salkeld Osmotherley (1702-63) was Vicar of Kirkby Fleetham (Y) 1729-63, and had a son Salkeld, said to have been a surgeon in the West Indies where he died unmarr., and daus. Mary (d. 1798, aged 61), wife of Abraham Mari Jonas De La Pierre, secretary to the French Ambassador; and Ann, wife of Watson Smith, of Kirkby Fleetham. The above mentioned William Osmotherley (d. 1618) bought Dubmill, Holm Cultram, and founded a branch of the family, which continued until John Osmotherley (d. 1741) left a dau. Frances who marr. 1733 Thomas Barwise, of Lowsay, and inherited the estate. The male line was continued by the descendants of her uncle Thomas (b. 1691), whose representatives in 1937 were John William Osmotherley, of Maryport, and John Osmotherley, of Flimby. *Arms.* Argent a fess Sable between three ravens Proper* (FCW). Harl. MS. No. 1536 and Machell give: Argent a fess between three martlets Sable (FVC; MMS vi 421). DSL gives for Sir William de Osmunderlaw, Sheriff 1402 and 1417: Argent a fess engrailed between three martlets Sable.

OSSOLINSKI, *anglicé* OSSALINSKY. Count Vladimir Boris Ossalinsky,† of Chestnut Hill, Keswick (d. 1859, aged 51), marr. 1839 Mary, dau. and heir of Edward Washington Jackson, *q.v.* Their son Capt Vladimir Boris Jackson Ossalinsky, of Skiddaw View, Main Street, Keswick, assumed his mother's surname in lieu of his own. *Arms.* The Polish Counts Ossolinski bore: Quarterly, 1 & 4, Gules a battle axe Argent hafted Or; 2 & 3, Per pale Argent and Gules an eagle displayed counterchanged; on a point in base,

* These arms, now almost indecipherable, with the initials of William and Frances Osmotherley, date 1682, and motto "Memento te esse mortalem" are on the lintel of the doorway to Dubmill.

† In 1843 his effects were sold under a writ of *fieri facias.*

Azure a lion rampant crowned Or. *Crest.* A demi lion rampant crowned Or holding in the paws a battle axe Argent hafted Or (RAG).

OSTLE – see SEWELL.

OWEN. GMS records the following, without specifying any place of residence, and without tinctures. *Arms.* A boar tied to a tree on a mount in base. BGA gives this coat for Owen, of Pembrokeshire.

OXFORD, University of. *Arms.* Azure an open book Proper leathered Gules with seven straps Or the pages inscribed 'Dominus illuminatio mea' the whole between three open crowns Gold (Shield on monument in Carlisle Cathedral to Richard Assheton, 1st Viscount Cross, *q.v.*).

PAKENHAM. Impaled by Vane on shield at Hutton-in-the-Forest; Col the Hon. William Lyonel Vane, D.L., J.P. (1859-1920), marr. 1904 Lady Katharine Louisa Pakenham (d. 1954), younger dau. of the 4th Earl of Longford. *Arms.* Quarterly Or and Gules in the first quarter an eagle displayed Vert.

PALEY. A family long settled at Langcliffe near Settle, the most distinguished member of which was the Ven. William Paley, D.D. (Cantab) (1743-1805), author of *A View of the Evidences of Christianity,* Rector of Musgrave 1775-77, Vicar of Dalston 1776-93, Vicar of St. Lawrence, Appleby, 1777-89, Prebendary of Carlisle 1780-95, Rector of Great Salkeld 1782-1805. *Arms.* Gules a bend Vair between six cross crosslets Argent. *Crest.* In front of a stag's head couped Proper a cross crosslet Or. *Motto.* Cervus non servus (BLG5).

PALMER, of Scaleby Hill. John Palmer, yeoman, of Scaleby Hill, died 1761, aged 86. *Arms.* . . . a chevron . . . between three palmers' scrips . . . (Gravestone, Scaleby churchyard).

PALMER, of Wallhead. John Palmer, of Wallhead, Crosby-on-Eden, yeoman (d. 1761), was father of William Palmer (d. 1735, aged 22). *Arms.* . . . on a bend sinister . . . between in dexter chief a mullet pierced . . . and in sinister base an escallop . . . a hound passant to the sinister . . . (Gravestone, Crosby-on-Eden churchyard).

PARISH. Commander Frank Reginald Woodbine Parish, D.S.O., R.N., of Tomkins Farmhouse, Martley, Worcs., marr. 1928 Millicent Dora, dau. and coheir of William Wybergh James, *q.v.,* and has two daus., Prudence Elizabeth Woodbine, marr. 1956 Major Peter Richard Heaton-Ellis, and Carolyn Angela Jane, actress, who is of Redmain Gill, Cockermouth. *Arms.* Argent on a chevron Sable between ten cross crosslets six in chief and four in base of the last a cross crosslet fitché of the first a chief Azure issuant therefrom a sun in splendour Or. *Motto.* Justem et tenacem (BLG18).

PARKE, of Whitbeck. Lawrence Parke (d. 1691), who was disclaimed by Dugdale 1665, was of a family long established in Whitbeck, and bought the manor and advowson of Whitbeck 1687. He marr. 1661 Agnes Latus (d. 1671), and was succ. by their son John Parke, of Whitbeck Hall, now Townend (1664-99). He marr. Dorothy Hudleston,* of Hutton John, and was succ. by their son Hudleston Parke (1689-1738). His grandson Charles sold the estate 1807 to Lord Lonsdale. From his younger brother Lt-Gen William Parke, of the Thickets, Jamaica (d. 1813), whose son Charles (1791-1860) bought the Henbury estate, Dorset, 1847, descended Richard Parke (b. 1905), the head of the family in 1937 (BLG15). *Arms.* Azure on a fess

* She later marr. John Warburton, Somerset Herald, the antiquary, for whom see DNB.

engrailed between three hinds trippant Or as many torteaux each charged with a pheon of the field. *Crest.* A stag's head couped Sable holding in the mouth a key Or. *Motto.* True and fast (BGA). MVC gives: *Arms.* Argent on a fess Sable three escallops of the field a canton Ermines.* *Crest.* A stag's head couped in its mouth a branch (FAC).

PARKER, of Old Town and of Warwick Hall. Christopher Parker, of Old Town, Hesket-in-the-Forest (d. 1686), was grandfather of Christopher Parker (d. 1776), who had issue, *int. al.,* Thomas (b. 1732) and John (b., 1737); from the latter descend the Parkers of Petterill Green, Skirwith Abbey, Warwick Hall and the Laithes, *q.v.* Thomas Parker (1732-1807) was father of Thomas Parker (1784-1828) who bought Warwick Hall from Robert Warwick, *q.v.,* and was High Sheriff of Cumberland for a few weeks in 1828. He was succ. at Warwick Hall by his brother William Parker, J.P. (1789-1856), who bought Skirwith Abbey 1822. Dying unmarr. he was succ. there by his kinsman the Rev. Christopher Parker (see Parker of Skirwith Abbey), and at Old Town and Warwick Hall by the latter's nephew Thomas Holme Parker. *Arms.* Azure two bars gemel Argent between three bucks' heads erased Or all between two flaunches of the last. *Crest.* A cubit arm vested Vert cuffed Argent holding in the hand the attire of a stag and a bow and arrow saltirewise all Proper (BGA).

PARKER, of Skirwith Abbey and Warwick Hall. The Rev. John Parker (1737-79), younger son of Christopher Parker, of Old Town, *q.v.,* was father of Christopher Parker, D.L., J.P., of Petterill Green (1775-1838), High Sheriff of Cumberland 1830, who was father of Robert Holme Parker, the Rev. Christopher Parker, and William Parker. Robert Holme Parker, J.P. (1812-47), succ. to Petterill Green and was father of Thomas Holme Parker, D.L., J.P. (1842-1901), who was High Sheriff 1873, and succ. his kinsman at Old Town (which he sold 1889) and at Warwick Hall, which his trustees sold. His son Major Cuthbert James Vere Holme Parker (1880-1966), the last of the family, died unmarr. The Rev. Christopher Parker, J.P., M.A. (Cantab) (1816-65), above mentioned, succ. to Skirwith Abbey and was succ. by his son Edward Wilson Parker, J.P. (1853-1932). His son Major Frederick Cyril Francis Parker (1888-1970), the last male descendant, was of Skirwith Abbey, Newbiggin Hall (W), and Beaumont, Penrith. His daus. were Pamela Mary Elizabeth (1922-67), marr. Victor Dunn; and Bridget Mariota, marr. Gerald Archer. *Arms* and *Crest.* As preceding entry. *Motto.* Virtutis alimentum honos (BLG17; FD7).

PARKER, of Carleton Hill and The Laithes. William Parker, D.L., J.P. of Carleton Hill, Penrith (1819-92), 5th son of Christopher Parker (d. 1838), see preceding entry, Parker of Skirwith Abbey and Warwick Hall, was father of the Rev. William Hasell Parker, M.A. (Oxon), of Carleton Hill (1855-1935), Vicar of All Saints, Cockermouth, 1881-1935 and Hon. Canon of Carlisle; of Edward Thomas Parker, J.P., of Carleton Hill (1862-1942); and of Christopher John Parker, D.L., J.P. (1859-1932), who bought The Laithes, Skelton. Christopher Miles Parker, his son (b. 1886), who was Master of the Brampton Harriers 1914-19, was father of Christopher Peter Parker, who is the only male descendant of Christopher Parker (d. 1686). *Arms* and *Crest.* As Parker, of Old Town and of Warwick Hall.

PARKER, of Moorhouse Hill. William Parker, of Moorhouse Hill, Hesket-

* Not Pean, as stated by Field (FAC).

in-the-Forest (1711-89), and Ann his wife (1710-76) had seven children – four sons and three daughters – between 1736 and 1752. By 1769 all were dead *s.p.* and William adopted his great-nephew Isaac Field (1765-1830) and left him his estate on condition that he assumed the surname Parker. Field (FAC) states that Isaac's dau. and heir [Mary] marr. (1) [Robert Sanderson] Milbourne and (2) [Christopher] Parker, but it is incorrect to call Mary Isaac's dau. and heir for he was father of Matthew Grave Parker (b. 1798) who had a son Isaac Ellison Parker (d. 1881, aged 39), and in any case Mary was the eldest of four daus. *Arms* (granted to Isaac Field, *post* Parker, 1790). Vert two bars ermine between three stags' heads erased Or. *Crest.* A mount Vert thereon a stag reguardant Proper collar and line reflexed over the back Or its dexter forefoot resting on a shield erect Azure charged with a garb Gold (CA xvii/266). *Motto.* Medio tutissimus ibis (FBC).

PARKER, of Parknook. The Parker family have lived at Parknook, Gosforth, for over 300 years. The estate descended to Timothy Parker (1748-1805) who marr. 1778 Ann (d. 1819, aged 57), dau. of Alexander Hoskins, of Broughton Hill. His 3rd son Captain Charles Parker, R.N. (1785-1872), was father of Captain Charles Allan Parker, R.M. (1813-54), whose son Charles Arundel Parker, J.P., M.D., F.R.C.S., F.S.A. (1851-1918),* was grandfather of the present head of the family, Charles Gordon Parker, of Parknook. *Arms.* Gules a chevron between three leopards' faces Or. *Crest.* A leopard's head erased and guardant Or ducally gorged Gules (BLG17; CW2 xviii 243-45; M.I., Melling church). *Motto.* Hurrah, hurrah (FBC).

PARKER, of Acorn Bank and Lattendales. William Parker, D.L., J.P. (d. 1879), a descendant of the Parkers of Parknook, *q.v.*, acquired *c.* 1835 Ware Park, Herts., where he was succ. by his son Commander John Harry Eyres Parker, J.P., R.N. (1845-88), whose son William Francis Parker, J.P. (1873-1929), succ. but moved in 1909 to Westmorland as tenant of Warcop House until 1913 when he went to Acorn Bank. His elder son John Warneford Parker succ. him in the tenancy and was there until 1934, when he bought Lattendales, Greystoke, where he lived until 1945 when he moved to Edenbrows, the house inherited by his wife, the dau. and heir of Norman Fletcher, *q.v.* He now lives in Penrith. His younger brother Francis Brian Everard Parker (d. 1977) was of Woodleigh, Southwaite. *Arms* and *Crest.* As Parker of Parknook, *q.v. Motto.* Sapere aude.

PARKER, of Tarn. This family descends from Thomas Parker, of Bootle (d. *c.* 1510). His descendant John Parker, of Tarn† (b. *c.* 1570), was ancestor of Richard Parker, of Tarn (1725-1805), father of John Parker (b. 1770) and the Rev. Richard Parker (1773-1826), Curate of Satterthwaite (L) 1816-26. The above John Parker (b. 1770) was father of Richard Parker, J.P., of Tarn and Flatts, and afterwards of Underwood House, Bootle (1812-92). His son John Parker, of Tarn and Flatts (1839-1907), marr. 1878 Mary (d. 1912), dau. and heir of Thomas Grindall. Their son John Parker (1883-1955) succ. to Tarn and Flatts and was later of Tarn Estate, Concession, Rhodesia. His son John Anthony Grindal Parker, I.C.D., of Mount Pleasant, Salisbury, Rhodesia, former member of the Council of the University of Rhodesia, and

* Author of *The Gosforth District,* 1904; new edition, revised by W. G. Collingwood, 1926.

† Mr. Michael Butler-Cole tells us that local tradition is that this house was built from materials from shipwrecks, and the saying is that "it came from the sea, and will go back to the sea," an allusion to the sea's inroads on the Bootle coast.

Permanent Secretary for Defence, is now head of the family. His eldest son, Trevor John Anthony de Grindall Parker, B.Ch.B. (Birm), D.M.R.D. (Eng), F.R.C.R., formerly Senior Registrar and Clinical Tutor, Royal Postgraduate Medical School, London, is now of A.M.A. House, West Perth, Western Australia (DX/640-1, R.O. Carlisle). *Arms.* Azure a cross quarterly Or and Ermine between four frets of the second. *Crest.* A crest-fan Azure thereon a fret Or. *Badge.* Two arrows the points enfiling a plain circlet all Or. *Mottoes.* Below the shield: Je maintiendrai; Above the crest: Fret not (CA 137/70).

PARKER. The Rev. Arthur Henry Neville Parker, M.A. (Dunelm) (1862-1922), Rector of Greystoke 1914-22, was descended from the Parker family, of Browsholme (L). *Arms.* Vert a chevron between three bucks' heads cabossed Or. *Crest.* A stag trippant Proper. *Motto.* Nec fluctu nec flatu movetur (BLG18).

PARKER. Irving Bell recorded the gravestones in Brampton Old churchyard of . . . Parker, of Brampton, 1759, and . . . Parker, of Brampton, butcher, 1771(?). *Arms.* . . . a stag's head cabossed . . . between two flaunches . . . (ABD).

PARKIN, of Skirsgill and The Laithes. For the earlier history of this family, see AWL. Hugh Parkin (1753-1838) was sent out to India by his kinsman John Robinson, M.P., and on his return acquired Skirsgill, Penrith; he was High Sheriff of Cumberland 1797. By his marr. to Sarah Margaret (1770-1858), dau. of William McDowall, he was father of, *int. al.,* James Parkin (1797-1860), who bought the Laithes estate, Skelton, 1840, when he was of Greenways, Penrith; the estate was sold to Christopher John Parker, *q.v.,* 1885. One of James's younger brothers, the Rev. Charles Parkin, M.A. (Oxon) (1799-1884), was father of Paxton William Parkin, J.P. of Sharrow Bay (1839-1912), whose youngest dau. Hilda Margaret (d. 1957) marr. 1914 Brigadier General Francis Henry Guy Stanton, R.A. (1873-1928), and lived at Lattendales, Greystoke. Another younger brother of James, above (1797-1860), was Anthony Parkin, of Sharrow Bay (1803-90). *Arms.* Argent an eagle displayed Sable langued Gules and in chief a label of three points of the second on a canton Or a fess dancetté between six billets also of the second each charged with an ermine spot. *Crest.* Out of a ducal coronet Or a pine cone Vert. *Motto.* Honeste audax (HMC). Two slightly different versions of the Parkin bearings are on the monuments in Dacre church to (1) James Parkin, above (1797-1860), and (2) his younger brother, Anthony Parkin, above (1803-90), viz. (1) *Arms.* Argent an eagle displayed Sable on a canton also Argent *(sic)* a fess engrailed Or between six billets Gules. *Crest.* A pineapple Proper. (2) *Arms.* . . . an eagle displayed . . . on a canton . . . a fess dancetté . . . between six billets . . . each charged with an ermine spot . . . .

PARKIN. The Rev. John Parkin, M.A. (Cantab), of Seaton (d. 1887), a native of Workington, was Vicar of Halton, Hastings, 1838-87. His eldest son John Samuel Parkin, M.A. (Cantab), of Seaton and of Low Wood Nook, barrister at law (1843-1931), was a Commissioner under the Universities of Oxford and Cambridge Act 1877. His brother Thomas Parkin, J.P., M.A. (Cantab), of The Tarns, Holme St. Cuthbert, and of Fairseat, High Wickham, Hastings (1845-1932), was Lieut, Royal Cumberland Militia (VAC). *Arms* (granted to John Samuel Parkin 1890). Argent an eagle displayed Sable charged on the breast with a cross pattée fitché Or two flaunches of the second each charged with as many billets paleways of the third. *Crest.* An eagle displayed Sable holding in each claw a cross pattée fitché Or and charged on each wing with a billet also Or (CA lxv/192). *Motto.* Honesta audax (FD7).

PARKIN-MOORE – see MOORE.

PARKINS. Harl. MS. 1536 shews John Parkins, of [?] Hudlo, or Hurtlow, as bearing *Arms.* Gules two chevrons between three escallops Argent. *Crest.* Out of a ducal coronet Or an unicorn's head Ermine crined bearded and armed Or (FVC; MVC).

PARR. Sir William Parr, K.G., of Kendal (1434-83), was High Sheriff of Cumberland 1471. For fuller details of this family, to which belonged Katherine Parr, Henry VIII's last wife, see AWL. *Arms.* Argent two bars Azure. These arms are on the ceiling of Carlisle Cathedral, and quartering Roos, they are on the tomb at Lanercost of Humphrey, Lord Dacre, who marr. the above Sir William Parr's sister Mabel. The family later bore: Argent two bars Azure a bordure engrailed Sable, which coat is given by Fuller for Sir William Parr (FWE), whilst DSL gives: Quarterly, 1 & 4, Or three water bougets Sable (L[d] [Roos] of Kendal); 2 & 3, Argent two bars Azure within a bordure engrailed Sable (Parre).

PARSABLE, of Row Beck. On the exterior wall of Dearham church is a tablet to John Parsable,* of Row Beck (d. 1802, aged 74), Sarah [Grisdale] his wife (d. 1769, aged 40), whom he marr. 1753, and other members of the family. Their son the Rev. William Parsable (1760-1837) was Perpetual Curate of Borrowdale 1804-37 and Vicar of Gilcrux 1826-37. The tablet also commemorates William Parsable, stone-cutter (d. 1841, aged 47), who marr. 1816 Sarah Allison, who in 1847 was a tea dealer at Dearham, and their son Henry, drowned in the river at Row Beck 1836, aged 9½. *Crest.* An arm in armour embowed grasping an arrow fesswise above the hand a fleur-de-lys. *Motto.* Disce vivere, pati mori (Tablet at Dearham church).

PARTIS, of Tallantire. Matthias Partis, tobacco merchant of Newcastle, and Sheriff of that city (d. 1718), marr. 1688 Anne (d. 1721, aged 53), dau. of Henry Fletcher, of Tallantire, *q.v.*, to which their son† Fletcher (1692-1758), High Sheriff of Cumberland, 1734, succ. He was succ. by his brother Henry Partis (1697-1766), a prominent Newcastle merchant, who was Sheriff of that city 1745, and Mayor 1752 and 1760. His son Henry Fletcher Partis‡ (d. unmarr. at Tallantire Hall 1775, aged 37) was succ. by his kinsman Hendry Hopper, of Durham, who sold the estate 1776 to William Browne, *q.v.* *Arms.* Per fess Argent and Gules three bucks' heads cabossed counterchanged (MSN). Field incorrectly quotes Denton Sheriffs as authority for: Per pale Argent and gules three bucks' heads cabossed counterchanged (FAC).

PARVYNG. Robert Parvyng was ordained by the Bishop of Carlisle 1299 and became Rector of Hutton-in-the-Forest. His relative and namesake Sir Robert Parvyng§ (d. 1343) became one of the most eminent of English

* He was of Dovenby and Great Broughton and appears in Bridekirk parish register in 1753 as John Passible!

† Thomas Partis, who was buried at Crosthwaite in 1747, having been "found dead in Mr. Laithes' park and stript naked," may have been their son.

‡ The *Newcastle Courant* said in 1775 "His nearest relative is a poor man who sells ballads in the streets."

§ Not Parning, as in DNB.

lawyers. He was a large landowner in Cumberland and was Knight of the Shire 1325, 1327-28 and 1331-32. He became Chief Justice of the King's Bench 1340, and was Chancellor of England 1341-43. His heirs were his sisters Joan (d. 1349), wife of John Pacock, and Emma, wife of John de Scaleby. The former's heir was her son Sir Adam Pacok (d. *c.* 1380-1), who assumed the name Parvyng and was Sheriff 1368-71 and Knight of the Shire 1357-58 and 1373. His son and heir Sir Robert Parvyng (d. *c.* 1405-6), Sheriff 1382, was the last male (CW2 xix). *Arms.* . . . three mullets . . . and a bordure engrailed . . . (MMD).*

PATRICKSON, of Ennerdale. Col Ralph P. Littledale in CW2 xxv traced the tangled history of many branches of this family, known as "Kings of Ennerdale." In 1514-15 John Patrickson paid 4d rent for a house on Kelton Common. In 1548 Henry, Marquess of Dorset, sold lands in Egremont and St. Bees to Anthony Patrickson, who in 1549 leased the tithes of Ennerdale and Kinniside and later Salter Grange, Lamplugh. He was the builder of Carswell How. His four sons Roger (d. 1583), William (living 1603), John and Anthony all founded families at Stawbank (Lamplugh), sold before 1622; at Carswell How; Weddiker (Arlecdon); and Stockhow (Lamplugh), respectively. Weddiker was sold by William Patrickson 1652, while Thomas Patrickson sold Carswell How in 1685. To the latter branch belonged John Patrickson (1611-52) who owned Calder Abbey, which descended to his son Richard Patrickson, J.P. (1647-1706), High Sheriff of Cumberland 1672, whose son Richard sold the property. Stockhow was inherited by William Patrickson (d. 1645), and descended to Thomas Patrickson (1670-1735), who sold the estate. His son Anthony was living in 1755, a bachelor and destitute. A junior branch was founded by Anthony Patrickson, of Scalegill, St. Bees (d. 1729). His male line failed with his son Thomas, merchant of Whitehaven (1701-46), who marr. Martha (d. 1762, aged 79), sister of Christopher Wilson, of Bardsey (L), see AWL, by whom he had an only son Anthony (1721-25). His heirs were his sisters Isabella (b. 1681), marr. 1712 John Ponsonby, of Haile, *q.v.*; Frances (1683-1767), marr. Isaac Langton, *q.v.*; Bridget (1692-1738), marr. 1721 John Benn; and Mary (b. 1694), marr. Capt William Braithwaite, of Col Cockran's Regt. *Arms.* At the Visitation of 1665, Thomas Patrickson recorded on behalf of his father Joseph Patrickson of Carswell How: Or a fess between three greyhounds courant Sable a crescent for difference. *Crest.* On a mount a stag courant reguardant all Proper unguled and attired Argent (FCW). At the same Visitation, Thomas Patrickson, of Stockhow, although apparently belonging to a branch junior to that of Carswell How, recorded an undifferenced version of the *Arms,* viz. Or a fess between three greyhounds courant Sable. *Crest.* On a mount a stag courant reguardant all Proper (FCW). Fleming recorded the same arms (FDC), as did Lysons who, however, recorded the *Crest* as: On a mount Vert a stag courant Proper hoofed and attired Or (LMC). Denton recorded also a variant of the *Arms:* Argent three greyhounds courant Sable terreted (DAC). On a monument in St. Bees church the arms formerly appeared as . . . a fess . . . between three greyhounds courant . . . ; impaling, . . . three wolves' heads . . . (Wilson)

* Field suggests that a coat on the ceiling of Carlisle Cathedral, which he blazoned as: Azure three stars within a bordure engrailed Or, may be for Parvyng or Waverton, *q.v.* (CW2 xxxiv 28-9).

(CWE, where, however, the impaled coat is wrongly said to have been Benn).*

PATRICKSON. Without stating any place of residence, Harl. MS 1536 gives the following *Arms.* Argent three birds Proper on a chief Azure the sun in his splendour (FVC).

PATRICKSON, of Houghton Town Head and Low Crosby. Hugh Patrickson, of Knells, Stanwix (d. 1712), was father of, *int. al.,* John (see Patrickson, of Knells), and of an older son William, whose grandson William (1746-1813) was of Houghton Town Head. He marr. 1790 Elizabeth Wilson of Low Crosby (d. 1794, aged 34), and apparently acquired that estate which was inherited by their son William (1793-1846). Sarah (b. 1753), aunt of the last named, marr. 1784 Thomas Phillips, *q.v.* In 1937, according to Field, the Houghton Town Head family was represented by Hugh Patrickson, of Chile (FAC). *Arms.* . . . a fess . . . between three hounds courant . . . (Monument to William Patrickson, above, d. 1846, in Crosby-on-Eden churchyard). Field quotes LMC as authority for: Or a fess between three greyhounds courant Sable. *Crest.* On a mount Vert a stag courant Proper hoofed and attired Or (FAC; LMC). *Motto.* Mente et manu (M.I. in Stanwix church).

PATRICKSON, of Knells. According to Field, this family owned land at Cargo in 1590. Hugh Patrickson, of Knells, was ancestor through his eldest son William of the Houghton Town Head family. A younger son John (1681-1771) was grandfather of Hugh, Captain 4th Light Dragoons (1759-1821). The latter had an only son Hugh Patrickson, D.L., J.P. (1781-1858), who was of Kirklinton Park, which he built 1822, and St. Mary Holme, Lanercost, which he acquired by marr. 1837 to Margaret, dau. of Thomas Tallentire and sister and heir of Thomas Calvert Tallentire. He left the former estate to Hugh, son of his first cousin Hugh Patrickson, saddler, of Scotch Street, Carlisle (d. 1867, aged 58). Hugh Patrickson, junior, J.P. (1843-97), was in early life a compositor on the *Penrith Observer* and the *Carlisle Express* and later a reporter on the *Carlisle Patriot.* In 1901 Kirklinton Park was owned by Hugh Patrickson, of Poplar House, Hayton. *Arms* and *Crest.* As Patrickson, of Houghton Town Head and Low Crosby.

PATTENSON, of Melmerby Hall. John Pattenson, a Penrith attorney (d. 1705), marr. 1672 Mary (1651-1738), dau. of Roger Sleddall, of Penrith (d. 1667), and sister and coheir of Roger Sleddall (d. 1697). Their younger son John was of Carleton Hall, Penrith (see Pattenson, of Carleton Hall); their eldest son Thomas (1673-1742) was of Breaks Hall, Ormside, and by his marr. (1) 1694 to Elizabeth (d. 1710), dau. and coheir of the Rev. William Thirkeld, of Melmerby Hall, *q.v.,* acquired that estate. He marr. (2) 1712 Deborah (d. 1741), dau. and coheir of Samuel Mottram, of Thorpe Hall, Lincs., and widow of Richard Crackanthorpe. He was succ. by his son the Rev. Lancelot Pattenson, B.A. (Cantab) (1706-59), Rector of Ousby 1735-59 and of Melmerby 1739-59, who marr. 1736 Margaret (d. 1777), 5th dau. and coheir of Charles Orfeur, *q.v.* Their son and heir Thomas (1747-1811)† was High Sheriff of Cumberland 1793 and marr. 1768 Barbara (d. 1781), dau. of John Grainger, of Bromfield, *q.v.* Their son John Pattenson, Bengal

* For the correct arms of Wilson, of Bardsea, see AWL.

† In his will he directed "Dinner at my funeral to be in the barn, cold roast beef, hot potatoes, cheese and plenty of racked ale, but no smoking for fear of fire".

C.S. (1774-1817), marr. 1801 Mary Anna Frances Antoinetta (d. 1837), eldest dau. of Stephen Harris, *q.v.*, and their son John Edward (1811-64) sold the Melmerby estate 1846. His younger brother, the Rev. Robert Cane Pattenson (1816-1904) was Rector of Melmerby 1843-81. *Arms.* Argent on a fess Sable three fleurs-de-lys Or (LMC). On hatchments in Melmerby church, the shield is also charged with a label of three points Gules. *Crest.* Out of a ducal coronet Or a camel's head Proper. *Motto.* Pie repone te.

PATTENSON, of Carleton Hall. John Pattenson, attorney (1681-1721), son of John Pattenson (d. 1705), see Pattenson, of Melmerby Hall, acquired Branthwaite Hall and Carleton Hall, Penrith. He marr. 1706 Elizabeth, dau. and heir of John Lough, of Blencarn, *q.v.* His only son Christopher Pattenson (d. 1756), succ. and was High Sheriff of Cumberland 1746.* His three sisters and coheirs were Elizabeth, marr. Thomas Simpson, *q.v.*; Dorothy, marr. John Raincock; and Mary, marr. William Adderton. *Arms, Crest* and *Motto.* As Pattenson, of Melmerby Hall.

PATTINSON. John Pattinson, of Harraby, gentleman, sealed his will (proved 1726) with the following *Arms.* . . . four mullets in fess . . . between two bars . . . (Record Office, Carlisle).

PATTINSON, of Alston and Salkeld Hall. Hugh Lee Pattinson, F.R.S., later of Scot's House, West Boldon (D), metallurgical chemist (1796-1858), was born at Alston, son of Thomas Pattinson, retail trader there. After working for some years as clerk and assistant to Anthony Clapham, soap-boiler, in Newcastle upon Tyne, he was appointed 1825 assay-master in Alston to the lords of the manor, the Greenwich Hospital Commissioners, *q.v.* He discovered a process for separating silver from lead-ore, and in 1834 established chemical works at Felling, later at Washington (D) (DNB). His grandson Major Hugh Lee Pattinson, of Scot's House and of Stotes Hall, Jesmond (1854-1924), was father of Air Marshal Sir Lawrence Arthur Pattinson, K.B.E., C.B., D.S.O., M.C., D.F.C., of Salkeld Hall (1890-1955) (VAC). *Arms.* Sable semé of drops of silver issuant from the base flames of fire Proper. *Crest.* In front of flames of fire a dexter hand bendwise holding an ingot of silver all Proper. *Motto.* Ex vile pretiosa (Granted in allusion to the discovery by Hugh Lee Pattinson of a process for the separation of silver from lead) (BGA).

PAULTON. Shield at Hutton-in-the-Forest; a Vane quartering. *Arms.* Or on a fess between three mullets Sable as many bezants.

PAYNE. Arthur Lavington Payne, J.P., of Staffield Hall, Kirkoswald (1860-1917), was 2nd son of Sir Salusbury Gillies Payne, 5th Bart.† His monument in Kirkoswald church says that it was "erected by friends and colleagues in business in the City of Manchester in appreciation of his character and kindly consideration at all times." His son James Ralph Salusbury Payne, Lieut Seaforth Highlanders, attached the Tank Corps, killed in action in France 1918, aged 30, is also commemorated in the church. *Arms.* Gules a fess between two lions passant Argent. *Crest.* A lion's jamb erased and erect Argent grasping a broken tilting spear Gules. *Motto.* Malo mori quam foedari (BGA; DPB; M.I., Kirkoswald church).

* As such it fell to him to see that the executions of the Jacobite prisoners of the 'Forty-Five were carried out.

† He died 1893, when his son and heir Charles Robert Salusbury Payne assumed the baronetcy, but he discontinued the use of the title *c.* 1900. For details of this disputed title, see DPB 1897.

PEACOCK. John Peacock, of Murrah, Greystoke (d. at Denton, Co. Durham, 1798, aged 87), was father of the Rev. Thomas Peacock (1756-1851), who was born at Caldbeck; he was Perpetual Curate of Denton (D) 1780-1835 and was father of the Very Rev. George Peacock, M.A., D.D. (Cantab) (1791-1858), Dean of Ely 1839-58. *Arms.* Sable three peacocks in their pride Argent a chief embattled Or (Window in St. Oswald's, Durham).

PEARCE – see MARTIN.

PEARS, of Brampton. Thomas Pears, of Brampton, maltster (d. 1747), had by Elizabeth his wife a son John, who was under 21 in 1747. *Arms.* . . . three pears stalks downwards . . . , two and one, and three crosses pommé with plain lower limbs . . . , one and two (ABD).

PEARS, of Brampton. John Pears, of Brampton, staymaker, died 1780, aged 61. *Arms.* . . . a chevron . . . between three pears . . . (Tombstone, Farlam churchyard).

PEARS,* of Walton. Thomas Pears, of Walton, died 1747, aged 52. *Arms.* . . . a chevron . . . between a cross pattée . . . in chief and a star of four points . . . in base. *Crest.* An escallop (Tombstone, Walton churchyard).

PEARS, *post* PEARS-ARCHBOLD. William Pears, of Carlisle, later of Fenham Hall, near Newcastle upon Tyne, obtained a grant of arms in 1870, as did his son James Archbold Pears, who in accordance with the will of Jane Archbold, of Gallowgate, Newcastle, then assumed the name and arms of Archbold. *Arms* (granted to William Pears). Gules two bendlets nebuly Or between two unicorns' heads erased of the last each charged with an estoile of the first. *Crest.* Upon a rock Proper a wyvern Vert gorged with a collar gemel Or supporting with the dexter claw an escutcheon also Or charged with an estoile Or (CA lvii/230). His son was granted the *Arms* of Archbold: Argent a lion rampant Sable holding between the paws a fret Azure in base a fleur-de-lys of the last on a chief also Azure two fleurs-de-lys of the first. *Crest.* Two lions' gambs erased each encircled with a wreath of oak Proper holding an escutcheon Argent charged with a fleur-de-lys Azure (CA lvii/238). *Motto.* Vi et virtute (FBC).

PEARSON, of Carlisle. John Pearson, of Castle Street, Carlisle, attorney (d. 1774), was Town Clerk of Carlisle 1740-73, serving during the occupation of the city by the Jacobite army in the '45. On the recapture of the city he was, on the orders of the Duke of Cumberland; arrested with Joseph Backhouse, the Mayor, and sent in custody to London; both were eventually released. He was an alderman of the city 1761-73. He marr. 1738 Elizabeth (d. 1777), sister and coheir of William Fothergill, *q.v.* His son Thomas Pearson succ. him as Town Clerk in 1773. *Arms.* Per fess embattled . . . and . . . three suns in their splendour. *Crest.* A dove close in its beak a sprig of olive (Seal of John Pearson).

PEARSON, of Cardew Lodge. John Barrington Pearson, O.B.E., of Cardew Lodge, Dalston (1883-1955), son of Richard Pearson, was managing director of Messrs. Cowans Sheldon, and was High Sheriff of Cumberland 1942. His dau. and heir Jean Leeper Pearson marr. 1951 David Cameron Smail, of The Trees, Ottoline Drive, Troon. *Arms.* Or a bend company Sable and Argent between two bull's heads cabossed of the second. *Crest.* A bull's head

* Field wrongly recorded this surname as PEARSON (FAC).

couped affronté Sable between two sprigs of heather Proper. *Motto.* Nec temere nec timide.

PEASE. Elinor Dorothea, Viscountess Rochdale, C.B.E., J.P., who marr. 1931 the 1st Viscount Rochdale, *q.v.*, is 2nd surviving dau. of Ernest Hubert Pease, of Lodge House, Bembridge, Isle of Wight, and of Mowden, Darlington (d. 1928). *Arms.* Per fess Azure and Gules a fess nebuly Ermine between two lambs passant in chief Argent and in base upon a mount Proper a dove rising Argent holding in the beak a pea-stalk the blossom and pods also Proper (BLG15).

PEILE. John Peile, J.P. (1776-1855), was for 37 years Lord Lonsdale's chief colliery agent and for 45 years a trustee of the town and harbour of Whitehaven. *Arms.* Argent a bend between two mullets Sable. *Crest.* A demi man in armour affronté sinister hand on hip in the dexter hand a sword. *Motto.* Malo mori quam foedari (Monument, St. James' church, Whitehaven).

PELHAM. Charles Pelham, of Brocklesby, Lincs., marr. (3) Elizabeth, dau. of Michael Warton and sister and coheir of Sir Michael Warton, *q.v.*, on whose death *s.p.* 1725 the Cumberland estates bequeathed to him by Henry Curwen, *q.v.*, passed to their son Charles Pelham (d. *s.p.* 1763), who left them to his great-nephew Charles Anderson (d. 1823, cr. Baron Yarborough 1794). *Arms.* Quarterly, 1 and 4, Azure three pelicans Argent vulning themselves Proper; 2 and 3, Gules two belts erect Argent decorated with buckles and studs Or (BP105).

PENNINGTON, Baron Muncaster. The history of this family has been admirably told by Joseph Foster in *Penningtoniana* (1878). Gamel de Pennington, Lord of Pennington *temp.* Henry II, who heads the pedigree, gave Pennington and Muncaster churches to Conishead Priory. To his descendant Alan, Richard de Lucy gave Ravenglass 1208. From him descended Sir Alan Pennington (d. 1415) who marr. Katherine, dau. and coheir of Sir Richard de Preston. Their son Sir John (d. 1470), High Sheriff of Cumberland 1427 and 1430, sheltered Henry VI after Towton 1461, and was given the Luck of Muncaster. His son John, High Sheriff 1434 and 1459, died *v.p.* His son Sir John (d. 1512), High Sheriff 1510, succ. and was succ. by his son John (d. 1516), whose dau. and heir Isabel marr. Thomas Dykes, *q.v.* His cousin John (d. 1522), High Sheriff 1522, succ. and was succ. by another cousin Sir William Pennington (d. 1532) who was High Sheriff 1528. His son William (d. 1573), High Sheriff 1552, 1558 and 1565, succ. He marr. Bridget, dau. of Sir John Hudleston, of Millom, *q.v.*, and widow of Sir Hugh Askew, *q.v.* Their son Joseph (d. 1641) was High Sheriff 1599 and 1610 and his son William (1590-1652) was High Sheriff 1639. His grandson William (*c.* 1655-1730) was cr. Baronet 1676, and was High Sheriff 1685. By Isabel (d. 1687) his wife, dau. and coheir of John Stapleton, of Warter (Y), he was father of Sir Joseph Pennington, 2nd Bart. (1677-1744), M.P. for Cumberland 1743-44, who marr. 1706 Margaret (d. 1738), dau. of John, 1st Viscount Lonsdale, and sister and coheir of Henry, 3rd and last Viscount, *q.v.* Their 2nd son Sir John Pennington, 3rd Bart, M.P. for Cumberland 1745-68, Lord Lieutenant of Westmorland, died unmarr. 1768, and was succ. by his brother, Sir Joseph, 4th Bart. (1718-93), who marr. 1739 Sarah (d. 1783). dau. and heir of John Moore, apothecary, of Bath. Their eldest son Sir John, 5th Bart. (1741-1813), M.P. for Westmorland 1806-13, was cr.

Baron Muncaster in the peerage of Ireland, 1783. He marr. 1778 Penelope (d. 1806), dau. and heir of James Compton. His dau. and heir Maria Margaret Frances (1783-1850) marr. 1811 James, 24th Earl of Crawford and 7th Earl of Balcarres (1783-1869), and their descendant Robert Alexander Lindsay, the 29th Earl of Crawford, is the representative of the Pennington family in the female line. Lord Muncaster was succ. in the barony under a special remainder by his brother General Lowther Pennington (1745-1818), who also succ. to the Baronetcy. He was succ. by his only son Lowther Augustus John (1802-38), who marr. 1828 Frances Catherine (1806-53), youngest dau. of Sir John Ramsden, 4th Bart., *q.v.* Their son Gamel Augustus, B.A. (Cantab) (1831-62), High Sheriff 1859, succ. but died *s.p.m.* and was succ. by his brother Josslyn Francis, F.S.A. (1834-1917), M.P. for West Cumberland 1872-80 and for Egremont 1885-92, and Lord Lieutenant of Cumberland 1876. In 1898 he was cr. Baron Muncaster of Muncaster in the peerage of the United Kingdom. He died s.p. when his honours became extinct, and the estates passed to his cousin Sir John Ramsden, Bart., *q.v.* (GECB; GEC; CW2 lxvi; JFP). *Arms.* Or five fusils conjoined in fess Azure (FFC; FVC; DVL). MMD gives: Quarterly, 1 & 4, Argent two bars Gules on a canton of the last a cinquefoil Or [Preston]; 2 & 3, Or five fusils conjoined in fess Azure. *Crest.* A cat-a-mountain passant guardant Proper. *Supporters.* Dexter, A lion guardant Proper charged on the breast with an oak branch Vert; Sinister, A horse reguardant Proper bridled Or. *Mottoes.* Vincit amor patriae; Firm, vigilant, active (BP58).

PENNINGTON, of Seaton. After the death of Sir Hugh Askew, *q.v.*, Bridget his widow, dau. of Sir John Hudleston, marr. 1563 William Pennington, of Muncaster (d. 1573), *q.v.*, and their 2nd son John (d. 1613) succ. to the Askew estates, including Seaton. These descended to Miles Pennington, aged 34 at the time of Dugdale's Visitation 1665, and High Sheriff of Cumberland 1668. His successor Robert Pennington, of Bishop Auckland (D), High Sheriff 1706, had a son George who had succ. by 1747. Administration of his estate was granted in 1752 to his sisters Margery (b. 1712), marr. 1753 Myles Sandys, of Graythwaite (L), and Elizabeth, who marr. 1757 Farrer Wren, of Binchester (D). In 1777 Myles Sandys and the Wrens sold Seaton to John Pennington, later 1st Lord Muncaster (CW2 xi; Deeds of the manor of Seaton). *Arms.* Or five fusils in fess Azure a canton Gules (FCW).

PENNINGTON-RAMSDEN – see RAMSDEN.

PENNY. John Penny, LL.D. (Oxon) (d. 1520), Abbot of Leicester, was Bishop of Bangor 1504-8 and Bishop of Carlisle 1508-20. *Arms.* BBE, quoting Burton's *History of Leicester* as authority, gives: Quarterly fretty and a canton Gules, with a query.

PENRETH. Sir John de Penreth* (d. 1322) was granted rents at Skelton by Robert de Clifford 1309. He owned the manor of Lamonby and had licence to settle it and other lands upon himself and Margaret his wife, and to alienate two acres in Penrith to the Augustinian Friary there 1318. In 1322 he was appointed Warden of the Marches of Northumberland. *Arms.* Gules a bend battely Argent (FFC; MKE). Papworth gives this as: Gules a bend embattled counterembattled Argent (OBA).

* Foster and Field give his name wrongly as Penzret, see FFC and FAC, and Papworth converts him into John Penserd, of Cumberland.

PENRITH Rugby Football Club. *Device* (on shield). Azure a saltire surmounted of a domed tower Argent.

PENRITH Rural District Council. The Council was granted the following in 1961. *Arms.* Gules on a bend wavy between three escallop shells and as many cross crosslets fitché Argent a bendlet wavy Azure. *Crest.* Out of a coronet composed of four ears of wheat and as many acorns leaved set alternately upon a rim Or a mount Vert thereon a stag reguardant Gules attired and unguled Or. *Motto.* Sine pavore sine favore.

PENRITH Urban District Council. The Council was granted the following in 1952. *Arms.* Per chevron Azure and gules issuant from the point of the chevron rays of the sun between two sheaves of corn Or and in base a triple-towered castle Gold. *Crest.* A saltire Argent fimbriated Azure enfiled by an ancient crown Or. *Motto.* Fide et fortitudino.

PENRUDDOCK, of Arkleby. This family, which took its name from Penruddock in Greystoke parish, were free tenants of the manor of Hutton John, retaining their holding until the end of the 17th century, though they lived at Arkleby. Robert Penruddock of that place marr. Agnes, dau. and heir of Sir William Leigh, and their grandson Robert, who made his will in 1579, was of Hale, Hants., and left his Cumberland and Westmorland estates to his nephew John, of Hale (1540-1601), son of Anthony Penruddock. His dau. Catherine marr. Sir Edward Musgrave, *q.v.,* and his dau. Elizabeth marr. Gawen Braithwaite, of Ambleside, see AWL. He was succ. by his son Sir Thomas (*c.* 1577-1628), whose kinsman Sir John Penruddock (d. 1676) was of Compton Chamberlayne, Wilts., which he built and was High Sheriff of that county 1643. His son Col John Penruddock (1619-55) joined the insurrection of 1655 against Cromwell, and was captured and beheaded at Exeter. His descendants owned Compton Chamberlayne until 1930 when it was sold by Capt George William Penruddocke, M.C. (1894-1947). The present head of the family is Col Norman Feilding Penruddocke, R.A.S.C. (BLG17; *ex inf.* the late Nigel Hudleston). *Arms.* The family now bears: Gules a bend embattled Argent (FD7; BLG17). FVC and FCW record: Quarterly, 1, Gules a bend raguly Argent; 2, Per chevron Sable and Ermine in chief two boars' heads couped [untinctured]; 3, Sable six annulets, two, two, and two, Or; 4, Azure a fess between three martlets Or. VEW (ii 46), however, states that the following were granted to George Penruddock, of Penruddock, 1548: Quarterly, 1, Gules a bend "in battell" Argent; 2, Per chevron Sable and Argent in chief two boars' heads [couped] Or; 3, Sable six annulets [two, two, and two] Or; 4, Azure a chevron between three martlets Or.* GMS records: Gules the trunk of a tree raguly and trunked in bend Argent. *Crest.* The family now bears: A lizard's head Azure armed and langued Gules between two wings Or (FD7; BLG17). FVC records: A demi dragon sans wings rampant Azure between two eagles' wings displayed Or. FCW contracts this to: A demi dragon between two eagles' wings displayed Or. LMC follows FVC but blazons the demi dragon as Vert. *Motto.* Gloria soli Deo (FD7). Field, however, quotes the Browne of Troutbeck MSS. as authority for: Ad lucem et laboram (FAC).

PENTNEY PRIORY, Norfolk. Founded by the Vaux family, it is thought that the Augustinian canons may have been brought from Pentney to

* In the illustration in the margin the field in the 2nd quartering is painted Sable and Ermine.

Lanercost *c.* 1200. *Arms.* Gules three baskets Or (Shield on curtains in Lanercost Priory).

PERCY, Earl of Northumberland. Henry de Percy (1341-1408), cr. Earl of Northumberland 1377, marr. (2) Maud, widow of Gilbert, Earl of Angus, dau. of Thomas, Lord Lucy of Egremont, and aunt and heir of Joan de Lucy, *q.v.* She died *s.p.s.* 1398, having settled her estates, including the castle and honour of Cockermouth, on her stepson, Sir Henry Percy, "Hotspur," on condition that the arms of Lucy were to be quartered with those of Percy. In addition to this, in spite of having no descent from the family of Lucy, the Earls of Northumberland added the Barony of Lucy to their style. Jocelyn, Earl of Northumberland, the last male heir, died 1670, his dau. and heir Elizabeth marrying Charles Seymour, Duke of Somerset, *q.v.* William Percy, D.D. (Cantab) (1428-62), a younger son of the 2nd Earl of Northumberland, was Chancellor of the University of Cambridge 1451-5 and Bishop of Carlisle 1452-62. A later member of this great northern family, Hugh Percy, M.A., D.D. (Cantab) (1784-1856), a younger son of Algernon, 1st Earl of Beverley, and grandson of the first Duke of Northumberland, was Bishop of Rochester 1827 and Bishop of Carlisle 1827-56. *Arms.* The original arms of Percy were: Azure a fess engrailed Or, later blazoned as: Azure five fusils conjoined in fess Or (Percy ancient). Henry, 1st Lord Percy (1273-1314), adopted: Or a lion rampant Azure (Percy modern). The family later bore: Quarterly, 1 & 4, Quarterly, i & iv, Percy modern, ii & iii, Gules three lucies hauriant Argent (Lucy); 2 & 3, Percy ancient (FFC; GEC). *Crest.* On a chapeau Gules turned up Ermine a lion statant Azure the tail extended. *Supporters.* Dexter, A lion rampant Azure; Sinister, A lion rampant guardant Or ducally crowned of the last gorged with a collar compony Argent and Azure.* *Motto.* Esperance en Dieu (BP, various editions; Achievement in house in Cockermouth). *Badges.* A crescent Argent; A shacklebolt Or within a crescent Argent; A lion passant Azure; A silver key crowned; A bugle horn without strings Azure garnished Or; A falchion hilted Or sheathed Sable; A unicorn passant Argent ducally gorged and lined Or; A boar statant Argent ducally gorged and lined Or; A leopard statant Argent semé of torteaux and hurts crowned Or (FDB). Bishop William bore for *Arms*: Quarterly, 1 & 4, Gules three lucies hauriant Argent; 2 & 3, Or a lion rampant Azure in a bordure (BBE).

PERCY. Thomas Percy, M.A. (Oxon), D.D. (Cantab) (1729-1811), famous as editor of *Reliques of Ancient English Poetry,* was born at Bridgnorth, Salop., the son and grandson of a grocer, the family name being Pearcy or Piercy, but he alleged descent from Sir Ralph Percy (d. unmarr. 1464), 7th son of the 2nd Earl of Northumberland. He was Vicar of Easton Maudit, Northants., 1753-82, Dean of Carlisle 1778-82, and Bishop of Dromore 1782-1811. *Arms.* Or a lion rampant Azure (BBE). Field gives: Quarterly, 1 & 4, Or a lion rampant Azure; 2 & 3, Gules three luces hauriant Argent. *Crest.* On a chapeau Gules turned up Ermine a lion statant tail extended Azure (FAC).

PERROTT, of Blitterlees. John Perrott, of Blitterlees, died 1809, aged 26.† *Arms.* Ermine on a bend Gules two naked arms issuing at the elbows out of

* Jefferson recorded the sinister supporter as: A unicorn Argent collared gobony Or and Azure (JAW).

† Not 126, as stated by Field (FAC).

clouds irradiated at either end of the bend the hands grasping a horseshoe. *Crest.* A hand cuffed and couped at the wrist and grasping a rapier. *Motto.* Praebare strenuum hominem (Tombstone at Holm Cultram).

PERSHALL – see KNIGHTLEY and CORBOILE.

PERSHALL. Shield at Hutton-in-the-Forest; a Vane quartering. *Arms.* Argent a cross pattée flory Sable on a canton Gules a wolf's head erased of the field.

PHILIPSON, of Irthington. John Philipson, of Irthington, yeoman, is mentioned in 1675 (HN 102/1). Anne, dau. of Thomas Philipson,* of Pateshill, was buried there 1746. *Arms.* . . . a chevron . . . between three boars' heads erased . . . (ABD).

PHILLIPS. Thomas Phillips, of the Middle Temple and Low Crosby (d. 1800, aged 65), was descended from the Phillips family of Hallsford. He marr. 1784 Sarah (1753-1831), dau. of William Patrickson, of Houghton Head, *q.v.,* and had sons John (d. 1836, aged 48) and Thomas (d. 1862, aged 68). *Arms.* . . . a lion rampant . . . . *Crest.* A lion rampant (Tombstone of Thomas Phillips, senior, in Stapleton churchyard).

PICKERING, of Scaleby. The large estates of the Moresbys in Cumberland and Westmorland descended to Anne, dau. and heir of Sir Christopher Moresby, *q.v.,* who marr. Sir James Pickering, of Killington (W). Their son Sir Christopher Pickering, of Scaleby Castle (1485-1516), succeeded and was succ. by his only dau. Anne (1517-82) who marr. (1) Sir Francis Weston, *q.v.,* (2) Sir Henry Knyvett, *q.v.,* and (3) John Vaughan. *Arms.* Ermine a lion rampant Azure crowned Or (TVN; NB i 263; Glass in Killington church). The arms, with the field plain, are on a memorial slab in St. Andrew's church, Penrith, commemorating Sir Christopher Pickering (d. 1516), and quartering Moresby (quartering Fenwick, Tilliol, and ?Asby and Lascelles). *Crest.* None of the older authorities record any crest for Pickering, but Chancellor Ferguson describes a token from Bankland Colliery dated 1760 as bearing the arms of Pickering, with *Crest.* A griffin's head erased (CW1 xv 399). *Supporters.* The Pickering shield above the entrance to Crosby Ravensworth Hall (W) is supported by: Dexter, A lion; Sinister, A unicorn.

PICKERING, of Threlkeld. Sir James Pickering, of Killington, see previous entry, had younger sons James and William, who marr. before 1513 respectively Elizabeth and Winifred, daus. and coheirs of Sir Lancelot Threlkeld, of Threlkeld, *q.v.* The latter couple inherited Threlkeld manor, which descended to their grandson Sir Christopher Pickering, of Ormside (W) (d. 1621, aged 75), who was knighted 1607. He was Sheriff of Cumberland 1590, 1606, 1607 and 1611. He was succ. by his illegitimate dau. Frances who marr. (1) 1620 John Dudley (d. 1623), and (2) Cyprian Hilton. His sisters and coheirs were Winifred, who marr. Henry Crackanthorpe, and Mary, who marr. Thomas Dalston. *Arms.* Ermine a lion rampant Azure crowned Or on the shoulder an annulet Argent for difference (TVN). In a window in the chancel of Greystoke church the arms appear as: Ermine a lion rampant Azure. Machell recorded: Ermine a lion rampant Azure crowned Or in dexter chief a crescent Argent for difference (MMS vi 423).

PIGOT. Geoffrey Pigot, of Melmerby, *temp.* Edward I, bore *Arms.* Sable three picks Argent (FFC). It seems almost certain, however, from the

* Not Phillips, as incorrectly rendered by Bell Irving (ABD).

pedigree of Pigot, of Clotherholme, near Ripon (Y), in FVY, that this refers to Melmerby, also near Ripon, not to Melmerby (C).

PINDER. The Rev. Francis Ford Pinder, M.A. (Cantab) (d. *s.p.* 1861, aged 58), son of Francis Ford Pinder and Elizabeth (Senhouse) his wife, was Rector of Gosforth 1835-61. His brothers, Col George Pinder, 15th Regt., of Hall Croft, Gosforth (d. *s.p.* 1881, aged 72), and the Rev. Humphrey Senhouse Pinder, placed a brass in his memory in Gosforth church. *Arms.* Quarterly, 1 & 4, Azure a chevron Argent between three lions' heads erased Ermine crowned Or (Pinder); 2 & 3, Azure a leopard rampant Proper (Hothersall) (JWC). *Crest.* A lion's head erased ducally crowned (Brass in Gosforth church).

PLANTAGENET, Edmund. Edmund of Woodstock, Earl of Kent (1301-30), 6th and youngest son of Edward I, marr. 1325 Margaret (d. 1349), dau. of John Wake, of Liddel, and sister and heir of Thomas Wake, *q.v.* Their dau. Joan (d. 1385) marr. Edward, the Black Prince, *q.v. Arms.* Gules three lions passant guardant Or a bordure Argent (FFC).

PLANTAGENET, Edward. Edward Plantagenet, styled "The Black Prince" (1330-76), eldest son of Edward III, marr. Joan, dau. of Edmund of Woodstock, Earl of Kent, and his wife Margaret Wake, *q.v.*, heiress of the Barony of Liddel. He died *v.p.* and was father of Richard II, see below. *Arms.* Quarterly, France (ancient) and England a label Argent (Clerestory window, Carlisle Cathedral).

PLANTAGENET, John. John of Gaunt, Duke of Lancaster (1340-99), 4th son of Edward III, was Governor of Carlisle, 1380-84. He marr. (2) 1371 Constance, dau. of Pedro I, King of Castile and Leon. *Arms* (as King of Castile in right of his wife). Quarterly, 1 & 4, Gules a Castle Or (Castile); 2 & 3, Argent a lion rampant Azure (Leon); impaling, Quarterly, France (ancient) and England a label Ermine (Clerestory window, Carlisle Cathedral).

PLANTAGENET, Richard. Richard Plantagenet, styled "of Bordeaux" (1367-1400), son and heir of Edward, the Black Prince, see above, succ. his grandfather Edward III as King Richard II 1377, and was deposed 1399. He marr. (1) Anne, dau. of Charles IV, King of Bohemia. *Arms.* Quarterly, France (ancient) and England; impaling, Bohemia, *q.v.* (Clerestory window, Carlisle Cathedral).

PLANTAGENET, Richard. Richard Plantagenet, Duke of Gloucester (1452-85), 3rd surviving son of Richard, Duke of York (killed 1460), and younger brother of Edward IV (d. 1483), was granted the Honour of Penrith 1471, and was Sheriff of Cumberland 1475. He came to the throne as Richard III 1483. *Arms.* Quarterly, France (modern) and England, with (as Duke of Gloucester) a label of three points. *Supporters.* Two boars Argent armed Or (Sign of the Gloucester Arms, Penrith). *Badge.* A boar passant [Argent armed Or] (Stone carving on Carlisle Castle). Fuller records the arms as: [Quarterly] France and England on a label of three points Ermine as many cantons Gules (FWE). DSL gives the label as Ermine, but without the cantons.

PLASKET, of Wigton. The Plaskets have long been established in Wigton, and the name appears in the parish registers as early as 1616. William Plasket marr. 1740 Isabel Bouch, of Bagwra (d. 1745, aged 41). Their son Thomas

Plasket (b. 1741) obtained in 1794, according to Field (FAC), a grant of *Arms.* Or on a cross invected Sable five escallops Erminois.

POCKLINGTON, *post* POCKLINGTON-SENHOUSE. Joseph Pocklington (1736-1817), son of William Pocklington, banker, of Newark (Notts.), was of Barrow House, Keswick, and the owner of Derwent Isle which became known as Pocklington's Island. He died unmarr. and Barrow House eventually came to his great-nephew Joseph Pocklington (b. 1804), who marr. 1835 Elizabeth, dau. and coheir of Humphrey Senhouse, *q.v.*, and assumed that surname 1842. *Arms.* Ermine three bends Azure on a chief Or three martlets Sable. *Crest.* A demi leopard rampant Proper holding in the dexter paw an ostrich feather Argent (BLG5).

PONSONBY, of Haile. Loelia, Duchess of Westminster, dau. of the Rt. Hon. Sir Frederick Edward Grey Ponsonby, 1st Baron Sysonby, has written: "The Ponsonbys came over from Picardy with the Plantagents and were granted the post of Hereditary Barber to the King."* It is clear that the founder of the family was Punzun, a Norman, who gave his name to the estate of Ponsonby. He was the ancestor of a long line of distinguished men, several of whom have been raised to the peerage. In 1334 Alexander de Ponsonby held Ponsonby, but before 1388 the estate had been acquired by the Stanleys. The manor of Haile descended to Agnes and Constance, daus. of Alexander de Haile. The latter (a widow before 1334) marr. William Ponsonby, and was mother of Alexander above. Haile was thus acquired and has continued in the family ever since. Sir John Ponsonby, M.P. (1608-78) was a Roundhead who acquired Irish estates, which passed to his 3rd son William (1657-1724), who was cr. Baron Bessborough 1721 and Viscount Duncannon 1722. His half brother John Ponsonby (*c.* 1638-1708) succ. to Haile, and was High Sheriff of Cumberland 1695. His son John (1678-1745) was High Sheriff 1718 and was succ. by his son John (1712-63) who was High Sheriff 1749. His son Miles Ponsonby, D.L., J.P. (1755-1814), High Sheriff 1809, was the last male of this line. His five sons died unmarr. Of his five daughters, three died unmarr., Mary marr. 1817 Edward Carr Knubley, *q.v.*, and Dorothy (1780-1852) marr. 1805 John Fisher, D.L., J.P. (d. 1848, aged 71). The latter, in accordance with Miles's will, assumed the name and arms of Ponsonby 1816. They were succ. at Haile by their son Miles Ponsonby, D.L., J.P. (1808-92), who marr. 1837 Barbara (d. 1874, aged 67), dau. of Christopher Wilson, of Rigmaden (see AWL). Their son Miles De Haile Ponsonby (1841-1915) succ.† and was succ. by his only son Ronsley Miles (1904-64), who sold Haile Hall to his kinsman, General Sir John Ponsonby, K.C.B., C.M.G., D.S.O. (1866-1952),‡ in 1922, but retained the estate. He died in Australia and is buried at Botany (PPF). *Arms.* At the Visitation of 1665, Dugdale recorded a pedigree of five generations, but no arms, stating "Respite given for exhibiting the Armes." Lysons, Milbourne and Burke record the arms which are on a monument in Haile church:

* *Grace and Favour,* 1961. She added: "In support of this bold assertion there are the three combs on our coat of arms, and if that is not enough, why then, let the sceptics prove something to the contrary."

† He migrated to Tasmania, leaving Haile Hall in the care of his sister Barbara. Their brother Henry, born in Paris in 1851, had a distinguished naval career. He mar. Jessie Bulteel and lived for a time at Haile, and latterly in the Isle of Man, where he died 1916.

‡ He was eldest son of General the Rt. Hon. Sir Henry Frederick Ponsonby, P.C., G.C.B. (1825-95), grandson of the 3rd Earl of Bessborough.

Gules a chevron between three combs Argent. *Crest.* On a ducal coronet three arrows one in pale and two in saltire points downwards Or feathered and pointed Argent entwined by a serpent Proper. *Motto.* Pro rege, lege, grege (LMC; MMD; BLG15).

PONSONBY, of Springfield and Egremont. William Ponsonby, of Egremont (d. 1766, aged 63), marr. 1736 Anne Gaitskell (d. 1788, aged 76). Their son John Ponsonby, of Springfield (d. 1783, aged 45), was a Whitehaven attorney who marr. 1775 Elizabeth Gale (d. 1782, aged 44). Their son Capt John Ponsonby, R.N. (1779-1841), was of Springfield and Barrow House, Keswick. He marr. Elizabeth (d. 1839, aged 56), dau. of William Browne, of Tallantire, *q.v.* Their son William Browne Ponsonby (1811-55), Bombay Army and Captain 7th Lancs. Rifles, marr. 1844 Eliza Anne, dau. and coheir of Capt Daniel Jones Skelton, *q.v. Arms* and *Crest*. As Ponsonby of Haile.

POOLE. Impaled by Irton, *q.v.*, on staircase window in Irton Hall; George Irton (*c.* 1667-1749) marr. Elizabeth, dau. of David Poole, of Knottingley and Sykehouse (Y). *Arms.* Argent* a fess between three leopards' faces Or.

POPHAM. Shield at Hutton John; a Hudleston quartering, brought in by Barantyne, *q.v. Arms.* Argent on a chief Or two bucks' heads cabossed Proper. *Sic*; correctly, Argent on a chief Gules two bucks' heads cabossed Or.

PORTER, of Allerby and Weary Hall. Thomas Porter, of Bolton (C), acquired Allerby by marr. to the dau. and heir of Thomas Lowther, of that place. His grandson Anthony Porter marr. Jane, dau. and coheir of Rowland Thornborough, of Osmotherley in Furness. Their grandson Thomas (living 1578) died *s.p.* and his widow took Allerby to her 2nd husband's family, the Eaglesfields. Thomas's half brother George Porter (d. 1587) was founder of the family at Weary Hall. His son Joseph (*c.* 1573-1649) had seven sons: from William descended the Porters, of Lowholme, *q.v.*, Eskdale Green, Longrigg, Gatehouse, Drigg and Egremont; from John came the family of Close in Bolton and Ireland; and from Nicholas the Porters of Usthwaite. The Weary Hall line was continued by the eldest son George Porter (*c.* 1599-1649), whose son Joseph (*c.* 1646-94) had a son George (d. 1697) who was succ. by his brother Joseph, who sold Weary Hall. He was living 1715 with his sister at Thackthwaite. *Arms* (of Porter, of Allerby). Gules on a fess Or three bells Azure within a bordure engrailed Argent.† *Crest.* An antelope's head erased Argent attired Gules gorged with two bends sinister Or (FCW; FVC; MMS vi 421). *Arms* (of Porter, of Weary Hall). Sable three church bells Argent. *Crest.* An antelope's head erased Argent attired Or gorged with a ducal coronet Gules (FCW).‡ MMD tricks the *Arms* of Porter, of Weary Hall, as: Gules a bordure invected Azure over all on a fess Or three bells of the second. Field records the Porters, of the Close, as bearing for *Crest*; A portcullis Argent chained Or. *Motto.* Vitam impendere vero (FAC).

* *Sic*; correctly, Azure.

† Dugdale made the following note: "These Armes he [i.e., Joseph Porter, who recorded the pedigree in 1665] affirmeth to be borne by his great grandfather, and that they are cut in stone very antient over the gates of his house at Wery-Hall."

‡ Curwen records: Gules on a fess Azure three church bells Or a bordure engrailed Argent (CW2 vi).

PORTER, of Low Holme. For full details of this family, see CW2 xiv. William Porter (b. before 1600, d. 1683), 2nd son of Joseph Porter, of Weary Hall, *q.v.*, settled at Low Holme, Eskdale, and was ancestor of a long line. John Porter (1751-1803) disinherited his eldest son John (1773-1841), in favour of his son William, but another son, the Rev. Joseph Porter, M.A. (Oxon) (1775-1833) bought the estate and re-instated John in possession. His grandson Joseph (1824-82) sold Low Holme 1880. The Porters of Gatehouse were also descended from this family, to which belonged Lancelot Salkeld Porter (1911-42), a poet of great promise, who was killed while serving with the Royal Corps of Signals in the Middle East. *Arms* and *Crest.* As Porter, of Weary Hall.

PORTLAND, Duke of – see BENTINCK.

POSTLETHWAITE, of The Hollins, formerly of Broadstone (L). Richard Postlethwaite bought Broadstone, Dalton-in-Furness, 1612 and the estate continued with his descendants for more than 250 years. William Postlethwaite (d. 1769, aged 61) was of Millwood and Broadstone, and was succ. by his son John (d. 1813, aged 61), whose eldest son William (1773-1805) died in Dominica. The 2nd son, the Rev. Thomas Postlethwaite, M.A. (Cantab) (1775-1815), was Curate of Rampside 1798-1800. His youngest brother John (1780-1854) eventually succ., and was succ. by his eldest son John (1813-78), solicitor, who sold Broadstone 1864, and bought The Hollins, Hensingham, 1870. He was in partnership in Scotch Street, Whitehaven, with his eldest son John (1843-86), later an iron ore proprietor. He died *s.p.* and was succ. by his brother Miles Postlethwaite, J.P. (1857-99), who died unmarr. at Mombasa, East Africa, and was succ. by his sister Elizabeth, wife of Thomas Thom, see p. 267. *Arms.* Argent a chevron Sable between three boars' heads couped . . . . *Crest.* On a ducal coronet a boar's head couped. *Motto.* Toujours prest (Seals in possession of L. C. R. Thom-Postlethwaite).

POSTLETHWAITE, of Millom. A pedigree of this family by Albert Hartshorne, F.S.A., a descendant, is in CW1 x, the line beginning with John Postlethwaite, of Bankside (d. 1595). His son John is called of Powhouse in 1605, and this estate, with Lacra and Lowscales, descended to his grandson John (d. 1680), whose son Miles (1668-1742) marr. 1735 Mary, dau. of Thomas Myers, of Groops, *q.v.* Their only son John, of Po House, solicitor of Kendal (1738-1813), died unmarr. leaving his estates to his cousin John Myers, *q.v.* From Matthew Postlethwaite, of Bankside (1607-82), younger son of John, of Powhouse in 1605, see above, descended a junior line. Matthew's son John Postlethwaite, M.A. (Oxon) (1650-1713), was headmaster of St. Martin's School, London, and High Master of St. Paul's School. His nephew Matthew, M.A. (Cantab) (1680-1745), became Archdeacon of Norwich. *Arms.* According to Hartshorne, John Postlethwaite, High Master of St. Paul's School, bore: Argent a bugle horn Sable stringed Gules a chief indented of the third in base a chevron of the last. Field, however, states that his seal displayed: A bugle-horn stringed between a fess dancetté and a chevron (FAC). Burke gives for Postlethwaite, but without specifying any county or town of origin: Argent a bugle horn Sable stringed Gules in base a chevron of the second a chief indented of the third (BGA).

POSTLETHWAITE, of The Oaks. John Postlethwaite, of Broughton House,

Broughton-in-Furness, mercer (d. 1789, aged 80), was succ. by his son John Postlethwaite (1744-1832), who marr. 1786 Margaret, dau. of Robert Hodgshon, of The Oaks, Millom. Their son Robert Postlethwaite, D.L., J.P. (1788-1859), succ. his father at Broughton and his uncle, William Hodgshon, J.P., at The Oaks, and was himself succ. at The Oaks by his 3rd son William Postlethwaite, D.L., J.P. (1829-1908), who was High Sheriff 1865, and was later of Rankapuka, Geraldine, New Zealand. His eldest son, Robert Hodgshon Postlethwaite (b. 1862), was living in California in 1902; his 2nd son, Hugh Wastel Postlethwaite, B.A. (Cantab) (b. 1867), was of San Francisco with a son Frank William Hylton (b. 1891); his 3rd son, Arthur Herbert Postlethwaite, J.P. (1869-1951), succ. to The Oaks where he lived until 1922 when he went to America, where he died (DPB; BLG5; *Ex inf.* the Hon. Miss Elinor Cross). *Arms.* Argent a chevron between three boars' heads couped Sable. *Crest.* On a ducal coronet Or a boar's head Sable. *Motto.* Semper paratus (BLG5; Window in Broughton-in-Furness church).

POSTLETHWAITE, *post* THOM-POSTLETHWAITE. Elizabeth (d. 1939), eldest dau. of John Postlethwaite, of The Hollins, Hensingham, *q.v.* marr. 1885 Andrew Thomas Thom (1848-1909), son of William Thom, and succ. her brother Miles Postlethwaite (see p. 266) at The Hollins 1899. In 1900 she and her husband assumed the additional surname Postlethwaite and received a grant of arms. She was succ. at The Hollins by her son Andrew Cecil Scott Thom-Postlethwaite, barrister at law (1888-1973), who was later of Armaside, Lorton. He marr. 1918 Gertrude Adele Roope, dau. and coheir of Sir Richard Roope Linthorne, *q.v.* His son and heir Humphrey Richard Miles Thom-Postlethwaite (b. 1919) died *v.p.*, leaving an only son, Ian Miles. In Cumberland the family is represented by his uncle, Lorne Cecil Roope Thom-Postlethwaite, of Armaside (b. 1922). *Arms* (of Thom). Or a bend chequy Gules and Argent. *Crest.* A dexter arm erect Proper holding a sword in pale also Proper hilt and pommel Or. *Motto.* Dum vivo spero. *Arms* (of Postlethwaite, granted 1900 to A. T. Thom). Per pale Argent and Sable two chevronels between as many boars' heads erased in chief and a boar statant in base and (for distinction) in the centre chief point a cross crosslet all counterchanged. *Crest.* Upon a mount Vert a boar's head erased Argent thereon an eagle preying Sable the boar's head charged for distinction with a cross crosslet also Sable. The arms and crest without the marks of distinction were granted to Mrs. Thom and their issue. *Motto.* Toujours prest.

de POTHONIER. Charles Sligo de Pothonier, of Upper Belgrave Square, London, whose ancestor was a French emigré, had a dau. and heir Vera Henrietta (1886-1967) who marr. 1906 John Anthony Spedding, *q.v. Arms.* Quarterly 1 & 4, Gules on a chevron Argent three mullets Azure, impaling, Or a lion rampant to the sinister Sable; 2 & 3, Quarterly, i, Argent two bones in saltire surmounted of a human skull Sable; ii & iii, Gules on a bend sinister Argent a pallet Vert; iv, Argent a garb Azure; in the fess point of the 2nd and 3rd quarters an anchor in bend Azure cabled Gules. *Crest.* An arm embowed in armour Proper garnished Or in the hand a scimitar also Proper hilt and pommel of the second (Painting in possession of Mr. George Spedding).

POTTER. Barnabas Potter, M.A., D.D. (1577-1642), Provost of the Queen's

College, Oxford 1616-26, Bishop of Carlisle 1629-42, was son of Thomas Potter, of Highgate, Kendal. *Arms.* BBE attributes to him the arms of his nephew Christopher Potter (for whom see AWL), viz. Argent on a pale Azure three pairs of wings of the first. Burke describes the pairs of wings as conjoined and elevated.

POTTER. Thomas Potter, of Lazonby, was father of the Rev. Robert Potter (1696-1768), Vicar of Stillingfleet (Y), and the Rev. William Potter, M.A. (Oxon) (1711-68), Vicar of Hemingbrough (Y) 1742-68, when he was succ. by his son the Rev. William Potter, M.A. (Cantab) (1742-96), who became Vicar of Brayton (Y) 1773. *Arms* (tricked by the Rev. William Potter in Lazonby and Hemingbrough parish registers). Argent on a pale Azure three pairs of wings conjoined and elevated of the first.* (BHH).

POTTINGER. Thomas Pottinger, of Mount Pottinger, Co. Down, marr. 1752 Frances (1732-1823), 3rd dau. of Eldred Curwen, of Workington, *q.v.* Their son Captain Henry Pottinger, 38th Regt (d. *s.p.* in the Isle of Man 1827, aged 70), was of St. Mary's, Carlisle, when he marr. 1792 Mary (b. 1773, d. at Stanwix 1832), dau. of Henry Birkett. *Arms.* Vert an eastern crown Or between three pelicans feeding their young Proper a canton Argent charged with a cross Gules. *Crest.* A dexter arm embowed in armour Proper garnished Or the hand gauntletted and grasping a sword also Proper hilted and pommelled Gold the arm encircled by an eastern crown Gules. *Motto.* Virtus in ardua (BP58).

POTTS, of The Limes. Ann, wife of John Potts, of The Limes, died 1726, aged 76. *Arms.* . . . a bend . . . between in chief a Passion cross, a merchant's mark (?), and a billet . . . and in base three roundles . . . (Lanercost tombstone).

POWELL. The Rev. Thomas Wade Powell, M.A. (Cantab) (1829-96), younger son of the Rev. Benjamin Powell, J.P., of Bellingham Lodge, Wigan (1792-1861), and brother of Sir Francis Sharp Powell, 1st and last Bart., was Vicar of Aspatria 1879-85 and Rural Dean of Maryport. His sister Elizabeth, who was coheir of her brothers, marr. 1862 John Wareing Bardsley, Bishop of Carlisle, *q.v.* *Arms.* Sable three escutcheons Argent each charged with a boar's head erased of the field all within a bordure Or. *Crest.* A lion rampant Sable gorged with a double chain Or therefrom pendent a pheon Argent and resting the sinister forepaw upon a shield Or charged with an eagle's head erased Azure. *Motto.* Omne bonum Dei donum (VAC; BP68).

PRATT. John Pratt, D.S.C., L.R.C.P.I., L.R.C.S.I., Surgeon, R.N. (1880-1935), 5th son of Robert Pratt, J.P., of Gawsworth, Co. Cork, and Knockane, Castlemartyr (1835-1910), was Medical Officer of Health, Millom, and was drowned while sailing his yacht in the Duddon estuary (BLG15). *Arms.* Gules on a fess between three elephants' heads erased Or tusked Argent as many mullets Sable. *Crest.* An elephant's head erased Sable tusked Or. *Motto.* Servabo fidem (Brass, St. George's, Millom; FD7).

PRATT. A tablet in Caldbeck church, erected by their surviving son, Capt John Backhouse Pratt (d. 1837), 4th Regt Bengal Native Infantry, commemorates Capt John Pratt, of Hurworth (D), late North York Regt, who died at Moffat, 1799, aged 38; his widow, Mary, dau. of John

* The Rev. Isaac Tyson, *q.v.*, a later Vicar of Hemingbrough, caustically noted that these were the wings and bearings of a goose.

Backhouse, of Caldbeck, died at Camberwell, 1815, aged 51; and their son, Capt George Pratt, R.N., died 1814, aged 25. *Crest.* A dragon's head couped.

PRESCOTT. Impaled by Blencowe on deed dated 1751 in the R.O., Carlisle; Henry Blencowe, of Blencowe (1712-65), *q.v.*, marr. Mary, only surviving dau. and heir of Alexander Prescott, of Thoby Priory, Essex. *Arms.* [Sable] a chevron between three owls [Argent]. See GA2.

PRESCOTT. The Ven. John Eustace Prescott, M.A., D.D. (Cantab) (1832-1920), son of George Prescott, of Gibraltar, merchant, was Fellow of Corpus Christi College, Cambridge, 1857, Vicar of St. Mary, Carlisle, 1877-79, Canon residentiary and Archdeacon of Carlisle 1883-1920, and Chancellor of the Diocese 1900-20. A notable scholar, his *Register of Wetherhal Priory*, 1897, and his *Statutes of Carlisle Cathedral* are works of great erudition.* He was a benefactor to Carlisle Diocese and Cathedral, and a learned and astute Chancellor. His son Harry Ernest Prescott, M.A. (Cantab), M.I.C.E. (1859-1944), marr. 1894 his cousin Lucy Beatrice Clarke, dau. of John Barrow Prescott, of the Manor House, Wilmslow Park (Ch.). His younger brother Cyril Arthur Prescott, B.A. (Cantab) (1864-1943), was an underwriter in London (VAC; CW2 xx). *Arms.* [Sable] a chevron between three owls [Argent]. *Crest.* A cubit arm erect vested Gules and cuffed Ermine holding in the hand a hand beacon fired. *Motto.* Dux mihi Deus (Brass, Carlisle Cathedral; Bookplate).

PRESTON (?). Field (FAC, p. 272) records a 15th century shield on a gable of Muncaster church, with *Arms.* . . . two bars . . . and on a canton . . . a fleur-de-lys . . . . It is possible that this is intended for Preston, Sir Alan de Pennington (d. 1415) having marr. Katherine, dau. and coheir of Sir Richard de Preston.

PRESTON – see CARUS.

PRESTON, Viscount – see GRAHAM, of Netherby (II).

PRESTON – see SIMPSON.

PREVOST. Col Thomas William Prevost, J.P., 21st Royal Fusiliers (1823-1911), son of Admiral Thomas James Prevost (1771-1855), was of Newtown House, near Carlisle 1850-56, of Stanwix House 1856-72, and later of Lowther Street, Carlisle. His elder son Edward William Prevost, Ph.D., M.A. (1851-1920), was author of *A Glossary of the Words and Phrases pertaining to the Dialect of Cumberland.* His elder son William Augustin John Prevost, Major, R.A., of Edinburgh (b. 1898), is the author of several papers in the *Transactions* of the Cumberland & Westmorland Antiquarian & Archaeological Society. *Arms.* Azure a dexter arm in fess issuing from a cloud in the sinister fess point the hand grasping a sword erect Proper pommel and hilt Or in chief two mullets Argent. *Crest.* A demi lion rampant Azure charged on the shoulder with a mural crown Or the sinister paw grasping a sword erect as in the arms. *Motto.* J'ai bien servi.

PROBY. Mary, Lady Inglewood, J.P., is eldest dau. of Sir Richard George Proby, 1st Bart., of Elton Hall, Peterborough, and marr. 1949 the 1st Baron Inglewood, *q.v.* *Arms.* Quarterly, 1 & 4, Ermine on a fess Gules a lion passant Or (Proby); 2 & 3, Argent two bars wavy Azure on a chief of the

* He was a Vice-President of the Cumberland & Westmorland Antiquarian & Archaeological Society and "rarely absent from the Council, where his word was of great weight."

last an estoile between two escallops Or (Allen). *Motto.* Manus haec inimica tyrannis (FD7).

PUDSEY. Florence, dau. of Henry Pudsey, of Barforth (Y), marr. (1) Sir Thomas Talbot, of Bashall (Y); (2) before 11 July 1511, as his 2nd wife, Henry, 10th Lord Clifford, "the Shepherd Lord," *q.v.*, by whom she had an only child Dorothy, who marr. Sir Hugh Lowther; and (3) Lord Richard Grey, son of Thomas, 1st Marquess of Dorset. *Arms.* Vert a chevron between three mullets pierced Or (Impaled by Clifford on shield in Gerard Lowther's house, now the Two Lions Hotel, Penrith).

PURDON. According to Burke (BGA and BLG 1847), James Purdon, of Kirklinton, went to Ireland *temp.* Henry VIII – a pedigree in the Record Office, Carlisle, says *temp.* Elizabeth, who gave him a large estate in Co. Louth. He marr. a dau. of the Earl of Montrose; their son Gilbert Purdon obtained in 1588 a confirmation by Ulster of the following *Arms.* Argent a leopard's face between a chief and a chevron Sable. *Crest.* A dexter arm embowed Proper holding a banner Gules fringed Or charged with a leopard's face Argent the staff broken above the hand. *Motto.* Pro aris et focis.

PUXLEY. The Rev. Herbert Boyne Lavallin Puxley, M.A., of Llethr Llestri, Carmarthenshire, and of Lavallin House, Tenby (1836-1908), later Rector of Catton (Y), was Curate of Cockermouth 1859-65 and Vicar 1865-73. *Arms.* Quarterly, 1 & 4, Gules on a bend cotised Argent five lozenges conjoined of the first in the sinister chief an annulet Or (Puxley); 2 & 3, Argent a fleur-de-lys Sable a chief engrailed Azure (Lavallin). *Crest.* An arm in armour embowed Proper charged with a lozenge between two annulets in pale Gules the hand grasping a dagger also Proper. *Motto.* Loyal en tout (BLG18).

PYEL. Shield at Hutton John; a Hudleston quartering. *Arms.* Argent a bend between two mullets Sable.

QUAYLE, of Crogga. Major James Spedding, D.L., J.P., of Summergrove, *q.v.* (1779-1863), had an eldest dau. Mary Jane Hamilton (1809-92), who became in her issue her father's heir. She marr. 1837 Mark Hildesley Quayle, of Crogga, Isle of Man (1804-79), Clerk of the Rolls, Chairman of the Magistrates, Member of the Legislative and Executive Council and twice Deputy Governor of the Island. Their seven sons all died *s.p.* Their 2nd son Mark Hildesley Quayle, M.A. (Cantab), of Crogga, solicitor (1842-1928), succ. to Summergrove on the death of his cousin, J. W. H. P. Spedding, *q.v.*, and was succ. by his brother, the Rev. Daniel Fleming Wilson Quayle, M.A. (Oxon), J.P., of Bridge House, Castletown, Isle of Man (1847-1929).* He was succ. by his sisters Emily and Edith (who marr. Latham Tomlin). In 1931 they sold the Summergrove estate to their kinsman, John Anthony Spedding, *q.v. Arms.* Argent on a chevron Sable gutté d'eau between three quails Proper two swords points upwards of the first in the centre chief point a pellet. *Crest.* Upon a mount Vert a quail between two bullrushes all Proper. *Motto.* Assiduitas (BLG13). The arms are on a tablet in St. Lupus church, Malew, Isle of Man, to Mary Jane Hamilton Quayle, impaling Spedding.

QUEENSBERRY. Marquess of – see DOUGLAS.

QUIN. Shield on font in Muncaster church; Louisa Mary Isabella (d. *s.p.*

* His mother, a descendant of the Flemings of Rydal, was dau. of Senhouse Wilson.

1872), eldest dau. of Sir John Ramsden, 4th Bart., and sister-in-law of the 3rd Lord Muncaster, marr. 1847 Lord George Quin (d. 1888), 2nd son of the 1st Marquess of Headfort. *Arms.* [Vert] a pegasus courant wings addorsed [Ermine] a chief [Or] a crescent for difference.

RADCLIFFE, Earl of Derwentwater. Sir Nicholas Radcliffe, living 1450, descended from the Radcliffes, of Radcliffe Tower (L), marr. *c.* 1417 Elizabeth, dau. and heir of Sir John Derwentwater, *q.v.*, and acquired Castlerigg, Lord's Island, Derwentwater and Tallantire. He was High Sheriff of Cumberland 1422 and 1426. His grandson John, living 1509, High Sheriff 1507, was partly disinherited. By Anne his wife, dau. and coheir of Sir Henry Fenwick, *q.v.*, he had a son* Sir John (d. 1529), High Sheriff 1514-16, 1518, 1523 and 1526. He marr. Alice (d. 1554), dau. of Sir Edmund Sutton or Dudley. *q.v.*, but died *s.p.* His uncle Sir Edward Radcliffe, who had succ. to the Derwentwater estate, marr. Anne, dau. and heir of John Cartington, of Cartington (N), and acquired Dilston Castle, which became the family's principal residence. His great-grandson Sir Francis Radcliffe (1563-1622) was involved in the Gunpowder Plot, and is described as "an obstinate, dangerous and not unlearned recusant." He was cr. Baronet 1620 and bought the manor of Alston 1619. His son Sir Edward Radcliffe, 2nd Bart. (1589-1663), who fought in the Civil War, marr. Elizabeth, dau. and heir of Thomas Barton, of Whenby (Y), and was succ. by his son Sir Francis (1624-96), who was cr. Earl of Derwentwater 1688. He marr. Katherine, dau. and coheir of Sir William Fenwick, of Meldon (N). Their son Sir Edward, 2nd Earl (1655-1705), marr. 1687 Lady Mary Tudor (d. 1726), natural dau. of Charles II. His son Sir James, 3rd Earl (1689-1716), was executed for his part in the '15. His only son John (d. 1731, aged 18), but for the attainder 4th Earl and 6th Bart., died unmarr., his sister and heir being Lady Anne Radcliffe, who marr. Robert James, 8th Baron Petre. Their uncle Charles, *de jure* 5th Earl and 7th Bart., was executed 1746 for his part in the '45. He marr. 1724 Charlotte Maria Livingston, Countess of Newburgh (d. 1755). Their son James Bartholomew Radcliffe (1725-86), but for the attainder 6th Earl and 8th Bart., succ. his mother as 3rd Earl of Newburgh and in the latter title he was succ. by his son Anthony James (1757-1814), who died *s.p.*, when the Derwentwater earldom and the Radcliffe baronetcy became extinct and the Earldom of Newburgh passed to a cousin (GEC). *Arms.* Argent a bend engrailed Sable (FFC; LMC; Brass in Crosthwaite church; Window in Bolton church (W)). Various authorities have at different times shewn these arms as differenced by a fleur-de-lys, a label, a crescent or a rose. *Crest.* On a ducal coronet Or a bull's head erased Sable. Burke gives: Out of a ducal coronet a bull's head Sable armed Or. *Supporters.* Two bulls Pean gorged with ducal coronets armed and chained Argent (BGA).†. The bookplate of Edward, 2nd Earl of Derwentwater, dated 1702, as illustrated in CW2 iv, displays the following. *Arms.* Argent a bend engrailed Sable. *Crest.* A bull's head couped Sable

* He also had a dau. Anne, who marr. John Radcliffe, or Rowell, and had a son John, whose dau. and heir Dorothy marr. Francis Dacre. They sold much of the estates they inherited from Sir John Radcliffe.

† In Keswick Museum is the so-called 'Lord Derwentwater's Chair' which has carved on the back a coat-of-arms: Quarterly, 1 & 4, . . . on a fess . . . a fleur-de-lys . . . ; 2 & 3, . . . on a chief . . . three (?) lions' heads erased . . . . *Crest.* A (?) lion's head. Although said to be the arms of Sir John Radcliffe (d. 1529), the coat in fact bears no resemblance to the arms of Radcliffe.

gorged with a ducal coronet and chained Argent. *Supporters.* Two bulls Sable gorged with ducal coronets and chained Argent.

RADCLIFFE, Baron and Viscount FitzWalter and Earl of Sussex. Elizabeth (b. 1430), dau. and heir of Walter, 5th Lord FitzWalter (1400-31), inherited Egremont Castle and a third of the Barony which she carried to her husband, John Radcliffe, of Attleborough, Norfolk, whom she marr. before 27 Oct. 1444, and who was killed 1461. Their son John, 6th Lord FitzWalter (1452-96), was succ. by his son Robert, 7th Lord FitzWalter (d. 1542), who was styled "Lord Fitz Water and Egremond" in 1524, though only a coheir to the latter title. He was cr. Viscount FitzWalter 1525 and Earl of Sussex 1529. In that year he and his son and heir Henry, later 2nd Earl of Sussex (*c.* 1506-57), sold Egremont Castle and the third part (the Middle Ward) of the barony to Henry, 6th Earl of Northumberland, and others* (GEC; CFF). *Arms.* Argent a bend engrailed Sable. *Crest.* On a chapeau Gules turned up Ermine two wings of the first which are connected by a nimbus pendent therefrom a fetterlock and surmounted by an estoile all Or. *Supporters.* Two bulls Sable gorged with ducal coronets armed and chained Argent. *Motto.* Virtus propter se (BGA).

RAILTON, of Carlisle. Thomas Railton, of Carlisle, obtained in 1733 a grant of the following *Arms.* Vert a buck trippant Argent attired and unguled Or a chief Vair (CA viii/171A).

RAILTON, of Throstle Hall. Field recorded the following tombstone at Caldbeck for the Railton family, living at Throstle Hall, Caldbeck, in 1759. *Arms.* . . . three lions' heads erased . . . . *Crest.* A demi lion rampant holding in its paws a roundle (FAC).

RAINBOW. The Rt. Rev. Edward Rainbow, M.A., D.D. (Cantab) (1608-84), son of the Rev. Thomas Rainbow, Rector of Blyton-in-Lindsey, Lincs., was Master of Magdalene College, Cambridge, 1642-50, when he was expelled by Parliament. Restored in 1660, he was Dean of Peterborough 1661-64, Vice-Chancellor of the University of Cambridge 1662-63, and Bishop of Carlisle 1664-84 (DNB). *Arms.* Ermine on a chief per pale Gules and Azure three estoiles Or (BBE).

RAINEFORD, of Cumberland. No other details given. *Arms.* Azure an eagle displayed Argent ducally crowned Or (BGA).

RAMSAY. Lady Ida Mary Ramsay, dau. of the 14th Earl of Dalhousie, marr. 1938 Sir George Frederick Johnson, of Castlesteads, *q.v.* *Arms.* Argent an eagle displayed Sable beaked and membered Gules. *Motto.* Ora et labora.

RAMSDEN, *post* PENNINGTON-RAMSDEN. Sir William Ramsden, 2nd Bart., of Byrom (Y) (1672-1736), marr. 1695 the Hon. Elizabeth Lowther (d. 1764), 2nd dau. of John, 1st Viscount Lonsdale, and sister and coheir of Henry, 3rd and last Viscount Lonsdale. Their descendant, Sir John William Ramsden, 5th Bart., D.L., J.P., M.A. (Cantab), M.P., Under Secretary for War (1831-1914), marr. 1865 Lady Helen Guendolen St. Maur (d. 1910), youngest dau. and coheir of Edward Adolphus, 12th Duke of Somerset. Their only son Sir John Frecheville Ramsden, 6th Bart., D.L. (1877-1958), succ. 1917 to the estates of his kinsman, the last Lord Muncaster, *q.v.*† His

* GEC says that he sold Egremont Castle to the King 1539. Lord Northumberland (d. 1537) had made the King heir to all his lands 1535, so perhaps the grant of 1539 was a confirmation of the sale in 1529.

† Frances Catherine, 4th and youngest dau. of Sir John Ramsden, 4th Bart., marr. 1828 Lord Muncaster's father, the 3rd Baron Muncaster.

elder son John St. Maur Ramsden (1902-48) died *v.p.,** leaving a dau. and heir Carola Eloise, who marr. 1961 George Fillmore Miller III, of New York City. The baronetcy was inherited by his brother Sir (Geoffrey) William Pennington-Ramsden, 7th Bart. (b. 1904), who was High Sheriff of Cumberland 1962. In accordance with the will of the last Lord Muncaster he assumed the surname Pennington 1925 and was granted the arms of that family (see below). He assumed the surname Pennington-Ramsden 1958. His elder dau. Phyllida Rosemary marr. 1955 Patrick Thomas Gordon-Duff, who assumed the additional surname Pennington 1955. *Arms.* Quarterly, 1 & 4, Argent on a chevron between three fleurs-de-lys Sable as many rams' heads couped at the neck of the field (Ramsden); 2 & 3, Quarterly, i & iv, Or five fusils conjoined in fess Azure a canton Sable (Pennington); ii & iii, Ramsden, as Quarters 1 & 4. *Crests.* 1, A cubit arm in armour Proper the gauntlet holding a fleur-de-lys Sable (Ramsden); 2, A mountain cat passant guardant Proper resting the dexter forepaw on a fleur-de-lys Sable (Pennington). *Motto.* Audaces fortuna juvat (DPB).

RANDLES. Sir John Scurrah Randles, J.P., of Bristowe Hill, Keswick (1857-1945), son of the Rev. Marshall Randles, D.D., Professor of Theology in Wesleyan College, Didsbury (1826-1904), was M.P. for Cockermouth 1900-6 and 1906-10. *Arms.* Per chevron Azure and Or in chief two mullets and in base the emblem of Mars all counterchanged. *Crest.* A dexter cubit arm erect Proper the hand grasping the emblem of Mars Sable. *Motto.* To seek, to strive, to find (FD7).

RAPER, *post* LAMPLUGH. John Raper, of Lotherton (Y), marr. 1750 Ann (b. 1729), 4th dau. of the Rev. Thomas Lamplugh, *q.v.,* Canon of York and Rector of Bolton Percy (Y), and sister and coheir of the Rev. Thomas Lamplugh, of Lamplugh, Rector of Copgrove (Y) and Prebendary of York. Their son John Raper, of Lotherton and Abberford (d. 1824), succ. his uncle as Lord of the Manor of Lamplugh 1783, and was succ. by his elder son John Lamplugh Raper (1790-1867), who assumed the name and arms of Lamplugh 1825. He was succ. by his brother Henry (1795-1867), who survived him less than a month, and was succ. by his great nephew Walter Lamplugh Brooksbank, grandson of his only sister Ann (d. 1857) who marr. 1815 James Brooksbank, *q.v.* (CW2 xxxviii 115-8). *Arms.* Per fess wavy Azure and Argent a pale counterchanged and three antelopes' heads erased Or.

RASHDALL. The Very Rev. Hastings Rashdall, M.A., D.Litt. (Oxon), M.A., D.C.L. (Dunelm), F.B.A. (1858-1924), was Chaplain of University College, Durham, and tutor in the University of Durham 1884, Canon of Hereford 1910-17, and Dean of Carlisle 1917-24. *Arms.* Sable an orle within four martlets and as many roses Argent barbed and seeded Proper alternating in orle. *Crest.* Upon a plate a martlet Azure.

RATHBONE, of Bassenfell. Samuel Greg Rathbone, of Bassenfell, formerly of Allerton (L) (b. 1823), was 2nd son of William Rathbone, J.P., of Greenbank, Liverpool. His 3rd son Robert Cuthbert Rathbone (1865-1943) was buried at St. John's, Bassenthwaite. *Arms.* Ermine on a fess Azure between two roses in chief Gules barbed and seeded and the Roman fasces erect in base Proper three bezants. *Crest.* The Roman fasces fessways in front

* He was murdered at his home in North-West Malaya.

of a lion's head Proper gorged with a collar Argent charged with two roses Gules. *Motto.* Suaviter et fortiter (BLG10; FLP).

RAUGHTON. Uchtred owned Raughton *temp.* William II. Reginald son of Uchtred was living 1202. According to Denton, one of the family marr. the dau. and heir of Adam de Crookdake and acquired half the hamlets of Gamelsby and Biglands, near Parton. John Raughton owned these lands, and other lands in Crookdake, Bromfield, Burgh, etc. in 1364. Denton says the estates descended to Catherine, wife of John Aspilon, of Buckinghamshire, who sold them to the Warcop family (DAC; CW2 x). *Arms.* ... on a bend ... two annulets .... Also: ... a bend ... cotised ... (MMD). DAC, however, states that the arms, or cognizance, were: "the sparrow hawk."

RAWLINSON, of Duddon Hall. Miss Frances Esther Millers left Duddon Hall to her cousin Capt William Sawrey Rawlinson (1835-75). His son William Millers Rawlinson (1863-97) succ. and had an only son William Gray Rawlinson (1890-1915), Lieutenant, D.C.L.I., who was killed in action in France. For fuller details, see AWL. *Arms.* Sable three swords paleways the centre one point downwards the other two points upwards Proper hilts and pommels Or a chief indented of the last. *Crest.* An armed arm couped at the elbow erect Proper grasping a sword as in the arms. *Motto.* Non mutandus (AWL).

RAWSON, of Wastdale Hall. Stansfeld Rawson, D.L., J.P., of Wastdale Hall (1778-1856), 2nd son of John Rawson, of Stonyroyd (Y), was succ. at Wastdale Hall by his 2nd son Charles Stansfeld Rawson, also of Gale Syke, Wastdale (1812-63). *Arms.* Per fess wavy Sable and Azure gutté d'Or a quadrangular castle with four towers Argent on a a chief Or three ravens' heads erased of the first. *Crest.* Issuant from an annulet Or a raven's head erased Sable gutté d'Or holding in the beak an annulet Gold. *Motto.* Laus virtutis actio (VEW xvi 109, 111).

REA, Baron Rea, of Eskdale. Daniel Key Rea, of Esk Villa, Eskdale (d. 1884), marr. Elizabeth (d. 1884), dau. of Joseph Russell, of Liverpool, and had issue *int. al.* a son James Hall Reay, J.P., who built Gate House, Eskdale, in 1896. After the death of his widow Jane the estate passed to his nephew, Walter Russell Rea, elder son of Russell Rea, P.C., M.P. (1846-1916), founder and senior partner of Messrs. R. & J. H. Rea, shipowners and merchants. Walter Russell Rea (1873-1948), who was Chief Liberal Whip 1931-35, was cr. Baronet 1935 and Baron Rea, of Eskdale, 1937. He was succ. by his elder son Sir Philip Russell Rea, P.C., O.B.E., D.L., J.P., M.A. (Oxon), 2nd Bart. and 2nd Baron. *Arms.* Or on a fess wavy Azure between three stags courant Gules a lymphad sails furled of the field. *Crest.* A stag at gaze Gules resting the dexter fore-leg on an anchor Or. *Supporters.* On either side a stag Gules each charged on the shoulder with a bezant thereon an anchor Azure. *Motto.* In omnia promptus (BP105). The crest and motto are carved in stone over the front door of Gate House.

READE. Robert Reade (d. 1415) was Bishop of Waterford 1394-96, Bishop of Carlisle 1396-97, and Bishop of Chichester 1397-1415. His seal carries the device of what seems to be a bee volant (BBE).

READE. Mary Spencer Revell, Lady Graham, C.B.E., J.P., wife of Sir Fergus Graham, Bart., *q.v.*, whom she marr. 1918, is dau. and heir of Major-General Raymond Northland Revell Reade, C.B., C.M.G., of Stutton

Manor, Ipswich (1861-1943). *Arms.* Quarterly, 1 & 4, Argent a saltire vairé Azure and Or between four Cornish choughs Proper (Reade); 2 & 3, Erminois on a chevron embattled Gules three estoiles Or all within a bordure engrailed Sable (Revell). *Motto.* Cedant arma togae (BLG17).

REAY, of The Gill. This family, descended in the female line from the Osmotherley and Barwis families, was long settled at Bromfield. John Reay (d. 1824) marr. 1769 Julian, dau. of John Jackson, of Crosby, Cross Canonby, and sister and coheir of the Rev. Thomas Jackson. Their 3rd son John Reay (d. 1850, aged 74) was Sheriff of London 1815. Their eldest son Jackson Reay was father of John Reay (1795-1867), who was a wine merchant in Mark Lane, London. In 1829 he built The Gill, which was inherited in turn by his sons* John William (d. 1882, aged 60), George, and the Rev. Thomas Osmotherley Reay,† M.A. (Oxon) (1834-1914), Vicar of Prittlewell, Essex (CW2 xvi 182-3; BLG 1847). *Arms.* Argent three bucks courant Gules. *Crest.* A buck at gaze Gules. *Motto.* In omnia promptus (BHI).

REDMAN. This family took their name from Redmain, Isel, and owned Levens (W) until 1562. Sir Richard Redman (*c.* 1355-1426), Speaker of the House of Commons 1415, was granted the Crown lands in Blencogo 1388 and in 1390 was entrusted with the supervision of the repairs to the castle, gates and walls of Carlisle. He was Sheriff of Cumberland 1389, 1393, 1396, 1398, 1401 and 1411. His descendant Edward Redman (*c.* 1456-1510) was M.P. for Carlisle 1477-78, Sheriff of Cumberland 1492 and M.P. for Westmorland 1495. He marr. Elizabeth (d. 1526), dau. of Sir John Hudleston, *q.v.*, and widow of Sir William Leigh, *q.v.* of Isel, and in 1509 he is described as of Isel. His son Richard (d. 1544) had issue, *int. al.*, a son Matthew (b. 1528) who sold Levens 1561. He appears to have died *s.p.* and it seems likely that his sisters were his coheirs; they included Matilda (d. 1624), who marr. (1) Christopher Irton, of Threlkeld, (2) Thomas Leigh, of Isel, *q.v.*, and (3) Sir Wilfrid Lawson, *q.v.* (GRL; CW2 lxii). *Arms.* Gules three cushions Ermine tasselled Or (NVY; FVY; NB i 204). *Crest.* Out of a ducal coronet a nag's head Gules (CW2 iii 304).

REDNESS. In 1406-7 Richard de Redness sealed a declaration assigning Redness Hall (later the Guildhall), Carlisle, to the Mayor and Citizens of Carlisle after the death of himself and his wife. *Arms.* . . . a fess . . . between in chief a spur . . . between a (?) whip or scythe . . . and a gemring . . . and in base a cross crosslet fitché . . . .

REED of Hassness. Frederic John Reed, D.L., J.P., of Hassness, Buttermere, (1808-1888), eldest son of John Reed of Bridgwater, Somerset (d. 1831) was High Sheriff of Cumberland 1878. He marr. 1835 Mary Ann (d. 1856), dau. of John Wood of Low House, Brackenthwaite, Lorton, and had a son Frederic (b. 1836), who went to America, and was lost sight of by his family, and a dau. Mary Wood (b. 1840), who marr. William George Sale, and had, *int. al.*, a son Frederic William Reed Sale (b. 1868), solicitor, of Carlisle, who was Deputy Official Receiver for Cumberland, and Deputy Coroner for East Cumberland. His son Geoffrey Stead Reed Sale, who is

* He was also father of Charles Reay (1825-86) and Joseph Reay (b. 1829), who both became Major-Generals in the Bengal Army.

† He played cricket for Surrey, Middlesex and Warwickshire, and wrote *A History of Surrey Cricket.*

now of Low House, Brackenthwaite, was formerly Headmaster of Rossall.* *Arms.* Argent a chevron Gules between three boars' heads erased Sable. *Crest.* A stag's head erased Sable semé of bezants. *Motto.* Faciam.

RENWICK. Impaled by Fisher in glass above staircase at Higham Hall; Joseph Fisher, J.P., of Higham Hall, *q.v.*, marr. 1875 Frances Mary (d. 1911), eldest dau. of John Nixon Renwick, of Newcastle upon Tyne. *Arms.* Argent a chief Ermine over all a lion rampant Azure.†

RESTWOLD, of Highhead. Ralph Restwold (d. 1383), M.P. for Westmorland 1336, marr. Juliana, dau. of William L'Engleys, of Highhead, *q.v.*, and so acquired that estate. His grandson Richard was M.P. for Cumberland 1419 and was succ. by his son Richard, M.P. for Cumberland 1421, and for Berkshire 1425. Though the family continued to be Cumberland landowners, they lived in the South, at La Vache, Chalfont St. Giles. Edward Restwold, aged 31 in 1522, sold Highhead to John Richmond, *q.v.*, 1542. His son Anthony was the last male of the family (CW2 xii). *Arms.* Quarterly, 1 & 4, Argent three bendlets Sable (Restwold); 2 & 3, Gules three lions rampant Argent ducally crowned Or (De la Vache) (CW2 xii 26). Field quotes the Visitation of Berkshire as authority for: Per saltire Ermine and Gules, and states that these arms are on the seal of Ralph de Restwold, 1362 (FAC).

REYNOLDSON. Isabella (d. 1739), dau. of (?Thomas) Reynoldson and niece of Isabel, widow of Erasmus Towerson, of Carlisle, marr. (1) 1678 as his 2nd wife Christopher Richmond, of Highhead Castle and Catterlen Hall (d. 1693), *q.v.*, and (2) before 1702 Matthias Miller‡ (d. 1705). *Arms.* Or two chevrons engrailed Gules on a canton of the second a lozenge Argent (Impaled by Richmond in Buck's View of Highhead Castle, 1739).

RIBTON. Alexander de Ribton, whose wife was Joan, owned the manor of Ribton and land in Eaglesfield 1308-9. One of the same name, with a wife Alice, owned lands in Upperby, Carleton, Dalston, Caldcoats, Carlisle and Burgh-by-Sands 1346-47. John Ribton bought the manor of Skelton from the Rev. Lancelot Southaick 1537; his son John sold a third part thereof to John Richmond 1544-5. Lands in Ribton were sold by John Ribton to Henry Tolson and Richard Symson 1558. The manor of Ribton was sold by William Ribton and Jane his wife to Christopher Curwen and others 1597. *Arms.* Quarterly, 1 & 4, Or three crescents Azure (Ribton); 2 & 3, Argent three birds' heads erased Sable (FVC). Burke gives for Ribton, of Ribton: Or three crescents Azure.§ *Crest.* Out of an Eastern crown Or a demi lion passant‖ Gules. Burke also gives for Ribton, of Ribton Hall: *Arms.* Or a

* Mr. Sale has a silver salver which, with a silver tea service, was given to Frederic John Reed "by a few mercantile firms of the City of London, as a testimonial of the high opinion they entertain of his professional exertions in obtaining the important decision of the Court of Exchequer (pronounced on the 12th November 1841) 'that executions founded on judgements on warrant of attorney are not protected by the Statute 2nd & 3rd Victoria Cap. 29'."

† The Renwick family now bears: Per chevron Sable and Argent in chief two lymphads of the second and in base on a mount Vert a horse courant of the first (BP105).

‡ To whom Field wrongly ascribes the Reynoldson arms (FAC).

§ Field suggests that a shield on the ceiling of Carlisle Cathedral displaying: Argent three crescents Azure, may be intended for Ribton (CW2 xxxiv 29).

‖ *Sic*, but clearly a slip, for Fairbairn gives the crest of Ribton, of Ribton, as: Out of an Eastern coronet Or a demi lion rampant Gules (FBC).

cross engrailed Gules in the dexter chief point a crescent Azure a bordure engrailed of the second (BGA).

RICE. A brass in Watermillock church commemorates Sir Cecil Arthur Spring Rice, P.C., G.C.V.O., G.C.M.G. (1859-1918),* Ambassador Extraordinary and Minister Plenipotentiary to the U.S.A. 1913-18, grandson of the 1st Baron Monteagle of Brandon, and of William Marshall, M.P., of Halsteads, Watermillock. His younger brother, Gerald Spring Rice, D.L. (1864-1916), was of Gowbarrow, and was Director for Cumberland Voluntary Aid. He was killed in action, serving with the Border Regt. He marr. 1905 Mary Isabella (d. 1937), dau. of John Bush, of Beauthorn, *q.v. Arms.* Quarterly, 1, Azure a lion rampant Or; 2, Per pale indented Gules and Argent; 3, Paly of six Argent and Azure a bend Gules; 4, Argent on a chevron between three mascles Azure as many mullets of the field. *Crests.* 1, A leopard's face ducally crowned; 2, A demi stag salient. *Motto.* Fides non timet (Brass, Watermillock church; bookplate of Gerald Spring Rice). The correct blazon is: *Arms.* Quarterly, 1 & 4, Per pale indented Argent and Gules (Rice); 2, Azure a lion rampant Or (Meredyth); 3, Argent on a chevron between three mascles Gules as many cinquefoils Argent (Spring). *Crest.* A leopard's face Gules ducally crowned Or (FD7; BP105).

RICHARDSON, or RICARDSON, *post* RANDAL, of Randalholme and Nunwick Hall. The Richardsons owned Randalholme, Alston, as early as 1664. From William Richardson (d. 1680) the estate descended to Thomas Richardson, of Penrith (d. 1708), who marr. a sister and in her issue coheir of Richard Hutton, of Penrith, *q.v.,* and had three daus. and coheirs – Anne (1692-1736), Mary and Frances. Anne marr. 1709 her cousin William Richardson, M.D., of Great Salkeld (1688-1769), son of Christopher Richardson, of Penrith (1650-1730). Their son Christopher Randall Richardson, or Ricardson, J.P. (1715-80), succ. and was also of Nunwick Hall. He directed his son William Randall Fetherstonhaugh Ricardson (1761-1807) to assume the additional name of Randall. The latter died *s.p.* and Nunwick passed to the relatives of his wife Jane† (d. 1810, aged 48), youngest dau. of Adam Wilkinson, of Nentsbury. *Arms.* Quarterly, 1 & 4, Per chevron . . . and . . . three lions' heads erased . . . in chief a label of two points‡ (Richardson); 2 & 3, . . . on a fess . . . three bucks' heads cabossed . . . (Hutton). *Crests.* 1, Issuing from a coronet§ a bull's head (Richardson); 2, Three arrows points downwards one in pale and two in saltire enfiled with a coronet‡ (Hutton). *Motto.* Virtute acquiritur honor (Achievement with date 1746 and initials C R R carved on north front of

* On 12 January 1918, barely a month before his death, on the last night which he spent in the British Embassy in Washington, he wrote the famous lines:

"I vow to thee my country – all earthly things above –
Entire and whole and perfect, the service of my love."

† She, described as "the most amiable and beautiful Miss Jenny Wilkinson", married him at Gretna Green 1780.

‡ Curwen and Field interpreted this as: Per chevron three bulls' heads erased, in chief a label of three points (CCT; FAC). The whole achievement is now very weathered, but we feel that the heads more closely resemble those of lions than of bulls, and can see no trace of horns; nor can we make out a third point on the labels. The seal of Christopher Richardson, of Penrith (1650-1730), mentioned above, certainly displays lions' heads.

§ The coronets seem to have on their rims strawberry leaves alternating with spikes capped with balls, and so to represent either Earls' or Marquess' coronets.

Randalholme). On the seal of the above Christopher Richardson, of Penrith (1650-1730), appears the motto: Bono vincc malum. The shield recorded by Hodgson (HHN II iii 65), formerly on the monument in Kirkhaugh church to W. R. F. R. Randal, as displaying: Argent on a fess Sable three bucks' heads Argent, is clearly that of Hutton. It should, however, be noted that W. R. F. R. Randal's father, the above Christopher Randall Richardson, or Ricardson, of Nunwick Hall, who marr. Sarah (d. 1805, aged 84), dau. of Matthew Fetherstonhaugh, of Featherstone Castle, and sister of Sir Matthew Fetherstonhaugh, 1st Bart. (d. 1774, aged 59) sealed his will dated 1780 with the following: *Arms.* Or on a fess Sable three bucks' heads cabossed . . . ; impaling, Gules a chevron Or between three feathers . . . (Fetherstonhaugh). *Crest.* Three arrows points down one in pale and two in saltire enfiled with a coronet. *Motto.* Toujours fide[le] (*Ex inf.* J. P. Godwin).

RICHARDSON. Anthony Richardson, descended from a family long settled at Byerstead, St. Bees, was born in Maryland, North America, 1738, and died 1787. A merchant in London, in partnership with his relative Anthony Bacon, M.P., he was father of Sir John Richardson, M.A. (Oxon) (1771-1841), barrister at law of Lincoln's Inn, Serjeant at Law 1818, and a Judge of the Common Pleas, who was knighted 1819. He marr. 1804 Harriet (1774-1839), 2nd dau. of Sir Charles Grave Hudson, 1st Bart.*; their eldest son Joseph John Richardson, B.A. (Oxon), barrister at law (1807-42), died unmarr. *Arms.* Sable on a chevron Argent three lions' heads erased of the first. *Crest.* On a mural crown Or a lion's head erased Sable celestially crowned of the first. *Motto.* Semper fidelis (Shields in the New Hall and Council Room of Lincoln's Inn; *Ex inf.* Mr. Roderick Walker, Librarian).

RICHARDSON, of Lowther and Penrith. John Richardson, of Lowther (W) (1766-1812), son of John Richardson, of Stanwix (d. 1806, aged 80), descended from an old Kirkandrews-on-Eden family, was principal agent to Lord Lonsdale, Receiver General of Westmorland, Clerk of the Peace for Westmorland 1799-1812, and Alderman of Carlisle. He marr. Lucy Sidebottom (d. 1829, aged 50); she built Abbot Bank, Penrith, which Lord Lonsdale later bought. Their eldest dau. Mary Anne (d. 1852, aged 41) marr. James Strachan, *post* Strachan-Davidson, merchant, of Manila and Madras, and had a son James Leigh Strachan-Davidson (1843-1916), Master of Balliol College, Oxford, 1907-16. *Arms.* Sable on a chief Argent three lions' heads erased of the field. *Crest* (now broken). A cubit arm erect vested and cuffed Argent (AWL). Bellasis gives this as: An arm embowed vested and cuffed the hand grasping a hammer all Proper (BWN).

RICHARDSON, of Denton Hall. William Richardson, of Denton Hall, Nether Denton, died 1782, aged 63. On a gravestone in Nether Denton churchyard there is a shield bearing a *Crest,* viz. On a wreath a mural crown issuing therefrom a cock's head. Field interpreted this as: On a wreath a mural crown therefrom issuing an eagle's head (FAC).

RICHARDSON, of Holmfoot. Joseph Richardson, of Holmfoot, Lanercost, died 1747,† aged 80, and William Richardson, of Holmfoot, died 1754, aged 81: *Arms.* . . . three chaplets . . . (Lanercost tombstone). Bell Irving,

* Son of Joseph Hudson, of Bowderbeck, Keswick.

† Field incorrectly gives this date as 1717.

however, recorded this as: . . . three annulets . . . (ABD), as did Field (FAC).

RICHMOND. Harl. MS. 1536 and Burke give the following for Richmond, of Cumberland, without further details. *Arms.* Argent a fess engrailed between six fleurs-de-lys Sable (FVC; BGA). DSL gives this coat for Christopher Richmond, of Highhead Castle, *q.v.*, High Sheriff 1691. GMS gives the same coat for Richmond, quarterly with: Or two bars Gules.

RICHMOND, of Corby. The Musard family filled the office of hereditary Constable of Richmond (Y), finally adopting the surname Richmond. Roald Fitz Alan (d. before 1266) marr. *c.* 1250 Isabella, Lady of Corby, who marr. (2) Alan de Lascelles. His son Sir Roald de Richmond, living 1287, was also known as son of Roald le Constable, or de Burton. His son Sir Thomas de Richmond released land in Warwick (C) to his relative John de Warwick 1302. He was present at Caerlaverock* and for his services was granted the Honour of Cockermouth. In 1316 he was killed in Jedburgh Forest by James, Earl of Douglas. His son Roald conveyed Corby to Sir Andrew de Harcla, *q.v.*, 1322 (CW2 xvi). *Arms.* Gules two bars gemel and a chief Or (FFC).

RICHMOND, of Highhead Castle and Catterlen. John Richmond† (d. 1575), who marr. Margaret, dau. of Sir Hugh Lowther, bought Highhead Castle from the Restwold family *temp.* Henry VIII. His son and heir John (d. 1597) was succ. by his son Christopher (d. 1644), High Sheriff of Cumberland 1630, who marr. Isabella Chaytor, *q.v.* Their son Christopher (1623-76), who recorded his pedigree at Dugdale's Visitation, 1665, marr. (1) Mabel, dau. and coheir of John Vaux, of Catterlen Hall, *q.v.*, and so acquired that estate, and (2) 1662 Magdalen (d. 1674), dau. of Andrew Hudleston, of Hutton John. His son and heir Christopher (d. 1693), High Sheriff 1691, marr. (1) Mary, dau. of Sir Wilfrid Lawson, Bart., *q.v.*, and had a dau. Jane (d. 1731), marr. 1696 William Stephenson, of Plumpton, and a son and heir Christopher (1671-1702) who succ. and marr. 1696 Elizabeth (d. 1740, aged 63), dau. and heir of Hugh Watson, of Holms in Allendale, by whom he had Elizabeth (1699-1768), and Isabella (1701-46) who marr. John Hutchinson, *q.v.*, of Durham; their descendants are the heirs general of the Richmond family. The above Christopher Richmond (d. 1693) marr. (2) 1678 Isabella Reynoldson, *q.v.*, by whom he had a son Henry Richmond

* His bravery is commemorated in the Caerlaverock Roll thus:

> Thomas de Richmond comes once more
> One gallant charge he led before;
> Vermillion clad: on vermeil field
> Gold chief with twice twin bars, his shield.
> Brave lances he again has brought
> And madly they the bridge have sought
> Thundering for entry; on each head
> Stones and cornues are fiercely shed.
> But recklessly de Richmond's band
> Drive back the stones with furious hand,
> While those within as madly pour
> On head and neck the ceaseless shower (JPP i 110).

† Field (FAC) calls him "a reputed cadet of the Richmonds of Yorkshire," and adds "There is a strong probability" that he is identical with a John Richmond, born at Wetheral, to whom the following arms were granted 31 Henry VIII: Argent on a bend between two leopards' heads Sable three cinquefoils Or on a chief of the second a bezant between two martlets of the field (Jackson, M.342). This coat impales Reynoldson, *q.v.*, in Buck's View of Highhead Castle.

(1690-1716) who succ. to the estates on his half-brother's death, and left them to his mother; and daus. Isabel (b. 1679), marr. Col Samuel Gledhill; Elizabeth (b. 1680), marr. 1718 Peter Brougham; Sarah (1681-1755), marr. (1) 1710 George Simpson, and (2) John Barker; Mabel (b. 1686), marr. 1713 Henry Brisco; Susanna (1688-1774), who succ. to the estates on her mother's death; and Margaret (1689-1759), marr. William Gale, *q.v.*, whose dau. Isabella, wife of Henry Curwen, inherited Catterlen Hall. Highhead Castle was parcelled out among the other descendants of the sisters and coheirs of Henry Richmond (JPP i; CW2 lxix). *Arms** (as certified by Christopher Richmond at Dugdale's Visitation, 1665, when he spelt his surname Richmund). Gules four barrulets Or a chief of the last† (FCW). This is more usually blazoned as: Gules two bars gemel and a chief Or (LMC). DSL gives for Christopher Richmond, High Sheriff 1630: Barry of six Or and Gules. *Crest.* A demi cat-a-mountain Proper grasping a helmet between its paws. *Motto.* Deo vivente juvante (OMH). The arms, crest and motto are to be seen at Catterlen Hall. There is a fine stone carving of the Visitation version of the arms, impaling: [Gules] fretty [Argent] a crescent for difference (Hudleston), over the entrance to Orthwaite Hall, with initials C[hristopher] R[ichmond] and date 1675 (CW2 lxix).

RICHMOND, Earl of. John, Duke of Brittany and Earl of Richmond, held the Honour of Penrith for a short time *temp.* Richard II (NB ii 398; LMC p. 144). *Arms.* Chequy Or and Azure a canton Ermine all within a bordure Gules powdered with lions passant guardant of the first (BGA; FAC).

RICHMOND. The Rev. Thomas Knyvett Richmond, M.A. (Oxon) (1833-1901), Canon residentiary of Carlisle 1883-1901, Vicar of St. Mary, Carlisle, 1883-1901, Vicar of Raughton Head 1874-78, and Vicar of Crosthwaite 1878-83, was eldest son of George Richmond, R.A., portrait painter (1806-96), and grandson of Thomas Richmond, miniature painter (1771-1837). He was father of Reginald Thomas Richmond, M.A. (Cantab), M.R.C.S., L.R.C.P., of Seascale (1869-1944) (DNB; WW). *Arms.* Azure two fleurs-de-lys in pale between as many pallets Argent. *Crest.* A demi lion Argent gorged with a collar and chain reflexed over the back Azure the collar charged with two annulets Or holding between the paws encircled by a chaplet of oak an escutcheon Azure thereon a fleur-de-lys Argent. *Motto.* Ancora imparo (FD7).

RIDLEY. Nicholas Ridley, of Willimotswick (N), marr. Alice (d. 1450), dau. and coheir of Sir Clement Skelton, *q.v.*, and her share of the manor of Orton (C) passed to her son Nicholas Ridley, aged 30 in 1450. His descendant of the same name sold it 1577 (CW2 xl). *Arms.* Argent on a mount Vert a bull statant Gules. *Crest.* A greyhound courant Argent collared Or (FVN).

RIDLEY, of Knorren Lodge. John Ridley, of Parkend (N) (d. 1865), marr.

* A Wiltshire family of Richmond, said to be a branch of the Cumberland family, bore the following: *Arms.* Argent a cross patonce azure between four estoiles Gules. *Crest.* A tilting spear Argent headed Or broken in three parts one erect the other two in saltire enfiled with a ducal coronet. *Motto.* Resolve well and persevere. This achievement may, however, have been adopted from a Webb heiress. A Lancashire branch of the Wiltshire Richmonds bore the same arms, crest and motto, but substituted mullets for estoiles in the arms (CW1 ii 109-10).

† And on an escutcheon of pretence: Gules a fess chequy Or and of the first between three garbs of the second, for Vaux, of Catterlen, *q.v.*

Bridget, dau. of Matthew Atkinson, of Temple Sowerby, and had issue, *int. al.,* Thomas Ridley, J.P. (1817-1900), who succ. to Parkend, and owned and occupied Knorren Lodge, Askerton, with his brother John Matthew Ridley, J.P., M.A. (Cantab) (1820-99), who rowed for Cambridge 1840-43. The former was succ. by the latter's son John Hilton Ridley, J.P., M.A. (Cantab) (1848-1904), who rowed for Cambridge 1869 and 1870. He was succ. by his son Charles Noel Ridley, Captain Northumberland Hussars Yeomanry (1884-1915), who died of wounds received in action. He was succ. at Parkend by his younger brother and at Knorren by his daus. and coheirs – Nancy Daphne, who marr. (1) Capt W. G. Collyer, (2) Capt John Vedder, and (3) John Metcalfe; Phyllis; and Jean Mary (BLG17). *Arms.* Gules on a chevron between three falcons Argent as many pellets. *Crest.* A bull passant the tail extended over the back Gules. *Motto.* Constans fidei (BLG8).

RIDLEY, in Batenbush. John Ridley, in Batinbush (now Batenbush), Kirkandrews-on-Esk, blacksmith, died 1731, aged 60. *Arms.* . . . three horseshoes . . . . *Crest.* A hand cuffed and couped at the wrist and holding a hammer (Gravestone in Kirkandrews-on-Esk churchyard).

RIDLEY, of Walton Rigg. Thomas Ridley, of Walton Rigg, marr. Sarah (d. 1744, aged 35), whom the inscription on her gravestone declares to have been "devout, meek, diligent, industrious and charitable." Field (FAC), wrongly states that she died aged 135! *Arms.* . . . a cross . . . (Gravestone, Walton churchyard).

RIGGE. A Cumberland family, of which no details are available. *Arms.* Ermine on a chevron Gules three annulets Or (Harl. MS. 1536, in FVC). Burke spells the name Rigg, and gives for *Crest.* A human heart Or charged with a rose Gules (BGA).

RILEY, of Ennim. Major Hamlet Riley, D.L., J.P., LL.B. (Cantab), of Ennim, Blencowe (1851-1922), 2nd son of James Riley, of Brearley House (Y), was High Sheriff of Cumberland 1901. His only son Lt-Col Hamlet Lewthwaite Riley, D.S.O., O.B.E., B.A. (Oxon), of the Rifle Brigade (1882-1932), had two sons – William Hamlet Riley (1927-63) and Major Timothy Richard Riley, the 3rd Green Jackets, who is of Burbank House, Blencowe. *Arms.* Or on a chevron between in chief two crosses pattée fitché Azure and in base on waves of the sea a ship in full sail Proper three bees volant of the field (BLG10; FD7; M.I., Greystoke church). BLG18, however, gives: Or a chevron between in chief two crosses pattée fitché and in base an ancient ship Azure on a canton gules nine billets of the field, three, three, two and one. *Crest.* A dragon's* head couped Sable bezanté in front thereof an anchor entwined with a cable fesswise Or. *Mottoes.* Sans Dieu rien (BLG10); Si nemo sequitor solus ibo (BLG18).

RIMINGTON, of Tynefield. This family takes its name from Rimmington (Y). William Rimmington, of Sedbergh, was father of Timothy Rimmington, of Castlegate, Penrith, who came to the town and established himself as a chairmaker *c.* 1735. His son Michael (d. 1814) was a grocer and banker and built Tynefield, Penrith, 1805. His son George Rimington, banker (b. *c.* 1784), was of Ludgate Hill, London, before settling at Tynefield, where he was succ. by his son Michael (1807-69), whose eldest son George Arthur

* A rather amusing misprint in BLG18 converts this into a dragoon's head.

Rimington,* J.P., M.A. (Oxon), barrister at law (1856-1931), was Chairman of Cumberland Quarter Sessions 1906-30 and a member of Cumberland County Council. He lived at the Mansion House, Penrith, and later at Tynefield. By Frances Dykes (d. 1928, aged 78), dau. of Sir Robert Brisco, Bart., *q.v.*, he had a youngest son Geoffrey Brisco Rimington† (1891-1952), administrator, Overseas Civil Service, Kenya. His son Geoffrey Philip Rimington, of Stoke Poges, Bucks., formerly Agricultural Officer, Overseas Civil Service, is now head of the family. *Arms.* Argent six barrulets Azure‡ a bend Gules. *Crest.* A cubit arm erect vested Gules cuff Argent holding in the hand a broken tilting-spear Proper. *Motto.* Avito viret honore (Bookplate of G. Philip Rimington).

RITSON. The Rev. Joseph Ritson (d. 1712), ordained in Carlisle 1695, was schoolmaster and Curate of Alnwick 1704-12. His son the Rev. Joseph Ritson (1710-58) was Curate of Brigham 1736, Vicar of Dearham 1736-58, Rector of Egremont 1737-58, and Schoolmaster of Cockermouth 1731-58. He marr. 1737 Mary (d. 1757), dau. and heir of the Rev. Thomas Jefferson, *q.v. Arms.* The Rev. Joseph Ritson, jun., sealed with what could be either: ... three birds' heads erased ... ; or perhaps: ... three lions' heads erased ... (Record Office, Carlisle, DRC 10).

ROBERTSON, of Cleator. William Robertson, of Cleator Mains, attorney (d. 1704), marr. 1688 Phoebe (d. 1745), dau. of John Lamplugh, of Lamplugh (d. 1689), *q.v.* Their son John (1691-1735) succ. He marr. Henrietta (d. 1733), dau. of Ferdinando Latus, *q.v.*, and widow of John Hudleston, of Egremont (d. 1733), but died *s.p.*, his heirs being his sisters Frances, who marr. 1711 William Savage, and Phoebe (b. 1697) (CCC). *Arms.* ... a chevron ... between three stags ... (Seal in Record Office, Carlisle).

ROBERTSON, of Rowrah. John Robertson, of Rowrah, died 1738, aged 71. His dau. Deborah (1699-1789) marr. Richard Skelton, of Rowrah. *Arms.* ... a fess ... between three stags statant .... *Crest.* A stag statant (Gravestone in Lamplugh churchyard). Field recorded the arms with tinctures, viz. Argent a fess Azure between three stags statant Gules (FAC).

ROBERTSON-WALKER – see WALKER.

ROBINSON, of Bothel. The tombstone of Anne (d. 1737, aged 69), wife of William Robinson, of Bothel, in Torpenhow churchyard, displays the following. *Arms.* ... on a chevron ... between three stags trippant ... as many cinquefoils ... ; impaling, Fletcher, *q.v. Crest.* A stag trippant. Field recorded these with tinctures, viz. *Arms.* Vert on a chevron between three

* His younger brother, Lt-Gen Sir Michael Frederick Rimington, K.C.B., C.V.O., B.A. (Oxon) (1858-1928), was commissioned in the Inniskilling Dragoons 1881, and won fame in the Boer War as the commander of Rimington's Guides (the "Tigers"). *The Times* said of him "Picturesque is the word that best describes him. He makes everyone else look hopelessly commonplace. His men admire him immensely, like him a good deal, and fear him a little. Generals ... sometimes find him a bit of a handful, that is, if their policy is at all a backward one."

† *The Times* described him as "one of the best known figures in the Kenya administrative service, whose name was almost legendary for turning wild animals into domesticated companions. ... He succeeded in training a zebra as a polo pony but regarded the harnessing of an ostrich to his rickshaw as his most spectacular achievement. ... His chimpanzee Mabel ... was his regular table companion, eating determinedly with knife, fork and spoon, and during office hours typing 'Mabel Rimington' on the typewriter."

‡ Perhaps intended to be: Barry of twelve Argent and Azure, etc.

stags trippant Or as many cinquefoils Gules. *Crest.* A stag trippant Or (FAC).

ROBINSON, of Whitbarrow Hall. This old yeoman family built up a large estate at Whitbarrow in Greystoke parish, chiefly through the purchases of the Rev. Isaac Robinson (1754-1819), son of Joseph (1722-92). He left the estate to his nephew, Lieut Joseph Robinson, R.N. (d. 1835), who conveyed Whitbarrow Hall to John Robinson (d. 1871, aged 77), who was either his half-brother or a cousin. He was succ. by his son Thomas (1825-1901), whose son and heir John Harrison Robinson, J.P. (1850-1935), left Whitbarrow when he was 19 for Blackpool, which he saw grow from a village of 5,000 inhabitants to a town of over 100,000. He retired from business in 1903 and returned to Whitbarrow; he was a member of Penrith Rural District Council and a Director of the Ullswater Steam Navigation Co. His son Roland Walkden Robinson, solicitor, of Blackpool (1876-1947), was father of Sir John Roland Robinson, 1st Lord Martonmere, P.C., K.C.M.G., M.A., LL.B. (Cantab), who was M.P. for Widnes (L) 1931-35, for Blackpool 1935-45, and for Blackpool South 1945-64, when he was cr. Baron Martonmere, of Blackpool in the County Palatine of Lancaster. From 1964 until 1972 he was Governor and Commander-in-Chief of Bermuda. *Arms* (granted to Isaac Robinson 1795, and to the descendants of John Robinson, his grandfather). Azure a flying fish in bend Proper on a chief Or a stag lodged between two cinquefoils Gules. *Crest.* An arm embowed vested Azure cuffed Argent in the hand a flying fish Proper. Though entitled to these arms, Lord Martonmere obtained a grant of the following: *Arms.* Argent a three masted merchant ship of early 18th century date the mainsails furled Proper on a chief Azure a portcullis chained between two roses Or. *Crest.* A lion's head erased Or in the mouth a crescent Gules. *Supporters.* Dexter, A lion Or collared flory counterflory Gules; Sinister, A stag Gules attired and unguled collared flory counterflory Or. *Motto.* Integrity and understanding (BP105).

ROBINSON, of Knopesfould. Elizabeth, wife of John Robinson, of Knopesfould, Lanercost, died 1729. *Arms.* . . . on a chevron . . . between three stags courant . . . three trefoils . . . (Gravestone, Lambley churchyard (N)).

ROBINSON. Cuthbert Robinson, merchant, of Carlisle, was grandfather of George Robinson, of Moore Place, Bucks., M.P. for Great Marlow, who in 1731 obtained a grant of arms for himself and the descendants of his grandfather. *Arms.* Argent on a chevron Azure embattled and counter embattled between three stags Proper a salmon naiant of the first. *Crest.* On a mural crown chequy Argent and Azure a stag's head cabossed Proper (CA viii/1156). *Motto.* Vincam malum bono (BGA).

ROBINSON. Henry Robinson, M.A., D.D. (Oxon) (d. 1616), a native of Carlisle, Principal of St. Edmund Hall, Oxford, 1576, Provost of the Queen's College, Oxford, 1581, was Bishop of Carlisle 1598-1616. *Arms.* Azure a flying-fish in bend Argent on a chief of the last three roses Gules. One authority tinctures the field Vert, and Guillim charges the chief with a rose between two torteaux (BBE).

ROBINSON, of Scalesceugh. John Robinson, yeoman (d. 1862), of Scalesceugh, Carleton, in 1829, had an only son, John Robinson, M.D., M.R.C.S., apothecary to Carlisle Dispensary (d. 1851, aged 24 or 25), and a dau. Frances (d. 1909), who marr. 1854 John Harrison, of Gaitsgill, and had a son John Robinson Harrison, of Scalesceugh, *q.v.* (*Ex inf.* Major A. J. R. Harrison and Mr. and Mrs. G. G. S. Richardson, of Wetheral). *Crest.* A stag trippant. *Motto.* Amicitia (M.I., Wetheral church;* Overmantel at Scalesceugh).

ROBINSON – see WILKINSON.

ROBINSON. An unusual notice appeared in the *Penrith Observer* of 30 September 1862, viz.: At Plumpton Low Street, on the 14th inst., Mr. John Robinson, in his 77th year. He was buried at the parish church of Hesket-in-the-Forest, the family burial place, on the 17th inst., the arms of whose ancestors were – "Argent a chevron between three escalop shells gules" – the bearing whereof was not only ancient but honourable.

ROBINSON, of Maryport. John Wilson Robinson, of Maryport and Highgate, Kendal (*c.* 1725-74), was Mayor of Kendal 1756-57. He marr. Margaret (1735-1812), dau. and coheir of the Rev. Thomas Mawdesley, of Mawdesley Hall (L). Of their children, Godsalve Thomas (b. 1757) was lost at sea *s.p.*; Wilson (b. 1759) died young; Mary (b. 1761) marr. Henry Bainbridge, M.D., of Sedbergh; and Margaret (1763-1808) marr. 1786 William Gibson, of Lune Villa, and Beck Head, Kirkby Lonsdale (1761-1843); from them descends Joseph Stephen Hollins-Gibson, of Sebergham, *q.v.* (CW1 xiv 454; AWL). *Arms.* Vert a chevron between three bucks at gaze Or (*Ex inf.* J. S. Hollins-Gibson).

ROBSON. The gravestones in Lanercost churchyard of Jeoffrey Robson, of Askerton, senior (d. 1726, aged 60); Elizabeth, . . . of Jeffery Robson, of Askerton (d. 1733, aged 24); Edward, son of John Robson, of the Side (d. 1751, aged 25); Elizabeth Robson, of the Side (d. 1753, aged 75, or perhaps 35); Thomas Robson, of Irthington Mill (d. 1753, aged 63); Thomas Robson, of the Tweedy Hill (d. 1763, aged 53); and John Robson, of Highstead Ash (d. 1763, aged 78); all bear the following *Arms.* . . . three boars' heads couped . . . . *Crest.* A boar's head couped. The gravestone in the same churchyard of John Robson, senior, of the Side (d. 1752, aged 83), bears: *Arms.* . . . three boars' heads couped contourné . . . . *Crest.* A boar's head couped contourné.

ROBSON, of Kirkandrews-on-Eden. Impaled by Robson on gravestone in Grinsdale churchyard; Thomas Sibson, of Grinsdale (d. 1726), *q.v.*, marr. 1690 Isabell, dau. of John Robson, of Kirkandrews-on-Eden. *Arms.* . . . a chevron . . . between three boars' heads couped . . . . The shield is very weathered and the boars' heads much resemble bears' heads; Bell Irving interpreted them as does' heads (ABD). Field states that the *Crest* on this stone, which is now indecipherable, is that of Robson, not of Sibson, viz. A demi boar.

ROBSON, of Pelahill. Jane, wife of Richard Robson, of Pelahill, Bewcastle, died 1732, aged 41. *Arms.* . . . three boars' heads couped . . . (ABD).

ROBSON. Charles Stewart Robson, J.P. (b. 1856), 3rd son of the Rev. Thomas William Robson, M.A. (Oxon), Rector of Marske-in-Swaledale (Y), descended from Thomas Robson (d. 1760), who sold his Heighington (D) estate, was tenant of Irton Hall *c.* 1911-25. *Arms.* Azure a chevron

* The inscription to Dr. Robinson is "a tribute to his private worth and valuable and benevolent services that he rendered to the poor during his official connexion with the Carlisle Dispensary."

Ermine between three boars' heads couped Or. *Crest.* Out of a mural coronet Azure a boar's head and neck Erminois (BLG5).

ROCHDALE, Baron and Viscount – see KEMP.

ROLLO. Major the Hon. Gilbert de Ste. Croix Rollo (1872-1932), 5th son of the 10th Baron Rollo, was of Highmoor, Wigton, from 1922 until his death. His only dau. Glory Evelyn marr. 1934 Capt Bernard Henry Esme Howard, of Johnby Hall, *q.v.*, and is now of The Garth, Greystoke. *Arms* (impaled by Howard on shield in hall of Greystoke Castle). Or a chevron between three boars' heads erased Azure.

ROLLO, Duke of Normandy. Shield at Hutton-in-the-Forest; a Vane quartering. *Arms.* Gules two lions passant guardant Or. Another shield displays: Gules two leopards passant Or pelletté. An unidentified shield at Hutton-in-the-Forest, displaying: Gules two lions passant Argent, may also be intended for Rollo.

ROLT. The Rev. Clarence Edwin Rolt, M.A. (Oxon) (d. 1918, aged 37), was Rector of Watermillock 1914-18. His sister Miss Agnes Louise Rolt (d. 1966, aged 81), was of Croft, Watermillock. *Arms.* Argent on a bend Sable three dolphins of the first ducally crowned Or. *Motto.* Cuspis fracta causa coronae (Shield in St. Paul, Deptford, Kent).

ROMILLI – see le MESCHIN.

ROOKE, of Akehead. John Rooke is mentioned in Wigton parish registers in 1604. John Rooke, of Akehead (d. 1716, aged 55), had a grandson John (1750-1817), marr. Peggy (d. 1838, aged 80), dau. of . . . Barnes, of Little Bampton. Their eldest son John Rooke (1780-1856), writer on economic topics, was scientist, mathematician, musician, geologist, and an advocate of free trade (DNB; CHW). *Arms.* Argent on a chevron between three rooks Sable as many suns Or. *Crest.* On a garb Or a rook feeding Proper. *Motto.* Efflorescent cornices dum micat sol (BGA).

ROOKE. Thomas Rooke of Kelsick, Dundraw, marr. 1660 Anne, dau. of John Henderson of Down Hall, Aikton. Their son William Rooke, attorney, Town Clerk of Carlisle* (d. 1731, aged 67), marr. Dorothy (d. 1733, aged 65) sister and co-heir of Charles Smithson, attorney, of Carlisle and Newcastle (d. 1732). Their son John obtained 1755 a grant of arms for himself and his father's descendants. From his brother Henry Rooke, Chief Clerk of the Records in the Tower of London (1711-75) descended Mortimer Rooke,† B.A. (Oxon), solicitor, of The Ivy, Chippenham, Wilts., and Eccleston Square, S.W.1 (1854-1942), whose 2nd son John Wentworth Rooke, O.B.E., Capt Wilts Yeomanry, of The Ivy (1887-1965), had four daus. and co-heirs – Rosalind Jane, marr. 1948 Richard Brian, Elizabeth Anne Seymour, marr. 1956 John Peter Henderson Werner, Portia Joan Peters, marr. 1958 John Michael Westhead, and Susan Freda. *Arms.* Argent on a chevron engrailed Azure between three rooks Proper as many suns in their splendour Or. *Crest.* A garb thereon a rook in a feeding posture all Proper. *Motto.* Nos pascit Deus. (*Ex inf.* Miss S. F. Rooke, of The Old Rectory, Little Langford, Salisbury; BLG13).

ROOS, or ROS. Robert de Roos, Lord of Helmsley (Y) (d. 1226-7), son of Everard de Roos, Lord of Helmsley (d. *c.* 1186) and his wife Roesia, dau. and coheir of William Trusbut, Lord of Warter (Y), and ancestor of the Barons Ros of Helmsley, Werk and Kendal, was Sheriff of Cumberland 1213. *Arms.*

* For an account of his acquittal on a charge of barratry 1713, see CW2 iv 64.

† He was the 7th child of a 7th child of a 7th child.

Gules three water bougets Argent (FFC; EDP; Shields on ceiling of Carlisle Cathedral). In the Musgrave window in Kirkoswald church the arms of Roos, of Yolton (Y), appear as: Or three water bougets within a tressure flory Gules.

ROOS, or ROSSE. John de Roos, or Rosse (d. at Rose Castle 1332), was Bishop of Carlisle 1325-32. *Arms.* Gules three water bougets Argent (BBE). Field states that he was son of Lord Roos of Hamlake but he is not in the pedigrees in EDP or BEP.

ROPER. Impaled by Howard on shield in hall of Greystoke Castle; Bernard Howard, of Glossop (1674-1735), marr. 1710 Anne (d. 1744), dau. of Christopher Roper, 4th Baron Teynham. *Arms.* Per fess Azure and Or a pale counterchanged and three bucks' heads erased of the second.

ROSS, of Staffield. Mary, eldest dau. of George Lowthian, *q.v.*, (d. 1735), and coheir of her brother Richard, marr. Alexander Ross, of Dumfries, and had a son George, whose son Richard Lowthian Ross succ. to Staffield Hall 1798 after the death of his uncle's widow. He much improved the estate, planting thousands of trees, and making the walks opposite Nunnery Walks. He sold Staffield 1837. *Arms.* Quarterly, 1 & 4, Gules three lions rampant Argent (Ross); 2 & 3, Lowthian, *q.v.* (John Atkinson's MS. notebook).

ROSS. Impaled by Coulthart in west window of Bolton church (C); William Coulthart, of Pasture House, also of Collyn, Dumfriesshire (1774-1847), *q.v.*, marr. 1801 Helen (d. 1860), 2nd dau. of John Ross, of Dalton, Dumfriesshire. *Arms.* Gules a water bouget Argent. Correctly, Gules three water bougets Argent (BLG4).

ROTHERY. Charles William Rothery (1823-77), elder son of John Rothery, of Leeds, merchant, was of Greta Hall, Keswick, *c.* 1858-63. *Arms.* Per bend Or and Gules two bends indented counterchanged. *Crest.* A tower Argent charged with two bendlets indented and issuing from the battlements thereof a demi lion Gules holding with his dexter paw three arrows one in pale and two in saltire Proper. *Motto.* Festina lente (BLG4).

ROUTLEDGE, of Bewcastle; and of Stapleton. Bell Irving recorded the tombstones of a number of members of the Routledge clan, of Bewcastle, who lived in the 18th and early 19th century at Flatt, Graham's Onset, Greenholme, Hillend, Kilstown, Kirkbeckstown and Park, all of which displayed the following *Arms* with slight variations: . . . a chevron . . . between in chief a garb . . . and a branch . . . and in base a rose . . . , in chief a sword fessways hilt to the dexter. The variations are the replacement of the rose in base by an escallop, an oak leaf, a cinquefoil, a fleur-de-lys, a heart voided, or a mullet; and the transfer of the sword from the shield to use as a crest. Bell Irving recorded a similar shield, with a mullet in base, and the sword displayed as a crest on a gravestone at Stapleton, on which the inscription had weathered away (ABD).

ROUTLEDGE, of Troughfoot and Smithsteads. Thomas Routledge, yeoman, of Troughfoot and Smithsteads, Stapleton (d. 1745), marr. 1697 Margaret, dau. and heir of Edward Forrester, of the latter place. The date of her death and age on her tombstone in Stapleton churchyard have been read as 172–, aged 52(?), but her burial is not recorded there between 1720 and 1729. Her son Edward Routledge (d. 1758, aged 54) succ. to Smithsteads; his dau. Eleanor (d. 1814, aged 73) marr. Reginald Armstrong. *Arms.* . . . an indecipherable charge* . . . and in chief three mullets . . . (Stapleton gravestone). Bell Irving added tentatively a bordure (ABD).

ROWLEY, of Glassonby Lodge. Edwin Rowley (1823-88), whose family came from Yorkshire, was of Glassonby Lodge, where he was succ. by his son William Edwin Rowley (d. 1904, aged 48). His son Major Guy Shafto Rowley, F.R.G.S., Major 8th King's Royal Irish Hussars (1889-1976), marr. 1935 Muriel Elizabeth, dau. and coheir of Robert McQueen Grant. Their son Guy Grant Rowley is now of Glassonby Lodge. *Arms.* Argent on a fess between three pierced mullets of six points Sable as many like mullets of the field. *Crest.* A sword bendwise Argent hilt and pommel Or passing through a pierced mullet of six points Sable. *Motto.* Faites bien et laissez dire (M.I. Addingham church).

RUDD, of Dovenby and Cockermouth. Mary A. Rudd in RRF traces the descent of the branch settled at Dovenby and Cockermouth from Robert (1599-1661), son of Robert Rudd, of The Hollins, Lorton. His descendant John Rudd, of Dovenby and Whitehaven (1714-62), marr. 1738 Ann (d. 1793), dau. and heir of Thomas Trohear, of Papcastle and Dovenby. Their son John Rudd, of Dovenby and Cockermouth (1741-1800), marr. 1770 Jane, dau. and coheir of William Thompson, of Workington, and had issue, *int. al.*,† the Rev. John Rudd, M.A. (Cantab) (1770-1834), Vicar of Blyth, Notts., and William Rudd, attorney, of Derwent House, Cockermouth (1780-1841), whose 2nd wife Marianne (d. 1842, aged 37) was dau. of John Head, of High Cross, Loweswater, and niece and coheir of the Rev. James Satterthwaite, *q.v.* The Rev. John Rudd's granddau. Mary Amelia (b. 1863) was author of the family history, RRF. The head of the family after 1922 was her nephew Douglas George Ferris Rudd (b. 1898). *Arms.* Argent on a canton Azure five martlets Or. *Crest.* A cross botoné. This achievement is on the tomb in Bridekirk churchyard of Thomas Rudd (d. 1833), uncle of the Rev. John Rudd, who, having enquired at the College of Arms, was told that these were the only Rudd arms registered. He therefore placed these arms on his uncle's tomb, though the family had earlier used: Azure a lion rampant and a canton Or. The family resumed the use of this latter coat, with *Crest.* A cross botoné Or. *Motto.* In cruce salus.

RUSSELL, of Roanlands. The Russells of Arnaby, Millom, descended from John Russell (d. 1608) whose grandson Matthew (1615-85) acquired Roanlands by marriage to a Taylor heiress. His grandsons were Robert Russell, of Roanlands (1682-1757), and Matthew, a merchant in Sunderland (1685-1760), who died *s.p.* and left his fortune to his brother's younger son William Russell (1734-1817) who bought Brancepeth Castle (D) and in 1803 succ. his brother Matthew (1733-1803) as owner of Roanlands, which he sold. He was said to be one of the richest commoners in England, with an income of £80,000 a year, derived chiefly from his collieries. He marr. Mary, dau. and coheir of Robert Harrison, of Sunderland, and was succ. by his son Matthew Russell, D.L. (d. 1822), M.P. for Saltash 1801-22, whose son William (1798-1850) died *s.p.*, leaving Brancepeth Castle to his sister Emma Maria (d. 1870); she marr. 1827 Gustavus Frederick, 7th Viscount Boyne (1797-1872), who

* Variously described by different authorities as: a trefoil figure; not unlike an escallop; three(?) garbs; and a doe's head facing to the sinister.

† His 2nd son Thomas Trohear Rudd (b. 1772) and Mary his wife were murdered by three of their slaves on their Skiddaw plantation, Portland, Jamaica, 1803.

assumed the additional surname and arms of Russell 1850 (BLG 1846; GEC). *Arms.* Argent on a chevron between three cross crosslets fitché Sable an escallop Or. *Crest.* A goat passant Argent (Hatchments, Brancepeth church; Shields, Brancepeth Castle; BGA).

RUSSELL, of Workington. Burke assigns to a family of Russell, of Workington, the following. *Arms.* Argent a lion rampant Gules on a chief Sable three roses of the field. *Crest.* A goat passant Argent attired Or.

RUSSIAN EMPIRE. Amongst the shields in the east window of Upperby church commemorating the Allies of World War I, is one presumably intended for the Russian Empire. *Arms.* Gules an eagle displayed with two heads wings inverted Sable on the breast an escutcheon of the first charged with a cross Argent.

RUTHVEN, OF FREELAND, Baroness. Bridget Helen, who succ. her father Major-General Walter Patrick, 10th Lord Ruthven, of Freeland, C.B., C.M.G., D.S.O. (1870-1956), as Baroness Ruthven, of Freeland, marr. (1) 1918 the 11th Earl of Carlisle, *q.v.,* and (2) 1947 the 1st Viscount Monckton, of Brenchley. *Arms.* Paly of six Argent and Gules a bordure Ermine. *Crest.* A goat's head couped Argent attired Or. *Supporters.* Two goats Argent attired maned and unguled Or gorged of collars Gules. *Motto.* Deeds shaw (BP105).

RYDER. John Oldham Ryder, merchant, of 35 Back Piccadilly, Manchester (d. at Irton Hall 1871, aged 38), marr. Elizabeth (1836-1911), eldest child of the Rev. Samuel Irton Fell, Incumbent of Ambleside, and granddau. of William Fell, of Market Street, Ulverston, who marr. 1787 Martha (b. 1766), youngest dau. of Samuel Irton (1714-66), *q.v.* Mrs. Ryder was first cousin once removed and god-daughter of Samuel Irton (1796-1866) who left her the Irton estates, which she sold for £65,100 in 1872, and moved to Rothay Bank, Grasmere, and later to Seedley Lodge, Pendleton, Manchester. Her four sons – Irton (who took the name of Irton 1885); John; the Rev. Charles Senhouse Ryder, M.A. (Cantab), Chaplain of St. George's church, Cannes, 1919-30 (d. there 1930); and Samuel – and three daus. all died *s.p.* (CW2 xli, lxxiv 212-14). *Arms.* Per chevron . . . and . . . three crescents . . . . *Crest.* Out of a mural crown a dragon's head (*Ex inf.* Mrs. H. S. Greg, of Kendal).

RYMER, of Calder Abbey. Thomas Rymer,* J.P., son of William Rymer, solicitor of Manchester, bought Calder Abbey from the Rev. Samuel Minton-Senhouse, *q.v.,* 1885. He was succ. by his nephew Thomas Harrison Rymer, J.P. (1852-1911), only son of William Rymer, of Manchester, who marr. Mary, dau. of Thomas Harrison, of Kendal. He was High Sheriff of Cumberland 1910. In 1887 he marr. Amy Elizabeth (1858-1961), dau. of Robert Falkner, of Kersal, Manchester, and had two daus. and coheirs. *Arms.* Vair a bordure Azure charged with seven bezants a chief arched Gules thereon an ear of rye leaved and slipped Proper between two crosses botoné Argent. *Crest.* In front of a cubit arm in armour holding a sword erect between four ears of rye leaved and slipped two on either side all Proper a cross botoné Gules. *Motto.* Ense animus major (FD7; Monument in Calderbridge church).

ST. ANDREWS, University of. *Arms.* Per saltire Or and Azure in chief an open book Argent in base a lion rampant Gules on a chief of the last a crescent reversed between two mascles Or (Shield on monument in Carlisle

* Affectionately known as "The Abbot of Calder."

Cathedral to Richard Assheton, 1st Viscount Cross, *q.v.*, who was Hon. LL.D., St. Andrews).

ST. AUGUSTINE. A window in Setmurthy church, erected in memory of Joseph Fisher, of Higham (1850-1921), and containing a representation of St. Augustine, displays the following *Arms.* Sable a cross Argent in the first quarter an archiepiscopal staff in pale Or surmounted of a pall Argent charged with five crosses pattée fitché Sable in the second quarter a lily slipped and leaved Proper.

ST. BEES PRIORY. Founded early in the 12th century by William le Meschin, *q.v. Arms.* The Priory used the arms of the Percy family, *q.v.*, as follows: Quarterly, 1 & 4, Or a lion rampant Azure; 2 & 3, Gules three lucies hauriant Argent (TVN; WEC).

ST. BEES SCHOOL. The school* was established as a grammar school by Archbishop Edmund Grindal, *q.v.*, in 1587 and was reconstituted in 1881. *Arms.* The school uses the arms of Archbishop Grindal as Archbishop of Canterbury in the following form: Dexter, Azure an archiepiscopal cross in pale Or surmounted by a pall Proper charged with four crosses pattée fitché Sable; Sinister, Quarterly Argent and Azure a cross quarterly Ermines and Or between four doves collared counterchanged; the whole ensigned with a bishop's mitre. *Motto.* Expecta Dominum (*Ex inf.* W. Fox, Bursar, St. Bees School, from information supplied by the College of Arms).

ST. BEES THEOLOGICAL COLLEGE. Founded in 1806 by George Henry Law, Bishop of Chester, the College was intended to provide "for the better instruction of those candidates for Holy Orders who were unable to obtain a University education." Its most generous benefactor was the 2nd Earl of Lonsdale, who endowed it with the vicarage of St. Bees and re-built the choir of the Priory for use as lecture room and library. The College ceased to exist 1896 (BPP). *Arms.* The College used those of the Priory, *q.v.* (St. Bees College Calendar, 1854).

ST. JOHN. The Rev. Henry St. Andrew St. John, M.A. (Oxon) (1796-1874), great-grandson of John, 10th Lord St. John of Bletsoe, was Vicar of Addingham 1834-38. To another branch of the same family belonged Canon Maurice William Ferdinand St. John, B.A., D.D. (Dunelm) (1827-1914), grandson of George Richard, 4th Viscount St. John and 3rd Viscount Bolingbroke. He was Curate of Drigg 1851-53. His great-grandson Kenneth Oliver Musgrave St. John is now the holder of the two titles. *Arms.* Argent on a chief Gules two mullets Or. *Crest.* A mount Vert thereon a falcon rising Or ducally gorged Gules. The Barons St. John bear the same, with the falcon belled Or. *Motto.* Of the Viscounts St. John and Bolingbroke: Nec quaerere nec spernere honorem. Of the Barons St. John: Data fata secutus (BP105).

ST. JOHN'S COLLEGE, Oxford. In window in St. John's-in-the-Vale church commemorating Henry Corrie Jackson, *q.v.*, Scholar of St. John's College, Oxford, who died at Boshof, South Africa, 1900, aged 20. *Arms.* Gules on a bordure Sable eight estoiles Or on a canton Argent a lion rampant Sable; an annulet Gold for difference.†

* W. G. Collingwood in *The Lake Counties* rather charmingly couples it and the bathing-beach at St. Bees as "the staples of the place."

† Geoffrey Briggs in CCH states that these arms "are of no authority" and blazons the canton as Ermine.

ST. MARY'S ABBEY, York. William le Meschin, *q.v.*, gave the church of St. Bees and the chapel of Egremont to St. Mary's Abbey, York. His son Ranulph le Meschin confirmed the grant and gave the priory of Wetheral to St. Mary's, which also held the parish of Workington until the Reformation. *Arms.* These are displayed on the ceiling of St. John's, Workington, as: Sable three birds Argent. This is Woodward's blazon, together with: Argent on a cross Gules a bezant figured Or in the dexter canton a key (WEC). For fuller versions of this second coat, see AWL.

ST. OWEN. Shields at Hutton-in-the-Forest; a Vane quartering. *Arms.* Gules a cross Argent in the first quarter an escutcheon Or charged with three chevrons of the first.

SALKELD, of Brayton. Thomas Salkeld (d. 1627), who bought Salter Grange 1584, was grandson of Lancelot Salkeld, of Whitehall, *q.v.* His son Thomas Salkeld, of Brayton (living 1649), marr. Isabel, dau. of Sir Edward Musgrave, and left three daus. and coheirs – Catherine, marr. *c.* 1641-2 Joseph Patrickson, of Carswell How, *q.v.*; Frances, marr. William Barwis; and Mary, marr. Thomas Wybergh *q.v. Arms* (as borne by Patrickson on an escutcheon of pretence at the Visitation of 1665). Or fretty Vert (FCW). The Wyberghs quartered for Salkeld: Vert fretty Argent a canton Gules, but this is the coat of Salkeld of Threapland.

SALKELD, of Little Salkeld and Corby. Richard de Salkeld, Knight of the Shire for Cumberland 1328, was granted the manor of Corby by Edward II and in 1332-33 bought half the manor of Little Salkeld from William and Joan de Arthuret. His younger son Hugh appears to have been ancestor of the Salkelds, of Whitehall, *q.v.*; his elder son John was father of Richard Salkeld (d. 1388-9), Knight of the Shire 1382. His descendant Sir Richard Salkeld (d. 1501) was High Sheriff 1457, 1461, 1465, 1470, 1483-85, and 1494. He marr. Joan, dau. and heir of Roland Vaux, of Triermain, *q.v.*; their daus. and coheirs were Christian, marr. William Dykes, *q.v.*; Anne, marr. before 1506 Lancelot Warwick; Margaret, marr. *c.* 1470 Thomas Blenkinsop, *q.v.*; Maude, marr. (1) Nicholas Fetherstonhaugh, (2) John Sandford; Agnes, marr. . . . Eaglesfield; and Katherine, marr. (1) her kinsman Thomas Salkeld, of Rosgill, (2) Sir Christopher Curwen (d. 1499), *q.v.*, and (3) before 1510 Richard Duckett. By her first husband Katherine had a son Thomas Salkeld (d. 1574) whose son Richard (d. 1575) owned the manors of Rosgill and Timperon, and half the manors of Corby and Little Salkeld, which descended to his dau. Barbara (1540-1626) who marr. before 1559 her kinsman George Salkeld, of Rosgill and Thrimby (d. 1597). Their son Thomas (1567-1639) was High Sheriff of Cumberland 1598 and sold his moiety of Corby to Lord William Howard 1625. His son Richard (1593-1630*) was succ. by his sister Dorothy Wormeley, widow. The Little Salkeld estate came to George Salkeld who sold it "for a song"† to Col Thomas Cholmley during the Civil War (CW2 xxi and lxvi). *Arms.* The original arms of the parent branch of the Salkeld family appear to have been Vert a fret Or, or Vert fretty Or (FFC; CW2 xxi 71). The monument of Sir Richard Salkeld in Wetheral church (d. 1501, see above) displays: . . . fretty . . . ; DSL ascribes to him: Vert a fret Argent. At the Visitation of Yorkshire 1563-4, the above Thomas Salkeld (d. 1574) recorded: Quarterly,

* Not 1631, as stated in error in AWL.

† Thomas Denton's MS. *History of Cumberland.*

1 & 4, Vert fretty Argent (Salkeld); 2, Argent fretty and a chief Gules (Salkeld); 3, Argent a bend chequy Or and Gules (Vaux) (NVY); Quarter No. 2 must be intended for Salkeld of Corby, and FVC (p. 12) records a similar coat, viz. Argent a fret and a chief Gules. Dykes, of Dovenby, quarters Salkeld, of Corby, as: Vert a fret Or (see p. 99, above). MMD and FVE give: Vert fretty Argent.

SALKELD, of Ranbeck and Holme Hill. Joseph Salkeld, of Penrith and Ranbeck, Kirkland (d. 1809), was father of Thomas, John, of Ranbeck (1763-1819), and Joseph, of Randalholme and Holme Hill (1765-1835), see below. Thomas Salkeld, J.P. (1760-1820), became Lt-Col, 27th Bengal Native Infantry, and was later of Eusemere (W), Abbey Street, Carlisle, and Holme Hill, Hawkesdale, which he bought 1810 from George Holme Sumner, *q.v.* He was High Sheriff of Cumberland 1819. In 1809 he marr. Abigail, youngest dau. and coheir of John Mitchinson, *q.v.*, but died *s.p.* and was succ. by his brother Joseph, above. He was succ. by his son Lt-Col Thomas Salkeld, D.L., J.P. (1806-78), of the Royal Westmorland Militia, who was High Sheriff of Cumberland 1850. His successor was his nephew Louis Carruthers Salkeld, J.P. (1857-1916), who was High Sheriff 1896, and was also of Hawkesdale Hall and Wormanbie, Dumfries. His son Major Carleton Salkeld, J.P. (b. 1880), succ. and was later of Mill Eden, Wetheral. He left five daus. *Arms.* Vert fretty Argent. *Crest.* A demi dragon rampant. *Motto.* Foy en tout (M.I.s, Kirkland and Dalston churches). Field blazons the crest vert (FAC).

SALKELD, of Threapland. John Salkeld, called in FVC of "Holmerock," a younger brother of Lancelot Salkeld, of Whitehall (d. 1610), *q.v.*, bought the manor of Threapland from Lancelot Skelton, of Armathwaite. He marr. Barbara, dau. of George Fletcher,* and was succ. by their son John (1613-66), who marr. Mary (d. 1673), dau. of the Rev. Thomas Fairfax, Rector of Caldbeck. Their son Henry (b. *c.* 1633) was buried at Lamplugh as of Bothel and Threapland 1725. His son John† (d. 1703) marr. 1698 Frances, dau. of John Williamson, of Snittlegarth. Their sons Henry (b. 1699), John (b. 1700), and Roger (b. 1703), all died between June and July 1705, and their dau. Frances (1698-1749), who was of Wigton, was the last of the family.‡ Her father's sisters were Mary (1664-1733), marr. 1687 Cuthbert Osmotherley, *q.v.*; Grace (d. 1732), marr. 1712 the Rev. David King, Rector of Lamplugh; Elizabeth (b. 1670), marr. 1700 William Smith; and Margaret (1684-1737), marr. 1732 Richard Barwis, of Workington, distiller, and later of Cockermouth (d. 1735) (*Ex inf.* the Rev. F. B. Swift; CW2 xvi; Haswell's MS. continuation of Pedigrees in FCW). *Arms.* Vert fretty Argent a canton Gules (FCW).

SALKELD, of Whitehall.§ The Salkelds of Whitehall apparently descend from Hugh Salkeld, son of Richard, of Corby and Little Salkeld, *q.v.* He was pardoned in 1369 for having acquired from his father without licence a life interest in the manor of Corby. He marr. Christian, dau. and heir of Sir

* Not Thomas Fletcher, as stated in the 1665 Visitation pedigree (FCW).

† See the footnote to Sykes.

‡ In her will of 1749 she mentions her dear mother Mrs. Frances Richardson, her loving sisters Mrs. Elizabeth, Mrs. Grace and Mrs. Mary Richardson, and her cousin Mr. Joseph Williamson. Her mother (d. 1755) marr. (2) 1708 John Richardson, of Blackhallwood, by whom she had the three daughters named above.

§ Said to be the Whiteladies of Scott's novel *Redgauntlet.*

John Rosgill, of Rosgill, and acquired that manor, which passed to his descendant, Thomas Salkeld (see Salkeld, of Corby). Robert Salkeld, of Timperon, a younger son of Hugh, was father of John Salkeld, of Gowbarrow, whose son Lancelot (living 1539) marr. before 1505 Margaret (b. *c.* 1479), dau. of Sir Richard Hudleston and sister and coheir of Richard Hudleston, of Millom, *q.v.* From their three grandsons Lancelot, Thomas and John descended the families settled at Whitehall, Brayton, *q.v.*, and Threapland, *q.v.* The first named was of Whitehall and died 1610, having marr. Elizabeth (d. 1616), dau. and coheir of Nicholas Bardsey, of Bardsea (L), *q.v.* Their son Francis (d. *s.p.* 1633) succ. and was succ. by his brother Nicholas (b. 1584) who also died *s.p.* when he was succ. by his brother Thomas (d. 1638) who was of Coniscliffe (D), and was described in 1625 as "a very dangerous Popish Recusant." His grandson Sir Francis Salkeld (d. 1702) was knighted 1660 and was High Sheriff of Cumberland 1662. His children included Thomas, see below, Roger who was out in the '15, and Margaret, who marr. Edward Charlton, of Hesleyside (N). Thomas Salkeld, the heir (d. 1711), was succ. by his son Thomas (1704-36), who was succ. by his brother Dr. Henry Salkeld* (d. *s.p.* 1749), the last male of the family. He marr. 1737 his cousin Margaret (1716-69), dau. of William Charlton. She was succ. in the Cumberland estates by her nephew William Charlton, *q.v. Arms.* Quarterly, 1, Vert fretty Argent; 2, Argent fretty Gules and a chief of the last; 3, Blank, but presumably intended for Hudleston, *q.v.*; 4, Per fess Gules and Argent six martlets, three and three, counterchanged (Fenwick) (FVC). Fleming recorded: Vert a fret Argent (FDC). Lysons gives: Vert fretty Argent a canton Gules; i.e. the differenced coat used by Salkeld, of Threapland (LMC). *Crest.* A demi dragon rampant (?Vert) (FAC).

SALMOND, of Waterfoot. William Salmond, of Seaforth, Antigua, agent for Antigua, and later of Carlisle (1737-79), marr. 1765 Jane (1745-1820), 2nd dau. of Edward Hasell, of Dalemain, *q.v.*, and had issue Major General James Hanson Salmond (1766-1837), who built Waterfoot, Ullswater, where he was succ. by his son Lt-Col James Salmond, J.P., B.A. (Oxon) (1805-80). His 4th son was father of Air Chief Marshal Sir William Geoffrey Hanson Salmond, K.C.B., K.C.M.G., D.S.O. (1878-1933), and of Marshal of the R.A.F. Sir John Maitland Salmond, G.C.B., C.M.G., C.V.O., D.S.O. (1881-1968). Waterfoot descended to his 3rd son Rear-Admiral Henry Salmond, R.N., J.P. (1838-95), whose widow succ., and after whose death 1945 the estate was sold. *Arms.* Azure three salmon hauriant Or. *Crest.* A naked arm Proper holding a spear Or. *Motto.* Optima sapientia probitas (BLG11; M.I.,† Dacre church). Elsewhere, Burke gives; *Arms.* Sable three salmon hauriant Or. *Crest.* A naked arm Sable holding a spear Or. (BGA). Field quotes Whellan as authority for: An arm in armour Sable holding a falchion Or (FAC). Sir John Maitland Salmond bore: *Arms.* Or three salmon hauriant Sable on a chief of the second two wings conjoined with a wreath of laurel of the first. *Crest.* Issuant from clouds a dexter arm embowed the hand Proper grasping a trident Sable (BLG17).

SALVIN. The Rev. Hugh Salvin, M.B. (Cantab) (1773-1852), 5th son of

* He was a Jacobite and was involved in the '45. He left a heavily encumbered estate.

† On the M.I. at Dacre church to James Salmond (1805-80), above, the crest appears as: Issuant from clouds a dexter arm embowed the hand grasping a . . . (now broken).

Anthony Salvin, of Sunderland Bridge (D), a cadet of Croxdale, was Vicar of Alston 1841-52. *Arms.* Argent on a chief Sable two mullets Or (FVD). *Crest.* A wyvern wings elevated and endorsed Vert. *Motto.* Je ne change qu'en mourant (SHD iv (II) 117-20; M.I. Alston church).

SANDEMAN. Ian Gordon Preston Glas Sandeman, of Station House, Millom, is 2nd son of Thomas Glas Sandeman, J.P., of Ellel Grange (L) (1877-1965), 3rd Barao de Sandeman in the Kingdom of Portugal. *Arms.* Argent the emblem of Truth, a naked woman standing on a terrestrial globe issuing out of the base in her dexter hand an open book in her sinister which is elevated above her head a branch of palm on her breast the sun in his splendour all Proper and a veil across her middle of the field within a bordure Gules charged with three fleurs-de-lys also of the first. *Crest.* A rock Proper. *Mottoes.* 1 (Over the crest), Stat veritas; 2 (Under the shield), Olim cruore nunc candore (BLG18).

SANDERSON, of Armathwaite Castle. William Sanderson (d. 1727), son of Christopher Sanderson, of Eggleston and Barnard Castle (D), bought Armathwaite Castle from the Skelton family and was succ. by his brother Robert Sanderson, F.S.A. (1660-1741), who was Clerk of the Chapel of the Rolls, London, Usher of the High Court of Chancery and joint editor of Rymer's *Foedera.* He died *s.p.* and Armathwaite was inherited by his great-nephew William Milbourne, *q.v. Arms.* At the Visitation of Durham, 1666, the above Christopher Sanderson claimed as his arms those of the Sandersons of Brancepeth, viz. Paly of six Argent and Azure over all on a bend Sable a sword Proper hilt and pommel Or; but Dugdale noted: ". . . this family can have no right thereto" (FVD).

SANDERSON, of Penrith. Dugdale's pedigree of the Bird family, of Brougham (W), shews James Bird, who certified the pedigree (aged 31 in 1668), as marr. to Dorothy, dau. of John Sanderson, of Penrith (FCW). *Arms.* Paly of six Argent and Azure a bend Sable (HMS v 149).

SANDERSON. Impaled with Curwen on monument in Ponsonby church; Thomas Curwen, of Sella Park (1590-1653), marr. Helena (1612-70), eldest dau. of Samuel Sanderson, Keeper of Brancepeth Castle (D). *Arms.* Paly of six [Argent and Azure] on a bend [Sable] a sword [Proper] hilt and pommel [Or].

SANDES, of Rottington. John Denton in DAC says "The Sands of Rotington (called in old writings de Sabulonibus) were originally seated upon Burgh Sands where they had their capital house at a place called to this day Sandsfield from whence they took their sirname." In 1377 Richard del Sandes was knight of the shire for Cumberland and Thomas del Sandes served in 1390 and 1394-5. In 1421 William Sandes and Sir Peter Tiliol acquired the manor of Rottington and lands in Dearham, Egremont and Derwent Fells. In 1486 Christopher Sandes, who was Lord of Rottington in 1474 and 1496, "servant to the King's most dear Mother," was appointed porter of the inner gate of Carlisle Castle. His son William had succ. by 1498. The estate descended to Robert Sandes (d. 1588), one of the first governors of St. Bees School 1585. He sold Rottington 1579* and his son Henry (1562-1614) appears to have been the last of the family. His dau.

* Denton (DAC, p. 25) says that he "being dissatisfied . . . with the loss of a mistress, sold his estate to Curwen of Workington and went to Ireland, where he died." This seems doubtful, since he was buried at St. Bees.

Dorothy (b. 1586) marr. 1605 Henry Ponsonby, of Haile (SBR; CCT; JPP). *Arms.* Richard del Sandes bore: Argent a fess dancetté between three cross crosslets fitché Gules (FFC). Thomas de Sandes, whose silver seal was found in Carlisle Castle, bore the same.

SANDES. Burke gives this family as of Cumberland and Surrey, 1512, without further details. *Arms.* Sable on a chevron between three men's heads couped sidefaced Or as many cross crosslets fitché Gules on a chief Argent three birds' legs erased of the first. *Crest.* An heraldic tiger Azure tufted maned collared and lined Or the line twisted around the body four times and falling behind the hind legs (BGA).

SANDES, or SANDS. Burke gives this family as of Lattimer, Bucks, and Cumberland, without further details. *Arms.* Argent a fess dancetté between three crosses pomel fitché Gules (BGA).

SANDFORD. Thomas Sandford, of Askham (W) (d. 1564), who was Sheriff of Cumberland 1546 and 1555, marr. Grace (1516-66), dau. of Anthony Crackanthorpe and niece and coheir of Ambrose Crackanthorpe, *q.v.* Their son and heir Thomas (1538-74) marr. Anne, sister and coheir of Thomas Hutton, *q.v.*, and later wife of John Middleton, *q.v.* (CW2 xxi). *Arms.* Per chevron Sable and Ermine two boars' heads in chief couped Or (FWE). DSL records an earlier member of the family, Robert de Sandford, as Sheriff of Cumberland *temp.* Edward II,* and bearing: Ermine on a chief indented Sable three boars' heads couped Or.

SANDFORD. Francis Berkeley Sandford, M.A. (Cantab), of Roselands, Ambleside (1864-1945), headmaster of Blencowe Grammar School 1896-1912, was 3rd son of the Rev. George Sandford, M.A. (Cantab) (1816-98), Vicar of Eccleshall, Sheffield, and a member of the Sandford family, of the Isle of Rossall, Salop. His eldest son, Sir George Ritchie Sandford, K.B.E., C.M.G., M.A. (Cantab) (1892-1950), had a distinguished career in the Colonial Service in East Africa and Palestine, culminating in his appointment as Governor and Commander-in-Chief of the Bahamas 1950; he died *s.p.*, and his nephew John Rossall Sandford, F.R.C.S. (Canada), of Oakville, Ontario, Canada,† now represents that line of the family. *Arms.* Quarterly, 1 & 4, Quarterly per fess indented Ermine and Azure (Sandford, of Sandford); 2 & 3, Per chevron Sable and Ermine two boars' heads couped close Or (Sandford, of the Isle). *Crests.* 1, A falcon wings endorsed preying on a partridge all Proper (Sandford, of Sandford); 2, A boar's head couped Or charged with a mullet and holding in the mouth a pheon fessways point to the sinister Argent (Sandford, of the Isle). *Motto.* Nec temere nec timide (BLG18). Fox-Davies adds a mullet to the second and third quarters of the arms, and gives the crest of Sandford of the Isle as: A boar's head couped Or with a broken spear Azure thrust through the mouth and charged with a mullet Sable (FD7).

SANDYS, of Redmain. Thomas del Sandes and Margaret his wife acquired the manor of Redmain in Isel 1384, and were still owners in 1406. The line ended in Elizabeth, dau. of Thomas Sandys, who marr. Christopher Curwen, of Camerton (living 1464), *q.v.*, and carried Redmain to that family. *Arms* (as quartered by Curwen). Argent a fess dancetté between

* Field states that he was acting Sheriff 16-17 Edward II (FAC).

† His sister Armine Margaret, wife of Norman Lewis Robinson, was a B.B.C. announcer and the first woman to read the news on television.

three cross crosslets fitché Gules (Wooden panel dated 1625 from Camerton Hall, now in Camerton church).

SARGENT. John Young Sargent, M.A. (Oxon) (b. 1829), Fellow of Hertford College, Oxford, 1877, lived for many years at Sella Park. He marr.* 1865 Anna Maria (d. 1871), 4th dau. of the Rev. Christopher Hilton Wybergh, Vicar of Isel, and their 3rd dau. Maud marr. 1902 Henry Herbert Williams, D.D., Bishop of Carlisle. *Arms.* . . . a chevron . . . between three dolphins naiant . . . ; impaling, Wybergh, *q.v.* (Shields on tombstone of Mr. and Mrs. Sargent in St. Clement's churchyard, Oxford).

SATTERTHWAITE. James Satterthwaite, of Helm, Undermillbeck (W) (will pr. 1800), was uncle of Lt-Col James Clarke Satterthwaite, J.P. (d. 1825, aged 83), who was Receiver General for Cumberland for nearly 30 years, Chairman of Cumberland Quarter Sessions, M.P. for Cockermouth 1784-90, elected for Carlisle 1790 but unseated, and M.P. for Haslemere 1791-1802. The Colonel, one of Lord Lonsdale's staunchest supporters, was of Papcastle and Arkleby Hall, later becoming tenant of the house in Cockermouth in which the poet Wordsworth was born. By Jane his wife (d. 1818, aged 74) he was father of the Rev. James Satterthwaite, M.A., D.D. (Cantab) (d. 1827, aged 54), who was Fellow of Jesus College, Cambridge, 1795-1806, Domestic Chaplain to Lord Lowther 1802, Rector of Whicham 1804-13, of Bootle 1807-13, of Lowther 1813-27 and of Aikton 1814-27. His coheirs were his nieces Jane, wife of the Rev. George Coventry, and Mary Ann (d. 1842), wife of William Rudd, *q.v.*; they were daus. of John Head, M.D., of High Cross, Loweswater. *Arms.* Ermine on a chief Sable three roses Argent; impaling, Sable three does trippant Argent. *Crest.* A lion's head erased gorged with a collar charged with three roses (Engraving of Arkleby Hall, HCC ii facing p. 350).

SATTERTHWAITE. James Satterthwaite, of Hawksead (d. 1786), settled in Cockermouth as a saddler and marr. 1732 Margaret, dau. and heir of Daniel Fearon, shoemaker. Their only son Daniel (1737-1825) was also a saddler in Cockermouth, and a landowner in Hawkshead, where he died eight days after his wife.† Their tombstone in All Saints' churchyard, Cockermouth, also commemorates their son John Thompson Satterthwaite, Capt 52nd Regt., who died at Chatham on his way to Madras (the year of his death is not given, and he is said to have been 15, presumably an error for 45); and their dau. Margaret Roberts died 1852, aged 75‡ (TWH). *Arms.* . . . two swords in saltire . . . surmounted by a bishop's mitre . . . in chief an Eastern crown . . . . *Crest.* An arm embowed in armour holding a sword. *Motto.* Domino confidimus (Tombstone in All Saints' churchyard, Cockermouth).

SAUL, of Carlisle. John Saul (b. 1698) was ancestor of Silas Saul, of Castle Street, Carlisle (1762-1844), founder of the well known firm of solicitors which, under the style of Saul & Lightfoot, still continues in Castle Street. He was joined by his sons George, J.P., of Brunstock House (1797-1853); Silas (1803-78), who was Under-Sheriff; and John (1815-68), see Saul, *post*

* His brother William Sargent, Fellow of the Queen's College, Oxford, marr. 1863 Isabella, eldest dau. of the Rev. C. H. Wybergh.

† The *Westmorland Gazette* says that they died "after a painful and lingering illness, which they bore with true Christian piety and resignation to the divine will and a bright example to their surviving relatives." The inscription on their tombstone says "They were interred here together in one grave November 11. Faithful in life they were and not separated in death."

‡ When her father made his will in 1814, she was wife of Joseph Wilkinson.

Kirklinton-Saul. Silas was, after the retirement of his brothers, joined by his eldest son Silas George (1836-1905), who was Under-Sheriff and Chapter Clerk. He was of Brunstock House, where he was succ. by his only son George Frederick Saul, J.P., solicitor and Under-Sheriff of Cumberland (1863-1925). His only son John Michael Saul (1908-75) was of Skinburness. His only dau. and heir is Eleanor Margaret Louise, who marr. 1975 John David Carlton Dix. The above Silas George's younger brother George Hodgson Saul (1837-1911) was of Crosby Lodge. *Arms.* Per chevron Gules and Argent two chevrons counterchanged (Bookplates of Silas George Saul and George Frederick Saul, the latter charged with a label of three points Argent). On monuments in Kirklinton church the arms are displayed as: Gules a chevronel between two chevrons Argent. *Crest.* A swan chained round the neck and wings expanded. *Motto.* Fideli certa merces.

SAUL, of Green Row and Carlisle. Joseph Saul (d. 1842) became headmaster of the famous Green Row Academy, Low Holme, in 1795. He was succ. by his son John, whose son Hugh was father of Alfred Tindal Saul, solicitor, of Highcroft, Carlisle (b. 1879), who had an only dau. and heir Mary Constance (d. 1977), marr. the Rev. J. A. Woodhead-Keith-Dixon, *q.v.* *Arms* (as borne by Joseph Saul). Argent a chevron between three ravens' heads erased Sable. His great-grandson A. T. Saul bore: Quarterly, 1, Saul, as above; 2, Argent a fess dancetté Gules between in chief a fleur-de-lys Azure between two crescents Gules and in base a crescent Gules between two fleurs-de-lys Azure (Tindal); 3, Per pale Argent and Sable three lions rampant counterchanged (Hetherington); 4, Argent three wolves' heads couped Sable langued Gules (Wilson, of Hayton, Aspatria) (*Ex inf.* the Rev. J. A. Woodhead-Keith-Dixon).

SAUL, *post* KIRKLINTON-SAUL, *post* KIRKLINTON. John Saul, J.P., attorney, of Anns Hill, Stanwix, of Kirklinton Hall, and of St. Alban's House, Brighton (1815-68), son of Silas Saul, attorney, of Carlisle, *q.v.*, marr. (1) 1842 Mary (d. 1851, aged 34), only child of Charles James Graham, of Anns Hill, *q.v.*, and (2) 1852 Mary Frederica (1814-91), dau. of Godfrey Mölling, *q.v.* He assumed the additional surname of Kirklinton and was succ. by his only son, George Graham Kirklinton, D.L., J.P., of Kirklinton Hall (1853-1927), who dropped the surname Saul, and was High Sheriff of Cumberland 1898. He marr. 1904 Mary Allison Dorothy (d. 1936), 4th dau. of Sir Thomas Fairbairn, 2nd Bart. *Arms.* Gules a chevronel between two chevrons Argent. *Crest.* A swan chained round the neck and wings expanded. *Motto.* Fideli certa merces (M.I., Kirklinton church).

CARR-SAUNDERS. Sir Alexander Morris Carr-Saunders, K.B.E., M.A. (Oxon and Cantab), LL.D. (Glasgow, Columbia and Natal), Litt.D. (Dublin and Liverpool), D.Litt. (Malaya), D.Sc. (London), F.B.A., J.P., of Bridge House, St. John's in the Vale (1886-1966), was Director of the London School of Economics 1937-56. He marr. 1929 Teresa, dau. of Major E. H. Molyneux-Seel, of Huyton Hey Manor, *q.v.* Their son, Dr. Edmund Carr-Saunders, is of Folly, Newby Cross, Carlisle. *Crest* (on Sir Alexander Carr-Saunders' bookplate). An elephant's head erased. *Motto.* En vertu la force.

SAUNDERS, *olim* RICHARDSON. Joseph Richardson, of Culgaith (1772-1844), marr. Eliza Euphemia Fisher (d. 1838, aged 58), niece and heir of Elizabeth Wilkinson who bequeathed Nunwick Hall to her. Her son

Randal Wilkinson Richardson (1816-66) succ. and in 1837 assumed the name of Saunders in compliance with the will of Joseph Richardson Saunders, merchant, of Ardwick Place, Manchester. His son Charles Ricardson Saunders (d. 1892, aged 50) succ. and continued breeding shorthorns at Nunwick until 1870 when the herd was sold. At the end of his life he went to live at Houghton Hall, near King's Lynn. *Arms* (granted 1837). Sable on a chevron Ermine between three bulls' heads cabossed Argent as many lions' heads erased Gules. *Crest.* A demi bull Gules the sinister foot resting on an inescutcheon Sable charged with a lion's head erased Or (CA xlii 213).

SAURIN. Impaled by Graham, *q.v.*, on brass in Stanwix church; Elizabeth Jane (1799-1865), dau. of James Saurin, D.D., Bishop of Dromore, marr. 1821 Major James Reginald Torin Graham. *Arms.* Argent out of a mount a tree Proper on a chief Sable a crescent Or between two mullets Argent. Burke blazons the arms: Argent out of a mount Vert an oak tree Proper on a chief Azure a crescent between two mullets of the first (BLG6).

SCAIFE, of Walton Rigg. William Scaife, of Walton Rigg, Walton (d. 1767, aged 39), was succ. by his son William (d. 1840, aged 74) who marr. 1797 Catherine Frances (d. 1830, aged 49), only dau. of the Rev. Hugh Nanney, Vicar of Haltwhistle. Their son Charles Mark Guy Scaife, of Haltwhistle, was father of Lewis Scaife, a police sergeant in Newcastle upon Tyne (d. *c.* 1911, aged 60), who had sons Lambert and Arthur Scaife. *Arms.* . . . on a chevron . . . between three wolves' heads erased . . . as many trefoils slipped . . . . *Crest.* An arm embowed in armour flourishing a battle axe. *Motto.* Medio tutissimus ibis (Tombstone, Walton churchyard).

SCALES. Impaled by Howard on shield in hall of Greystoke Castle; Sir Robert Howard (d. *v.p.* 1398) marr. Margery, dau. of Robert, Lord Scales (d. 1369). *Arms.* Gules six escallops Argent, three, two, and one.

SCOTT, of Brunstock. Mason Thompson Scott, of Brunstock, Carlisle (1865-1916), was 4th son of Sir Walter Scott, 1st Bart., of Beauclerc, Bywell St. Andrews (N) and of Newcastle upon Tyne (1826-1910), and grandson of Samuel Scott, a publican of Holm Cultram (d. 1833, aged 42). *Arms.* Per chevron Azure and Or in chief two bees volant and in base a crescent all counterchanged. *Crest.* A crescent Sable issuant therefrom a bee volant Proper. *Motto.* Invitum sequitur honor (VEW xviii 201, 203; BP105).

SCOTT, of Crookburn. John Scott, of Crookburn, Bewcastle, died 1760. *Arms.* . . . on a bend . . . a mullet . . . between two decrescents . . . (ABD). Field recorded this as: Or on a bend Azure a mullet between two crescents of the field (FAC), but as the coat is on the tombstone in Bewcastle churchyard, it is almost certain that tinctures are not given.

SCOTT, of Oak Bank. John Scott, of Albyfield, Cumrew, farmer (d. 1858), by Mary (Gibson) his wife was father of John Scott, J.P. (1811-99), a landowner in Cumrew and Wetheral, where, between 1869 and 1871, he built Oak Bank, a mansion now called Killoran. He also lived at Albyfield, Bickley, Kent. His son and successor, the Rev. Alfred Scott, M.A. (Oxon) (d. 1933, aged 83), was vicar of St. Mary, Paddington, 1884-1900, and a licensed preacher in the diocese of Carlisle 1900-33, during which period he lived at Albyfield, Wetheral. He was succ. by his son John Linton Scott (1887-1971) (*Ex inf.* Mr. and Mrs. G. G. S. Richardson, of Wetheral). *Arms.* Argent on a bend between six estoiles Azure an escallop between two crescents Or. *Crest.* In front of a stag's head erased Proper gorged with a collar gemel Or three crescents Gold. *Motto.* Obstando supera (BGA).

SCOTT, of Rattenrow. John Scott, of Rattenrow, Caldbeck (1781-1858), was father of John Scott, J.P. (1813-79), who died at Gravenhurst, Beds. *Arms* (on gravestone in Caldbeck churchyard). . . . a fess . . . between in chief two mullets . . . and in base a crescent . . . .

SCOTT. Mrs. Anne Katharine Sibella Morton, A.R.I.B.A., wife of Jocelyn Wiseman Fagan Morton, of Jenny Hill, Matterdale, is younger dau. of Sir Samuel Haslam Scott, 2nd Bart. (see AWL). *Arms.* Azure a greyhound courant Argent collared Gules and attached by a line of the second to a sphere in chief Or.

SCOTT, *post* SCOTT-NICHOLSON. Benjamin Scott (d. 1846, aged 83), descended from a Caldbeck family, founded in 1799 in English Street, Carlisle, a printing and bookselling business, which eventually became one of the leading firms in the city and is now a branch of the Metal Box Co. The founder retired in 1832, and was succ. by his nephew Hudson Scott (d. 1891, aged 83), who gave his name to the firm. In 1868 his sons Sir Benjamin Scott (1841-1927) and William Hudson Scott took over its management. The former, a magistrate, was of Linden House, Stanwix, and was six times Mayor of Carlisle; he was knighted 1904. His only dau. Maud Hope, J.P. (b. 1875), marr. 1900 Edwin Nicholson, J.P., A.R.I.B.A., of Barn Close, Carlisle. They assumed the name of Scott-Nicholson. Their only son Christopher Scott-Nicholson (1906-45), Major Lanarkshire Yeomanry, was murdered in Damascus, while serving on General Spears' mission to Syria; he left two daus. *Arms.* Quarterly, 1 & 4, Sable a chevron Argent charged with a chevronel wavy Azure between three stags' attires within each a cross botoné fitché Or (Nicholson); 2 & 3, Or upon a mount issuant from the base a cross pattée Gules between four human hearts of the second the mount charged with a like heart of the field in the centre point (for distinction) an ermine spot Gold (Scott). *Crests.* 1, A falcon close Sable hooded Azure armed and belled Or between two crosses botoné fitché Gold (Nicholson); 2, A stag's head Gules attired and semé of human hearts Or holding in the mouth a gillyflower of the first leaved and slipped Proper and charged (for distinction) with an ermine spot Gold (Scott). *Motto.* Age quod agis (FD7).

SCOTT. The Rev. William Scott (d. 1776) was Curate of St. Bees 1734-39, and Minister 1739-76, and headmaster of St. Bees School. His son the Rev. Robert Scott (d. 1804, aged 59), Headmaster of St. Bees 1773-88, was Minister of St. Bees 1776 and Rector of Whicham 1794-1804. *Arms.* . . . an eagle displayed . . . (Seal in Record Office, Carlisle, DRC 10).

SCREMBY, SKREMBY. Field quotes *Notes and Queries,* 1874, as authority for William de Skremby, said to have held lands in Cumberland *temp.* Richard II. *Arms.* Azure three bars and a bend Or (FAC). Burke gives an alternative: Azure two bars and a bend Or (BGA).

SCROPE. Richard Scrope (d. 1468), Rector of Fen Ditton, Cambs., and of Wensley (Y), younger son of Richard, 3rd Lord Scrope of Bolton, was Bishop of Carlisle 1464-68. *Arms.* Azure a bend Or (BBE; EDP). These arms were, according to the evidence of William, Prior of Lanercost, in the celebrated case of Scrope v. Grosvenor 1385-90, in windows in the Priory both plain and differenced by a bordure Or; and the undifferenced arms were also at that time in a chapel at Kirkoswald (VCHC ii 159).

MOLYNEUX-SEEL. Teresa, Lady Carr-Saunders, of Bridge House, St. John's-in-the-Vale, widow of Sir Alexander Carr-Saunders, K.B.E. (1886-1966), *q.v.*, is dau. of Major E. H. Molyneux-Seel, of Huyton Hey Manor (L). *Arms.* Quarterly, 1 & 4, Per fess potent counter-potent Pean and Azure three wolves' heads erased counterchanged (Seel); 2 & 3, Azure a cross moline Or a canton Argent (Molyneux).

SEGRAVE. A Howard quartering, brought in by Mowbray, *q.v.*, on shields in Greystoke Castle and Naworth Castle; John, Lord Mowbray (1340-68), marr. *c.* 1349 Elizabeth (b. 1338), dau. and heir of John, Lord Segrave (d. *s.p.m.* 1353). *Arms.* Sable a lion rampant Argent crowned Or. On the shield at Greystoke, the lion is not crowned.

SEGRAVE. Shield at Hutton John. A Hudleston quartering, brought in by Barantyne and Drayton, *q.v.* Called Segrave in the Visitation of Oxfordshire, this coat appears on all the Drayton tombs in Haseley Church, Oxon. *Arms.* Ermine two bars Gules in chief a demi lion rampant issuant Gules.

SELBY, Viscount, of Carlisle – see GULLY.

SELBY. Impaled by Curwen in window in Workington Hall; Sir Patricius Curwen, of Workington (1601-64), marr. 1620 Isabella (d. 1667), 4th dau. and coheir of Sir George Selby, of Whitehouse (D). *Arms.* Barry of ten Or and Sable.

SENHOUSE, of Hames Hill and The Fitz. Patricius Senhouse (d. 1682), 4th son of John Senhouse, of Netherhall (d. 1667) (see Senhouse, *post* Pocklington-Senhouse), marr. 1655 Elizabeth, dau. and heir of Thomas Bromfield, of Hames Hill, Cockermouth, and so acquired that property and The Fitz. Their great-grandson Humphrey Senhouse (1759-1829) was Major in the Royal Cumberland Militia and marr. 1784 Isabella, dau. and coheir of William Ponsonby, of Whitehaven. Their elder son Humphrey (1788-1839) had three sons – Humphrey (1811-75), William Ponsonby (1813-56) and John (1816-49), who all died *s.p.* Their only sister Isabella (1817-88) marr. 1857 Richard Bell,* M.D., J.P., of Cockermouth (1805-87), who assumed the surname Senhouse on his wife's succeeding to The Fitz 1875. They were succ. by their only son Humphrey Patricius Senhouse, J.P., M.A. (Oxon) (1860-1914), who was succ. by his only son Humphrey Patricius Senhouse, M.C., of The Fitz (1894-1970), who was High Sheriff of Cumberland 1947. He marr. 1927 Ethel Florance Nancy (d. 1975), dau. of Joseph Anthony Steele Dixon, of Lorton Hall, and sister and heir of Anthony Thomas Steele Dixon, *q.v.* Their only son Humphrey Patricius Senhouse, M.A. (Oxon) (b. 1928), who was High Sheriff of Cumberland 1968, is now of The Fitz. *Arms.* At The Fitz is a carved stone, dated 1665, and extremely weathered and difficult to decipher, but apparently displaying; Quarterly, 1, A popinjay; 2 & 3, Three eagles displayed (Eaglesfield); 4, A popinjay in chief a (? difference mark). *Crest.* A popinjay. *Motto.* Vae victis. In 1947 Humphrey Patricius Senhouse, sen., obtained a grant of the following *Arms.* Or a popinjay Proper a bordure

* Eldest son of James Oliphant Bell, surgeon, of Whitehaven (d. 1831), who, after studying at the University of Edinburgh, began practising in Cockermouth in 1797.

Tenné. *Crest.* Upon a billet fesswise Or charged with three roses Gules barbed and seeded a popinjay Proper. *Motto.* Vae victis.

SENHOUSE, of Seascale I. This family takes its name from Sevenhouse=Seven hills, now called Hall Senna, in Gosforth. About 1200 Alan de Copeland gave a fifth part of Bolton there to Walter de Sevenhouse, which remained with his descendants for 500 years, and the family acquired the manor of Newton *c.* 1270. To this family belonged William Senhouse (d. 1505), Abbot of St. Mary, York, who became Bishop of Carlisle 1495 and Bishop of Durham 1502. Another member of the family, Simon Senhouse, was Prior of St. Mary's, Carlisle, in 1505 and 1518. He is believed to have been brother of Thomas Senhouse, of Seascale (b. *c.* 1477), who arranged in 1528 that his son and heir John (d. 1568) should marry Elizabeth, dau. of Gawen and Mabel Eaglesfield and sister and coheir of Richard Eaglesfield, *q.v.* By this marriage the manors of Alneburgh (Netherhall) and Eaglesfield came into the family. The former passed to John's son John (d. 1604), see Senhouse, *post* Pocklington-Senhouse, of Netherhall, while the latter manor was sold to John Eaglesfield 1559. Seascale descended to John Senhouse (1599-1669) who marr. 1634 Anne, dau. of John Bimpson, of Shevington (L), and niece and coheir of Sir Edward Wrightington, of Wrightington (L). Their son Wrightington Senhouse (1639-67) died *v.p.* and Seascale was inherited by his son John (1660-1738) who marr. Elizabeth Bellingham. He was High Sheriff 1703, but by 1707 he had lost the family estates which he had mortgaged, the new owner being Robert Blaicklock, *q.v.* He retired to Penzance and in 1730 published a translation of the *Satires of Persius.* He was also of Little Salkeld and of St. Sepulchre, London. In 1738 his heir at law was his granddau. Elizabeth Ditchburn, widow, presumably the dau. of his eldest son. A younger son, Alan Senhouse (b. 1695), was of Snow Hill, London, distiller, with sons Alan (aged 14 in 1730) and John (b. 1724). No further information concerning them is available (CW1 xii). *Arms.* On the table-tomb of Prior Simon Senhouse, see above, in Carlisle Cathedral, appears: Per pale Argent and Gules dexter a popinjay Proper.* *Crest.* A popinjay Proper. *Motto.* Lothe to offend. At the Visitation of 1665, Wrightington Senhouse recorded, on behalf of his father: *Arms.* Quarterly, 1 & 4, Or a parrot Proper (Senhouse); 2 & 3, Gules three eagles displayed Or (Eaglesfield). *Crest.* A parrot Proper (FCW). *Badge.* A rose Gules. FVC and MVC recorded the arms as: Per pale Argent and Gules dexter a popinjay Vert beaked and membered Gules. Portraits at Isel Hall display: Per pale Or and Gules dexter a popinjay Proper. MMD gives: Quarterly Argent and Gules in the first and fourth quarters a popinjay Vert beaked and membered Or.

SENHOUSE, of Seascale II. In 1800 the manors of Seascale and Newton were bought by Samson Senhouse, of Ponsonby Parsonage (d. 1855, aged 78), son of William Senhouse (d. 1800), who was appointed surveyor General of Barbados and the Leeward Islands 1770 and was son of Humphrey Senhouse, of Netherhall (d. 1770), *q.v.* Samson sold Seascale Hall to his mother and at her death in 1835, aged 79, his brother Capt Sir Humphrey le Fleming Senhouse, K.C.H., K.B., R.N., bought the estate for £11,000. He died on board H.M.S. *Blenheim* 1841 and was buried at

* Not: Or a popinjay Proper or Vert, as recorded by Field (FAC).

Macao.* The estate was then sold. He marr. 1810 Elizabeth (1783-1865), dau. and coheir of Admiral John Manley, and had two daus. and coheirs, Elizabeth Manley, marr. 1843 Capt John Charles Pitman, R.N.;† and Rose Mary le Fleming Senhouse, of Galeholm, Gosforth (1828-1903), whose history of the Seascale family is in CW1 xii. *Arms.* As Senhouse of Seascale I. *Crest.* A parrot [Proper] issuing from the beak a label inscribed "Deo Gratias" (Brass, Gosforth church).

SENHOUSE, *post* POCKLINGTON-SENHOUSE, of Netherhall. The Netherhall Senhouses descend from John Senhouse, of Seascale, *q.v.*, who marr. the heiress of Alneburgh Hall or Netherhall, inherited by their younger son John Senhouse (d. 1604), the friend of Camden, the antiquary, and a noted scholar with a great interest in the Roman antiquities on the estate.‡ His son Peter (d. 1654) was High Sheriff of Cumberland 1626. His descendant John Senhouse (1660-94), who marr. Jane (d. 1720), dau. and heir of Richard Lamplugh, of Dovenby, was succ. by his six daus. and coheirs§ who sold Netherhall 1716 to their uncle Humphrey Senhouse (d. 1738, aged 69), the nephew and adopted son of Joseph and Bridget Hudleston, of Millom. He was High Sheriff 1714. His son Humphrey (d. 1770, aged 65) was High Sheriff 1742.‖ He marr. 1731 Mary (d. 1790), eldest dau. and coheir of Sir George Fleming, 2nd Bart., Bishop of Carlisle. Their son Humphrey Senhouse, M.A. (Cantab), Fellow of Pembroke College, Cambridge (1731-1814), was Lt-Col Cumberland Militia and M.P. for Cockermouth 1786 and for Cumberland 1790.¶ His son Humphrey, M.A. (Cantab) (1773-1842), was High Sheriff 1826. He marr. 1803 Elizabeth Frances (d. 1844), dau. and coheir of Robert Charles Greaves, *post* Ley, of Ingleby Hill (Dy). His only son Humphrey (1809-34) died unmarr. and *v.p.*, and his daus. and coheirs were Elizabeth (1805-90), marr. 1835 Joseph Pocklington, D.L., J.P. (1804-74), *q.v.*; Catherine (d. 1853), marr. at Gretna Green 1844 Thomas Smith, M.D., of Brigham (d. 1849); and Ellen (d. 1838), marr. 1837 Lt-Col John Taubman Goldie Taubman, of the Nunnery, Isle of Man. The eldest dau. Elizabeth succ. to Netherhall and she and her husband, who was High Sheriff 1846, assumed the name and arms of Senhouse 1842. They were succ. by their son Humphrey Pocklington-

* The *Cumberland Pacquet* said of him "As we happened to differ with him in some of his views . . . we frequently felt it our duty . . . to cross his path, but we should be ashamed of ourselves if one spark of ungenerous feeling should prevent us from doing justice to his public character as a gentleman of probity and honour, and as a brave, gallant and meritorious servant of his country, who by his valour and praiseworthy conduct had won his way to honour and distinction in his country's service."

† Their eldest dau. Elizabeth Gertrude le Fleming Pitman (1846-1936) was of The Ferns, Seascale.

‡ His son Richard Senhouse, M.A., D.D. (Cantab) (d. unmarr. 1626), was Dean of Gloucester 1621-24 and Bishop of Carlisle 1624-26.

§ Mary (b. 1682), marr. (1) 1699 Francis Skelton, *q.v.*, of Branthwaite, and (2) Richard Butler, of Rawcliffe (L); Jane (b. 1687), marr. 1704 John Stephenson, Speaker of the Manx House of Keys; Frances (b. 1689); Grace (1691-1755), marr. 1721 Richard, 2nd Viscount Shannon; Isabella (1693-1774), marr. 1717 John Fletcher, of Clea, *q.v.*; and Elizabeth (b. 1695).

‖ He founded the port which he named Maryport in honour of his wife.

¶ His brother William (1740-1800) was ancestor of the Senhouses of Seascale II, *q.v.* Another brother, Sir Joseph Senhouse, H.E.I.Co.'s naval service (1743-1829), was of Hensingham Hall and Arkleby Hall, and Ashby St. Ledgers, which he acquired by marr. 1787 to Mary (d. 1850, aged 70), dau. and heir of Joseph Ashley, *q.v.* Their son William (d. 1885) left the property to Humphrey Pocklington-Senhouse, see above. On 4 May 1785 Sir Joseph paid E. Parker of Oxford Street, London, £4 4s. for engraving his quartered arms on red cornelian and gold.

Senhouse, D.L., J.P. (1843-1903), High Sheriff 1892.* His four sons died unmarr., Humphrey, the eldest (1880-89), being killed in a riding accident, and Oscar William, the 3rd, 2nd Lieut Coldstream Guards (1891-1915), being killed in action. The 2nd son, Col Guy Joseph Pocklington-Senhouse, D.L., J.P., T.D. (1882-1952), High Sheriff 1913 and 1946, succ. and was succ. by his youngest brother Roger Henry (b. 1899), man of letters and publisher. He was succ. by his great-nephew, Patrick Joseph Scott-Plummer, grandson of his elder sister Dorothy Elizabeth (d. 1962) who marr. (1) 1904 Lt-Col Joseph Walter Scott-Plummer (d. 1909), and (2) 1923 Francis Henry Meade, C.B.E. Her sister Blanche Violet Florence marr. 1911 Capt Thomas Rupert Clutterbuck, Coldstream Guards (d. 1932) (BLG17; NCL). *Arms.* At the Visitation of 1665 John Senhouse recorded: Quarterly, 1 [Or]a parrot Proper (Senhouse); 2, Gules a chevron between three combs Argent (Tunstall); 3, Gules three eagles displayed Or (Eaglesfield); 4, Azure on a chevron Or between three dolphins Argent five cinquefoils Gules (Blennerhasset). *Crest.* A parrot Proper (FCW). The Pocklington-Senhouses originally bore: *Arms.* Quarterly, 1 & 4, Or a parrot Proper a canton Sable (Senhouse); 2 & 3, Pocklington, *q.v.* They later omitted the canton from the 1st and 4th quarters. *Crests.* A parrot as in the arms with a label in its beak inscribed 'Deo gratias' (Senhouse); 2, Pocklington, *q.v.* *Motto.* Vae victis (BLG 1846; BLG17; FD7).

SENHOUSE, or SEVER. William Senhouse, or Sever (d. 1505), was Abbot of St. Mary's York, 1485-1502; Bishop of Carlisle 1495-1502; and Bishop of Durham 1502-5. *Arms.* Quarterly Gules and Argent in the first and fourth quarters a dove close of the second (BBE; OBA).

SENHOUSE, *post* MINTON-SENHOUSE, of Calder Abbey. By marriage to Sarah, only child of John Tiffin, *q.v.*, Joseph Senhouse,† of Wigton, acquired the Calder Abbey estate. He was succ. by his son John, High Sheriff of Cumberland 1758-59, who was succ. by his only son Joseph Tiffin Senhouse (1760-1805), of the 3rd Regt of Foot Guards. He marr. (1) 1781 Elizabeth (d. *s.p.* 1790, aged 27), dau. and coheir of Robert Watters, of Whitehaven, and (2) Sarah (1762-1807), dau. of Thomas Sunderland, of Bigland Hall (see AWL). By the latter he had four daus. and coheirs – Mary (1793-1884), who succ. to Calder Abbey, and marr. Capt Thomas Irwin, *q.v.*; Eleanor (1794-1883), marr. Samuel Irton, *q.v.*; Sarah, who succ. her sister Mary at Calder Abbey; and Jane Elizabeth (d. 1857, aged 45), marr. 1837 James Quirk (d. 1851), acting Attorney General of the Isle of Man and High Bailiff of Douglas. Miss Sarah Senhouse left Calder Abbey to her kinsman, the Rev. Samuel Minton, M.A. (Oxon), who was descended from Eleanor, dau. of the above Joseph Senhouse, who marr. 1775 Joseph Hoskins. Mr. Minton took the name of Senhouse 1884 and was ancestor of the family of that name, of which Cyril Minton-Senhouse (b. 1909), his great-grandson, is now head. *Arms,* of Senhouse (as borne by Capt Thomas Irwin on an escutcheon of pretence in east window of Calderbridge church). Or a popinjay Proper in sinister chief a cross crosslet fitché Sable. *Arms,* of Minton. Vert three garbs Or within two bars Ermine between two

* He rowed for Oxford 1865 and 1866.

† BLG 1846 states that he was descended from Leonard Senhouse, of Wigton, son of John Senhouse, of Netherhall (d. 1604), but no such son is mentioned either in the will of John Senhouse or in that of his widow Annas, 1609.

heraldic tigers passant one in chief and another in base of the second. *Crest.* Upon a mount Vert an heraldic tiger as in the arms the dexter paw resting on a garb erect Proper. *Motto.* Pro Deo et patria (FD7).

SETON. Sir John de Seton (d. 1299), whom G. W. S. Barrow in *Robert Bruce* describes as a Yorkshire Knight,* bought much landed estate in Cumberland, including a third of the manor of Skelton, and a share of the barony of Kirklinton, from William Lockard. He marr. Ermina, dau. and heir of Thomas Lascelles, *q.v.*, and acquired further estates in the county, which descended to their son Sir Christopher Seton (1278-1306), whose estates also included a share of the manor of Kirkandrews-on-Eden. He marr. Christian Brus (d. 1356-57), dau. of Robert, Earl of Carrick, and sister of King Robert of Scotland, and widow of Gratney, 7th Earl of Mar. In 1306 he was involved in the rebellion of Bruce, and was present when the latter murdered John Comyn, he himself killing Comyn's uncle, Sir Robert Comyn. For this he was drawn, hanged and beheaded at Dumfries, and all his English estates were forfeited.† His son Sir Alexander Seton (d. 1347), Governor of Berwick upon Tweed, was succ. by his only surviving child Margaret, who marr. Alan de Wyntoun, who took the name of Seton. Their descendants include the Earls of Seton, the Marquesses of Huntly and the Dukes of Gordon. *Arms.* Or three crescents Gules. King Robert granted to Sir Alexander Seton the double tressure of Scotland, so that his descendants bear: Or three crescents within a double tressure flory counterflory Gules. The King also granted him a coat of augmentation: Gules a sword supporting an imperial crown (NSH pp. 183, 237).

SEWELL. Thomas Sewell, of Boonwood, Cumrew, was father of the Rev. William Sewell, M.A. (Oxon) (1721-1800), Rector of Headley, Hants., 1765-1800, four of whose grandsons, sons of Thomas Sewell, solicitor, of Newport, Isle of Wight, are in DNB, including the Rev. William Sewell, M.A., D.D. (Oxon) (1804-74), the founder of Radley College, and of St. Columba's College, Ireland, and the Rev. James Edwardes Sewell, M.A., D.D. (Oxon) (1810-1903), Warden of New College, Oxford, 1860-1903. Another brother, Henry, was first Prime Minister of New Zealand. *Arms.* Sable a chevron between three bees volant Argent. *Crests.* 1, A dexter arm embowed in armour Proper garnished Or holding an acorn Gold; 2, In a chaplet of roses Argent leaved Vert a bee volant Or (BGA).

SEWELL, of Brandlingill. William Miller Sewell, of Hayborough House, Dearham, had a son Frederic Robertson Sewell, D.L., J.P. (1839-1907), Lt-Col commanding the 3rd Batt. The Border Regiment, who marr. 1867 Jane, dau. and heir of Joseph Ostle, of Brandlingill. Their son William Woodville Robertson Sewell, B.A. (Cantab) (b. 1868), practised as a solicitor in Cockermouth before becoming a fruit grower in Jersey. His younger brother, Hubert Woodville Sewell, J.P., B.A. (Cantab) (1872-1925), practised in Carlisle as a partner in the firm of Messrs. Sewell & Butler, solicitors. His son was Hubert Frederick Rimington Sewell (b. 1912). *Arms.* Quarterly, 1 & 4, Gules a chevron Argent between two bees volant in chief Proper and a chaplet in base Argent; (Sewell); 2 & 3, Argent a fess nebuly Sable between a mullet of eight points in chief and a

* Said to have been descended from Alexander Seton who witnessed a grant of Roxburghshire lands *c.* 1150.

† His brother John was drawn and hanged at Newcastle upon Tyne a little later.

fleur-de-lys in base Azure (Ostle). *Crest.* Upon a mount vert a bee volant Proper within a chain in arch Or. *Motto.* In labore quies (FD7).

SEYMOUR, Baron Cockermouth, Earl of Egremont, Duke of Somerset. Charles Seymour, 6th Duke of Somerset (1662-1748), "the proud Duke," acquired the Percy estates in Cumberland by marriage 1682 to Elizabeth, dau. and heir of Joceline, Earl of Northumberland, *q.v.* Their 2nd but 1st surviving son, Algernon Seymour, 7th Duke of Somerset (1684-1750), was cr. Baron Cockermouth and Earl of Egremont 1749, but died *s.p.m.s.* The Dukedom passed eventually to Edward Adophus, 12th Duke, K.G., P.C. (1804-85), who died *s.p.m.s.* His daus. and coheirs were Lady Jane Hermione St. Maur (d. 1909), marr. 1852 Sir Frederick Ulric Graham, Bart., *q.v.*; Lady Ulrica Frederica Jane (d. 1916), marr. 1858 Lord Henry Frederick Thynne; and Lady Helen Guendolen (d. 1910), marr. 1865 Sir John William Ramsden, Bart., *q.v.* *Arms.* Quarterly, 1 & 4, Or on a pile Gules between six fleurs-de-lys Azure three lions of England; 2 & 3, Gules two wings conjoined in lure the tips downwards Or. *Crest.* Out of a ducal coronet Or a phoenix Gold issuing from flames Proper. *Supporters.* Dexter, A unicorn Argent armed maned and tufted Or gorged with a ducal collar per pale Azure and Gold to which is affixed a chain of the last; Sinister, A bull Azure ducally gorged chained hoofed and armed Or. *Motto.* Foy pour devoir (BP, various editions). The arms are quartered by Ramsden on a shield at Muncaster Castle. On a shield at Hutton John the arms appear as: Gules two wings conjoined in lure Or, Sir John Hudleston, K.B. (d. 1547), having marr. Joan, dau. of Sir John Seymour.

SHARPE. At the 1619 Visitation of Leicestershire William Sharpe, of Rolleston, Leics., a 37 years old bachelor, registered his pedigree, stating that his great-great-grandfather was John Sharpe, of Baydon in Cumberland, whose son Hugh was of the same place. Hugh's son William Sharpe, of Wing, Rutland, was grandfather of the above named William. *Arms.* Azure a pheon Argent within a bordure of the last charged with eight torteaux in dexter chief a crescent for difference. *Crest.* On a ducal coronet Or a peacock sitting Proper in the beak an ear of wheat of the first charged on the breast with a crescent for difference (Harl. Soc. Vis. Leics, 1619, p. 89).

SHARPE. William Henry Sharpe Sharpe, J.P., of St. Bees, Ensign 1st (The Royal) Regiment 1844 and Captain and Adjutant of the Royal Cumberland Militia from 1852, had issue, besides a younger son, Henry Birch, of whom below, an elder son James William Sharpe, M.A. (Cantab) (1852-1917), assistant master at Charterhouse 1877-91, and Senior Fellow of Gonville and Caius College, Cambridge; his son William Henry Sharpe Sharpe was born 1885. Henry Birch Sharpe, barrister-at-law (1855-1926), was father of John York Birch Sharpe, of London (b. 1904). *Arms.* Argent three roses fesswise Gules leaved barbed and seeded Proper between as many eagles' heads erased Sable. *Crest.* In front of a wolf's head erased per pale Sable and Or gorged with a collar Vair three roses fessways as in the arms. *Motto.* Knowledge is power (FD7).

SHAW. Monuments in Crosby-on-Eden church commemorate the Rev. Henry Shaw, J.P. (d. 1791, aged 69), Rector of Scaleby 1759-91, and Vicar of Crosby-on-Eden 1758-91; Jane Harrison, his wife (d. 1808, aged 82); and the Rev. William Shaw (d. 1785, aged 32). *Arms.* Or a chevron wavy between three eagles displayed Sable; impaling, Harrison, *q.v.*.

SHAW, of Rampsbeck. Thomas Wood Shaw, later of Culmington Manor, Salop (1852-1934), eldest son of William Shaw, of Heaton Bolton (L) (1819-72), was tenant of Lazonby Hall until 1911. His younger brother Charles Henry Shaw, J.P. (1860-1933), was tenant of Eden Hall, before moving to Rampsbeck, Watermillock; he was High Sheriff of Cumberland 1916. His eldest son, Ronald Herbert Moseley Shaw, was born 1901 (BLG15). *Arms.* Argent a chevron Ermines between in chief two talbots' heads erased and in base a griffin's head erased Azure. *Crest.* Upon a mount Vert a talbot passant Sable eared Or resting the dexter forefoot on an escutcheon Argent charged with a chevron Ermines (FD7). *Motto.* Respice finem (Seal).

SHAW, of Quarry Hill. Geoffrey Edward Shaw, V.R.D., of Quarry Hill, Mealsgate (b. 1921), was 2nd son of Major John Edward Durrant Shaw, T.D., J.P., of Wellburn Hall (Y), High Sheriff of Yorkshire 1939. *Arms.* Azure three lozenges in chevron between as many talbots' heads erased Argent. *Crest.* A talbot passant Argent charged on the neck with three lozenges conjoined and resting the dexter paw upon an escutcheon Azure charged with a rose also Argent barbed and seeded Proper (BLG18).

SHEEPSHANKS. The Rev. William Sheepshanks, M.A. (Cantab) (1741-1810), son of Richard Sheepshanks, of Linton-in-Craven (Y), was Curate of Sebergham 1777-1808 and Prebendary of Carlisle 1795-1810. *Arms.* Azure a chevron Erminois between in chief three roses and in base a sheep passant Argent. *Crest.* On a mount Vert a sheep passant Argent. *Motto.* Perseverando (BLG8).

SHEFFIELD. Sir William and Sir Thomas de Sheffield are mentioned as Cumberland knights in 1310 and 1311 (CW2 iii). Sir Thomas de Sheffield, said to be of Cumberland, was living 1396, and bore *Arms.* Or a fess between six garbs Gules (FFC). His seal bears these arms untinctured (BM 13330).

SHEFFIELD, sometime OLIPHANT-SHEFFIELD. Robert Stoney Sheffield, J.P., of Broadfield House, Southwaite (1864-1937), 2nd son of Capt John Charles Sheffield, 21st Fusiliers (1834-1903), who was 3rd son of Sir Robert Sheffield, 4th Bart.,* marr. 1901 Mary Beatrice (d. 1933), dau. and heir of George Henry Hewitt Oliphant-Ferguson, of Broadfield (see Hewitt), and assumed the additional surname of Oliphant. He was succ. by his only son Edmund George Sheffield (1913-76), formerly Lieut R.N.V.R., who discontinued the use of the surname Oliphant. He was succ. by his eldest son John Robert Sheffield. *Arms.* Argent a chevron engrailed between two garbs in chief Gules and in base a sheaf of five arrows Proper banded also Gules. *Crest.* A boar's head erased at the neck Or between two arrows points downwards Proper. *Motto.* Comiter sed fortiter (BLG15).

SHELTON-AGAR – see AGAR.

SHERLOCK. Francis George Sherlock (1870-1943), eldest son of Capt Francis George Sherlock, 72nd Highlanders, descended from the family of Sherlockstown, Co. Kildare, bought Irton Hall 1929, and was succ. there by his son Walter Nugent Sherlock (b. 1897), who was later of Mount

* Sir Robert's granddau. Gwendoline Sophia Alice (d. 1921) was 1st wife of Lancelot Edward, 6th Earl of Lonsdale.

Pleasant, Holmrook. *Arms.* Per pale Argent and Azure three fleurs-de-lys counterchanged. *Crest.* A pelican in her piety Proper (BGA).

SHERWEN. The Rev. Samuel Sherwen (1790-1870), son of John Sherwen, of Seascale How, became Curate of Dean 1823, and having bought the advowson, presented himself to the Rectory 1825, and was Rector till his death. He was succ. by his nephew, the Rev. William Sherwen, M.A. (Oxon) (1831-1915), who was Hon. Canon of Carlisle 1887-1902, and Archdeacon of Westmorland 1902-15. His brother, Samuel Sherwen, was of Lonsdale Place, Whitehaven, and Woodbank,* Beckermet. The Archdeacon's son, the Rev. William Basil Sherwen, M.A. (Oxon) (1869-1949), was Curate of Dean 1907-15, and Rector 1915-43. Another member of the family, the Rev. William Sherwen Sherwen, B.A. (Cantab) (b. 1872), was incumbent of Thwaites 1916-47, and was later of Eskside, Ravenglass, now the home of his dau. Dora and her husband, the Rev. Murray Knowles Hodges, B.A. (Cantab), vicar of Muncaster 1945-75 and of Waberthwaite 1957-75. *Crest.* On the gateway of Woodbank was formerly displayed: A demi man in armour holding a dagger in his right hand. Cut in stone above the entrance to Samuel Sherwen's other house, 9 Lonsdale Place, Whitehaven, was this crest: A demi savage holding a sword in the dexter and a staff in the sinister hand. Fairbairn gives for the Rev. William Sherwen: A demi man holding in his dexter hand a sword and in his sinister a staff all Proper (FBC).

SHORT. The Rev. Hugh Martin Short, J.P., M.A. (Dunelm), of Newham Hall, Stokesley (Y), and of Aislaby Lodge, Whitby (Y) (1817-98), was Vicar of Thornthwaite 1858-81. He was youngest son of the Rev. Lawrence Short, of Ashover (Dy), and Charlotte Eleanora (Holwell) his wife. *Arms.* Quarterly, 1 & 4, Azure a griffin segreant Argent a chief Ermine (Short); 2, Or on a bend Gules three goats trippant Argent (Holwell); 3, Sable a stag's head couped Or between three bugle horns also Or stringed and garnished Azure (Thurston). *Crest.* A griffin's head couped between two wings (BLG9).

SHORTRIDGE, of Bewcastle. William Shortrigg, of Rulewater, Roxburghshire (1698-1753), settled in Bewcastle and was succ. at Rowantrees by his eldest son William Shortrigg (1723-1811), who marr. (2) Mary Newton. Their son William Shortridge, of Kingcreahill, Rowantrees, and Moss Side (1768-1867), was father of, *int. al.,* William, of Hewstown, Stapleton, and George Howe, of Abbeyholme. *Arms.* Argent a fess gules between three thistles Vert flowered of the second. *Crest.* A dexter hand holding a scimitar Proper. *Motto.* Pro aris et focis (CW2 xxxix 35-41).

SIBSON, of Arkleby. A tablet in Plumbland church commemorates Captain John Sibson, of the parish of St. Anne's, Limehouse, and a native of Plumbland (d. 1760, aged 61). *Arms.* Per fess embattled Gules and Azure three elephants' heads erased Or (Sibson); impaling, Per fess Azure and Gules a fess between three sheldrakes Argent.

SIBSON, of Grinsdale and Carlisle. Interesting details of this old Grinsdale family are in CW2 xxii. In 1560, an award was made in favour of George Sibson concerning a tenement in Grinsdale, the parties to the dispute being enjoined to "live on friendly terms as good neighbours and Christian people

* Not Woodbeck, as in FAC, p. 272.

ought to do." From George descended Thomas Sibson (1664-1726) who marr. 1690 Isabell (d. 1754, aged 84), dau. of John Robson, of Kirkandrews-on-Eden. They are buried in Grinsdale churchyard with their eldest son George (d. 1713, aged 23). The line was continued by their second son John (1693-1739), who marr. Ruth, dau. of the Rev. Thomas Story, of Kirkbampton. His grandson Thomas (b. 1779) was father of *int. al.* John and George (1808-74), solicitor of Fisher Street, Carlisle. John (1807-72) was grandfather of Thomas Sibson (1871-1944), partner in the firm of Bendle, Sibson and Davidson, solicitors, of Carlisle. His son Thomas Liddle Sibson, of Myresike, Wetheral, is now the head of the firm. His sister Mary K. Sibson, of 5 Croft Road, Carlisle, was a member of Carlisle City Council 1951-74, Mayor of Carlisle 1967-68, and the last chairman (1969-74) of the Joint Archives Committee for Cumberland, Westmorland and Carlisle. *Arms* (on tombstone of Thomas and Isabell Sibson, above, in Grinsdale churchyard). . . . a fess indented . . . and in chief three decrescents . . . ; impaling, Robson, *q.v. Crest.* Field states that the crest on the tombstone, which is now so weathered as to be indecipherable, is that of Robson, i.e., a demi boar, and that the Sibsons bore: A falcon rising. *Motto.* Nunquam obliviscar (FAC).

SIBTHORP. Col Charles de Laet Waldo Sibthorp, M.P., 4th Dragoon Guards (1783-1855), well known opponent of Catholic emancipation and of the Reform Bill, was of Barco Lodge, Penrith, where his son Henry Arthur Mainwaring Sibthorp (d. 1908), was born 1821. *Arms.* Quarterly, 1 & 4, Argent two bars gules a bordure Sable (Sibthorp); 2 & 3, Or a bend Azure between three leopards' faces Gules (Waldo). *Crests.* 1, A demi lion rampant erased Argent collared and holding in the dexter paw a fleur-de-lys Sable (Sibthorp); 2, A demi leopard guardant Proper debruised with two bendlets Azure (Waldo). *Motto.* Nil conscire sibi (BLG17).

SIMPSON, of Orthwaite and Carleton. The history of this family has been narrated by the Rev. F. B. Swift in CW2 lxix. . . . Simpson, of Yorkshire, was father of Hugh Simpson, of Allerthwaite (Orthwaite) (d. 1645), whose son Hugh (d. 1675) was aged 50 in 1665. He and his son Lancelot (d. 1711), who was 22 in 1665, sold Orthwaite Hall *c.* 1664. Lancelot marr. 1662 Mary (1638-1703), dau. and coheir of William Musgrave, *q.v.*, of Musgrave Hall, Penrith, and Fairbank, Plumpton, and so acquired those properties. Their son Hugh became Clerk of the Peace for Cumberland 1710. He marr. 1699 Jane, dau. and coheir of Thomas Addison, *q.v.* Their son Lancelot (1703-68) was of Musgrave Hall, and their younger son Thomas (1706-68), an attorney, who was Clerk of the Peace for Cumberland 1730-68, became agent to the Duke of Somerset 1747, and was later agent to Lord Egremont and the Duke of Portland. He marr. Elizabeth, sister and coheir of Christopher Pattenson, of Carleton Hall, *q.v.*, and acquired that estate. Their son Hugh (b. 1733) succ. but survived his father less than two months, and was succ. by his sister Elizabeth (b. 1741), who marr. 1767 James Wallace, *q.v. Arms.* None exhibited at the Visitation of 1665, but on an escutcheon of pretence on the tablet to James Wallace in St. Andrew's, Penrith, they appear as: Per bend wavy Or and Sable two lions rampant in sinister chief and in dexter base counterchanged.

SIMPSON, of Lonninghead. John Simpson, of Lonninghead (d. 1767, aged 54), was father of John Simpson, of Lonninghead (d. 1771, aged 37); the latter's youngest son, Robert Simpson, M.D., of St. Petersburg, Russia, died there 1822, aged 71. Another member of the family, Lancelot, was father of the Rev. John Simpson, ordained in 1781 to the curacy of Mosser, and later Curate of Felkirk (Y); his brother, the Rev. Joseph Simpson (1758-1830), was ordained in 1786 to the curacy of Monkwearmouth and was Curate of Tanfield (D) until his death. *Arms.* . . . on a chief . . . three crescents . . . . *Crest.* A dove. *Motto.* Alis nutrior (M.I., Sebergham church, where the motto appears as: Alas nutrior).

SIMPSON, of Murrah. Barbara (1731-1830), eldest dau. and coheir of Christopher Simpson, of Murrah, Greystoke (d. 1756), marr. John Bell, of Low Lonning, Farlam (1727-1800), *q.v.* *Arms.* . . . on a chief . . . three crescents . . . (*Ex inf.* the late E. J. B. Irving).

SIMPSON, of Stoneknow. George Simpson, yeoman, of Stoneknow, Scaleby, died 1767, aged 85. *Arms.* . . . on a chief . . . three crescents . . . (Gravestone at Scaleby). Bell Irving recorded this as: Per fess . . . three crescents in chief . . . (ABD). Field blazoned the arms as: Ermine on a chief Sable three crescents Or, and wrongly attributed them to Preston (FAC).

SIMPSON. Impaled by Irving, *q.v.,* in window in Bowness-on-Solway church; Peter Irving, of Port Carlisle (1804-69), marr. Jane (1808-90), dau. of Thomas Simpson, of Fishers Gill, Aikton. *Arms.* Argent on a chief Azure three increscents of the field.

SIMPSON, *post* SYMPSON. The Rev. Joseph Simpson, later Sympson, a friend of Wordsworth, was Reader of Highhead chapel 1738-41 and Curate 1741-45, Curate of Mungrisdale 1745-49, Curate of Skelton 1749-52, Curate of Irthington 1752, and Curate of Wythburn 1757 until his death in 1807, aged 92. He came of a Great Salkeld family. His son the Rev. Joseph Sympson, B.D. (Cantab) (1753-1807), was also Curate of Wythburn. *Arms* (as borne by a descendant, Edward Mansel Sympson, of Deloraine Court, Lincoln). Or a lion rampant Sable between two cranes' heads erased Proper in chief and a serpent nowed Vert in base. *Crest.* A lion rampant Or gutté-de-poix holding between the forepaws a maunch Sable and resting the dexter hind paw on a serpent nowed Vert. *Motto.* Laetus sorte mea (Bookplate; FBC).

SISSON. This family, which appears to have had its roots in Greystoke and Dacre, became linked with Westmorland when Cuthbert Sisson (d. 1609) bought Kirkbarrow (W) from Lord and Lady Arundel 1583. He spent the last years of his life with his dau. Eleanor and her husband Joseph Hudleston, *q.v.,* at Hutton John. He disinherited his eldest son Edmund, who died in the Fleet Prison, London, 1627, and gave Kirkbarrow to his 2nd son William, from whom it descended to Francis Sisson (d. before 1686), who acquired Celleron in Barton 1636. Celleron was bought 1711 by Edward Sisson, of Stainton, Dacre, who granted it to William Sisson 1713. (For the later descent of Kirkbarrow, see AWL). To this family belonged George Sisson, of Dacre and Townhead, Penrith (d. 1710, aged 75), who marr. 1666 Dorothy (1636-1722), dau. of Andrew Hudleston, of Hutton John. Their dau. and in her issue heir, Dorothy (1674-1707), marr. 1696 Henry Blencowe, of Blencowe, *q.v.* *Arms.* . . . three lions rampant . . . (Impaled by Hudleston on stone tablet at Hutton John and by Blencowe on brass in St. Andrew's church, Penrith). These arms are also on seals on the wills of

Edward Sisson, of East Sleekburn (D), Master Gunner of Tynemouth Castle, 1720, who left 5s. to Mr. Christopher Blencow "to bar his claim and demand to my real or personal estate," and John Sisson, of Newcastle upon Tyne, excise officer (will pr. 1745), who owned lands at Celleron.

SISSON. Burke has an entry for a family of Sisson, Sysum, Sison or Session, said to be originally from Normandy, settled at an early period in Ireland, afterwards of Penrith, with *Arms.* Per fess embattled Or and Azure three griffins' heads erased counterchanged. *Crest.* A griffin's head erased Or. *Mottoes.* Hope for the best; Si sonent tubae paratus (BGA). Papworth (OBA) makes no mention of Penrith, and it is certain that the Sissons of Penrith, *q.v.,* came from Dacre and that their arms were completely different.

SITLINGTON, or SUTTLINGTON, of Wigton. William Sitlington, son of John Sitlington, of Wigton, applied for a grant of arms 1748, and stated that his "mother coming thro' the forest of Westward to Wigton fell in labour and was there on 21 July 1722 at 6 p.m. delivered of said William, as appears by register of Wigton was baptised 20 Sept. following." He desired to have arms showing the accident and his travels round the globe. He was christened as son of John Suttlington, who was baptised at Wigton 1690, son of John Suttleton, of Lessonhall. *Arms.* Azure on the ecliptic circle Or the sign of Libra Sable in chief a terrestrial globe in a stand all Proper and in base on a mount Vert a male child extended in bend sinister Proper. *Crest.* A Holy Lamb reguardant Ermine accoiled with a laurel branch Vert holding the banner Proper (CA ix/271). *Motto.* Have mercy on us, good Lord (BGA).

SKELTON, of Armathwaite Castle. In CW2 xii 11-19 F. H. M. Parker traced the descent of this family from Hugh de `Skelton, whose son Thomas (d. 1366) left a son and heir Sir Clement (b. *c.* 1345), M.P. for Cumberland 1378, 1382, 1393 and 1396, who marr. Joan (b. *c.* 1345), dau. and heir of Giles de Orton and left daus. and coheirs Agnes, marr. Sir Willliam Leigh, *q.v.*; Joan, marr. (1) Ralph Blennerhassett, and (2) Sir John Middleton; and Alice, marr. (1) Nicholas Ridley, and (2) John Bellasis. Parker conjectured that Clement Skelton probably had a younger brother Thomas, who marr. a dau. and coheir of Sir Henry Malton, *q.v.,* and acquired the manor of Threapland. Their son John, later knighted, was granted Morton, Hesket, Nunclose, Wooloaks and Blabberthwaite in Inglewood Forest 1399. He was Sheriff of Cumberland 1404, 1408 and 1431, and his son John (d. 1458) was Sheriff 1440, 1445 and 1450, and was succ. by his son John (b. *c.* 1438) who marr. Joan, dau. and coheir of Sir Henry Fenwick, *q.v.,* and in 1461 acquired Armathwaite, which descended to their son John (d. 1544), Sheriff 1511, who was succ. by his grandson William Skelton (1516-85), whose son Lancelot heads the 1665 Visitation pedigree. The latter's son John (1579-1652) was Sheriff 1632 and was succ. at Armathwaite and Southwaite Hall by his son Richard (1600-71), who rebuilt and endowed Armathwaite chapel. He marr. 1623 Lettice, dau. of Robert Burdett, *q.v.,* and sister of Sir Thomas Burdett, Bart. Their grandson Richard (b. 1651) sold Armathwaite Castle 1712 and in 1721 was of Wycliffe (Y). He had ten sons, including John, his heir, and Richard, who was of Barrockside 1721, and Nicholas (1691-1766), a priest, for whom see AWL (CW2 xii, xxxiii, xl; SS 175). *Arms.* Clement de Skelton bore: Azure a fess Gules between three fleurs-de-lys Or (FFC). At the Visitation of 1665 John Skelton recorded: Azure on a fess* between three fleurs-de-lys Or a Cornish chough Proper beaked and legged Gules. *Crest.* A peahen's head erased Sable in the beak an acorn Or stalked and leaved Vert (FCW). At Southwaite Hall, in panels with initials R S L and date 1628, the arms appear as: . . . a fess . . . between three fleurs-de-lys . . . ; impaling, . . . two bars . . . the upper one charged with three martlets . . . and the lower with one martlet . . . (Burdett). On Richard Skelton's seal, 1668, the fess is charged with a chough, as in the Visitation version of the arms (D/Lons/L/Letter/ Viscount Lowther 1668, bundle in R.O., Carlisle).

SKELTON, of Branthwaite. This branch of the Skelton family descends from Hugh de Skelton, whose son John (d. before 1343) was father of Thomas Skelton (1328-65), who marr. Joan, dau. and heir of Robert de Whitrigg, Lord of Little Bampton, *q.v.* Their son Richard (1355-1432) held the manors of Branthwaite and Kirkbampton and lands in Skelton. These estates descended to Richard Skelton (1460-1526) who also owned the manor of Hensingham and a third of the manor of Skelton, which came to his grandson Thomas (1512-63). The estate descended to Thomas Skelton, a recusant (d. 1679), who marr. Alice Christian, of Unerigg, and had four sons – Henry (d. *s.p.* 1689); John (d. *s.p.* 1696); Thomas (d. *s.p.*); and Francis (d. 1704) who marr. 1699 Mary, dau. and coheir of John Senhouse, of Netherhall, *q.v.* She inherited Branthwaite and marr. 1708 Richard Butler, of Rawcliffe (L) (d. 1715). There is no mention of her after 1724, nor is it clear how the estate passed to General Henry Skelton (d. 1757) who was commissioned in the army 1708, served at Fontenoy and Dettingen, and left Branthwaite to James Jones, see Skelton, *olim* Jones. *Arms.* Azure a fess Argent between three fleurs-de-lys Or (TVN).† Fleming recorded: Vert a fess between three fleur-de-lys Or (FDC), as did Machell (MMS vi 417). MMD and DSL give: Azure a fess between three fleurs-de-lys Or. The arms, much worn, are at Branthwaite Hall.

SKELTON, of High House. At the Visitation of 1665 Richard Skelton, of High House, Hesket-in-the-Forest, was aged 62, and registered a pedigree of four generations, beginning with his great-grandfather William Skelton, of Appletreethwaite, said to be descended from the Skeltons of Branthwaite. Richard was twice married – to (1) Dorothy Thwaites, of Thwaites, by whom he had a dau. Dorothy (18 in 1665); and (2) Eleanor Hudleston, of Hutton John (b. 1622), by whom he had four daus. of whom the eldest Mary was aged 12 in 1665. *Arms.* Azure a fess Gules cotised Argent between three fleurs-de-lys Or (FCW). Burke gives: Azure a fess cotised between three fleurs-de-lys Or (BGA).

SKELTON, of Loweswater. Capt. Thomas Skelton, 59th Regt (1779-1856), descended from the Skeltons of Loweswater, marr. Agnes (d. 1854), dau. and coheir of John Dodson, of Woodland Hall, Kirkby Ireleth. The estate was inherited by Major James Brougham, J.P. (b. 1845), only son of James Lindsey Brougham by his marr. to Mary, 3rd dau. and coheir of Joseph Skelton, of Loweswater. His only child Auriol Margaretta marr. 1913 Viscount Ipswich (1884-1918) and was mother of John Charles William, 9th Duke of Grafton (1914-36). *Arms.* Quarterly, 1 & 4, Azure a fess between

* LMC blazons the fess Argent.

† For the quartering, Argent a bend dancetté Azure, recorded by Tonge, see Whitrigg.

three fleurs-de-lys Or (Skelton); 2 & 3, Or on a bend Sable three lions passant guardant of the field (Branthwaite);* impaling, Dodson, *q.v.* (M.I.s, Loweswater church and churchyard). *Crest.* An eagle's head erased in the beak an acorn stalked and leaved (FLP).

SKELTON, of Petterilwray. Field (FAC) says that the sisters and coheirs of Clement Skelton, of Petterilwray, living *temp.* Henry VII, marr. Robert Brisco, of Crofton, . . . Glaister, and Ralph Dacre. The first marriage is recorded in the 1665 Visitation, the bride's name being Katherine, dau. and heir of Clement Skelton. Since her great-great-grandson died 1583, it would seem that the marr. was probably before the reign of Henry VII. We have been unable to trace details of the other two marriages and it will be noted that Katherine is called dau. and heir. In 1518 Clement Skelton conveyed the manor of Petterilwray with lands in Ullock and Hensingham to George Skelton and Marion his wife (FOF). *Arms.* (as quartered by Brisco at 1665 Visitation). Azure a fess Sable between three fleurs-de-lys Or (FCW). The fess in the quartering was later blazoned Or.

SKELTON. Richard Skelton was Sheriff of Cumberland 1405-6. *Arms.* Vert a fess between three fleurs-de-lys Or (FWE). DSL, however, attributes to him: Azure a fess between three fleurs-de-lys Or.

SKELTON, *olim* JONES, of Branthwaite and Papcastle. On the death in 1757 of Gen Henry Skelton, *q.v.*, Branthwaite Hall was inherited by Capt James Jones, 3rd Regt of Foot Guards (b. 1720), who had saved his life on the battlefield by shooting an enemy dragoon as he was about to cut him down. His son Arnoldus Jones, M.P., of Branthwaite Hall† and Papcastle, 3rd Guards (d. 1793, aged 42), assumed the surname and arms of Skelton 1774. He marr. 1775 Elizabeth, dau. and coheir of William Hicks, of Whitehaven, and acquired the Papcastle estate. His elder son Major Henry Skelton, D.L., J.P., 19th Lancers (d. *s.p.* 1836, aged 59), was succ. by his brother Capt Daniel Jones Skelton, R.A. (1786-1859), who was the last male, his sons predeceasing him. His daus. and coheirs were Anne Eliza (d. 1860), marr. 1844 Capt William Browne Ponsonby, H.E.I.C.S. (d. 1855), *q.v.*; Maria, marr. 1844 the Rev. James Burrow; Mary Dorothea, marr. 1849 Lt-Gen Henry Grove, 23rd Dragoons; Frances, marr. 1845 Major George Hutchins Bellasis, H.E.I.C.S.; and Sophia Henrietta (BHC). *Arms* (granted 1774). Azure a fess between three fleurs-de-lys Or. *Crest.* A chough's head erased in the beak a slip of oak Proper. *Motto.* Forever (CA xiii/29).

SKINNER. Impaled by Fetherstonhaugh, *q.v.*, on shield at The College, Kirkoswald; Sir Timothy Fetherstonhaugh (1899-1969) marr. 1933 Anne Gladys, dau. of Sir Henry Ross Skinner, of Tarland, Aberdeenshire (1867-1943). *Arms.* Argent a koodoo bull at gaze Proper on a chief Azure a thistle leaved and slipped between two astronomical symbols of the planet Mars all Or.

SLACK, of Cockermouth. John Slack, tanner, of Cockermouth, died 1833. *Arms.* Azure a cross pattée throughout per bend sinister Ermine and Or in fess point a quatrefoil counterchanged. *Crest.* An arm embowed in armour

* The 2nd and 3rd quarters are obviously intended to shew a descent from the Skeltons of Branthwaite, but there is no proof of such descent and the Skeltons of Branthwaite quartered: Argent a bend dancetté Azure (TVN).

† Branthwaite was bought by J. C. Curwen 1798.

holding a sword wavy by the blade fessways (Tombstone, All Saints' churchyard, Cockermouth).

SLACK, of Derwent Hill. From Henry Slacke, of Browside, Glossop, Deputy Forester of Ashope 1525, descended William Slack, of Derwent Hill, Keswick (1774-1830). He was succ. by his 3rd son Robert Slack, M.D. (1822-93), whose 2nd son Robert Slack (b. 1857) succ. He marr. 1894 Maude, 2nd dau. and coheir of Lt-Col Sir Edmund Yeamans Henderson, K.C.B., R.E., and had two daus. and coheirs – Anne Elizabeth Henderson, marr. 1920 Major-General Ernest Ord Lewin, C.B., C.M.G., D.S.O.; and Elizabeth Angela Henderson (BLG13). *Arms.* Quarterly, 1 & 4, Azure on a cross formé throughout Ermine between four crescents Or a human heart Gules; 2 & 3, Argent a cross Vert (Upton); on an escutcheon of pretence, Per bend indented Sable and Or on a chief Argent a rose Gules barbed and seeded Vert between two ermine spots a bordure Gules (Henderson). *Crest.* In front of a crescent Or a snail Proper. *Motto.* Lente sed certe (FD7).

SLACK, of Fawcett Lees. Luke Slack, yeoman (d. 1739), whom Ferguson and Field wrongly call Black, marr. Isabel, sister and heir of John Forster, of Fawcett Lees, Lanercost, and so acquired that property. Their son Thomas bought from John and Thomas Forster, in Ireland, another messuage in Lanercost 1728. *Arms.* (on tombstone in Stapleton churchyard). . . . on a bend . . . two rows of billets . . . (ABD). Ferguson wrongly says the monument is at Kirklinton, and records the arms as: . . . a bend sinister chequy of five pieces . . . (CW1 xii 74). Field copies him, omitting five pieces (FAC).

SLEE. John Slee, of How, Mungrisdale, "a substantial yeoman," died 1629, leaving sons John (d. 1686), Thomas and Richard, and a dau. Elizabeth (d. 1686), who marr. *c.* 1637 Thomas Mark, of Mosedale (d. 1682). *Arms.* Vert a lymphad oars in action Argent sails furled Or flags and pennon flying Gules. *Crest.* On a chapeau Sable a plume of three ostrich feathers (BQS).

SLEE. Thomas Slee, of Dalemain, sealed his will dated 1738 with the following. *Arms.* . . . three (?) swans . . . . *Crest.* A pick axe.

SMALRIDGE. The Rt. Rev. George Smalridge, M.A., D.D. (Oxon) (1663-1719), was Dean of Carlisle 1711-13, Dean of Christ Church, Oxford, 1713-14, and Bishop of Bristol 1714-19. *Arms.* Argent a cross engrailed Azure between four bustards respecting each other Sable (BBE).

SMALWOOD. Thomas Smalwood, of Egton (Y), was father of the Rev. Alan Smalwood, M.A., D.D. (Cantab) (1608-86), Vicar of Norton (D) 1661-63, and Rector of Greystoke 1663-86. His elder son, the Rev. Gabriel Smalwood, M.A. (Cantab) (1650-98), was Vicar of St. Lawrence, Appleby, 1681-98; his younger son Charles Smalwood, of Little Salkeld (1651-1716), marr. 1687 Mary Sandford, of Askham. Their son Alan, of Little Salkeld (1690-1734), was father of the Rev. Charles Smalwood, B.A. (Cantab) (1721-71), who was vicar of Ainstable 1749-71 and of Kirkoswald 1761-71. He marr. 1753 Joyce (d. 1778, aged 50), dau. of Heneage Fetherstonhaugh, and sister and coheir of Timothy Fetherstonhaugh, *q.v.* Their only surviving son Charles Smalwood (1762-1839) was of the East India House, and assumed the surname and arms of Fetherstonhaugh 1797 (see further under that family). *Arms* (as impaled by Sandford on M.I. in Askham church). . . . a lion rampant . . . . On the bookplate of Admiral Tatham (see AWL) they are quartered as: Gules a lion rampant Or holding in the dexter forepaw a cup Sable. The Rev. Alan Smalwood, above, however, sealed in 1666 with what appears to be: . . . three griffins' heads erased . . . (.R.O. Carlisle. D/Lons/L/ Threlk. 13). An entirely different coat is painted on the hall ceiling at The College, Kirkoswald, viz.: Chequy Argent and Sable on a canton of the second a sword bendways of the first hilt and pommel Or point upwards.

SMITH. Sir Thomas Smith, M.A., LL.D. (Cantab), D.C.L. (Padua) (1513-77), statesman and scholar, was Regius Professor of Civil Law at Cambridge, Vice-Chancellor 1544, and Secretary of State, and was knighted 1548. He became second Dean of Carlisle when Dean Salkeld was ejected by Edward VI, was deprived by Queen Mary, and restored by Queen Elizabeth and held the deanery until his death, though he seldom visited Carlisle (DNB). *Arms.* Sable on a fess dancetté between three lions rampant each supporting a castle all Argent seven billets of the field (BGA). Field gives: Sable a fess indented Argent billetté of the field between three lions rampant guardant of the second each supporting an altar Or flaming Proper. *Crest.* A salamander in flames Proper (FAC).

SMITH. Thomas Smith, M.A., D.D. (Oxon) (1614-1702), was Prebendary of Carlisle 1660-61, Prebendary of Durham 1661-84, Dean of Carlisle 1671-84, and Bishop of Carlisle 1684-1702. *Arms.* Or a chevron between three crosses pattée fitché Sable. Another coat: Sable three bars and in chief as many crosses pattée fitché Or (BBE). *Crest.* A cubit arm erect and vested holding in the hand a cross pattée fitché (Gravestone in Carlisle Cathedral).

SMITH, of Cockermouth. Field (FAC, p. 339) states that Richard Smith (living 1780) marr. Mary Wordsworth, aunt of the poet, and that their son Richard Wordsworth Smith marr. Martha Fell, of Ulverston. In fact, as AWL shows, it was John Smith, of Bleansley, Broughton-in-Furness (1755-1807), grandson of William Smith, of Bleansley (d. 1781, aged 90), who marr. 1789 Mary, dau. of Richard Wordsworth, and first cousin, not aunt of the poet. Their son Richard Wordsworth Smith (1793-1832), Capt H.E.I.Co.'s maritime service, marr. 1820 Martha Fell. The poet's uncle, the above Richard Wordsworth, had a dau. Mary (1780-1867) who marr. (1) William Peake, R.N., who was killed in action 1813, and (2) 1816 William Proctor Smith, Paymaster, R.N., who was born in North America 1774 and died at Coniston 1853. Their son Wordsworth Smith, a Lieutenant in the army, was born at Ide, Devon, and died 1880 aged 63, and was buried at Grasmere. It is not known if these two families of Smith were related, nor whether William Proctor Smith had any connection with Cockermouth. *Arms* (of Smith, of Cockermouth). Sable on a fess engrailed Or between three squirrels sejant Argent each holding a marigold slipped Proper as many fountains (BGA). *Crest.* On a mount Vert a squirrel as in the arms charged on the body with a fountain (FAC).

SMITH, of Gamelsby and Thursby. John Smith, of Gamelsby, Aikton (d. 1759, aged 72), and his wife Martha (d. 1725) have a tombstone in Aikton churchyard, which also commemorates their son John (d. 1796, aged 84), his wife Ann (d. 1805, aged 75), and son John (d. 1797, aged 27). *Arms.* . . . on a fess engrailed . . . between three squirrels sejant . . . each holding a marigold slipped . . . as many fountains (Carving on lintel of farm at Gamelsby dated 1771, and on doorway at farm at Moorend, Thursby, with initials J S A for John and Ann Smith and date 1772. On a painting given to C. Roy

Hudleston by the late Mr. John Toppin, of Hazelrigg, Gamblesby, near Penrith, these arms appear as: Sable on a fess engrailed Or between three squirrels sejant Argent each holding a marigold slipped Argent seeded Gules as many fountains. The picture has on the back, in Mr. Toppin's hand: "This is the Smiths Crest given by the Heraldry Office for bravery in the Face of the Enemy about 1600. It is hereditary for all the Smiths of the North."

SMITH, of Thirlwall Gate. Nicholas Smith, of Thirlwall Gate, Lanercost, farmer, died 1782, aged 75. Mary, his wife, was buried at Lanercost 1762, and Nicholas, son of Nicholas Smith, of Thirlwall Gate, was buried there 1797, aged 2. *Arms.* ... on a chevron ... between three roundles ... as many crosses erect ... (ABD). The same arms are on the tombstone at Lanercost of Edward Smith, freeman of London, buried 1761.

SMITH, of Pygon's Hill, Lydiate (L), originally of Whitehaven. See pedigree in BLG4. *Arms.* Pean on a fess engrailed Or between three squirrels sejant Argent each holding a marigold slipped Proper a stag's head erased Azure between two fountains. *Crest.* On a mount Vert a squirrel as in the arms charged on the body with a fountain Proper. *Motto.* In medio tutissimus (BGA).

BROADLEY-SMITH. A brass in St. Michael's, Workington, commemorates Alan Broadley-Smith (1876-1915), Major 5th Battn. (TF) the Border Regt., killed in action near Hooge. *Arms.* Or an eagle's talon couped Gules* on a chief indented Azure a mullet Argent between two plates. *Crest.* A popinjay Vert beaked Gules charged on the breast with a mullet Or. *Motto.* Non nobis solum.

SNOWDEN. The Rt. Rev. Robert Snowden, D.D. (Cantab) (d. 1621), son of Ralph Snowden, of Mansfield Woodhouse, Notts., was ordained in 1599 and was Prebendary of Southwell 1599-1616, Chaplain to James I, and Bishop of Carlisle 1616-21. His brother the Rev. Richard Snowden, M.A. (Cantab) (d. 1620), ordained 1584, was Vicar of St. Oswald, Durham, 1602-20, and Prebendary of Carlisle 1617-19. *Arms.* Azure a lion salient Or (BBE).

SOMERI. Shield at Hutton-in-the-Forest; a Vane quartering. *Arms.* Or two lions passant Azure.

SOMERI – see DUDLEY.

SOPER. Burke gives this family as of Cumberland, with no further details. *Arms.* Argent a saltire engrailed between twelve billets Sable. *Crest.* A demi lion rampant holding between his paws a billet all Sable (BGA).

le SOR. Robert le Sor gave to Lanercost Priory the advowson of Grinsdale, which he acquired in marr. to a dau. and coheir of Asketil de Grinsdale. Their grandson William le Sor was in possession of half the manor of Grinsdale in 1270-71. *Arms.* Chequy Or and Gules a fess Azure (FAC).

SOMERSET. Mrs. Mary Felicia Studdert, wife of Thomas Copland Studdert, M.D., B.S. (Dunelm), F.R.C.P., of Crinkle Hill, Newby West, is dau. of Squadron Leader the Hon. Wellesley FitzRoy Somerset (1887-1969), and granddau. of the 3rd Baron Raglan. *Arms.* Quarterly, 1 & 4, Azure three fleurs-de-lys Or; 2 & 3, Gules three lions passant guardant in pale Or; all

* Not Sable, as given in FAC.

within a bordure compony Argent and Azure. *Motto.* Mutare vel timere sperno.

SOUTHAIK, of Skelton. Gospatrick, ancestor of the Curwens, had a younger son Gilbert, who became known as de Southaik from Southwick, Galloway. His grandson Gilbert (d. 1307) was of age in 1291. He marr. Isabel, sister and coheir of Richard Boyvill, Lord of Kirklinton, and so acquired, *int. al.*, a third of the manor of Skelton. William Southaik (d. 1559) owned this third which descended to his son Robert (b. *c.* 1534). John Southaik (d. 1580) appears to have succeeded. He bought half the manor of Morland 1570/1. His son John* (d. 1601), who was aged 40 and over in 1580, succeeded. He bought, with Richard Tolson, the manor of Little Bampton (C) 1582 and was High Sheriff of Cumberland 1591. His son and heir Francis (b. *c.* 1575) sold the advowson of Skelton to Corpus Christi College, Oxford, 1607. He was pardoned 1609 for alienating land in Skelton to Robert Southaik, who in 1618 sold lands there, including Scales, to Henry Brougham. He died 1623 owning one ninth of Skelton and leaving a son John then aged 30 and more (*Ex inf.* Dr. Christopher Kitching; CW1 v 40-43; CW2 lxvii). *Arms.* Machell recorded (without tinctures): A fess dancetté from the sinister chief a dexter arm issuing from clouds and extended towards a human heart between two spear heads pointing inwards in base a cross crosslet fitché (MMS vi 413). MMD gives: Argent a fess dancetté Sable in base a cross crosslet of the last on a chief Or dexter a human heart sinister a hand couped fessways Gules. Lysons gives: Argent a fess dancetté Gules in chief a human heart Proper between two nails Sable meeting in point on the summit of the fess in base a cross crosslet fitché of the last. *Crest.* Out of clouds Azure a cubit arm erect vested Gules the cuff Argent the hand holding a human heart erect Proper (LMC). At the Visitation of London, 1568, John Sowdeak, eldest son of William Sowdeak *alias* Sowtheake of Cumberland recorded: Argent a fess dancetté Gules from the sinister chief an arm issuing from clouds Proper vested gules touching in the chief point a heart of the last between two spear heads Sable pointing inwards. *Crest.* A dexter arm erect couped at the elbow vested Gules cuffed with a frill Argent holding in the hand a heart all Proper. His younger brother George, citizen and grocer of London, 5th son of the above mentioned William, recorded the same arms and crest each charged with an annulet Or for difference (BGA).

SOUTHEY. Robert Southey, D.C.L. (Oxon) (1774-1843), son of Robert Southey, of Bristol, linen draper, became Poet Laureate 1813. For many years he and his family lived at Greta Hall, Keswick, as tenants of William Jackson, *q.v.* He was elected M.P. for Downton, Wilts., 1826, but was unseated. He is buried in Crosthwaite churchyard, where there is a monument to him, and there is also a monument in the church. His eldest son the Rev. Charles Cuthbert Southey, M.A. (Oxon), was assistant curate of Cockermouth and Perpetual Curate of Setmurthy 1844-51 and Vicar of Askham (W) 1885-89. *Arms.* Sable a chevron between three cross crosslets

* He was perhaps the John Southaik, of Barwise Hall, who marr. between 1593 and 1599 Alice, dau. of Sir Henry Knyvett and widow of Christopher Dacre, *q.v.* See SUDWICK in AWL. The Brougham pedigree, always open to doubt, says that Peter Brougham (d. *c.* 1570) marr. Anne, heir of John Southaik, and so acquired Scales. This cannot be correct.

Argent.* *Crest.* A cubit arm erect vested and cuffed and holding a cross crosslet fitché. *Motto.* In labore quies (Bookplate of the poet, engraved by Thomas Bewick, 1813; BGA).

SOWERBY, of Dalston Hall. According to the Rev. Edmund Carr, Vicar of Dalston, John Sowerby (b. 1745) began life as a poor, barefooted boy, who ran bricks for the building of a barn at Cummersdale. He was sent to London to work in an insurance office, and there made a fortune† (PHY). He bought Dalston Hall from the Davison family, and was succ. by his 9th‡ son George Sowerby, D.L., J.P. (1794-1868), who bought the manor of Dalton Ryal (Y) and was succ. by his son George Sowerby, J.P., Lt-Col Durham Militia (1832-88). His eldest son, Thomas George Sowerby, J.P., of The Manor House, Lilley (1866-1938), sold Dalston Hall at the beginning of the 20th century. *Arms.* Barry of six Sable and Gules on a chevron between three lions rampant Argent as many annulets of the second. *Crest.* A lion rampant Argent langued Gules (PHY).

SOWERBY, of Sleetbeck. Daniel Sowerby, of Sleetbeck (d. 1667), a rich yeoman, who asked in his will to be buried in Bewcastle church "in my ancestors' burial place," owned land in that parish and at Botcherby and Harraby. He was succ. by his son William (d. 1729) who was succ. by his great niece Anne (d. 1780, aged 67), granddau. of John Sowerby, of Brampton, and dau. of Daniel Sowerby, of Sunderland (1688-1721). She marr. 1734 William Greenwell, *q.v.*, merchant adventurer of Newcastle upon Tyne. They built the present house at Sleetbeck 1744. Their arms and initials and date are over the door. *Arms* (borne by Greenwell on an escutcheon of pretence). Barry of six . . . and . . . on a chevron . . . between three lions rampant . . . as many annulets . . . (Shield at Sleetbeck).

SPEDDING, of Armathwaite and Mirehouse. Edward Spedding, of Whitehaven (d. 1706), marr. *c.* 1684 Sarah (d. 1716), dau. and coheir of Lancelot Carlisle, of Cairns, *q.v.*, and had *int. al.* sons John and Carlisle (see Spedding, of Summergrove). The former (1685-1758) was father of James Spedding (1719-59) who bought Armathwaite Hall from the Highmores 1748 and died there while he was High Sheriff. He marr. 1744 Susanna (b. 1722), dau. and heir of Wilfrid Irton, of Threlkeld Hall, and acquired that estate which came to their son John Spedding (1747-81) who was High Sheriff 1772. His son John, Captain in the Irish Brigade (1770-1851), sold Armathwaite Hall to Sir Frederick Fletcher-Vane. He inherited Mirehouse from Thomas Story 1802. Of his sons, Thomas Story Spedding succ. to Mirehouse; John Spedding was ancestor of the Speddings, of Windebrowe, *q.v.*; and James Spedding, M.A. (Cantab) (1808-81), was well known as an author and as the friend of Tennyson (DNB). The above Thomas Story Spedding, LL.B. (Cantab) (1800-70), was High Sheriff of Cumberland 1855. His son Henry Anthony Spedding, D.L., J.P., B.A. (Cantab) (1846-

* Field quotes Burke and the poet's monument as authority for: Gules a chevron between three cross crosslets Argent. BGA, however, distinctly blazons the field of the poet's arms as Sable, and the shield on the monument in Crosthwaite church is neither coloured nor hatched. A stained glass shield in Bristol Reference Library also has the field Sable.

† An East Indiaman was supposed to be lost with a valuable cargo, and heavily insured, the insurance was paid and the ship sold to Sowerby. Three weeks later she arrived with her cargo safe, and Sowerby sold her for £700,000. He bought Putteridge Park, Herts., and Lilley Manor, Beds.

‡ He had 10 sons and 6 daughters.

87), was High Sheriff 1884. He marr. 1882 Lady Jane Charlotte Stewart (d. 1897), dau. of the 9th Earl of Galloway, and had two daus. and coheirs, Blanche Frances (b. 1884) and Mildred Emma (b. 1885). They were succ. at Mirehouse by their cousin John Henry Fryer Spedding, of Windebrowe, *q.v. Arms.* Gules on a fess engrailed between three acorns slipped Or a mural crown between two roses of the first. *Crest.* Out of a mural crown Or a dexter arm embowed in armour the hand grasping a scimitar and the arm charged with three acorns one and two and entwined by a branch of oak fructed all Proper. *Motto.* Utile dulci (TSF; BLG18).

SPEDDING, of Storms. John Anthony Spedding, J.P., of Storms, Keswick (1878-1940), younger son of John James Spedding, of Windebrowe, *q.v.*, was called to the Bar 1901 and went the Northern Circuit. He was High Sheriff of Cumberland 1930. He marr. 1906 Vera Henrietta Sligo (d. 1969, aged 83), dau. and heir of Charles Sligo de Pothonier, *q.v.* Their son and heir Charles Anthony Spedding (1907-61) succ. and was succ. by his younger brother George John Frederic de Pothonier Spedding (b. 1919), who is now of Storms. *Arms,* etc. As Spedding of Armathwaite and Mirehouse.

SPEDDING, of Summergrove. Carlisle Spedding (1695-1755), 4th son of Edward Spedding, of Whitehaven (see Spedding, of Armathwaite, etc.), was agent to Sir James Lowther, and a leading mining engineer, with inventions to his credit. He was killed in a colliery accident. He marr. 1716 Sarah (d. 1771, aged 74), dau. of Edward Towerson, and had sons James (1720-88) and Thomas (1722-83). The latter was Vicar of St. James, Whitehaven. The former, James, bought Summergrove, Hensingham, from Anthony Grayson 1761. He marr. (2) 1779 Elizabeth (1745-1821), dau. and coheir of Thomas Harrington, *q.v.* Their son James Spedding, D.L., J.P. (1779-1863), was Capt 1st Foot Guards and Major Royal Westmorland Militia. His son James Dykes Spedding, Capt Westmorland Militia (1810-51), marr. 1848 Emily, dau. of the Hon. William Frederick Wyndham, *q.v.* Their son James Wyndham Harrington Percy Spedding* (1849-1924) succ., but dying unmarr. in Capri, Summergrove passed to his cousin Mark Hildesley Quayle, *q.v.*, and was later sold to John Anthony Spedding (see Spedding, of Storms). The family is now represented by Joseph Carlisle Harrington Spedding (b. 1905), formerly a tea planter in Ceylon, and now of Harts, Nether Compton, Sherborne, Dorset, whose son and heir is John Carlisle Spedding (b. 1951). *Arms,* etc. As Spedding of Armathwaite and Mirehouse.†

SPEDDING, of Windebrowe and Mirehouse. John Spedding, M.A. (Cantab), of Newcastle upon Tyne, banker (1806-39), 2nd son of John Spedding, of Mirehouse, *q.v.*, was father of John James Spedding, D.L., J.P., M.A. (Cantab), Col 1st Volunteer Battn The Border Regt (1834-1909), who was of Windebrowe or Greta Bank, Keswick, which was inherited by his eldest son Brigadier General Edward Wilfrid Spedding, C.M.G., O.B.E., R.A. (1867-1939). He was High Sheriff of Cumberland 1927 and was succ. by his son Lt-Col James Eustace Spedding, O.B.E. (1900-69), who was

* His younger brother Carlisle James Scott Spedding (1852-1915) was Private Chamberlain of the Sword and Cloak to Popes Leo XIII and Pius X.

† The following arms on Fairladies Farm, St. Bees, are probably intended for James Spedding, of Summergrove (1720-88) and his wife Elizabeth Harrington: . . . a fess engrailed Or between three acorns . . . , impaling . . . a fret. . . . .

High Sheriff 1956. His son Major John Henry Fryer Spedding, M.A. (Cantab), the Royal Green Jackets (retired 1969), barrister at law, succ. and is now of Mirehouse. *Arms,* etc. As Spedding of Armathwaite and Mirehouse. Field, however, states that Brigadier General Edward Wilfrid Spedding, as Sheriff 1927, bore the following on his seal: *Arms.* Gules on a fess engrailed between three acorns leaved and slipped Or a cross pattée .... *Crest.* Between two acorns leaved and slipped an arm in armour embowed and flourishing a sword (FAC).

SPENCER – see CAVENDISH, Duke of Devonshire.

SPENCER, *post* SPENCER-BELL, of Fawe Park. Jeremiah Spencer, of South Lodge, Cockermouth, was father of Jeremiah Spencer, whose sister and heir Mary Anne marr. James Bell, of Fawe Park, Keswick. They assumed in 1866 the surname and arms of Spencer and were parents of James Frederick Spencer Spencer-Bell (1863-86), an undergraduate of Magdalen College, Oxford, and a student of Lincoln's Inn, who was drowned in Derwentwater. Their dau. Adelaide Eliza (1859-1922) marr. Samuel Middleton Fox, *q.v. Arms.* Quarterly, 1 & 4, Ermine on a chief Sable an escallop between two bells Argent (Bell); 2 & 3, Quarterly Argent and Gules in the second and third quarters a fret of the first over all on a bend Sable three escallops also of the first (Spencer). *Crests.* 1, A beaver statant Ermine (Bell); 2, Out of a ducal coronet Or a griffin's head Argent collared Gules between two wings expanded of the second (Spencer). *Motto.* Dieu defend le droit (Spencer).

SPOONER. Cecile, dau. of the Rev. George Woodberry Spooner, B.A. (Oxon) (d. 1907, aged 94), Vicar of Inglesham, Wilts., 1857-1907, marr. 1907 William Nanson Donald, *q.v. Crest* (on silver cradle presented to Mr. and Mrs. Donald, when Mayor and Mayoress of Carlisle 1908, when their son was born). A boar's head couped pierced through the neck with a spear.

SPROAT, of Farlam. Bell Irving (ABD) deciphered no other details, but Field gave the Christian name as John, "An 18th century statesman" (FAC). *Arms.* ... a lion rampant ... (Gravestone at Farlam).

SPROT. Cecilia Doriel, younger dau. of Major Mark Sprot, D.L., J.P., Royal Scots Greys, of Riddell, Roxburghshire, marr. 1943 William Stephen Ian Whitelaw, M.P., of Ennim, *q.v. Arms.* Per fess Gules and Azure three salmon hauriant in pale each with a ring in his mouth Or in base a boar's head erased of the last langued of the first. *Motto.* Parce qu'il me plait (BLG17).

STACKHOUSE. The Rev. John Stackhouse, M.A. (Cantab) (1813-93), son of Anthony Stackhouse, of Stainforth, was Perpetual Curate of Thwaites 1849-74. *Arms.* Argent three saltires couped Gules chevronwise between a stackhouse or shed for the stacking of grain in chief Proper and in base a garb Vert. *Crest.* A saltire raguly Erminois charged with a pellet. *Motto.* Si Dieu veult (SSF).

STAFFIELD. A family of this name once owned part of the manor of Staffield. John de Staffol was a witness *c.* 1230, and John de Staffield held a moiety of Staffield 1270 and lands in Cliburn 1281, and was a juror 1292. John de Staffield was commanded to bring men to Carlisle for Edward I's Scottish expedition 1307; he was apparently a verderer in Inglewood Forest and died 1316. Another John is mentioned 1349. Adam Staffield was a witness 1373 (CW2 xvi). Denton says that the family ended in heiresses, married to Chamber, Mulcaster and Blennerhasset. *Arms.* Argent a pale Or (MMD) – a dubious ascription.

STAFFORD, Earl of Stafford and Duke of Buckingham. The Staffords were prominent amongst the ancestors of the Howards, Dukes of Norfolk, *q.v.* Ralph, Earl of Stafford (1301-72), marr. (2) 1336 Margaret, dau. and heir of Hugh, Lord Audley, Earl of Gloucester, *q.v.*, and from them descended Humphrey, Earl of Stafford (killed *v.p.* at the 1st Battle of St. Albans 1455) who marr. Margaret, dau. of Edmund Beaufort, Duke of Somerset, and sister and coheir of Henry Beaufort, Duke of Somerset, *q.v.* Their son Henry Stafford, Duke of Buckingham (1455-83), marr. Katherine, dau. of Richard Wydville, *q.v.*, and was father of Edward Stafford, Duke of Buckingham (1478-1521), whose dau. Elizabeth (*c.* 1497-1558) marr. as his 2nd wife Thomas Howard, Duke of Norfolk (1473-1554), *q.v. Arms* (impaled by Howard at Greystoke castle). Or a chevron Gules. These arms are also in a window and on the ceiling of Carlisle Cathedral, perhaps for Humphrey, 1st Duke of Buckingham (d. 1460), great-grandfather of the above Edward, who marr. Anne (d. 1480), dau. of Ralph Neville, 1st Earl of Westmorland, *q.v.* The arms are also on a shield at Hutton-in-the-Forest. Another shield there adds a crescent for difference, and a third displays: Gules six martlets Argent, three, two and one.

STAGG. "A geneaological correspondent" in the *Daily Telegraph* of 7 April 1960, contributed a pedigree of the Stagg family, of Stanwix, ancestors of the Earl of Snowdon. John Stagg *fl.* 1332 and in 1565 and 1575 Ingram and Anthony Stagg willed that they should be buried in Stanwix churchyard with their fore-elders. Thomas Stagg, of Stainton (d. 1706), was father of Thomas Stagg, of Sowerby Hall, whose grandson Rowland Stagg (1813-69) was a partner in Messrs. I. & R. Morley and marr. 1837 Jane (d. 1874), dau. of Robert Armstrong, of Haltwhistle. Their dau. Jane Margaret (1841-69) marr. 1867 Sir Owen Roberts, D.C.L. (Oxon) (d. 1915), and had a dau. Margaret Elizabeth (1868-1943), who marr. 1893 Robert Jones, M.D., F.R.C.P., F.R.C.S. (d. 1943), who assumed the additional surname Armstrong 1913 and was knighted 1917. Their grandson Antony Charles Robert Armstrong-Jones, G.C.V.O., marr. 1960 H.R.H. the Princess Margaret and was cr. Earl of Snowdon and Viscount Linley 1961. *Arms.* Or a chevron between two stags' heads erased Azure. *Crest.* A stag's head cabossed Or between the horns a cross pattée.

STALKER, of Sebergham. Gerard Stalker, of Sebergham Lonning Head, "householder and yeoman, formerly possessed of a great estate there," was buried at Sebergham 1794, aged 78. His 2nd son Daniel was a London merchant; his 3rd son Joshua (1763-1816) was a schoolmaster at Maryport, and then a shipbroker, and was later of Flimby. His son Foster Stalker (1798-1857) was a Colonel in the Bombay Army, and his son Thomas (1800-61) was a Captain in the same service. His dau. Mary (1789-1852) marr. Joseph Sharpe. *Arms.* Per saltire Vert and Argent two doves in fess of the first. *Crest.* A dove (M.I., Sebergham church).

STAMER. Major Arthur Cowie Stamer, C.B.E., of Faverdale Hall, Darlington (1869-1944), 5th son of the Rev. Sir Lovelace Tomlinson Stamer, 3rd Bart., had an only dau. Joan Eleanor, who marr. 1933 Sir William Howard Lawson, *q.v. Arms.* Quarterly Gules and Azure a cross Ermine charged with the sword of the city of Dublin in its scabbard in pale

Proper in the first and fourth quarters on a fess dancetté Argent a lion passant Gules in the second and third the cap of justice Or between three castles Argent. *Mottoes.* Jubilee; Virtute et valore (FD7).

STANCLIFFE. George Hall Stancliffe, of Lane Head, Boltongate, Captain, Reserve of Officers (b. 1899), is younger son of Percy Stancliffe, J.P., of Sion Hill, Thirsk (Y) (1867-1949), descended from John de Stancliffe, of Shibden (Y), living 1274. *Arms.* Argent a pallet dancetté cotised plain Gules on a chief arched of the last three roses of the first. *Crest.* In front of a stag's head erased Proper two mascles interlaced fesswise Sable. *Motto.* Juste et droit (BLG17).

STANDISH, *olim* STEPHENSON, of Scaleby and Brackenhill Tower. Maria Cecilia (d. 1817), dau. of Charles Strickland, of Sizergh (W), see AWL, and sister of Thomas Strickland, later Standish, marr. 1786 Edward Stephenson, of Farley Hill, Berks., and of Scaleby Castle (1759-1833), *q.v.* Their son Rowland Stephenson, of Scaleby Castle and Holm Cultram (d. 1843), assumed the name and arms of Standish 1834, and was father of Rowland Edmond Walter Pery Standish, D.L., J.P., of Scaleby Castle, and of Marwell Hall, Hants. (1820-93), who died *s.p.* and was succ. by his nephew William Pery Standish, O.B.E., J.P., of Scaleby Castle, Brackenhill Tower, Longtown, and Marwell Hall (1860-1922), High Sheriff of Cumberland 1902. His son Edward William Standish (1903-33) was succ. at Scaleby by his wife Sheila Margaret, dau. of Col Richard Byron, who sold it 1946. The present representative of the family is their son, Edward Anthony Byron Standish, of Inwood Farm, Seale, Surrey. *Arms* (granted 1834 to Rowland Stephenson, above, and Lady Lucy his wife, dau. of Edmund Henry, Earl of Limerick). Sable three standishes, two and one, Argent and for distinction a canton Ermine. *Crest.* An owl Argent beaked and legged Or charged for distinction on the breast with a rose standing on a mouse Proper (CA xl/187). These arms, with *Motto,* Nobilitas virtus, are at Brackenhill Tower. The family now bears the arms and crest undifferenced (FD7; BLG18*).

STANGER – see LEATHES.

STANHOPE. The Hon. Dudley Henry Eden Stanhope (1859-1928), who became 9th Earl of Harrington in 1917, marr. 1883 Kathleen, dau. of Joseph Carter Wood, of Warwick Hall, and was tenant of Whitefield House, Ireby, *c.* 1894-1901. *Arms.* Quarterly Ermine and Gules in the centre a crescent on a crescent for difference. *Crest.* A tower Azure a demi lion rampant issuant from the battlements Or holding in the paws a grenade fired Proper. *Supporters.* Dexter, A talbot guardant Argent gutté-de-poix; Sinister, A wolf Erminois; each gorged with a chaplet of oak Proper. *Motto.* A Deo et rege (BP58).

STANLEY, Earl of Derby. The Stanley family, Earls of Derby since 1485, held the manor of Bassenthwaite from the end of the 14th century until 1714 (NB ii 93; SBB). *Arms.* Argent on a bend Azure three stags' heads cabossed Or. *Crest.* On a chapeau Gules turned up Ermine an eagle wings extended Or preying on an infant in its cradle Proper swaddled Gules the cradle laced Gold. *Supporters.* Dexter, A griffin wings elevated; Sinister, A stag; each Or and ducally collared with line reflexed over the back Azure. *Motto.* Sans changer (BP105).

* Both these authorities substitute a rat for the mouse in the crest.

STANLEY, of Dalegarth (formerly Austhwaite). John de Stanelawe witnessed a grant by Benedict de Eaglesfield (*fl.* 1313-55) of a grange in Greysouthen, where he is said to have bought lands 1355-56, but when he acquired lands in Brackenthwaite in Braithwaite 1335, he is called son of John de Stanlawe of Greysouthen. His grandson Nicholas de Stanelawe (living 1392) marr. before 1354 Constance, dau. and heir of Adam de Austhwaite, *q.v.* of Austhwaite, and so acquired that estate, now known as Dalegarth. His great-grandson Thomas Stanley (living 1503) was M.P. for Carlisle 1446-47. His descendant Edward Stanley (*c.* 1573-1647) marr. 1591 Anne, dau. and coheir of Thomas Briggs, of Cowmire Hall (W). Their grandson Edward Stanley (1639-1714) was High Sheriff of Cumberland 1688, and was succ. by his son John (*c.* 1662-1730) who built Ponsonby Old Hall and removed there from Dalegarth; he was High Sheriff 1719. His son Edward Stanley, D.L., J.P. (1690-1751), was High Sheriff 1731. He marr. 1737 Mildred (d. 1789, aged 71), dau. and coheir of Sir George Fleming, 2nd Bart., Bishop of Carlisle, *q.v.* Their son George Edward Stanley, D.L., J.P. (1748-1806), who was High Sheriff 1774, built the new Ponsonby Hall. He marr. (1) 1774 Dorothy (d. 1786), dau. of Sir William Fleming, 3rd Bart. and sister and in her issue coheir of Sir Michael le Fleming, 4th Bart.; their dau. and heir Elizabeth (b. 1781) marr. 1805 John Cumberland Hughes and was ancestress of the Hughes-le Flemings of Rydal Hall. He marr. (2) 1789 Elizabeth (d. 1817), dau. of Morris Evans, and was succ. by his son Edward Stanley, D.L., J.P. (1790-1863), High Sheriff 1823 and M.P. for West Cumberland 1832-52. He was succ. by his son William Stanley, D.L., J.P. (1820-81), who marr. 1859 Caroline (d. 1919, aged 84), dau. of Sir George Musgrave, Bart. Their two elder sons Edward Stanley, D.L. (1859-94) and William Stanley, D.L., J.P. (1861-1928) (who was of Southwaite Hill 1898-1912), died unmarr. and their brother Philip (1870-1940) succ. and was succ. by his son Lt-Col Nicholas Austhwaite Stanley, O.B.E., D.S.O., Indian Army (retired), of Dalegarth, who was High Sheriff 1973. He sold Ponsonby Hall to the Home Office 1951. In 1947 he bought Dalegarth, which had been sold by his uncle Edward to Lord Muncaster 1888 (Stanley muniments in Record Office, Carlisle). *Arms.* Argent on a bend Azure cotised Vert three stags' heads cabossed Or. *Crest.* A stag's head Argent attired Or collared Vert (FCW). FVC gives: A stag's head Argent attired Or gorged with a bar Azure and charged on the neck with a crescent for difference. *Motto.* Sans changer (BLG17).

STANLEY, of Pipe. Shields at Hutton-in-the-Forest; a Vane quartering. *Arms.* Argent on a bend Azure three stags' heads cabossed Or.

STANLEY, of Arnaby. Nicholas Stanley, see Stanley, of Dalegarth, is said in FVC, p. 9, to have had by Constance Austhwaite, his wife, a younger son John, of Hall Thwaites, whose descendant John Stanley was of Arnaby, Millom. He had three sons, Christopher, Thomas and Richard, of whom the first named may be the Christopher Stanley, of Arnaby, who was buried at Millom 1610, having had a son John baptised there 1605. Thomas Stanley* was of Leigh in Fittleworth, Sussex, and was knighted 1604. He died *s.p.* and was succ. by his brother Richard* (d. 1629), who was succ. by his son Thomas

* The authority for saying that these brothers were sons of John Stanley of Arnaby is FVC p. 10. In the pedigree in the 1634 Visitation of Sussex they are said to have been sons of John Stanley, of Dalegarth.

Stanley (d. 1639), whose daus. and coheirs were Mary, marr. 1630 John Stanley, of Dalegarth, Dorothy and Anne. The line was continued by their uncle John Stanley, of Fittleworth, whose grandson George Stanley, of Poulton, Hants., who committed suicide 1734, marr. 1719 Sarah (1696-1764), elder dau. and coheir of Sir Hans Sloane, 1st Bart. Their son the Rt. Hon. Hans Stanley, M.P. (1720-80), was a Lord of the Admiralty, Ambassador to France 1761, and Cofferer to the Royal Household 1766. He died* *s.p.* and his sisters and coheirs were Anne (d. *s.p.* 1803, aged 78), marr. Welbore, 1st Baron Mendip, and Sarah (d. *s.p.* 1821, aged 96), marr. Christopher Doyley (DCS; BSG; DNB; Sussex County Magazine, iv 821-26). *Arms.* Field quotes FVC as authority for the following: Argent on a bend Azure three stags' heads cabossed Or within a bordure engrailed Gules. *Crest.* A stag statant Gules attired and unguled Or. This achievement is certainly blazoned and illustrated in FVC, without however being specifically attributed to this branch of the family; Burke gives the same arms and crest for Stanley, of Arnaby (BGA). FVC gives for Stanley, of Lee, in Sussex: *Arms.* Or on a bend Azure cotised Vert three stags' heads cabossed of the field. *Crest.* A stag's head Argent attired Or gorged with a bar Vert and charged on the neck with a crescent.

STANWIX BOWLING CLUB. The Club, founded *c.* 1893, uses the following *Device.* Azure a fess dancetté Gules between three trefoils slipped Or on a chief Argent the word STANWIX. The shield ensigned with a mural crown Or.

STANWIX, of Carlisle. A pedigree of nine generations of this family was entered by Thomas Stanwix, of Carlisle (b. 1630), at the Visitation of 1665, beginning with a namesake living in the city 1461-62. A descendant of the same names, a captain of a foot company in Sir Philip Musgrave's regiment, was killed fighting for the King in 1648. From him was descended another Thomas, LL.D. (Cantab) (d. 1725), who was a Brigadier General and fought in Marlborough's campaigns. He was M.P. for Carlisle 1702-21, Mayor 1715 and Governor of Gibraltar 1710. His heir was the son of Matilda Roos (d. 1740), his sister, John Roos, who was enjoined to change his name to Stanwix in his uncle's will. He entered the army 1706, rising to be a Major-General. He was M.P. for Carlisle 1746-60, and for Appleby 1761-66. In 1752 he became Governor of Carlisle. He, his wife, and only dau., were lost when the *Eagle,* in which they were returning from Ireland to England, foundered in 1766.† (DNB; CWM). *Arms.* Azure a fess dancetté Gules between three crosses botonné fitché Or (FCW). LMC blazons the field Argent. The above Major-General John Stanwix bore on his seal: Or a fess dancetté . . . between three cross crosslets fitché . . . (R.O. Carlisle, D/S/Corr Box 2).

STAPLETON, of Edenhall. William de Stapleton (d. 1362), younger son of John Stapleton, of Stapleton, *q.v.,* marr. (1) before 1330 Juliana (b. 1314, d. before 1362), younger dau. and coheir of Robert de Turp, and acquired half the manor of Edenhall, which descended to his son William (1336-80), who acquired the other half by an exchange with his cousin John, *q.v.* He was Sheriff of Cumberland 1378 and was succ. by his son William (1364-1432), who was Sheriff 1414 and 1420-22. He marr. the dau. of Thomas de Blencowe, *q.v.,* who marr. Elizabeth, dau. of Nicholas de Veteripont, and

* He cut his throat with a penknife in the woods at Althorp.

† The untimely deaths of the family gave rise to a law suit in order to determine which of the three was likely to have survived longest.

sister and coheir of Robert de Veteripont, *q.v.* His son and heir William (*c.* 1393-1457) marr. Margaret (d. 1468), dau. and heir of another Nicholas de Veteripont. She in 1467 held lands in Stapleton of John de Stapleton. Their heirs were their daus. Joan (b. *c.* 1414), who marr. Thomas Musgrave (d. *v.p.* before 1457), *q.v.*, and Mariota (b. 1420), who marr. (1) William Hilton, *q.v.*, and (2) Richard Musgrave (CW2 xi, xiii). *Arms.* Argent three swords conjoined at the pommel Gules (FFC; brass and windows in Edenhall church; and quartered by Musgrave).*

STAPLETON, of Stapleton and Edenhall. A family who took their name from Stapleton (C) owned half the manor and advowson. John Stapleton, whose forbears may have been Derman and Stephen de Stapleton, living 1290, was owner of half the manor in 1329 and presented to the living 1338. His sons John (b. *c.* 1312) and William (see Stapleton, of Edenhall) marr. Joan† and Juliana (b. 1314), daus. and coheirs of Robert de Turp (d. 1314) and acquired the manor of Edenhall. In 1362 John and his cousin William agreed that in consideration of the former relinquishing his moiety of Edenhall, the latter would give up his fourth part of the manor of Stapleton. In 1485 John Stapleton held half the manor and in 1525 a man of these names of Rouncton, Sussex, sold to Thomas, Lord Dacre, twelve messuages in Stapleton with the advowson, and lands in Great and Little Fenton and Stanwix (HN 143). *Arms.* Field's suggestion that the ring found in Lanercost in 1883 (CW1 ix), bearing: . . . a lion rampant queue fourché . . . , may have belonged to one of this family, a similar coat having been used by Robert de Stapleton (*Charles Roll, c.* 1290), seems unlikely for Robert doubtless belonged to the unrelated Stapleton family who came from Stapleton-on-Tees. It seems probable that the Stapletons of Stapleton (C) bore the same arms as the Stapletons of Edenhall: Argent three swords conjoined at the pommel Gules.‡

STAPLETON. Shield at Hutton John, a Hudleston quartering; Sir John Hudleston (d. 1512) marr. *c.* 1485 Joan (d. 1518), dau. and coheir of Sir Miles Stapleton, of Ingham, Norfolk. *Arms.* Argent a lion rampant Sable. The same arms are impaled by Irton, *q.v.*, in staircase window in Ireton Hall, John Ireton (d. 1539) having marr. Elizabeth, dau. of Sir Christopher Stapleton, of Wighill (Y).

STAVELEY, of Renwick. Adam de Staveley, Lord of Dent and Sedbergh, received a grant of Renwick from Henry I; his descendant Thomas Staveley held it 1291/92. *Arms.* MMD records: Argent on a chevron Sable between three fusils Gules as many stags' heads erased Or. The Rev. W. S. Calverley stated that the family "bore arms fretty in some form" (CW1 xii 171).

STEAD, of Dalston Hall. William Stead, of Waverbridge (1747-1810), descended from a Yorkshire family, was grandfather of John Stead, of Cummersdale and of Eden Lodge (d. 1892), whose son Edmund Wright Stead, J.P., of Dalston Hall (1862-1934), was High Sheriff of Cumberland 1909. His elder son Arthur Stead died in Canada 1967, aged 67, and the head of the family is his son Christopher Stead. *Arms.* Or on a chevron engrailed Sable between three bears' heads couped Gules muzzled Argent five roses of the last barbed and seeded Proper. *Crest.* A reindeer Proper armed and

* Fuller gives for the above William Stapleton, Sheriff 1378: Argent a lion rampant Sable (FWE).

† She marr. (2) Robert de Leyburn.

‡ This coat is on the tombstone in Kirkby Ravensworth churchyard (Y) of Samuel Stapylton, senior, died 1760, aged 77.

collared Or and tethered by a thong to a post on the dexter both also Proper. *Motto.* Constancie (FD7).

STEEL, of Derwent Bank. Joseph Steel, of Cockermouth, marr. 1785 Dorothy (d. 1799, aged 37), dau. of John Ponsonby, of Haile Hall. His eldest son John Steel, J.P., solicitor, of Derwent Bank, Papcastle (1788-1868), was M.P. for Cockermouth 1854-68. The said Joseph's 3rd son Col James Steel, C.B. (1792-1859), 67th Bengal Native Infantry, left descendants (BLG4; HBO). *Arms.* Col Steel's monument in All Saints', Cockermouth, displays: . . . a bend Ermine* in sinister chief an eagle's head erased . . . on a chief . . . three pennons points to the sinister . . . . *Motto.* Vincit veritas. Burke gives: Argent a bend chequy Sable and Ermine between two lions' heads erased Gules on a chief Azure three billets Or. *Crest.* A lion's head erased Gules (BGA).

STEPHENSON, of Crosslands. Henry Stephenson, of Crosslands, Alston, was father of John Stephenson (d. 1761, aged 76), Alderman of Newcastle, and co-patron of the living of Alston, whose eldest son Henry marr. his first cousin Sarah, dau. and coheir of Sir William Stephenson (d. 1774), Lord Mayor of London 1764-65. Henry's dau. and heir Elizabeth marr. 1782 John Savile, 2nd Earl of Mexborough. Henry's brother Matthew Stephenson, Sheriff of Newcastle 1759, was of Walworth Castle (D) (MOM; HHN II iii 85). *Arms* (confirmed to Sir William Stephenson, 1764). Gules on a bend Erminois three leopards' faces Vert. *Crest.* A garb Erminois (CA xi/37).

STEPHENSON, of Scaleby. Edward Stephenson, of Keswick, descended from the Stephensons of Bannisdale, was father of Edward Stephenson, M.P., of Keswick (1691-1768), Governor of Bengal 1728. He bought Scaleby Castle and other estates in Cumberland and died *s.p.* worth upwards of £500,000. He was succ. by his brother John (1700-71), whose son Edward died 1782, aged 44. His cousin Rowland Stephenson (1728-1807), M.P. for Carlisle 1787-90, marr. Elizabeth Anne (1738-82), dau. of Francis Drinkel, of Kendal, by Frances, dau. and coheir of Richard Wilson, of Black Hall, Kendal. Their son Edward (1759-1833) was father of Rowland Stephenson, later Standish (see that family), and of Mary Eliza (1787-1821) who marr. 1807 her kinsman Rowland Stephenson, M.P. (1782-1856). From them descends the present head of the family, Rowland Macdonald Stephenson, solicitor, of Chapters, Silverton, Devon. *Arms.* On brasses in Crosthwaite church to Edward Stephenson, his brother John and nephew Edward, these appear as: Gules on a bend Or three leopards' faces [Vert].† On the brass to John Stephenson, the arms impale: Argent a chevron engrailed between three crosses pattée Gules (Forward). *Crest.* A garb. The arms are on Buck's View of Holm Cultram Abbey and on R. M. Stephenson's bookplate, where the crest is Or.

STEPHENSON, *post* FETHERSTONHAUGH. John Stephenson, of Nentsberry, Alston (d. 1752), was father of Joseph Stephenson, of Nentsberry, joiner (1737-85), who had issue, *int. al.,* Thomas, of Worcester, and Mary (1772-1847), who marr. (2) Richard Fetherstonhaugh and was mother of Alexander Stephenson Fetherstonhaugh, of Hopton Court, Worcs.

* The bend is so divided into compartments that the hatching could represent: Compony Ermine and Ermines, or Erminois and Pean.

† On the tombstone of Rowland Stephenson in All Hallows churchyard, Tottenham, these arms impale: . . . a wolf rampant . . . on a chief . . . three mullets . . . , i.e. Wilson. This coat was presumably used by Elizabeth Anne Stephenson, née Drinkel, whose mother was Frances Wilson, of Black Hall, Kendal, see above. See also AWL.

(1798-1875), and Joseph Fetherstonhaugh, of Hopton Court (1806-77). Thomas Stephenson, of Worcester, above (bap. 1777), was father of the Rev. Thomas Nash Stephenson (d. 1876), whose son Lt-Col Shirley Arthur Stephenson, J.P. (1861-1949), inherited Hopton Court from Joseph Fetherstonhaugh, above, and in 1882 assumed the name and arms of Fetherstonhaugh (CW2 lxx 280-82). *Arms.* Quarterly, 1 & 4, Gules two chevronels engrailed between three feathers within a bordure also engrailed Argent in the centre chief point a cross crosslet of the last for distinction (Fetherstonhaugh); 2 & 3, Gules on a bend nebuly Erminois between six ears of wheat, three and three, one in pale and two in saltire banded Or three leopards' faces of the first (Stephenson). *Crests.* 1, An heraldic antelope's head erased Gules surmounted by two feathers in saltire Argent charged on the neck for distinction with a cross crosslet Or (Fetherstonhaugh); 2, In front of a garb Or a cornucopia fesswise Proper (Stephenson). *Motto.* Ne vile velis (FD7).

STERNE. Richard Sterne, D.D. (Cantab) (d. 1683), son of Simon Sterne, of Mansfield, Notts. and great-grandfather of Laurence Sterne, the novelist, was Master of Jesus College, Cambridge; Chaplain to Archbishop Laud, whom he attended on the scaffold; Bishop of Carlisle 1660-64; and Archbishop of York 1664-83. *Arms.* Or a chevron between three cross crosslets Sable (BBE). Burke gives as variant: Or a chevron between three crosses pattée Sable. *Crest.* A cock starling Proper (BGA).

STEWARD, *post* FALCON-STEWARD, of Newton Manor. John Steward, of Chapel House, Hensingham (d. 1848, aged 81), marr. Margaret Cecilia, dau. of Anthony Benn, of Hensingham House, *q.v.*, and was father of Anthony Benn Steward, J.P., of Newton Manor, Gosforth* (1805-81), who bought the manor of Seascale after the death of Sir Humphey le Fleming Senhouse 1841. He was High Sheriff of Cumberland 1858, and was succ. by his nephew, the Rev. Robert Stewart Falcon, M.A. (Oxon) (1829-87), son of Robert Falcon, M.D., of Whitehaven (1789-1859), by Margaret Steward his wife. He assumed the additional surname and arms of Steward 1883, and was succ. by his nephew (the son of his younger brother, the Rev. Thomas William Falcon, M.A. (Oxon) (1832-83), of Clifton House, Workington), William Watts Curwen Falcon (1881-1911), who assumed the surname Steward 1902. His only son Commander Hugh William Falcon-Steward, R.N., is now of Newton Manor. *Arms* (as borne by Anthony Benn Steward). Or a fess chequy Argent and Azure within a bordure Ermine. *Crest.* A stag Proper gorged with a collar chequy Argent and Azure (BLG4). On a tablet in Moresby church, the stag is gorged with a crown. *Arms* (granted to the Rev. Robert Steward Falcon, 1883). Quarterly 1 & 4 Or a fess engrailed chequy Azure and Argent between two stags' heads cabossed in chief and a round buckle in base of the second all within a bordure Ermine (Steward); 2 & 3, Sable a chevron between two falcons close in chief and an annulet in base all Argent (Falcon). *Crests.* 1, A stag Or charged on the body with a buckle as in the arms and resting the dexter fore leg on a stag's head cabossed Proper (Steward); 2, On a rock Proper and within an annulet in front thereof Sable a falcon close Argent (Falcon).

STEWART. Impaled by Graham on hatchment in Arthuret church; Sir James

* Which he built 1835.

Graham, 1st Bart, of Netherby, *q.v.*, marr. 1782 Catherine (d. 1836), dau. of John Stewart, 7th Earl of Galloway. *Arms.* Or a fess chequy Argent and Azure surmounted of a bend engrailed gules within a double tressure flory counterflory of the last. These arms are also borne on an escutcheon of pretence by Marshall on a brass in St. John's, Keswick; Reginald Dykes Marshall, D.L., J.P., of Castlerigg, *q.v.*, marr. (2) 1864 Mary Jane (d. 1925), eldest dau. and coheir of Rear-Admiral the Hon. Keith Stewart, C.B., R.N. (1814-79), and granddau. of George, 8th Earl of Galloway.

STIRLING. The Rt. Rev. John Stirling, D.D., of Craigie, Ayrshire (d. 1844), Moderator of the General Assembly of the Church of Scotland 1823, was father of John Stirling, D.L., J.P., of Fairburn, Muir of Ord (1820-1907), one of the pioneers of the Cleator iron ore industry, and owner of the Montreal Mines, Cleator Moor. He marr. 1852 Marion (d. 1907), dau. of John Hartley, of Moresby, and was succ. by his eldest son William Stirling, D.L., J.P., of Fairburn and Monar (1859-1914) (CCC; BLG18). *Arms* (as impaled by Ainsworth, *q.v.*, at the Flosh, Cleator). Argent on a bend Azure three buckles of the field.

STOBART. John William Stobart, M.B.E., of Farlam Ghyll, is elder son of Henry Gervas Stobart,* J.P., of The Old Hall, Brompton (Y), a descendant of the Stobarts of Pepper Arden (Y). *Arms.* Barry of twelve Argent and Azure three lions rampant Purpure. *Crest.* A cubit arm grasping a dagger point downwards all Proper.

STODDART. The Rev. Charles Stoddart, M.A. (Cantab) (d. 1790, aged 85), Vicar of Chollerton (N) 1733-90, was Vicar of Brampton 1773-90. *Arms.* Sable three mullets and a bordure Argent (LAE).

STONEY. Percy Butler Stoney, L.R.C.P. (Edin) (1871), M.R.C.S. (1870), of Holborn Hill, Millom, a descendant of the family of Portland Park, Co. Tipperary, practised for over 40 years in Millom, and was Medical Officer to Millom U.D.C., Coroner for the Lordship of Millom, and Medical Officer to the Hodbarrow Mining Co. Of his sons, Elkin Percy Stoney (1880-98) died on his way to India, and Malcolm Percy Stoney (b. 1883) was in 1905 an undergraduate at Harvard. *Arms.* Or on a bend cotised Azure three escallops of the field. *Crest.* Out of a mural crown Proper a demi lion Or holding between the paws a spur erect Argent winged Gules. *Motto.* Nunquam non paratus (BLG6).

STORDY, of Moorhouse. The Stordys, a Quaker family, are said to have been at Moorhouse, Kirkbampton, since the early 17th century, when Thomas Stordy died. Stonehouse, their home, has the date 1706 on a mantelpiece with the initials W S T. It was in this house that Bonnie Prince Charlie slept on 9 November 1745, when the owner was presumably William Stordy (d. 1794, aged 81), whose 3rd son Capt Robert Stordy, 31st Foot, of Abbey Street, Carlisle (d. 1816, aged 64), had a dau. and heir, Mary Tirzah, who marr. 1814 John Dixon, of Carlisle. To a junior branch belonged Thomas Stordy (d. 1788), ancestor of Thomas Stordy, of Thurstonfield, Burgh-by-Sands (b. 1844), whose son John Stordy, of Beech House, Thurstonfield (1892-1959), was father of Thomas Stordy, now of The Beeches. John's younger brother Thomas Johnston Stordy, of Thurstonfield (b. 1896), was father of John Stordy and of Henry George Stordy, who is now of Lough House, Thurstonfield. *Arms.* Argent a

* His sister Miss Amy Stobart (d. 1934) lived for many years at Lattendales, Greystoke.

chevron Azure between three escallops Sable. *Crests.* 1, An escallop Sable between two wings erect Or; 2, An arm embowed in armour Azure flourishing a knotted club Sable. *Motto.* Fortis in arduis.

STORY. Edward Story (d. 1502) was Bishop of Carlisle 1468-78, and Bishop of Chichester 1478-1502. *Arms.* Per fess Argent and Sable a pale and three storks counterchanged (BBE).

STORY, of Joses Town. Thomas Story, of Joses Town, Kirklinton, yeoman, died 1746, aged 65; his son Richard died 1746, aged 21. Their gravestone in Kirklinton churchyard bears the words "Here lieth the father and the son." *Arms.* ... three birds ... (probably intended to be storks, but not really resembling these birds). Field recorded ... three storks ... and in chief as many bells or escallops ... (FAC).

STORY, of Justicetown. Thomas Story, of Justicetown, Kirklinton (d. 1632),* was succ. there by his son Thomas (1630-1721) who marr. 1658 Thomasin (d. 1675), dau. of the Rev. George Constable,† Rector of Arthuret 1639-73. Their eldest son, the Very Rev. George Story, D.D. (1660-1721), was Chaplain to the Dowager Countess of Carlisle, Rector of Kirklinton 1681-94, and, as an Army Chaplain, was present at the Battle of the Boyne. He was Rector of Carrickfergus 1694, Dean of Connor 1694-1705, and Dean of Limerick 1705-20 (DNB). For a few weeks he owned the Justicetown estate, which was sold in 1722 by his widow to his brother Thomas Story, a lawyer (1670-1742), who became a member of the Society of Friends and travelled widely in Britain and America, exercising his ministry. It has been said of him that he was, next to his friend William Penn, the leading Friend of his generation. He died *s.p.*, his heir being his sister Anne (d. 1747) who marr. (1) 1687 Arthur Forster, of Kingfield, and (2) Robert Elliot of Dinlabyre, Roxburghshire, who was buried as of Justicetown at Arthuret 1732. Ann was buried there from Carlisle, "late of Justicetown." For some of her descendants, see CW2 lxviii (TWS). *Arms.* Quarterly of six: 1, 3 & 5, A stork;‡ 2 & 4, Vair; 6, A bend. *Crest.* A stork's head (M.I., Arthuret church).

STORY, of Knowe. Mary, wife of David Story, of Knowe, died 1767. *Arms.* Quarterly of 6: 1, 3 & 5, A stork; 2, A cross flory;§ 4, Vair; 6, A bend (ABD).

STORY, of Kirkland House. William Story, of Kirkland House, Wigton (d. 1873), was descended from the Storys of Cargo. His son John Story, J.P., of Kirkland House (1844-1921), had two daus. and coheirs, Mary Sarah (b. 1878), and Amy Elizabeth (b. 1880), who marr. Charles William Wilson (see Wilson of The Gale) (SOO). *Arms.* Per fess Argent and Sable a pale and three storks all counterchanged. *Crest.* A whelk shell Or a stork

* Emily E. Moore, in TWS, says that he is commemorated at Kirklinton thus:

Under this stone lyes Thomas Story
Whose soul is gone to Heavenly glory
Admirable for wisdome and well so approved
In England and Scotland by rich and poor loved.
Had sixteen sons and four daughters fair
Which Anna his loving wife him bare
1632.

† He was a poor relation of Sir Richard Graham, Bart., who presented him to Arthuret.

‡ Bell Irving recorded this as: A swan contourné (ABD).

§ Field recorded this as: A pale flory (FAC).

standing thereon Proper. *Motto.* Fabula sed vera (Window in Wigton church).

STORY, of Lake. Francis Story, schoolmaster, of Lake, Kirklinton, died 1697, aged 61. Elizabeth, dau. of George Story, of Length . . . , died 1711, aged 10. *Arms.* . . . a crescent . . . between in chief two mullets . . . and in base a (?) billet fessways . . . (Tombstones in Kirklinton churchyard). Bell Irving interpreted the (?) billet as: A cornet mouth to the sinister (ABD). Field interpreted it as: An object like a blunt shaped wedge which was probably meant for a stork (FAC).

STORY, of Penrith. Richard Story, M.D. (d. 1821, aged 82), was a surgeon and apothecary in Penrith for many years. He marr. 1766 Margaret, dau. of Robert Dawson, of Penrith, *q.v.*, and had a son Col David Story, R.A. (1781-1841), whose daus.* and coheirs were Margaret, marr. George Henry Carleton Sunderland, of Swarthdale; and Charlotte, mar. 1843 Capt Pentyre Anderson-Morshead, R.A. (CPK). *Arms.* Argent a lion rampant Vert within a bordure Azure; impaling Dawson, *q.v.* *Motto.* Tout pour l'amour rien par force (Tombstone, St. Andrew's churchyard, Penrith).

STOURTON. Shield at Hutton-in-the-Forest; a Vane quartering. *Arms.* Sable a bend Or between six fountains.

STREATFEILD. William Edward Streatfeild (d. 1915, aged 53), son of the Rev. William Streatfeild, marr. Avis, dau. of the Rev. Bernard Edward Watkins *q.v.* She lived for many years at Welbank, Mosedale, and their dau., Miss Ruby A. G. Streatfeild, is now of Brantgate, Mosedale. *Arms.* Per fesse Gules and Sable three bezants (BLG18).

STRICKLAND. William Strickland (d. 1419), of the Sizergh family, see AWL, and perhaps a younger son of Sir Thomas Strickland, of Sizergh (d. 1376), was Bishop of Carlisle 1400-19. His dau. and heir Margaret (d. 1449) marr. *c.* 1391 Sir Robert Lowther, of Lowther. *Arms.* Sable three escallops Argent (HSS). The Lowthers, however, quarter for Strickland: Sable three escallops within a bordure engrailed Argent (FCW).

STRIVELYN. Sir John de Strivelyn (d. 1378), Constable of Edinburgh Castle 1337, marr. before 1327 Barnaba (b. *c.* 1292, living 1357), dau. and coheir of Sir Adam de Swinburne, *q.v.* In 1357 the King, on account of the good services done by her husband, restored to her all her lands in Cumberland and pardoned her for all felonies committed by her father and ancestors. *Arms.* Sable crusilly and three covered cups Argent (FFC). In another version this is: Sable crusilly fitché and three covered cups Argent, which version is carved on stone on a shield at the Demesne Farm, Bewcastle, formerly over the gate of Bewcastle Castle, of which Canon James Wilson wrote that it was "one of the most ancient coats of arms, sculptured in stone, in existence in the county of Cumberland" (*Scottish Historical Review,* 1918).

STRONG, of Rattenrow. Field stated (FAC) that the court rolls of the manor of Blackhall showed that Edward Strong was admitted to a customary tenement called Rattenrow, near Durdar, *c.* 1600, and added that the property was farmed by succeeding generations† until the death of John

* T. A. Trollope met these two girls at the home of their uncle John de Whelpdale in Bishop Yards, Penrith. See his *What I Remember,* ii 42, for a delightful reference to them.

† The will of John Strong of Rattenraw (d. 1765) leaves to his nephew Christopher Wannop younger of Newby his watch and violin, and his German flute to another nephew John eldest son of Samuel Strong. He also left £3 a year "towards keeping a school for the learning of poor peopl's children in Blackwel High and Low bound." He had an only dau. Sarah.

Strong (d. 1842, aged 37) and that in 1937 his great-grandson James Rowland Strong, of Yew Tree, Thursby (b. 1897), owned it. He was son of John Timothy Strong (d. 1919, aged 58) and died *s.p.* 1966. His uncle Thomas Slack Strong (1863-1947) was a partner in the Carlisle legal firm of Messrs. Wright, Brown & Strong, and was succ. by his son Thomas Strong, M.A. (Cantab) of Buckabank, who was admitted a solicitor 1926 and is the present head of the family. His sons are Peter Strong and Michael Timothy Strong. *Arms.* Gules an eagle displayed within a bordure engrailed Or. *Crest.* A demi eagle displayed issuing from a mural coronet Or. *Motto.* Strong is the truth (FAC).

STRUTT. Impaled on bookplate of Thomas Angelo Irwin, D.L., J.P., of Lynehow, *q.v.*, who marr. 1879 Lucy Frances, dau. of George Henry Strutt, D.L., of Bridgehill, Belper (Dy). *Arms.* Per pale Gules and Azure two chevronels engrailed between three cross crosslets fitché Or.

STUART. Impaled by Howard on shield at Greystoke Castle; Henry Frederick, Earl of Arundel, Surrey and Norfolk, Lord Mowbray (1608-52), marr. 1626 Elizabeth (d. 1674), dau. of Esme Stuart, 3rd Duke of Lennox. *Arms.* Quarterly, 1 & 4, Azure three fleurs-de-lys Or within a bordure Gules semé of buckles Argent; 2 & 3, Or a fess chequy Azure and Argent a bordure engrailed Gules; over all on an escutcheon Argent a saltire engrailed between four roses Gules.*

STUART. The Very Rev. Henry Venn Stuart, M.A., D.D. (Cantab) (1864-1933), was Prebendary of Lichfield 1905-24, and Dean of Carlisle 1924-33. *Crest.* A pelican in her piety Proper.

STUDDERT – see SOMERSET.

STUDHOLME. Denton gives a pedigree of eight generations of this family, beginning with William Studholme who bought lands in Grinsdale from John de Kirkanders 1336-37. Joseph Studholme, of Hole House (d. 1755, aged 73), was great-grandfather of John, of Studholme, Abbey Town, and afterwards of St. Nicholas and Morton Head (1787-1847), who sold the last of the family estates. His eldest son Joseph (1827-1904) settled in Ireland; his 2nd son John (1829-1903), with his younger brothers Paul (1831-99) and Michael (1833-86), emigrated to New Zealand 1851, where John, a magistrate, was of Merevale, Christchurch, and Coldstream, Ashburton Co., Canterbury. He was a member of the House of Representatives 1867-74 and 1878-82. His son William Paul Studholme, J.P., M.A. (Oxon), of Perridge House, Devon (1864-1941), was High Sheriff of Devon 1936, and was succ. by his 2nd son Sir Henry Gray Studholme, C.V.O., M.A. (Oxon), cr. Baronet 1956; he was M.P. for Tavistock 1942-66 and Vice-Chamberlain of H.M. Household 1951-56. (DAC; BLG17). *Arms.* Vert a horse statant Argent caparisoned Or on a chief of the second three mullets of six points pierced Gules. *Crest.* A horse's head Argent bridled and charged on the neck with a spur Or. *Motto.* Semper paratus (BP105).

STUTEVILLE. T. H. B. Graham in CW2 xiii 33-54 has provided an account of this family from Robert de Stuteville, named Grundebeof, imprisoned for life by Henry I 1106. His grandson and namesake was a justice itinerant in Cumberland 1169-70, and was father of William (d. 1203), Sheriff of

* These arms are also in glass in the library of The Queen's College, Oxford, Katherine Stuart (1640-1702), granddaughter of the above Esme, Duke of Lennox, having marr. (2) Sir Joseph Williamson, *q.v.*

Cumberland 1198 and 1200, and Nicholas (d. *c.* 1206), who obtained a grant of Liddel barony. The male line failed with his grandson Eustace de Stuteville in 1241. His heir was his cousin Joan (d. 1276), dau. of Nicholas de Stuteville II (d. 1233). She mar. (1) *c.* 1229 Hugh Wake, *q.v.*, and (2) Hugh Bigod (d. *c.* 1265). *Arms.* Joan de Stuteville, widow of Hugh Wake, sealed with: Barruly . . . and . . . (Brit. Mus. 6719). DSL gives for William de Stuteville, above: Barry of ten Argent and Gules a lion rampant Sable.

SUDWICK – see SOUTHAICK.

SUMNER. William Brightwell Sumner, Bengal Civil Service, of Hatchlands, Surrey (*c.* 1730-96), marr. Catherine (1736-71), dau. of John Holme, of Holme Hill, *q.v.*, and niece of Thomas Holme (1712-94), after whose death the estate passed to his great-nephew George Holme Sumner, M.P., J.P., Col 1st Royal Surrey Militia (b. 1760). He assumed the additional name of Holme, and sold Holme Hill to Col Thomas Salkeld, *q.v.*, 1810. *Arms.* Quarterly, 1 & 4, Ermine two chevrons Or (Sumner); 2 & 3, Holme, *q.v. Crest.* A lion's head erased Argent ducally gorged Or (BLG5). BGA gives: A lion's head erased Argent ducally crowned Or.

SURTEES. Impaled by Salvin, *q.v.*, on tablet in Alston church; the Rev. Hugh Salvin, Vicar of Alston, marr. 1840 Julia Alice (1810-80), dau. of Anthony Surtees, of Milkwelburn. She was buried at Bywell St. Andrews (N). *Arms.* Ermine on a canton Gules an orle Argent. The same arms are borne by Isabel Susan Ann, only dau. of Major Robert Lambton Surtees, O.B.E., J.P., of Redworth Cottage, Littlestone-on-Sea, Kent, who marr. 1944 Major Charles Spencer Richard Graham, *q.v.*

SUTTON. Francis Sutton, of Coundon (D), and later of Lancaster, died at Greystoke parsonage 1760, aged 83, and was buried in the churchyard with his wife Teresa (d. 1764, aged 77) (HDR). *Arms.* . . . a chevron . . . between three annulets . . . (Gravestone, Greystoke churchyard).

SUTTON. The Rev. Alfred Sutton, C.B.E., J.P., M.A. (Cantab) (1851-1938),* Hon. Canon of Carlisle, son of James Sutton, of Shardlow Hall (Dy), was Curate of St. James, Whitehaven, 1879-81, Vicar of Bridekirk 1881-1938, and Rural Dean of Maryport. He was Chairman of Cumberland County Council 1914-38. His only son Air Marshal Sir Bertine Entwisle Sutton, K.B.E., C.B., D.S.O., M.C. (1886-1946), was Commandant of the R.A.F. Staff College 1941, and Air Member for Personnel 1942-45. *Arms.* Argent a wolf passant Sable on a chief arched Azure an annulet between two crosses flory of the first. *Crest.* Three annulets interlaced, one and two, Argent between two wings Sable each charged with a cross flory of the first (BLG18).

SUTTON. In a window in Scotby church commemorating Geoffrey Storrs Sutton, M.C., Captain, 19th Battn King's Liverpool Regt, killed at St. Quentin 1918, aged 23, appears the following *Crest.* On a chapeau Gules turned up Ermine an eagle wings expanded Or preying on an infant in its cradle Proper, i.e. the crest of the Stanleys, Earls of Derby.

SWINBURNE. Sir John de Swinburne, of East Swinburne (N), was Sheriff of Cumberland 1277 and at that time bought the manor of Bewcastle, which descended to his son Sir Adam Swinburne (d. before 1327), who also

* In 1877-79 he helped, with General Gordon, to suppress slave dealing in Darfur.

acquired the manor of Lanerton. Sir Adam forfeited Bewcastle because of his attachment to John Balliol, late King of the Scots, but later regained it. His son Sir Henry (1296-?1326) died *s.p.,* his sisters and coheirs being Barnaba (b. *c.* 1292, living 1357), marr. Sir John de Strivelyn, *q.v.*; Christina, marr. Sir John de Widdrington, *q.v.*; and Elizabeth, marr. Roger Heron (CW2 xxii, xxvi, lix). *Arms.* The family bore two coats, viz. Gules three boars' heads couped Argent; and, Argent on a cross Gules five garbs Or (FFC; HBN). DSL, however, attributes to Sir John de Swinburne, Sheriff 1277: Per fess Gules and Argent three cinquefoils counterchanged. See next entry.

SWINBURNE, of Huthwaite. Alan Swinburne, a younger son of Sir William Swinburne, of Capheaton (N), doubtless came to Cumberland in the train of the Percy family, and marr. the heir or coheir of the Huthwaites of Huthwaite, *q.v.* In 1398 he held half Huthwaite and Brigham and lands in Dunthwaite and Branthwaite of Matilda, Countess of Northumberland. In 1454 John Swinburne was a retainer of the Earl, Receiver in Cumberland and Bailiff of Allerdale. A later John Swinburne in 1537 saved Robert Wetlay, one of the assistants to Dr. Leigh, when he was surveying the Cumberland monasteries. Wetlay was seized by a mob of 500 men, and taken to Cockermouth market, where the crowd wanted to behead him. John Swinburne persuaded the mob to spare his life. In 1544 he sold his land at Chollerton (N) to his kinsman William Swinburne, of Capheaton. He was succ. by John Swinburne (d. 1618) who in 1581 set up the inscription* over the doorway of Huthwaite Hall. His descendant Richard Swinburne (*c.* 1636-1715) in 1699 joined with his wife Eleanor (Bouch), his son John (b. 1661) and Winifred (Lawson) his wife, in selling for £800 the manor of Huthwaite and 1,100 acres. Richard Swinburne is said by Col Haswell to have died a pauper. His son had a large family between 1683 and 1693 and descendants have been traced at Flimby until 1757. *Arms.* Quarterly, 1 & 4, Gules three boars' heads couped Argent crined Or between nine cross crosslets of the second; 2 & 3, Per fess Gules and Argent three cinquefoils counterchanged a crescent for difference. *Crest.* A boar's head erect couped Argent (FCW).

SWINNERTON. Shield at Hutton-in-the-Forest; a Vane quartering. *Arms.* Argent a cross couped fleury Sable. This should be: Argent a cross flory Sable.

SWYLLIARD. Said by Burke to be of Cumberland; no other details. *Arms.* Sable a cross Argent on a chief of the first (*sic*) a fleur-de-lys Or (BGA).

SYKES, of Sykes Dyke. Dugdale in the Visitation of Yorkshire, 1665, traces the descent of the Sykes family, of Leeds and Spofforth, later of Kirk Ella (Y), from Richard Sykes, of Sykes Dyke, near Carlisle, whose younger son William left Cumberland, settled in Leeds, and was ancestor not only of the present Baronets of Sledmere (Y), but also of William Sykes, lord of the manor of Leeds (d. 1652) who owned the manor of John de Chappell, Carlisle. His son Richard Sykes, of Leeds (1627-94), had a 3rd dau. and

* Iohn Swynburn esquire & elsabth his wyfe did make coste of this Work in the dais of ther lyfe
The inscription is accompanied by two shields, one displaying the Royal arms (Quarterly, France Modern and England), and, . . . three cinquefoils . . . . The latter shield is inverted.

coheir Anna marr. Ralph Thoresby, F.R.S., the antiquary.* Although Clay pours cold water on this descent, Dugdale added: "See the Visit. of Cumberland for the Armes." *Arms.* Argent a chevron Sable between three sykes or fountains Proper (CVY; FMG).

SYMPSON – see SIMPSON.

TAIT. The Most Rev. Archibald Campbell Tait, P.C., M.A., D.C.L., D.D. (Oxon), F.R.S. (1811-82), youngest son of Crauford Tait, of Harvieston, Clackmannanshire, and Cambodden, Argyll, was Headmaster of Rugby 1842-50, Dean of Carlisle 1850-56, Bishop of London 1856-68, and Archbishop of Canterbury 1868-82. To the same family belonged John Tait, of Ashbank House, Great Corby (d. 1945), descended from the Taits of Ludquharn, Aberdeenshire. His son Canon Reginald Campbell Tait, M.A. (Oxon), was Curate of Crosthwaite 1928-32, Rector of Grasmere 1945-73, and Hon. Canon of Carlisle 1958-73. *Arms.* Quarterly, 1 & 4, Argent a saltire and a chief engrailed Gules (Tait); 2 & 3, Argent two ravens hanging paleways Sable suspended by an arrow in fess piercing both their heads Proper (Murdoch) (BBE; POA). *Crest* (of Tait, of Harvieston). A dexter hand grasping a dagger Proper. *Mottoes.* Over the crest: Virtute; below the arms: Pro rege et patria (BGA).

TALBOT. Impaled by Howard on shield in hall of Greystoke Castle; Thomas Howard, Earl of Arundel, Surrey and Norfolk (1585-1646), marr. 1606 Alethea (d. 1654), dau. and eventually sole heir of Gilbert Talbot, 7th Earl of Shrewsbury. *Arms.* Gules a lion rampant within a bordure engrailed Or.

TALLENTIRE. Jonathan Tallentire, of Outhwaite, Renwick, gent. (*fl.* 1786), was a member of a well known Renwick family. *Crest.* A ram passant (Haresceugh deeds).

TARRANT. The Very Rev. Charles Tarrant, M.A., D.D. (Oxon) (1722-91), was Dean of Carlisle for a few months in 1764, and was then appointed Dean of Peterborough. *Arms.* Field suggests that they may have been: Argent a chevron between three eagles displayed Gules (FAC).

TATE, of Clarkstown. David Tate, of Clarkstown, householder, died 1756, aged 62. *Arms.* . . . a chevronel . . . between three boars' heads erased . . . all within a bordure . . . . *Crest.* A hand holding a javelin point to the sinister (Gravestone, Kirkandrews-on-Esk churchyard).

TATTERSHALL. Impaled by Howard on shield in hall of Greystoke Castle. Charles Howard, of Greystoke (d. 1713), younger brother of the 5th and 6th Dukes of Norfolk, *q.v.*, marr. Mary (d. 1695), eldest dau. and coheir of George Tattershall, of West Court, Finchampstead, Berks.; and his younger brother Bernard Howard (1641-1717) marr. 1672 Catherine (d. 1727), widow of Sir Richard Lichford, and 2nd dau. and coheir of the said George Tattershall. *Arms.* Sable a chevron between three tigers passant Or.

TATTESHALL. Shield at Hutton-in-the-Forest; a Vane quartering. *Arms.*

* In *A Reminiscence of Threapland Hall* (JPP i 187), Jackson describes a visit which Thoresby paid to Cumberland in 1694 to discuss a proposed marriage between his sister-in-law Deborah Sykes and John Salkeld, jun., of Threapland, *q.v.* The projected marriage came to nothing; Deborah married John Hough and died 1705. The Rev. F. B. Swift comments that some of Jackson's statements are to be questioned. The Threapland Salkelds belonged to the Church of England and were not in financial straits. Jackson's account should be read in conjunction with Thoresby's diary, and two letters written by Archdeacon (later Bishop) Nicolson in vol. i of *Letters of Eminent Men addressed to Ralph Thoresby, F.R.S.*

Chequy Or and Gules a chief Ermine. DSL gives these arms for Robert de Tateshale, Sheriff of Cumberland 1198.

TAYLOR. When Thomas Taylor, of Battersea, applied for a grant of arms in 1600 he stated that he was "descended of Thomas Taylor of Carlile gent whose issue fell down in the right line to John Taylor of London esq., his Arms being Sable a Lyon passant Argent." He was granted these Arms with the difference of an annulet in the dexter point Or. *Crest.* An ownce statant Proper with due difference aforesaid (CA xi/632).

TAYLOR, of Dockwray Hall. William Taylor, a surgeon, of Greenwich Hospital, who marr. 1754 Grace (1725-1801), elder dau. of John Fletcher, of Clea, *q.v.*, had, *int. al.*, a dau. Isabel who marr. a cousin, William Taylor, who appears to have bought the manor of Oulton and Dockwray Hall. This descended to their son John who was High Sheriff of Cumberland 1831. *Crest.* Field records his seal as bearing: Issuing out of a coronet a lion's head (FAC).

TAYLOR. Shield at Hutton John; William Hudleston, C.S.I., J.P., I.C.S., of Hutton John (1826-94), marr. 1856 Laura Henrietta (d. 1917), dau. of George Ledwell Taylor, of London (1788-1873).* *Arms.* Ermine on a chief Gules a fleur-de-lys Argent between two boars' heads erased and erect Or armed of the third.

TEASDALE, of Mumps Hall. Mumps Hall, Gilsland, made famous by Scott in *Guy Mannering,* was the home of the Teasdale family, who kept an inn there. Margaret Teasdale (d. 1777, aged 98) was the original of Tib Mumps in Scott's novel. The last of the family, John Teasdale, yeoman (d. 1788), left a sister Elizabeth, wife of William Carrick, of Mumps Hall. *Arms.* . . . a fess . . . surmounted of three piles . . . issuing from the chief and meeting in base point (Gravestone of John Teasdale, above, in Over Denton churchyard). On the gravestone of Bridget Teasdale, of Mumps Hall (d. 1779, aged 59), are the same arms with a canton; and on those of George Teasdale, of Mumps Hall (d. 1753, aged 25), and of the above Margaret Teasdale, the same arms with an escutcheon in dexter chief.

TEMPEST. Iris Mary, widow of Richard Whiteside Leeming, of Skirsgill Park, Penrith, whom she marr. 1949, is only dau. of Brigadier-General Roger Stephen Tempest, C.M.G., D.S.O., of Broughton Hall, Skipton-in-Craven (d. 1948). *Arms.* Argent a bend between six martlets Sable (BLG18). These arms are on a shield at Hutton John; Sir John Hudleston, of Millom (d. shortly before Nov. 1398), marr. Katherine, dau. of Sir Richard Tempest, of Bowling (Y).

TEMPLE. The arms of William Temple (1881-1944), Archbishop of York 1929-42 and Archbishop of Canterbury 1942-44, impaled with those of the See of York, are on the ceiling of St. John's, Workington. *Arms.* The See of York, *q.v.*; impaling, Quarterly, 1 & 4, Or an eagle displayed wings inverted Sable; 2 & 3, Argent two bars Sable each charged with three martlets Or.

TENDRING. Impaled by Howard on shield in hall of Greystoke Castle; Sir John Howard (d. 1436) marr. (2) Alice, dau. and heir of Sir William Tendring, of Tendring. *Arms.* Azure a fess between two chevrons Argent.

* He was a well known architect responsible for laying out much new development in the London of his day, such as Westbourne Terrace, Chester Place, and parts of Hyde Park Square and Gloucester Square (see DNB), and also for the restoration of Hutton John.

TENNANT, of Roachburn. Anne, wife of John Tennant, of Roachburn, died 1787, aged 46. *Arms.* ... a chevron ... and in base a rose ... a chief ... (Tombstone at Farlam).

TERRIBY. This family derived its name from Tarraby, Carlisle. Henry de Terriby gave land in Ainstable to Wetheral Priory 1230-1. Sir John de Terriby (probably d. 1298-99) was a juror 1268, and was exempted from serving as Sheriff for three years. He marr. Mary (b. *c.* 1250), dau. and heir of Robert de Whitfield; their dau. presumably marr. her cousin Richard de Whitfield and carried Tarraby to him. It later passed to the Aglionbys, *q.v.* (CW2 xxvii). *Arms* (as quartered by Aglionby). Argent an estoile Gules on a chief Azure three water bougets Or (FVC). FFC records for John Terby, or Tereby: Argent an estoile Or on a chief Azure three water bougets of the second; and Machell recorded these arms, with the points of the rays Gules, for Eglonby (*recte* Aglionby) (MMS vi 415).

THIRKELD. Anthony Thirkeld, of Evenwood (D) (d. *c.* 1615), was father of John Thirkeld (d. 1663), who settled in Cumberland at Dale, where he was succ. by his eldest son Anthony, whose younger brother Edward Thirkeld, of Durham, recorded a pedigree at the Visitation of Durham 1666, when he was aged 48. To the same family presumably belonged the Rev. William Thirkeld, or Threlkeld, who was sub Curate of Brancepeth (D) until he died 1675. His son William, M.A. (Edin) (d. 1701), was Vicar of Bishopton (D) 1681-86, and Rector of Melmerby 1685 until his death. He marr. before 1673 Anne (d. 1707), eldest dau. and coheir of Lancelot Threlkeld, of Melmerby, *q.v.*, and had a dau. and heir Elizabeth, who marr. Thomas Pattenson, *q.v.*, and took Melmerby Hall to that family. *Arms.* Argent a maunch Gules within a bordure Sable a crescent Azure for difference. *Crest.* A Turk's head Proper (FVD).

THIRLWALL. John Thirlwall, member of a Northumberland family, was also a Cumberland landowner. He marr. before 1375 Christian ... and was Sheriff of Cumberland 1384-86. He settled Middlesceugh and Alstonby 1396; these properties descended with a Thirlwall heiress to the Huttons of Hutton John, *q.v.* Philip Thirlwall, of Temmon, Denton and Eamont Bridge, marr. 1711 Mary Wybergh, of Clifton. Their descendant Thomas Thirlwall died at Newcastle upon Tyne 1822, aged 74. William Thirlwall, of Thirlwall Castle (N), marr. Lucy, dau. of Thomas Warwick, of Warwick Hall, and had a dau. and heir Eleanor (d. 1777), who was of Warwick Hall 1724. She marr. Matthew Swinburne and they sold Thirlwall to Lord Carlisle 1748. *Arms* (quartered by Hutton on stone slab at Hutton John). ... a chevron ... between three boars' heads erased .... The shield is protected by a griffin, presumably because John Thirlwall, living 1369, had as supporters two griffins, in consideration of the baronial rank claimed by his family (CW2 xxx 76; HHN II iii 144). DSL gives: Gules a chevron between three boars' heads couped Argent. Hodgson (*op. cit.*) gives the following for Thirlwall, of Thirlwall: *Arms.* Sable a chevron Argent between three boars' heads Or. *Crest.* On a chapeau Gules turned up Argent a boar's head couped at the neck of the second Argent (*sic*). Another, On a chapeau Gules turned up Ermine a wolf's head Argent.

THIRLWAY. A family of this name, of whom no details are known, bore *Arms.* Per fess Gules and Argent three cinquefoils counterchanged a crescent for difference (FVC). MVC shews the cinquefoils as pierced. These are the arms of the Swinburne family of Capheaton (N), which were quartered by the Swinburnes, of Huthwaite, *q.v.*

THOMAS. The Rev. John Thomas, B.A. (Oxon) (*c.* 1684-1747), son of George Thomas, of Carlisle, was ordained 1707, and was Curate of Holm Cultram 1708 and Vicar of Brampton 1721-47. His son the Rt Rev. John Thomas D.C.L. (Oxon) (1712-93), was Dean of Westminster 1768 and Bishop of Rochester 1774-93. *Arms.* Or a fess dancetté between three choughs Sable (BBE). *Crest.* A demi leopard rampant Proper holding in both feet a baton erect Or (BGA).

THOMLINSON, of Blencogo. Canon Bouch in CW2 xliv deals with the early history of this family, which was originally of Hawksdale, and shows that a supposed descent from the Co. Durham Visitation family is untenable. Richard Thomlinson (b. 1625) and Isabel his wife – their initials are over the front door of Blencogo Hall – were parents of, *int. al.*, the Rev. John Thomlinson, M.A. (Cantab) (1651-1720), Rector of Rothbury (N), who died *s.p.*; William (d. 1743, aged 86) who succ. to Blencogo; and the Rev. Robert, M.A., D.D. (Oxon) (1669-1748), Rector of Whickham (D) and Prebendary of St. Paul's. William's eldest* son, the Rev. John Thomlinson,† M.A. (Cantab), Rector of Glenfield, Leics. (1692-1761), had an only son John (1734-65), who marr. Anne,‡ dau. and heir of the Rev. William Plaskett, Vicar of Brampton. Their elder son John Thomlinson, of Brisco Hill (d. *s.p.* 1811, aged 50), was High Sheriff of Cumberland 1807. His heirs were his nieces, daus. of his brother Col William Thomlinson,§ 18th Light Dragoons (d. 1810) – Anne (d. 1835, aged 37), marr. (1) 1819 Capt Samuel Wyndowe (d. 1829), 1st Dragoons, *q.v.*, and (2) 1834 James Jardine; and Catharina Elizabeth (d. 1840), marr. 1830 John Swann (CW2 xliv, lxv; BLG 1846). *Arms.* Per pale Argent and Vert three greyhounds courant in pale counterchanged. *Crest.* A demi man holding with both hands a spear in bend point downwards (Brass in Bromfield church). Burke gives: *Arms.* Per pale wavy Argent and Vert three greyhounds courant [in pale] counterchanged a chief indented Azure. *Crests.* 1, A greyhound per pale wavy as in the arms; 2, A savage wreathed about the middle Proper holding in both hands a spear headed at each end Or (BLG 1846; BGA).

THOMLINSON, of the Gill. Nicholas Thomlinson, of Stonehall, Hawksdale (d. 1615), ancestor of the Thomlinsons of Blencogo, *q.v.*, had a younger son Robert (1575-1637), who was parish clerk of Dalston, and was of the Gill, where his descendants remained for several generations. The last of the family, Jane (d. at Greensyke, Dalston, 1858, aged 68), marr. John Ashbridge and their son William (1814-56) assumed the additional surname Thomlinson. His eldest son John Ashbridge Thomlinson, cotton manufacturer (1834-1908), built the Atlas Works, Nelson Street, Carlisle. His eldest son William Ashbridge Thomlinson, marine engineer, of Eden Grove, Armathwaite (1863-92), died *v.p.*, leaving a son William Ashbridge Thomlinson (b. 1891). *Arms.* Robert Thomlinson, of the Gill (1649-1717),

* His youngest son Robert, of New England, died unmarr. in Antigua 1758.

† His amusing, if scandal-mongering diaries were printed by the Surtees Society, Vol. cxviii.

‡ She marr. (2) the Rt. Rev. John Law, Bishop of Elphin.

§ He marr. Anne, dau. and coheir of the Rev. William Plumbe, of Aughton, Liverpool, by Catharina his wife, dau. and heir of Samuel Kirk.

bore: Azure a cross moline Argent on a chief Gules three cinquefoils Or. *Crest.* A bear's head erased Proper (*The Gaitsgill Chronicle,* iv 37).*

THOMPSON, of Arkleby. Richard Thompson, of Kilham (Y), aged 28 in 1665 (d. 1713), was father of the Rev. Gustavus Thompson, M.A. (Cantab) (1670-1710), Rector of Bolton and Plumbland 1702-10. His son Gustavus Thompson, of Arkleby Hall (d. 1756, aged 60), was High Sheriff of Cumberland 1728. He marr. 1720 Joanna (d. 1771), dau. of Humphrey Senhouse, and had an only son the Rev. Gustavus Thompson, M.A. (Oxon) (d. 1749, aged 28), Chaplain to Bishops Fleming and Osbaldeston, and Vicar of Penrith 1748-49. The line was continued by the descendants of his uncle Richard Thompson, ancestor of Vice-Admiral Thomas Boulden Thompson (1766-1828), who was cr. Baronet 1806. His descendant Sir Lionel Tennyson Thompson, 5th Bart., is the present holder of the title. Of the same family was the Rev. Edward Thompson, B.A. (Cantab) (1811-38), 3rd son of George Lowther Thompson, of Sheriff Hutton Park (Y); a son-in-law of Bishop Percy, he was Rector of Moresby 1835-37, and Vicar of Aspatria 1836-38. *Arms.* Per fess Argent and Sable a fess embattled counter-embattled between three falcons counterchanged (Tablets in Carlisle Cathedral and Crosscanonby church, and glass in Aspatria church). *Crest.* An arm in armour embowed flourishing a sword (Tablet, Cross Canonby church). Over the entrance of Arkleby Hall† the crest appears as: An arm in armour embowed holding a broken tilting spear. Burke (BLG4 and BGA) gives the crest of the Sheriff Hutton family as: An arm embowed in armour quarterly Or and Azure the gauntlet Proper holding a truncheon of a broken lance of the first. *Motto.* Je veux de bonne guerre.

THOMPSON, of Farlam. John Thompson, surveyor (d. 1787, aged 67), who was employed on Lord Carlisle's Morpeth estate, came to Cumberland to lay out farms and was of Farlam Hall, where he was succ. by his son Thomas (1765-1838), who was father of James (1794-1851), who entered Lord Carlisle's colliery office in 1808, and became colliery agent in 1819. In 1838 he became lessee of Lord Carlisle's collieries. On his death the firm was continued by his widow Maria and his sons, one of whom, Lt-Col Thomas Charles Thompson, J.P. (1832-88), was of Milton Hall, Brampton. He marr. 1856 Gertrude (1834-1904), dau. (and perhaps heir) of Richard Lacy, *q.v.* Their son Charles Lacy Thompson, D.L., J.P., B.A. (Cantab), of Farlam Hall (1857-1920), was High Sheriff 1900. His son Capt Thomas Alexander Lacy Thompson, D.S.O., M.C. (b. 1895), is of Woody Hyde, Grayshott, Hindhead, Surrey; he marr. 1917 Vera Mabel Florence, younger dau. and coheir of Thomas Dixon, of Rheda, *q.v.* *Arms.* Or on a fess dancetté Azure three estoiles Argent on a canton of the second a sun in splendour Or. *Crest.* An arm erect vested Gules cuffed Argent holding in the hand five ears of barley. *Motto.* In lumine lucem (Pedigree in possession of Capt T. A. L. Thompson).

THOMPSON, of Inglewood. For the earlier history of this family, see Thompson of Grayrigg and Underley in AWL. James Thompson, of

* The family later bore arms similar to, or the same as, those of Thomlinson, of Blencogo, for the same authority states (iv 77): "I have not the arms of the Thomlinsons in recent times by me at present, but there seems, I think, some connection between the modern shield and that of the Patricksons of Stockhow."

† Where the arms are carved in stone as: Quarterly, 1, Thompson; 2, Senhouse; 3, Godbold; 4, Eaglesfield, *q.v.*

Moresdale Hall (1800-46), was father of, *int. al.*, Robert Thompson, J.P., of Inglewood, near Penrith, who marr. 1876 Mary, only dau. of Richard Metcalfe Winn, of Bowerbank, Pooley Bridge, and had issue, Robert; Ella Mary, who marr. the Rev. Christopher William Wordsworth, *q.v.*; William; Madeleine Elizabeth, who marr. Capt John Henry Loftie, R.N.; and Henry Fothergill Thompson. *Arms.* Azure a lion passant guardant Or within a bordure Argent (HSW). The lion is sometimes depicted as passant only and as passant reguardant. *Crest.* A lion rampant Or. *Motto.* Spectemur agendo (M.I., Kirkby Lonsdale church; carvings and glass at Underley; BGA; HMC).

THOMPSON, of Nunwick Hall. Richard Heywood Thompson, J.P. (1850-1935), son of Samuel Henry Thompson,* D.L., J.P., of Thingwall Hall (L), acquired the Nunwick Hall estate in the 1890's and was High Sheriff of Cumberland 1904. Dying *s.p.*, he left the estate to his nephew Lt-Col Cecil Henry Farrer Thompson, O.B.E., D.S.O., Croix de Guerre, T.D., J.P., B.A. (Cantab) (1882-1975), son of Richard's elder brother George Rodie Thompson, D.L., J.P., of Lynwood, Ascot (1846-1915). Col Thompson, who was called to the Bar 1910, served with the London Rifle Brigade in World War I. He was High Sheriff of Cumberland 1940. *Arms.* Per fess Argent and Azure on a fess nebuly between three falcons all counterchanged a lure fessways Or. *Crest.* A lion rampant per fess nebuly Argent and Sable holding between the paws a lure Or (BLG17). Field recorded Richard Heywood Thompson's seal as High Sheriff as displaying: *Arms.* Per pale Argent and Sable on a fess nebuly between three falcons a . . . counterchanged. *Crest.* A lion rampant holding between the paws a . . . (FAC). Col C. H. F. Thompson's seal as High Sheriff displays: *Arms.* Per fess Or and Sable a fess embattled counterembattled between three falcons counterchanged. *Crest.* A lion rampant.

THOMPSON, of Workington. Benjamin Thompson, of Workington (1769-1839), solicitor and agent to John Christian Curwen, marr. 1793 Sarah Udale and had 19 children. Of these William (1805-73), described in 1837 as a banker, succ. him as agent to the Curwens. He marr. (1) 1837 Jane Agnes (d. 1839, aged 19), dau. of William Lomas, *q.v.*, and (2) 1854 Mary Thompson (1822-1900), by whom he had 5 children, who all died unmarr. *Arms.* Or on a fess indented Azure three estoiles Argent on a canton of the second a sun in his splendour. *Crest.* A cubit arm vested Gules cuffed Argent holding in the hand Proper ears of wheat fessways Or (Window, Aspatria church).

THOMPSON. Edmund Thompson, of Yanwath Gate, was father of Thomas Richardson Thompson, of whom below; William Thompson, of Brunswick Square, Penrith (1863-1950), manager of the Penrith branch of the Carlisle & North Western Counties Savings Bank; and Nathan Thompson, C.B.E., I.S.O., Inspector-General of H.M. Waterguard (Customs and Excise), London (d. 1947). Thomas Richardson Thompson, of Yanwath Gate and Carlisle (d. 1912), was father of William Jameson Thompson, of 71 Ashley Street, Carlisle (1906-69), whose son Miles Thompson is of Yanwath, Portreeve Close, Llantrisant, Glam. *Arms.* Argent fretty Azure a griffin

* His eldest son, Henry Yates Thompson (1838-1928), proprietor of the *Pall Mall Gazette*, had the best private collection of illuminated Mss. in the world, valued at a quarter of a million pounds.

passant Erminois on a chief engrailed Gules a cross formy Or between two estoiles of six points Argent. *Crest.* A griffin sejant Erminois langued Azure wings erect Argent fretty Azure. *Motto.* Hold fast unto good.

THOMPSON. The Rev. Thomas Thompson (1731-1804), a native of Patterdale,* Curate of Mungrisdale 1755-67 and of Patterdale 1767-1804, was father of the Rev. Thomas Thompson (1770-1858), who was Perpetual Curate of Allhallows 1812-58. He marr. Ann Clark. *Arms* (formerly in glass in Allhallows Old Church). Or on a fess indented Azure three mullets Argent on a canton of the second a sun in his splendour; impaling, Or on a bend engrailed Azure a mullet Argent in dexter chief (Clark).

THOMSON. John Thomson, of King Street, Whitehaven, draper (d. 1878), was father of the Rt. Rev. William Thomson, M.A., D.D. (Oxon) (1819-90), Provost of the Queen's College, Oxford, 1855-61, Bishop of Gloucester 1861-63, and Archbishop of York 1863-90. *Arms.* Azure a lion rampant Argent (BBE; Brass in St. Nicholas', Whitehaven).

THORNTHWAITE. Said by Burke to be of Cumberland, without further details. *Arms.* Per pale Argent and Gules a chevron between three lions' heads erased all counterchanged on a chief Or a thorn tree Proper. *Crest.* A lion's head erased Gules in the mouth a thorn sprig Vert fructed Proper (BGA).†

THORNTON. On an escutcheon of pretence in Dacre church; James Parkin, of the Laithes (1797-1860), *q.v.*, marr. a dau. of Bonnell Thornton (RWH). *Arms.* Quarterly, 1 & 4, Quarterly i & iv, Or a chief indented Azure; ii & iii, Gules three covered cups Or; 2, Argent a chevron Sable between three trees eradicated Proper fructed Gules; 3, Argent a fess between three eagles' heads erased Sable.

THRELKELD, of Melmerby. JPP (ii 282-329) contains a splendid account of this branch of the Threlkelds of Threlkeld. By the latter part of the 14th century they owned the manor of Melmerby which descended to Humphrey Threlkeld (d. 1526), whose brother Roland (d. 1565) was Rector of Melmerby, Great Salkeld and Kirkoswald, and of Dufton (W) and Halton (L), and Provost of the Colleges of Kirkoswald and Greystoke. His nephew Christopher (*c.* 1495-1569) was Lord of Melmerby for 43 years. The last male was Lancelot Threlkeld (1615-73) who marr. 1640 Katherine, dau. of Nicholas Whitfield, of New Shield, Alston Moor.‡ Their daus. and coheirs§ were Anne (d. 1707), wife of the Rev. William Thirkeld, *q.v.*; Catherine, marr. Richard Studholme; Mary (d. 1719), marr. 1674 Thomas Crackanthorpe, of Newbiggin (1637-1715), for which family see AWL; Dorothy (d. 1683), marr. (1) 1673 Anthony Dale, of Durham (d. 1681), and (2) Thomas Denton (1638-98), *q.v.*; and Margery (d. 1737), marr. Thomas Denton, son of the aforesaid Thomas by his first wife. *Arms.* Argent a

* A pedigree of five generations of the family, beginning with Thomas Thompson, of Hartsop Hall (d. 1715), is given in the Rev. W. P. Morris's *The Records of Patterdale,* 1903.

† John Thornthwaite, the younger, of Boltongate, sealed a deed selling Birkmire, 1737, with a griffin's head erased.

‡ Not Katherine Whelpdale, as stated in JPP ii 289.

§ The Rev. Richard Singleton, Rector of Melmerby, in 1677 gave the Rev. Thomas Machell many interesting details of this family. Of Anne Thirkeld he says, "The young lady is one of the Viragoes of our age and possesseth the Spirit as well as the estate of her warlike ancestors." He adds that Margery, the youngest sister, "is yet to be married and at your service."

maunch Gules (FCW). FVC and MVC shew the maunch charged with a trefoil for difference. *Crest.* A woman's bust Proper habited Gules (FCW).

THRELKELD, of Threlkeld. Randulf *filius* Ivo de Threlkeld gave land in Threlkeld to Fountains Abbey *c.* 1220-30. Henry de Threlkeld acted as Sheriff of Westmorland in 1292 and Henry Threlkeld acted in 1324. The latter was son of William Threlkeld, whose marr. to Isabel Hastings brought large estates at Yanwath, Crosby Ravensworth, Tebay and Rounthwaite into the family. The male line failed with Sir Lancelot Threlkeld* (d. between 1506 and 1510), who left three daus. and coheirs – Grace, marr. Thomas Dudley, *q.v.*; Elizabeth, marr. James Pickering; and Winifred, marr. William Pickering, *q.v.* (CW1 ix; CW2 xxiii). *Arms.* Argent a maunch Gules. In 1341 William de Threlkeld bore: . . . a maunch . . . in chief six annulets . . . . In 1344 he sealed a charter with a shield displaying: . . . three maunches . . . (D/Lons/Early deeds/T22). MS. Ashmole 834 gives: Ermine a maunch Gules (AWL). DSL gives for William de Threlkeld, Sheriff of Cumberland 1355-6: Argent a maunch Sable.

THRUSTON. Margaret, dau. and coheir of Lt-Col Edmund Heathcote Thruston, D.L., J.P., by Lucy (d. 1942), 3rd dau. of Sir Wilfrid Lawson, 2nd Bart., *q.v.*, marr. 1941 Richard Arthur Austen-Leigh and succ. her mother as Lady of the Manor of Hesket, and her cousin Sir Hilton Lawson, 4th and last Bart., as owner of Isel Hall. *Arms.* Sable three bugle horns stringed Or garnished Azure in the middle chief point an ermine spot Argent (BLG17).

THURNAM, of Carlisle. Field says (without giving an authority) that this family was of Yorkshire origin. Timothy Thurnam, M.D., marr. Dorothy (1768-99) dau. of William Graham, surgeon, of Carlisle (d. 1782). Their eldest son William Graham Thurnam (1792-1823) was Major in the Bombay Army, and his younger brother Charles (1796-1852), a native of Scotland, founded in 1816 at 5 English Street, Carlisle, the printing, bookselling and bookbinding firm which is still carried on in his name. His son William Graham Thurnam (d. at Rome 1859, aged 23) later carried on the firm with his brother James Graham Thurnam (d. 1872, aged 34). In 1937 the family was represented by William Rowland Thurnam, of Hampstead. *Arms.* Field gives these, from information received from the family, as: Argent three thorn-trees eradicated Proper (FAC). On the silver base of a box deposited in the Record Office, Carlisle (reference CC Misc.) the arms are engraved as: . . . three thorn-trees eradicated . . . , one and two. *Crest.* A tower. *Motto.* Probitas verus honos.

THWAITES, of Thwaites and Unerigg. It is generally supposed that the Thwaites family, which owned the manor of Thwaites from the 13th century, were near of kin to their overlords the Hudlestons. John de Thwaites was a witness 1271, and his successor William flourished until about 1300. A namesake was a witness 1334-65, and by 1435 the family had acquired the manor of Unerigg. In that year William Thwaites senior and Joan his wife and William Thwaites junior and Katherine his wife made a settlement of the manor. Glover's Visitation of Yorkshire 1584-5 has a pedigree of five generations, beginning with William Thwaites, of Lound

* He said: "I have three noble houses – one for pleasure, Crosby, where I have a park full of deer, one for profit and warmth wherein to reside in winter, Yanwath, and the third, Threlkeld, well stocked with tenants to go with me to the wars."

(Y), who marr. Margaret, dau. or sister of Sir Henry Bellingham. The head of the family in 1584 was William Thwaites, but in Cumberland the line seems to have been continued by Anthony Thwaites (d. 1585), whose son and heir Joseph (b. *c.* 1572) is described in Sandford's *Cursory Relation* as "one of wittest, brave monsirs for all gentile gallantry, hounds, haukes, horse courses, boules, bowes & arrowes, and all games whatsoever: play his £100 at cards, dice and shovelboord . . . and had not above £200 p an. yet left his children pretty porcions & dyed beloved of all parties." His son John Thwaites sold Thwaites to Sir John Lowther 1627 and Unerigg to Richard Barwis (CW2 iv). *Arms.* FFC records for Thomas Thwaites, of Coupland, *temp.* Edward III: Argent a cross Sable fretty of the field. TVN and FVY give: Quarterly, 1 & 4, Argent a cross Sable fretty Or; 2 & 3, Sable a crowned lion rampant Argent charged on the shoulder with three billets Sable.* VN and FCW give this same quartered coat, with the crown in the second and third quarters Or. Machell recorded: Argent a cross Sable fretty Or (MMS vi 421). Thomas Denton recorded: Vert a cross Argent fretty Gules (JAW). John Denton recorded: . . . a cross Argent fretty Gules (DAC). NB ii 15 give: Or a cross Argent fretty Gules. Lysons give: Argent a cross Sable fretty Or (LMC). MMD gives: Quarterly 1 & 4, Argent a cross Sable fretty Or; 2 & 3, Sable a lion rampant Argent crowned Or. *Crest.* A demi falcon displayed Azure charged on the neck with two bars indented and on each wing with a goutte Or and holding in the beak a marigold slipped Proper (VN ii 35).

TICKELL. The Rev. Richard Tickell, B.A. (TCD) (d. 1692), son of Thomas Tickell, of Whitehaven,† was Rector of Egremont 1673-92, Vicar of Bridekirk 1680-85, and Rector of Distington 1685-92. He marr. Margaret, dau. and coheir of William Layton, of Dalemain, *q.v.* Their son Thomas Tickell, M.A. (Oxon) (1686-1740), a native of Egremont, was well known as a poet and became Professor of Poetry at Oxford in 1711. In 1724 he was made Secretary to the Lords Justices of Ireland (DNB). *Arms* (granted 1726). Quarterly, 1 & 4, Gules a maunch Argent; 2 & 3, Sable on a bend Argent three escallops Gules (Layton). *Crest.* An arm couped below the elbow and erect vested Gules charged with three fleurs-de-lys Or cuffed Argent holding in the hand Proper a fleur-de-lys Gold (BGA).

TIFFIN, of Calder Abbey. John Tiffin, of Cockermouth (d. 1751), bought Calder Abbey 1730. His dau. and heir Sarah marr. Joseph Senhouse, of Wigton, *q.v.*, and carried Calder Abbey to that family. *Arms.* Argent on a chevron between three lions' heads erased Gules as many battle axes of the field. *Crest.* A lion rampant collared and holding a battle axe (Hudson Scott's reprint 1877 of Buck's View of Calder Abbey; FD7, *sub* Irwin). Field, however, recorded Buck's View of Calder Abbey, 1739, as shewing the same crest as that recorded in the next entry for Tiffin, of Whitrigg. *Motto.* Patria fidelis (FAC).

TIFFIN, of Whitrigg. John Tiffin, of Cockermouth, was described as "Officer of Workington" in 1739 when he marr. Mary, dau. of John Ribton, of Cockermouth. His only surviving son, Joseph Tiffin, of Whitrigg, Bowness-on-Solway, obtained a grant of arms in 1770 which was identical with those blazoned in the previous entry; we have not, however,

* TTV omits the billets.

† Not of the Rev. John Tickell, of Penrith, as in DNB.

succeeded in establishing any relationship between the two families. *Arms.* Argent on a chevron between three lions' heads erased Gules as many battle axes of the field. *Crest.* A demi lion rampant Gules gorged with a collar flory counterflory Or holding a battle axe Proper.

TILLIOL, of Scaleby. Richard de Tilliol or Ridere was succ. by his grandson Peter de Tilliol (d. 1183). From him descended Peter de Tilliol, Sheriff of Cumberland 1327-30. Robert de Tilliol (d. 1367) was sheriff 1356-58, 1361, and 1366, and his son Sir Piers (or Peter) Tilliol, of Scaleby Castle (d. 1435), served 1387, 1394 and 1403; he marr. Elizabeth, dau. and coheir of Sir Robert Mulcaster, *q.v.* Their son Robert (1415-35) was of unsound mind and his sisters and coheirs were Isabel (1406-38), who marr. John Colvill, *q.v.*, and Margaret (1410-59), who marr. (1) Sir Christopher Moresby, *q.v.*, and (2) Thomas Crackanthorpe. *Arms.* Gules a lion rampant Argent a baston Azure (FFC; MMD; Stone shield at Scaleby Castle).

TILNEY – see TYLNEY.

TIMPERON. Matthias Timperon, of West Newton, Bromfield (d. before 1801), whose ancestors were said to have been established there for many generations, was father of Joseph Timperon, a London merchant, who obtained in 1801 a grant of the following *Arms.* Argent on a fess wavy Azure between two bucks trippant in chief Proper attired Or and in base two sugar canes in saltire surmounted by a cutting bill also Proper three estoiles Gold. *Crest.* On a mount vert a greyhound couchant Argent collared gemel Azure supporting with his paws a shield Or charged with a fess thereon three estoiles as in the arms (CA xxi/260).

TINNISWOOD, of Waygill Hill. An old Talkin family, the Tinniswoods were settled at Waygill Hill from early times. From Robert (*fl.* 1570) descended Robert, a customary tenant in Talkin in 1603. His descendant George (1643-63) was chosen to go with Lord Carlisle, when he was appointed Ambassador to Moscow, where he killed a fierce wild boar.* From his elder brother descended Robert (d. 1772, aged 70), who was succ. by his grandson Robert (d. 1820, aged 69), who got into debt, and Waygill Head was sold to the Grahams of Edmund Castle after his death. A descendant Thomas Tinniswood (1879-1953) was of Penrith and Kirkby Stephen, and was father of the present representative of the family, John Mounsey Tinniswood, of Wood End, Greystoke. Of this same family, Robert Tinniswood farmed Rose Bank, Dalston, where he was succ. by his son Richard Harrison Tinniswood (b. 1877); another son, Robert Westgarth Tinniswood, was formerly of the Crown Hotel, Eamont Bridge, and is now of the Old Rectory, Greystoke. *Arms.* Argent a chevron Vert between three trees Proper. *Crest.* A cubit arm in armour couped fessways holding in the hand a sword erect enfiled with a boar's head all Proper. *Motto.* Nihil sine labore (*Ex inf.* J. M. Tinniswood).

TINNISWOOD, of Penton. Joseph Tinniswood, of Brampton, marr. 1801 Ann, sister of John Hodgson, of Abbey Street, Carlisle, and Penton House, Nichol Forest (d. 1847), *q.v.* Their son George Tinniswood, M.D. (Glas) (d. 1877), succ. his uncle in Abbey Street and Penton House, where he lived 1849-59. He also practised at York, Gateshead, and at Harland House, Norton (D), where he died. His son was John Hodgson Tinniswood

* He never saw Cumberland again; on his way home, he fought a duel in Lincoln, killing his opponent, but he was treacherously stabbed to death.

(b. 1856). *Crest* (in Eaglesfield House, Abbey Street, Carlisle). A cubit arm in armour couped fessways holding in the hand a sword erect enfiled with a boar's head all Proper.

TOLSON, of Bridekirk. Henry Tolson was granted the manor of Bridekirk, which belonged to Gisburn Priory (Y), 1543. His son Henry, of Woodhall (d. 1585), was High Sheriff of Cumberland 1575, and had sons Richard, and John (1576-1644), Provost of Oriel College, Oxford. The former died 1650 and was succ. by his son Henry Tolson (1593-1663), High Sheriff 1647, who marr. 1618 Margaret, dau. and heir of Henry Savile, of Wath-upon-Dearns (Y). Their son Richard Tolson, J.P. "an utter barrister" (1622-90), was M.P. for Cumberland 1646-48 and for Cockermouth 1660-61, and High Sheriff 1666. His son Henry (1651-1724) marr. 1666 Frances (d. 1695), dau. of Sir Wilfrid Lawson, of Isel.* He or his son Henry sold Woodhall 1707. The descent is obscure but Lt-General Richard Tolson (1746-1815) claimed to be heir at law and heir in entail of Henry, and in 1824 the General's son Major Richard Henry Tolson, F.S.A., of Woodland Lodge, Som., 2nd Life Guards (b. 1776), announced that he was about to petition the Attorney General, claiming the barony of Darcy, and in 1827 he attempted unsuccessfully to claim the Woodhall estate. He had an only child, Jane Dinnis Tolson,† who marr. 1819 Richard Harcourt Symons (CW2 lx; *Carlisle Patriot;* BLG 1846.‡ *Arms.* Quarterly, 1 & 4, Vert on a chief Azure three martlets Or all within a bordure of the third pelletté§ (Tolson); 2, Quarterly, i & iv, Argent on a bend Sable three owls Argent (Savile), ii & iii, Argent a cross moline Sable a crescent for difference (Copley); 3, Argent three bars Azure in chief as many lozenges Vert (Fleming, of Wath). || *Crest.* Out of a ducal coronet Or a lion's gamb Ermine holding two ostrich feathers Vert and Azure (FCW). *Motto.* Ferro comite (BLG 1846).

TONI. Shield at Hutton-in-the-Forest; a Vane quartering. *Arms.* Argent a maunch Gules.

TOPPIN. John Toppin, of Musgrave Hall, Skelton, yeoman (d. 1857), marr. 1833 Anne (1802-71), dau. of John Castlehow, of Askham, and was succ. by their son John Castlehow Toppin (b. 1834), whose sons were John Henry, of Musgrave Hall (b. 1862); Charles, M.A. (Cantab) (1864-1928), a cricket blue, assistant master at Malvern 1886-1928; Frederick, J.P., of Musgrave Hall (b. 1867); and Herbert Castlehow (b. 1874). *Arms.* Argent a cross engrailed between four herons' heads erased Sable. *Crest.* In front of a rising sun a heron wings expanded holding in the beak a luce or pike all Proper. *Motto.* Deo patriae amicis (FD7).

TORRIANO. Captain Charles Torriano, R.A. (d. 1791), grandson of Charles

* Their 5th son Francis, b. 1686, marr. at Piscataway, Prince George's County, Maryland, 22 Sept. 1707 Mary, dau. of Robert Clark of that place. Their dau. Frances (1710-*c.* 1741) marr. Butler Stonestreet (1703-55). From them descends Donald A. Schuder, of Woodland, California.

† See *Observer* 10 September 1820 for an account of an action at Somerset Assizes, in which Mrs. Dod, "an eminent milliner and dressmaker" at Taunton, sued Major Tolson. His daughter, then aged 20, it was claimed, in 1819 employed the plaintiff to make her trousseau, the cost being £358, which the Major, who only had £200 a year, "though highly respectable," refused to pay. Miss Tolson ordered 35 dresses but only two pairs of stockings.

‡ The pedigree there given must be used with caution.

§ Fuller gives: Vert on a chief Azure three martlets Or; i.e., without the bordure (FWE). DSL gives: Vert on a chief Azure three martlets Or all within a bordure Argent.

|| FVC and MVC record, for Fleming, of Wath: Azure two bars Argent on a chief of the last three lozenges Gules.

Torriano and Rebecca (Paravicini) his wife, was of Carlisle in the 1750's. His dau. Elizabeth marr. 1786 Peter Nathan Roberts; their grandson Major Herbert Champion Roberts, Madras Army (1828-1904), had, *int. al.,* daus. and coheirs Emma Marie (d. 1898, aged 41), marr. 1894 Andrew John Hudleston, *q.v.,* and Alice Margaret Caroline (1859-1931), marr. 1894 Ferdinand Hudleston, *q.v. Arms.* Quarterly, 1 & 4, Azure two sceptres in saltire Or surmounted by a castle Gules on a chief of the second an eagle displayed Sable (Torriano); 2 & 3, Azure a swan Argent beaked and legged Or (Paravicini). *Crest.* An eagle displayed Sable (BGA; MS. history of the Torriano family).

TOWERSON. William Towerson, a Cumbrian from Copeland, who became a citizen and merchant of London, trading to Russia, Spain, Portugal and the "East parts," was an Elizabethan adventurer, who fought several battles at sea against the French and Portuguese – he had great conflict "with the Portugalles and Nigroes." He obtained from Norroy a confirmation of his family arms, and a grant of an honourable augmentation in recognition of his heroism at sea, 1581. *Arms.* Gules a fess between three boars' heads couped Ermine on a canton Argent a ship Sable with all equipage and furnitures. *Crest.* A demi negro Proper prepared to the conflict with dart and pavice Gold (MS. Ashm. 834. 1. *f.* 53, printed in Harl. Soc. lxxvii (1926) 198-200).

TOWERSON. Edward Towerson, of Whitehaven, had a dau. Sarah (1696-1771) who marr. 1716 Carlisle Spedding, *q.v.* Their son set up a monument to them in Holy Trinity church, Whitehaven, with the arms of Spedding, impaling Towerson. No description of the coats of arms seems to have survived, and since the demolition of the church, the monument appears to have disappeared. *Arms.* Burke gives for Towerson, of Cumberland: Gules a fess between three boars' heads couped Ermine (BGA). See also Irwin.

TOWRY, of Croglin Hall. George Towry, of Grindalyth (Y) (d. *c.* 1644), was father of George Towry, J.P., of Croglin Hall (*c.* 1629-1717), who marr. Anne, dau. and heir of William James, of Carlisle. Their son George (1664-1717) marr. 1687 Mary (b. 1672), dau. of John Grey, of Acton (N). Their son Admiral John Towry (d. *s.p.* 1757), Commissioner of the Navy at Port Mahon, inherited Shipley Lane (N) which he left to his nephew Henry John Phillips (son of David Phillips and Mary Towry), who took the name Towry 1760 and died unmarr. 1762 when he was succ. by his brother Capt George Phillips, R.N., who likewise assumed the name. His son Capt George Henry Towry, R.N. (1767-1809), died unmarr., and the heir was the dau. Anne (1769-1843) who marr. 1789 the 1st Baron Ellenborough, *q.v. Arms.* Azure a tower domed Argent a crescent for difference (FCW). Burke gives: Azure a tower triple-towered and domed Argent. *Crest.* A griffin passant per pale Or and Argent (BGA). Papworth gives for Towers, of Crollinghall, Cumberland: *Arms.* Argent three towers triple-towered Gules (OBA).

TREVENEN. Sydney William Trevenen, of Portland Square, Carlisle, a Cornishman (d. 1901, aged 56), was admitted a solicitor 1868, and came to Carlisle as managing clerk to John Nanson, Town Clerk. He became a partner of Nanson's former partner, Richard Henry Clutterbuck, *q.v.,* 1877, and was deputy Coroner for East Cumberland, and solicitor to the Old Brewery Co., Carlisle, and to the County Hotel Co. He marr. Jessie, dau. of

Thomas King Atkinson, J.P., of Carlisle and Reston Hall (W), and had issue Sydney Vyvyan Trevenen (b. 1894) and Irene, marr. 1923 Lt-Col Noel Stanley Clutterbuck, *q.v.* *Arms.* Argent on a fess Gules between two chevrons Azure an escallop between two fleur-de-lys of the field. *Crest.* A stag quarterly Vert and Erminois attired Or. *Motto.* In se teres (FD7).

TREWARTHEN. GMS records the following, without specifying any place of residence. *Arms.* Argent a boar statant Gules armed and bristled Or.

TRIMBLE, of Green Lane. An unpublished pedigree by the late W. Percy Hedley shows that this family, whose name was originally Tremmell, was long settled in Holm Cultram. John Tremmell, of Abbey Town (d. 1730), was father of George Tremble, of Abbey Town and Calvo (b. 1700), whose son George (1728-85) was of Moor End, Thursby. His eldest son George (b. 1752) marr. Ann Rumney and was ancestor of the Trimbles of Watermillock, who changed their name to Rumney. The 4th son, Edward Trimble,* of Moor End, Thursby, and Cardew Hall (1763-1841), was father of Robert Trimble, of Green Lane, Dalston (1792-1859), founder of the Dalston Brewery, who was succ. by his son Edward (1826-80), whose son William Tennant Trimble, J.P. (b. 1866), was an early pioneer in Florida, returning to Green Lane on the death of his brother. He was a director of Maryport Brewery and an alderman of Cumberland County Council.† His youngest son, William Steuart Trimble, High Sheriff in 1971, is now of Green Lane. *Crest.* A bull passant. *Motto.* Audaces fortuna juvat (Seal of W. S. Trimble, as High Sheriff).

TRIVERS – see ESTRIVERS.

TROUTBECK, of Blencowe. It has been said, although we have not found an authority, that this Blencowe family takes its name from Troutbeck (W) and not from its Cumberland namesake. The Rev. Edward Troutbeck, B.A. (Oxon) (d. 1606),‡ went from Carlisle diocese to be Rector of Whitfield (N) 1571.§ The Rev. Robert Troutbeck (d. 1637) was incumbent of Newton Reigny 1594-1637. His son the Rev. George Troutbeck, B.A. (Cantab) (1614-91), was Vicar of Alston 1638 and Rector of Bowness-on-Solway 1660-91. His son the Rev. Robert Troutbeck, B.A. (Cantab) (d. 1706), was ordained in Carlisle 1668 and was Vicar of Corbridge 1685-1706. He left sums of £50 to the poor of Dacre|| and Bowness, the interest to be distributed annually by a Troutbeck. The line was continued by George Troutbeck, of Great Blencowe (1713-80), father of William Troutbeck, of Ennim Bank (1743-1819), whose grandson the Rev. John Troutbeck, M.A., D.D. (Oxon) (1832-99), was Vicar of Dacre 1858-64, and Minor Canon of Westminster Abbey (where he is buried) 1869-99. His eldest son John Troutbeck, M.A., B.C.L. (Oxon) (1860-1912), Coroner for

* His dau. Isabella (b. 1759) marr. 1793 the Rev. John Mayson (d. 1845), Curate of Thursby and Rector of Great Orton. Their granddau. was Mrs. Beeton, of cookery fame.

† In 1935 he published *The Trimbles and Cowens of Dalston, Cumberland.*

‡ In his will dated 1602 he left 2s. 6d. for the "reparation of Dalmain bridge when it is builded that a laden horse may go over the same without danger."

§ Rober Troutbeck (d. 1631), ordained at Carlisle 1622, was Rector of Whitfield 1623-31.

|| John Troutbeck by will 1787 left the interest of £200 "to be distributed every Easter, on the family tombstone in Dacre Churchyard, provided the day be fine, by the hands, and at the discretion of a Troutbeck of Blencowe, if there should be any living, those next in descent having prior right of distribution. If none should be living that would distribute the money, then by a Troutbeck as long as one could be found that would take the trouble of it."

Westminster and South West London and Deputy High Bailiff for Westminster, was buried at Dacre. *Arms.* Azure three trouts fretted in triangle Argent. *Crest.* A Moor's head couped at the shoulders (Brasses, Newton Reigny and Dacre churches).

TRUSBUT – see ROOS.

TUBMAN. Robert Tubman, mercer (d. 1727), a member of a leading Cockermouth family, marr. Frances (d. 1729), dau. and coheir of the Rev. George Lamplugh, Rector of Lamplugh. Their son Robert (d. 1745) was a merchant with an interest in the Virginia trade, and was of Cockermouth Castle. He marr. 1723 Martha (1698-1763), 9th dau. of Ewan Christian, of Unerigg. Their sons Richard (b. 1726) and Robert (b. 1735) died *s.p.*, leaving a sister and heir Frances (1731-1802), who marr. (1) 1752 Samuel Irton, *q.v.*, and (2) 1770 the Rev. Reginald Brathwaite, Vicar of Hawkshead, the builder of Belmount in that parish. *Arms.* Azure on a bend between six lozenges Or five escallops Sable (Shield on the Irton altar frontal, dated 1768, and worked by Frances Irton, née Tubman; now the property of Mrs. H. S. Greg of Kendal).

TUDOR. The arms of King Henry VIII are on the Salkeld screen in Carlisle Cathedral. The same arms, being those of his dau. Queen Elizabeth I, are on the keep of Carlisle Castle, with date 1577, and also above the entrance to Huthwaite Hall, with date 1581. *Arms.* Quarterly, 1 & 4, Azure three fleurs-de-lys Or (France, modern); 2 & 3, Gules three lions passant guardant in pale Or (England). *Supporters.* Those of Henry VIII on the screen in Carlisle Cathedral are: Dexter, A dragon; Sinister, A greyhound. Those of Queen Elizabeth at Huthwaite Hall are: Two hounds.*

TUDOR. Miss Christine Elizabeth French Tudor, B.Sc. (Dunelm), of Rigg End, Blencarn, is dau. of Frederick Edward Tudor, of Aldenham, Herts. (1880-1958), by his wife Constance Margaret Thomson (1883-1960), and granddau. of Frederick Sidney Scripps Tudor, of Wyton Hall, near Hull (Y) (1839-82), by his wife Rosa (1842-1918), dau. of Edward Francis French, of Cheshire and Galway, son of George French, of Galway, and his wife Dorothy Platt. *Arms.* Quarterly, 1 & 4, Or a lion passant between three annulets Sable (Tudor); 2, Azure a bend engrailed between two dolphins embowed Argent (French); 3, Azure on a chevron between three escallops Argent as many leopards' faces Gules (Platt); over all, on an escutcheon of pretence, Quarterly 1 & 4, Argent a buck's head cabossed Gules on a chief wavy of the last a lozenge between two mullets of the field; 2 & 3, Or a lymphad Sable; all within a bordure Gules (Thomson). *Crests.* 1, On a mural crown a serpent nowed (Tudor); 2, A demi lion supporting with his paws a tilting spear thereto attached a standard charged with a fleur-de-lys (French); 3, A cat-a-mountain salient (Thomson). *Motto.* Malo mori quam foedari (Wooden overmantel at Rigg End).

TUFNELL. William Tufnell, M.P., of Langleys, Essex (1769-1809), marr. 1804 Mary (d. 1829), dau. of Thomas Carleton, agent to Lord Monson, and niece and coheir of Lough Carleton (d. 1792), see Lough. Through this marr. the Tufnells acquired lands in Blencarn and Kirkland, which passed to

* At Yanwath Hall (W) Queen Elizabeth's supporters are carved on a chimney overmantel more correctly as: Dexter, A lion rampant; Sinister, A dragon (CW1 i 57).

their elder* son, the Rt. Hon. Henry Tufnell, D.L., M.P., B.A. (Oxon) (1805-54), Chief Liberal Whip, a Lord of the Treasury 1835-40, and Secretary to the Treasury 1846. His dau. and eventual coheir Caroline marr. 1870 Lt-Col Alfred Molyneux Cranmer-Byng, *q.v.* (TFT). *Arms.* Quarterly, 1 & 4, Azure on a fess Argent between three ostrich feathers erect Proper as many martlets Sable (Tufnell); 2 & 3, Gules a cross botoné Argent charged at the ends with twelve escallops Sable (Humfreys). *Crest* (granted 1708). A dexter arm embowed in armour brandishing a falchion the edge embrued all Proper adorned with a scarf tied above the wrist Azure. *Mottoes.* Esse quam videri; Manus haec inimicia tyrannis (TFT).

TULLIE. The ancestor of this family was Thomas Tullie, of Blindcrake, Isel, whose will was proved 1569. His descendant George Tullie, of Carlisle, marr. 1614 Thomasine Hechstetter and had issue, *int. al,* Timothy, of whom below; Thomas (1620-76), Dean of Ripon 1675-76; and Isaac, Mayor of Carlisle, and the author of the *History of the Siege of Carlisle 1644-45.* The eldest son Timothy, M.A. (Oxon) (1615-1700), was Rector of Cliburn 1639-56, and Rector of Middleton-in-Teesdale 1660-1700. His son the Rev. Thomas Tullie, M.A. (Oxon), LL.D. (Lambeth) (1656-1727), was Chancellor of Carlisle 1683-1727, Prebendary of Carlisle 1684-1716, Rector of Aldingham 1694-1727, Vicar of Crosthwaite 1710-27, and Dean of Carlisle 1716-27. He was the builder of Tullie House, Carlisle, where he was succ. by his eldest son Jerome (1694-1756), High Sheriff 1744. Dying *s.p.* he was succ. by his brother William, of Gray's Inn (b. 1697, will dated 1765, pr. 1767). Their youngest brother Thomas, LL.B. (1701-42), was Vicar of Aldingham 1727-42 and Prebendary of Carlisle 1728-42. Their sisters Anne, who marr. William Cornthwaite, and Isabella, who marr. 1728 the Very Rev. John Waugh, *q.v.,* were their coheirs. *Arms.* Argent on a chevron engrailed Gules three escallops Or in chief a lion passant guardant Azure (DSL). *Crest.* A demi dragon rampant (Buck's View of Wetheral Abbey, 1739). These arms are on a shield in the Old Library, St. Edmund Hall, Oxford, and on a silver tankard, hall marked 1675-6, now in Carlisle Museum and given to Carlisle Corporation by Thomas Tullie, Principal of St. Edmund Hall,† with *Crest.* A dragon's head couped, and *Motto.* Non solum nobis nati sumus. Burke gives for Tully, of Wetheral Abbey: *Arms.* Argent on a chevron Gules three escallops Or in chief a lion passant Vert. *Crest.* A cupid with his bow and quiver all Proper (BGA).

TURNER, of Gap. Thomas Turner, of Gap, or Closegap, died 1730, aged 59. *Arms.* . . . a chevron . . . between in chief a crescent reversed . . . and in base a star of four points . . . (Gravestone, Kirkandrews-on-Esk). Bell Irving gives almost the same arms for Thomas Turner, of Breahead, Kirkandrews-on-Esk, 1766: . . . a chevron engrailed . . . between in chief a crescent reversed . . . and in base a star of four points . . . all within a bordure . . . (ABD). Jane, dau. of Thomas Turner, from Wragmire, "beyond Carlisle," and her mother Jannet were both buried at Kirkandrews-on-Esk in 1766.

* Their younger son Edward Carleton Tufnell (1806-86) marr. 1846 Honoria Mary (1824-77), dau. and heir of Col William Macadam, K.H., who marr. Honoria, dau. of John Hudleston, H.E.I.C.S., *q.v.*

† R. S. Ferguson gives an inaccurate description of the arms in *Old Church Plate in the Diocese of Carlisle,* p. 282.

TWEDALE, of Whitehill. Elizabeth, wife of John Twedale, of Whitehill, was buried at Lanercost 1753, aged 28. *Arms.* ... three trefoils slipped* ... (Lanercost tombstone).

TYES. Burke recorded the following, without further details, for Tyes, of Cumberland and Northumberland, *temp.* Henry I (*sic*). *Arms.* Argent a chevron Gules (BGA).

TYLNEY. Impaled by Howard on shield in hall of Greystoke Castle, and quartered on shield in Naworth Castle; Thomas Howard, Duke of Norfolk (1443-1524), famous for his victory, when Earl of Surrey, at Flodden, 1513, marr. (1) 1472, Elizabeth (d. 1497), widow of Sir Humphrey Bourchier, and dau. and heir of Sir Frederick Tylney, of Ashwellthorpe, Norfolk. *Arms.* Argent a chevron between three griffins' heads erased Gules armed Or.

TYSON. The Rev. Isaac Tyson (1766-1821), son of Jacob and Jane Tyson, of Wath in Cleator, was Vicar of Hemingborough (Y) 1793-94, and Vicar of Adlingfleet (Y) 1794-1821. His son the Rev. Edwin Coleman Tyson, M.A. (Cantab) (d. at Lazonby 1863), was of Milburn (W) without cure 1855-63. His brother the Rev. William Daniel Tyson, M.A. (Cantab) (d. 1865, aged 60), held the living of Milburn 1858-65. *Arms.* On the tablet to the Rev. Isaac Tyson's youngest dau. Elizabeth (d. 1829, aged 19) in Bridlington church, these appear as: ... three lions rampant ... (BHH).

TYSON. Thomas Tyson, of Seathwaite (C), was father of John Tyson, clerk of the Survey in H.M.'s Dockyard, Woolwich, who in 1803 represented to the College of Arms that his family had used the arms of Tyson as registered at the 1687 Visitation of London,† but was unable to prove his descent, and a grant was made to him of the following *Arms.* Per chevron Gules and Vert the last gutté d'eau three lions rampant Erminois ducally crowned Argent. *Crest.* A sinister arm embowed vested Or bearing an antique shield lined per chevron Gules and Vert the last gutté d'eau the straps of the shield Argent (CA xxii/149).

TYSON. Edward Tyson, solicitor, of Maryport (d. 1892), had an eldest son Edward Thomas Tyson, J.P., solicitor, of Wood Hall, Bridekirk (1847-1923), who was High Sheriff of Cumberland 1914. *Arms.* Vert gutté d'eau three lions rampant Argent each holding in the dexter paw a torch erect fired Proper. *Crest.* A demi lion rampant Vert gutté d'eau holding in the dexter paw a torch as in the arms and resting the sinister on a rose Gules barbed and seeded Proper. *Motto.* Fortiter et vigilanter (BGA; FD7).

UCHTRED. Shield at Hutton-in-the-Forest; a Vane quartering. *Arms.* Sable on a cross patonce Or five mullets of the field.

ULLSWATER, Viscount – see LOWTHER.

UMFRAMVILLE, Earl of Angus. Gilbert de Umframville, Earl of Angus, Baron Umframville (aged 15 in 1325, d. 1381), marr. between 1350 and 1369 Maud (d. 1398), only dau. of Thomas, 2nd Baron Lucy, and sister of Anthony, 3rd Baron, and aunt and heir of Joan, Baroness Lucy, *q.v.* He had

* Field (FAC) recorded this as three hunting horns (!).

† The pedigree was registered by Dr. Edward Tyson, Physician to Bethlehem Hospital, a descendant of Nicholas Tyson, of Birket (C). Dr. Tyson's nephew, Samuel Tyson, of Woodland Green, Glos., being unable to justify his right to the arms, obtained in 1709 a grant of the following *Arms.* Vert three lions rampant reguardant Argent crowned Or. *Crest.* A sinister arm in mail Or the hand Proper defended by an antique shield Or lined Vert with braces Gules (CA v/336).

no issue by her and she marr. (2) before October 1383 Henry Percy, 1st Earl of Northumberland, *q.v.* (HNF; GEC). *Arms.* Gules crusilly and a cinquefoil Or (FFC; Shield on Cockermouth Castle).

URIELL, of Cockermouth. A pedigree of six generations of this family was certified by Richard Uriell, of Cockermouth, then aged 45, at Dugdale's Visitation of 1665. George Uriell, of Cockermouth and later of "Metchlopatam" (?Masulipatam), made his will in 1677 and died before 1681. His nephew Dalston Uriell, of Sebergham, had a son William (b. 1727). *Arms.* Argent on a chief three plates a crescent for difference (FCW). No tincture is given for the chief, and Dugdale added: "Respite given for proofe of these armes." Burke gives: Argent on a chief (sometimes a fess) Sable three plates (BGA).

USHER. The Most Rev. James Usher, or Ussher, M.A., D.D. (TCD) (1581-1656), son of Arnold Usher, one of the six clerks in chancery, in Ireland, became Vice-Chancellor of Trinity College, Dublin, 1617, Bishop of Meath 1621, and Archbishop of Armagh 1625. In 1642 he was appointed Bishop of Carlisle *in commendam,* holding the see until September 1643, when Parliament abolished the episcopacy. *Arms.* Quarterly, 1 & 4, Azure a chevron Ermine between three billets Or; 2 & 3, Sable three lions' gambs erased and erect Argent (BBE). Burke gives: Quarterly, 1 & 4, Azure a chevron Ermine between three batons Or; 2 & 3, Argent three lions' gambs couped and erect Sable armed Gules (BGA).

USHER – see CROFTON.

UVEDALE. A Howard quartering, on shield in Great Hall of Naworth Castle; Edward, 2nd Earl of Carlisle (d. 1692), marr. 1668 Elizabeth, dau. and coheir of Sir William Uvedale, of Wickham, Hants. *Arms.* Argent a cross moline Gules.

VANE-FLETCHER, post FLETCHER-VANE, of Hutton-in-the-Forest. After much litigation it was agreed in 1717 that if Thomas Fletcher, of Moresby, *q.v.,* died *s.p.* – as he did – the estates to which he succ. in 1712 on the death of Sir Henry Fletcher, 3rd Bart., *q.v.,* should go to Sir Henry's sister's son Henry Vane (b. 1689), 2nd son of Lionel and Catherine Vane, of Long Newton (D). On succeeding Henry, who was High Sheriff of Cumberland 1741, assumed the surname Fletcher. Dying unmarr. 1761, he was succeeded by his brother Walter (d. 1775, aged 82), whose son Lionel Wright Fletcher-Vane (1723-86) was cr. Baronet 1786, less than a month before his death. He was succ. by his son Sir Frederick Vane-Fletcher, later Fletcher-Vane (1760-1832), High Sheriff 1788, M.P. for Winchelsea 1792-94, for Carlisle 1796-1802, and for Winchelsea 1806-7. His son Sir Francis Fletcher-Vane (1797-1842), High Sheriff 1837, was succ. by his son Sir Henry Ralph Fletcher-Vane, D.L., J.P. (1830-1908), High Sheriff 1856 and Vice-Lieutenant 1880. Dying *s.p.* he was succ. in the title, but not the estates (which passed eventually to Lord Inglewood, *q.v.*), by his cousin Sir Francis Patrick Fletcher-Vane, J.P., 5th and last Bart. (1861-1934). *Arms.* Or three sinister gauntlets Azure a canton Gules (BP58). DPB (1897) gives: Quarterly, 1 & 4, Or three gauntlets Azure a canton Gules; 2 & 3, Azure three gauntlets Or. *Crests.* 1, A dexter gauntlet erect holding a sword all Proper hilt and pommel Or (BP58); 2, An armed arm embowed couped at the shoulder grasping a sword all Proper (LMC).

FLETCHER-VANE, Baron Inglewood, of Hutton-in-the-Forest. William

Morgan Fletcher-Vane, D.L., T.D., M.A. (Cantab), of Hutton-in-the-Forest, only son of Col the Hon. William Lyonel Vane, D.L., J.P. (1859-1920), and nephew of the 9th Baron Barnard, assumed the surname Fletcher-Vane in lieu of Vane 1931. He was M.P. for Westmorland 1945-64, and was cr. Baron Inglewood, of Hutton-in-the-Forest, 1964. *Arms.* Azure three sinister gauntlets Or. *Crest.* A dexter hand in armour couped at the wrist Proper holding a sword Argent pommel and hilt Or (BP105). *Supporters* (granted 1970). On either side a roebuck Proper collared and pendent from the collar a pheon Argent. *Motto.* Faithful unto death.

VANSITTART. The Rev. William Vansittart, M.A., D.D. (Oxon) (1779-1847), Rector of Shottesbrook and White Waltham, Berks, son of Arthur Vansittart, D.L., J.P., D.C.L., of Shottesbrook and Clewer, Berks. (1726-1806), was Prebendary of Carlisle 1824-47. His nephew, the Rev. Charles Vansittart, M.A. (Oxon) (1820-78), later Rector of Shottesbrook, son of Arthur Vansittart, D.L., J.P., of Shottesbrook and Clewer (1775-1829), was Perpetual Curate of Wetheral and Warwick 1847-48. *Arms.* Ermine an eagle displayed Sable on a chief Gules a ducal coronet Or between two crosses pattée Argent. *Crest.* An eagle's head couped at the neck between two wings elevated and displayed Sable the whole resting on two crosses pattée Argent. *Motto.* Fata viam invenient (BLG15). In a window in Carlisle Cathedral, commemorating the Rev. William Vansittart, above, the shield is charged with a mullet Argent for difference, and the crest appears as: In front of a demi Eagle displayed Sable two crossess pattée Argent.

VARTY. There does not appear to be any connected pedigree of this well known Penrith family. Monumental inscriptions in St. Andrew's churchyard, Penrith, record, *int. al.,* John Varty (d. 1757), "an upright laborious man who was providentially warned to flee from destruction when a stone quarry in which he had been working just before suddenly fell in." His eldest son William Varty (d. 1771, aged 67) was Under Librarian of Lincoln's Inn; another son Jonathan, a shoemaker (d. 1789, aged 79), is described as "mild, sweet, serene and tender in his mood, not grave with sternness nor with lightness free against example resolutely good fervent in zeal and warm in charity." Of Hannah (d. 1755) his wife it is said "She willingly gave up her all to meet her Lord leaving her husband with six little children, pledges of their mutual Love." Of these children, William Varty, skinner, was father of Jonathan (b. 1775) who may have been father of Thomas Varty, of Stagstones,* Penrith (b. 1816). His dau. Annie Elizabeth Waring (d. 1967, aged 94) marr. 1901 Alfred Gilbert Crafter (d. 1931). *Arms.* Gules three crosses moline Or a chief vairé Sable and Ermine. *Crest.* A man's head full-faced Proper ducally crowned Or (BGA).

VAUX, of Brownrigg. Caldbeck parish registers contain entries relating to this family down to 1760. Robert Vaux (1642-1721), who was born, lived and died at Brownrigg, "being the 13th Robert sprung from that family," was father of Robert, "the 14th of that name" (1678-1747). His sister Barbara survived until 1760. Their uncle, the Rev. George Vaux, B.A. (Oxon) (1660-1715), was Rector of Courteenhall, Northants., 1708-15, when he was succ. by his son the Rev. Robert Vaux, B.A. (Oxon) (1697-1753), whose son, the Rev. Robert Vaux, M.A. (Oxon) (d. 1792, aged 70), was Rector 1754-92. He is the "young couzen" who was a beneficiary and

* The mansion was demolished in the 1930's.

executor of the will of the above Robert Vaux (d. 1747). *Arms.* . . . a fess compony counter-compony . . . and . . . between three garbs . . . (Shield at High Brownrigg; Seal on Robert Vaux's will 1747).

VAUX, of Catterlen. Hubert de Vaux, 1st Lord of Gilsland, *q.v.*, acquired the manor of Catterlen *temp.* Henry II. It passed before 1170 to Sir John Vaux, whose descendant William is said to have marr. Margery, dau. and heir of . . . Vaux, of Triermain, and had a son William, *fl.* 1351. The marriage may have taken place, but Margery was not heir of Vaux of Triermain, though the Catterlen family quartered the arms of Vaux, of Triermain. William Vaux, *fl.* 1481, marr. Isabel, the heiress of the Delamores, *q.v.* Their descendant Roland (d. 1586) built 1577 the Elizabethan wing of Catterlen Hall. John Vaux, his grandson (1583-1652), who fought in the Royalist army, was the last of the family. He marr. 1616 Isabel (b. *c.* 1579), dau. and heir of Thomas Musgrave, of Hayton, *q.v.*, and widow of John Musgrave. Their daus. and coheirs were Mabel, marr. Christopher Richmond, of Highhead Castle, *q.v.*, and Mary, marr. William Graham, of Nunnery (d. 1661), *q.v.* (JPP i 103-6; CW2 vii). *Arms.* . . . a fess chequy . . . and . . . between six garbs . . . (Shields in Newton Reigny churchyard and at Catterlen Hall, one of the latter quartering, . . . a cross flory . . . , for Delamore, *q.v.*). Curwen blazoned this as: Or a fess chequy Or and Gules between six garbs of the last banded of the first (CW2 vii 115). At the Visitation of 1665, Richmond bore Vaux, of Catterlen, on an escutcheon of pretence as: Gules a fess chequy Or and of the first between three garbs of the second (FCW). NB (ii 394) give: Or a fess chequy Or and Gules between three garbs Gules banded Or; and LMC the same, without blazoning the bands. FVC gives a quarterly coat, viz. Quarterly, 1, Or a fess chequy Gules and of the field between three garbs of the second (Vaux, of Catterlen); 2, Gules a fess chequy of the field and Or between six garbs of the last (Vaux, of Catterlen); 3, Argent a bend counter-compony Or and Gules (Vaux, of Triermain); 4, Vert a cross moline Or (Delamore, of Cumberland). *Crest.* An eagle's head erased Sable beaked and gorged with a collar Or (MVC). Machell recorded the arms as: Sable a fess compony counter-compony Or and Gules between three garbs Argent (MMS vi 417). For the various versions of the arms and crest at Conishead Priory, Ulverston parish church, and St. Ninian's church, Brougham, see AWL.

VAUX. Thomas Vaux of Calthwaite and Kirkby Stephen (d. 1588), a younger son of William Vaux of Catterlen, was grandfather of Lancelot Vaux of St. Dunstan's-in-the-East, London, baker (*c.* 1559-1617) who, in 1614, bought on behalf of his cousin John Vaux of Catterlen, the estates forfeited by William Vaux. Lancelot's descendant George Vaux, Citizen and Surgeon of London (1721-1803), was father of *int. al.* Jeremiah (1747-1829) and James Vaux, see below. The former was ancestor of the Rev. George Bowyer Vaux, M.A. (Oxon), (1850-1943), Rector of Carshalton, Surrey, whose 3rd, but eldest surviving son, Stephen Vaux (b. 1888) is now head of the family. Also descended from Jeremiah Vaux was Calvert Vaux (1824-95), who went to America 1850, and was for 30 years landscape architect of the Department of Public Parks, New York City. He helped to lay out the Smithsonian grounds, Washington, and designed Central Park, New York, and many other parks. His great nephew Brigadier Peter Alfred Lincoln Vaux, O.B.E. (b. 1916) is of 10 Greenways, Fleet, Hants. The above James Vaux (1748-1842) went to Philadelphia 1771 and bought a 300 acre plantation which he named Vaux Hill. Here red clover was first cultivated in America. His son George Vaux (1779-1836), Counsellor at Law, was a great horticultural enthusiast, and laid out and planted Washington Square, Philadelphia. His grandson George Vaux IX (1863-1927) of Bryn Mawr, Philadelphia, was a lawyer and keen mineralogist, whose collection is now in Bryn Mawr College. His elder son George Vaux X (b. 1908), of 320 Caversham Road, Bryn Mawr, Pa., is now head of the family in the U.S.A. *Arms.* As Vaux of Catterlen. William S. Vaux (1872-1908), brother of George Vaux IX bore Checky Argent and Gules on a chevron Azure three roses of the first. *Crest.* An eagle's head. *Motto.* Hodie non cras.

VAUX, of Corby. The following shield is in Harl. MS. 1536, with no other details. *Arms.* Argent a bend company counter-company Gules and Or (FVC).

VAUX, of Gilsland. Hubert de Vaux or Vallibus* (d. 1165), whose family owned much land in East Anglia in 1086, was granted the Barony of Gilsland in 1158. His son and heir Robert (d. *s.p.* 1195), the founder of Lanercost Priory, was Sheriff of Carlisle 1174 and of Cumberland 1175-85. He was succ. by his brother Ranulph (d. 1198), whose son Robert was under age 1199. His son Hubert was succ. by his dau. and heir Maud, who marr. Thomas de Multon (d. before 12 January 1270-1), *q.v.* (GEC; CW2 xlii). *Arms.* Chequy Or and Gules (DAC; LMC). The arms were so quartered by Dacre and Howard. Camden (*Britannia*) gives: Chequy Argent and Gules, as does DSL for Robert de Vaux, Sheriff 1175-85. NB (ii 488) gives: Argent a bend chequy Or and Gules. Robert, 4th Lord of Gilsland, is said to have sealed his grant of Triermain to Roland de Vaux, *q.v.*, with: . . . a bend chequy . . . a bordure . . . charged with eight roundles . . . (CW1 iii 176).

VAUX, of Triermain. Among the lands acquired by Hubert de Vaux, 1st Lord of Gilsland, *q.v.*, was the manor of Triermain, made famous by Sir Walter Scott's *Bridal of Triermain.*† It passed to his sons and grandson, the 2nd, 3rd and 4th holders of the Barony, and was given by Robert, 4th Lord, to his (?bastard) brother Roland, who was living 1212. His descendant Roland de Vaux (d. 1363), High Sheriff of Cumberland 1338, obtained a licence to crenellate Triermain 1340. His descendant Roland, living 1490, was Knight of the Shire 1452-53 and High Sheriff 1451, 1461-63 and 1466-68. He was the last of his family, and was succ. by his dau. and heir Joan, wife of Sir Richard Salkeld, *q.v.*‡ *Arms* (as quartered by Salkeld).§ Argent a

* Field translated "de Vallibus" as "of walls" (FAC), but the name is derived from *vallis* = valley, and not from *vallum* = wall. The theory that the arms are punning ones, i.e. that the chequy field represents the masonry of a wall, is therefore untenable.

† Scott writes:

> "Sir Roland de Vaux he hath laid him to sleep,
> His blood it was fever'd, his breathing was deep.
> He had been pricking against the Scot,
> The foray was long, and the skirmish hot;
> His dinted helm and his buckler's plight
> Bore token of a stubborn fight."

‡ The Vaux family, of Catterlen, *q.v.*, quartered the arms of Vaux, of Triermain, but it is clear that if William Vaux did marry a Triermain cousin, she was not, as has been asserted, an heiress.

§ On the monument of Sir Richard Salkeld and his wife Joan in Wetheral church the latter's arms are impaled as what appears to be: . . . four pallets lozengy . . . .

bend chequy Or and Gules (FCW). Vaux, of Catterlen, quartered this as: Argent a bend counter-compony Or and Gules (FVC). DAC, NB and LMC all give for Vaux, of Triermain: Vert a bend chequy Or and Gules. FFC, however, records for Roland de Vaux, *temp.* Henry III: Argent a bend chequy Argent and Gules. The version quartered by Salkeld is displayed at Conishead Priory, Ulverston parish church, and St. Ninian's, Brougham, see AWL.

de VERE. Impaled by Howard on shield in hall of Greystoke Castle; Sir Henry Howard, *styled* Earl of Surrey (*c.* 1517-47), executed for high treason *v.p.*, marr. Frances, dau. of John de Vere, Earl of Oxford. *Arms.* Quarterly Gules and Or in the first quarter a mullet Argent.

VERNON. Shields at Hutton-in-the-Forest; a Vane quartering. *Arms.* Or a fess Azure. Another shield displays: Or fretty Gules; which seem to be the arms of Verdon.

VERNON, *olim* JENKIN. The Rev. Charles Vernon, formerly Jenkin, J.P., M.A., B.D. (Cantab), of Wherstead Park, Great Thurlow Hall, and Herringswell, Suffolk (1790-1863), assumed the surname Vernon on succeeding to that family's estates in Suffolk 1860. He marr. in Carlisle Cathedral 1862 Sarah Grace, dau. of John Fawcett, of Petterill Bank, *q.v.*, and widow of Edward L. Haworth. He was buried in Upperby churchyard. *Arms.* Or on a fess Azure three garbs of the field in chief a cross crosslet of the second. *Crest.* A demi Ceres Proper vested Azure holding in the dexter hand a sickle and in the sinister arm a garb about her head a wreath of wheat all Proper charged on the vest with a cross crosslet Or. *Motto.* Semper ut te digna sequare (Upperby tombstone; BGA).

VENABLES-VERNON, *post* VERNON-HARCOURT. The Hon. Edward Venables-Vernon, later Vernon-Harcourt, P.C., D.C.L. (1757-1847), 3rd son of George, 1st Lord Vernon, by his 3rd wife, Martha, dau. of Simon Harcourt, was Prebendary of Gloucester 1785-91, Bishop of Carlisle 1791-1807, and Archbishop of York 1807-47. *Arms.* Quarterly, 1 & 4, Gules two bars Or (Harcourt); 2, Argent a fret Sable (Vernon); 3, Or on a fess Azure three garbs of the field (Vernon) (BBE).

VESCI. A shield on the ceiling of Carlisle Cathedral may be intended for Vesci. *Arms.* Or a cross Sable. Field, however, read this as: Or a cross Azure, without identifying it (CW2 xxxiv 28).

VESEY. The Most Rev. John Vesey, D.D. (1637-1716), Archbishop of Tuam, had seven sons, from the eldest of whom, the Rev. Sir Thomas Vesey, 1st Bart., descends Viscount de Vesci; from the 6th son, the Rev. George Vesey (d. 1737), was descended the Rev. Thomas Agmondisham Vesey (1848-1922), Rector of Marske in Swaledale (Y), whose son Canon Norman Agmondisham Vesey, M.A. (Dunelm), of Howe Rigg, Portinscale (1889-1976), was ordained by the Bishop of Jarrow 1912, and was Rector of Whitby 1948-54, Vicar of St. Mary with St. Nicholas, Beverley, 1954-58, and Vicar of Cumwhitton 1958-61. He was appointed Canon of York 1953 and Canon Emeritus 1958. *Arms.* Or on a cross Sable a patriarchal cross of the field. *Crest.* A hand erect in armour holding a laurel-branch all Proper. *Motto.* Sub hoc signo vinces (FD7).

VETERIPONT. The history of this junior branch of the great baronial family has been written by the Rev. F. W. Ragg in CW2 xi 259-320. Its founder Ivo de Veteripont (d. 1239) was brother of Robert, Lord of Appleby, ancestor of the Clifford family (d. 1231), see AWL. King John confirmed to Ivo in 1209 the grant made to him by William, King of Scotland, of Alston, Elrington and Kirkhaugh. Ivo also inherited his mother's estate of Maulds Meaburn and he owned lands in Ireby, Blencarn, Ainstable, Waverton and Carlisle. His descendant Robert (1300-71) marr. Margaret, heiress of Ukmanby and Middlesceugh, and had a son Nicholas whose son Robert died *s.p.* 1369, aged 18, his coheirs being his sisters Elizabeth (b. *c.* 1346), marr. Thomas de Blencowe, *q.v.*, and Joan (b. *c.* 1349), marr. William de Whitlaw. *Arms.* The Cliffords quartered Veteripont as: Gules six annulets Or, three, two, and one, see AWL, and these arms are on the ceiling of Carlisle Cathedral.* Windows in Edenhall and Kirkoswald churches display for Veteripont, of Alston: Or six annulets Gules, three, two, and one.

VICARS. No place of residence stated. *Arms.* Argent on a cross flory Sable five mullets of six points of the field on a chief Gules three roses Or. *Crest.* A dove close Argent beaked and membered Gules bearing in its mouth a laurel branch Vert. *Motto.* My Lord and my God (FVC).

VILLIERS. The Rt. Rev. Henry Montagu Villiers, M.A., D.D. (Oxon) (1813-61), was 5th son of the Hon. George Villiers, and grandson of the 1st Earl of Clarendon. He was Canon of St. Paul's 1847-56, Bishop of Carlisle 1856-60, and Bishop of Durham 1860-61. *Arms.* Quarterly, 1 & 4, Argent on a cross Gules five escallops Or a crescent for difference (Villiers); 2 & 3, Azure a chevron between three lozenges Argent on a canton Gules a lion rampant between three cross crosslets [Or] (Hyde) (BBE). *Crest.* A lion rampant Argent ducally crowned Or. *Motto.* Fidei coticula crux (BP105).

VIPOND. John Vipond, of Annatwalls, "an affectionate husband, a tender parent," died 1758, aged 82. *Arms.* . . . six annulets . . . (Tombstone, Alston churchyard). *Crest.* Field recorded this as: ?A quatrefoil or cross crosslet (FAC).

VIPONT. Thomas Vipont was Bishop of Carlisle 1255-56. *Arms.* Or six annulets Gules (BBE).

WADHAM. Arthur Edward Montague Wadham, J.P., of Cockermouth (1863-1925), Capt Westmorland and Cumberland Yeomanry, was elder son of Edward Wadham, D.L., J.P. (1828-1913), see AWL, who marr. 1860 Mary Elizabeth (1838-1932), dau. of Montague Ainslie, see AWL. His younger dau. Joan marr. 1935 William Walker, of Greenlands, *q.v.* The present head of the family is her brother, Lt-Col Edward Wadham, of Dairy Cottage, Corton, Wilts. *Arms.* Gules a chevron between three roses Argent. *Crest.* Between the attires of a stag Or a rose Gules. *Motto.* Spero meliora.

WAKE, of Liddel. Joan (d. 1276), dau. of Nicholas de Stuteville, *q.v.* succ. to the Barony of Liddel 1241. She marr. (1) Hugh Wake (d. 1241) and (2) Hugh Bigod (d. 1266), and was succ. by her son Baldwin Wake (d. 1282). His son John (d. 1300) succ. and was succ. by his son Thomas (d. *s.p.* 1349), the last male of the family, whose heir was his sister Margaret (d. 1349), who marr. Edmund of Woodstock, Earl of Kent, see Plantagenet. Their dau. Joan marr. the Black Prince, see Plantagenet, and the Barony eventually came to the Crown (GEC; SEB). *Arms.* Or two bars Gules in

* Owing to incorrect painting, the arms appear on certain shields on the triptych from Appleby Castle, now in the Record Office, Carlisle, as: Or six annulets three, two, and one Sable, i.e. the arms of Lowther.

chief three torteaux (FFC). Curwen gives: Or a fess Gules in chief three torteaux (CW2 vi).

WAKE. Captain Drury Wake, 17th Dragoons (d. 1787, aged 43), 2nd son of Sir William Wake, 7th Bart., was a Royalist officer in North America and was later of St. Bees, where he was buried. His son Baldwin Wake, M.D. (1774-1842), was physician to York Lunatic Asylum from 1815 till his death, and also a physician to York County Hospital. He marr. Sarah (d. 1856, aged 75), dau. of James Spedding, of Summergrove, *q.v.*; her sister Anne marr. 1807 Charles Wake, M.D. (d. 1852), younger son of the above Drury Wake (BP105; Foster's Peerage). *Arms.* Or two bars Gules in chief three torteaux (M.I. to the above Sarah Wake in Crosthwaite church).

WAKEFIELD. Lt-Col Arthur William Wakefield, M.B., B.Chir., M.A., M.D. (Cantab), M.R.C.S., L.R.C.P., of Applecote, Keswick (1876-1949) was 5th son of William Wakefield, of Birklands, Kendal, see AWL. He served as a trooper in the Boer War, was M.O. to the Royal National Mission to Deep Sea Fishermen in Labrador 1908-14, and served in World Wars I and II. He was a member of the Everest Expedition of 1922. *Arms.* Argent two barrulets Sable between three owls Proper. *Crest.* A bat displayed Proper charged on each wing with a crescent Argent (BLG17).

WALBY. In 1660 Grace Walby sealed her will (proved at Carlisle 1661) with the following *Arms.* . . . a chevron Ermine between three roundles . . . each charged with a cross . . . .

WALDEGRAVE. The Rt. Rev. and Hon. Samuel Waldegrave, M.A., D.D. (Oxon) (1817-69), 2nd son of William, 8th Earl Waldegrave, was Canon of Salisbury 1857-60, and Bishop of Carlisle 1860-69. *Arms.* Per pale Argent and Gules. *Crest.* Out of a ducal coronet Or a plume of five ostrich feathers per pale Argent and Gules. *Motto.* Passes avant (BP105). The arms are on the Bishop's tomb in Carlisle Cathedral. The Bishop's hatchment, formerly in Dalston church and later in Dalston Hall, is no longer to be seen there.

WALKER,* of Boothby. Christopher Walker, yeoman (d. 1774), was of Abbey Lanercost 1762 (will) and later of Boothby, and owned lands at Guards Hill and Thornymoor in Walton parish. John Walker, yeoman, his "nephew or cousin", is mentioned in a deed of 1772 (HN). *Arms* (on tombstone in Walton churchyard) . . . on a fess . . . three roundles . . . in chief as many mullets . . . .

WALKER, of Greenlands. Herbert Wilson Walker, of Wasdale Hall (d. 1934), was Lord of the Manor of Derwentwater and Castlerigg. His son William Walker, J.P., of Greenlands, Irton, one of the last Aldermen of Cumberland County Council, was High Sheriff 1963. *Arms.* Argent on a chevron Gules three roses of the field barbed and seeded Proper in chief two cross crosslets fitché Sable. *Crest.* A demi lion Gules holding in the dexter paw a cross crosslet fitché Or the sinister paw resting on a rose Argent barbed and seeded Proper.

WALKER. John Walker, of Whitehaven, mercer, marr. 1796 Frances (d. 1812), dau. of Drury Wake, *q.v.,* and had a son Admiral Sir Baldwin Wake Walker, K.C.B., R.N. (1803-76), who served as an admiral in the Turkish Navy as Yaver Pasha, and also as admiral in the British Navy and was Comptroller of the Navy 1847-60. He was cr. Baronet 1856. His son and successor Vice-Admiral Sir Baldwin Wake Walker, 2nd Bart., C.V.O.,

* Field recorded the name as ?Walton (FAC).

C.M.G., R.N. (1846-1905), marr. 1877 Fanny Augusta (d. 1951), eldest dau. of Captain Cowper Coles, C.B., R.N.* The present holder of the title is Sir Baldwin Patrick Walker, 4th Bart., hereditary Pasha of the Ottoman Empire. *Arms.* Gules on a chevron between three cross crosslets Argent an anchor Sable on a chief of the second three stags' heads cabossed Proper a canton Azure thereon a representation of the diamond decoration appropriate to the rank of Pasha of the Ottoman Empire, which was conferred on Sir Baldwin Wake Walker by the Sultan for his gallant and distinguished services in Syria. *Crest.* Out of a naval crown Azure a stag's head Proper gorged with an eastern crown Or. *Motto.* Ready and faithful (BP105).

ROBERTSON-WALKER. William Walker, whose family came from Grasmere, settled as a merchant in Whitehaven and acquired a fortune. In 1809 he built Gilgarran in Distington parish, and in 1819, with his sister Anne, he went to Italy to buy ornamental trees for his grounds. The ship in which they were travelling was attacked by a Spanish gun-boat, and Walker was killed. His sister was brought home in a frigate commanded by Capt James Robertson, J.P., R.N. (d. 1858), whom she marr. 1824. He assumed the additional surname Walker on marriage and was High Sheriff of Cumberland 1841. Dying *s.p.*,† he was succ. by his nephew James Robertson, J.P., B.A. (Oxon) (1850-1927), who assumed the surname Walker 1893. His son James Francis Austin Robertson-Walker, J.P., B.A. (Oxon) (1877-1940), succ. and was succ. by his son Lt Ian Murdo Robertson-Walker, R.N. (1918-41), who was killed in action on board H.M.S. *Gloucester* at the Battle of Crete. His brother and successor, Austin Thomas Robertson-Walker (b. 1921), gave up residence at Gilgarran in 1951 (*Whitehaven News*, 22 Nov. 1951). *Arms.* The Robertsons used the arms of the Robertsons, of Struan, clearly without authority, viz.: Gules three wolves' heads erased Argent armed and langued Azure; with a wild man chained lying under the arms as a compartment. *Crest.* A dexter arm and hand erect holding a regal crown all Proper. *Motto.* Virtutis gloria merces (BLG4).

WALLACE, Baron Wallace of Knaresdale. Thomas Wallace, attorney, of Asholme (N) (1697-1737), settled at Brampton. He marr. Dulcibella Sowerby (who marr. (2) the Rev. William Plaskett) and had a son James Wallace (d. 1783, aged 52), born at Brampton, who was M.P. for Horsham 1770-80, Solicitor General 1778, and Attorney General 1780-83. He marr. 1767 Elizabeth (d. 1811), dau. of Thomas Simpson, of Carleton Hall, *q.v.*, and sister and heir of Hugh Simpson, and so inherited the estates of that family, which descended to their only son, the Rt. Hon. Thomas Wallace, M.A., D.C.L. (Oxon), who was born at Brampton 1768 and died *s.p.* at Featherstone Castle (N) 1844. He marr. 1814 Jean, dau. of John, 2nd Earl of Hopetoun, and widow of Henry, 1st Viscount Melville. He was cr. 1828 Baron Wallace of Knaresdale and in that year sold Carleton Hall and the

* He was the designer of H.M.S. *Captain*, which went down off the French coast 1870 with a loss of 481 lives, including the Captain, Hugh Talbot Burgoyne, V.C., R.N., who marr. 1864 Evelyn Laura (d. 1889), dau. of the above Sir Baldwin Wake Walker, and his brother-in-law Charles Sinclair Walker, (b. 1849). Mrs. Burgoyne marr. (2) 1874 Wilson Fox, see AWL p. 126.

† Mrs. Robertson-Walker's heir at law was John Wilson, husbandman, of Bootle (C), who in 1867 owned land at Goody Bridge, Grasmere.

other Simpson estates. Though he had Wallace cousins, he devised his estates to his wife's nephew, Col the Hon. James Hope (d. 1854, aged 46), who assumed the additional name of Wallace (GEC; HCC; HHN). *Arms.* Gules a lion rampant Argent within a bordure company of the second and Azure. *Crest.* Out of a ducal coronet Or an ostrich's head and neck Proper holding a horse-shoe in the beak.* *Supporters.* Dexter, A lion per bend dovetailed sinister Sable and Or murally crowned and charged on the shoulder with a cross flory Gold; Sinister, An antelope Proper ducally gorged and chained and charged on the shoulder as the dexter (BGA).

WALLACE. Shield at Hutton John. William Hudleston, Madras Civil Service (1793-1855), marr. 1820 Annette Claire (1802-88), dau. of John Wallace, H.E.I.C.S. (1777-1814);† and his brother Josiah Andrew Hudleston, Madras Civil Service (1799-1865), marr. her sister Susan Eleanor Wallace (d. 1837). *Arms.* Gules a lion rampant Sable (*sic*) charged on the shoulder with a ?ermine spot Argent.

WALPOLE. Lady Catherine Walpole‡ (1797-1867), 7th dau. of Horatio, 2nd Earl of Orford, marr. 1822 Henry Hawes Long, of Hampton Lodge, Surrey. Their eldest dau. Charlotte Caroline Georgiana (1823-96) marr. 1849 Henry Howard, of Greystoke Castle and Thornbury Castle, Glos. (1802-75), *q.v.* From Horatio, 1st Baron Walpole, of Wolterton (1678-1757), younger brother of the 1st Earl of Orford, was descended Sir Hugh Seymour Walpole, C.B.E., of Brackenburn, Borrowdale, novelist (1884-1941), elder son of George Henry Somerset Walpole, Bishop of Edinburgh (1854-1929). *Arms.* Or on a fess between two chevrons Sable three cross crosslets of the first (Shield in library at Greystoke Castle). *Crest.* The bust of a man in profile couped at the shoulders Proper ducally crowned Or from the coronet flowing a long cap turned forwards Gules tasselled and charged with a catherine wheel Gold. *Motto.* Sibi constat (BP105).

WALSH, Baron Ormathwaite – see BENN.

WALTON, of Alston. W. H. D. Longstaffe, in a note to the pedigree of Hilton, Baron of Hilton (D), stated that the Waltons, of Alston, gave "the coat of Hilton", i.e. Argent two bars Azure, "surmounted by *a red lion rampant*" (TVN).

WARDEN. Capt George Archibald Warden, 19th and 66th Foot, of Wansfell, Seascale (1841-90), marr. 1863 Isabella Maria (d. 1871), eldest dau. of the Rev. Quintin Dick Hume. He retired 1868 and was later Captain, Carlow Rifles. *Arms* (in brass on family bible). Or a chevron Gules between three pears (Warden); impaling, Quarterly, 1 & 4, Vert a lion rampant Argent (Hulme); 2 & 3, Argent three ravens Vert. *Crest.* Out of a crescent Argent an arrow erect point upwards Sable barbed and flighted Or. *Motto.* Industria et spe (AWL).

WARENNE. A Howard quartering, on shields in Naworth and Greystoke Castles, and elsewhere in Cumbria; Edmund FitzAlan, Earl of Arundel (1285-1326), marr. 1305 Alice (d. *c.* 1338), dau. of William de Warenne

* Field recorded a brass formerly in St. Andrew, Penrith, as showing a snake, not a horsehoe, in the beak (FAC).

† Their son William Hudleston (1826-94) succ. to Hutton John, see Hudleston, of Kelston and Hutton John.

‡ She was a well known novelist.

(d. *v.p.* 1286), and sister and heir of John de Warenne, Earl of Surrey (d. 1347). *Arms.* Chequy Or and Azure.

WARREN, Baron de Tabley. Shield in library at Greystoke Castle; Sir Arthur Keppel Cowell-Stepney, *q.v.*, marr. 1875 the Hon. Margaret Leicester Warren, 4th dau. of George, 2nd Baron de Tabley (1811-87). *Arms.* Chequy Or and Azure on a canton Gules a lion rampant Argent; with the badge of Ulster.

WARTON. Catherine (d. 1710), dau. of Michael Warton, of Beverley (Y), marr. 1658 Eldred Curwen (d. 1673), *q.v.*, and their son Henry Curwen (1661-1725) left the manors of Seaton, Rottington and Stainburn to his cousin Sir Michael Warton (d. *s.p.* 1725, aged 73), who bequeathed them to his great-nephew Charles Pelham, *q.v.* *Arms.* Or on a chevron Azure a martlet between two pheons of the field. *Crest.* On the stump of a tree couped and sprouting a squirrel sejant all Proper holding in his paws a nut Or (CVY). Burke records the squirrel as collared Gold (BGA).

WARWICK, of Warwick. According to FCW, Ranulph de Meschines gave the manor of Warwick to Odard, who also got the manor of Corby from Hubert and Robert de Vaux. Odard, sometimes called de Corkeby, was living 1130. His son William (d. *c.* 1195), gave the advowson of Warwick to Wetheral Abbey. His descendants adopted the surname Warwick. Thomas Warwick (d. *v.p.* 1624-25) was Mayor of Carlisle. His grandson Thomas (1643-89) was father of John Warwick (d. 1720), who was agent to Lord Carlisle. He marr. Mary (d. 1729), dau. of Francis Howard, of Corby, and had a son Francis Warwick (d. 1772), the last male.* He marr. 1736 his cousin Jane (1715-88), dau. of Thomas Howard, of Corby; she entertained Prince Charles Edward Stuart at Warwick Hall in 1745 (CW2 lix). The estates passed to Francis Warwick's kinsman, Ralph Maddison (1744-78), 2nd son of the Rev. Thomas Maddison, of Gateshead (1700-72), who was son of John Maddison and Mary Warwick, his wife. The above Ralph Maddison and his younger brother John (1749-84) assumed the surname Warwick. Their sister and heir Sarah (1741-74) marr. 1763 Thomas Bonner (1720-98), of High Callerton (N), and their son Robert Bonner (b. 1766), High Sheriff of Cumberland 1803, succ. to the estates and assumed the surname Warwick 1792. He became bankrupt 1822 and the Warwick Hall estate was sold to Thomas Parker, *q.v.*, for £45,000. His eldest son Francis Warwick (1802-57), Bengal Army, was killed in the Indian Mutiny; his 3rd son John (1805-81) succ. to Callerton Hall, and was succ. by his only son Robert Maddison Warwick, M.A. (Cantab) (1853-1931). *Arms.* Azure three lions rampant Argent.† *Crest.* A dexter arm embowed in armour the hand gauntletted holding a battle axe (FCW). Lysons record this as: A dexter arm couped at the shoulder in armour holding in the gauntlet a battle-axe all Proper (LMC).

* His sister Ann died at Warwick unmarr. 1774. The *Newcastle Courant* described her as "an ancient maiden lady of the Roman Catholic persuasion but always much respected for her candour, moderation and charitable disposition towards those who differed from her in religious principles."

† On the monument in Carlisle Cathedral to Jane (d. 1832, aged 32), widow of Sir Frederick Treise Morshead, Bart., *q.v.*, and Anne (d. 1823, aged 21) 2nd & 3rd daus. of Robert Warwick (formerly Bonner), above, the arms appear quarterly, as follows: Quarterly, 1, Warwick; 2, Gules a lion passant between two escallops in pale [Argent] (Bonner); 3, Or two battle axes in saltire [Sable]; 4, Argent a chevron between three martlets Sable (Maddison). MMD records for Warwick: Vert a lion rampant Argent (?Ermine).

WARWICK, of Warwick Bridge. In Harl. MS. 1536 the quartered coat of this family appears as follows. *Arms.* Quarterly, 1 & 4, Argent three leaves Vert; 2 & 3, Vert a lion passant Argent (FVC).

WARWICK, of Holmegate and Clarkshill. Helen Warwick, gentlewoman, wife of Thomas Warwick, of Holmegate, Warwick, was a recusant in 1589. Thomas Warwick bought Clarkshill, Lanercost, 1729, and it descended to James Warwick (d. 1763, aged 56), whose brother Thomas Warwick (d. *s.p.* 1768, aged 66) was of Holmegate, where he was succ. by James's son Thomas (d. 1780, aged 45). Clarkshill descended to another son, James, who sold it 1784. *Arms.* . . . three lions rampant . . . . *Crest.* A hand holding a battle axe blade to the dexter and downwards (Tombstones at Warwick and Lanercost).

WARWICK, of Irthington. George Warwick, junior, of Irthington, yeoman, died 1776, aged 58. *Arms.* . . . three lions rampant . . . . *Crest.* An arm embowed in armour holding a battle-axe blade to the sinister and upwards (Gravestone, Irthington churchyard).

WARWICK – see BONNER.

WASDALE. James Wasdale, of Kirkoswald, a native of Wasdale Head, where his family is said to have lived for several generations, had an only son, Dr. John Wasdale, of Carlisle, and of St. Martin's in the Fields, London, who in 1803 obtained a grant of *Arms.* Argent on a chevron Gules between two garbs Vert in chief and a lion's head erased Ermines in base three cross crosslets fitché Or. *Crest.* A demi lion Argent holding in his paws a staff entwined by a serpent Proper (CA xxii/277).

WASHINGTON, of Dacre Lodge. Lt-Col Timothy John Clulow Washington, M.C., 9/12th Royal Lancers, of Dacre Lodge, son of Peter Washington, of Pine Farm, Wokingham, Berks., marr. Margaret Helen, younger dau. and coheir of Major Edward William Hasell, *q.v.* *Arms.* Argent two bars Gules in chief three mullets of the second. *Crest.* Out of a ducal coronet Or an eagle wings endorsed Sable. *Motto.* Volo valeo.

WATERTON. The Very Rev. Canon George Webb Waterton, M.R. (1842-1911), was youngest son of Henry Waterton, of Wansford Lodge (Ch), and a descendant of Sir Thomas More. Ordained 1866, he was priest at the Roman Catholic chapel in Chapel Street, Carlisle, and was later from 1879 until 1907 Rector of the Church of Our Lady and St. Joseph, Warwick Road, Carlisle, which was built during his ministry. He was Canon of Hexham from 1886. Retiring in 1907 he was chaplain at St. Joseph's Home, Botcherby, of which he was the founder, and where he died. *Arms.* Barry of six Ermine and Gules over all three crescents Sable. *Crest.* An otter passant holding in its mouth a pike all Proper. *Motto.* Better kinde frembd than frembd kyen (BLG6).

WATKIN. Field recorded the following for this name on a tombstone at Bridekirk, without further details. *Arms.* Azure a wolf rampant Argent. *Crest.* A lion's head erased (FAC).

WATKINS. Robert Arundel Watkins (d. Penrith 1946, aged 91), one of the 20 children of the Rev. Bernard Edward Watkins, M.A. (Oxon), of Lawkland Hall (Y). Rector of Treeton (Y) 1846-77, was for many years agent to the Gorst family at Castle Combe, and lived for several years at Redmire, Troutbeck (C). His son Rear-Admiral Geoffrey Robert Sladen Watkins, R.N., D.S.O. (1885-1950), was Chief Naval Staff Officer at Gibraltar in

1939, and later British Naval Liaison Officer to the C. in C., French naval forces in the Mediteranneann.* His son Geoffrey Robert Gordon Watkins, R.N. (retd.) (b. 1910), is of Manoir de Kerville, Reux 14130, Pont l'Evêque, Calvados, France. *Arms.* Gules on a cross fleuretté between four demi griffins Or five pierced cinquefoils Azure. *Crest.* A cubit arm erect the hand grasping a tilting spear in bend sinister Proper. *Motto.* Spes tutissima coelis. (*Ex inf.* Mrs. Rosemary Methuen, elder daughter of the above named Rear-Admiral Watkins).

WATSON, of Alston and Castle Carrock. John Watson, of Snappergill, Alston Moor (d. 1748), was grandfather of John Watson, of Snappergill and Garth Foot, Castle Carrock (1759-1835), who marr. 1789 Margaret (d. 1832), dau. and coheir of James Hodgson, of Garth Foot. Their son Joseph (1789-1866) inherited Snappergill and Garth Foot, and was of Penn Manor, Bucks. Co., Pennsylvania. His grandson John, of San Antonio, Texas (1868-1944), succ., but died *s.p.* John Watson (1790-1880), brother of the above Joseph, was of Talkin, and his son John (1818-71) was of Bombay, and of Orton Park, Orton, and Gelt Hall, Castle Carrock. He was succ. by his son, the Rev. Alfred Ralph Watson, M.A. (Cantab), of Orton Park (1856-1900), whose grandson Arthur Ralph Cecil Watson, M.A. (Cantab), is now head of the family. *Arms.* Per fess Ermine and Azure three crescents in fess between as many martlets Or. *Crest.* A griffin's head erased Argent gorged with an antique crown and holding in the beak a lotus flower slipped Or. *Motto.* Mea gloria fides.

WATSON, of Braystones. Henry Hough Watson, J.P., F.C.S., of Braystones, St. Bees (1810-86), eldest son of John Watson (d. 1851), was born at Bolton-le-Moors. He marr. 1852 Jane, dau. of William Atkinson, of Sellafield, and had sons John Dalton Watson, J.P., of Carleton Green, Drigg (1853-1903), and William Henry Watson, J.P., F.G.S., of Braystones and Steelfield Hall, Gosforth (1859-1934). *Crest.* A dexter arm in armour embowed holding in the gauntlet a palm branch all Proper. *Motto.* Veritas (FBC).

WATSON, of Easton. Christopher Watson held land at Easton of Sir Leonard Dacre in 1581. Simon Watson, of Easton, marr. 1748 Deborah James, of Scaleby, and was grandfather of Christopher Watson, of Marsh House (d. 1859, aged 68), who farmed 210 acres at Easton. His 4th son, the Rev. Howard Watson, B.A. (Cantab)† (1841-1911), Vicar of Water Orton, Warwickshire 1871-1911, was father of the Rev. Sydney Montague Watson (1874-1962), Rector of St. Maurice, Winchester, whose dau. Kathleen marr. Frederick Rusden Newell, *q.v.* *Crest.* An arm embowed in armour holding in the gauntlet a palm branch Vert. *Motto.* Fiat justitia (*Ex inf.* the Rev. G. F. W. Newell).

WATSON, of Stoneraise. John Watson, of Stoneraise, Westward, a Captain of Foot at the seige of Carlisle in Charles I's army, descended from John

* Much of his service was in submarines. When he sank a German U-boat in 1917 it was the first time one submarine had torpedoed another. He ended World War I by receiving the surrender of the German submarines, and did the same thing a generation later. The *Daily Telegraph* said of him: "At Toulon he was the only British official for five days when France collapsed. Collecting all the ships he could find, he sent home stranded Britons and himself escaped to Algiers in a flying boat with only minutes to spare. He liberated nine British ships the French were holding for the purpose of bargaining with the Germans".

† He rowed for Cambridge in 1864, and weighed twenty-four stone.

Watson, of Carlisle, *temp.* Henry VIII, was father of Jonathan Watson, J.P., of Pall Mall Court, London (d. 1722), who obtained a grant of arms 1720. He left his Cumberland estate at Lownthwaite to his sister Alice Asbridge in trust for his sons Jonathan and John. The former marr. Elizabeth, sister and heir of Lt-Col Jonathan Bullock, of Faulkborn, Essex (d. 1809), and had a son Jonathan Josiah Christopher Watson (d. 1832) who assumed the name and arms of Bullock 1810. His descendant Walter Henry Bullock (1861-1924) sold Faulkborn (BLG17, *sub* Parker, of Radwinter; BBF). *Arms.* In his application for a grant of arms, Jonathan Watson stated that his ancestors bore: Argent a fess Gules in chief two crosses bottoné of the second; and for *Crest.* A dexter arm embowed in armour Proper holding a broken shackbolt Sable. He was granted: *Arms.* Argent a fess embattled and two crosses bottoné in chief Gules. *Crest.* A dexter arm embowed in armour Proper garnished Or holding a palm branch Vert (CA vii/41).

WATSON, of Cumberland, Kent and London. No other details given. *Arms.* Argent a fess Gules in chief three crosses bottoné of the second. *Crest.* On a mount Vert a palm tree Or (BGA).

WATTS. Richard Watts, J.P. (d. 1864) was of Clifton House (which he built 1824), Great Clifton. He marr. 1827 Mary (b. 1792), dau. of Thomas Falcon, and was succ. by her nephew, the Rev. Thomas William Falcon (see Steward). *Arms.* Azure three arrows points downward Argent on a chief Or as many negroes' heads couped Sable. *Crest.* A greyhound passant Proper collared Sable holding in the dexter paw an arrow in bend point downwards Argent (*Ex inf.* Cdr H. W. Falcon-Steward).

WATTS, of Hawkesdale Hall. The long pedigree of the Rev. William Watts, J.P. (1716-89) in WCW states that he was son of Capt Charles Watts, Royal Life Guards (d. 1745), for whom the claim is made that he was descended from Sir John le Fleming (d. 1320-21), Lord of Wath on Dearne (Y), whose descendant John was known as de Wath or Wathes. The Rev. William Watts' ordination papers, however, show that he was son of Thomas Watts, of Penrith, where he was baptised 1716. He was Curate of Bolton (W) 1743 and of Holy Trinity, Whitehaven 1747-57, and Rector of Moresby 1754-89. He marr. 1750 Mary (d. 1782, aged 61), dau. of Clement Nicolson, of Whitehaven, and niece and heir of John Nicolson, of Hawkesdale Hall, Dalston. Their son the Rev. Clement Watts, B.A. (Oxon) (1756-96), was Vicar of Holm Cultram 1783-96 and had a son John Nicolson Watts (1782-1815), who was in the Madras Civil Service from 1796 until his death. He was succ. by his eldest son John James Watts, of Hawkesdale Hall (b. 1803, living 1860), who had a dau. and heir Mary (WCF). *Arms.* Quarterly, 1 & 4, Argent a fess and in chief two cross crosslets Gules; 2 & 3, Ermine on a chief Gules a bezant between two billets Or. *Crest.* A lozenge Gules between two wings elevated Or (BGA). Whellan gives three cross crosslets in Quarters 1 & 4, and for *Crest.* A dexter arm embowed in armour Proper grasping in the gauntlet an amphisboena Or langued Gules (WCW). On a shield in the billiard-room at Brunstock House, the arms appear as: Quarterly, 1 & 4, Argent a fess and in chief two cross crosslets fitché Gules; 2 & 3, Ermine on a chief Gules an annulet between two billets Or.

WAUGH. John Waugh, of Scattergate, Appleby, yeoman (d. 1690), was father of the Rt Rev. John Waugh, M.A., D.D. (Oxon) (1655-1734), who was Rector of St. Peter, Cornhill, 1704-34, Dean of Gloucester 1720, and

The arms of John Whelpdale, dated 1580, over the door of the Gloucester Arms, Penrith

Bishop of Carlisle 1723-34. His only son the Very Rev. John Waugh, M.A., D.C.L. (Oxon) (*c.* 1703-65), was Rector of Caldbeck 1727-65, Vicar of Stanwix 1727-65, Prebendary of Carlisle and Chancellor 1727-65, and Dean of Worcester 1751-65. In 1728 he marr. Isabella, dau. of the Very Rev. Thomas Tullie, *q.v.*, and coheir of her brothers, from whom she inherited Tullie House, Carlisle, and Wetheral Abbey. Their only son the Rev. John Waugh, M.A. (1730-77), was vicar of Bromsgrove, Worcs., and Prebendary of Carlisle 1768-77. His coheirs were his sisters who played an important part in the social life of Carlisle, entertaining at Tullie House and at Wetheral; they were Judith (1731-99), Isabella (1735-1809), Elizabeth (1737-1814), Mary (1739-1815), and Margaret (1743-1803). *Arms.* BBE gives two coats: Ermine a cross pattée Argent; and, Argent on a chevron Sable three bezants. Both Burke and Field give: Argent on a chevron Gules three bezants (BGA; FAC); as does Henry Wagner in his pedigree in CW1 xiii.

WAVERTON. Denton says that the de Wavertons were descendants of the Lords of Wigton, and owned Great and Little Waverton. They were benefactors of Holm Cultram, and the Abbey register records a gift of land by Lambert, son of Gillestephen de Waverton. Adam, son of Gamel de Waverton, was living in the early 13th century, and the family became extinct in the male line *temp.* Edward II, the heiress Agnes, dau. of Hugh Waverton, of Waverton, marrying William Dykes, *q.v. Arms* (as quartered by Dykes and tricked in MMD). Argent three estoiles within a bordure engrailed Gules.*

WELLS. The Rev. William Wells, B.A. (Oxon) (*c.* 1649-99), son of Thomas Wells, of Windermere, was Headmaster of Millom and Whicham Free Grammar School from *c.* 1669 and Vicar of Millom 1670 until his death by drowning on Duddon Sands. He marr. Elizabeth (b. 1651, d. shortly before April 1744), dau. of Thomas Hudleston, of Salthouse, Millom (1606-63), and sister and heir of Barrentine Hudleston, of Salthouse (1642-1720). Their children were Hudleston Wells (1672-1745); Margaret (b. 1676), presumably marr. James Morris and had a dau. Elizabeth (d. *s.p.* before 1747); and Dorothy (1686-1730), marr. 1714 John Bigland, of Bigland (1690-1747). *Arms* (as wrongly quartered with those of Bigland on Dorothy Bigland's monument in Cartmel Priory). Argent a chevron voided Azure between three flames of fire Proper.

WERE. Thomas Were, of Burrington, Devon, had a dau. and heir Mary, who marr. Richard Hall Clarke, whose son John Were Clarke, *q.v.*, was father of Eliza Were, wife of Timothy Fetherstonhaugh, *q.v. Arms* (as quartered by Clarke in The College, Kirkoswald, and Kirkoswald church). Argent on a bend Vert between six cross crosslets fitché Gules three croziers Or. In Kirkoswald church the croziers are Argent.

WESSEX. Shield at Hutton-in-the-Forest; a Vane quartering. *Arms.* Gules a griffin segreant Or.

WEST. The Rev. Lewis West, M.A. (Cantab) (d. 1667), 3rd son of Francis

* Field suggests that a coat on the ceiling of Carlisle Cathedral, which he blazoned as: Azure three stars within a bordure engrailed Or, may have been intended for Waverton, having originally been: Or three stars of six points and a bordure engrailed Gules (FAC; MMD). It is admittedly very difficult to record the coats on the ceiling accurately owing to their situation, but the present writers interpreted this coat as: Sable three mullets and a bordure engrailed Or, i.e. Wigton, *q.v.*

West, of Hunskelf (Y), was Vicar of Addingham 1635-46 and 1661-67, Prebendary of Carlisle 1636-67, and Archdeacon of Carlisle and Rector of Great Salkeld 1660-67. *Arms.* Argent a fess dancetté between three leopards' faces Sable a crescent for difference (FVY). Burke gives the arms quartered by Fenton, of Underbank (Y), as: Argent a fess dancetté in chief three leopards' heads Sable (BLG 1847; BLG4).

WESTOLL. James Westoll, of Sunderland (d. 1895), had an only son James Westoll, J.P., of High Coniscliffe and The Cloisters, Sunderland (1860-1929), who was father of James Westoll, J.P., B.A. (Cantab) (1889-1969), who settled at Glingerbank, Longtown, and was High Sheriff of Cumberland 1933. His elder son James Westoll, D.L., J.P., M.A. (Cantab), barrister at law, of Dykeside, Longtown, was High Sheriff 1964. He was the last Chairman of Cumberland County Council, serving from 1958 until 1974, and the first Chairman of Cumbria County Council. *Arms.* Per fess Sable and Argent on a fess dovetailed Or a fess Gules charged with three roses Argent barbed and seeded Proper between in chief a horse courant of the second and in base a falcon close of the first belled Or. *Crest.* Between two cinquefoils Or a cubit arm erect vested Azure cuffed Argent holding in the hand a falcon close Proper belled Or. *Motto.* Nisi Dominus frustra.

WESTON. Sir Francis Weston, of Sutton Place, Surrey (?1511-36), marr. Anne, dau. and heir of Sir Christopher Pickering, *q.v.*, and was beheaded on a charge of misconduct with Queen Anne Boleyn. His son Sir Henry sold his moiety of Scaleby Castle 1586. A descendant, John Joseph Webbe-Weston (1784-1840), marr. 1811 Caroline, dau. and heir of Charles Graham, of Netherby, *q.v. Arms.* Ermine on a chief Azure five bezants. *Crest.* A Saracen's head couped the tongue protruding Proper wreathed about the temples Argent and Azure (BGA).

WHARTON. The Wharton family, of Wharton (W), for fuller details of which see AWL, acquired the manor of Croglin (C) by marr. *temp.* Edward I to a dau. and coheir of Philip Hastings, of Croglin. It remained in the family until after the death *s.p.m.s.* 1731 of Philip, Duke of Wharton (NB ii 433). *Arms.* Sable a maunch Argent* and (as an augmentation granted to the 1st Lord Wharton, 1553) a bordure engrailed Or charged with lions' gambs erased in saltire Gules armed Azure (FCW; NB i 561; MMS vi 397; GEC). *Crest.* A bull's head erased (NB). Burke gives this as: A bull's head erased Argent attired Or ducally gorged per pale Gules and Or. See also the monument to the 1st Lord Wharton in Kirkby Stephen church. Burke also gives: A Moor kneeling in coat of mail all Proper ducally crowned Or stabbing himself with a sword of the first hilt and pommel Gold. *Supporters.* Dexter, A bull Argent ducally gorged per pale Or and Gules the dexter horn of the last the sinister Gold; Sinister, A lion Gules fretty Or (BGA). *Motto.* Pleasur in acts darmys (GEC).

WHELPDALE, of Skirsgill and Penrith. This family took its name from a place in the Barony of Liddell. In CW2 xliii Col Haswell has given an account of the family, but it is necessary to counsel caution in using this paper, for it contains many serious misprints. Gilbert de Whelpdale was a juror in 1380 and is perhaps the man whose heirs owned land at Hornsby, Cumwhitton, 1485. Roger Whelpdale, born at or near Greystoke, was

* This unaugmented coat is on a shield on the ceiling of Carlisle Cathedral.

Bishop of Carlisle 1419-22, and there is a brass in Greystoke church to John Whelpdale, LL.D. (d. 1526), who was master of the College there after 1518 until death and Rector of Caldbeck 1488, succeeding a namesake. In Penrith John Whelpdale (d. 1596), one of the original governors of Queen Elizabeth Grammar School 1564, lived in Dockray Hall, now the Gloucester Arms, where his initials and date 1580 and coat of arms are still to be seen; Susan his wife (d. 1604) appears to have been a Carleton (see *Arms*, below). Their descendant William Whelpdale (1576-1652) marr. (2) Bridget (d. 1636), dau. of Robert Burdett, *q.v.* Their son John Whelpdale (b. 1611) succ. to Dockray Hall and appears to have acquired the Skirsgill estate, but when he made his will (proved 1664) in 1663, he was of Whinmore (Y), the home of his 2nd wife Sarah Lodge. His son and heir Andrew (d. 1716) was father of, *int. al.,* William, his heir, and Thomas, of whom below. William (d. 1773, aged 82) was succ. by his son Andrew, attorney (1735-78). His freehold estates were ordered to be sold peremptorily by order of the Court of Chancery 1787; they were presumably bought by his brother Col Thomas Whelpdale, 25th Foot (d. 1792, aged 57), who was High Sheriff of Cumberland 1787, and the last of the family to live at Skirsgill. His son Andrew, of Battersea (1773-1830), was clerk to the Government Tax Office. His son Walter Hutchinson Whelpdale (1817-86) succ. his kinsman John de Whelpdale (see *post*) but rapidly dissipated his fortune, and in 1848 it was said of him that he "is a ruined man and there will not be sixpence for him to live upon after payment of interest upon the monies he is owing." In 1849 he wrote to his trustees saying that he had changed his name to W. H. Willis "to avoid recognition." He was the last of the family and died *s.p.* The above mentioned Thomas Whelpdale (1695-1756), son of Andrew (d. 1716), was a prosperous Penrith attorney and moneylender and was steward to the Duke of Portland 1721-56. He was the builder of the house in Penrith known as the Mansion House. His dau. and heir Elizabeth (1722-94) marr. without his consent John Richardson,* attorney, of Penrith (1725-80), and their son John Richardson, D.L., H.E.I.C.S. (1760-1844), assumed the surname Whelpdale 1794, later calling himself de Whelpdale. He was Lt-Col of the Loyal Leath Volunteers and in 1809 Lt-Col Commanding the Penrith regiment of the Cumberland Militia. He was High Sheriff 1804, and in addition to his large estate in and around Penrith, owned Armathwaite Hall in Hesket-in-the-Forest parish. He died *s.p.*, leaving his fortune and estates to his kinsman Walter Hutchinson Whelpdale, see above (Whelpdale family papers in Record Office, Carlisle; CW2 lii). *Arms.* Argent three greyhounds courant in pale Gules collared Or (MMS vi 421; FVC; LMC; Brass, Greystoke church, where the collars are belled; Lintel, Gloucester Arms, Penrith†). BBE records two coats for Bishop Whelpdale, viz. Argent three wolves passant in pale Gules on the first a mullet Or; and, Argent three greyhounds courant in pale Gules collared Azure. *Crest.* Field recorded the seal of John de Whelpdale as Sheriff, 1804, as bearing: A stag trippant (FAC).

* Son of William Richardson, of Halton (L).

† In the Gloucester room of the Gloucester Arms, the arms of Whelpdale are in plaster on the ceiling, impaling: Ermine on a bend sinister . . . three pheons . . . . This is clearly intended for Carleton, and since the achievement apparently dates from the time of John Whelpdale (d.1596), it seems probable that his wife Susan was a Carleton. The artist blundered and reversed the bend.

WHINNOW. This family took their name from Whinnow in Thursby parish. Simon and Isabella de Quynhou occur in 1304 (CW2 xxv 318). Sir Gilbert Whinnow* had a dau. and heir Margaret, who marr. Sir John Crofton, of Crofton, *q.v.*; their dau. and heir marr. Isold Brisco (FCW). *Arms.* Per pale Argent and Sable a fleur-de-lys counterchanged (FVC).

WHINYATES. General Sir Edward Charles Whinyates, K.C.B., R.A. (1782-1865), 3rd son of Major Thomas Whinyates, Bengal Army, lived for a time at Hayton, Carlisle, when he commanded the Royal Artillery, Northern District, 1840-51 (1851 Census; DNB; HBO). *Arms.* Paly of six Or and Azure a bordure gobony of the first and Gules on a chief Ermine a lion passant Gules between two spur rowels upwards Gules. *Crest.* In front of an anchor erect Sable a cubit arm holding a sword Proper pommel and hilt Or. *Motto.* Loyal en tout (FD 1895).

WHITE. The Rt. Rev. Francis White, M.A., D.D. (Cantab) (*c.* 1565-1638), was Dean of Carlisle 1622-26, Bishop of Carlisle 1626-29, Bishop of Norwich 1629-31, and Bishop of Ely 1631-38. *Arms* On a portrait of Bishop White when Dean of Carlisle, aged 59, these appear as: Argent a chevron Azure between three boars' heads couped .... BBE gives: Gules a chevron between three boars' heads couped Argent. Burke gives the same, with the addition of a bordure engrailed Argent (BGA).

WHITE, of Eskbank. John White, of Eskbank, died 1708, aged 52. *Arms.* ... three roses in fess ... between three boars' heads erased ..., one and two, the one in chief to the sinister, the two in base turned outward (Gravestone, Kirkandrews-on-Esk churchyard).

WHITE, of Keswick. Isaiah White, of Keswick (d. 1793, aged 67), marr. Ann, dau. of William Key, *q.v.*, and had a son William White (1753-1811), who is described on a monument in Crosthwaite church as late of Bombay. *Arms.* Per pale Or and Azure on a fess engrailed Argent between three greyhounds courant counterchanged a fleur-de-lys between two lozenges Gules. *Crest.* An arm embowed Or banded at the wrist and elbow Gules (Monument in Crosthwaite church).

WHITE. Robert le Rougetel White, B.Arch. (Liverpool), A.R.I.B.A., A.M.T.P.I., L.R.A.M., of Cross Gates, Lorton, son of Robert Prosser White, M.D. (Edin) (1855-1934), is descended from Joseph White, of Sutton Hall (Ch) (1736-1818). *Arms.* Argent two escallops in fess Sable and in base a buck trippant Proper attired Or on a chief azure a bezant between two bees volant also Proper. *Crest.* On a mount Vert a buck trippant per pale Argent and Proper attired Or the dexter foreleg bearing a flagstaff in bend sinister also Proper thereon hoisted a banner Gold fringed and charged with an escallop Gules. *Motto.* Sedule et prospere (BLG15; Window in Crosby-on-Eden church).

WHITEHAVEN, Town of. The town uses, without authority, a differenced version of the arms of Lowther, *q.v.*, and an undifferenced version of their crest. *Arms.* Or six annulets, three, two, and one, Sable within a bordure Argent. *Crest.* A dragon passant Argent. *Motto.* Consilio absit discordia.

WHITEHAVEN, CLEATOR & EGREMONT RAILWAY. Incorporated 1854, amalgamated with the Furness and London & North Western Railways 1878. *Device.* Four shields with the fields Vert, portraying (1) A

* Papworth misprints the name as Whitrow.

2–2–2 well tank locomotive; (2) A three-masted sailing ship; (3) A garb; and (4) An ironworks; all Proper (DRH).

WHITEHEAD. The Rev. Robert Whitehead, M.A. (Oxon), of Ormside Lodge (W) (d. 1851, aged 88), was Rector of Musgrave 1807-11, and of Ormside 1811-51, and Perpetual Curate of Hensingham, in succession to his son, 1831-51. He marr. 1789 Jane, only dau. of Christian Albert de Passow, Danish Consul, and had issue, *int. al.*, Jane (d. 1816, aged 24), marr. 1812 Edward Hasell, of Dalemain, *q.v.*, and the Rev. George Davenport Whitehead, M.A. (Oxon) (d. 1864, aged 73), Perpetual Curate of Hensingham 1817-31. *Arms.* Gules a fess between three fleurs-de-lys Argent (Impaled on Edward Hasell's hatchment formerly in Dacre church).

WHITEHEAD – see LAWSON.

WHITELAW, of Ennim. The Rt. Hon. William Stephen Ian Whitelaw, P.C., C.H., M.C., D.L., B.A. (Cantab), of Ennim, formerly Major, Scots Guards, has been M.P. for Penrith and Border since 1955. He was Lord President of the Council and Leader of the House of Comons 1970-72, and Secretary of State for Northern Ireland 1972-73, and has been Deputy Leader of the Opposition since 1975. He is a descendant of Col Samuel Lacy, *q.v.* *Arms.* Sable a chevron engrailed Or between three boars' heads couped Argent armed and langued of the second. *Crest.* A bee erect Proper. *Motto.* Solertia ditat.

WHITFIELD, of Clargill. Ralph Whitfield, descended from the Whitfields, of Whitfield (N), marr. Mary (b. *c.* 1609), dau. of John Teasdale, of Clargill (d. 1627), and apparently thus acquired the estate, which descended to Thomas Whitfield (d. 1773),* High Sheriff of Cumberland 1747, who was known as the 'Earl' of Clargill, and who marr. 1724 Anne (bap. 1702), dau. of George Mowbray, of Allenheads (N). Their only dau. and heir Anne, 'Countess' of Clargill (d. 1796), marr. 1777 Thomas Graham, M.D. (d. 1789). She died *s.p.*, her heirs being her Mowbray cousins. *Arms.* Machell recorded for Whitfield, of Whitfield, Cumb. (*sic.*): Or a bend Sable between two bendlets engrailed of the last (MMS vi 415).

WHITRIGG. Robert de Whitrigg occurs 1291, and a man of the same names, living 1346, marr. *c.* 1320 . . . , dau. and heir of . . . Branthwaite, and acquired the manor of Branthwaite, which passed to his son Sir Thomas, living 1362, who also owned Little Bampton (C). He marr. Elena, sister and coheir of Robert le Brun, *q.v.*, but died *s.p.* and was succ. by his sister Joan, who marr. (1) Thomas Skelton (1328-65) and took Branthwaite to that family (see Skelton, of Branthwaite), and (2) 1367 John Denton. Sir Thomas Whitrigg and Elena are mentioned in the will of Robert Whitrigg (d. 1362), no relationship being specified. Robert also mentions Alice, wife of John de Bampton, *q.v.*, and Robert de Bampton, who were no doubt relatives. *Arms.* Glover's *Ordinary* states that Sir Thomas Whitrigg bore: Argent fretty and a canton Gules, but he may have used the arms of his mother, heiress of the Branthwaite family. Undoubtedly John Denton, *supra*, impaled his wife's arms as: . . . a bend dancetté . . . , see grave slab in Ainstable church, and the Skeltons used as a quartering, almost certainly for Whitrigg: Argent a bend dancetté Azure (TVN).

* The *Newcastle Courant* says that he was buried at Alston "with great funeral pomp, according to the custom of the country: above 700 persons were invited and dined at the house and attended the body to the church."

WIDDRINGTON. Sir John de Widdrington, of one of the oldest Northumbrian families, marr. Christina, dau. and coheir of Sir Adam de Swinburne, *q.v.*, and so acquired Lanerton. Their son Roger settled the manors of Denton and Lanerton in 1367 on his son John (d. *s.p.*) when he married (CW2 lix). *Arms.* Quarterly Argent and Gules a bend Sable (FFC; FVN).

WIGRAM. Oswald Lewis Wigram, of Eden Brae, Armathwaite (1878-1960), was son of Lewis Wigram, M.A. (Oxon) (1844-1915), a descendant of Sir Robert Wigram, 1st Bart., and marr. 1914 Lucy Clare Elaine, dau. of Canon Thomas Wilkinson Stephenson, Vicar of Addingham. Their son, Major Michael Lewis Wigram, R.A. (T.A.), of Lyndhurst Avenue, Mill Hill, London, was educated at St. Bees. *Arms.* Argent on a pale Gules three escallops Or over all a chevron engrailed counterchanged on a chief waves of the sea thereon a ship representing an English vessel of war of the 16th century with four masts sails furled Proper colours flying Gules. *Crest.* On a mount Vert a hand in armour in fess couped at the wrist Proper charged with an escallop and holding a fleur-de-lys erect Or. *Motto.* Dulcis amor patriae (BP105).

WIGTON. Odard de Logis, the Sheriff, living 1130, acquired the mesne manor of Wigton from Waldeve son of Gospatrick. It descended to Odard de Wigton (d. 1238) who also owned the manors of Melmerby, Stainton, Blackhall and the hamlet of Warwick. His grandson John (1264-1315) was the last male of the family. He was unhappily marr. to Dionisia de Luvetot, whom he divorced 1312 because of her pre-contract with John Paynel, but an attempt to declare illegitimate their only child Margaret (1293-1349) failed. She died *s.p.*, having marr. (1) John de Crookdake (d. 1305), *q.v.*; (2) John de Denum; (3) John Gernon (d. 1334); and (4) John de Weston (d. 1343) (CW2 xxvii, xxix). *Arms.* Walter de Wigton, probably of this family, bore at Caerlaverock 1300: Sable three mullets and a bordure indented Or. Another coat gives this as: Sable three mullets and a bordure engrailed Or;* and another as: Sable three fleurs-de-lys and a bordure engrailed Or (FFC).

WILDRY, of Penrith. No other details given. *Arms.* Azure on a chevron between three martlets Or five gouttes Sable (MVC). Burke gives these arms for a family called Wildy (BGA). Field blazoned the gouttes as ermine spots (FAC).

WILKINSON, of Carlisle. Joseph Wilkinson, of Carlisle and Berners Street, London, was father of the Rev. Joseph Wilkinson, B.A. (Oxon) (d. 1831), who was Curate of Irthington and later Perpetual Curate of Monkwearmouth (D) 1793-98, and Rector of East and West Wretham, Norfolk. His son Joseph Wilkinson (b. 1796) was a solicitor of Norwich. The Rev. Joseph's sisters were Elizabeth (d. 1833, aged 71), marr. 1784 William Richard Dacre (see APPELBY); Frances, marr. 1796 George Losh; and Alice, marr. 1798 William Losh. The two last named were sons of John Losh, *q.v. Arms.* . . . a fess Vair between three unicorns passant . . . (Gate-pillars at Woodside).†

* This coat is on the ceiling of Carlisle Cathedral, presumably for Wigton, but it should be noted that Field read it as: Azure three stars within a bordure engrailed Or, and suggests that it may originally have been intended for Parvyng, *q.v.*, or Waverton, *q.v.*

† Field states that the arms on the gate-pillars are: Gules a fess Vair between three unicorns passant Or (FAC), but in fact they are neither hatched nor coloured. These are the arms of Wilkinson, of Wateringbury, Kent, whose crest Field also ascribes to Wilkinson, of Carlisle.

WILKINSON. The Rev. Robert Wilkinson (1752-1839), son of Thomas Wilkinson, of Cockermouth, was Master of Dovenby School 1770-1, Assistant Master of Hipperholme School (Y) 1771, Perpetual Curate of Lightcliffe (Y) 1782, Headmaster of Heath School, Halifax, 1789, and Vicar of Darton 1790. He marr. 1782 Sarah Robinson, of Hipperholme (d. 1833, aged 73). *Arms.* Azure a chevron between three whelks Argent (Wilkinson); impaling, Sable three falcons . . . (Robinson). *Crest.* A demi lion rampant issuant from a mural crown. *Motto.* Unitas (CW2 lxxii 339-40).

WILLIAMS, of Johnby. Roger Williams (d. 1664), who came from St. Nicholas, Glamorgan, became the "learned steward" of the baronies of Greystoke and Burgh, and *c.* 1650 bought Johnby Hall, where he was succ. by his son William (d. 1680), who also succ. him as steward. In his young days he fought for King Charles I. By his wife Barbara, dau. of Miles Halton, *q.v.*, he had four daus. and coheirs: Dorothy (b. 1666), marr. 1696 Sir Edward Hasell, *q.v.*; Lettice (b. 1668), marr. (1) John Winder, *q.v.*, and (2) Joshua Blackwell; Mary (1671-1722), marr. 1697 the Very Rev. Thomas Gibbon, Dean of Carlisle, *q.v.*; and Barbara (1674-1724), marr. 1712 Joseph Relf, of Cockermouth, attorney (d. 1723). *Arms.* On the monument of William Williams in Greystoke church, the arms appear as: Argent a chevron between three fleurs-de-lys Sable; impaling, Argent a lion rampant Gules (presumably for Halton, *q.v.*). The Williams coat is also impaled by Hasell on a monument in Dacre church. In the modern window in Greystoke church on the south side of the sacrarium the arms appear as: Sable a bend between three fleurs-de-lys, two and one, Argent.

WILLIAMSON. The Rev. Joseph Williamson, Vicar of Bridekirk 1625-34, was father of the famous Sir Joseph Williamson, P.C., M.A., LL.D. (Oxon), F.R.S., M.P. (1633-1701), who was born at Bridekirk and educated at St. Bees and Westminster Schools. He was Fellow of the Queen's College, Oxford, Clerk in the Secretary of State's Office, Keeper of the King's Library, and founder of the *London Gazette.* Knighted in 1672, he was Secretary of State 1674-79 and a Commissioner of the Admiralty (DNB). *Arms.* Sir Joseph originally bore: Argent on a chevron engrailed Azure between three trefoils slipped Sable as many crescents Or. In 1670 he received a grant of: Or a chevron engrailed between three trefoils slipped Sable. *Crest.* Out of a ducal crown a demi eagle Gules winged Sable holding in his beak a trefoil slipped also Sable. In 1683 he received as an augmentation a grant of supporters and of a further coat to be quartered with the foregoing, viz. Azure a saltire Argent on a chief Gules a lion passant guardant Or. *Supporters.* Dexter, An eagle close Proper gorged with a ducal coronet beak legs tongue and claws Gules; Sinister, A crane Proper gorged with a like coronet beaked and legged Gules (LNK).* *Motto.* Sub umbra tuarum alarum (BGA).

WILLIAMSON, of Milbeck. John Williamson died 1544, owning the Manor

* A number of variants of the arms are given by various authorities, viz. Argent on a chevron engrailed Azure between three trefoils Vert as many crescents Or (FDC); Sable a chevron engrailed between three trefoils slipped Or (BGA); Argent a chevron engrailed between three trefoils slipped Sable (FAC). A stone achievement on the wall of Beech Cottage, Tallentire, which has clearly been removed there from elsewhere, was probably intended for the above Rev. Joseph Williamson, Vicar of Bridekirk 1623-34. *Arms.* Or a chevron Gules between three trefoils slipped Sable. *Crest.* A griffin's head erased.

of Crosthwaite and houses and lands there and in Keswick, Thornthwaite, Portinscale, Braithwaite and Cockermouth which descended to his son John Williamson (*c.* 1508-58) who was succ. by his son Thomas (b. *c.* 1536). Milbeck descended to Nicholas Williamson (d. 1592), who may have been his son. An inscription over the door of Milbeck apparently refers to his death. A pedigree at p. 144 of FCW gives four generations of this family, which agrees with the details given above, the first John (d. 1544) being shewn as marr. to Isabel, dau. and heir of John Thirkeld, of Mehere or Motherd. In the Braithwaite pedigree at p. 18 of FCW, the latter name appears as Milberton, in Cumberland; Robert Braithwaite, of Ambleside, marr. Alice, dau. of the second John Williamson, above (*c.* 1508-58). *Arms.* Machell recorded the arms of Williamson, of Milbeck, as impaled in a window at Burneside Hall (W): Argent on a chevron engrailed* between three trefoils slipped [Sable] as many crescents Or (CW1 vi 104-5).

WILLIAMSON, of Snittlegarth. Roger Williamson, of Snittlegarth, Torpenhow, marr. 1734 Barbara, dau. of Roger Gregg, of Mirehouse, and sister and coheir of Joseph Gregg. Before 1768 the Gregg estates were divided between the Williamsons and the Storys, Barbara's sister Ann having marr. the Rev. John Story. Threapland Hall became the property of the Williamsons. Roger Williamson was High Sheriff 1776, but Whellan (WCW p. 259) says that "Mr Williamson became embarrassed" *c.* 1816. *Arms.* . . . a chevron engrailed . . . between three trefoils slipped . . . .† *Crest.* A griffin's head erased (Tombstone, Torpenhow churchyard).

WILLIAMSON. Sir Hedworth Williamson, 5th Bart., of Whitburn (D) (d. 1788), High Sheriff of Co. Durham 1747-88, acquired the Lordship of Millom by marr. 1747 to Elizabeth (d. 1793), dau. and co-heir of William Hudleston, of Millom (d. 1745), *q.v.*, and retained it until 1774. *Arms.* Or a chevron Gules between three trefoils slipped Sable. *Crest.* Out of a mural crown Gules a wyvern's head wings endorsed Or (BP105).

WILLIAMSON, of Bankhead. John, son of Thomas Williamson, of Bankhead, Bewcastle, died 1765. *Arms.* . . . a bend . . . (Bewcastle tombstone).

WILLIAMSON, of Brampton. No other details deciphered. *Arms.* . . . two stags' heads erased . . . in dexter base and sinister fess (ABD).

WILLIAMSON. Harl. MS. 1536 gives for Williamson, of Cumberland, with no other details. *Arms.* Argent on a chevron between three trefoils slipped Sable as many crescents Or all within a bordure engrailed of the second (FVC).

WILLIAMSON, of New Hall. No other details given. *Arms.* Argent on a chevron engrailed between three trefoils slipped Azure as many crescents Or (BGA).

WILLIAMSON, of Keswick. No other details given. *Arms.* Or a chevron engrailed between three falcons' heads erased Azure on a chief Gules a fleur-de-lys enclosed by two suns of the first. *Crest.* A falcon's head Or between two wings expanded Azure on each wing a sun Gold (BGA).

WILLIAMSON, of Whitehaven. Field recorded the following for Thomas

* The illustration in EAH depicts the chevron as invected.

†The arms on the tombstone are neither coloured nor hatched, despite Field's blazon of them as: Or a chevron engrailed between three trefoils slipped Sable (FAC). For this coat, see previous entry.

Williamson, of Whitehaven (d. 1745). *Arms.* Or a chevron engrailed Sable between three trefoils slipped (Tombstone, Trinity church, Whitehaven; FAC).

WILLIS. Joseph Willis, of Kirkoswald, shoemaker (d. aged *c.* 46), was father of Richard Willis (1777-1855), a prominent Australian colonist. *Arms* (as used by the family in Victoria). Or on a chevron between three mullets of six points Gules a cross formé of the first. *Crest.* A hind trippant holding in the mouth an oak branch leaved and fructed Or charged on the shoulder with a mullet of six points Or. *Arms* (as used in New South Wales). . . . a chevron . . . charged with three mullets . . . . *Crest.* A hind charged with a mullet (BCG).

WILMER. David Wilmer, of Leamington Priors, Warwick, and Highgate, London, marr. 1834 Isabella (1816-90), 3rd dau. of Capt John Ponsonby, R.N., of Springfield, Egremont. Their son Charles Ponsonby Wilmer (1838-1903) is commemorated in Crosthwaite church by a window given by his widow. He was of Heathfield House, Wimbledon Common, solicitor, and was clerk to the governors of Highgate School 1876-98. *Arms.* Gules a chevron Vair between three eagles displayed Or; impaling, Azure two lions rampant combatant Argent supporting a tower triple-towered of the last (Kelly) (Window, Crosthwaite church).

WILSON, of Demainholm. John Wilson, of Demainholm in Liddesdale, died 1756, aged 69, and was buried at Bewcastle; and Eleanor, his wife, died 1758, aged 73. *Arms.* Bell Irving recorded these on the gravestone as: . . . a chevron . . . between three roses . . . in chief a hound . . . (ABD). Field interpreted the hound as a wolf passant, and gives the place of residence incorrectly as Demesne (FAC).

WILSON, of Evening Hill. John Wilson marr. Tamar Robinson and had a son John (d. 1830) who marr. 1769 Sarah, dau. of Edward Knubley, of Finglandrigg, *q.v.* Their son Lt-Col John Knubley Wilson, D.L., J.P., of Gillhead, near Whitehaven (1785-1862), Royal Cumberland Militia, was later of Evening Hill, Thursby, which he built *c.* 1836. He marr. (1) 1823 Harriet (d. 1828), 8th dau. of Walter Chambre, of Whitehaven, *q.v.,* and (2) 1831 Mary (d. 1875, aged 86), dau. of Henry Jefferson, of Whitehaven, but died *s.p. Arms.* Sable a wolf salient and in chief three estoiles Or. *Crest.* A demi wolf salient Or. *Motto.* Res non verba (BLG 1846).

WILSON, of Flatt. Thomas Wilson, of Flatt, Bewcastle (1723-73), succ. his father John Wilson as owner of that property and of Harvest Bank, Upper Field and Matthew Croft. He marr. 1741 Ann Graham, of Ryehill, but *c.* 1746 he left Bewcastle alone and went to Leghorn, Italy, where he established himself as a ropemaker and ship's chandler. He prospered and owned property in Leghorn and a house in Pisa. His heirs were his daus. Elizabeth (1741-1807), who marr. 1758 James Nixon, of Flatt (d. 1827, aged 92); and Jane (d. 1765), who marr. 1762 John Cleathing, *q.v.,* secretary to the British Consul in Leghorn. Elizabeth's son Thomas Nixon (1763-83) was his chief beneficiary, and in 1773 he assumed the name Wilson. His heir was his brother John Wilson Nixon (b. 1780) who settled in Indiana *c.* 1818 and died there *s.p. c.* 1857. In 1773 Thomas Nixon, on assuming the name Wilson, was granted the following *Arms.* Sable a wolf rampant per fess Ermine and Erminois in chief three estoiles Or. *Crest.* A demi wolf as in the arms (CA xii/273). On Thomas Wilson's monument in the old British

Cemetery, Leghorn, the arms appear as: . . . a wolf salient Or in chief three mullets . . . .

WILSON, of The Gale. The Rev. John Wilson, Rector of Welton, Northants., was father of Ashley Henry Wilson (d. 1854, aged 38), who marr. 1835 Mary (b. 1814), dau. of Richard Jackson, of Moss-side, Holm Cultram, *q.v.* Their only son William Fletcher Wilson, of The Gale, Abbey Town (1840-1922), was, by Esther his wife (d. 1917), father of Charles William Wilson* (1879-1939), who marr. 1911 Amy Elizabeth, dau. and coheir of John Story, of Kirkland House, Wigton, *q.v.*, and had issue Ashley Fletcher Story Wilson of Buckland Newton, Dorset, and Barbara Mary Story Wilson, of Kirkland House, Wigton. *Arms.* Per pale Argent and Azure three lions' gambs erased fessways in pale counterchanged. *Crest.* A lion's head erased Argent gutté de sang (Window in Holm Cultram church).†

WILSON. George Wilson, surgeon and apothecary, of Wigton, was father of the Rev. John Wilson, M.A. (Oxon) (1789-1857), who was Fellow of The Queen's College, Oxford, 1824-36, Tutor 1825-35, Dean 1829 and Bursar 1830, and Rector of Holwell, Dorset, 1835-57. *Arms.* Argent three wolves' heads erased Sable (Shield in window of The Queen's College).

WILSON, of Moot. A gravestone in Arthuret churchyard commemorates George, son of George Wilson, in Moot (d. 1693, aged 29). *Arms.* . . . three wolves' heads couped . . . . *Crest.* A crescent enflamed.

WILSON, of Thornthwaite Grange. Isaac Whitwell Wilson, J.P., of Castle Lodge, Kendal (1833-81), for whose ancestry see AWL, had *int. al.* a 6th son Anthony Bagster Wilson, J.P., M.I.M.E., of Thornthwaite Grange, Keswick, Lord of the Manor of Thornthwaite (b. 1871). His eldest son Anthony Comar Wilson, of Oakley Manor, Basingstoke, Hants. (b. 1903), was father of Struan Wilson, now representative of this branch of the family. *Arms* (of Wilson, of High Wray). Argent a wolf salient Vert on a chief Sable a fleur-de-lys between two estoiles Or. *Crest.* A demi wolf rampant Vert. *Mottoes.* Providentia et labore; Ovium qui velatus (FLP; BGA). Burke also records the following variant: *Arms.* Sable a wolf's head salient (*sic*)‡ Or in chief three mullets of six points Argent. *Crest.* A demi wolf as in the arms. *Motto.* Res non verba (BLG 1851).

WILSON. Impaled by Ponsonby on tablet in Haile church; Miles Ponsonby, D.L., J.P., of Haile Hall (1808-92), *q.v.*, marr. 1837 Barbara (d. 1874, aged 67), 3rd dau. of Christopher Wilson, of Rigmaden (see AWL). *Arms.* Argent a wolf rampant [Sable] on a chief of the last a fleur-de-lys between two estoiles [Or].

WILSON, *post* MORLEY. The Very Rev. Thomas Wilson, M.A., D.D. (Cantab) (d. 1778), was ordained 1742, was Vicar of Torpenhow 1743-78, Prebendary of Carlisle 1743-64, and Dean 1764-78. He marr. 1744 Margaret, younger dau. of John Morley, of Beamsley Hall, and sister and, in her issue, coheir of Josias Morley, of Beamsley. Their elder son the Rev. Thomas

* See SFE.

† Burke records these as the arms and crest of Wilson, of Penrith, Cumberland, and Welborne, Lincs., granted 24 March 1586 (BGA). Field recorded Burke's entry as: *Arms.* Per pale Argent and Azure three lions' gambs erased fesswise counterchanged in the dexter chief a wolf's head erased Sable. *Crest.* On a mount Vert a lion's gamb erased fessways Argent thereon a lion's head couped Erminois (FAC).

‡ This should probably read – a demi wolf salient.

Wilson, M.A. (Oxon) (1748-1812), was Vicar of Corbridge 1773-84, Rector of Distington 1785-1812 and Vicar of Brigham 1797-1812. He succ. to the manors of Clapham and Rathmell on the death of his uncle 1783 when he took the name of Morley. *Arms.* . . . a wolf salient . . . in chief three mullets or estoiles . . . (Seal of Dean Wilson).

WILSON, *post* WALTON-WILSON. John Wilson, of Carrshield, Allendale, was father of John Wilson, of Nent Hall (see below), and of Jacob Wilson, of Alston House (1770-1858),* whose son Joseph Wilson, of Crackenthorpe Hall (1801-76), marr. 1832 Ann, dau. of Joseph Bowstead, of Beckbank (C) and had an eldest son Sir Jacob Wilson, for whom see AWL. The above named John Wilson (1761-1838), proprietor of lead mines, bought Shotley Hall (N), and was ancestor of the Wilson, later Walton-Wilson family of that place, the last of whom, Hugh John Craufurd Walton-Wilson, Lieut R.N. (b. 1915), died on active service 1939. *Arms.* In a window in Shotley church, these appear as: Per pale, Dexter, Purpure a chevron Argent and in chief three mullets Or; Sinister, Argent a wolf rampant Proper. Above the entrance to Nent Hall, they are carved as: . . . a wolf rampant . . . in chief three mullets of six points . . . . *Crest.* A demi wolf rampant Proper (Window, Shotley church; M.I., Alston church). *Motto.* Semper vigilans. In 1880 John Wilson Walton (son of Thomas Walton by Maria, dau. of the above named John Wilson, d. 1838) assumed the additional surname Wilson and obtained grants of arms for Walton and for Wilson: *Arms.* Quarterly, 1 & 4, Sable a wolf salient Argent holding in the mouth an arrow in bend sinister Proper within an orle of ten mullets of six points of the second (Wilson); 2 & 3, Argent three pellets each charged with an ermine spot of the first on a chief dovetailed Gules as many pallets Ermine (Walton). *Crests.* 1, A demi wolf Proper gorged with a collar and chain reflexed over the back Or supporting an arrow in pale also Proper (Wilson); 2, Two arrows in saltire surmounted by another in pale transfixing a stag's head cabossed all Proper (Walton) (CA lxi/57 and 61; Tablet, east end of Shotley church). *Mottoes.* Semper vigilans (Wilson); Possunt quia posse videntur (Walton).

WILTSHIRE. The Rev. Edward Wiltshire, M.A. (Cantab) (d. 1730), was Rector of Kirkandrews-on-Esk 1685-1730. *Arms.* . . . a chevron . . . in chief six crosses pattée, four and two, . . . all within a bordure . . . (Tombstone, Kirkandrews-on-Esk churchyard). The bordure may, however, be intended to be only the outline of the shield, for in 1704 the Rev. Edward Wiltshire sealed with: . . . a chevron . . . in chief six crosses pattée, four and two, ...

WINDER, of Lorton. Peter Winder, of Lorton (living *c.* 1649), was father of John Winder, of Lorton and of Cockermouth (1627-96). His eldest son John Winder, of Gray's Inn, barrister-at-law (d. 1699, aged 47), marr. Lettice, dau. and coheir of William Williams, of Johnby Hall, *q.v.*, and had a son Williams Winder (1690-1766), merchant and Consul at Barcelona 1723-34. *Arms.* Chequy Or and Vert a fess Gules. *Crest.* Out of a ducal coronet Or a bull's head Ermine holding in the mouth a cherry branch slipped and

* His dau. Betty (d. 1883) marr. 1831 Thomas Fair, of Frenchfield, Penrith (d. 1848, aged 53). Their son the Rev. Thomas Wilson Fair, M.A. (Cantab) (d. 1911, aged 68), was Vicar of Eskdale 1904-11. His dau. Mary Cicely Fair (d. 1955, aged 80) was for many years a leading member of the Cumberland & Westmorland Antiquarian & Archaeological Society, to whose *Transactions* she was a prolific contributor. The authors of this book acknowledge with gratitude the financial help they have received from her estate.

fructed all Proper (Plaster overmantel in bedroom at Lorton Hall dated 1630 with initials of Peter and Ann Winder; AWL; John Winder's monument in All Hallows, Barking, dated 1699).

WINDSOR, of Farlam.* Halden, Lord of Catterlen, had a son Uchtred, who succ. him, and also owned Farlam, both of which estates he forfeited because of his adherence to Stephen. He had at least three sons – William de Kersuniere, living 1201, and Walter and Alexander de Windsor. Walter must have regained Farlam, for he gave the church to Lanercost. Denton suggested that from him descended Adam de Farlam, living 1294, but it seems likely that the de Farlams were sub-feoffees of the Windsors, for Solomon de Farlam *c.* 1220 gave land in Farlam to Wetheral Priory, Walter de Windsor being a witness (CW2 xix 92, lxiv 106). William de Windsor was Sheriff of Cumberland 1367. *Arms.* Argent a saltire Sable (DAC). Lysons give: Gules a saltire Argent between twelve cross crosslets Or (LMC). William de Windsor, the Sheriff, bore: Gules a saltire Argent (DSL).

WINTER, of Penrith and Kendal, *post* WINTOUR. . . . Winter, of Penrith, marr. Cecile, dau. and coheir of Mrs. Mary Grame, of Dockray Hall, Penrith* (d. 1659), and had a son Edward Winter, of Elderbeck, Pooley Bridge, mercer (d. 1655), who became a member and treasurer of the Committee for the Propagation of the Gospel in the four Northern Counties 1650, and is described as "a maintainer of Malignant Ministers" (ECW). His son Thomas (1649-89) was a Penrith merchant, and was father of Thomas Winter (b. 1684), a Kendal ironmonger who was Mayor of Kendal 1719. He marr. 1708 Anne, dau. and heir of Lancelot Forth (see p. 394, and had a son Forth Winter, of Ovenden House, Kent, ironmaster (1717-90), whose eldest son Thomas (b. 1754) had changed the spelling of his name to Wintour when he proceeded M.A. (Oxon) 1779. His descendant is Miss L. Marjorie M. Wintour, of Bristol. *Arms.* Sable a fess Ermine. *Crest.* A cubit arm erect habited holding in the hand three ostrich feathers (Seal). Burke gives these arms and crest for Winter, of Glos. and Worcs. (BGA).

WINTER, of Alston. No other details given. *Arms.* Sable a fess Ermine in chief a crescent Argent (BHI, *sub* GRAY).

WISEMAN. Impaled by Salkeld, *q.v.*, on the tablet in Kirkland church commemorating Joseph Salkeld, of Holme Hill (1765-1835), and his wife, Margaret Wiseman (d. 1872, aged 83). *Arms.* Sable a chevron Ermine between three chessrooks.

WITHAM. Impaled by Howard, *q.v.*, on seals at Corby Castle; Philip Howard, of Corby Castle (1730-1810), marr. 1754 Ann (d. 1794), eldest dau. of Henry Witham, of Cliffe (Y). *Arms.* Or a bend Gules between three pewits Sable.

WOLFRIC. Shield at Hutton-in-the-Forest; a Vane quartering. *Arms.* Azure a chevron between three swans' wings elevated Argent.

WOLLASTON. Jefferson states that the surname of Elizabeth (d. 1419), who marr. Sir Richard Musgrave, was probably Wollaston, since the arms of that family are quartered by the Musgraves. *Arms.* Argent three mullets Sable (JLW pp. 411-3).

* There seems no ground for Field's statement that this family was a cadet branch of the south country Windsors.

* Now the Two Lions.

WOOD. Abigail Wood (d. 1741), presumably dau. of Henry Wood, of Woodend, Lamplugh, and baptised there 1709, marr. 1732, when she is described as of High Cross, Loweswater, Daniel Dickinson, of Streetgate, *q.v.* *Arms* (impaled by Dickinson on silver cup at Redhow). Argent an oak tree fructed [Proper]. *Crest.* Issuing from clouds a sinister hand holding a leaf slipped.

WOOD. Impaled by Senhouse in photograph of portrait in the Record Office, Carlisle (D/Crerar/77F22); Humphrey Senhouse, of Netherhall (1731-1814), *q.v.*, marr. 1768 Catherine, dau. of Thomas Wood, of Beadnell (N). *Arms.* Azure on a bend Argent three fleurs-de-lys Sable each charged with as many bezants.

WOODFORD. The widow of Lord William Gordon (see Conway) gave in 1834 his Derwentwater estate,* including the house called Derwent Bay, Portinscale, to his nephew Major General Sir John George Woodford, K.C.B., K.C.H., Grenadier Guards (1785-1879), a Peninsular veteran. He was son of Col John Woodford (d. 1800), who marr. 1778 Susan, eldest dau. of the 3rd Duke of Gordon, and widow of John, 9th Earl of Westmorland (GEC; TGG). *Arms.* Sable three leopards' faces reversed jessant-de-lys Argent.† *Crest.* A naked savage wreathed about the head and waist in the dexter hand a club in the sinister a palm branch in bend all Proper. *Motto.* Libertate quietem (BGA).

WOODHALL. John Woodhall, of Papcastle (d. 1728), marr. Elizabeth (1685-1727), dau. of Richard Lamplugh, of Ribton (d. 1705), *q.v.*, and in her issue heir of her nephew Richard Lamplugh (1707-64). Their only child Frances (1711-40) marr. 1731 John Brougham, of Cockermouth (1705-82), by whom she had Peter Brougham, later Lamplugh, *q.v.*, who died *s.p.*, and Mary (d. 1785), who marr. 1769 Frecheville Dykes, *q.v.* *Arms.* Burke gives for Woodhall, of Cockermouth: Argent a cross moline Gules in the first quarter an ermine spot Sable (BGA). Dykes, however, quarters for Woodhall: Per fess indented Or and Azure two bars between three crescents counterchanged (see p. 99, above).

WOODHEAD-KEITH-DIXON – see DIXON.

WOODHEAD. At Lorton Hall there is a copy of the grant of arms dated 1898 to Henry Woodhead, of The Gardens, Cape Town, Cape of Good Hope, Major in the Duke of Edinburgh's Own Volunteer Rifle Corps, eldest son of Sir John Woodhead, late of Holm Firth, Sea Point, Cape Town, Mayor of Cape Town 1887, 1889, 1894 and 1897. *Arms.* Per chevron nebuly Argent and Azure two oak trees in chief and in base an African bush buck's head and neck affronté and erased all Proper. *Crest.* An African bush buck's head couped Proper gorged with the battlements of a tower Or between on the dexter side an oak branch fructed Proper and on the sinister a rose Argent stalked and leaved Vert. *Motto.* Aequo animo.

WOODHOUSE. William Woodhouse (b. 1788) marr. 1817 Sarah Dorothy (b. 1797), 2nd dau. of the Rev. Humphrey Hervey, Vicar of Bridekirk, and had a son Capt William Hervey Woodhouse, of Armathwaite Castle, and Irnham Hall, Lincs. (1823-59), whose dau. and heir Isabel Hervey (d. 1911)

* Part of the estate, called Brandlehow Park and covering 108 acres, was acquired by the National Trust in 1902 – its first Lake District property (TLD).

† Elsewhere Burke gives this as: Sable three leopards' faces reversed Gules swallowing as many fleurs-de-lys Argent (BEB).

marr. 1889 Capt John Wolrige-Gordon. *Arms.* Per pale Or and Gules two chevronels engrailed between three cinquefoils all counterchanged. *Crest.* A demi griffin couped Azure semé of cinquefoils Or and holding with its claws a bird bolt Proper. *Motto.* Virtus in arduis (BLG11).

WOODROUFFE SMITH. On an escutcheon of pretence on a tablet in Stanwix church commemorating Maria Woodrouffe (d. 1854, aged 59), wife of George Head, of Rickerby House, *q.v.*, and dau. and heir of Thomas Woodrouffe Smith, of Stockwell Park, Surrey. *Arms.* . . . on a chevron . . . three stags' heads erased . . . a chief . . . charged with five billets . . . .

WOOLEY. John Wooley, M.A., Dean of Carlisle 1577-95, is described as Esquire and not in Holy Orders. He was buried in St. Paul's Cathedral (NB ii 304). *Arms.* Field gives, quoting BGA as authority: Argent on a chevron Sable an eagle with two heads displayed of the field. The entry in BGA assigns these arms to Wolley, of Leigh, Dorset, and Pirford, Surrey. In his unpublished TS., *Surrey Coats of Arms*, Field quotes Dugdale's *History of St. Paul's* as authority for: Argent on a chevron Sable an eagle displayed of the first, as authority for the arms of Sir John Wolley, Dean of Carlisle (d. 1596).

WORDSWORTH. John Wordsworth, of Cockermouth, attorney (1741-83), steward to Lord Lonsdale and coroner for the seignory of Millom, was father of William Wordsworth, poet laureate (1770-1850), who was born in the house now known as Wordsworth House, Cockermouth. His eldest son, the Rev. John Wordsworth, M.A. (Oxon) (1803-75), ordained 1828, was Rector of Moresby 1829-34, Vicar of Brigham 1832-75, and Rector of Plumbland 1840-75. His 3rd son, the Rev. John Wordsworth (1837-1927), was Curate of Brigham 1870-75, and of Harrington 1875-76, Vicar of Ennerdale 1876-78, Rector of Gosforth 1878-95, and Vicar of All Hallows 1895-1925. His son John Stanley Curwen Wordsworth (1873-1929) was father of the present representative of the family, William Derrick Wordsworth (b. 1912), whose uncle the Rev. Christopher William Wordsworth, M.A. (Oxon) (1879-1965), was father of Mrs. Mary Winn Henderson, of Rydal Mount, wife of Alexander James Henderson. For further particulars of the family, see AWL. *Arms.* Argent three church bells Azure. *Crest.* A stag's head erased Argent (BLG5). Burke also gives: An antelope's head erased Argent (BGA), which appears on the bookplate of the poet's son William. *Motto.* Veritas (BLG5; Bookplate).

WORKINGTON, Borough of. The Borough formerly used: *Arms.* Per pale, Dexter, the arms of Curwen, *q.v.*, with a label of five points issuant from the chief; Sinister, The representation of a blast furnace; on a chief, On waves of the sea a steam- and sailing-ship of two funnels and four masts. *Crest.* That of Curwen. *Motto.* Floreat castellum et oppidum (SGH, 1st edn.). In 1950 the Borough obtained a grant of the following: *Arms.* Sable between two piles Or billetté Azure a garb of the second. *Crest.* Issuant from a mural crown Or a unicorn's head Argent holding in the mouth an anchor in bend Sable. *Supporters.* Dexter, A representation of Vulcan with hammer and anvil all Proper; Sinister, A representation of Themis wearing a robe Azure and having in her right hand a cornucopia and in her left hand a pair of scales all Proper. *Mottoes.* Floreat oppidum laborans; Levavi oculos meos in montes (SGH; CCH).

WREN, of Birkettbank. There was long a branch of the Wren family at

Birkettbank, Crosthwaite. John Wren (d. 1784, aged 47), Elizabeth his wife (d. 1797, aged 61), and John their son (d. 1811, aged 28), are all buried in St. John's-in-the-Vale churchyard; Elizabeth was perhaps Elizabeth Gaskarth, of Threlkeld, and married to John at Crosthwaite 1778. *Arms.* Gules a pale dancetté between three wrens two to the dexter and one to the sinister . . . . *Crest.* A hound passant (Tombstone, St. John's-in-the-Vale churchyard).

WREN, of Castlerigg. Gawen Wren, of Castlerigg (d. 1738, aged 86), belonged to an old established Crosthwaite family. His son Gawen Wren died *v.p.* 1726, having marr. Alice Tatham, of Rydal Hall (W), a granddau. of Sir Daniel Fleming. He had two daus. and coheirs, Barbara (1718-72), marr. 1746 John Langton, *q.v.*, and Anne (b. 1720), who succ. to Castlerigg. *Arms.* On the monument to Gawen Wren (d. 1738), above, in Crosthwaite church, these appear as: Argent a pallet indented Or over all six wrens, three, two and one, also Or. Field suggests that this should be: Per pale indented Argent and Sable six wrens counterchanged (FAC).

WRIGHT, of Meadhope. In 1740 David Wright, of Meadhope, Kirkandrews-on-Esk, sealed his will with the following *Arms.* . . . seven lozenges, three, three, and one, . . . *Crest.* Indecipherable.

WRIGHT. Impaled by Dixon on hatchment at Lorton Hall; James Dixon, of Millom, marr. 1911 Margaret (d. 1951), dau. of James Wright, of Glossop (Dy). *Arms.* Sable on a chevron Argent three spearheads Gules in chief two unicorns heads of the second erased of the third armed and maned Or in base on a pile Gold issuing from the chevron a unicorn's head erased Sable.

WRIGHTSON. Mrs. Ann Winby White, wife of Robert le Rougetel White, of Cross Gates, Lorton, *q.v.*, is younger dau. and coheir of Wilfrid Ingram Wrightson, J.P., M.A. (Cantab), of Steeple Ashton, Wilts. (1876-1949), and granddau. of Sir Thomas Wrightson, 1st Bart., of Neasham Hall (D). *Arms.* Or a fess invected chequy Azure and Argent between two eagles' heads erased in chief Sable and a saltire couped in base Gules. *Motto.* Veritas omnia vincit (BP105).

WRIGLEY. James Wrigley (d. 1846), who went from Shropshire to found paper mills at Bury (L), was father of, *int. al.*,* Thomas Wrigley, D.L., J.P., of Wansfell, Ambleside (1808-80), High Sheriff of Lancashire 1872, whose son Frederick Wrigley (d. 1928) was father of John Basil Wrigley, of Steelfield, Gosforth (1882-1963), High Sheriff of Cumberland 1932. *Arms.* The above Thomas Wrigley, as High Sheriff of Lancashire, bore: Argent on a chevron Sable three mullets of the field (Shield in Shire Hall, Lancaster). His grandson John Basil Wrigley, above, bore: Argent on a chevron Sable three mullets of the field between two flaunches Gules each charged with a stag's head erased also of the field. *Crest.* A stag's head erased semé of mullets and holding in the mouth a trefoil slipped. *Motto.* Acquirit qui tuetur (Seal).

WYBERGH, of St. Bees and of Borrans Hill. William Wybergh, of St. Bees, marr. 1365 Eleanor, dau. and heir of Gilbert Engaine, of Clifton Hall (W), and acquired that estate, which remained in the family until sold in 1919. Thomas Wybergh (b. 1628) marr. 1657 Mary, dau. and coheir of Thomas Salkeld, of Brayton, and his grandson Thomas (1685-1753), Town Clerk of Appleby, marr. 1713 Mary, dau. and heir of Christopher Hilton, of Burton and Ormside, by whom he had twenty children. The eldest son William

* From his dau. Sarah (b. *c.* 1816), who marr. William Grundy, is descended Captain Mark Phillips, husband of H.R.H. Princess Anne.

(1726-57) marr. 1754 Mary, dau. and coheir of Thomas Crakeplace, *q.v.* Their son Thomas (1757-1827) marr. 1786 Isabella, dau. of John Hartley, of Whitehaven, and sister of Anne, wife of Sir Wilfrid Lawson, 10th Bart., who died *s.p.* 1806, leaving his Cumberland estates to his wife's nephew, Thomas Wybergh, who assumed the name Lawson, but died *s.p.* 1812, when he was succ. by his brother Wilfrid, who also took the name Lawson and was cr. Baronet 1831 (see Lawson, *olim* Wybergh). Another brother John Wybergh, J.P., was of Isel Hall and The Mount, Papcastle (1789-1873); another, the Rev. Christopher Hilton Wybergh (1799-1876), was Vicar of Isel and Bromfield; and another, Cdr Peter Wybergh, R.N. (1794-1848), was ancestor of the present head of the family, Archibald Henry d'Engayne Wybergh, J.P., of Borrans Hill,* High Sheriff of Cumberland 1960. *Arms.* Field states that "their ancient coat" was: Sable three bars between as many mullets, two in chief and one in base, Or; and this coat is given by FVC, FDW and NB i 417. However, FFC records William de Wybergh, 38 Edward III, as bearing: Sable three bars Or in chief two estoiles of the last. At the Visitation of 1665, Dugdale recorded: Or three bars Sable on a chief of the first [*sic*] two mullets of the last (FCW); which LMC more correctly blazons as: Or three bars Sable and in chief two mullets of the second. Machell gives: Barry of six Or and Sable three mullets of the first (MMS vi 407). A tablet in Clifton church (W) displays: Or three bars Sable in chief mullets of the last pierced Gules. FD7 gives: Sable three bars Or in chief two estoiles of the second (see above), and BLG17: Or three bars Sable in chief two estoiles of the last. *Crest.* A griffin's head erased Or (BLG 1851). The family now uses: A griffin's head erased per pale Or and Argent charged with a mullet of six points Sable. *Motto.* Hominem te esse memento (BLG17; FD7).

WYDVILLE, Earl of Ryvers. A series of shields from Thornbury Castle, Glos., now in Greystoke Castle, illustrating the medieval ancestry of the Howards, includes one for Wydville; Katherine, dau. of Richard Wydville, Earl of Ryvers (executed 1469), marr. (1) Henry Stafford, Duke of Buckingham, *q.v.* *Arms.* Argent a fess and a canton Gules. This coat is also on a shield on the ceiling of Carlisle Cathedral.

WYND. Caleb Wynd, of Whitehaven, sealed a letter dated 29 November 1728 to John Spedding, of Whitehaven, with the following *Arms.* . . . a fess . . . between three mascles . . . . *Crest.* A griffin's head erased (R.O., Carlisle).

WYNDHAM, Earl of Egremont. The Rt. Hon. Sir William Wyndham, 3rd Bart., of Orchard Wyndham, Som. (d. 1740), marr. Lady Katherine Seymour, dau. of Charles, 6th Duke of Somerset, and sister of Algernon, 7th Duke, who was cr. Earl of Egremont 1749, with special remainder to his nephew Charles Wyndham (1710-63). Charles succ. his father as 4th Bart., and his uncle as 2nd Earl of Egremont 1750, inheriting also his large estates in Cumberland. He was M.P. for Appleby 1742-47, and Vice-Admiral of Cumberland. He was succ. by his son George O'Brien Wyndham, F.S.A., 3rd Earl of Egremont (1751-1837), for whose descendants, see Wyndham, Baron Leconfield and Egremont. He was succ. as 4th Earl of Egremont by his nephew George Francis (1785-1845), son of the Hon. William Frederick Wyndham (d. 1828, aged 65). He died *s.p.* and the titles became extinct. His

* Whither the family removed early in the 19th century.

half-sister Emily (d. 1899) marr. (1) 1848 James Dykes Spedding, *q.v.*, and (2) 1859 Major George Charles Degen Lewis, R.E., and his half-brother Col Arthur Wyndham, H.E.I.C.S. (d. 1874), marr. (1) 1828 Ann Magdalene, only dau. of Capt Samuel Stalker Burns, 80th Foot, and had a son Capt William Wyndham, R.A. (b. 1842); and (2) 1856 Emily Frances Ballantine (1821-1904), sister of the above J. D. Spedding. *Arms.* Azure a chevron between three lions' heads erased Or. *Crest.* A lion's head erased within a fetterlock Or the bow company counter-company Gold and Azure. *Supporters.* Dexter, A lion rampant Azure winged Or; Sinister, A griffin Argent gutté de sang. *Motto.* Au bon droit (BGA; LMC). The arms are impaled by Spedding in the west window of St. Bees church, and on a shield in the possession of Mr. George Spedding.

WYNDHAM, Baron Leconfield and Egremont. George O'Brien Wyndham, 3rd Earl of Egremont, *q.v.*, marr. 1801 Elizabeth, dau. of the Rev. . . . Iliffe, by whom he had six children born before the marriage. The eldest son George (b. 1787) eventually inherited his father's estates in Cumberland and Sussex and was cr. Baron Leconfield, of Leconfield in the East Riding of Yorkshire 1859. The title and estates, including Petworth, and over 11,000 acres in Cumberland, descended to Charles Henry, G.C.V.O., J.P., 3rd Baron Leconfield (1872-1952), who was succ. by his brother Hugh Archibald, 4th Baron (1877-1963), whose successor was another brother, Edward Scawen, D.S.O., 5th Baron (1883-1967). He was succ. by his son John Edward Reginald Wyndham, M.B.E., J.P. (1920-72), who was private secretary to Mr. Harold Macmillan 1957-63. He was cr. Baron Egremont, of Petworth, Co. Sussex, 1963, by which title he preferred to be known after he had become 6th Baron Leconfield. He was succ. by his son John Max Henry Scawen Wyndham, B.A. (Oxon), who also prefers to be known as Lord Egremont. *Arms.* Azure a chevron between three lions' heads erased Or within a bordure wavy of the last. *Crest.* A lion's head erased Or within a fetterlock the lock Gold and the bow counter company Or and Azure the head charged with a saltire wavy Gules. *Supporters.* Dexter, A lion Azure winged inverted and plain collared Or; Sinister, A griffin Argent gutté de sang plain collared Gules. *Motto.* Au bon droit (BP105).

WYNDOWE. Captain Samuel Wyndowe, 1st or Royal Dragoon Guards (d. 1829), son of Samuel Wyndowe, of Stroud, later of Kingsdown, Bristol (d. 1813), marr. 1819 Anne, eldest dau. and coheir of Col William Thomlinson, of Blencogo, *q.v.*, and was succ. by his eldest son Oliver Thomlinson Wyndowe, of Blencogo Hall and Coventry Street, London (d. 1854). *Arms.* Azure a fess embattled counterembattled between three lions' paws erased Or. *Crest.* A lion's paw erased Azure holding a cross crosslet fitché Or (BLG 1846).

WYVILL, of Johnby Hall. William Wyvill, of Johnby Hall, Greystoke (d. 1658), 3rd son of Christopher Wyvill, of Burton Constable (Y), marr. 1637 Mary, dau. and heir of Leonard Musgrave, of Johnby Hall, where his son and heir Christopher (1638-75) was born. Not long before his death William bought the Winderwath estate (W) from Thomas Braithwaite, of Burneside. His son Christopher was of Johnby Hall and Winderwath. At the latter he was succ. by his son Timothy Wyvill, of Penrith (1672-1724), whose son Anthony (1700-27) was father of Anthony Wyvill, of Penrith (1726-59), father of Marmaduke (1752-71), whose coheirs were his sisters

Dorothy (1751-1831), marr. 1776 John Coupland, merchant, of Lancaster;* Mary (b. 1754); Elizabeth (b. 1755); and Margaret (1756-1820), marr. Robert Delap, merchant, of Belfast. They sold Winderwath to Edward Hasell, of Dalemain, 1787 (BEB; Winderwath title deeds). *Arms.* Quarterly of six, 1 & 6, Gules three chevrons interlaced vairy Argent and Gules a chief Or a mullet Argent for difference (Wyvill); 2, Sable three mallets Argent a crescent for difference;† 3, Azure a chief indented Or (FitzRandolph); 4, Azure a bend Or a label of three points Argent (Scrope); 5, Azure six annulets Or, three, two and one, a cinquefoil for difference (Musgrave). *Crest.* A wyvern wings elevated Or nowed Vert (FCW). At the Visitation of Yorkshire, 1665, the above named William Wyvill's nephew, Sir Christopher Wyvill, recorded the crest as: A wyvern with the wings addorsed Argent breathing flames Proper (CVY). In a window in Greystoke church, the arms appear as: Gules three chevrons interlaced vairy Or, Gules and Azure a chief Or.

YARKER. The Yarker family claims descent from Reinhold Yarker, of Leyburn (Y), whose son Thomas was buried at Wensley 1549, see AWL. John Yarker, schoolmaster of Swindale (1809-75), was father of John Yarker, of Withington (L) (b. 1833), author of *Genealogy of the Surname Yarker,* 1882; his grandson John Yarker died of trench fever in World War I. Another member of the family, Edward Harrison Yarker, of Carlisle (1898-1966), was father of Kenneth Yarker, of Thursby, and Edward Harrison Yarker, of Ulverston. *Arms.* Gules on a chevron between three unicorns passant Or as many human hearts of the field. *Crest.* A stork rising Argent collared beaked and legged Gules reposing the dexter claw on a human heart as in the arms and holding in the beak an oak-branch fructed Proper. *Motto.* La fin couronne les oeuvres (BLG 1851).

YATES. The Rev. Francis‡ Yates, a native of Donington, Salop., was ordained 1686, and was incumbent of St. Nicholas, Whitehaven, 1693 until he died 1720, and Rector of Moresby from 1711. His son, the Rev. Francis Yates, B.A. (Oxon), LL.B. (Cantab) (1699-1762), was incumbent of St. Nicholas, Whitehaven 1726-38, Rector of Moresby 1729-35, and later Rector of Slaidburn and Vicar of Gargrave (Y). He marr. 1725 Anne, eldest dau. and coheir of Charles Orfeur, of Plumbland Hall, *q.v.* Their 3rd son, the Rev. Dr. Lowther Yates (d. unmarr. 1798, aged 68), was Master of Catherine Hall, Cambridge, and their youngest son, John Orfeur Yates (d. at Hutton Hall, Penrith, 1818, aged 85), who spent many years in India, built Skirwith Abbey§ in 1768 and was High Sheriff of Cumberland 1783. He marr. Mary (d. 1816, aged 66), sister and coheir of Christopher Aglionby, of Nunnery, *q.v.,* and had issue Francis Yates (1777-1840), M.P. for East Cumberland, who assumed the name of Aglionby as did his nephew Charles Yates, son of John Yates (TEV). *Arms.* . . . a chevron . . . between three gates . . . (M.I., St. Nicholas, Whitehaven; Shield at Wigton Hall).

YEATS. Thomas Yeats, of Carlisle, sealed a letter in 1767 with the following

* One of his daughters, living in Penrith with her mother, ran away with . . . Hutchinson, a play actor. William Coupland Hutchinson, who died at Broughton-in-Furness 1868, aged 53, was presumably a son.

† In the Visitation of Yorkshire, 1612, this quarter appears as: Or three pickaxes Sable a crescent for difference (Pigot) (FVY).

‡ Not William as in FAC.

§ Sold in 1822 to William Parker by Francis Aglionby (Yates) when he moved to Nunnery.

Arms. Argent a fess chequy* . . . between three gates . . . . *Crest.* Out of a baron's coronet a (?) scaling ladder† (*Ex inf.* J. P. Godwin).

YORK, See of. Shields on ceiling of St. John, Workington, and elsewhere in Cumberland. *Arms.* Gules two keys in saltire the sinister surmounting the dexter Argent in chief the Imperial crown Or.

ZOUCHE. Shield at Hutton John, said to be for Zouche, and brought in by the marr. of Sir John Popham, *q.v.*, to a Zouche heiress. *Arms.* Azure a chevron Or between ten bezants.‡

ZOUCHE. Ann, dau. and heir of James Zouche, M.D., of Whitehaven, marr. as his 2nd wife William Fletcher, of Field Broughton and St. Andrew Moor (d. 1730), see AWL. *Arms.* Gules ten bezants, four, three, two, and one (Henry Fletcher Rigge's MS. notes entitled *The Older Monuments in Cartmel Priory Church*, 1876).

* The chequers could perhaps be intended to be hatching for Sable.
† This is little more than a guess, for the crest is almost indecipherable.
‡ The bezants resemble leaves a great deal more closely than roundles.

UNIDENTIFIED HERALDRY

BRUNSTOCK HOUSE. A shield in the billiard room displays: Argent on a fess between three hunting horns Azure stringed Or an escallop of the last.

BRUNSTOCK HOUSE. A small hatchment brought there from elsewhere, bears: *Arms.* Azure a lion rampant Or. *Crest.* A lion rampant Or. *Motto.* Intro ut exeam.

HESKET-IN-THE-FOREST. A shield on an imposing Victorian monument in the churchyard, from which the inscription has disappeared, displays (perhaps for Bickley): . . . a chevron embattled counter-embattled . . . between three griffins' heads erased . . . ; impaling, . . . a chevron (? Or) between three cross crosslets fitché . . . .

HUTTON-IN-THE-FOREST. A shield displays: Azure a chief Gules over all a lion rampant Or on a canton of the last a chevron of the second.

LAYTON HOUSE, Greystoke (the home of Mr. H. C. Gill). Shields in stained glass, said to come from Switzerland or Germany, display the following:

1. *Arms.* Gules in chief two ermine spots Argent headed Or and each enfiled with a crown also Or in base a fleur-de-lys of the last.

2. *Arms.* Quarterly Argent and Gules in fess a baton fessways Sable surmounted of an annulet Or. *Crest.* A baton fessways Sable surmounted of an annulet Or.

55A CASTLEGATE, PENRITH. Shields discovered in 1908, when the charges on the impaled coat were described as annulets. In 1948, when seen by C.R.H., they were roundles.

1. . . . a saltire engrailed . . . ; impaling, . . . six roundles, three, two, and one, ...

2. . . . a (?) rose . . . ; impaling, . . . six roundles, three, two, and one . . . .

The field in each case is now Azure, or Sable, and the charges are Or.

ST. CATHERINE'S ROMAN CATHOLIC CHURCH, PENRITH. A shield displays the following: Gules a mountain in base Proper and in chief three fleurs-de-lys, one and two, Or.

A SUPPLEMENT TO AN ARMORIAL FOR WESTMORLAND AND LONSDALE

ADDITIONS AND CORRECTIONS

(The page numbers in brackets refer to those of the original book)

ABRAHALL, HOSKYNS- (p. 1). The Rt Rev. Anthony Leigh Egerton Hoskyns-Abrahall, Bishop Suffragan of Lancaster from 1955, resigned 1975.

AINSLIE, of Over Kellet and Grizedale (pp. 3-4). *Arms.* On the bookplate of Dr James Ainslie, of Carlisle and Kendal, in Viscountess Wolseley's collection of bookplates, Hove Area Library, the arms appear as: Argent [*sic*] a cross patonce Or.

AINSLIE. (pp. 3-4). On the death *s.p.* of Ernest Henry Ainslie, B.A. (Cantab), of Elleray Bank, Windermere (1856-1919), son of the Rev. Henry Ainslie, Vicar of St Mary Windermere, his brother Canon Richard Montague Ainslie, T.D., M.A. (Cantab) (1858-1924), Vicar of Childwall (L) 1903-24, became head of the family. He was succ. by his younger son Henry Ainslie (1896-1927), whose daus. and coheirs are Constance Patricia (b. 1923), wife of Aquiles Gomes, and Barbara Helen (b.1925), wife of Harold Lomax, of Rugby. Wilfred Ainslie, F.R.I.B.A. (1859-1936), became the male representative on his nephew's death and was succ. by his only son Montague Ainslie (1924*-75), who served in World War II with the Intelligence Corps in Palestine and in India with the 2nd Gurkhas. He was subsequently a teacher in Spain, and died in Palma, Majorca. The present head of the family is Denys Malcolm Lafone Ainslie, of Bentleys, North Holmwood, near Dorking (b. 1921), who is great-grandson of William George Ainslie, M.P., of St. Mary's Mount and Brogden House, Ulverston (1832-93), younger brother of the above named Rev. Henry Ainslie.

ALEXANDER. (p. 5). Francis Marie Alexander, née Callow of Field Head, Windermere, died 10 October 1975, aged 76.

ANDREW. Shield in window of Thurland Castle for Sara Andrew (d. 1689), 2nd wife of James Lees, of Clarksfield (d.1679). *Arms.* Gules a saltire parted and fretty Or.

von ANGLOCH. The arms of Bernhart von Angloch, a knight of the Order of St John, Grand Bailiff of Somenthür in Locarno and of Rotweil, are in Swiss glass dated 1595 in Sizergh Castle which was brought by the National Trust from Wasdale Hall; the colours are very faded and indistinct. *Arms.* Quarterly, 1 & 4, Per fess Argent and Sable a demi boar salient couped and counterchanged; 2 & 3, Per bend sinister Sable and Or a Danish hatchet [?Proper]. The glass also contains two other shields: *Arms.* Quarterly, 1 & 4, Or a goat rampant Sable; 2 & 3, Argent three (?) strawberries slipped Vert. And *Arms.* Argent a cross Sable. *Motto.* Lang ist nit ewig.

ASHBURNER, of Gleaston and Scales (p. 8). *Arms.* For "bore three crescents on the fess," read "bore three mullets on the fess."

* Not 1920, as in AWL.

ASPINALL. The bookplate of Thomas Dawson, of Allan Bank, Grasmere (1812-95) (p. 98), shows Dawson impaling the arms of Aspinall; he marr. 1834 Martha, dau. of William Aspinall, of Liverpool. *Arms.* Or a chevron between three griffins' heads erased Sable.

ATKINSON, of Burton-in-Kendal (p. 11). The arms blazoned were granted 1810 to William Atkinson, of Grays Inn, London, and of Burton-in-Kendal (d. 1825), only son of William Atkinson, of Haverbrack, Beetham, deceased (CA xxvi/64).

ATKINSON, of Temple Sowerby and Morland (p. 12). This family at one time used the following *Arms.* Gules an eagle displayed with two heads Argent on a chief of the second three mullets of the first. *Crest.* A falcon wings expanded (BLG4).

ATKINSON, of Winderwath (p. 12). HSW records the *Arms* of James Atkinson, as High Sheriff 1870, as: Gules an eagle with two heads displayed Argent on a chief of the last three mullets of six points of the field.

ATON. Curwen gives for this family, without stating whether of Westmorland or Cumberland: *Arms.* Or three bars Azure on a canton Gules a cross patonce Argent (CW2 vi 211). As a Clifford quartering on the Countess of Cumberland's tomb in St. Lawrence, Appleby, the arms appear as: Or two bars Gules on a canton Sable a cross patonce Or.

ATTON. Quartered by Boynton, *q.v.*, in a window at Levens Hall. *Arms.* Or a cross Sable.

AUDLAND (p. 13). Brigadier Edward Gordon Audland died at Ackenthwaite, 22 October 1976, aged 79.

BACKHOUSE, of Morland (p. 14). *Crest.* NB (i 448) blazon the eagle in the crest as displayed Vert.

BACKHOUSE, of Morland (p. 14). The Rev. Robert Backhouse, M.A. (Oxon and Cantab) (b. 1693), son of Edward Backhouse, of Morland, was Vicar of Newbold Pacey, Warwickshire. He was a benefactor to The Queen's College, Oxford. *Arms.* Per saltire Or and Azure a saltire Ermine (Shield in glass in The Queen's College Hall).

BAGENAL. Timothy Bracegirdle Bagenal, M.A. (Cantab), F.Inst.Biol., of 5 Bankfield, Kendal, Principal Scientific Officer, Freshwater Biological Association, is descended from Philip Bagenal, formerly Newton, of Benekerry, Co. Carlow (1796-1856), and from John Bagnall, Mayor of Newcastle-under-Lyme (St.) five times between 1519 and 1533. *Arms.* Barry of four Ermine and Or a lion rampant Azure. *Crest.* An heraldic antelope sejant Vert attired unguled ducally gorged and chained Or (IFR).

BAKER. Impaled by Sackville (see AWL, p. 258) on triptych from Appleby Castle, now in the Record Office, Carlisle; Thomas Sackville, Baron of Buckhurst and Earl of Dorset (d. 1608), marr. 1555 Cicely (d. 1615, aged 80), dau. of Sir John Baker, of Sissinghurst, Kent. *Arms.* Azure a fess between three swans' heads erased Or.

BARNARDISTON. Quartered by Boynton, *q.v.*, in window at Levens Hall. *Arms.* Azure a fess dancetté between six cross crosslets fitché Argent.

de BARRETO. Baron Henry De Barreto, D.L., J.P., F.R.S.L., K.G.C.S. (1818-90), a landowner in Long Sleddale, was younger son of James Aldridge, D.L., by Elizabeth, dau. of William Bliss, and succ. to the title and Portuguese estates of his cousin Baron Alreyo by permission of the King of Portugal in 1855. He also succ. to Spanish estates on the death of Col

Carlo Antonio Barreto, and assumed that surname 1869. In 1868 he marr. Catherine Eliza (b. 1845), dau. of the Rev. Robert Duncan Baker and niece of Edward Wilson, of Rigmaden. Their eldest son Baron Henry Edward Ernest Victor Bliss, J.P. (b. 1890), assumed the surname Bliss in lieu of de Barreto 1919. *Arms.* Per bend Sable and Gules a bend lozengy Argent and Azure between four fleurs-de-lys two and two Or. *Crest.* A dexter cubit arm erect the hand grasping a crossbow in bend and two arrows in bend sinister all Proper. *Motto.* Deus nobiscum quis contra? (BHI).

BARROW. The Rev. William Barrow, M.A., D.C.L. (Oxon) (1754-1836), was 2nd son of John Barrow, of Sedbergh. He was proprietor of the Soho Square Academy,* and became Prebendary of Southwell 1815 and Archdeacon of Nottingham 1830. At the 1826 Westmorland election he voted as owner of a freehold in Birkbeck Fells. His brother James Barrow died at Gaythorne Hall, Appleby, 1836, aged 80 (SSR; Letters of Richard Radcliffe and John James, 1755-83). *Arms.* Sable two swords in saltire points upwards between four fleurs-de-lys Argent. *Crest.* A squirrel sejant cracking an acorn slipped and leaved (Bookplate of the Rev. W. Barrow).

BARROW. James Barrow, linen draper of Kendal (*c.* 1775-1817), bought Hill Top, Ambleside, from his brother-in-law, the Rev. John Knipe, of Hamburg. *Arms.* . . . two swords in saltire . . . between four fleurs-de-lys . . . (Seal of James Barrow).

BAYLEY – see WALLER.

BAYNES (pp. 15-16). The keystone bearing the Baynes arms, viz. A shinbone in pale crossed by another in fess, found near Sellet Hall and mentioned by W. H. Chippindall (*A History of Whittington,* p.68) as having been removed to The Biggins for better preservation, has recently been built into a wall at Biggins Grange, the home of Major and Mrs. J. G. W. Skipwith.

BECK, later ALCOCK-BECK (p. 24). In addition to the arms recorded, the bookplate of Thomas Alcock Beck (1795-1846) bears another shield displaying: Argent two bars wavy Azure over all on a bend Gules three plates. It seems highly probable that these arms were intended for Beck.

BELLINGER. Edmund Bellinger arrived in South Carolina 1674 from Westmorland, and became a Landgrave 1698 and Receiver of Public Monies 1700. He marr. in Westmorland Elizabeth Cartwright; their eldest son Edmund Bellinger was the second Landgrave and was succ. by his son Edmund. *Arms.* Argent a saltire engrailed Sable between four roses Gules. *Crest.* A stag's head (NQ clxvii 14).

BELLINGHAM, of Levens (pp. 26-7). The arms and crest of Bellingham are carved under the eaves of No. 7 Stramongate, Kendal, now occupied by Mr. and Mrs. J. P. Kelly, with the inscription: Baron 1546 of K[irkbie] K[endall], the whole within a lozenge.† *Arms.* Argent three bugle horns stringed Sable. *Crest.* A stag's head couped Gules. The arms, ensigned with a coronet, and with initials IB and date 1774, are carved on the door of a built-in cupboard in the house.

* Boswell, whose son went to the Academy, said that he was a coarse North Countryman, but a very good scholar.

† The house was restored in 1863 by John Broadbent, grandson of William Bellingham (d. 1794). He then set up the arms on the outside of the house.

BENNETT, of Heysham Tower (p. 27). *Motto.* De bon vouloir servir le roi (Bookplate of Miss Bennett in Viscountess Wolseley's collection).

CAVENDISH-BENTINCK (p. 29). In the footnote, delete the words "and there is a crescent for difference in the Cavendish quarters;" and insert the words "double-queued" after "two lions."

BERRY (p. 29). On the north front of Croftlands, Caton, which was built by Thomas Berry in 1745 and restored by Richard Sparling-Berry, 1833, the *Crest* appears as: A demi lion rampant holding in the dexter paw a cross crosslet fitché. *Motto.* In hoc signo vinces.

BENT. Mrs Nancy Baldwin Darlington, wife of Colonel Henry John Darlington, of Melling, see AWL, is dau. of Baldwin Harry Bent, of Wray House, formerly of Heysham Lodge (1861-1941). *Arms.* Azure on a fess Or between six bezants three torteaux. *Crest.* A demi lion Azure holding between the paws a bezant. *Motto.* Nec temere nec timide.

BETHOM, BETHAM (p. 30). A pedigree of the Betham family in the possession of Mrs Margaret Sarah Hollett, wife of Ronald Frederick Grix Hollett of Greenbank, Sedbergh, and dau. of Aubrey Dover Betham, of Greenbank, Sedbergh, shews a second *Motto* above elephant's head crest, viz. Salus in periculo.

BIGLAND, of Bigland Hall (p. 31). In the blazon of the *Crest, delete* the word rampant.

BINDLOSS. Philip Bindloss, of Park House, Heversham (d. 1802, aged 35), was father of Thompson Bindloss, ironmonger, of Castle Green, Kendal (d. 1850, aged 52), who was Mayor of Kendal 1838 and 1844, and marr. Elizabeth (d. 1881, aged 78), dau. of Edward Kitching, *q.v.* His nephew Alderman William Bindloss (d. 1895, aged 69), son of Robert Bindloss, of Rowell, Milnthorpe, succ. him at Castle Green and in the business and was Mayor six times between 1880 and 1895. He contributed £7,000 towards the enlargement of Kendal Town Hall, and in his will left £3,000 for the Town Hall Carillon. He marr. 1869 Agnes Sarah (d. 1894, aged 74), dau. of Dr John Kitching, *q.v.,* but died *s.p. Arms.* Quarterly per fess indented Or and Gules on a bend Azure a cinquefoil between two martlets Or (Clerestory window in Kendal Parish Church). These arms, now very weathered and difficult to decipher, are also on the west facade of Kendal Town Hall.

de BISCHINSEN – see de FINGERLEN.

BISSELL. (p. 34). The Rev. William Bissell's bookplate depicts his *Arms.* Gules on a bend Argent three escallops Sable. *Motto.* Verum atque decens (Viscountess Wolseley's collection of bookplates).

BLACKBURN, See of. The Hundred of Lonsdale South of the Sands lies in the Diocese of Blackburn. *Arms.* Per fess Gules and Or two keys in saltire wards downwards Argent in chief and a rose barbed and seeded Proper in base (CCH).

BLACKBURN – see WALLER.

BLAKE. Hugh McKellar Blake, M.A. (Cantab), is lecturer in Medieval Archaeology in the Department of Classics and Archaeology of the University of Lancaster. *Arms.* Argent a fret Gules. *Crest.* A mountain cat passant guardant proper. *Motto.* Virtus sola nobilitat (Bookplate of George Frederick Blake, H. M. Blake's grandfather).

BLISS – see de BARRETO.

BLÜCHER von WAHLSTADT or BLÜCHER de WAHLSTATT, (p. 36). Rietstap records the arms as: Quarterly, 1 & 4, Argent the Eagle of Prussia; 2, Or a Prussian marshal's baton and a sword Argent in saltire enfiled with a crown of laurel Vert: 3, Or an Iron Cross: overall an escutcheon, Gules two keys endorsed Argent (RAG).

BODDINGTON. (p. 36). Humphrey West Boddington's elder son Humphrey Cyril Bindloss Boddington died at Sandwich 4 February 1976, aged 65; his younger son Michael Christopher Bindloss Boddington, D.F.C., D.F.M., Squadron Leader R.A.F., of Ramsteads, Outgate, died 22 February 1977.

BOLD – see STANLEY.

BONSOR. Major John Michael Charles Bonsor, of Bracken Hall, Grayrigg (b. 1927), is son of Alexander John Bonsor, nephew of Sir Cosmo Bonsor, 1st Bart. He served in the Royal Navy 1945-47, and was commissioned in the 9th Queen's Royal Lancers in 1948, serving with 9/12th Royal Lancers (Prince of Wales's) from 1960 until 1969, when he retired. *Arms.* Per fess Azure and Argent a pale counterchanged and three lions' heads erased Or a crescent Sable charged with a mullet Or for difference on a chief indented Erminois three roses Gules barbed and seeded Proper and a label of three points Sable. *Crest.* A staff raguly fessways Sable thereon a wolf passant Sable collared and chained Or the dexter paw holding a rose as in the arms (Painting in possession of Major Bonsor).

BOURCHIER. Shield on triptych from Appleby Castle, now in the Record Office, Carlisle; William Bourchier, Earl of Bath (1557-1623), marr. (2) 1583 Elizabeth Russell (d. 1605), 2nd dau. of Francis, 2nd Earl of Bedford. *Arms.* Argent a cross engrailed Gules between four water bougets Sable.

BOWDLER. William Audley Bowdler, M.R.C.S., L.R.C.P., Major R. A. (1884-1969), M.P. for Holderness 1922-23, son of William Henry Bowdler, of Kirkham (L), was of Brathay Fell and Oakhow, Coniston. His son John Christopher Audley Bowdler is of Tunbridge Wells. *Arms.* Argent two Cornish choughs in pale Proper beaked and legged Gules. *Crest.* A dexter arm embowed holding in the hand an arrow all Proper. *Motto.* Innocue ac provide (BGA).

BOWEN. Millicent Jane, dau. of Dr Thomas Graham Mathews, of Green Close, Kirkby Lonsdale, see AWL, marr. 1937 Col Charles Guy Bowen, O.B.E., Lancashire Fusiliers (1908-67), and is now of Lilac Cottage, Kirkby Lonsdale. *Arms.* Argent a chevron Sable between three Cornish choughs Proper. *Motto.* Secret and hardy.

BOWRING (p. 43). Geoffrey Price Bowring, D.L., M.C., T.D., M.A. (Oxon), of Halton Park, 2nd son of Henry Illingworth Bowring, J.P., of Whelprigg, was High Sheriff of Lancashire 1976.

BOYLE. Shield on triptych from Appleby Castle, now in the Record Office, Carlisle; Richard Boyle, Earl of Cork (1612-98), marr. 1634 Elizabeth (1613-91), Baroness Clifford, dau. and heir of Henry, 5th Earl of Cumberland. *Arms.* Per bend crenellé Argent and Gules.

BOYNTON (p. 44). The arms of Boynton are also on shields at Sizergh Castle, with the following quartering for Old Boynton: Or on a cross Sable five bulls' heads cabossed Argent. Alice (d. 1595), dau. of Nicholas Tempest, of Stella and Stanley (D), marr. (1) Christopher Place, of Halnaby

(Y) (d. *c.* 1555); (2) 1561 Walter Strickland, of Sizergh (d. 1569); and (3) Sir Thomas Boynton, of Barmston (Y) (d. 1581) (HSS).

BRADSHAIGH. Henry Fletcher Rigge in his MS. *The Older Monuments in Cartmel Priory Church,* 1876, recorded the arms of Bradshaigh as impaled by Preston on the monument of Sir William Lowther, of Holker, 1st Bart. (d. 1705); Thomas Preston, of Holker (d. 1696, aged 50), marr. (2) Elizabeth (d. 1732, aged 81), dau. of Sir Roger Bradshaigh, 1st Bart., of Haigh (L). *Arms.* Argent two bendlets between as many martlets Sable.

BRAITHWAITE, of Stock Park. Col G. E. Braithwaite in TBC shows that a branch of the family flourished for many generations at Stott or Stock Park, Finsthwaite. In the churchyard is the gravestone of George Braithwaite (d. 1761, aged 92) and of his sons John (d. 1736, aged 29) and James (d. 1754, aged 25). George's widow Deborah died 1769 leaving the property to her son George, whose three children – George (d. 1814), Hannah (d. 1827) and Mary (d. 1833) – were all unmarried and the last named left the estate to her cousin, the Rev. Richard Lucas, M.A (Cantab) (1787-1846). He was succ. by his son George Vere Lucas, J.P. (1822-95), who thereupon assumed the surname and arms of Braithwaite, in accordance with the terms of Mary Braithwaite's will. His two sons died *s.p.* and the family is now extinct in the male line. *Arms.* Gules on a chevron Argent three cross crosslets fitché Sable a mullet for difference. *Crest.* A greyhound couchant Argent collared and chained Gules charged with a mullet for difference (BGA).

BRANDON. Impaled by Clifford on triptych from Appleby Castle, now in the Record Office, Carlisle; Henry, 2nd Earl of Cumberland (d. 1570), marr. (1) 1537 Eleanor (d. *s.p.m.s.* 1547), youngest dau. and coheir of Charles Brandon, Duke of Suffolk (*c.* 1484-1545), by his 3rd wife Mary, Queen Dowager of France, 3rd dau. of King Henry VII. *Arms.* Barry of ten Argent and Gules a lion rampant Or ducally crowned per pale of the first and second.

BRAOSE. Impaled by Clifford on triptych from Appleby Castle, now in the Record Office, Carlisle; Walter de Clifford (d. 1263/4) marr. Margaret, widow of John de Braose. *Arms.* Azure semé of cross crosslets a lion rampant Or.

BRETHERTON (p. 50). Mrs. Dorothy Unthank died 27 November 1976, aged 86.

BROWN, of Kirkby Lonsdale. Edmund Brown, of Kirkby Lonsdale, yeoman, son and heir of Edmund Brown, of Clifton (W), tailor, deceased, sold a messuage and tenement in Clifton 1731. *Arms.* . . . . three swans . . . . *Crest.* An axe erect blade to the sinister (Seal on deed in R.O., Carlisle, D/Lons/L/Clifton 1/11).

BRYDSON. (p. 58). Paul Reginald Benson Brydson, of Water Park, died 22 May 1977.

BUTLER – see STANLEY.

BUTLER, of Infield (p. 63). Theobald FitzWalter Butler, D.L., J.P., of Infield (1845-1914), was 6th and youngest son of James Blake Butler, J.P., of Glenwilliaim, Co. Clare (1799-1849), and was descended from Peter, or Piers, Butler, known as *Piers na mBuile,* or "Wild Piers", of Grallagh, Co. Tipperary (*c.*1521-77), 2nd. son of James, 9th Lord of Dunboyne. The said T. W. Butler's 3rd and youngest son, Major Francis James Butler, M.C. (d. unmarr. 1945), was of Tytup Hall, Dalton-in-Furness (IFR).

BUTLER. The Rev. Theobald Butler, B.A. (TCD), of Drom, Co. Tipperary, marr. 1815 Anne, dau. of James Kearney, of Blanchville, Co. Kilkenny, and had *int. al.* a son, the Rev. Theobald Butler, M.A. (TCD), of Bellshow, Windermere (1822-1904). His nephew Charles James Butler assumed the additional surname of Kearney 1876. *Arms.* Or a chief indented Azure and three escallops in bend counterchanged. *Crest.* Out of a ducal coronet Or a plume of five ostrich feathers Argent issuant therefrom a demi falcon also Argent. *Motto.* Timor Domini fons vitae.

BUTLER-COLE (p. 63). A fine carved wooden armorial panel, now above the entrance to the Grill Room of the Royal Hotel, Kirkby Lonsdale, but at one time forming part of the head of an old four-poster bed at Beaumont Cote (see also STANLEY),* displays the arms of Butler-Cole, as follows: *Arms.* Quarterly of ten, 1 & 10, Quarterly, i & iv, [Azure] a chevron between three covered cups [Or] (Butler); ii & iii, [Vert] on a fess [Argent] three lions' heads erased [Gules] (Cole); 2, [Azure] three escallops in pale [Or] and two flaunches [Ermine] on a chief [Argent] three lions rampant [of the first] (Clarke); 3, Per pale nebuly [Azure and Or] five [correctly, six] martlets [counterchanged], one, two and two, a canton [Argent] (Fleetwood); 4, [Vert] a chevron between three stags' heads cabossed [Or] (Parker, of Browsholme); 5, [Argent] a chevron [correctly, three chevrons Gules] between three martlets [Sable] (Singleton); 6, [Azure] on a chevron between three covered cups [Or] as many mullets [of the first] (?Jackson); 7, [Argent] a chevron [correctly, three chevrons Gules] and in dexter chief a mullet [of the last] (Langton); 8, [Argent] on a bend [Sable] three bugle horns [of the first] stringed [Or] (Greenhalgh); 9, [Or] a chevron between three bugle horns stringed [Sable] (Foster, or Forster). The whole impaling, [Argent] a griffin segreant [Sable ducally] crowned beaked and legged [Or] (Grimshaw). *Crests.* 1, A horse statant [Argent] pelleté bridled and reined [Sable] (Butler); 2, A lion's head erased [Gules] pierced in the neck by an arrow [Argent] (Cole). *Motto.* Deum cole regem serva. Thomas Butler, of Kirkland (d. *s.p.* 1864 aged 68), son of Thomas Butler (d. 1824, aged 55) and his wife Susan Clarke, of Liverpool, assumed the additional surname Cole 1816, and marr. Louisa (d. 1851). dau. of John Grimshaw, of Preston.

CALVERT (p. 65). *Arms.* GMS records for Calvert, without specifying any place of residence: Sable an inescutcheon Ermine within an orle of owls Argent.

CARDWELL. Shield in window of Thurland Castle for Elizabeth, dau. of Thomas Cardwell, of Lytham, marr. 1843 John Livesey, *q.v. Arms.* Argent a chevron Sable between three maidens' heads erased at the bust Proper crowned Or.

CECIL. Impaled by Clifford on triptych from Appleby Castle, now in the Record Office, Carlisle; Henry, 5th Earl of Cumberland (1592-1643), marr. 1610 Frances (1593-1644), dau. of Robert Cecil, 1st Earl of Salisbury. *Arms.* Barry of ten Argent and Azure over all six escutcheons Sable, three, two, and one, each charged with a lion rampant of the first.

CHAMPAIN, BATEMAN-, of Halton Park (p. 72). *Arms* (of Currie). For "in the centre point" read "in chief".

* The achievement was obviously a 19th century addition to the original bedhead, which seems to date from the 16th or 17th century. We are grateful to Mr. R. F. C. Butler-Cole, of Fell End House, for drawing our attention to these arms and to those described under STANLEY.

CHESTER (p. 75). *Arms.* In Quarters 1 & 4, insert "Gules" between "engrailed" and "bezantée."

CHEVERS. Michael John Chevers, of Fountain House, Ulverston, marine nuclear engineer with Vickers Armstrong, eldest son of Hyacinth Edward Joseph Chevers, of Southborne, Bournemouth, is descended from Sir William Chevre who accompanied Strongbow on his invasion of Ireland in 1172. *Arms.* Gules three goats salient Argent. *Crest.* A demi goat Argent as in the arms collared Gules horned and unguled Or. *Motto.* En Dieu est ma foi (IFR).

CHOLMELEY. Shield on triptych from Appleby Castle, now in the Record Office, Carlisle; Sir Richard Cholmeley, of Roxby and Whitby Abbey (Y) (d. 1583), marr. (2) Lady Katherine Clifford (d. 1598), widow of John, Lord Scrope of Bolton, and eldest dau. of Henry, 1st Earl of Cumberland. *Arms.* Gules two esquires' helmets in chief Proper garnished Or and in base a garb of the last.

CLIBURN, of Cliburn (p. 79). *Arms.* GMS records: Argent two chevronels and a chief Sable.

CLIFFORD (p. 80). *Arms.* The senior line of the Clifford family bore: Chequy Or and Azure a bend Gules (Shields on triptych from Appleby Castle, now in the Record Office, Carlisle).

CLIFFORD (p. 80). An unidentified quartering on the Countess of Cumberland's tomb in St. Lawrence, Appleby, displays the following *Arms.* Sable three murthering chain shots Or. Curwen records this as: Azure three murdering chain-shots Or (CW2 vi).

COCK. Shield in window of Thurland Castle for Mary Cock, wife of John Lees, of Clarksfield (1695-1750). *Arms.* Gules three cocks Argent combed and wattled Or.

COLENSO. Shield in window of Thurland Castle for Frances Ellen Colenso, godmother of Dorothy Neville Lees (b. 1886). *Arms.* Azure a saltire Argent in chief an estoile of the last.

COLTON. The Rev. William Colton, B.A. (Oxon) (d. 1802), was Curate of St. Mary, Lancaster *c.* 1780-1802 and Curate of Over Kellet in 1795. His only son, William Butterfield Colton, was a wine-broker in Liverpool. *Arms.* Argent a saltire between four crescents Azure. *Crest.* A demi talbot Argent ducally crowned Or (William Colton's bookplate described by Major P. Raban in *The Coat of Arms* i 273 f.).

COMPTON. Shield on triptych from Appleby Castle, now in the Record Office, Carlisle; James Compton, 3rd Earl of Northampton (1622-81), marr. (1) 1647 Isabella (1622-61), 2nd dau. and coheir of Richard Sackville, Earl of Dorset (d. 1624). *Arms.* Sable a lion passant guardant Or between three esquires' helmets Argent.

CONEY (p. 83). John Coney, formerly of Appleby Castle, is now of Garth House, Brampton.

COOKSON. Shield in window of Thurland Castle for Rebecca Cookson, of Ribby, marr. 1811 Thomas Cardwell, of Lytham, *q.v.* *Arms.* Per pale Argent and Gules two legs in armour fessways in pale couped at the thigh Proper.

COOPER. The Ven. John Cooper, M.A. (Cantab) (1813-96), son of Samuel Cooper, of Tranby (Y), was Fellow of Trinity College, Cambridge 1837-59, Vicar of Kendal 1858-96, Hon. Canon of Carlisle 1861-83, Canon Residentiary 1883-96, and Archdeacon of Westmorland 1865-96. *Arms.* His seal as Archdeacon of Westmorland displays: [Argent] on a cross [Sable] a mitre with labels [Or] (The See of Carlisle); impaling (in chief), [Argent] two bars and on a canton [Gules] a lion passant [Or] (Lancaster), and (in base), . . . a bend . . . between two lions' heads erased . . . (Cooper).

COWARD. Members of the Coward family, describing themselves as yeomen, succeeded each other at Stonedykes, Ulverston, and Woodyeat, Lowick, from the time of John Cowherde (1498-1574). His descendant, John Coward (1743-1819), was Innkeeper of the Hare and Hounds Inn, Skelwith Bridge, as was his son, Jeremiah Coward (1789-1871), father of Jackson Coward, bobbin turner, of Skelwith Bridge (1834-91). His son Jackson Coward, of Hawkshead (1872-1941), a powderman at the Langdale Gunpowder Works, later Head Gardener at Wray Castle, was grandfather of Harry Coward, of 2737 Abbott Road, Regina, Saskatchewan, Canada, engineer. The latter, whose only son is Stewart Anthony Coward, in 1974 obtained a grant of the following *Arms.* Vert three Guernsey cows' heads cabossed Proper on a chief Or a rose Gules barbed and seeded Proper slipped between and the three stalks conjoined with two maple leaves slipped Gules. *Crest.* Two anchors in saltire Proper surmounted by a rose Gules barbed and seeded Proper. *Motto.* Safe in my ancestral strength.

COWPER, *post* COWPER-ESSEX. Christopher Swainson Cowper-Essex (b. 1903) died at St. Richard's Hospital, Chichester, 13 February 1976, and was buried in Hawkshead churchyard. His son Peter Thomas Cowper-Essex (b. 1930), is now head of the family.

CRACKANTHORPE, of Newbiggin (p. 87). Some very old carved wood recently discovered at Newbiggin Hall bears, in addition to the initials I C, probably for Sir John Crackanthorpe, High Sheriff of Cumberland 1477-83 and 1512-14, the arms of Crackanthorpe flanked on either side by a unicorn passant. These may have been intended for supporters, or perhaps only for decoration, and this applies also to the two (?) wyverns which support the Crackanthorpe arms on an overmantel in the hall. *Arms.* Lysons recorded: Or a chevron between three mullets pierced Sable (LMC).

CRAMLINGTON (p. 88). Further research has shown that BGA erred in describing this family as of Westmorland, instead of as of Cramlington (N), the last male being William Cramlington, whose dau. and coheir Agnes (*c.* 1395-1466) carried the estates to her 2nd husband William Lawson, of Bywell and Cramlington, whom she marr. in or before 1425. From them descended the Lawsons, baronets, of Brough (Y), see p. 200, and James Lawson, who acquired Nesham Abbey (D) 1540. His descendant James Lawson (1568-1631) was father of Frances, who marr. 1617 Richard Braithwaite, of Burneside (NCHN xiii 380-9; SHD iii 264). *Arms.* Barry of six Argent and Azure in chief three annulets of the last (FVN). Machell saw among other coats at Burneside Hall one showing Braithwaite impaling, Quarterly, 1 & 4, Lawson, 2 & 3, Cramlington (EAH p. 102). Curwen wrongly attributes the Cramlington arms to Lawson (CW2 vi).

CUDWORTH. Shield in window of Thurland Castle for Ralph Cudworth, of Werneth, Lord of the Manor of Oldham, marr. 1465 Betty, dau. of Alex Lees, of Lees. *Arms.* Azure a fess Erminois between three demi lions rampant Or.

CUNDI. Impaled by Clifford on triptych from Appleby Castle, now in the Record Office, Carlisle; Walter de Clifford (d. 1222/3) marr. Agnes, dau.

and heir of Roger de Cundi, of Covenby and Glentham, Lincs., by Alice, dau. and heir of William de Cheney. *Arms.* Argent a fess between three martlets Gules.*

DALSTON, of Acornbank (p. 94). Some fine armorial glass at Acornbank, some of it presumably removed there from Dalston Hall, displays the Dalston arms, with quarterings and impalements, as follows:

1. Argent on a chevron engrailed between three daws' heads erased Sable beaked Or a mullet of the last for difference (Dalston); impaling, Or six annulets Sable, three, two and one (Lowther). Christopher Dalston, of Acornbank (*c.* 1530-1604), Sheriff of Cumberland 1596, see p. 84, above, marr. Mabel, dau. of Sir John Lowther.

2. Quarterly, 1, Argent a chevron between three daws' heads erased Sable beaked Or (Dalston); 2, Sable three covered cups Argent (Warcop); 3, Argent a fess dancetté between three cocks' heads erased Sable combed and wattled Gules (Tamworth); 4, Azure a chevron between three escallops Or a bordure engrailed of the last (Colby); in the centre of the quarters, the badge of Ulster. The whole impaling, Quarterly, 1, Azure on three dishes Or as many boars' heads couped Argent a mullet Or for difference (Bolles, ancient); 2, Argent a chevron Gules between three mullets Sable on a chief of the last a lion's head erased between two lozenges Or (Bolles, of Osberton); 3, Argent on a fess Gules between three eagles' or hawks' heads erased Sable as many crosses moline (?recercely) Argent† (Watts); 4, Gules a wyvern‡ wings displayed Or on a chief Argent a label of three points Ermine (Brent). Sir William Dalston, 1st Bart., of Dalston (C), see p. 83, above, marr. Anne (d. 1639), dau. of Thomas Bolles, of Osberton, Notts.

3. Quarterly, 1, Bolles, ancient, 2, Bolles, of Osberton, 3, Watts, 4, Brent, as above; impaling, Or a bend Gules between three martlets (correctly, pewits) Sable (Witham). Thomas Bolles, above, marr. Mary§ (d. 1662), dau. of William Witham, of Ledston (Y).

Another window displays a series of crests:

4. A boar's head couped Argent (Warcop).

5. An arm embowed in armour Proper garnished Or holding in the gauntlet a sword Argent pommel and hilt gold (Colby).

6. Out of a ducal coronet a daw's head Sable beaked Or (Dalston).

7. A cock Proper (Bolles).

A fine oak overmantel, formerly in the hall and now in a bedroom, displays five shields:

8. *Arms.* Dalston, a mullet for difference. *Crest.* Dalston.

9. Dalston; impaling, Lowther.

10. Dalston; impaling, . . . three hawks close jessed and belled . . . . ||

11. Dalston; impaling, [Argent] on a fess [Sable] three stags' heads cabossed

* OBA gives these arms for Cheyney, of Buckinghamshire.

† The colours are badly faded, and the fess is now of a golden hue, but it is certainly not Vert, as stated by Dr. F. Haswell (CW2 x 222-3); and indistinct as the crosses are, they resemble crosses moline, recercely, or even pattée, much more closely than cross crosslets, as interpreted by Dr. Haswell.

‡ Not a cockatrice, as stated by Dr. Haswell.

§ Said to have been created a baroness in her own right (CW2 x 221).

|| Dr. Haswell recorded this as: . . . three sparrows . . . , for Phillip; Thomas Dalston, of Acornbank (d. 1611), marr. 1580 Jane, dau. of James Phillip, of Brignall (Y).

[Or] (Hutton). Sir Christopher Dalston, of Acornbank (1586-1634), marr. 1603 Anne, dau. of Sir William Hutton, of Hutton Hall, Penrith.

12. Dalston; impaling, ... three escallops ..., one and two, on a canton ... a boar's head couped ... (Fallowfield). John Dalston, of Acornbank and Millrigg (1611-92), marr. Lucy, dau. and heir of Richard Fallowfield, of Great Strickland.

DANSON (p. 95). Lt-Col John Raymond Danson died 18 June 1976.

DAVISON. *Arms.* Two variants of what may be the arms of Davison are impaled by Tatham on the funeral hatchments in Hornby church of Admiral Sandford Tatham, see AWL, and his wife Ann (d. 1842), viz. Or a fess wavy between three cinquefoils Gules; and, Or a fess wavy between six cinquefoils Gules. Another variant is in a window in Melling church: Or a fess wavy between six cinquefoils Azure.

DAWSON, of Allan Bank (p. 98). On the wall of Glenthorne, Grasmere, is a stone shield with the initials T M D for Thomas and Martha Dawson, and date 1837 (?), with *Motto.* Toujours Propice.

FINCH-DAWSON (p. 99). Miss Ruth Felicia Finch-Dawson is 2nd, not eldest, dau. and coheir of Gerard Finch-Dawson.

de FINGERLEN de BISCHINSEN – see FINGERLEN.

de la SEE – see SEE.

de la WARR – see WEST.

DENT, of Flass (p. 100). The arms of Dent, quarterly with those of Wilkinson, of Flass, are engraved and hatched on glass at Flass, as follows. *Arms.* Quarterly, 1 & 4, Argent on a bend Sable three lozenges ermine (Dent); 2 & 3, Azure on a chevron between three whelk-shells barways Or a leopard's face Gules between two mascles Sable (Wilkinson). *Crests.* 1, A heraldic tiger's head erased (Dent); 2, A unicorn's head erased gorged with a collar thereon a leopard's face between two mascles (Wilkinson). The arms are carved in stone on the west front of the house, with date 1853, and the crests are on the gate pillars, but that of Wilkinson has lost its horn and has thus been converted into a horse's head.

DICKSON, of Abbots Reading (pp. 101-2). George Frederick Dickson, of Abbots Reading, had an eldest surviving son Frederick Cartwright Dickson (b. 1814), who was of Chapel House, Staveley (L). He was father of Frederick Maurice Dickson, J.P., of Levenside, Haverthwaite (1853-1929), and of Helene Jeanne Dickson (b. 1877), who was of Chapel House till her death. *Arms.* A shield on Chapel House displays these as: ... three mullets ... on a chief Or as many pallets Gules. *Motto.* Fortes fortuna juvat.

DIXON. The Rev. Thomas Dixon, M.A., D.D. (Oxon) (d. 1722), son of Thomas Dixon, of Orrest Head, Windermere, matriculated from The Queen's College, Oxford, 1665, aged 15; he was elected a Scholar of the College 1669 and a Fellow 1674, and was Rector of Weyhill, Hants., 1682-1772 (HHW). *Arms.* Sable a cross between four hinds' heads erased Or (Window in the College chapel, to which he was a benefactor).

DUCKETT. (p.105). *Arms* Curwen records these as having been, prior to the reign of Richard II: Quarterly Azure and Sable a bend Gules. He also records the following quarters; Azure a bend cotised between six crosses pattée Or (Bingham); Sable a chevron Or between three griffins' heads erased Argent (Skinner); Argent a chevron Ermine between three cocks Sable beaked and legged Gules (Henshaw); Argent a chevron Gules between three hearts . . . (Baskerville); Lozengy Or and Azure on a chief Gules a lion passant Or (Kipping); Ermine a cross flory Or between four annulets Azure (Ward); Azure a fess Erminois between three sheldrakes Proper (Jackson); Azure on a fess Or between three saltires Argent an annulet Sable (Goldstone); Azure three arrows erect Or (Chaldecot); Ermine a lion rampant Gules crowned Or (Turberville).

DUDLEY, Earl of Warwick (pp. 105-6). Ambrose Dudley, Earl of Warwick (*c.*1528-90), marr. (3) 1565 Anne (1548-1604), dau. of Francis Russell, 2nd Earl of Bedford, and the arms of Dudley impaling Russell are on the triptych from Appleby Castle, now in the Record Office, Carlisle.

DURANT. In 1912 the arms below were granted to Mrs Rosa Ryder Openshaw, née Durant, widow of James Alfred Openshaw, *q.v.,* to be borne by her and her descendants. *Arms.* Sable a cross crosslet saltirewise between two annulets in pale and as many fleurs-de-lys in fess Or (Original grant in possession of Mr John R. Hurrell, of Hutton, Brentwood, Essex).

ECHLIN, (p. 106). The present head of the family is Loris Godfrey Bertram Gilbert Leyborne Echlin, of Ickenham, Uxbridge.

ECROYD, (p. 107). Alizon Margaret Farrer, widow of Sir Arthur Cutforth, died in London 26 May 1976, aged 79.

EDWARDS. George Thomas Edwards, a cadet of Edwards, of Old Court, Co. Wicklow, who lived at Lake View, Bowness, in 1876, was grandfather of Col Arthur Wayman Edwards, O.B.E., M.C., formerly of Ladstock, Thornthwaite, Keswick, and now of 4 Almond Court West, Barnton, Edinburgh. His 2nd son, Lt Denis Wayman Edwards, R.N. (Rtd.), is of White House, Knock. *Arms.* Vert a stag trippant Or attired and unguled Argent on a chief of the last three falcons Proper. *Crest.* A lion's head erased Ermines between two palm branches Proper. *Motto.* Heb Dduw heb ddim, Duw a digon.

ETON COLLEGE. Shield in a window of Tunstall church. *Arms.* Azure three lilies slipped and leaved Argent on a chief per pale Azure and Gules dexter a fleur-de-lys and sinister a lion passant guardant Or.

EVERARD. Shield in window of Thurland Castle for Penelope Everard (1751-1836), marr. 1779 John Collins, of Fulham and Staines (d. 1807, aged 64); they were great-grandparents of Lt-Col Edward Brown Lees, see AWL. *Arms.* Argent on a chief Gules three mullets pierced of the field.

EVERARD (p. 109). Captain James Everard, of Lowick, had a son James Everard, R.N., who was drowned at sea, and daus. and coheirs Eleanor, marr. Edward Proudfoot Montagu (see AWL, p. 207); Mary, marr. the Rev. Isaac Gaskarth, Perpetual Curate of Lowick; Louisa Blencowe, marr. John Warnes and had a dau. Susanna, marr. the Rev. Charles George Calvert, see p. 50, above; Fanny, wife of . . . Fisher; and Anna, marr. Dr. Walter Scott.

EWYAS. Impaled by Clifford on triptych from Appleby Castle, now in the Record Office, Carlisle; Roger de Clifford, son of Walter de Clifford (d. 1222/3), marr. Sibill, dau. and coheir of Robert de Ewyas. *Arms.* Argent a fess Gules between three mullets Sable.

EXETER COLLEGE, Oxford. *Arms.* See p. 104, above. A variant is in a window of Tunstall church: Argent two bendlets nebuly Sable on a bordure of the last eight pairs of keys endorsed and interlaced in the bows Or wards upwards; impaling, Gules on a bend Or between two escallops Argent a

Cornish chough Sable beaked and membered Gules between two cinquefoils Azure on a chief Or a rose Gules barbed and seeded Proper between two fleurs-de-lys also Gules.

FALLOWFIELD (p. 111). *Arms.* Another authority for: Sable three escallops Or, is Machell (MMS vi 399).

FAYRER (p. 113). Sir Joseph Herbert Spens Fayrer, 3rd Bart., D.S.C., died 23 July 1976, aged 76, and was succ. by his son, Sir John Lang MacPherson Fayrer, 4th Bart.

FERGUSON INDUSTRIAL HOLDINGS Ltd., of Appleby Castle. In 1976 Mr. Denis Stewart Vernon, of Appleby Castle, Chairman of Ferguson Industrial Holdings Ltd., obtained on behalf of the Board of Directors a grant of arms for the Company, whose registered office is at Appleby Castle. *Arms.* Vert within an orle of eight towers Argent a builder's trowel blade upwards Or. *Crest.* A sea horse Proper supporting over the dexter shoulder a builder's hod Or. *Supporters.* Dexter, A peregrine falcon perched upon a branch of apple leaved and flowered; Sinister, A snowy owl perched upon a branch of grey alder leaved and flowered; all Proper. *Badge.* In front of a pomme ensigned by a length of wall with three crenels Argent a builder's trowel blade upwards Or. *Motto.* Fides inter honestos.

de FINGERLEN de BISCHINSEN. Impaled with Deincourt and Strickland on hatchment at Sizergh Castle; Thomas Strickland, of Sizergh and Borwick (1792-1835), marr. 1824 Gasparine Ursule Ida (1805-46), youngest dau. of the Baron de Fingerlen de Bischinsen. *Arms.* Quarterly, 1 & 4, Or issuing from a cloud in base Proper a cubit arm vested Gules the forefinger also Proper pointing upwards; 2, Azure a demi man in armour holding in the dexter hand a curved sword all Proper; 3, Azure four mullets of six points Argent, one, two, and one; over all an escutcheon of pretence, Per fess Argent and Gules in chief a demi horse rampant Proper in base a bezant.

FITZGIBBON. Maurice FitzGibbon, F.R.I.C., F.C.S., of Haverbreaks, Lancaster, formerly managing and technical director, Lunevale Products Ltd., Halton, is son of Maurice FitzGibbon, M.A., M.D., of 10 Merrion Square, Dublin, and of Howth, Co. Dublin, medical practitioner,* and grandson of the Rt. Hon. Gerald FitzGibbon, P.C., Q.C., LL.D. (TCD), of 10 Merrion Square, Dublin, and of Howth (1837-1909), Lord Justice of Appeal in Ireland. *Arms.* Ermine a saltire Gules on a chief argent three annulets of the second. *Crest.* A boar passant Gules charged on the body with three annulets fessways Argent. *Motto.* Nil admirari.

FITZWILLIAM. Shield on triptych from Appleby Castle, now in the Record Office, Carlisle; William FitzWilliam, Earl of Southampton (*c.* 1490-1542), marr. 1513 Mabel (d. 1550), dau. of Henry, Lord Clifford (d. 1523). *Arms.* Lozengy Argent and Gules a mullet Sable for difference.

FLEETWOOD (p. 118). A variant of the arms of Fleetwood is above the entrance to Lindeth Lodge, Silverdale. *Arms.* Per pale wavy Azure and Or six martlets, two, two, and two [counterchanged]. *Crest.* A wolf† passant reguardant. *Motto.* Homo homini lupus.

FLETCHER, of Field Broughton (p. 121). *Arms.* Henry Fletcher Rigge, in his MS. *The Older Monuments in Cartmel Priory Church,* 1876, records the arms as:

* He helped to defend Trinity College, Dublin, in the 1916 uprising.

† Which gives the house its present name of Wolf House.

Argent a cross Sable between four pellets each charged with a pheon of the first.

FLETCHER, of Crow How (p. 120). Sir Frank Fletcher was Headmaster of Charterhouse 1911-35, not 1911-15; his brother Clement had one Christian name only.

FLINT. A Clifford quartering on the Countess of Cumberland's tomb in St. Lawrence, Appleby. *Arms.* Sable three flint stones Argent. Curwen records this as: Vert three flint stones Argent (CW2 vi).

FORMBY. John Formby, D.L., J.P., B.A. (Cantab), of Formby Hall (L) (1852-1933), was also of Far Close, Arnside. *Arms.* Argent a lion rampant Gules on a chief Azure two doves Proper. *Crest.* A dove Proper. *Motto.* Semper fidelis (BGA).

FORTH, of Kendal. The Forths were well known pewterers in Kendal. Hugh Forth was father of Lancelot Forth (d. 1717), who was Mayor of Kendal 1684 and 1708. He owned the White Hall in Highgate, and though he had a large family, at his death only his dau. Anne, who marr. 1708 Thomas Winter, Mayor of Kendal 1719 (see p. 372), survived. *Arms* (as quartered by Winter on seal). Gules a lion rampant holding a staff raguly [Or].

FOTHERGILL, of Ravenstonedale (p. 125). George Fothergill was the builder of Armathwaite *Chapel,* not *Castle.*

FULLER-MAITLAND – see MAITLAND.

FURNESS ABBEY (p. 128). The Abbey's arms are carved on the 14th century font in St. Mary's church, Dalton-in-Furness. *Arms.* [Sable] on a pale [Argent] a crozier [of the first]. They are also on the font in Holy Trinity, Millom (C), and are illustrated in HCC i 523.

GARRATT (p. 131). *Crest.* Henry Fletcher Rigge in his MS. *The Older Monuments in Cartmel Priory church,* 1876, records this as: A tower.

GATHORNE (p. 132). The earliest known ancestor of this family, Richard Gathorne, who was married at Kirkby Lonsdale 1585, owned land at Holmscales, Old Hutton. His grandson John Gathorne (1608-79), who was buried at Burton-in-Kendal, had two sons, from the younger of whom, John, the Gathornes of Kirkby Lonsdale and the Earls of Cranbrook descend. The elder son and heir, Edward, was ancestor of Edward Gathorne, the last male of the senior line, who died at Allonby 1795. In the female line the family is represented by the Remingtons of Worthing, the Todds of The Green, Lambrigg, the Barrows, formerly of The Ghyll. Bradleyfield, and the Atkinsons, formerly of The Homestead, Kendal, descendants of his aunts (*Ex inf.* Dr. T. G. Fahy, of Shaw End).

GHIKA. H.S.H. Princess Alexandrine H. Ghika built Brackenhill, Kendal, in the 1920's and lived there for some ten years. *Arms.* The Princes Ghika, of Greece, Moldavia and Wallachia, bore: Gules an eagle displayed Or charged on the breast with an escutcheon quarterly 1 & 4, Argent an eagle displayed Sable, 2 & 3, Argent an eagle displayed Sable* (RAG).

GIBSON, of Bampton (p. 134). The arms of John Gibson (d. 1730), Provost of The Queen's College, Oxford, 1717-30, are in a window of the College chapel. *Arms.* Azure three storks rising, two and one, Proper; impaling, Azure a chevron between three talbots' heads Argent collared Sable ringed

* *Sic*; should the escutcheon perhaps be blazoned: Quarterly Argent and Sable four eagles displayed counterchanged?

Or (Alexander*). *Crest.* A lion's paw Gules issuing out of a ducal coronet clasping a spiked club Or.

GIBSON, of Quernmore Park (p. 135). Charles Gibson, of Quernmore Park (1790-1832), was father of, *int. al.*, a 6th and youngest son, the Rev. George Gibson, M.A. (Cantab) (1831-1921), who had two daus. and coheirs – Barbara Childeroy Gibson (1885-1963), marr. Harry Llanover Davies and had a son who was killed in action in World War II; and Mary Childeroy Gibson, of Furners, Henfield, Sussex, who is now the family's representative in England.

GILBERT. The Rev. Thomas Morrell Gilbert, M.A. (Cantab) (1835-1928), youngest son of Ashurst Turner Gilbert, Bishop of Chichester, was Vicar of Heversham 1866-1921 and Hon. Canon of Carlisle 1877-1928. *Arms.* Gules an armed leg couped at the thigh . . . between two spears erect . . . (BBE).

GRAHAM, of Smardale. George Graham, of Nunnery (see p. 137, above) was father of *int. al.* 2nd and 3rd sons Richard and George Graham, who were of Smardale. According to Machell, the latter marr. Susan, dau. of Robert Barton, of Breeks (see AWL), adding "He was a very stout little man in the Civil Wars, but never had the fortune to be rich." *Arms.* See p. 137, above.

GRAHAM (p. 139, footnote). The tablet in the sanctuary of St. Lawrence, Appleby, is of wood, not stone (*Ex inf.* Martin R. Holmes).

GREEN. The arms of Green are on shields on the ceiling of the Parr chapel, Kendal parish church;† Sir Thomas Parr, of Kendal (d. 1517), marr. Maud (d. 1531), dau. and coheir of Sir Thomas Green, of Green's Norton, Northants. *Arms.* Quarterly, 1 & 4, Azure three stags trippant Or (Green); 2 & 3, Azure a chevron between three cross crosslets Or on a chief of the last a lion passant Gules (Maplethorpe).‡

GRESLEY – see WEST.

GRESSINGHAM. What are said to be the *Arms* of the de Gressingham family, which held land in Gressingham until the time of Alice (dead by 1404), dau. of Thomas de Gressingham, and wife of Adam de Southworth, are on a stone on the Over Hall, or Crowtrees, Gressingham, viz. . . . a hunting horn with baldrick . . . (CHG).

GRINDALL. Quartered by Boynton, *q.v.*, on shields at Sizergh Castle and Levens Hall. The coat is attributed to Grindall in FVY, but H. Hornyold-Strickland identified it as Monceux. *Arms.* Gules a cross moline Or.

HALHEAD, of Kendal. A clerestory window in Kendal parish church was given by Hilton Halhead, of Liverpool, merchant, at the restoration of 1850-52, in memory of his father John Halhead, of Kendal (d. 1830). *Arms.* Barry of ten Argent and Gules three escutcheons Or. *Crest.* A falcon wings expanded Proper.

HALNABY. Quartered by Boynton, *q.v.*, in a window at Levens Hall. *Arms.* Argent a fess engrailed§ between six fleurs-de-lys Sable.

HARKER – see TINNISWOOD.

HARRISON, of Hare Appletree (p. 150). The family is now represented in Cumbria by John Kirk Harrison, of Whinthwaite House, Levens, late vice-

* The Provost marr. 1717 Mrs. Alexander, of St. Giles, Oxford.

† As are those of FitzHugh, Lancaster, Marmion, Parr and Roos, for which see AWL.

‡ The colours are very dull and faded and difficult to interpret. Whitaker recorded this quarter as: Gules a chevron between three crosses botony Or on a chief a lion passant Argent (WHR ii 327).

§ The fess should be plain, see FVD.

chairman of Thomas & James Harrison Ltd., shipowners, of Liverpool and London (the Harrison Line), son of John Harrison, of Hinderton (Ch) (d. 1914), who was son of John Harrison, of Batty Hill, Cockerham (1819-67), and grandson of James Harrison, of Batty Hill (1781-1862), by his wife Ann Hodgson, of Yealand.

HERBERT, Earl of Pembroke and Montgomery (p. 155). The arms of Herbert, impaling Vere, are on the triptych from Appleby Castle, now in the Record Office, Carlisle; Philip Herbert, Earl of Pembroke and Montgomery (1584-1650), who marr. (2) Lady Anne Clifford, dau. of George, 3rd Earl of Cumberland, marr. (1) 1604 Susan (1587-1629), 3rd dau. of Edward Vere, 17th Earl of Oxford. *Arms.* Per pale Azure and Gules three lions rampant Argent. The arms, with a crescent for difference, are impaled by Lowther, *q.v.,* on a funeral hatchment now in Lowther church; St. George Henry, 4th Earl of Lonsdale (1855-82), marr. 1878 Constance Gladys (d. 1917), 3rd dau. of Sidney, 1st Baron Herbert of Lea, and sister of the 13th Earl of Pembroke. Their dau. and heir Lady Gladys Mary Juliet Lowther (1881-1965) marr. (1) 1903 Sir Robert George Vivian Duff, 2nd Bart. (killed in action 1914), and (2) 1919 Major Keith Trevor. Her mother marr. (2) 1885 the 2nd Marquess of Ripon.

HILL. Shield in stained glass on staircase at Plumpton Hall, Ulverston; William Sawrey, of Plumpton (d. 1727), see AWL, marr. . . . dau. of . . . Hill. *Arms.* Argent a chevron Or* between three lozenges Sable.

HILTON, of Hilton and Burton (p. 158). *Arms.* GMS records for Hilton, of Hilton (W): Sable a fess between in chief two saltires Argent and in base three plates.

HOGHTON – see STANLEY.

HOLKER. Shield in window of Thurland Castle for Dorothy Holker, of Euxton (L), marr. 1805 Thomas Livesey, of Hoghton. *Arms.* Per chevron embattled Argent and Azure three lions rampant counterchanged.

HOLME. George Holme, of Waterhead, Monk Coniston (1592-1630), was father of Capt Thomas Holme (1624-95), Surveyor General of Pennsylvania 1682-95, in which capacity he laid out the city of Philadelphia. *Arms.* Argent a chevron Azure between three chaplets Gules on a bordure . . . . . . roundles . . . (CW2 xxiii 78-83).

HOLMES, of Castle Bank (p. 161). Delete M.A. (Oxon) after Martin Rivington Holmes. Mr. M. R. Holmes was Mayor of Appleby-in-Westmorland 1975-76.

HOLT. Stone shield at Newbiggin Hall; Montague Hughes Crackanthorpe, formerly Cookson, of Newbiggin Hall (1832-1913), marr. 1869 Blanche Alethea Elizabeth (d. 1928), youngest dau. of the Rev. Eardley Chauncy Holt, M.A. (Oxon). *Arms.* [Argent] on a bend engrailed [Sable] three fleurs-de-lys [of the field].

HOLY ROMAN EMPIRE, The. The arms of the Holy Roman Empire, ensigning those of the Swiss Forest Canton of Uri, *q.v.,* which was at one time part of the Empire, are in glass dated 1640 at Sizergh Castle which was brought by the National Trust from Wasdale Hall. *Arms.* Or an eagle displayed with two heads Sable behind each head a halo.

HORNYOLD-STRICKLAND, of Sizergh. Henry Hornyold, J.P., F.S.A., K.C.S.G. (1890-1975), only son of Alfred Joseph Hornyold, of the family of

* Correctly, Gules; it may have been so originally, and faded to Or.

Blackmore Park, Worcs., marr. 1920 the Hon. Mary Constance Elizabeth Christina Strickland, see AWL, and in 1932 assumed the additional surname and arms of Strickland after the conveyance to him of the Sizergh estate. He was High Sheriff of Westmorland 1937 and Lord Lieutenant 1957-65. He was succ. by his son, Lt-Cdr Thomas Henry Hornyold-Strickland, D.L., D.S.C., of Sizergh, Count della Catena, High Sheriff of Westmorland 1973. *Arms.* Quarterly, 1 & 4, Sable three escallops Argent (Strickland); 2 & 3, Azure on a bend embattled counter-embattled Argent a wolf courant between two escallops Sable (Hornyold). *Crests.* 1, A holly tree fructed Proper (Strickland); 2, A demi unicorn Gules crined and armed Or (Hornyold). *Mottoes.* Sans mal (Strickland); Fidem tene (Hornyold).

HUDDLESTON, of Elterwater. David Huddleston, of Low Birkhow, Little Langdale, slate getter and yeoman (d. 1795), was father of David, John and Miles Huddleston, from whom many bearers of the surname are descended. David Huddleston (1766-1831), the eldest son, became a clerk in the Kendal Bank *c.* 1793, and was made a partner in 1810, retiring in 1823 to Elterwater Hall, now the Eltermere Hotel. He founded the gunpowder works at Elterwater and was succ. by his son John Huddleston (1803-41) whose son William Huddleston, of Kirkby, Liverpool (1829-80), was the last to live at Elterwater Hall. His grandson William Steel Huddleston, Major R.A. (b. 1896), was killed in action 1940. His son Miles Huddleston is now head of the family. (CFB). *Arms.* Gules a fret Argent. *Crest* and *Motto.* As Hudleston, of Millom, see p. 171 (Engraved on watch in the possession of Mrs. Elfrida Nelson, only dau. of David Huddleston, of Brantholme, Lonsties, Keswick).

HUGHES. Impaled by Clifford on triptych from Appleby Castle, now in the Record Office, Carlisle; Francis, 4th Earl of Cumberland (1559-1641), marr. 1589 Grisold, or Grizell (d. 1613), widow of Edward Neville, Lord Abergavenny, and dau. of Thomas Hughes, of Uxbridge. *Arms.* Per fess Or and Argent a lion rampant reguardant Sable.

HUTTON, of Thorphinsty (p. 170). Henry Fletcher Rigge, in his MS. *The Older Monuments in Cartmel Priory Church,* 1876, records the following *Crest.* On three arrows plumed Argent a coronet Or.

JOHNES (p. 174). *Arms.* Henry Fletcher Rigge in an illustration in his MS. *The Older Monuments in Cartmel Priory Church* hatches the arms as: Ermine a chevron Sable.

JONES. Shield in window of Thurland Castle for Betty (d. 1847), dau. of Joseph Jones, of Hope House, Oldham, marr. (1) Joseph Harrop and (2) James Lees, of Higher Clarksfield House (1759-1828). *Arms.* Azure on a cross raguly Argent between in the first and fourth quarters a pheon and in the second and third a cross moline Or five mullets pierced Gules.

KEIGHLEY – see STANLEY.

KELK. Quartered by Boynton, *q.v.,* on shields at Sizergh Castle and Levens Hall. *Arms.* Sable a bend flory counterflory Argent.

KENDAL, Earls of (p. 176). See also PLANTAGENET, Earl of Kendal.

KENDAL GRAMMAR SCHOOL. The school uses the following variant of the *Arms* of the town of Kendal: Quarterly, 1 & 4, Gules three wool hooks Proper; 2 & 3, Vert three teasels Proper; the shield ensigned with a ducal coronet Or. *Motto.* Nisi Dominus frustra.

KENWORTHY. Shield in window of Thurland Castle for Mary (1725-80), dau. of William Kenworthy, of Quick, Saddleworth (Y), and wife of John Lees, of Clarksfield (1720-68). *Arms.* Argent a fess counter-compony Or and Gules between three eagles displayed Sable.

KESSELRING. The arms of Thomas Kesselring, Hereditary Steward of the Lordship of Liebenfels and Altenklingen and High Steward of the Lordship of Weinfelden from 1585 to 1610, and of his son Kilian Kesselring, Major General and Treasurer of the County of Thurgau in Switzerland, 1632, are in a window in Sizergh Castle which was removed by the National Trust from Wasdale Hall. *Arms.* Sable a lion rampant contourné Or holding between the forepaws a yoke Gules. *Crest.* A demi lion Or crowned Gules and holding between the forepaws a yoke also Gules. *Motto.* Gott erkens in gnaden.

KITCHING. John Kitching, of The Nook, Shap (d. 1811, aged 83), was father of Edward Kitching, surgeon, of Flowerden, Milnthorpe (1756-1815), who had a dau. Elizabeth* (d. 1881, aged 78), wife of Thompson Bindloss, *q.v.*, and a son John Kitching (d. 1879, aged 83) who practised as a surgeon in South Audley Street, London, until 1830, when he returned to Milnthorpe and practised there till his death. His only dau. Agnes Sarah (d. 1894 aged 74) marr. 1869 Alderman William Bindloss, *q.v.* She left Flowerden, Milnthorpe, to Annie Marjorie Harrison, who took the name Kitching 1910. *Arms.* . . . a chevron . . . between three bustards . . . (Shield on west facade of Kendal Town Hall).

KNIPE (p. 179). *Arms.* Henry Fletcher Rigge, in his MS. *The Older Monuments in Cartmel Priory Church,* 1876, records the arms on a brass as: Argent two bars Gules in chief three wolves' heads couped . . . .

KNIPE, of Warton. James Knipe, of Warton, had a son Christopher Knipe, of London, who in 1616 had a confirmation of his arms, and the grant of a crest. *Arms.* Gules two bars Argent in chief three wolves' heads couped of the same. *Crest.* A wolf's head Argent shot through the neck with a broad arrow Or (Grant in possession of the Rev. W. G. D. Fletcher, printed in Harl. Soc. lxxvii (1926), p. 126).

KRUPP. Shield in window of Thurland Castle for Friedrich Alfred Krupp, godfather of Maud Lees (1880-1967). *Arms.* Argent out of a mount in base Vert a palm tree encircled by a serpent Proper. Another shield, for Margarethe Krupp, godmother of the Rev. Ronald Lees (1882-1959), shews these arms impaling: Or a wolf rampant Sable.

LAMB. Edward Lamb, of High Green, Sandford, Warcop, yeoman (d. 1748), was father of, *int. al.*, the Rev. Matthew Lamb, M.A., D.D. (Oxon) (1732-97), who was Fellow of The Queen's College, Oxford; Principal of Magdalen Hall, Oxford, 1786-88; Prebendary of Lichfield 1772 and of Worcester 1775-97; and Chancellor of the Diocese of Oxford. He was also Vicar of Banbury and Rector of Harvington, Worcs., and of Chipping Warden, Northants. *Arms.* Azure on a fess wavy Or between two lions rampant in chief and a lamb passant in base Argent supporting with its dexter forefoot a pennon of the last charged with a cross of St. George three crosses pattée Gules. *Crest.* A mount Vert thereon in front of a gate Sable a lamb passant Argent supporting a pennon as in the arms the staff entwined with an olive branch Proper (M.I., Chipping Warden church).

* She gave the Kitching Memorial Reading Rooms in memory of her brother, whose daughter built the Kitching Memorial Hospital to his memory.

LANCASTER. The Rev. William Lancaster, M.A. (Oxon) (1650-1717), was born at Sockbridge Hall, Barton, and was schoolmaster at Barton before going up to Oxford as tutor to Sir John Lowther 1670. He became Rector of St. Martin-in-the-Fields 1694; Provost of The Queen's College, Oxford (to which he was a most generous benefactor) 1704; Archdeacon of Middlesex 1705; and Vice-Chancellor of Oxford 1706-10. *Arms.* Various versions of the Provost's arms are in windows of the chapel of The Queen's College: 1, Argent three bars Azure on a canton Gules a chaplet Or; 2, Argent two bars Gules on a canton of the second a mullet of the first; 3, Argent two bars and a canton Gules on the last a lion passant guardant Or; impaling, Gules a chevron Vair between three eagles displayed Or (Wilmer); 4, As 3, without the impalement but with *Crest.* A demi sea horse maned Or.

LANCASTER, City of (p. 182). The arms of the City of Lancaster are carved in stone on the building in Windermere now occupied by the National Westminster Bank, but formerly by the Lancaster Banking Company. The arms are also carved on the doors of the Company's former premises, now known as Old Bank Chambers, in Lake Road, Ambleside.

LANG. The Rev. Robert Lang, M.A. (Cantab) (1840-1908), was Curate of Kendal 1863-65. *Arms.* Per pale indented Argent and Sable three lions' heads erased counterchanged on a chief indented Ermine a dolphin naiant of the second. *Crest.* A boar's head erased Proper between two fleurs-de-lys Or. *Motto.* Virtuti fortuna comes (FD7).

LANGTON (pp. 183-4). Robert Langton (d. 1524), a native of Appleby and nephew of Thomas Langton, Bishop of Winchester, was Prebendary of Lincoln 1483-1517, Archdeacon of Dorset 1486-1514, Treasurer of York Minster 1509-14 and Prebendary 1514-24. *Arms.* A shield in a window in the chapel of the Queen's College, Oxford, displays: Per pale Gules and Azure the letter Tau Argent and a plummet Or in pale between an escallop and a catherine wheel of the fourth on a chief of the last a cross patonce of the first between two torteaux the dexter charged with a key the sinister with a dagger in bend Or. J. R. Magrath in QCO describes a coat-of-arms in a window in the College chapel as for Langton: Argent a fret [*recte* fretty] Gules a chief of the second. This also occurs with a tun Or ensigned with the letter R in the fess point.

LATHAM. A Stanley quartering on shield on Hornby church tower. *Arms.* [Or] on a chief indented [Azure] three plates.

LA TROBE. The Rev. John Antas La Trobe, M.A. (Oxon) (1799-1878), son of Christian Ignatius La Trobe (1758-1836), was Vicar of St. Thomas, Kendal, 1840-65, Hon. Canon of Carlisle 1858-78, and a well known writer on music (DNB). *Arms.* Argent on a fess Azure a fleur-de-lys between two escallops Or. *Crest.* Out of clouds a dexter cubit arm Proper the hand grasping an anchor fessways Or (BGA, *sub* Bateman).

LAWSON. Impaled by Standish on a hatchment at Sizergh Castle; Thomas Strickland Standish, of Sizergh, Standish and Borwick (1763-1813), marr. (1) 1789 Anastasia Maria (1769-1807), elder dau. and coheir of Sir John Lawson, 5th Bart., of Brough (Y). *Arms.* Argent a chevron between three martlets Sable.

LEACH. The Rev. Thomas Leach, B.A. (Cantab) (1818-75), Vicar of Thornton-in-Lonsdale 1848-75, marr. 1847 Ann Elizabeth, only dau. of Richard Lodge, of Keen Ground, Hawkshead, surgeon. Their younger son

Richard Ernest Leach, M.A. (Cantab) (d. 1929, aged 72), was Headmaster of Appleby Grammar School 1891-1901 and Mayor of Appleby 1899. *Arms.* Azure a lion rampant Argent gorged with a collar nebuly of the field a chief nebuly of the second, thereon a crown vallary between two mascles Gules. *Crest.* In front of a dexter cubit arm the hand grasping a serpent head upwards Proper three mascles Or. *Motto.* Finis coronat opus (FD7).

LEATHAM. Mrs. Priscilla Helen Wynne, of The Old Rectory, Great Musgrave, widow of Major Graham Chamley Wynne (see AWL, p. 334), is 2nd dau. of Vice-Admiral Eustace La Trobe Leatham, C.B., of Hemsworth Hall (Y) (1870-1935). *Arms.* Per saltire Ermine and Or on a chief engrailed Azure three bezants each charged with a saltire Gules. *Motto.* Virtute vinces (BLG18).

LEIGHTON. Henry Gerard Mather Leighton, M.A. (Oxon), F.S.A., of 9 Bathwick Hill, Bath, is son of Wilfrid Leighton, J.P., F.S.A., who marr. 1931 Margaret, 4th dau. and coheir of Harold Mather, *q.v.* They now own a large part of Mr. Mather's estate at Staveley. *Arms.* Quarterly per fess indented Or and Gules in the second and third quarters a crescent of the first. *Crest.* A wyvern Sable armed and legged Or charged on the shoulder with an escutcheon of the arms. *Motto.* Dread shame (BLG17).

LEY. Brigadier Hugh Marlborough Hale Ley, C.B.E., D.L., of the Dower House, Burrow, formerly of Treworgan Vean, Cornwall, late the 3rd Carabiniers (Prince of Wales Dragoon Guards), son of Lt-Col Arthur Edwin Hale Ley, late Indian Cavalry (1879-1963), is descended from Hugh Ley, of Milor and Treworgan Vean, Cornwall, in 1655. *Arms.* Argent a chevron Sable between three seals' heads couped Proper.* *Crest.* A lion sejant Or the dexter forepaw raised. *Motto.* Vincendo victus.

LEYBURNE, of Cunswick (pp. 189-90). *Arms.* TVN gives: Quarterly, 1 & 4, Gules six lions rampant Argent; 2 & 3, Argent on a bend Sable three annulets of the field in chief a trefoil slipped of the second.

LIVESEY. Shields in windows of Thurland Castle; Lt-Col Edward Brown Lees, D.L., J.P. (1843-96), marr. 1877 Dorothy (d. 1912), dau. of John Livesey, of Blackburn (L) (1810-86). *Arms.* Argent a lion rampant Gules between three trefoils slipped Vert.†

LOFTIE (p. 191). Lt-Cdr William Henry Paule Loftie, D.S.C., R.N. (Rtd), died at Bowerbank 16 May 1976, aged 57.

LOWRY, of Kendal. Richard Lowry, of Kendal, was father of the Rev. John Lowry, M.A. (Oxon) (*c.* 1709-84), who was Fellow of The Queen's College, Oxford, 1734, Proctor 1741, Whyte Professor of Moral Philosophy 1742, and Rector of Charlton-on-Otmoor 1753. *Arms.* The father sealed a deed of 1719 with the following: ... a chevron ... between three birds .... The son's shield in a window in the Hall of The Queen's College, however, bears: Sable a cup Or issuing therefrom two branches Vert.

LOWTHER, Earl of Lonsdale (p. 192). On the funeral hatchment now in Lowther church of St. George Henry, 4th Earl of Lonsdale (1855-82), the *Arms* of Lowther, Or six annulets Sable, are charged with an inescutcheon, Argent on waves of the sea Proper a three-masted ship with sails set flags and pennons flying also Proper, to denote his office of Hereditary Admiral of the Coasts of Cumberland and Westmorland.

* Burke gives for Ley, of Treworgan Vean: Argent three pine trees Vert (BGA).

† In one shield the trefoils are incorrectly shewn as Gules.

MACAN. Thomas Townley Macan, M.A., Ph.D. (Cantab), of Stevney, Outgate, Hawkshead, scientist and author (b. 1910), is elder son of Col Thomas Townley Macan, C.B., of Axminster, Devon (b. 1860). From 1935 to 1977 he was naturalist with the Freshwater Biological Association, Windermere, and was Deputy Director 1946-77. He was formerly General Secretary of the International Association of Limnology, and during World War II he served as Major, R.A.M.C. *Arms.* Azure fretty Or on a fess Argent a boar passant Gules. *Crest.* A salmon naiant Proper. *Motto.* Virtus sub pondere crescit.

MACHELL, of Penny Bridge (p. 197). *Motto.* For Mauvais chien, read Mauvais chiens.

McKAY (p. 197). Sir George Mills McKay was of Glen Rothay, Rydal, when he bought Rothay Bank, Ambleside, now known as Rothay Manor, 1913. The property was sold after his death.

MACMILLAN. Shield in window of Thurland Castle for Emma Macmillan, godmother of Dorothy Neville Lees (b. 1886). *Arms.* Or a lion rampant Sable in chief three mullets Azure pierced Argent; impaling, Vignatel, *q.v.*

McNAUGHT. James McNaught, of Kendal, was son of James McNaught (d. 1810) and grandson of Alexander McNaught, of Milton Park, Kirkcudbrightshire, descended from the McNaughts, of Kilquharity. *Arms.* Sable a fess chequy Argent and Azure between three lions' heads* erased of the second langued Gules. *Crest.* Out of a ducal coronet Or a lion's head as in the arms. *Motto.* Post praelia praemia (BLG4, p. 298).

FULLER-MAITLAND. John Alexander Fuller-Maitland, M.A. (Cantab), Hon. D.Litt. (Dunelm), F.S.A., of Borwick Hall (1856-1936), son of John Fuller-Maitland, was music critic of *The Times.* He was the author of a number of books on musical subjects, and joint editor in 1931 of John Lucas' *History of Warton* (CW2 xxxvi 240). *Arms.* Quarterly, 1 & 4, Or a lion rampant within a tressure flory counterflory Gules† (Maitland); 2 & 3, Quarterly i & iv, Argent on a cross Sable five crescents of the field; ii & iii, Argent three bars Gules a canton of the last (Fuller); over all in fess point a crescent Argent for difference. *Crests.* 1, A lion sejant affronté Argent crowned Or holding in either forepaw a sword Proper hilt and pommel Or*; 2, A beacon Or fired Proper. *Motto.* Consilio et animis (Stained glass in door panels at Borwick Hall).

MAPLETHORPE – see GREEN.

MARSHALL, of Aynsome (p. 200). *Arms.* Henry Fletcher Rigge in his MS. *The Older Monuments in Cartmel Priory Church,* 1876, records the arms as impaled by Fletcher, of Field Broughton, see AWL, as: Argent three bars Sable a canton Ermine. In an illustration, he hatches the arms on the chandelier as: Quarterly, 1, Per pale Or and Purpure a lion rampant Argent; 2 & 3, Argent three bars Sable a canton Ermine; 4, Or three chevronels Gules a label of five points Argent; impaling, Johnes, *q.v.*

WYKEHAM-MARTIN. Charles Alan Wykeham-Martin (1864-1942), son of Commander Cornwallis Wykeham-Martin, J.P., R.N., was for some years

* Burke incorrectly records them as boars' heads.

† The lion rampant of the Maitlands is normally depicted as couped in all its joints and within a double tressure flory counterflory; and the tressure is double on a shield above a back door at Borwick Hall. The lion sejant in the crest is usually represented holding a fleur-de-lys in the dexter paw.

the Rydal Hall estate agent, and lived at Loughrigg Holme. *Arms.* Quarterly, 1 & 4, Gules a lion rampant within an orle of cross crosslets and mullets alternately Or (Martin); 2 & 3, Argent two chevronels Sable between three roses Gules barbed Vert seeded Or (Wykeham). *Crests.* 1, A martin entwined by a serpent Proper in the beak a cross crosslet fitché Or (Martin); 2, A buffalo's head erased Sable armed Or charged on the neck with two chevronels Argent (Wykeham). *Motto.* Manners makyth man.

MATHER. Harold Mather, J.P., A.C.A., of Sidegarth, Staveley (W) (1862-1941), was son of William Mather, of Eagley (L). His family acquired a large estate in Nether Staveley in the middle of the 19th century, chiefly to obtain the ash cuttings from its coppices to supply their bobbin mill on the banks of the River Gowan. Later the family settled in Staveley, first at Middle Fairbank and then at Sidegarth, which Mr. Mather built. His four daus. and coheirs were Constance (1892-1967), marr. Canon C. H. Ellison, Vicar of St. Anne's-on-Sea; Hilda, marr. Leslie W. Black, of the Western Telegraph Co.; Alice Kathleen (1895-1958); and Margaret, marr. 1931 Wilfrid Leighton, J.P., F.S.A., of The Manor House, Burnett, Som. (d. 1967), for whose son, see LEIGHTON (BLG17). *Arms.* Per fess embattled Gules and Argent in chief three eagles' heads erased Or and in base as many arrows paleways points downwards Sable (Bookplate of H. G. M. Leighton).

MATHEWS (p. 202). Dr. Richard Graham Mathews, of Green Close Cottage, Kirkby Lonsdale, died on 16th April 1977.

MATHEWS. Shield in window of Inlaid Chamber, Sizergh Castle; Henry Hornyold-Strickland, *q.v.*, was son of Alfred Joseph Hornyold (1850-1922) by his wife Marie Louise Geneviève Alice (d. 1943), dau. of Julien Francois Bertrand de La Chere, of Paris, and his wife Mary Mathews (d. 1890), dau. of Henry Mathews, of Belmont, Herefordshire (1789-1828), and sister and heir of Henry, 1st and last Viscount Llandaff (1826-1913). *Arms.* Or a lion rampant reguardant between two flaunches Sable each charged with a mullet Argent.

MILLER, of Bampton – see p. 228, above.

MILLER. Armorial glass from Fell Foot, originally set up by George John Miller Ridehalgh, of Fell Foot, now in the possession of Mrs M. E. Forrest, of Broughton Lodge Farm House. *Arms.* Argent a fess wavy Azure between three wolves' heads erased Gules. *Crest.* A wolf's head erased Proper gorged with a collar wavy Azure.

MILNE, Shield in window of Thurland Castle for Abram Crompton Milne, godfather of Dorothy Neville Lees (b. 1886). *Arms.* Sable on a millrind Argent between two flaunches Or a lion rampant of the field.

MOLYNEUX – see STANLEY.

MONCEUX – see GRINDALL.

MONTE ALTO – see p. 230, above.

MÖTELIN – see WÖTELIN.

MOUNSEY (p. 211). For the arms of this family, see p. 234, above.

NEVILLE, Quartered by Strickland on shields at Sizergh Castle; Sir Walter Strickland, of Sizergh (*c.* 1497-1528), marr. *c.* 1515 Katherine, eldest dau. and coheir of Ralph Neville, of Thornton Bridge (Y). *Arms.* Gules on a saltire Argent a mullet pierced Sable.

NEWTON, Shield in window of Thurland Castle for Sara Newton (d.

1743), wife of John Lees, of Clarksfield (d. 1724). *Arms.* Azure three eagles displayed Argent.

NORTH, of Newton Hall (pp. 217-8). Richard Coulthurst North, of Newton Hall, died 9th August 1976, aged 43.

NORTH, of Newton (pp. 217-8). *Arms.* A window in Thurland Castle displays: Azure a lion passant between in chief two fleurs-de-lys and in base a quatrefoil pierced all Argent.

OLIVIER, (p.220). Lt-Col Henry Arnould Olivier died 22nd April 1976, aged 72.

OPENSHAW, James Alfred Openshaw, of Exeter, and of Park Side, Kendal, marr. Rosa Ryder, dau. and heir of . . . Durant, *q.v.* In 1912, when she was living a widow at Southbridge Manor, Streatley, Berks., she obtained a grant of arms to be placed on any monument or otherwise to the memory of her husband and borne by his descendants, and also a grant of arms for herself and her descendants, see DURANT. *Arms.* Per fess Vert and Or in chief three keys in fess erect the wards downwards and to the dexter and in base as many oak trees couped also in fess counterchanged. *Crest.* A squirrel sejant Gules supporting a woodman's axe Or. *Motto.* Felix laborans (Original grant in possession of Mr. John R. Hurrell, of Hutton, Brentwood, Essex).

ORDE. John Bertram Orde, of Longridge, Norham, Major 2nd Dragoon Guards (1783-1863), was of Soulby, Kirkby Stephen, in 1848 when his dau. Harriet (b. 1824) marr. the Rev. Charles Charlton; another dau. Eliza Jane marr. 1849 the Rev. John Romney, of Whitestock Hall, see AWL, and her nephew William Beresford Orde died in infancy at the Hall in 1859. *Arms.* Sable three salmons hauriant Argent. *Crest.* A stag's head erased Proper. *Motto.* Fortis in se ipso (RND).

PARKINSON, *alias* FETHERSTONE. In 1566 James Parkinson, *alias* Fetherstone, of Westmorland in the Barony of Kendal, "a younger brother . . . being uncertain" of his ancestors' crest, obtained a grant of the following *Crest.* On a torse Silver and Gules "a demy teager" Silver holding in his paws a sword broken the hilt and pomell Gold and about his neck a collar Sable studded and ringed Gold (Cotton MS Faustina E1 f. 18b, Harl. Soc. lxxvii (1926) 167-8). BGA gives for Fetherston, *alias* Perkinson, the following *Arms.* Gules on a chevron between three ostrich feathers Argent as many pellets.

PHILIPSON (pp. 231-2). *Arms.* GMS records: Gules a chevron between three boars' heads erased Argent.

PHILIPSON. The 1568 London Visitation contains a pedigree headed by Mathew Philipson, of Kendal in Com Ebor [*sic*]. His son Robert was living 1568 (Ex inf. Dr. T. G. Fahy, of Shaw End). *Arms.* Sable a chevron Ermine between three bats' wings expanded Argent. *Crest.* A horse's head couped Or crined Sable holding in the mouth an oak branch Vert acorned Or (Harl. Soc).

PLACE. Quartered by Boynton, *q.v.*, in window at Levens Hall. *Arms.* Azure on a chief Argent three quatrefoils* Gules.

PLANTAGENET, Earl of Cambridge. Shield on triptych from Appleby Castle, now in the Record Office, Carlisle; Richard Plantagenet, Earl of

* Correctly, chaplets.

Cambridge (b. *c.* 1375, executed 1415), marr. (2) *c.* 1414 Maud (d. *s.p.* 1446), divorced wife of John Neville, Lord Latimer, and dau. of Thomas, Lord Clifford (d. 1391). *Arms.* Quarterly, France Modern and England, all within a bordure Or semé of lions passant Gules.

PLATT, of Huntingstile (p. 234). General Sir William Platt died in London in November 1975.

PLATT. In 1737 Mrs. Ellen Beaumont, widow, of Kendal, formerly of Appleby, sealed her will (pr. 1737) with what seem to be the arms of Platt. This was perhaps her maiden name, for although she mentions her "brother" John Harrison, she could have meant "brother-in-law". She seems to have been twice married, for she also mentions her son Thomas How. *Arms.* . . . on a chevron . . . between three escallops . . . as many leopards' faces . . . . *Crest.* A stork holding in its beak an escallop.

POSTLETHWAITE, of Abbots Reading. Richard Postlethwaite, of Abbots Reading, Colton (d. 1787, aged 95), was father of Miles Postlethwaite (d. *s.p.* 1788, aged 67), who succ., and was in turn succ. by his sister's son, Arthur Benson, see AWL p. 27. *Arms.* Gules a fess counter-compony . . . and . . . between three birds . . . . *Crest.* A (?) dove holding in the beak a sprig (Seal on will of Miles Postlethwaite).

PURTON. Impaled by Livesey, *q.v.*, on shield in Thurland Castle for Susan Livesey, godmother of Ethel Lees (1884-1969). *Arms.* Argent on a chevron Gules three pears Or.

RAWLINSON, of Cark Hall (p. 242). *Arms.* Curwen transposes the tinctures and records: Argent two bars gemel between three escallops Gules (CW2 vi).

CADOGAN-RAWLINSON (p. 244). Commander Cadogan-Rawlinson's Christian names are Kenneth Roger Brooke.

READE. Armorial glass from Fell Foot, now in the possession of Mrs. M. E. Forrest, of Broughton Lodge Farm House; George John Miller Ridehalgh, of Fell Foot, marr. 1856 Fanny Rosa, dau. of George Reade, of Congleton (Ch). *Arms.* Gules a saltire between four garbs Or. *Crest.* On the stump of a tree a falcon rising Proper belled and jessed Or.

REYNELL. Henry Willock Reynell, of Kendal and Scalthwaiterigg, Superintending Surveyor of Taxes (d. before 1847), marr. 1807 Elizabeth, dau. of John Thwaites, of Appleby, and had *int. al.* daus. Eliza, born at Kendal 1808, who was of High Street, Appleby, 1851; Anna (b. 1810), Harriet (b. 1815), and Jane (b. 1817), all in Kendal. *Arms.* Masonry Argent and Sable a chief indented of the second. *Crest.* A fox passant Or. *Mottoes.* Murus aheneus esto; Indubitata fides (BLG1846).

RICHARDSON, of Rownehead, or Ronhead. Thomas Richardson, of Rownehead, or Ronhead, Dalton-in-Furness (will pr. 1717), sealed in 1688 and 1693 with *Arms.* . . . on a chief . . . three lions' heads erased . . . . This is given in the Barrow Naturalists' Field Club *Proceedings* xvii 54 as: Argent on a chief three lions' heads erased Sable.

RICHARDSON. William Richardson, of Brampton (W), was father of the Rev. Michael Richardson, M.A., D.D. (Oxon) (b. *c.* 1708), who was fellow of The Queen's College, Oxford, 1741 and Rector of Sulhampstead, Berks. *Arms.* Per fess Argent and Azure a lion rampant counterchanged (Shield in glass in The Queen's College Hall).

RIDEHALGH (pp. 248-9). In an armorial window from Fell Foot and a painting in the possession of Mrs. M. E. Forrest, of Broughton Lodge Farm House, the *Crest* is: A demi lion rampant Erminois holding between the paws a garb Azure.

Mrs. Ethel Ridehalgh, widow of William Smith Ridehalgh, died 1st October 1975, leaving two daus. and co-heirs, Mrs. Marjorie E. Forrest, and Mary, who marr. 1945 the Hon. Greville Reginald Howard, 3rd son of the 19th Earl of Suffolk.

RIGG, of Little Strickland (p. 249). *Arms.* The correct blazon of Machell's version of the arms is: Ermine on a chevron Sable five annulets Argent (MMS vi 399). GMS records: Ermine on a chevron Sable five plates.

ROBINSON, of Newby Bridge. The Robinson family, which was of Newby Bridge for some generations, failed in the male line on the death *s.p.* 1788, aged 83, of John Robinson, who left the Newby Bridge estate to his widow, Emma (d. 1791, aged 77); she left the estate to her brother, Thomas Machell, of Aynsome, see AWL. *Arms.* Vert on a chevron Or between three harts trippant Argent as many cinquefoils . . . . *Crest.* A hart's head couped (Henry Fletcher Rigge, MS. *The Older Monuments in Cartmel Priory Church,* 1876).

ROSSELLS, or RUSSELL, of Newton (Y). Quartered by Boynton, *q.v.,* on shields at Sizergh Castle and Levens Hall. *Arms.* Argent a chevron Azure between three roses Gules.

ROWLEY (p. 255). For ROWELY, read ROWLEY.

ROTHWELL, of Hawkshead (p. 254). Christopher Myles Rothwell, the present male representative, is son of Richard Myles Rothwell, not of Rainshaw Norris Rothwell.

RUSSELL (p. 257, footnote). The arms of Russell are also on the triptych from Appleby Castle, now in the Record Office, Carlisle.

RYLANDS (p. 258). George Chapman Rylands, T.D., D.L., J.P., C.C. (Ch), of Woodstock, Stretton, was appointed O.B.E. in the Queen's Birthday Honours List, 1976.

SACKVILLE – see WEST.

SADLEIR. Capt Blount Sadleir, of London, 6th son of Richard Sadleir, of Sopwell, Herts (1569-1624), and grandson of Sir Ralph Sadleir, P.C., of Standon, Herts. (1507-87), bought the manor of Beetham 1652. A later member of the family, Philip Archer Sadleir, M.I.Mech.E., now of Karlstad, Sweden, descended from Capt Sadleir's elder brother, Thomas Sadleir, of Sopwell Hall, Co. Tipperary, was a turbine designer with Vickers Armstrong at Barrow-in-Furness 1946-51 (FRK ii 236; IFR). *Arms.* Or a lion rampant per fess Azure and Gules. *Crest.* A demi lion rampant Azure ducally crowned Or. *Motto.* Servire Deo sapere (IFR; BGA).

ST. JOHN (p. 258). On two shields in Appleby Castle the *Arms* are impaled as: Argent on a chief indented Gules two mullets pierced Or.

ST. MARY'S ABBEY, York (p. 258). For a variant of the *Arms,* see p. 290.

SALKELD (p. 259). Dorothy, sister and heir of Richard Salkeld (d. 1630), marr. (1) . . . Wormeley, nor Morley.

SALMOND (p. 260). For a fuller version of the *Arms,* see p. 292.

SANDERSON (pp. 260-1). Another *Motto.* Sans Dieu rien (Window in Halton church, containing the arms of Sanderson and of the Diocese of Blackburn, given 1977 by Robert Tunstall Sanderson).

SANDFORD, of Howgill (p. 261). What seem to be intended for the arms of

Sandford are on a pipe head at Howgill Castle, one of a pair* dated 1733. *Arms.* ... three boars' heads couped .... Curwen gives the arms as: Per chevron Sable and Ermine on a chief Argent two boars' heads couped of the first (CW2 vi).

SANDFORD, of Howgill (p. 261). The tablet in the chancel of St. Lawrence, Appleby, is of wood, not stone (*Ex inf.* Martin R. Holmes).

SCHERBIN. The arms of Frau Susanna Scherbin, wife of Kilian Kesselring, *q.v.,* are in Swiss glass dated 1632 in Sizergh Castle, removed there by the National Trust from Wasdale Hall. *Arms.* Or issuing from clouds in chief Proper a cubit arm vested Azure cuffed Argent extended downwards and holding in the hand also Proper a pair of spectacles Sable the lenses Argent. *Crest.* Between two wings Azure a cubit arm erect vested of the last cuffed Argent holding in the hand Proper a pair of spectacles Sable the lenses Argent.

SCHRIBER, or SCHREIBER. The arms of Johann Joachim Schriber, or Schreiber, are in Swiss glass dated 1619 in Sizergh Castle, removed there by the National Trust from Wasdale Hall. *Arms.* Gules on grass in base a chamonix rampant all Proper. *Crest.* A demi chamonix Proper.

de la SEE. Quartered by Boynton, *q.v.,* on shields at Sizergh Castle and Levens Hall. *Arms.* Azure two bars† wavy Argent.

SHARP. Sir Milton Sharp, B.A. (Cantab) (1880-1941), who succ. his father as 2nd Bart. 1924, lived at Swarthbeck Point, Howtown. His younger brother Charles George Gordon Sharp (1885-1961) was of Kirk Hey, Kents Bank, Grange-over-Sands. The present holder of the title is Sir Milton's only son, Sir Milton Reginald Sharp. *Arms.* Azure on a fess engrailed Argent between two plates a torteau between two pheons Gules. *Crest.* In front of a pheon Sable an eagle's head erased Azure charged with a cross crosslet Or. *Motto.* Nitor donec supero (BP105).

SHERBORNE – see STANLEY.

SHUTTLEWORTH (p. 271). Sir Charles Ughtred John Kay-Shuttleworth, 4th Baron Shuttleworth, died 5th October 1975, aged 58, and was succ. by his eldest son Charles Geoffrey Nicholas Shuttleworth.

SISSON (p. 272). *Arms.* Curwen gives: Bendy of six Argent and Gules (CW2 vi).

SMARDALE, of Smardale. Nigel de Smardale and Eva his wife are mentioned 1202-3, and Henry de Smardale was a witness 1230. Guido de Smardale occurs 1250, and in 1291 he or another of this name had a grant of the manor of Smardale, which by 1292 had passed to Michael de Harcla, whose son Sir Andrew presumably forfeited it. By 1388 it had become the property of Thomas, son of John de Warthcopp, in right of Katherine his wife. It is always said that the Warcops acquired Smardale by marriage to a Smardale heiress, and they certainly quartered the arms of that family, and sometimes used them instead of their usual coat. *Arms.* TVN, NVY and FVY all shew the Warcops as bearing: Argent on a fess Gules three cushions, or lozenge-cushions, of the field. It seems clear, however, that these were the arms of Smardale, which they sometimes used instead of their own, and sometimes quartered.

* The other bears the *Crest* of Honywood: A wolf's head erased.

† There are three bars on one shield in the Boynton Room, Sizergh Castle.

SMITH, of Tent Lodge (p. 275). The 5th son of the Rev. William Smith (1630-75) was the Rev. Joseph Smith, M.A., D.D. (Oxon) (1670-1756), Provost of The Queen's College, Oxford, who marr. Mary (d. 1745), youngest dau. and coheir of Henry Lowther, of Ingleton Hall, also of Cockermouth and of Lowther, Co. Fermanagh, see p. 231, above. *Arms* (on tablet outside chapel of The Queen's College). Quarterly, 1 & 4, Azure on a mount in base Vert a castle Argent on a chief Or three storks' heads erased Gules; 2 & 3, Argent on a bend between two horses' heads erased Azure maned Or three lozenges of the last each charged with an ermine spot; over all, on an escutcheon of pretence (for Lowther), Or six annulets, three, two and one, Sable.

SOUTHWORTH. Impaled by Preston, of Holker, see AWL, on wooden tablet in Cartmel Priory; Christopher Preston, of Holker (d. 1594), marr. Margaret Southworth. *Arms.* Argent on a chevron Sable three cross crosslets of the field.

SPARLING (p. 279). The *Arms* of Sparling are on a stone fireplace at Croftlands, Caton, as: Or three sparlings hauriant . . . a crescent for difference.

SPINKS. Shields in window of Thurland Castle for Elizabeth Spinks, godmother of Major Eric Brown Lees, J.P. (1878-1918), and for S. L. Spinks. *Arms.* Azure a cross masculy Argent between four eagles displayed Or.

STANDISH (p. 281). On the banner of Gerald, 1st and last Baron Strickland, see AWL p. 286, now at Sizergh Castle, which formerly hung in the Chapel of the Order of St. Michael and St. George in St. Paul's Cathedral, the following coat is quartered for Old Standish, in addition to the usual Standish arms: Argent a saltire and a bordure engrailed Sable.

STANLEY. A fine carved wooden bed-head, apparently dating from the 16th or 17th century and formerly part of a four-poster bed at Beaumont Cote (see also BUTLER-COLE, p. 387, above) but now in the Grill Room of the Royal Hotel, Kirkby Lonsdale, displays the arms of Stanley and other prominent Lancashire families, as follows:

2 1 3

Fyrste at thy rysyng & last at thi rest be
thou gods srvand for yt hold I best

4 5 6 7

1. *Arms.* Quarterly, 1 & 4, Quarterly, i & iv, [Argent] on a bend [Azure] a [correctly, three] buck's head cabossed [Or] (Stanley); ii, [Or] on a chief indented [Azure] three plates (Lathom); iii, Chequy [Or and Azure] (Warren); 2 & 3 [Gules] three legs in armour [Proper garnished and spurred Or] flexed and conjoined in triangle at the upper part of the thigh (The Lordship of Man); over all, on an escutcheon of pretence, [Azure] a lion rampant [Or] (Monhalt). The shield is surrounded by a Garter, with a corrupt version of the *Motto*: Hony male quy tuoiy pena. *Crest.* An eagle wings expanded [Or] preying on an infant in its cradle [Proper] swaddled [Gules] banded [Gold].

2. *Initials* (above shield. R[ichard] M[olyneux]. *Arms.* [Azure] a cross moline pierced with a lozenge [Or]. *Motto.* Prai for nb (?Nicholas Butler).

3. *Arms.* Quarterly, 1 & 4, [Sable] three bars [Argent] (Hoghton); 2 & 3, [Argent] a mullet [Sable] (Ashton). *Crests.* Two bulls' heads [Argent].

Initials (below shield). R[ichard] H[oughton].

4. *Arms.* [Quarterly, 1 & 4, Vert] an eagle displayed [Argent; 2 & 3, Argent] a lion rampant [Vert]. *Initials* (below shield). R[ichard] S[herborne].

5. *Arms.* [Argent] a griffin segreant [Sable] beaked and legged [Or]. *Initials* (below shield). R[ichard] B[old].

6. *Arms.* [Azure] a chevron between three covered cups [Or]. *Initials* (below shield). N[icholas] B[utler].

7. *Arms.* [Argent] a fess [Sable]. *Initials* (below shield). H[enry] K[eighley].

STEPHENSON, STEVENSON. Shield on stone fireplace in Croftlands, Caton. *Arms.* Gules on a bend Or three leopards' faces . . . .

STOKES. The Rev. Cosby Hudleston Stokes (1881-1932) was father of Mrs. Barbara Glencairn Armstrong, who marr. (1) 1933 Rupert Newborn and (2) 1963 the Rt. Rev. Mervyn Armstrong, O.B.E., of Glen Brathay, Skelwith Fold, Ambleside, formerly Bishop of Jarrow. *Arms.* Gules a demi lion rampant double queued Argent a bordure Sable entoque of bezants. *Motto.* Ire in adversa (IFR).

STOREY (p. 285). Alan Thomas Trevor Storey died at Stellenbosch, South Africa, 28th December 1975.

STRICKLAND, of Sizergh (p. 286). For the Hon. Mary Constance Elizabeth Cristina Strickland, read Mary Constance Elizabeth Christina Strickland.

SURTEES. Quartered by Boynton, *q.v.*, in window at Levens Hall. *Arms.* Ermine on a canton Gules an orle Or.

TALBOT. Impaled by Clifford on triptych from Appleby Castle, now in the Record Office, Carlisle; Henry, 1st Earl of Cumberland (1493-1542), marr. (1) Margaret, dau. of George Talbot, 4th Earl of Shrewsbury. *Arms.* Gules a lion rampant and a bordure engrailed Or.

TANKARD. The arms of this Yorkshire family were formerly impaled by Lancaster in plaster on a ceiling in Sockbridge Hall; Lancelot Lancaster, of Sockbridge, marr. Frances, eldest dau. of Thomas Tankard, of Boroughbridge (Y) (d. 1597). *Arms.* [Argent] on a chevron between three escallops [Gules] as many annulets [of the field] (CW1 ii 37).

TAYLOR. Samuel Taylor, of Moston (L), was father of Col Samuel Taylor, J.P., of Eccleston Hall and Moston (d. 1820), who was Grand Master of the Loyal Orange Institution of England and during the invasion scare of 1811 raised and commanded a regiment of volunteers, which became the Manchester Regiment. His son Samuel Taylor, D.L., J.P., of Ibbotsholme, Windermere (1802-81), was father of Samuel Taylor, D.L., J.P. (b. 1826), who died *v.p.* 1880, having marr. 1857 Maria, dau. of the Rev. Samuel Irton Fell, incumbent of Ambleside. Their son Samuel Taylor, D.L., J.P., M.A. (Cantab), barrister at law, of Birkdault, Haverthwaite (1859-1935), was Vice-Chairman of Lancashire Quarter Sessions, and a member of the Royal Commission on Local Government 1925. His eldest son the Rev. Samuel Taylor, M.A. (Cantab) (1884-1956), a distinguished antiquary, a Vice-President of the Cumberland & Westmorland Antiquarian & Archaeological Society, and a contributor to *Transactions,* was Vicar of Flookburgh 1915-26, of Holy Trinity with St. Barnabas, Carlisle, 1926-30, of Millom 1935-44, and of Burneside 1944-49, Hon. Canon of Carlisle 1947-49, and Canon Emeritus 1949-56. He lived in retirement at Field Beck,

Cartmel. His brother* Geoffrey Fell Taylor, M.B.E., T.D., J.P., of Cark-in-Cartmel, Major 4th Battn Royal Lancaster Regiment (1890-1949), was father of Samuel Geoffrey Taylor, J.P., of Rowancrag, Finsthwaite, Major, Indian Army (Rtd.), the present head of the family. *Arms.* Ermine on a chief dovetailed Gules a mallet between two escallops Or. *Crest.* A demi lion Sable semé of mallets Or holding between the paws an acorn Gold slipped Vert. *Motto.* Annoso robore quercus (BLG6). The bookplate of one of the above Samuel Taylors, however, displays a completely different achievement, viz. *Arms.* Per bend Argent and Azure on a bend engrailed Vert between two lions rampant . . . three annulets of the first. *Crest.* A demi griffin segreant. *Motto.* Freodom andmin eaeder edel.

TAYLOR. Armorial glass from Fell Foot, now in the possession of Mrs. M. E. Forrest, of Broughton Lodge Farm House; George Lewis Ridehalgh, of Polefield House (L), see AWL, marr. Sarah, dau. of Dr. Edmund Taylor, of Oldfield Road, Salford (L), and had an only son George John Miller Ridehalgh, of Fell Foot. *Arms.* Ermine on a chief indented Sable† a ducal coronet Or between two escallops Argent. *Crest.* A demi lion rampant Ermine holding between the paws a ducal coronet Or.

TEMPEST. Impaled by Strickland and by Boynton on shields at Sizergh Castle; Walter Strickland, of Sizergh and of Thornton Bridge (Y) (1516-69), marr. 1561 Alice (d. 1595), dau. of Nicholas Tempest, of Stella (D), and widow of Christopher Place, of Halnaby (Y). *Arms.* Quarterly, 1 & 4, Argent a bend engrailed between six martlets Sable (Tempest); 2 & 3, Gules a cinquefoil within an orle of eight crosses patonce‡ Or a crescent for difference (Umfraville).

THOMPSON, of Grayrigg and Underley (p. 293). Denniss William Denniss-Thompson, of Summerdale House, Preston Patrick, died 16 April 1977.

THWAYTES (p. 296). HSW records the *Arms* as: Argent a cross and a bordure Sable fretty Or.

TINNISWOOD. Thomas Tinniswood, of Penrith and Kirkby Stephen (1879-1953), see p. 341, was father of Nancy, who marr. 1939 Geoffrey Berry Harker, solicitor, of The Manor House, Kirkby Stephen. *Arms.* See p. 341.

TOLSON, of Tolson Hall (p. 297). Deeds in the possession of Mr. J. A. Cropper, of Tolson Hall (for whom, see AWL), indicate that the 17th and 18th century form of this name was TOWSON or TOWNSON.

PAGET-TOMLINSON (p. 298). Dermot Hugh Thomas Paget-Tomlinson, of Summerfield, died 15 August 1976, aged 60, and was succ. by his elder son, Michael Lloyd Dermot Paget-Tomlinson, of Abbot Hall, Kirkby Lonsdale.

TONI. Impaled by Clifford on triptych from Appleby Castle, now in the Record Office, Carlisle; Walter de Clifford, 2nd son of Richard Fitz Pons, *temp.* Richard I, acquired Clifford Castle, Herefordshire, by marr. to Margaret, dau. of Ralph de Toni. *Arms.* Argent a maunch Gules.

* To their sister Nancy, now of 4 Little Aynam, Kendal, who marr. 1916 Hugh Stuart Greg, J.P., of Woodcroft, Haverthwaite (1869-1942), see AWL, we are indebted for much helpful advice and information.

† The black has faded to a reddish hue, but a painting of the arms in Mrs. Forrest's possession shews that the chief was originally Sable.

‡ Correctly, cross crosslets.

TOWNELEY (p. 299). The arms of Towneley, of Towneley, are on hatchments at Sizergh Castle; Charles Strickland, of Sizergh (1734-70), marr. 1762 Cecilia (d. 1814), dau. of William Towneley, of Towneley. She marr. (2) 1779 Charles' cousin, Jarrard Strickland, of York (1741-95).

TOWNLEY of Hardcragg. Thomas Townley, a cadet of the Townleys of Townhead, marr. his cousin Jemima, dau. of Richard Blomley Postlethwaite, and thus acquired the Hardcragg estate in Grange-over-Sands, which descended to their son William Gresham Marshall Townley (d. 1929), whose widow sold it. Their son Charles Joseph Marshall Townley d. 1974; his sisters and co-heirs are Cicely Maureen, widow of Benedict Craven, Monica Mary Bernadette, of Hazelbank, Grange-over-Sands, Mary Pamela, widow of Alfred Macaulay Atkinson and Katharine Amice Mary, wife of Anthony Garret Hayes. *Arms* in glass at Hardcragg: Argent on a fess Sable a rose Gules in chief three pierced mullets of the second. *Crest*. On a perch in front of a nest with two eggs a hawk close all Proper. *Motto*. Tenez le Vraye. (*Ex inf.* Miss M. M. B. Townley and Mr. K. L. Bocock.)

TUFTON, Earl of the Isle of Thanet (pp. 310-2). The 'modern' version of the *Arms* of Tufton was granted to Sir Nicholas Tufton, Earl of the Isle of Thanet, by Sir William Segar, Garter, in 1628, as follows: Quarterly of six, 1 & 6, Sable an eagle displayed Ermine within a bordure Argent (Tufton); 2, Gules a cross Argent a label of five points Azure (Hever); 3, Gules a chevron between three lions' paws erased within a bordure Argent (Browne); 4, Azure a chevron Or between three swans Argent (Charleton); 5, Per bend sinister Sable and Or a lion rampant counterchanged (Francis). *Crest*. A lion dragonett sitting Argent (Harl. MS. 1470 f. 199, printed in Harl. Soc. lxxvii (1926) 200-1). Another *Motto*. Fiel però desdichado (EHM; FBC).

TUNSTALL, of Thurland castle (p. 302). *Crest*. A window in Thurland Castle displays this as: A cock Argent beaked and membered Or combed and wattled gules in the beak a label inscribed DROIT.

UMFRAVILLE – see TEMPEST.

URI, The Canton of. The arms of the Swiss Forest Canton of Uri, ensigned by those of the Holy Roman Empire, *q.v.*, are in glass dated 1640 at Sizergh Castle which was removed there by the National Trust from Wasdale Hall. *Arms*. Or a bull's head cabossed Sable ringed Gules. *Motto*. Das Loblich Landt Uri.

VAUGHAN. An escutcheon of pretence on the arms of Stanley on Hornby church tower; Sir Edward Stanley, K.G., 1st Lord Monteagle, see AWL, marr. (2) *c.* 1501 Elizabeth (d. 1515), widow of John, Lord Grey, of Wilton, and dau. of Sir Thomas Vaughan, of Tretower, Co. Brecon. *Arms*. . . . a lion rampant . . . .

VERE (p. 305). The arms of Vere are impaled by Herbert on the triptych from Appleby Castle, now in the Record Office, Carlisle; Philip Herbert, Earl of Pembroke and Montgomery (1584-1650), who marr. (2) Lady Anne Clifford, dau. of George, 3rd Earl of Cumberland, marr. (1) 1604 Susan (1587-1629), 3rd dau. of Edward Vere, 17th Earl of Oxford. *Arms*. Quarterly Gules and Or in the first quarter a mullet Argent.

VESCI – see BROMFLETE (AWL p. 54).

VIGNATEL. Shield in window of Thurland Castle for Lucy Vignatel, godmother of Maud Lees (1880-1967). *Arms*. Or three jugs Sable.

WALLER. Mrs Beryl Bayley, B.A. (Cantab), wife of Christopher Spencer Bayley, of Durham Ox, Old Town, Kirkby Lonsdale, is dau. of Major Robert Jocelyn Rowan Waller, D.S.O., of Littlestone, Kent (1882-1968), and is descended from Richard Waller (will pr. 1688), who held a commission in Sir Arthur Loftus' Regiment in Cromwell's army in Ireland and obtaining a grant of land at Cully, Newport, Co. Tipperary, settled there 1642; he was descended from the Warrens, of Poynton (Ch). From him also descend Mrs. Gundred Eva Young, wife of Lt-Col Richard Arthur Allicocke Young, of Bowfell, Bowness-on-Windermere, and Mrs. Margaret Harriet de Warrenne Blackburn, wife of Wilfrid Evelyn Blackburn, T.D., F.C.A., of Baddeley Mount, Bowness-on-Windermere, daus. and coheirs of Henry Trench FitzArthur de Warrenne Waller, F.C.S., A.R.C.M. (1873-1911). *Arms.* Chequy Or and Azure on a canton Gules a lion rampant double queued of the first. *Motto.* Honor et veritas (IFR).

WALMSLEY. Sir Joshua Walmsley, J.P. (1794-1871), was a pupil at Richard Aislabie's school at Eden Hall, Kirkby Stephen, in 1807 and was later an assistant in the academy, leaving in 1813 to become usher in a school at Liverpool, where he was later in business. He was Mayor of Liverpool 1838, was knighted 1840, and was M.P. for Bolton 1849-52 and for Leicester 1852-57 (*Penrith Observer* 5 and 12 October 1954). *Arms.* Gules on a chief dancetté Ermine a bee volant Proper between two hurts. *Crest.* A lion passant Ermine on the head a crown vallary Or and his dexter forepaw resting on a knight's helmet Proper (BGA).

WARCOP (p. 309). Robert de Sandford, Lord of the Manor of Sandford, died before 1403, leaving two daus. and coheirs Katherine, marr. Thomas Warcop, Vicar of Kirkby Stephen (d. 1452), and Margaret (b. *c.* 1395), marr. Christopher Bardsey (CW2 viii, xxii).

WARD. Quartered by Strickland on shields at Sizergh Castle; Sir Walter Strickland, of Sizergh (*c.* 1497-1528), marr. *c.* 1515 Katherine, eldest dau. and coheir of Ralph Neville, of Thornton Bridge (Y), by Anne, dau. and coheir of Sir Christopher Ward, of Newby and Givendale (Y). *Arms.* Azure a cross patonce Or. HHS (p. 81) gives: Azure a cross botony Or. Another dau. and coheir, Joan, marr. Sir Edward Musgrave, of Hartley, and NB (i 595) records the arms as: Azure a cross moline Or. Curwen gives: Azure a cross flory Or (CW2 vi).

de la WARR – see WEST.

WARREN. A Stanley quartering on shield on Hornby church tower. *Arms.* Chequy [Or] and [Azure].

WAY. A stone shield at Lily Mere House,* with date 1838 and initials T U E, displays the arms of Way; Thomas Upton, of Ingmire Hall (1800-43), marr. 1829 Eliza (d. 1870), 2nd dau. of Benjamin Way, of Denham Place, Bucks. *Arms.* Azure three lucies hauriant in fess Argent.

WELCH, of Leck Hall (p. 313). *Arms.* Azure six mullets pierced Or, three, two, and one (Window, Thurland Castle).

WEST, Lord De La Warr. The arms of West are impaled by Bindloss on an overmantel dated 1629 originally in Borwick Hall, now in the Bindloss Room at Sizergh Castle; and, with quarterings, on a hatched shield on the entrance porch of Sizergh Castle. Sir Francis Bindloss, of Borwick, see

* Probably taken there from Ingmire Hall.

AWL, marr. Cecilia West, dau. of Thomas, 3rd Baron De La Warr (1557-1618). Their descendant, Gerald, Lord Strickland, see AWL, marr. (1) 1890 the Lady Edeline Sackville (1870-1918), eldest dau. of Reginald Windsor, 7th Earl De La Warr. *Arms* (on overmantel). [Argent] a fess dancetté [Sable]. The shield on the porch displays: Quarterly, 1, West; 2, Gules a lion rampant between eight cross crosslets fitché in orle Argent (De La Warr); 3, Quarterly Or and Gules over all a bend Vair (Sackville); 4, Vairé Ermine and Gules (Gresley).

WESTROPP (p. 315). Canon R. M. L. Westropp resigned the living of Natland 1975 and is now of Inglewood, Kirkby Lonsdale.

WHILE (pp. 316-7). The family bears the following *Arms*. Per chevron Azure and Sable in chief two cross crosslets and in base a salamander reguardant in flames all Or. *Crest*. A demi griffin Sable beaked and membered Gules holding between the claws a hawk's lure Or. *Badge*. Two hawks' lures the lines interlaced in a Heneage knot Or. *Motto*. Animus omnia superat (Painting in possession of Mr. D. A. While, of Birkdault).

WILDMAN, of Hornby. Thomas Wildman, of Lincolns Inn, London, and James Wildman, of Kingston, Jamaica, obtained in 1776, for themselves and for the descendants of their father Edward Wildman, of Hornby, a grant of the following *Arms*. Azure on a chevron Ermine between two eagles displayed in chief and a lion passant in base three estoiles Or. *Crest*. Out of a mural crown chequy Or and Azure a demi lion rampant Argent maned and tufted Sable in the paws a battle axe erect blade imbrued Proper staff gold (CA xiii/247).

WILSON, of Burtergill. John Wilson, of Burtergill, Warcop, yeoman (1742-1820), marr. 1778 Mary Breeks (1760-1836). The youngest of their thirteen children was Richard Wilson (1800-69), who joined his cousin Stephen Cleasby, a Russian broker, in business in London, eventually becoming an oil broker on his own account, and one of the leading and most respected merchants in the city.* He was Mayor of Brighton 1863, and was of Molesworth House there and of Chiddingly. His daus. and coheirs were Emma (d. 1933) who marr. 1865 Mr. Justice Grantham and Mary wife of . . . Brooksbank. *Arms*. Argent a chevron between a quatrefoil between two mullets in chief and a cart wheel in base all Gules. *Crest*. A demi lion Gules between the paws an escutcheon Argent charged with a cart wheel as in the arms and holding in the mouth three cinquefoils slipped Vert (BGA).

WILSON, of Kendal (p. 325). In 1976 Lt-Cdr Paul Norman Wilson was raised to the peerage as Baron Wilson, of High Wray. He received a grant of the following *Supporters*. Dexter, A Herdwick ram; Sinister, A sea-wolf;† both Proper.

WORDSWORTH (p. 331). For Richard (*c.* 1680-1762), read Richard (1690-1760).

The Rev. Christopher William Wordsworth (d. 1965) was born at Gosforth 1879.

* "His name is now, after a retirement of nearly 20 years, looked upon almost as a household word . . . as an example of one, who throughout his career, was always accurate, and preserved without once wavering, integrity and honour of the strictest character, in all his transactions."

† It is thought that this example of the use of a sea-wolf as a supporter is unique in British heraldry.

Motto. The family later used: Veritas in caritate (*Ex inf.* Donald P. Sewell, of Frizington).

WORTHINGTON. Charles James Worthington, of The Holme, Hawkshead (b. 1843), was 3rd son of Robert Worthington, of Sale Hall (Ch) (1805-68). His 2nd son, Lt-Col Frank Worthington, O.B.E., D.S.O. and Bar, B.A., B.Chir., M.B. (Cantab), R.A.M.C. (b. 1880), served with distinction in World Wars I and II. *Arms.* Or three acorns chevronwise Proper between as many tridents Sable. *Crest.* In front of a trident erect Sable a goat passant Argent in the mouth an acorn as in the arms (BFR). *Motto.* Mihi parent aequoris undae (FBC).

WÖTELIN.† The arms of Frau Elizabeth Wötelin, wife of Thomas Kesselring, *q.v.*, are in glass dated 1632 in Sizergh Castle, removed there by the National Trust from Wasdale Hall. *Arms.* Or on rocks in base Purpure a raven Proper. *Crest.* Out of a crown rocks Purpure thereon a raven Proper.

WRIGHT. Shield in window of Thurland Castle for Betty (d. *s.p.* 1808), dau. of Robert Wright, and 1st wife of James Lees, of Clarksfield (1759-1828). *Arms.* Argent two bars Azure on a chief of the last three leopards' faces of the field.

WYATT (p. 333). For boars' heads couped, read boars' heads erased.

YOUNG – see WALLER.

ZOUCHE (p. 337). *Arms.* Henry Fletcher Rigge in his MS. *The Older Monuments in Cartmel Priory Church,* 1876, records these as: Gules ten bezants, four, three, two, one, in pile.

ABBREVIATIONS AND AUTHORITIES (p. xviii). BFR – For A. B. Burke read A. P. Burke.

ABBREVIATIONS AND AUTHORITIES (p. xx). Add: HSW = G. N. Higgin, *The Heraldry of the High Sheriffs of Westmorland.* 1938. MS. volume in Record Office, Kendal.

ABBREVIATIONS AND AUTHORITIES (p. xx). LCB – For C. B. Tracy, read W. B. Tracy.

UNIDENTIFIED. Stone tablet built into wall at Roose Farm, Barrow-in-Furness, with initials R E B. *Arms.* Per chevron . . . and . . . three fleurs-de-lys . . . .

UNIDENTIFIED. Painted stone tablet at Barwick Hall, Middleton (W), with initials I W and date 1692. *Arms.* Vert a cross patonce Argent. Possibly, Watson.

UNIDENTIFIED. Stone shield in courtyard at Capernwray Hall. *Arms.* . . . on a chevron . . . between three crosses patonce . . . as many fleurs-de-lys . . . .

UNIDENTIFIED. Shield on stone fireplace at Croftlands, Caton. *Arms.* Vert three greyhounds courant in pale . . . . Perhaps, Tomlinson.

UNIDENTIFIED. Shield on stone fireplace at Croftlands, Caton. *Arms.* Sable on a bend engrailed between two cotises also engrailed Argent three garbs . . . the whole between five garbs . . . .

UNIDENTIFIED. Stone shield on tower of Tunstall church. *Arms.* . . . a chevron . . . between three (?) squirrels sejant . . . the two in chief respectant.

† This could perhaps be read as MÖTELIN.

UNIDENTIFIED. Wooden shield on choirstalls in St. Wilfrid's chapel, Brougham. *Arms.* . . . three roses, one and two, ...

UNIDENTIFIED. Overmantel in dining-room at Broughton Tower; almost certainly continental in origin. *Arms.* Quarterly, 1, Argent a spur rowel Gules; 2 & 3, Argent three bars Gules; 4, Argent a lion rampant Gules. *Supporters.* Dexter, A winged sphinx; Sinister, A winged lion with an eagle's head.

UNIDENTIFIED. Lintel of door in hall at Broughton Tower; almost certainly continental in origin. *Arms.* Per fess Azure and chequy Or and Gules in chief a fleur-de-lys of the second. *Motto.* Laus tibi Domino.

UNIDENTIFIED. Oak chairs from Chatsworth in Cartmel Priory choir, given by the Duke of Devonshire, 1867. *Arms.* Two shields – Dexter, . . . an eagle displayed . . . suspended from its beak by a riband . . . an escutcheon . . . charged with a lion rampant . . . ; Sinister, . . . three bendlets sinister wavy Purpure. *Supporters.* Two eagles reguardant.

UNIDENTIFIED. Quartered by Lowther at 1665 Vis., also on monuments in Lowther church. *Arms.* Sable three martlets volant Argent.

UNIDENTIFIED. Stained glass in east window of Tunstall parish church; brought from Flanders last century, probably late 15th century and from a hospital served by the canons of St. Anthony. *Arms.* Per fess Or and Argent in chief a demi eagle displayed issuant Sable charged on the breast with an escutcheon of the first thereon a St. Anthony's cross Argent and ensigned with an imperial crown also of the first, in base on a bend sinister (untinctured) a mullet of six points Or in sinister base a fleur-de-lys (also untinctured).

UNIDENTIFIED. Carved in stone, free standing above a gate at Wynlass Beck, Windermere; said to have been brought from an inn at Troutbeck Bridge. *Crest.* A dolphin naiant.

UNIDENTIFIED. Stone tablet outside The Grange, Windermere. *Arms.* Quarterly, 1 & 4, . . . a bend Ermine between six martlets . . . 2 & 3, . . . a fess . . . between three gouttes . . . ; on an escutcheon of pretence, . . . a talbot passant . . . on a chief . . . three martlets . . . . *Crest.* A three-barred gate.

UNIDENTIFIED. Early Tudor bedstead from Crackenthorpe Hall, described in *Country Life,* 5 July 1946; also, stained glass at Longmire, Troutbeck, home of Dr. & Mrs. F. T. Madge. *Arms.* . . . three clarions or wool-hooks . . . .

UNIDENTIFIED. A fine carved wooden mantelpiece in No. 7 Stramongate, Kendal,* now occupied by Mr. and Mrs. J. P. Kelly, displays two shields, with *Arms:* . . . three chevrons couped . . . . Beneath the shields on each side of the fireplace are the following *Badges* or *Devices:* Left side, A horse forcene; An escallop; A demi dragon wings expanded. Right side, A Tudor rose; A horse forcene; A vase issuing therefrom a five petalled flower.

* Once owned by the Bellingham family.

AGLIONBY

ARMSTRONG

ASKEW

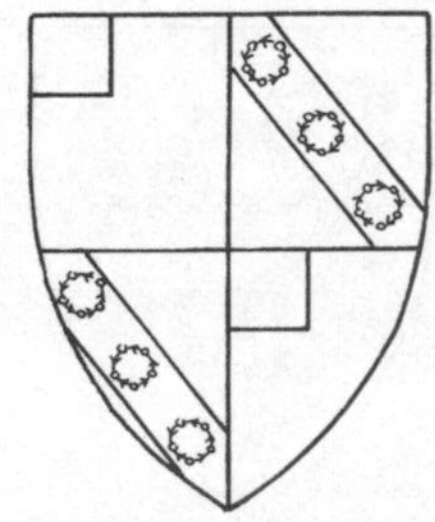
BLENCOWE

BLENNERHASSET

BOUCH

BOUMPHREY

BRISCO

BURGESS

CITY OF CARLISLE

CHRISTIAN

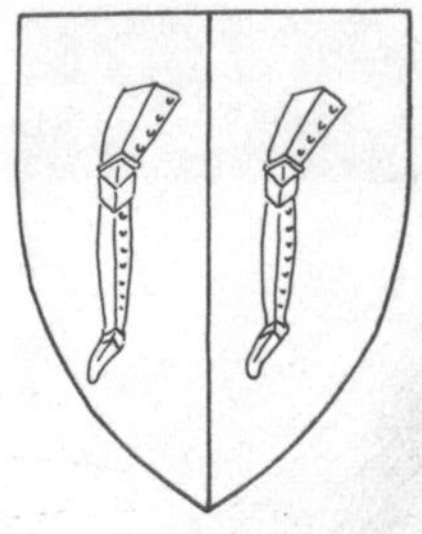
COOKSON

CURWEN

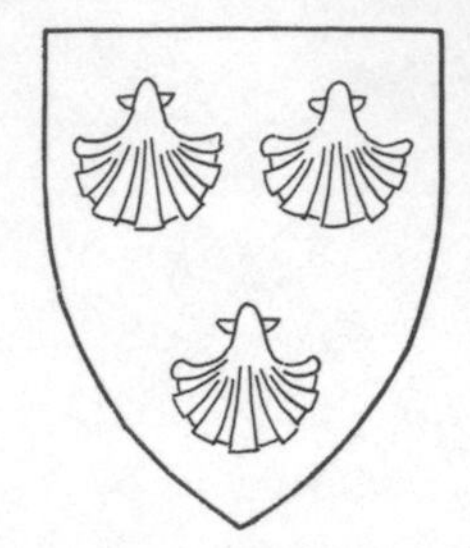

DACRE

DALSTON

DENTON

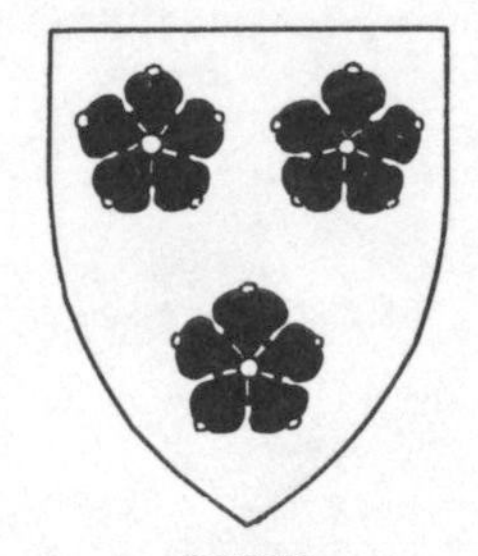

DYKES

EAGLESFIELD

FERGUSON

FETHERSTONHAUGH

FLETCHER

GRAHAM

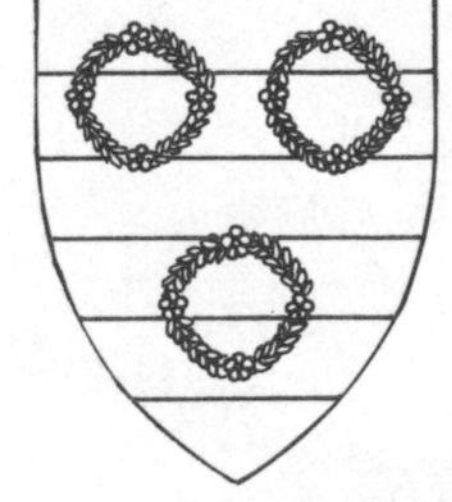

GREYSTOKE

HARCLA

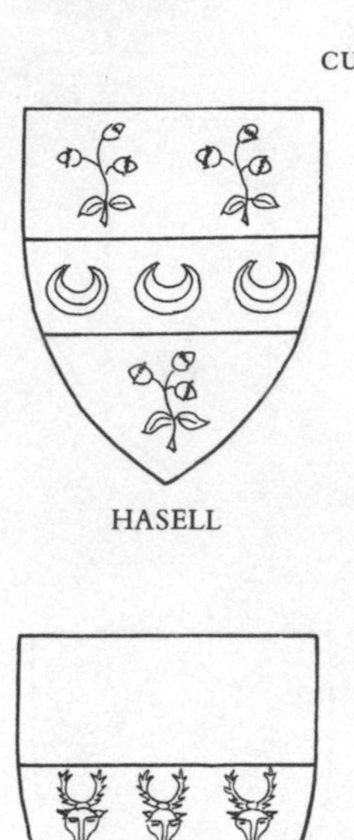

HASELL

HOWARD

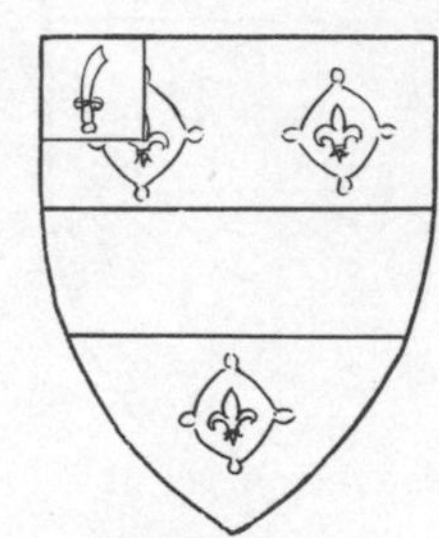

HUTTON,
of Hutton John

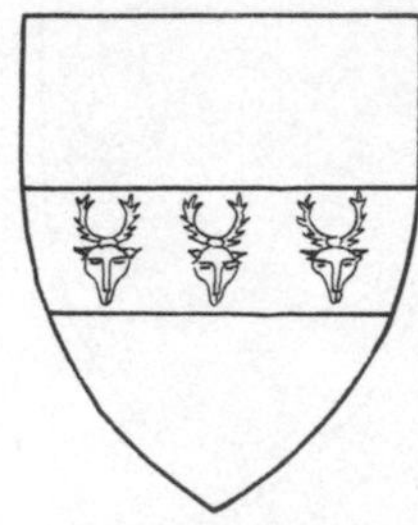

HUTTON,
of Hutton Hall, Penrith

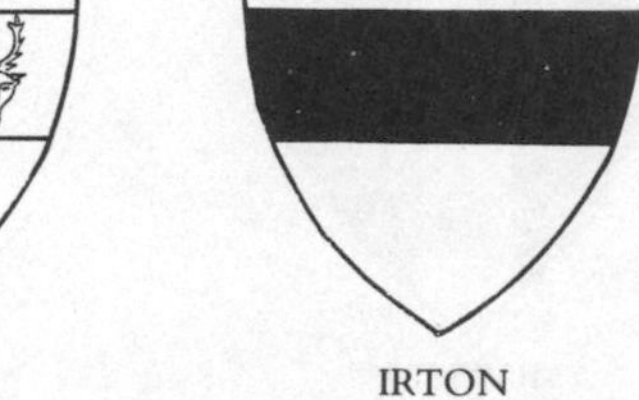

IRTON

IRVING

JAMES

KIRKBRIDE

LAMPLUGH

LAWSON,
of Isel & Brayton

LAWSON
olim WYBERGH

LAYTON

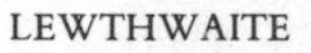

LEWTHWAITE

LOWTHER

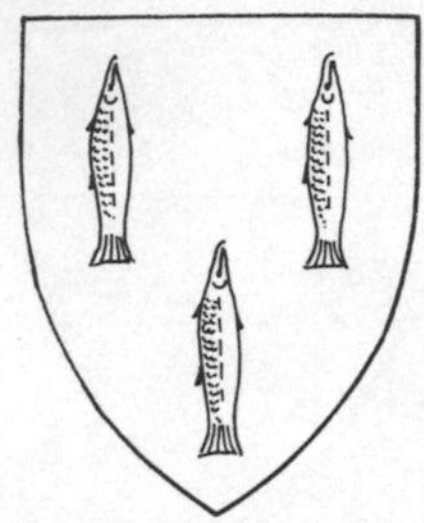

LUCY

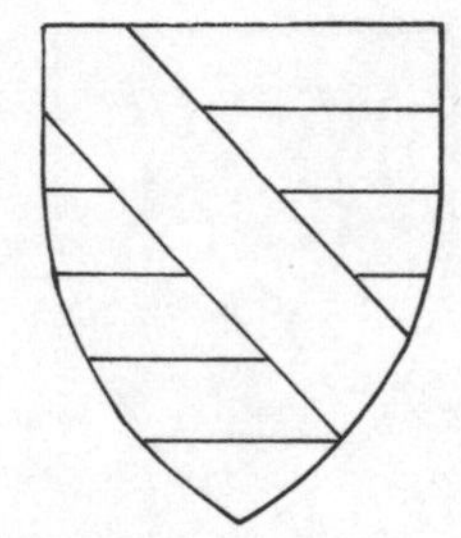

MARTINDALE

MORESBY

MUSGRAVE

ORFEUR

PARKER

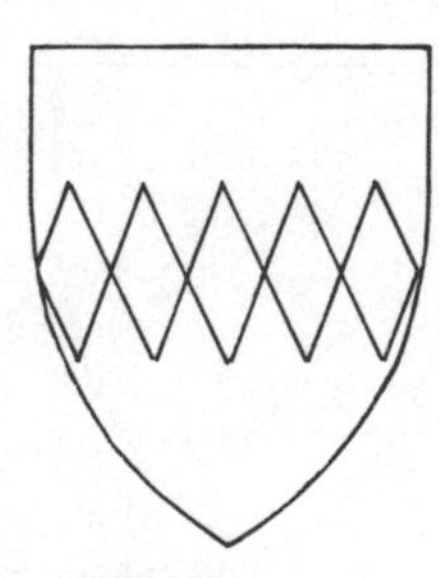

PENNINGTON

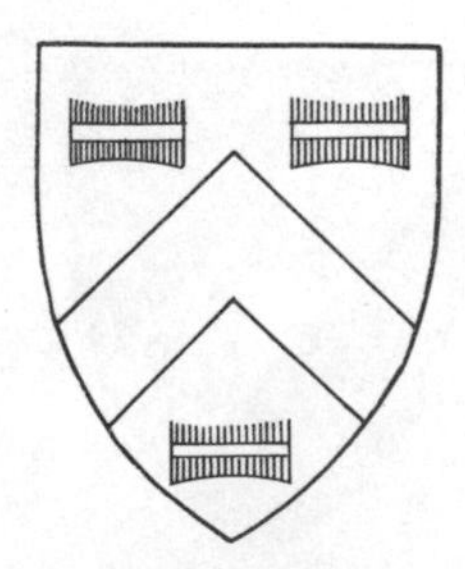

PONSONBY

PORTER

RADCLIFFE

RICHMOND
SALKELD
SENHOUSE
SKELTON
SOUTHEY
STANLEY
THRELKELD
TULLIE
VANE
VAUX
WARWICK
WORDSWORTH

APPENDIX

LETTER FROM RALPH BIGLAND, CLARENCEUX KING OF ARMS, TO GEORGE DALTON, D.L., OF CARLISLE (DIED 1784, AGED 45), IN REPLY TO HIS ENQUIRY *RE* A GRANT OF ARMS (see p. 84) (In Record Office, Carlisle).

Heralds Office, London, 7th Octr 1776

Sir

In acknowlegement of your Request by Mr Garnat who lately waited on me on your behalf, I am to Inform you that the Fees for a legal Establishment of Arms and Crest by Patent granted by the Kings of arms are £42.7.6. There are but two methods of bearing arms either to shew a Connection with some Family whose Right to arms is established or by having Arms granted as aforesaid as there doth not appear that any Arms are settled to y^{r} Family, like many others in the same Predicament. We generally devize two different Sketches for Gent^{n} to please their Fancy some like one Emblem some another perhaps in allusion to some Event or Anecdote in a Family, but whatever is concluded upon must not interfere with the arms of another Family, which we shall take care of. As no Arms can be established in this Kingdom but by the Authority of the Earl Marshal of England 'Tis customary for every Gent^{n} on these applications to sign a memorial addressed in like manner as I have herein inclosed, but if it should not suit your Stile Place or Residence you'll please to alter it accordingly. You see I have not only settled it you & your Issue, but also to the Issue of your Father in order that the Patent may take in any Brothers or Sisters, otherwise you can alter it, by saying to your Memorialist & his Descendants. You will please to signify what kind of Bearing you wou'd like and I will devize something suitable. I shall like to have the Christian Name of your Mother and whose Daughter she was, her Father's Residence. Your signing the memorial and sending me the same is all the Trouble you will have in this Affair. And when the Patent is done, which will phaps be in about 14 days Time I will transmit the same to you. If you have any Cousin of your Surname and w^{d} like to have such taken in, you'll please give me his Name & Residence. I shall have a Pleasure in proving my Self

Sr your most obedient Servant
RALPH BIGLAND.
Clarenceux King of Arms.

George Dalton, Esqr

SUBSCRIBERS TO THE EDITION-DE-LUXE

Atkins, M. G. de St. V., The Courtyard, Kirkby Lonsdale (No. 47).
Bewley, Mrs. G. P., Town Head, Dean, Workington, Cumbria CA14 4TJ (No. 26).
Borron, J. R. E., 98 King Street, Knutsford, Cheshire (No. 39).
Bridgewater, R. D., Braggington House, Braggington, Stratford-upon-Avon CV37 8BB (No. 32).
Burgess, Sir John, D.L., J.P., Cumbria Newspapers Group Ltd., Dalston Road, Carlisle (No. 15).
Carlisle Library, Tullie House, Carlisle (No. 50).
Carruthers, Mrs. Dorothy C., Cornerstones, Aglionby, Carlisle (No. 42).
Carter, Sir Charles F., Vice-Chancellor of the University of Lancaster, Emmanuel House, Brettargh Drive, Lancaster LA1 5BN (No. 3).
Clough, T. H. McK., Rutland County Museum, Catmos Street, Oakham, Rutland LE15 6HW (No 46).
Cumbria Newspapers Group Ltd., Dalston Road, Carlisle (No. 16).
Curwen, S. R., 6 Markall Close, Cheriton, Alresford, Hampshire (No. 17).
Dacre, John C., Tuakau Road, Pukekohe, New Zealand (No. 23).
Dawson, Miss Nan, 8 Barras Close, Morton Park, Carlisle CA2 6PR(No. 35).
Dickson, E. Mylrea, Cherry Holt, Harris Lane, Abbots Leigh, Bristol B88 3QX (no. 9).
Dykes, Joseph Ballantine, M.C., Redmain Lodge, Redmain, Cockermouth (No. 4).
Ferguson, Major R. S., M.V.O., Manningford Bruce House, Pewsey, Wilts. (No. 33).
Fetherstonhaugh, T. R., The College, Kirkoswald, Penrith (No. 10).
Finlay, Michael, The Plains, Wetheral, Carlisle (No. 49).
Greenwood, G. B., Whittington Hall, Whittington via Carnforth (No. 13).
Greg, The Rev. John K., Sandsfield Vicarage, 3 Housesteads Road, Carlisle CA2 TXF (No. 43).
Hall, Mrs. A. R. P., The Old Hall, Oughterside, Aspatria, Cumbria (No. 41).
Heysham, Mounsey-, G. H., Castletown, Carlisle (No. 24).
Howard, The late Lt. Col. the Hon. H. A. C., C.M.G.* (No. 27).
Hudleston, John A., c/o World Health Organisation, Avenue Appia 1211, Geneva 27, Switzerland (No. 44).
Hudleston, Mrs. Mary, Cayton Hall, South Stainley, Harrogate (No. 18).
Hudleston, Dr. W. I. S., 57 Inverleith Row, Edinburgh (No. 29).
Hurrell, John R., Brundon, 1 Burses Way, Hutton, Brentwood, Essex CM13 2PL (No. 12).
Jefferson, David, The Vyne, Deep Field, Datchet, Berks. 5L3 9J5 (No. 37).
Lancaster, Arthur E., The Cottage, Edenhall, Penrith CA11 8SX (No. 40).
Leeming, A. R., M.A., D.Phil., Skirsgill Park, Penrith (No. 25).

* Henry Howard who was born in 1913 and died on 19 Oct. 1977 was the 4th son of the 1st Lord Howard of Penrith. A man greatly loved, he spent the closing months of his life in Cumberland, and lies in the churchyard at Matterdale, a village for which he had a great affection.

C. R. H.

MacMichael, Nicholas Hugh, 28 Little Cloister, Westminster Abbey, London SW1 (No. 6).
Mawson, D. J. W., Calees, The Banks, Brampton, Cumbria (No. 36).
Murray, D. W., Inglesham, Etterby Scaur, Carlisle (No. 48).
Parker, Dr. T. J. A. de G., c/o Messrs. Barclays International, 1 Cockspur Street, London SW1 (No. 20).
Postlethwaite, Thom-, L. C. R., Armaside, Lorton, Cockermouth (No. 45).
Richmond, Vice-Admiral Sir Maxwell and Lady, No. 4 Rural Delivery, Whangarei, New Zealand (No. 19).
Rowling, Mrs. Marjorie A., The Eyrie, Heathwaite Manor, Windermere, Cumbria LA23 2NQ (No. 30).
Sandys, M. E. M., Graythwaite Hall, Ulverston, Cumbria (No. 7).
Senhouse, H. P., The Fitz, Cockermouth (No. 31).
Sidaway, Pallant-, G. E., 20 Danes Road, Staveley, Cumbria LA8 9PW (No. 38).
Smith, Jabez-, A. R., 21 Upper Phillimore Gardens, London W8 7HF (No. 34).
Smith, R. E., 55 Edith Road, West Kensington, London W14 0TH (No. 28).
Spedding, G. J. F. de P., Storms, Keswick, Cumbria (No. 21).
Strong, T., Buckabank, Dalston, Cumbria (No. 14).
Thornburgh, Frederick Harcourt, Box 1053, 561 Via Media, Palos Verdes Estates, California 90813, U.S.A. (No. 2).
Thornburgh, Robert Grant, M.D., 1066 Atlantic Avenue, Long Beach, California 90813, U.S.A. (No. 1).
Trimble, William Steuart, Green Lane, Dalston, Carlisle (No. 5).
Wakefield of Kendal, The Lord, The Old House, Kendal, Cumbria (No. 22).
Walker, William, Greenlands, Holmrook (No. 11).
Wilson, Tryon-, Brigadier C.E., C.B.E., D.S.O., D.L., Dallam Tower, Milnthorpe, Cumbria LA7 7AG (No. 8).

SUBSCRIBERS TO THE ORDINARY EDITION

Agar, Mrs. Lillian Hetherington (née Raven), 19 Ancaster Road, Leeds.
Aglionby, Francis, 36 Bark Place, London W2.
Ainsworth, Mrs. Mary, 41 Bongate, Appleby-in-Westmorland.
Allan, Adrian R., The Golden Fleece, Carleton, Carlisle.
Ancestry Research Achievements Ltd., Northgate, Canterbury, Kent.
Antiquaries of London, Society of, Burlington House, Piccadilly, London W1 V OHS.
Armitt Library, Ambleside.
Askew, I. V., Wellingham House, Lewes, Sussex.
Australia, National Library of, Canberra.
Banks, Allan P., Flat 23, Chesterwood Drive, Sheffield.
Barratt, R., Cowmire Hall, Crosthwaite, Kendal.
Bassenden, Robert L., Starkers, Wray, Lancaster.
Beattie, Mrs. Esther E., 134 Blackwell Road, Carlisle.
Behrens, G. A., Low Gables, Vicarage Lane, Burton-via-Carnforth, Lancs.
Berry, M. R. W., Crag House, Grasmere.
Bewley, Miss Kathleen Spedding, 43 Stonehouse Park, Thursby, Carlisle.
Birmingham Public Libraries, Central Libraries, Birmingham.
Bishopsgate Institute, 230 Bishopsgate, London EC2.
Black, J. A., The Gables, Fairbank, Kirkby Lonsdale.
Black, John Mather, Chessenden House, Smarden, Kent.
Bolton, The Central Library (BSU Dept.), Le Mans Crescent, Bolton, Lancs.
Bottomley, E. M., High Lickbarrow, Windermere.
Boumphrey, David S., P.O. Box 907, Brooks, Alberta, TOJ OJO, Canada.
Boumphrey, Francis S., Apartment 307, 155 Balliot Street, Toronto M46 1C4, Ontario, Canada.
Boumphrey, Miss Janet S., Town End Cottage, Kirkby Lonsdale.
Boumphrey, Leslie, Yeavering, Monkhill, Burgh-by-Sands.
Boumphrey, Mrs. Naomi E., Town End Cottage, Kirkby Lonsdale – 2 copies.
Boumphrey, Robin S., 1 Harper Street, MacGregor ACT 2615.
Bowman, Mrs. J., 8 Mitchelgate, Kirkby Lonsdale.
Brathay Field Study Centre, Old Brathay, Ambleside.
Brisco, Sir Donald G., Bart., J.P., Longworth, Box 165, Haverlock North, New Zealand.
Bristol and Gloucestershire Archaeological Society (Miss Elizabeth Ralph, F.S.A., Hon. Secretary).
Brocklebank, The late A. F., Allendale House, Armathwaite, Carlisle.*
Brocklebank, Ralph Wilfrid, Orland, Clint, Worcestershire.
Brown, G. I., Soillerie, 18 Belah Road, Carlisle.
Brownrigg, John and Ida, Brownrigg Road, RD1, Feura Bush, New York 12076, U.S.A.
Bryer, T. P., 85 Lythe Fell Avenue, Halton, Lancaster.

* Alan Francis Brocklebank, I.S.O., B.A., was a co-founder and Chairman of the Council of the Cumbria Family History Society. He died, greatly lamented, on 8 January 1978.

Buchanan, Mrs. H., 79 Ashridge Crescent, Shooters Hill, London, SE 18.
Bulman, Dr. Robert, 150 Abingden Terrace, Didcot, Oxfordshire.
Bunney, Mrs. Charlotte, Hwith, Ravenstonedale.
Bush, Mr. and Mrs. Herbert, Gatesgarth, Watermillock, Penrith.
Calvert, F. R., 31 Hospital Road, Keighley, Yorks.
Cartmell, Mr. and Mrs. J., 8 Regent House, Lansdown Road, Cheltenham.
Cave-Browne-Cave, B. W., Birket Houses, Winster, Windermere.
Chetham's Library, Long Millgate, Manchester.
Chorley, The late Lord, Q.C.*
Cline, Loree Shaw, 1336-A Cansler Avenue, Gadsden, Alabama 35901, U.S.A.
Cockerill, T. J., Old Mill House, Weston Colville, Cambridge.
Cole, M., LL.B., Melrose House, Snitter, Thropton, Morpeth.
Cole, Clarke-Butler-, R. F., Fell End House, Hale, Milnthorpe.
Cook, Mrs. J. M. E., 12 Two Saints Close, Hoveton, Norwich.
Cookson, Sawrey-, Major John Henry Crackanthorpe, Newbiggin Hall, Westmorland.
Coward, Harry, 2737 Abbott Road, Regina, Saskatchewan S4N 2J7, Canada.
Cowley, Mrs. Dorothy I., 16 Ingleton Close, Cheadle, Cheshire.
Cox, Mrs. Audrey, Nurse's House, Kirkby Lonsdale.
Cropper, J. A., Tolson Hall, Kendal.
Cumbria County Library, 1 Portland Square, Carlisle – 40 copies.
Cumbria Newspapers Group Ltd., Dalston Road, Carlisle.
Cumbria Record Office, Alma Block, The Castle, Carlisle.
Curwen, S. J., 32 St. Lawrence Boulevard, Radcliffe-on-Trent, Nottingham.
Curwen, Archives Trust, Record Office, County Hall, Kendal.
David, Mrs. Joan E., Perwick, 7 Oaks Field, Ambleside.
Dawson, Finch-, Miss F., Orchard House, Kings Meaburn, Penrith.
Day, Alfred Neville Bloxsome, 41 Queen's Gate Gardens, London SW7.
Denyer, C. M., 18 Hillside Avenue, Woodford Green, Essex.
Dickinson, The Rev. J. C., Yewtree Cottage, Barngarth, Cartmel.
Dickinson, R. F., D.L., J.P., B.A., Red How, Lamplugh, Workington.
Dixon, Charles J., Hodge Hill Common, Hodge Hill, Birmingham.
Donald, J. C. N., School House, Raughton Head, Carlisle.
Dove Cottage, The Trustees of, Grasmere.
Downes, Miss Mary, 3 Park Terrace, Maryport.
Duckworth, Mrs. Dorothy, 2 Chapman Road, Hoddlesden, Darwen, Lancs.
Durham University Library, Palace Green, Durham.
Duxbury, Arthur Braithwaite, Hartley, Kirkby Stephen.
Ecroyd, Edward Peter, Low House, Armathwaite, Carlisle.
Elwes, Mrs., Warwick Hall, Carlisle.
Embleton, The Rev. Harold, Q.H.C., M.A., R.N. (retired), The Vicarage, Bognor Regis, West Sussex.
Fagg, T. W., Blencathra, Kirkby Lonsdale.
Fahy, Dr. T. G., Shaw End, Patton, near Kendal – 2 copies.
Falcon, Mrs. D. G., Irton, Nottage, Porthcawl, Mid Glamorgan.
Falcone, Alberto Girardi, Policastro-Bussentino, (SA) Italy.
Farquharson, Mrs. Joan, 6 Alexander Drive, Winston Park, P.O. Gillitts, Natal 3600, S. Africa.

* Lord Chorley, one of Westmorland's most distinguished sons, died aged 82, January 1978.

Fell, Miss C. I., Friar Cote, Sandside Milnthorpe.
Ferguson Industrial Holidays Ltd., Appleby Castle, Appleby-in-Westmorland.
Fleming, John, Hare Hall, Dunnerdale, Broughton-in-Furness.
Fletcher, Guy C., 402 'B' Street, Washington, Kansas 66968, U.S.A.
Forsyth, Lewis, M.B.E., 3 Jennet Croft, Wetheral, Carlisle.
Fox. W., M.A., J.P., High House, St. Bees.
Fraser, Miss C. M., B.A., Ph.D., F.R.Hist.S., 39 King Edward Road, Tynemouth, North Shields.
Fraser, G. M. and K. M., The Bungalow, Baldrine, Isle of Man.
French, T. W., M.A., F.S.A., 8 Water End, Clifton, York.
Fulford, Roger, Barbon Manor, Carnforth.
Garnett. M. E., Saddlers Cottage, Frisby-on-theWreake, near Melton Mowbray, Leics.
Garnett, Major W. F., Quernmore Park near Lancaster.
Garrod, R. P., The Rookery, Watton Road, Little Melton, Norwich, Norfolk NR9 3PB.
The Genealogical Society of the Church of Jesus Christ of Latter Day Saints, Inc., 50 East North Temple, Salt Lake City, Utah 84150, U.S.A.
Gibson, Hollins-, J. S., Church Town House, Sebergham, Carlisle – 2 copies.
Gibson, Miss M. C., Furners, Henfield, West Sussex.
Gibson, Metcalfe-, R., Town Head House, Ravenstonedale.
Giles, Morgan-, R. F., Carlecotes Hall, Dunford Bridge, Sheffield.
Godwin, Jeremy, 15 Drovers Lane, Penrith.
Gray, Mrs. Rosemarie, Eggleston Hall, Barnard Castle, Co. Durham.
Gresson, Lieut. Cdr. J. D., Fountain House, Kirkby Lonsdale.
Guildhall Library, London EC2.
Halton M. C., 24 Monks Way, Orpington, Kent.
Hare, Anthony E. C., The Old Rectory, Great Ormside, Appleby.
Harris, Mrs. G. Arden, Bowscar, Penrith.
Harrison, Major A. J. R., Wreay Hall, Wreay, Carlisle – 5 copies.
Harrison, John Vincent, 1 Summerleaze Avenue, Bude, Cornwall.
Harwood, Mrs. Annette M. T., Pytts House, Fulbrook, Burford, Oxfordshire.
Haselden, The Misses L. and E., Flat 8, Manor House, Alexandra Drive, Liverpool.
Heelis, Brigadier J. E., Netherley, Milburn, Penrith.
Heraldry Today, Parliament Piece, Ramsbury near Marlborough – 6 copies.
Hetherington, Brigadier General Travis M., U.S.A.F. (retired), 202 Glentower Drive, San Antonio, Texas 78213, U.S.A. – 2 copies.
Hill, Alan, C.B.E., 56 Northway, London, NW11 and New House, Rosthwaite near Keswick.
Hodge, E. W., Elterwater Hall, Westmorland.
Hodges, The Rev. M. K., Eskside, Ravenglass.
Hodson, Miss Irene, 11 Hala Hill, Scotforth, Lancaster.
Holdsworth, Fred, Bookseller, Central Buildings, Ambleside.
Holme, J. B., Main Street, Greenodd, near Ulverston.
Houlson, Mrs. M. E., 18a Fairfield Crescent, Oakwood, Hexham.
Housden, Miss Maxine, 6 King Alfred Place, Winchester.
Housden, Miss Pam, 70 Pattison Road, London NW2.
Howard, Nicholas S., Johnby Hall, Penrith.

Howe, M. S., 31 King's Court North, Kings Road, Chelsea, London SW3.
Huckell, R. W., M.A., 15 Christian Street, Maryport.
Huddleston Mr. and Mrs. W., 10 Roedean Drive, Glebe Park, Eaglescliffe, Cleveland.
Hudleston, C. A., Grove Cottage, St. James Street, Yarmouth, Isle of Wight.
Hudleston, C. Roy, Far Oak Bank, Ambleside, Westmorland – 2 copies.
Hudleston, Mrs. M. L., End House, 56 Salkeld Road, Penrith.
Hudleston, Roland Andrew, Hutton John, Dacre, Penrith.
Hughes, J., F.S.A., 20 Killington Drive, Heron Hill, Kendal.
Humphreys, Norman, M.I.R., Greenriggs, 45 Sandgate, Kendal — 2 copies.
Huntingdon, The Henry E. Library and Art Gallery, San Marino, California 91108, U.S.A.
Hyde, Mrs. Joan (née Hudleston), Bream Bay Drive, Ruakaka, Northland, New Zealand.
Inglewood, The Lord, Hutton-in-the Forest, Penrith.
Institute of Historical Research, University of London, Senate House, London WC1.
Iredell, Godfrey, Woodlands, Braithwaite, Keswick.
Irving, J. B., Angerton Farm, Kirkbride, Carlisle.
Jay, Mrs. Eileen, Croft Foot, Colthouse, Ambleside.
John Rylands University Library of Manchester, Oxford Road, Manchester.
Johnson, Miss Phoebe, Low Fold, Grasmere.
Kay, Miss E. M., 40 Linton Avenue, Leeds.
Kipling, Miss C., Miller Ground, Windermere – 2 copies.
Knipe, W. Dixon, Bailiff Ground, Kirkby in Furness.
Lancashire County Library, Preston – 6 copies.
Lancashire Record Office, Bow Lane, Preston.
Lancaster University Library, Lancaster.
Leeds, The Reference Library, Central Library, Calverley Street, Leeds.
Leeds, University of, The Brotherton Library.
Le Fleming, F., Viaduct Farm, Chappel, Essex.
Leighton, Henry Gerard Mather, F.S.A., 9 Bathwick Hill, Bath.
Leresche, Miss E. J., 26 Greenside, Kendal.
Lewis, O. B., 12a Old Mill Close, Bestwood Colliery, Nottingham.
Ley, Brigadier Hugh M. H., The Dower House, Burrow, via Carnforth.
London Library, The, 14 St. James's Square, London SW1.
Loveday, Dr. L. C., 24 Mount Pleasant Gardens, Wigton.
Lynn, Miss E. C., Fernleigh House, High Seaton, Workington.
Macalpine, Miss R., Gillside, Grasmere.
McCollum Miss M., Department of Palaeography, University of Durham, South Road, Durham City.
McCosh, Mr. and Mrs. Bryce, Dalemain, Penrith.
McCosh, Robert Hasell, Dalemain, Penrith – 2 copies.
Macdonald, M. A., Highside, Lorton, Cockermouth.
Macleod of Suardal, Norman, 2 Pimlico, Durham City.
Macpherson, Cdr. R. J. G., 19 Church Street, Modbury, Ivybridge, Devon.
MacPherson, Miss Sheila J., Haygarth, Docker, Kendal, Westmorland.
Manchester Public Libraries, Central Library, Manchester.
Manx Museum, The Library, Douglas, Isle of Man.
Martindale, C. B., F.R.I.B.A., Bradwell House, Milton Keynes, Bucks.

Mathews, Mrs. E., Green Close Cottage, Kirkby Lonsdale.
Messenger, F. O., Crag End, Braithwaite, Keswick — 2 copies.
Messenger, J. L., Stonehaven, Wormley, Godalming, Surrey.
Minns, Mrs. V. A., 116 Montrose Avenue, Edgware, Middlesex.
Mossop, Clement J., Mossop Family Foundation, 2899 Walnut Hill Avenue, Philadelphia, Pa 19152, U.S.A.
Myers, John, 19 Grand Rue, 1204 Geneva, Switzerland – 2 copies.
Naylor, T. P., The Clock House, Far Sawrey, Ambleside.
Nelson, Mrs. Elfrida V., A.T.D. (neé Huddleston), Hedgefield Cottage, Muirfield Road, Inverness, Highland Region.
Newcastle upon Tyne, University of, Dept. of Adult Education, Newcastle upon Tyne.
Newell of Staffa, The Rev. Gerald Frederic Watson, Lashmars House, 31 High Street, Steyning, Sussex.
Northumberland Record Office, Melton Park, North Gosforth, Newcastle upon Tyne.
Ogden, Lt. Col. R. H., M.B.E., Fairthwaite Park, Cowanbridge, Carnforth.
Oliphant, Mrs. Helena, Curzon Cottage, Temple Sowerby, Penrith – 2 copies.
Ord, Blackett-, His Honour Vice-Chancellor A. J., Helbeck Hall, Brough, Kirkby Stephen.
Ormathwaite, The Lord, Penybout Hall, Llandrinodd Wells, Powys.
Palaeography and Diplomatic, Dept. of, University of Durham, The Prior's Kitchen, The College, Durham City.
Palmer, Mrs. Jean L., Scaleby Hall, Carlisle.
Parker, John R., Stone Raise, 42 Lakeland Park, Keswick.
Parker, O., Boaylchbrym, Kirk Andreas, Isle of Man.
Peskett, Hugh, Debrett Ancestory Research, 78 Parchment Street, Winchester.
Phillips, Mrs. Constance M., 1 The Green, Leathley, Otley, Yorks.
Pike, Cdr. B. H., R.N., Lambrigg Foot, Grayrigg, Kendal.
Postlethwaite, The Rev. A. J., The Vicarage, Oak Bank, Whitehaven.
Postlethwaite, Thom-, L. C. R., Armaside, Lorton, Cockermouth – 2 copies.
Prevost, W. A. J., 26 Coates Gardens, Edinburgh.
Public Record Office, The Library, Chancery Lane, London WC2.
Puttock, Mrs. Sara E. C., 39 Meadow Way, Heathfield, Sussex TN21 8AJ.
Pye, Mrs. Anna, The Fox, The Green, Steeple Morden, Royston, Herts.
Quin, Joyce G., St. Mary's College, University of Durham, Durham City.
Rawlinson, Cadogan-, Commander K., 8 Creek Lane, Emsworth, Hants.
Reckitt, Lt. Col. B. N., Haverbrack, Milnthorpe.
Relph, James T., Holly Cottage, Crosby Ravensworth, Penrith.
Richardson, Miss E. Petty, Stockbridge House, Ulverston.
Richardson, Lawrence Bouskell, Bridge Cottage, Upton, Langport, Somerset.
Richmond, Lady, R. D., 4 Whangarei, New Zealand.
Rimington, G. Philip, Southcroft, Duffield Road, Stoke Poges, Slough.
Robins, Miss Pam, Church Style Corner, Kirkby Lonsdale.
Rooke, Miss S. F., The Old Rectory, Little Langford, Salisbury, Wilts.
Routledge, J. B., Glaxo Malaysia, Sdn Berhad, P.O. Box 11, Petaling Jaya, Malaysia.
Rowling, Mrs. Marjorie A., The Eyrie, Heathwaite Manor, Windermere.
Russell, Mrs M. M., Ulpha, 32 Granada Road, Denton, Manchester.
Rutter, D. T. S., Cleveland House, Gainford, Darlington.

Sanderson, Robert Tunstall, Carus Lodge, Lancaster.
Sawrey, W. R., 20 Boorea Avenue, Lakemba, N.S.W. 2195, Australia.
Schuder, Donald A., Rt. 1 Box 1155, Woodland, California 95695, U.S.A.
Seelen, M. A. M., Rennemigstraat 10, Heerlen 5200, Netherlands.
Shaver, Chester L., 265 East College St., Oberlin, Ohio, U.S.A. 44074.
Sibson, Miss M. K., 5 Croft Road, Carlisle.
Sibson, Thomas L., Miresyke, The Plains, Wetheral, Carlisle.
Slowe, P. St. P., Low Graythwaite Hall, Newby Bridge.
Spedding, John, Mirehouse, Keswick.
Stanford University Libraries, Stanford, California 94305, U.S.A.
Steward, Falcon-, H., Newton Manor, Gosforth, Seascale.
Strickland, Hornyold-, Lt. Cdr. T., Sizergh Castle, Kendal.
Studholme, Sir Henry, Bart., C.V.O., Wembury House, Plymouth.
Suessmann, Fraulein Ilse, 69 Heidelberg, Bergstrasse 15, W. Germany.
Swift, The Rev. F. B., 5 Westhaven, Thursby, Carlisle.
Sykes, Mrs. P. F., Stonethwaite, Elterwater, Langdale.
Tait, The Rev. Canon R. C., Highways, Clapham Old Road, Ingleton, via Carnforth.
Taylor, S. G., J.P., Rowancrag, Finsthwaite, Ulverston.
Thompson, Miles (of Carlisle), Yanwath, 2 Portreeve Close, Llantrisant, Mid Glamorgan.
Thompson, Miss P. A., 123a Lee Park, Blackheath, London SE3.
Thompson, T. A. Lacy, Woody Hyde, Grayshott, Hindhead, Surrey.
Thornburgh, Robert G., M.D., 1066 Atlantic Avenue, Long Beach, California 90813, U.S.A. – 2 copies.
Thornburrow, Robert William, 8 Crossway, Havant, Hants.
Tinniswood, J. M., Wood End, Greystoke, Penrith.
Tinniswood, R. D., Cockbridge House, Mealsgate, Carlisle.
Todd, H., 3 Fairbank Crescent, Sherwood, Nottingham.
Todd, John M., M.A., Redbourn House, St. Bees.
Todd, J. W., 67 Ford Well Road, Stockton-on-Tees, Cleveland.
Torbock, Commander R. H., R.N., Crossrigg Hall, Cliburn, Penrith.
Towill, Major J. M., Moorhouse Hall, Moorhouse, Carlisle.
Tudor, Miss Christine E. F., B.Sc., Rigg End, Blencarn, Penrith.
Turner, Constance Parker, Realands, Eskdale.
Turner, Ian D., Warrendene, 222 Nottingham Road, Mansfield, Notts.
Vane, The Hon. Christopher J. F., Hutton-in-the-Forest, Penrith.
Vaux, George, 320 Caversham Road, Bryn Mawr, Penna 19010, U.S.A.
Vaux, Brigadier P. A. L., 10 Greenways, Fleet, Hants.
Virginia Historical Society, Boulevard and Kensington Avenue, P.O. Box 7311, Richmond, Virginia 23221, U.S.A.
Walker, Mrs. Ida Stagg B., School Bank Cottage, Askham, Penrith.
Washington, G. S. H. L., M.A., F.S.A., 17 Eltisley Avenue, Cambridge.
Washington, Lt. Col. and Mrs., Dacre Lodge, Dacre, Penrith.
Westoll, J., Dykeside, Longtown, Carlisle.
Whitaker, E. M., Dykelands, Ulverston.
Whittaker, Bruce B., O.B.E., M.A., F.R.I.C.S., Thurston House, Tobermory, Isle of Mull, Argyll.
Wildridge, J. D. J., 41 Ellerbeck Lane, Workington.
Williams, D. J. W., 3 Lansdowne Grove, Devizes, Wilts.

Williams, D. M., Glenside, Morecambe Road, Ulverston.
Wilson, Dr. Alan, 46 Plynlimon Road, Christchurch, New Zealand.
Wilson, B., 16 Ulverston Road, Swarthmoor, Ulverston.
Wilson, Miss Olive, Crag View, Storrs Park, Windermere.
Wilson, P. A., Oak Hill, Lorton, Cockermouth.
Wilson, Messrs Titus and Son Ltd., 28 Highgate, Kendal.
Winter, G. H., 70 Dunmail Drive, Carlisle.
Woof, R. S., 4 Burdon Terrace, Newcastle upon Tyne – 2 copies.
Wright, Mrs. Vivian, Fennelsyke, Raughton Head, Carlisle – 3 copies.
Yale University Library, Newhaven, Connecticut 06520, U.S.A.